The Bradt Story

The first Bradt travel guide was written by Hilary and George Bradt in 1974 on a river barge floating down a tributary of the Amazon in Bolivia. From their base in Boston, Massachusetts, they went on to write and publish four other backpacking guides to the Americas and one to Africa.

In the 1980s Hilary continued to develop the Bradt list in England, and also established herself as a travel writer and tour leader. The company's publishing emphasis evolved towards broader-based guides to new destinations – usually the first to be published on those countries – complemented by hiking, rail and wildlife guides.

Since winning *The Sunday Times* Small Publisher of the Year Award in 1997, we have continued to fill the demand for detailed, well-written guides to unusual destinations, while maintaining the company's original ethos of low-impact travel.

Travel guides are by their nature continuously evolving. If you experience anything which you would like to share with us, or if you have any amendments to make to this guide, please write; all your letters are read and passed on to the author. Most importantly, do remember to travel with an open mind and to respect the customs of your hosts – it will add immeasurably to your enjoyment.

Happy travelling!

Hilary Bradt

Hilary Bradt

19 High Street, Chalfont St Peter, Bucks SL9 9QE, England
Tel: 01753 893444 Fax: 01753 892333
Email: info@bradt-travelguides.com Web: www.bradt-travelguides.com

Switzerland
Rail • Road • Lake
THE BRADT TRAVEL GUIDE
Second Edition

Anthony J Lambert

Bradt Publications, UK
The Globe Pequot Press Inc, USA

First published in 1996 by Bradt Publications.
This second edition published in 2000 by Bradt Publications,
19 High Street, Chalfont St Peter, Bucks SL9 9QE, England
web: www.bradt-travelguides.com
Published in the USA by The Globe Pequot Press Inc, 246 Goose Lane,
PO Box 480, Guilford, Connecticut 06475-0480

British Library Cataloguing in Publication Data
A catalogue record for this book is available from the British Library
ISBN 1 84162 014 9

Library of Congress Cataloging-in-Publication Data
Lambert, Anthony J.
    Switzerland : rail, road, lake : the Bradt travel guide / Anthony J.
    Lambert. — 2nd ed.
        p. cm.
    Rev. ed. of: Switzerland by rail. 1996.
    Includes bibliographical references and index.
    ISBN 1-84162-014-9
    1. Switzerland—Guidebooks. 2. Railroad travel – Switzerland –
    Guidebooks. I. Lambert, Anthony J. Switzerland by rail. II. Title.
DQ16.L35 2000
914.9404'74—dc21

00-056205

Photographs
Front Autumn view of Brienz (Adrian Baker/Photobank)
Text Anthony J Lambert (AL), Switzerland Tourism (ST)
Illustrations Isabel Fallow
Maps Alan Whitaker, with regional maps compiled from Philip's 1:1,000,000
Europe mapping (www.philips-maps.co.uk)

Typeset from the author's disc by Wakewing
Printed and bound in Spain by Grafo SA, Bilbao

Author

Anthony Lambert has been visiting Switzerland since childhood and has written 14 books about railways and travel. He has contributed to the AA's *Train Journeys of the World* and the *Insight Guide to Pakistan* and written about travel and railway journeys for such newspapers and magazines as the *New York Times*, *The Daily Telegraph*, *The Sunday Times*, *Wanderlust* and *World*. He was consultant editor to the nine-volume partwork, *The World of Trains*, and has travelled on the railways of over 40 countries.

Anthony's part-time work for the National Trust reflects an interest in architecture and cultural history, and he is also a keen cyclist and walker. He has talked to a wide range of audiences on railways and travel, including the Royal Geographical Society, of which he is a Fellow.

DEDICATION
For Gabriel,
in the hope that this book will still be in print
by the time he is old enough to use it.

For Marilyn,
hoping she might concede that the outcome justified the deed.

LIST OF MAPS

Basel centre	220	Neuchâtel centre	233
Basel & the Northwest	214	Neuchâtel & Jura	230
Bern centre	100	Northeast	72
Bernese Oberland	154	St Gallen centre	76
Eastern Bernese Mittelland	112	Southeast Vaud & Valais	300
Fribourg	146	Switzerland	IFC
Geneva centre	261	Switzerland Regions	2
Geneva & Lausanne	256	Ticino	336
Graubünden	360	Vevey & Montreux	278
Lausanne centre	273	Western Bernese Mittelland	130
Lugano centre	341	Yverdon centre	247
Luzern centre	176	Zürich centre	38
Around Luzern	186	Around Zürich	48

Contents

Acknowledgements   VII

Introduction   IX

PART ONE   GENERAL INFORMATION   I
Chapter I   Planning a Holiday   3

Chapter 2   Getting There   9
               By rail 9, By air 13, By car 15

Chapter 3   Swiss Travel System   15

Chapter 4   Crossing the Country   25
               William Tell Express 23, Stresa Express 23,
               Zermatt Express 23, Golden Pass route 23,
               Golden Pass Panoramic 26, Glacier Express 26,
               Palm Express 26, Bernina Express 27,
               Heidiland-Bernina Express 27, Engadin Star 27,
               Voralpen Express 27

Chapter 5   Walking and Cycling   27
               Walking 27, Cycling 31, Maps and guides for walking
               and cycling 33

PART TWO   THE GUIDE   37

Chapter 6   Zürich   39

Chapter 7   Around Zürich   49
               Lake Zürich (Zürichsee) 49, Zürich HB–Uetliberg 49,
               Zürich HB–Sihlbrugg 50, Zürich HB–Zug 50,
               Zug–Arth-Goldau 52, Zug–Zürich HB via Affoltern 52,
               Zürich HB–Brugg 53, Dietikon–Wohlen 54,
               Lenzburg–Rotkreuz 55, Zug–Luzern 56,
               Zürich HB–Ziegelbrücke 56, Ziegelbrücke–Linthal 57,
               Zürich HB–Rapperswil 60,
               Rapperswil–Pfaffikon–Arth-Goldau 62,
               Wadenswil–Einsiedeln 62, Rapperswil–Winterthur 64,
               Zürich Stadelhofen–Esslingen 65,

Zürich HB–Hinwil/Rapperswil 65,
Wetzikon–Effretikon 66, Zürich HB–Winterthur 66,
Winterthur–Bulach–Koblenz 69,
Zürich HB–Niederweningen–Bulach–Schaffhausen 70,
Zürich–Baden 70

Chapter 8   **The Northeast**   **71**
Winterthur–St Gallen 71, St Gallen–Trogen 75,
St Gallen–Wattwil–Rapperswil 77,
St Gallen–Romanshorn 78, St Gallen–Gais–Appenzell 78,
Gais–Altstatten Stadt 81,
Wasserbrau–Appenzell–Herisau–Gossau 81,
Gossau–Sulgen 83, Wil–Nesslau-Neu St Johann 84,
St Gallen–Rorschach 85, Rorschach–Heiden 86,
Rorschach–Schaffhausen 87, Schaffhausen–Erzingen 93,
Schaffhausen–Thayngen 93, Schaffhausen–Winterthur 94,
Winterthur–Etzwilen/Stein am Rhein 94,
Winterthur–Romanshorn 94, Frauenfeld–Wil 96,
Wil–Weinfelden–Kreuzlingen 96, Rorschach–Sargans 97,
Rheineck–Walzenhausen 98

Chapter 9   **Bern**   **99**

Chapter 10   **The Eastern Bernese Mittelland**   **111**
Bern Zytglogge/Theaterplatz–Worb Dorf 111,
Bern–Worb Dorf 113, Bern–Solothurn 113,
Solothurn–Moutier 117,
Solothurn–Niederbipp–Langenthal 118,
Solothurn–Olten 118, Oensingen–Balsthal 120,
Solothurn–Burgdorf 120,
Burgdorf–Konolfingen–Thun 121, Bern–Olten 122,
Langenthal–St Urban Ziegelei 124, Bern–Luzern 124,
Langnau–Burgdorf 126, Ramsei–Huttwil 127,
Wolhusen–Huttwil–Langenthal 127

Chapter 11   **The Western Bernese Mittelland**   **129**
Bern–Biel/Bienne 129, Lyss–Buren an der Aare 132,
Biel/Bienne–Neuchâtel 134,
Biel/Bienne–La Chaux-de-Fonds 134,
Sonceboz-Sombeval–Moutier 135,
Biel/Bienne–Delemont 135, Biel/Bienne–Solothurn 136,
Biel/Bienne–Ins 137,
Lyss–Murten–Payerne–Palézieux 137,
Bern–Neuchâtel 143,
Ins–Murten–Courtepin–Fribourg 143,
Bern–Lausanne 143, Flamatt–Laupen 149,
Fribourg–Payerne–Yverdon 149, Romont–Bulle 150,
Bern–Schwarzenburg 151

Chapter 12   **The Bernese Oberland**   **153**
Bern–Belp–Thun 153,
Bern–Thun–Spiez–Interlaken Ost 155, Interlaken 158,
Lake Thun 160,
Interlaken–Zweilütschinen–Lauterbrunnen 161,
Wilderswil–Schynige Platte 163,
Lauterbrunnen–Grutschalp–Mürren 164,
Lauterbrunnen–Kleine Scheidegg 166,
Kleine Scheidegg–Jungfraujoch 168,
Zweilutschinen–Grindelwald 170,
Grindelwald–Kleine Scheidegg 171,
Spiez–Zweisimmen 171, Spiez–Brig 172

Chapter 13   **Luzern**   **177**

Chapter 14   **Around Luzern**   **185**
Lake Luzern 185, The Swiss path 189, Vitznau–Rigi 189,
Arth–Rigi 192, Luzern–Lenzburg 192, Luzern–Olten 194,
Zofingen–Lenzburg 195, Luzern–Stans–Engelberg 196,
Luzern–Meiringen 200, Alpnachstad–Pilatus 204,
Meiringen–Innertkirchen 205, Meiringen–Interlaken 205,
Brienz–Rothorn 207, Luzern–Ariolo 208

Chapter 15   **Basel and the Northwest**   **215**
Basel 215, Basel–Rodersdorf 221, Basel–Delémont 222,
Delémont–Porrentruy–Boncourt 223, Porrentruy–Bonfol
224, Basel–Olten 224, Liestal–Waldenburg 225,
Sissach–Olten 226, Olten–Brugg 226,
Aarau–Menziken-Burg 228, Aarau–Wettingen 228,
Basel–Brugg 229

Chapter 16   **Neuchâtel and Jura**   **231**
Neuchâtel 231, Neuchâtel–Boudry 234,
Neuchâtel–La Chaux-de-Fonds 235,
La Chaux-de-Fonds–Le Locle 237,
Le Locle–Les Brenets 238,
La Chaux-de-Fonds–Glovelier 239,
Le Noirmont–Tavannes 240,
La Chaux-de-Fonds–Les Ponts-de-Martel 241,
Neuchâtel–Travers–Buttes 241, Neuchâtel–Yverdon 244,
Yverdon–Ste-Croix 248, Yverdon–Lausanne 250,
Chavornay–Orbe 250, Cossonay–Vallorbe 251,
Vallorbe–Le Day–Le Brassus 253

Chapter 17   **Geneva and Lausanne**   **255**
Geneva 255, Lac Léman 265,
Genève-Eaux-Vives–Annemasse–La Roche-sur-Foron 266,
Geneva–La Plaine 266, Geneva–Lausanne 266,
Nyon–La Cure 269,

Morges–Biere/L'Islemailont-la-Ville 269, Lausanne 270,
Lausanne-Flon–Ouchy 275,
Lausanne–Echallens–Bercher 276, Lausanne–Vevey 276

Chapter 18   Vevey and Montreux   279
Vevey 279, Vevey–Mont Pelerin 281,
Vevey–Puidoux-Chexbres 382, Vevey–Les Pléiades 282,
Blonay–Chamby 283, Vevey–Montreux 283,
Montreux 284, Montreux–Rochers-de-Naye 286,
Montreux–Zweisimmen–Lenk 288,
Montbovon–Gruyères–Bulle–Palézieux 294,
Bulle–Broc 296, Montreux–Aigle 297

Chapter 19   Southeast Vaud and the Valais   301
Aigle 301, Aigle–Leysin 302, Aigle–Les Diablerets 303,
Aigle–Champery 304, Aigle–Martigny 306,
Bex–Bévieux–Villars 308, Villars–Col-de-Bretaye 310,
St Maurice–St-Gingolph 311, Martigny–Vallorcine 311,
Martigny–Orsières'Le Chable 313, Martigny–Brig 315,
Brig–Domodóssola 321, Brig–Zermatt 322,
Zermatt–Gornergrat 326, Brig–Andermatt 327,
Realp–Gletsch 331, Andermatt–Goschenen 332,
Oberwald–Meiringen 332, Oberwald–Airolo 333,
Airolo–Andermatt 333, Andermatt–Furka–Oberwald 333

Chapter 20   The Ticino   335
Airolo–Lugano 335, Lugano 340, Lake Lugano 343,
Around Lugano 345, Lugano–Ponte Tresa 346,
Lugano–St Moritz 347, Luino–Cadenazzo 348,
Bellinzona–Locarno 348, Locarno 349, Lake Maggiore 350,
Around Locarno 352, Locarno–Domodóssola 353,
Lugano–Chiasso 357, Capolago–Generoso 358

Chapter 21   Graubünden   361
Andermatt–Chur 361, Disentis–Biasca 365,
Chur–Arosa 365, Chur–St Moritz 367,
St Moritz–Scuol–Tarasp 372,
The Swiss National Park 376,
St Moritz/Samedan–Tirano 377, Filisur–Davos–Chur 381,
Chur–Ziegelbrücke 384

Appendix 1   Language   387

Appendix 2   Useful Addresses   391

Appendix 3   Further Reading   393

**Appendix 4   Railway and Postbus Routes by Timetable
                  Number   394**

Index   397

Acknowledgements

Inevitably a book of this nature depends upon the help of numerous people in providing advice, information and hospitality. To the following I extend my thanks for their kindness:

Peter Anderegg, Ernst Bachmann, Eveline Bandi, Erich Bapst, Ernst Baumberger, Corinne Baume, Patrick Belloncle, Helmut Biner, Christa Branchi-Müller, Robert Brookes, Dominic Brühwiler, Frank Bumann, Daniel Burckhardt, Lisbeth Cardis, Claudia Cattaneo, Alison Chambers, Corinne Chappuis, Corinne Chevallaz-Chappuis, Barbara Compton, Paola Corazza, Stefano Crivelli, Dr Hans P Danuser, Kurt A Diermeier, Urs Eberhard, Douglas Ellison, H-P Ernst, Olivier Federspiel, Ursula Fischer, Sandrine Foschia, Hans Peter Frank, Anina Fromm, Hugo Furrer, Robert Gander, Bruno Gantenbein, Cécile Gardaz, Oliver Garnett, Barbara Gasser, Raymond Gertschen, Andrew Gordon, Robi Guglielmetti, Monika Haecki, Toni Hählen, Peider Härtli, Christine Hartmann, Philipp Heinzelmann, Ines Hentz, Philipp Hermann, Andrea Herzog, Isabelle Hesse, Roland Huber, I Jeckelmann, Ursula Känel, Karin Kelly, Xavier Kempf, Samuel Kocher, Roswitha Koller, Christian Kräuchi, Lisa Krummen, Philippe Kühne, Jrène Küng-Schmocker, Hansueli Kunz, Claudia Lansel, Peter Lehner, Peter Lemmey, Danny Löwensberg, Rolf Luethi, Andrea Lüthi, Cornelia Mainetti, Barbara Marti, Peter Mills, Jean-François Morerod, Dominique Moritz, Sabine Moser, Monica Müller, Barbara Mürner, Hans and Sylvia Neururer, Sir John and Lady Osborn, Adrian Ott, Eddy Peter, Amadé Perrig, Beat Pfammatter, Sylviane Putallaz, Beni Rach, Willy Raess, Sylvia Reinert, Robert Reich, Heidi Reisz, Véronique Robyr, Biba Roesti, Kathrin Rohrbach, Reto Rostetter, Stefanie Rother, Monika Rüthermann, George Saudan, René Schaetti, Urs Schenk, Jean-Louis Scherz, Max Schlumpf, Susy Schuppli, Dorle Schürmann, Jan Steiner, Andrea Stettler, Edith Strub, Barbara Thommen, Jurg Tschopp-James, W Twerenbold, A Ulrich, Hans van Well, Myriam Vils, Carol Voeffray, Corinne von Allmen, Michael Whitehouse, Rolf Wild, Hans Wismann, and Roland and Heidi Wyss.

In particular I would like to thank people at the London office of Switzerland Tourism: Eva Brechtbuehl, who was Director while the research was being done and whose advice and enthusiasm for the project were a great help and encouragement; Evelyn Lafone, without whose indefatigable help and organisation the book would never have been written; Edwin Schmid, the former Deputy Director, whose knowledge of Swiss railways was invaluable;

Roland Minder and Russell Palmer for particular help with the second edition; and the current director, Dino Dulio.

Many thanks to the editor of the book, Tricia Hayne, for her guidance on expanding the content for the second edition and to the publisher, Hilary Bradt, for having the confidence in the book to keep it in print. My thanks, too, to Sally Brock for the design, and to Alan Whitaker for the maps.

Finally, behind many an author of non-fiction there is a long-suffering family whose members have to live with the physical accumulation of research material and the mental absence of its perpetrator. My publisher could not have had a better fifth column: the questions 'When are you going to finish the book?' or 'How many pages have you written today?' have been an almost daily refrain from my small son. So my thanks to Marilyn and Gabriel for putting up with it for so long.

Gstaad station on the railway from Montreux to Zweisimmen and Lenk

Introduction

Switzerland is synonymous with some of the most beautiful mountain landscapes on earth. Over 12 million people a year visit Switzerland, primarily to see sights like the Jungfrau, Eiger and Matterhorn. Tourism promotion is the catalyst for most visitors, but curiously it was mainly the writings of poets and playwrights which encouraged the early tourists to visit the country – the third canto of Byron's *Childe Harolde*, Schiller's *Wilhelm Tell* and Rossini's opera based on it did more for Swiss tourism in the first half of the 19th century than any official promotion. This celebration of the country's natural beauty by writers and painters has, however, distorted the view of what Switzerland has to offer.

Because the landscape dominates most visitors' perceptions of the country, its architectural and cultural attractions have been relatively neglected. The principal art galleries, for example, have collections of paintings that would hold their own with most capital cities. The country has thousands of fine museums, castles, mansions and outstanding churches, as well as delightful vernacular buildings. The country's cities are a pleasure to visit, largely because the impact of motor traffic has been minimised. In a 1999 ranking of world cities for quality of life, the Swiss cities of Zürich, Bern and Geneva occupied second, fourth and sixth place, making Switzerland the most successful country in the world.

Switzerland is a paradise for those who prefer peace and solitude to noise and crowds. Even in high summer it is easy to escape the throng on summits of mountains like Pilatus and the Stanserhorn by walking for five minutes. Equally there are many relatively undiscovered places that would be major tourist attractions in countries less well endowed with natural beauty.

This book is a guide to exploring the country by public transport, describing every railway line and what there is to see from each station, as well as connecting journeys by steamer, postbus, funicular, cableway, bicycle and on foot. It does not attempt to provide a history of the country – though there is much history in it – nor to portray its character; books to be read before a visit, such as the *Insight Guide to Switzerland*, are suggested in *Further Reading*.

Why choose public transport?

Three factors combine to make public transport the best way to travel round Switzerland: the country has much of Europe's finest alpine scenery, a good part of which thankfully cannot be reached by road; it has without question the best national public transport system in the world; and the Swiss Pass that entitles visitors to unlimited travel over most of the system, and discounts on almost all the rest, is very good value. This combination is enough to persuade many tourists to rely wholly upon public transport, but there are other compelling reasons for doing so.

Principal amongst the positive reasons is the pleasure of travelling by train in Switzerland. For those accustomed to public transport systems starved of investment, it will be something of a revelation: every aspect of the system seems to be designed and operated to a standard rather than a price. Most trains are modern, clean and punctual. Stations of any size are staffed and offer facilities that smooth the traveller's path, such as luggage forwarding, cycle hire, money changing and a restaurant or buffet that is often used by locals because of its quality.

But what probably impresses visitors most is the way that Swiss public transport is planned to offer a seamless, integrated service. Trains connect with each other, buses meet and feed trains, and both are timed to complement a boat or funicular service. At each station timetables give clear information about all local transport, walks are signed from most stations and many offer cycling routes.

Then there is the view from the window. Some suburban lines apart, it is quite hard to find a train journey that does not offer attractive scenery, and Switzerland has more than its fair share of the world's really spectacular train journeys. Although the best-known are deservedly popular, there are some little-known journeys through equally fine landscapes to provide that sense of surprise which is part of the joy of travel.

Eco-tourism and sustainable transport

Concern about the impact of tourism on environments has focused largely on developing countries, but there are equally strong if different reasons why the principles of eco-tourism should be applied to developed countries. The impact of climate change is nowhere more evident than in the Alps where glaciers are in steady retreat, forest trees show increasingly severe evidence of atmospheric pollution and ski resorts on the margins of dependable snow grow more worried by the year. Recently research scientists have discovered that global warming is having a potentially catastrophic effect on Europe's permafrost: air temperature increases are being magnified fivefold underground. This will increase the instability of mountain sides and undermine the foundations of buildings at high altitude, including most of the skiing industry infrastructure.

The impact of vehicle pollution along Swiss transit corridors – turning entire valleys into 'traffic centres asphyxiated by pollution' as one Swiss writer put it – was the principal reason why the Swiss have voted in favour of measures to carry by rail all transit freight by 2005. But transport remains the fastest growing source of carbon dioxide and some other greenhouse gases. As Anna Pavord wrote in a series of articles on eco-tourism in the *Independent*, the first lesson is not to hire a car. Still worse is to drive your own car across Europe.

Green reasons aside, there are other disadvantages to using a car. Driving requires total concentration from the driver, especially on twisty mountain roads, so he or she will obtain little or no pleasure from the scenery. Unless you are experienced in driving on snow or ice, the roads in winter present a particular hazard. As travel insurance statistics show, traffic accidents are *the* major killer of travellers, whereas travelling by train is statistically safer than staying in your own home.

There is probably no other railway in the world that can boast such an environmentally friendly source of power. Not only is most of the electricity used by Swiss railways generated by water, but the technical sophistication of Swiss railway engineering (a function of investment levels) is reflected in the high proportion of trains equipped with regenerative braking. This exploits the steep gradients of many Swiss railways to combine braking with electrical generation; traction motors are turned into dynamos to feed current back into the overhead lines while checking the speed of the train. As a rule of thumb, two descending trains provide enough power for one to climb the gradient.

Public transport in Switzerland remains good value, and, as one US writer put it, 'the word "excellent" doesn't begin to describe the Swiss rail and bus system'. For the sake of Switzerland, its people and its visitors, let us hope it remains worthy of such praise.

Using this book

Place names in headings that are in upper and lower case indicate the starting or finishing points of the train service but the section describes only the part of the line between places in capital letters (eg: LUZERN–AIROLO–Lugano–Chiasso). Place names in **bold** in the text refer to stations. Cross-referencing is usually by table, and a list of tables and page numbers is given on page 394.

Part One

General Information

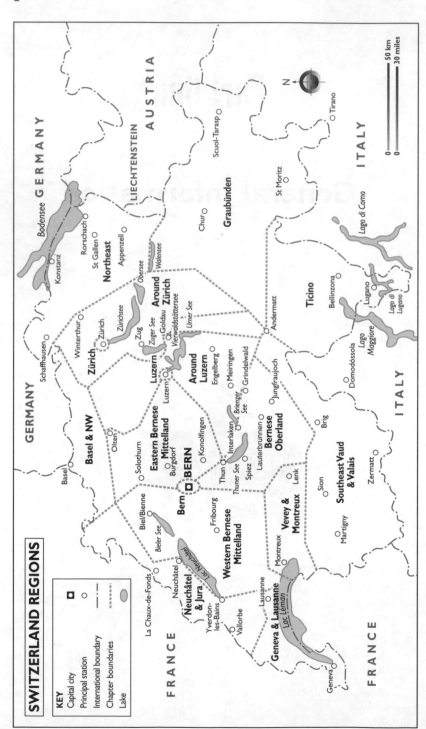

Planning a Holiday

For a first visit to any country there is a great temptation to try to see as much as possible in the time available. Even if it means that there is little time to savour the atmosphere of a place or explore anywhere in detail, this approach has much to commend it. If you don't expect to return to the country, then at least you will have seen as many different areas as time permits; if it is intended to be the first of a number of visits, a whistle-stop tour is a good way to decide which parts of the country appeal most and where you would like to spend more time on the next occasion.

Switzerland is not a large country, and the speed and frequency of main line trains makes it easy to traverse the whole country in a matter of hours – Geneva to St Gallen, or Basel to Lugano, for example, takes about four hours. Moreover, armed with a Swiss Pass, there is no additional cost for intensive use of the Swiss Travel System.

Ardent travellers excepted, however, most visitors prefer to be selective, or at least to pause for two or three nights at carefully chosen bases. Choices are obviously subjective affairs, but it is easy to explore regions like the Bernese Oberland or the Ticino from a single base.

Great railway journeys

In terms of Switzerland's great railway journeys, it is easy to recommend something of a hierarchy. The popularity of the Glacier Express between Zermatt and St Moritz is wholly deserved and is probably *the* journey not to be missed. Other outstanding and well-known scenic journeys are:

Montreux–Zweisimmen
Luzern–Interlaken
Interlaken–Jungfraujoch
St Moritz–Tirano
Locarno–Domodóssola

But there is a host of other lines, some used by hardly anyone except local people, that would warrant inclusion in a pantheon of great railway journeys for most other countries:

St Gallen–Gais–Altstätten
Gais–Appenzell–Wasserauen
Luzern–Bern

Luzern–Engelberg
Luzern–Andermatt–Lugano
St Moritz–Scuol-Tarasp
Martigny–Vallorcine
Bex–Villars
Aigle–Les Diablerets
Yverdon-les-Bains–Ste-Croix
Neuchâtel–Buttes
La Chaux-de-Fonds–Glovelier

That said, there are very few lines in Switzerland that are actually dull, blessed as the country is with a profusion of picturesque landscapes.

Maps

For planning a holiday based on use of the Swiss Travel System (see Chapter 3), Kümmerly + Frey's map of the railway and postbus networks is invaluable. The most detailed maps of the country are produced by the Swiss equivalent of Britain's Ordnance Survey, the Federal Office of Topography, and are to 1:25,000 scale. Most visitors will find the 1:50,000 series adequately detailed, and the Office also produces specialised maps showing hiking routes (see Chapter 5), ski routes, cultural heritage, museums, castles. It should be noted that Federal Office of Topography symbols and signs are explained in a separate free A5 leaflet 'Conventional Signs'.

These maps can be obtained from Stanfords, 12–14 Long Acre, Covent Garden, London WC2E 9LP. For the mail order service, tel: 020 7836 1321; fax: 020 7836 0189; email: sales@stanfords.co.uk

Cultural attractions
Art galleries

Collections of international repute may be found in Baden, Basel, Bern, Lugano, Winterthur and Zürich. Collections of largely Swiss interest or lesser European works are in Geneva, Lausanne, Locarno and Solothurn.

Castles

The country has numerous castles; amongst the finest that still have military pretensions are Aigle, Bellinzona, Burgdorf, Chillon, Grandson, Hagenwil, La Sarraz, Lenzburg, Lucens, Morges, Munot (Schaffhausen), Nyon, Oron, Porrentruy, Sion, Soyhières and Thun.

Country mansions

Amongst the most attractive houses open to visitors are some that were once castles, but have been so rebuilt that they retain only symbols of their defensive origins: Bottmingen, Brig, Bubikon, Chur, Colombier, Coppet, Gruyères, Hallwil, Jegenstorf, Kyburg, Landshut, Oberhofen, Spiez, Tarasp and Werdenberg.

Architecture

There is so much good vernacular and ecclestiastical architecture in Switzerland that it is invidious to select a few places for special mention. Some indication of the significance of a town or village is inevitably reflected by the length given to it in the book.

When to go

There is almost no time in the year when a visit to Switzerland is inadvisable. Perhaps the only month to be avoided is November; not only is the weather poor, but many of the mountain cableways and funiculars close, either for the winter if the area is not suitable for skiing, or for up to a month's maintenance work prior to reopening for winter sports. It is wrong to think of Swiss alpine resorts in winter as being devoted solely to the needs of skiers: about 40% of winter visitors are non-skiers, though most participate in other outdoor activities such as hiking, snowshoe trekking, paragliding or sledging.

Skiing at the higher resorts can be good right into April, after which follow two to three months of spring flowers when the mountain slopes can be a mass of colour. Rainfall in spring and autumn is generally higher than during the winter or summer, but rain often serves to clear the air, producing a clarity that is rare in summer when haze can obstruct views. The Jura region, in particular, is noted for its high spring rainfall. Although some hotels close for the winter in late September or October, the autumn can be a delightful time: the summer crowds are gone, the colours of the trees are glorious and the views can be much clearer than during the summer.

The mountain ranges that criss-cross the country often separate two very different sets of weather conditions; the passage of the Gotthard Tunnel can mark a transition from grey skies to bright sunshine. South of the Alps hours of sunshine are longer and precipitation lower, so those wanting warmth during a holiday at the margins of the summer may want to consider a few days in Ticino.

Hotels and other accommodation

Swiss hotels reflect the high standards which characterise most aspects of Swiss public services. Whether a 5-star hotel or a simple country inn, standards seldom disappoint. Swiss hotels are given the customary ranking of up to five stars, but a small number of hotels are deemed to have 'unique' qualities that make conventional star ranking inappropriate. Equally inns or small hotels without even a single star should not be considered in any way sub-standard; they will have fewer facilities and simpler furnishings, but may well have a homely quality that will appeal to anyone whose holiday won't be ruined by the absence of a trouser press.

For those in search of character and atmosphere, the number of large, grand hotels put up for the huge influx of Victorian visitors has diminished steadily since World War I: hotels like the Schreiber on Mount Rigi, Axenfels in Morschach and the Bristol in Lugano have succumbed to a sea-change in tourist requirements. None the less there are still some magnificent hotels redolent of the days when the Gotthard Express was steam-hauled and guests often stayed for months.

A selection of hotels near each station is to be found throughout the book. An '(H)' after the hotel name indicates that its building has historic interest or character. In addition, several books devoted to hotels and inns are listed in *Further Reading*, and the Swiss Hotels Association publishes the annual *Swiss Hotel Guide*, with illustrations of many of the establishments listed.

There are huge differentials in the highest and lowest prices charged by hotels within the same star ranking, partly reflecting the difference between high and low season rates and between 'fashionable' resorts and equally attractive, but less pretentious, resorts. Per night prices are given in Swiss francs for two people sharing a room:

Star	Top	Bottom
5	1,750	235
4	1,050	150
3	440	110
2	260	80
1	240	80
B&B	100	65

A service charge of 15% is added to hotel, restaurant and bar bills by law so tipping is neither expected nor desirable.

An enterprising initiative by the Federation of Rural Tourism of French Switzerland covers the southwest and is marketed under the name of Country Holidays. The illustrated brochure (in English) offers a mix of furnished apartments, mountain chalets and bed and breakfast accommodation, all in rural locations. Some are on working farms with animals, including ponies and horses that can be ridden by guests. (Fédération du Tourisme Rural de Suisse Romande, Office du Tourisme, CH-1530 Payerne; tel: 026/660 61 61; fax: 026/660 71 26; email: tourisme.payerne@mcnet.ch; web: www.tourismrural-payerne.ch)

The largest agency offering apartments or chalets for rent is Interhome, with over 4,000 properties available throughout Switzerland at a cost from £8 per person per night. Minimum rental periods are five nights in low season, seven nights in high season. The free brochure describes and illustrates all properties on offer. If you are going to Switzerland at short notice, it is worth contacting Interhome on a Saturday when a sale of rentals at up to half price is held for the week commencing the following Saturday; this can produce some real bargains out of season. Interhome also represents some Swiss hotels. (Interhome Ltd, 383 Richmond Road, Twickenham, Middlesex TW1 2EF; tel: 020 8891 1294; fax: 020 8891 5331; web: www.interhome.co.uk)

Youth hostel accommodation is available to visitors up to 25 years of age, but older people are accepted if room is available. A membership card of the national organisation in the visitor's country of residence must be shown, and intending visitors should check with youth hostels just as they would for a hotel. A list of Swiss youth hostels is available from Switzerland Tourism offices. A list of national organisations, and membership details, can be obtained from Youth Hostels Association, Trevelyan House, 8 St Stephen's Hill, St Albans, Hertfordshire AL1 2DY; tel: 01727 855215. Hostelling International, Suite 400, 205 Catherine Street, Ottawa, Ontario K2P 1C3; tel: (613) 237-7884. Hostelling International, 733 15th Street NW, Suite 840, Washington DC 20005; tel: (1) (202) 783 6161.

Saving money

Switzerland no longer deserves the reputation of being an expensive country to visit, as the exchange rates have been consistently favourable to visitors from Britain and the US for some years. None the less, there is a number of ways to save money:

- Although the Swiss Pass is discussed in Chapter 3, it is worth emphasising here that it represents excellent value for money if you are on a touring holiday. There are few places you cannot reach with it.
- Avoid the busiest months if you can, usually July and August, when prices of accommodation are highest.
- Eating in a mountain restaurant, perhaps on an open terrace overlooking a panorama of surrounding peaks, is part of the Swiss experience, but the prices can be high for the very good reason that it costs a lot to bring in the provisions. If you are on a tight budget, it is worth buying the ingredients for a picnic at a grocery before departure.
- Hotels just outside the main resorts and towns are often considerably cheaper than those near the centre; with a Swiss Pass there is no additional cost in travelling in from an outlying station. Many resorts have created 'Guest cards' which are issued to hotel guests and which entitle residents to discounts at a wide range of shops and services.
- Renting an apartment or chalet can also save money, especially if it is at a discounted rate (see the section on Interhome in *Hotels and other accommodation*, above).

Car-free resorts

Switzerland has nine car-free resorts that have formed the Society for Car-free Swiss Holiday Resorts. Some have made a virtue out of necessity, turning the near impossibility of road access into an asset, but the developed environmental conscience of many Swiss makes the absence of cars more than simply a cause of clean air and safety for children. The nine resorts are Bettmeralp, Braunwald, Mürren, Riederalp, Rigi-Kaltbad, Saas Fee, Stoos, Wengen and Zermatt.

Zermatt is the largest of these resorts and exceptional in that road access could have been feasible; however, local people felt that the quality of life and character of the place would have been ruined by the work necessary to accommodate cars. As the road up the valley from St Niklaus was gradually enlarged, a referendum was taken in Zermatt to determine whether the last stage from Täsch into Zermatt should be widened; 92% voted against it. Consequently the decision was taken to operate a rail shuttle service from

Täsch. Most freight to Zermatt also travels by train, and movement within Zermatt is largely by electric vehicles, the only exceptions being rubbish collection, ambulances and snowploughs. Even police vehicles are electric.

Towards the arrival time of trains, the square outside the station is lined with small electric vehicles, slightly smaller than British milkfloats, which each serve a particular hotel. The drivers wear identifying caps, and load the luggage on to the back platform while passengers seat themselves in the cab. The two 5-star hotels have horse-drawn buses or open carriages, which are lavishly decorated with flowers for newly married couples.

The measures taken in the other resorts to carry luggage and fulfil other services are similar but smaller in scale.

Travel and access for the disabled

Switzerland caters well for disabled travellers, though difficulties do arise from the low platform levels common throughout much of the Continent. Larger stations have hoists that will elevate a wheelchair to the level of the coach floor, and wheelchairs are available at a smaller number. Swiss Federal Railways produces a booklet giving details of stations with facilities and the appropriate course of action to obtain help ('*Informations et conseils pour les handicapés qui voyagent en train*').

The Royal Association for Disability & Rehabilitation (250 City Road, London EC1V 8AF; tel: 020 7250 3222) produces a guide to European accommodation facilities, and Switzerland Tourism can provide information; hotels of three stars and above can be expected to have a lift.

Provision for disabled access inevitably varies widely on mountain cableways and railways. Chairlifts and gondola lifts, which are usually boarded while in continuous motion, are obviously difficult if not impossible, but modern or rebuilt cablecars can sometimes accept wheelchairs.

Tourist information

The principal source of information in the UK is the Switzerland Travel Centre, Swiss Centre, Swiss Court, London W1V 8EE; tel: 00800 100 200 30; fax: 00800 100 200 31; email: stc@stlondon.com; web: www.MySwitzerland.com

Contact details for other Switzerland tourism offices around the world are given on page 391. More specialised information can be obtained from regional tourist offices:

Basel Tourism Schifflände 5, Basel CH-4001. Tel: 061/268 68 68; fax: 061/268 68 70; email: office@baseltourismus.ch; web: www.baseltourismus.ch
Bernese Oberland Tourism Jungfraustrasse 38, Interlaken CH-380. Tel: 033/823 03 03; fax: 033/823 03 30; email: info@berneroberland.com; web: www.berneroberland.com
Central Switzerland Alpenstrasse 1, Luzern CH-6002. Tel: 041/418 40 80; fax: 041/418 40 81; email: info@Central Switzerland.ch; web: www.CentralSwitzerland.ch
Eastern Switzerland Regio-info-Centre, Bahnhofplatz 1a, St Gallen CH-9001. Tel: 071/227 37 37; fax: 071/227 37 67; email: info@ostschweiz-i.ch; web: www.ostschweiz-i.ch

Pays de Fribourg Avry-le-Pont CH-1644. Tel: 026/915 92 92; fax: 026/915 92 92; email: info.tourisme@paysdefribourg.ch; web: www.pays-de-fribourg.ch

Geneva Tourism Rue du Mont Blanc 18, Postfach 1602, Geneva 1 CH-1211. Tel: 022/909 70 70; fax: 022/909 70 75; email: info@geneve-tourisme.ch; web: www.geneve-tourisme.ch

Graubünden Holiday Alexanderstrasse 24, Chur, CH-7001. Tel: 081/254 24 24; fax: 081/254 24 00; email: contact@graubuenden.ch; web: www.graubuenden.ch

Jura Tourism 1 rue de la Gruère, Postfach 364, Sagnelégier CH-2350; tel: 032/952 19 52; fax: 032/952 19 55; web: www.jura.ch

Office du tourisme du Jura bernois Av de la Liberté 26, Case postale, Moutier CH-2740. Tel: 032/493 64 66; fax: 032/493 61 56; email: information@jurabernois.ch; web: www.jurabernois.ch

Tourisme neuchâtelois – Littoral Hôtel des Postes, Postfach 1374, Neuchâtel CH-2001. Tel: 032/889 68 90; fax: 032 889 62 96; email: tourisme.neuchatelois@ne.ch; web: www.ne.ch

Schweizer Mittelland Tourism c/o Bernese Tourism, Postfach, Bern CH-3001. Tel: 031/328 12 28; fax: 031/ 311 12 22; email: info@smit.ch; web: www.smit.ch

Ticino Tourism Via Kugano 12, Postfach 1441, Bellinzona CH-6501. Tel: 091/825 70 56; fax: 091/825 36 14; email: ett@www.tourism-ticino.ch; web: www.ticinoinfo.ch

Valais Tourism Rue Pré-Fleuri 6, Postfach 1469, Sion CH-1951. Tel: 027/327 35 70; fax: 027/327 35 71; email: info@valaistourism.ch; web: www.valaistourism.ch

Zürich Tourism Bahnhofbrücke 1, Zürich CH-8023. Tel: 01/215 40 00; fax: 01/215 40 44; email: information@zurichtourism.ch; web: www.zurichtourism.ch

Canton Vaud Postfach 164, CH-1006 Lausanne. Tel: 021/613 26 26; fax: 021/613 26 00; email: information@lake-geneva-region.ch; web: www.lake-geneva-region.ch

Useful facts
Languages
German is spoken in north, central and eastern Switzerland, French in the west, Italian in the south and Romansch in the southeast.

Electric current
220V, 50Hz. Most appliances set for 240V will operate on 220V, but alter the setting if possible.

Weights and measures
Metric, using a comma rather than a decimal point and denoting thousands by a full point rather than a comma (eg: 1,6kg = 1.6kg).

Shops
Hours are usually 08.00–12.15, 13.30–18.30 on weekdays; 08.30–16.00 on Saturdays. Monday morning is often a half day.

Banking and money
Banks are open Mon–Fri 08.30–16.30 as a rule. The currency is the Swiss franc. Notes are available in denominations of SFr 10, 20, 50, 100, 500 and 1,000. Currency can be changed at airports and large stations daily 08.30–22.00.

Travellers' cheques may be cashed at banks and large hotels (though at an inferior rate). Although all major travellers' cheques are acceptable, the 'instant replacement' policy of American Express, Thomas Cook or Visa may be an advantage. Keep numbers of travellers' cheques in a separate wallet. American Express has offices in Basel, Bern, Geneva, Lausanne, Luzern and Zürich.

Post offices
Core hours are usually Mon–Fri 07.30–12.00, 13.45–18.30, Sat 08.00–11.00. Mail sent 'Poste restante' to a post office is held for 30 days and surrendered on production of a passport.

Telephones
Some large post offices have telephone sections where you pay for a call after making it. Phonecards of SFr 5, 10 and 20 are available. Calls made from hotel rooms are likely to be more expensive, since the hotel determines the rate. Lower rate calls obtain between 17.00 and 07.00.

Emergency numbers
Police 117
Fire brigade 118
Ambulance 144

English-speaking information line
Anglo-Phone is a 24-hour English-speaking information line. Dial 157-5014 from anywhere in Switzerland and someone will even be able to provide advice on finding an English-speaking babysitter, as well as events, excursions and activities.

Health and insurance
Since there is no state health service in Switzerland, nor reciprocal agreements for free treatment with other countries, it is imperative to take out health insurance, especially if you are taking part in sports or mountain walking.

Switzerland has very high standards of hygiene so neither food nor tap water should pose any hazard, but it is not advisable to drink from mountain streams, however clear they may look.

Embassies

Australia Tel: 157 5 60 05
Austria Tel: 031/356 52 52
Belgium Tel: 031/351 04 62
Canada Tel: 031/357 32 00
Denmark Tel: 031/350 54 54
Finland Tel: 031/351 30 31
France Tel: 031/359 21 11
Germany Tel: 031/359 41 11
Great Britain Tel: 031/359 77 00
Holland Tel: 031/350 87 00
Hungary Tel: 031/352 85 72

Ireland Tel: 031/352 14 42
Italy Tel: 031/352 41 51
Japan Tel: 031/300 22 22
Luxembourg Tel: 031/311 47 32
Norway Tel: 031/310 55 55
Poland Tel: 031/352 04 52
Portugal Tel: 031/351 17 73
Spain Tel: 031/352 04 12
Sweden Tel: 031/328 70 00
USA Tel: 031/357 70 11

Getting There

BY RAIL

The Channel Tunnel and Eurostar services to Lille, Paris Gare du Nord and Brussels have transformed the rail map of Europe, opening up new possibilities for both practical day and overnight journeys. The cross-platform interchange at Lille will enable progressively more connections to be made with TGV (*Train à Grande Vitesse*) services to a range of European cities. At present, no TGV services leave Lille for Switzerland, but by crossing Paris to catch a TGV from Gare du Lyon, you can reach Bern in 4½ hours or Lausanne in 4 hours from the French capital. These times will be reduced by construction of TGV Est, which will also increase the number and range of TGV services to Switzerland.

For those combining a visit to Switzerland with other countries, the range of trans-European trains is impressive. The following principal stations in Switzerland are linked by direct services with the cities that follow:

Basel Amsterdam, Berlin, Bologna, Bonn, Brussels, Cologne, Dortmund, Florence, Frankfurt, Hamburg, Hannover, Innsbruck, Leipzig, Luxembourg, Lyon, Milan, Paris, Rome, Strasbourg, Vienna
Bern Amsterdam, Barcelona, Bonn, Cologne, Florence, Frankfurt, Milan, Paris (TGV), Rome
Chur Amsterdam, Brussels, Hamburg
Geneva Barcelona, Irún, Lyon, Marseille, Milan, Paris (TGV), Toulouse, Valence, Venice, Zagreb
Lausanne Barcelona, Milan, Paris (TGV), Zagreb
Zürich Barcelona, Bucharest, Brussels, Budapest, Dresden, Frankfurt (ICE), Hamburg (ICE), Innsbruck, Leipzig, Milan, Munich, Paris, Prague, Salzburg, Stuttgart, Vienna, Zagreb

High-speed rail links with France

TGVs (the French high-speed trains) operate two daily return trains between Paris and Bern, a single return service to Zürich and five return workings with Lausanne.

High-speed rail links with Italy

Rail links with Italy were improved by the introduction of high-speed Pendolino tilting trains on various services to and from Milan. Marketed as the

Cisalpino, the train links Montreux, Lausanne and Geneva with Milan, reducing the time between Milan and Geneva to 3 hours 20 minutes. The Cisalpino sets also run from Milan over the BLS line to Bern, continuing to Basel, and also between Milan, Zürich and Stuttgart.

European rail passes

For those planning extensive rail travel in countries neighbouring Switzerland it may be sensible to think of a rail pass for Europe. Youth tickets are available to persons under 26; proof of age is required when purchasing tickets.

Eurail Pass

This offers unlimited first-class travel over the national railways of 17 European countries, with a choice of passes for 15 or 21 days or for 1, 2 or 3 months' consecutive travel. The countries covered are: Austria, Belgium, Denmark, Finland, France, Germany, Greece, Hungary, Italy, Luxembourg, Netherlands, Norway, Portugal, Republic of Ireland, Spain, Sweden and Switzerland. If you wish to stay for several days at various places en route, you can buy a Eurail Flexipass, which offers unlimited first-class rail travel for either 10 or 15 days within a 2-month period.

Special youth rates are available for both types of Eurail Pass in standard class, and there are also special rates for children aged 4–11 and for 2–5 people travelling together.

Europass

The pass covers fewer countries than the Eurail Pass, being valid in France, Germany, Italy, Spain and Switzerland. It offers unlimited first-class travel on 5, 6, 8, 10 or 15 days within a 2-month period. Add-ons are available: Austria/Hungary; Belgium/Netherlands/Luxembourg; Greece (including ADN/HML ferry services between Italy and Greece); and Portugal. A second-class Europass is available for those under 26, and group discounts are also available for 2–5 people travelling together.

Eurodomino/Freedom Pass

Ideal for exploring a neighbouring country, these passes are available for unlimited travel on the trains of the national railway operator and sometimes by private operators. The basic pass is valid for 3 days within a 1-month period, with an option to purchase up to 5 days additional travel. Up to 26 European countries can be chosen, the price naturally increasing with each country added. Youth passes are not available for first-class travel. The ticket covers virtually all high-speed train supplements, but there are a few exceptions so it is wise to check. Some of the better appointed overnight trains also call for a supplement.

The countries covered by the Freedom Pass are Austria, Belgium, Bulgaria, Croatia, Czech Republic, Denmark, Finland, France, Germany, Greece, Hungary, Italy, Luxembourg, Macedonia, Netherlands, Norway, Poland, Portugal, Romania, Slovakia, Spain, Sweden, Switzerland, Turkey, Yugoslavia and on the ADN/HML ferry services between Italy and Greece.

InterRail/InterRail 26+

Available for young people up to 26, the InterRail pass is structured on a zonal basis that allows a choice of up to eight zones. It allows unlimited travel on standard-class services provided by the national operator and reductions on some other trains. The pass brings with it discounts on certain shipping services and on some privately owned railways, particularly in Switzerland, and free admission to various transport museums. A valid passport and proof of residence in Europe for at least six months are required to purchase a pass, but the country of residence is excluded from the pass.

The zones are made up as follows:

A United Kingdom, Republic of Ireland
B Finland, Norway, Sweden
C Austria, Denmark, Germany, Switzerland
D Croatia, Czech Republic, Hungary, Poland, Slovakia
E Belgium, France, Luxembourg, Netherlands
F Morocco, Portugal, Spain
G Greece, Italy, Slovenia, Turkey (including ADN/HML ferry services between Italy and Greece)
H Bulgaria, Macedonia, Romania, Yugoslavia

Supplements for travel on many of the fastest train serices are required, and scat, couchette and sleeper reservations are extra.

Arrangements for the InterRail 26+ pass are identical but fares are about one-third higher.

Rail Europe Senior

Anyone over 60 qualifies for this pass which gives discounts of up to 30% in 25 different countries.

Useful addresses

Eurostar Group Eurostar House, Waterloo Station, London SE1 8SE. Tel: 0990 186186 (UK), 0044 123 361 7575 (from outside UK); fax: 020 7922 4499; web: www.eurostar.com

European Rail Ltd Tavistock House North, Tavistock Square, London WC1H 9HR. Tel: 020 7387 0444; fax: 020 7387 0888. Booking service for rail tickets throughout Europe except former USSR, Yugoslavia and Albania.

French Railways (SNCF) The Rail Shop, 179 Piccadilly, London W1V 0BA. Tel: 08705 848848. Motorail booking, tel: 08702 415 415. Also sells rail tickets to 5,000 European stations.

German Railways (DB) 18 Conduit Street, London W1R 9TD. Tel: 020 7317 0919 (information), 0870 6000778 (bookings); fax: 020 7491 4689; web: www.bahn.de

Swiss Railways (SBB) Switzerland Travel Centre, Swiss Court, London W1V 8EE. Tel: 0800 100 200 30; fax: 0800 100 200 31; email: stc@stlondon.com

See also the travel companies listed on page 21.

BY AIR

The easiest connections between air terminal and railway station are at Zürich and Geneva where the two facilities are adjacent. Both have frequent services to many parts of Switzerland.

From the UK

The Swiss airline **Crossair** offers the following direct services:

Birmingham–Basel, Bern (via Basel, Brussels or Paris), Geneva (via Basel or Zürich), Lugano (via Zürich), Zürich
Belfast–Basel
Bristol–Basel (via Amsterdam or Paris)
Cardiff–Basel (via Amsterdam or Paris
Dublin–Basel (via Manchester or Zürich), Bern (via Brussels), Geneva (via London or Zürich), Lugano (via London or Zürich), Zürich
Dundee–Basel (via Manchester)
Edinburgh–Basel (via Manchester or Paris)
Glasgow–Basel (via Manchester)
Guernsey/Jersey–Basel (via Zürich), Geneva (via Zürich), Lugano (via Zürich), Zürich
London City–Basel, Bern (via Paris or Basel), Geneva, Lugano, Zürich
Manchester–Basel, Bern (via Basel)

London City Airport is reached by a dedicated bus from Liverpool Street station running every 20 minutes and taking about 25 minutes; a new Docklands Light Railway link to the airport will open in 2004. If you hate crowds, City Airport should be your choice: the modest number of flights and the limit placed on the size of planes by the length of the runway combine to give a relaxed atmosphere to the departure areas. Moreover the Crossair service is excellent: their planes have leather seats, and smoked salmon croissants are offered for breakfast with champagne to follow. Tel: 0845 607 3000; web: www.crossair.com
    Other airlines are as follows:

Swissair flies from London Heathrow to Geneva and Zürich, and from Manchester to Zürich. Tel: 0845 601 0956; fax: 020 8762 7199; email: swissair.uk@e-mail.com; web: www.swissair.com
British Airways flights from London Heathrow serve Basel, Geneva and Zürich, and there is a direct flight from Manchester to Geneva. LinkLine, tel: 0345 222747; First Class, tel: 0345 222100
EasyJet flies to Geneva from Luton, Stansted, Gatwick and Liverpool and to Zürich from Luton. Tel: 0870 6000000; web: www.easyjet.com

From North America

Swissair flies from Atlanta, Boston, Chicago, Los Angeles, Miami, Montréal, New York, Newark and Washington.

United States

The toll-free reservation number for Swissair, unless otherwise stated, is 1 800 221 4750.

Atlanta 3391 Peachtree Road, NE Suite 210 (Buckhead), Atlanta, Georgia 30326
Boston Statler Office Building, 20 Park Plaza, Suite 1409, Boston, Massachusetts
02116. Tel: 1 800 221 6644
Chicago 150 N Michigan Avenue, Chicago, Illinois 60601. Tel: 1 800 221 6644
New York Swiss Center, 608 Fifth Avenue, New York 10020. Tel: 1 800 221 6644
Washington 1717 K Street, NW, Suite 1100, Washington DC, 20006

Canada
Toll-free number: 1 800 267 9477 (except Montréal)

Montréal Confederation Building, Suite 950, 1253 McGill College Avenue, St
Catherine, Montréal H3B 2Z7. Tel: (514) 954 5600
Toronto Tel: 1 416 360 7992

BY CAR
Thanks to the Channel Tunnel, it is easy to reach Switzerland in a day by car. In
common with many European countries, access to Swiss motorways has to be
paid for, by purchasing a vignette (available from Switzerland Tourism).
Although a Green Card is not compulsory, motorists are strongly advised to
acquire one, since the protection offered by most motor insurance policies is only
to a minimum requirement. Drivers are required to show a vehicle registration
certificate at the border and a full driving licence must be carried at all times.

The minimum driving age in Switzerland is 18, and children under 12 must
travel in the rear seats. A warning triangle must be carried, and police radar
speedtrap detectors are illegal. On-the-spot fines can be collected for failing to
wear a seat belt or for exceeding the speed limits of 120km/h (75mph) on
motorways, 80km/h (50mph) on other roads (unless otherwise signed) and
50km/h (31mph) in built-up areas whether or not there are signs indicating
this speed.

The driver should not expect to be able to enjoy the scenery, as mountain
roads in particular require vigilance. Some roads across the higher or more
exposed passes are closed during the winter months, though tunnels or car-
carrying trains substitute on the principal arteries.

There are 23 alpine passes and tunnels with varying dates of opening and
different tariff systems. Tickets for tunnels are purchased from booths on the
approach road.

Car hire
Car hire is generally cheaper if it is arranged before departure, and special rates
are available through Switzerland Tourism (see page 8).

In Switzerland, car hire is also available from the larger Swiss Federal
Railway stations and through Hertz by freephone (within Switzerland only).
Tel: 155 1234.

Itineraries
Outside the cities, Switzerland has innumerable scenic routes, though they are
not signposted as such. If you are armed with a good road map, these routes

are waiting to be explored. The postbus network outlined in this book covers some of the most attractive of these roads, and those seeking off-the-beaten path itineraries could well follow their example.

The famous Kapellbrücke in Luzern

Swiss Travel System

Switzerland has the densest network of public transport in the world. For two-thirds of Swiss people it is less than five minutes' walk from their homes to the nearest public transport; 97.5% live less than a kilometre away. Besides just over 5,000km (3,125 miles) of state- and privately owned railways, there are 660 postal-coach routes and over 600 funiculars, cablecars, rack railways and chairlifts. With local transport and steamer services, this amounts to a public transport network of about 20,500km (12,812 miles).

Only Japanese railways are used more frequently per person than those in Switzerland. With at least an hourly service on most Swiss routes, the national average is an astonishing 74 passenger trains a day, so a long wait is a rare occurrence.

Most of the standard-gauge network is operated by Swiss Federal Railways, which is abbreviated on coach sides to SBB/CFF/FFS, standing for Schweizerische Bundesbahnen, Chemins de Fer Fédéraux Suisses or Ferrovie Federali Svizzere in the three main languages of the Swiss Confederation. In addition there are 65 private railway companies, most of which operate narrow-gauge railways.

Many countries have a good public transport infrastructure, but all too often multiple ownership militates against the evolution of an integrated, complementary network within and between different modes of transport. Switzerland not only has the finest public transport infrastructure in the world, it also has the most integrated, making it fully deserving of the term 'system'. Despite multiple ownership, trains, buses, steamers, funiculars and cable railways are carefully timetabled to connect with admirable precision.

The benefits of this would be of reduced value if time-keeping was poor; in fact, it is extremely rare for any form of public transport to deviate from the timetable. This dependability, the frequency of services (except on the remotest of postal bus routes) and the ease of connections makes public transport a pleasure to use and the most stress-free way to travel.

Rail cards and passes

A range of passes has been created to suit the travel requirements of most visitors. These not only make use of the system much easier; they also represent excellent value:

The **Swiss Pass** entitles the holder to unlimited travel for 4, 8 or 15 days or one month on more than 16,000km (10,000 miles) of railway, boat and postal

256   Palézieux–Châtel-St-Denis–Bulle–Gruyères–**Montbovon** ⑩

→

Lausanne				553		ᚷ6 14	**7 10**	8 14	8 53	**10 10**	10 53	**12 10**		12 14	12 53
Palézieux	o			615		ᚷ6 32	**7 25**	8 38	9 14	**10 25**	11 14	**12 25**		12 38	13 14

		542	544	546	548	550	552	554	556	558	562	566	568	572
Palézieux				ᚷ6 18		ᚷ6 54	7 36	8 43	9 36	10 30	11 36	12 28	Ⓐ12 57	13 36
Granges (Veveyse)	x			6 20		6 56	7 38	8 45	9 38	10 32	11 38	12 30	12 59	13 38
Bossonnens				x 6 22		6 58	7 40	8 47	9 40	10 34	11 40	12 32	13 02	13 40
Tatroz	x			6 23		6 59	7 42	8 48	9 41	10 35	11 41	12 33	13 03	13 41
Remaufens	x			6 24		7 01	7 44	8 50	9 43	10 37	11 43	12 35	13 05	13 43
Au Moulin	x			6 26		7 03	7 46	8 52	9 45	10 39	11 45	12 37	13 07	13 45
Châtel-St-Denis	o			ᚷ6 29		7 05	7 49	8 54	9 47	10 41	11 47	12 38	Ⓐ13 11	13 47
Châtel-St-Denis			ᚷ6 05			7 11	7 54	8 56	9 50	10 44	11 50	Ⓐ12 49		13 50
Prayoud	x		6 08			7 15	7 57	8 59	9 53	10 47	11 53	12 52		13 53
Semsales			x 6 12			7 19	8 01	9 03	9 57	10 51	11 57	12 56		13 57
La Verrerie			x 6 15			7 22	8 03	9 05	10 00	10 53	11 59	13 00		14 00
Le Crêt	x		6 18			7 25	8 06	9 08	10 02	10 56	12 02	13 02		14 02
Les Ponts	x		6 20			7 29	8 09	9 11	10 05	10 59	12 05	13 05		14 05
Vaulruz-Sud	x		6 22			7 31	8 10	9 12	10 06	11 00	12 06	13 08		14 06
Les Colombettes	x		6 24			7 33	8 12	9 14	10 08	11 02	12 08	13 10		14 08
Vuadens-Sud			6 27			7 36	8 14	9 16	10 10	11 04	12 10	13 14		14 10
Planchy	x		6 29			7 38	8 16	9 18	10 12	11 06	12 12	13 16		14 12
Bulle	o		ᚷ6 34			7 42	8 20	9 22	10 16	11 10	12 16	Ⓐ13 20		14 16
Bulle		x 5 27	6 39		7 08		8 32	9 27	10 17	11 17	12 17	13 27		14 32
La Tour-de-Trême	x	5 30	6 42		7 11		8 35	9 30	10 20	11 20	12 20	13 30		14 35
Le Pâquier-Montbarry	x	5 32	6 44		7 13		8 37	9 32	10 22	11 22	12 22	13 32		14 37
Gruyères	o	5 33	6 45		7 14		8 38	9 34	10 24	11 23	12 23	13 34		14 38
Gruyères		5 34	6 46		7 15		8 39	9 35		11 24	12 24	13 35		14 39
Estavannens	x	5 37	6 49		7 18		8 42	9 37		11 27	12 27	13 37		14 42
Enney	x	5 38	6 50		7 19		8 43	9 38		11 28	12 28	13 38		14 43
Grandvillard		x 5 42	6 54		7 23		8 47	9 42		11 32	12 32	13 42		14 47
Neirivue	x	5 45	6 57		7 26		8 50	9 45		11 35	12 35	13 45		14 50
Albeuve	x	5 47	6 59		7 28		8 52	9 47		11 37	12 37	13 47		14 52
Lessoc	x	5 49	7 01		7 31		8 54	9 49		11 39	12 39	13 49		14 54
Montbovon	o	x 5 54	7 06		7 37		8 59	9 54		11 41	12 44	13 54		14 59
Montbovon		Ⓐ6 00			7 46		9 04			11 46	**13 04**			**15 04**
Château-d'Oex 120	o	Ⓐ6 16			8 04		9 19			12 04	**13 19**			**15 19**

Lausanne		14 10			15 14	16 14		17 10	18 14	19 10		21 10
Palézieux	o	14 25			15 38	16 38		17 25	18 38	19 25		21 25

		34 ⓡ(♀) PA Ⓒ	574	38 ⓡ(♀) PA Ⓒ	576	580	592 ⓡ ✕ PA	582	588	590	📷 590	594
Palézieux		14 30		15 43	16 43			17 36	18 43	19 36		21 36
Granges (Veveyse)	x	14 32		15 45	16 45			17 38	18 45	19 38		21 38
Bossonnens		14 34		15 47	16 47			17 40	18 47	19 40		x 21 40
Tatroz	x	14 35		15 48	16 48			17 42	18 48	19 41		21 41
Remaufens	x	14 37		15 50	16 50			17 44	18 50	19 43		21 43
Au Moulin	x	14 39		15 52	16 52			17 46	18 52	19 45		21 45
Châtel-St-Denis	o	14 41		15 54	16 54			17 49	18 54	19 47		21 47
Châtel-St-Denis		14 44		15 56	16 56			17 54	18 58	19 50		21 50
Prayoud	x	14 47		15 59	16 59			17 57	19 01	19 53		21 53
Semsales		14 51		16 03	17 03			18 01	19 05	19 57		x 21 57
La Verrerie		14 53		16 05	17 05			18 03	19 07	20 00		x 21 59
Le Crêt	x	14 56		16 08	17 08			18 06	19 10	20 02		22 02
Les Ponts	x	14 59		16 11	17 11			18 09	19 13	20 05		22 05
Vaulruz-Sud	x	15 00		16 12	17 12			18 10	19 14	20 06		22 06
Les Colombettes	x	15 02		16 14	17 14			18 12	19 16	20 08		22 08
Vuadens-Sud		15 04		16 16	17 16			18 14	19 18	20 10		x 22 10
Planchy	x	15 06		16 18	17 18			18 16	19 20	20 12		22 12
Bulle	o	15 10		16 22	17 22			18 20	19 24	20 16		22 16
Bulle		📷14 38		📷16 18	16 27	17 27	📷17 55	18 32	19 27		20 22	
La Tour-de-Trême	x				16 30	17 30		18 35	19 30		ᵗ²22 026	
Le Pâquier-Montbarry	x				16 32	17 32		18 37	19 32		ᵗ²22 028	
Gruyères	o	📷14 44		16 23	16 36	17 34	18 01	18 38	19 34		ᵗ²22 030	
Gruyères				16 24	16 37	17 35	18 02	18 39	19 35		ᵗ²22 031	
Estavannens	x				16 40	17 37		18 42	19 37		ᵗ²22 036	
Enney	x				16 41	17 38		18 43	19 38		ᵗ²22 038	
Grandvillard					16 45	17 42		18 47	19 42		ᵗ²22 041	
Neirivue	x				16 48	17 45		18 50	19 45		ᵗ²22 044	
Albeuve	x				16 50	17 47		18 52	19 47		ᵗ²22 046	
Lessoc	x				16 53	17 49		18 54	19 49		ᵗ²22 048	
Montbovon	o			📷16 43	16 59	17 54	📷18 35	18 59	19 54		20 53	
Montbovon					**17 04**			**19 04**				
Château-d'Oex 120	o				**17 19**			**19 19**				

■ SUPERTRAIN DU CHOCOLAT
SUPERPANORAMIC-EXPRESS
③ du 3 août – 19 oct

■ FONDUE-TRAIN
⑤ du 5 nov-17 déc, 7 jan-25 mars
ᵗ² Les arrêts sont déplacés en bordure de la route cantonale

Voie étroite. Classe unique

GFM, Fribourg

---

bus networks and on the municipal transport systems of 36 towns and cities. It also entitles the holder to a reduction of 25% on many mountain railways and aerial cableways. Prices range from a four-day 2nd class pass at £98 to a one-month 1st class pass at £323.

The **Swiss Flexipass** is ideal for those wanting to walk or cycle from a few

THE TRAIN TIMETABLE

The Swiss train timetable is a model of clarity. Each service is given a three-digit number; these numbers are given alongside the headings for the route descriptions throughout this book. They also appear alongside the synoptic map at the beginning of the timetable and alongside the route on the Kümmerly + Frey railway map.

At the beginning of the timetable is a list of all places served by any form of public transport. To the right of the name, bold (three-digit) numerals (300) refer to the train service, a number like 300.40 to the connecting bus service, four-digit numbers beginning with 2 to cableways, and four-digit numbers beginning with 3 to steamer services.

The bold arrows beneath the number of the timetable tell you in which direction to turn the page(s) to find the times of services in the opposite direction.

If the operation is seasonal (as for many cableways), the dates are given. Times given alongside stations are departure times unless a circle precedes the time, in which case it is the arrival time.

A number beside a station name indicates the table number of the main connecting service. A numeral in a box beside a station name indicates how many minutes you should allow to change trains.

At the head of the column of times is the train number; this number is used on the boards that indicate the location of carriages on the train (see below). Fast trains are in **bold** type; regional (stopping) trains are in normal type.

A dotted vertical line to the right of the service indicates that a supplementary charge is made (a rare stipulation). A wavy line to the left means that the train does not run every day, so a careful check should be made.

A small 'x' beside a station name means that it is a request stop at which passengers have either to tell the guard that they wish to alight, or if they are at the station, to inform the driver that they wish to board the train by depressing a button on the platform (see below).

The timetable is issued once a year at the end of May and may be purchased from railway stations and offices of Switzerland Tourism. Free pocket timetables are available for individual lines from Swiss stations.

centres: choose any three days within a 15-day period and enjoy the same benefits as the Swiss Pass.

If between two and five adults are travelling together, a 15% saving can be gained on the Swiss Pass and Flexipass through the **Saver Program** introduced in 2000.

The **Swiss Card** is valid for one month and provides a round-trip ticket from the border point or airport to any Swiss resort. It gives the holder unlimited half-fare trips on all other train, bus and steamer services, as well as excursions to most mountain tops. It is available only from Switzerland Tourism.

The **Swiss Transfer Ticket** is of particular benefit to winter sports travellers who will be likely to obtain a ski pass of some kind covering local transport, but would not wish to go further afield. The Transfer Ticket covers a one-day transfer from a border station or airport to any station in Switzerland and back. It is available only from Switzerland Tourism.

Holders of the Swiss Pass, Swiss Card or Swiss Transfer Ticket may also obtain a **Family Card** which allows children under 16 to travel free providing they are accompanied by at least one adult. The Family Card is available free to holders of these cards, providing they are bought outside Switzerland.

Regional passes

There is a wide range of regional passes which usually cover trains and buses, but the precise scope and conditions should be checked. The passes are available from railway and steamer stations in the areas concerned and from local tourist offices. Covering 7 or 15 days, some are also available from bus stations.

Appenzellerland-Toggenburg A 7-day pass covering the region.

Bernese Oberland Available between May and the end of October, it is valid for 7 or 15 days, during which you can choose 5 days for unlimited free travel on 450km (281 miles) of rail, bus and boat routes. The pass provides for 50% or 25% discounts on a further 1,000km (625 miles) of mountain railway, cablecar, chairlift and bus routes throughout the 15 days. Children up to 16 travelling with their parents have free travel while those between 16 and 25 (providing they are unmarried) travel at half price.

Chablais Regional Pass The network of narrow- and standard-gauge branch lines that leave the section of main line between Montreux and St Maurice is covered by this pass, as is the main line itself. Available for 7 days, it allows unlimited journeys on 3 days with a 50% discount on the others.

Regional Pass Lake Geneva Region Covers a large area of southwest Switzerland, extending as far east from Geneva as St Maurice and Gstaad, and as far north as Avenches and Concise. It includes all the branch lines in the area. The 7-day pass offers 3 days of unlimited free travel and four days of reductions at 25–50%.

Tell-Pass The pass covers 800km (500 miles) of railway, ship and bus routes in the area around Vierwaldstättersee. The pass is available for 7 or 15 days, and a map is provided showing the core routes on which unlimited travel is available for 2/5 days (within the 7 or 15 days) and a 50% discount on the other 5/10 days. A second category of routes is shown on which a 50% discount is available throughout the 7 or 15 days.

Passes are also available for Graubünden, Locarno/Ascona, Lugano, and Montreux/Vevey.

Useful addresses

European Rail Ltd Tavistock House North, Tavistock Square, London WC1H 9HR. Tel: 020 7387 0444; fax: 020 7387 0888; email: sales@europeanrail.demon.co.uk; web: www.european rail.com Railway travel specialists.

Ffestiniog Travel Harbour Station, Porthmadog, Gwynedd LL49 9NF. Tel: 01766 512340; fax: 01766 514715; email: info@festtravel.demon.co.uk; web: www.festtravel.co.uk Owned by the Ffestiniog Railway (so travel profits help to support the railway) with 20 years' experience of specialised help with rail travel. Organises escorted and unescorted railway-based tours.

Great Rail Journeys Ltd 71 The Mount, York YO24 1GX. Tel: 01904 679969; fax: 01904 679961. Organises escorted railway-based tours.

Rail Europe Travel Shops 179 Piccadilly, London W1V 0BA. Tel: 08705 848848. Motorail booking, tel: 08702 415415. Also sells rail tickets to 5,000 European stations.

Fly-Rail

This marvellous facility enables you to send your bags from any airport in the world right through to certain destinations when you check in to fly to Switzerland, or from the station of departure when you begin the journey home. The charge is £8.50 per item.

A special green label obtainable from Switzerland Tourism and Swissair offices should be attached to the case before it is checked in abroad. This label also serves as a customs declaration. You next see your case at the station in your Swiss destination.

On the return, cases (but not bicycles or unwieldy objects) can be sent from one of 125 Fly-Rail stations via Geneva or Zürich (or sometimes Basel) through to the airport at home. All you need is an OK confirmation on your ticket.

Another facility for the return journey is the opportunity for rail passengers at 23 stations to check in up to 24 hours before take-off and reserve a seat long before other passengers. To obtain a boarding card, you need to show your train ticket, airline ticket with OK status, and passport. The facility applies to most airlines.

The 23 stations in the scheme are Aarau, Arosa, Basel SBB, Bern, Biel/Bienne, Davos Platz, Davos Dorf, Fribourg, Geneva, Interlaken Ost, Interlaken West, Lausanne, Locarno, Lugano, Luzern, Montreux, Neuchâtel, St Gallen, St Moritz, Solothurn, Thun, Zug and Zürich.

Station facilities

The majority of Swiss stations are staffed, which makes it easier to provide a good range of facilities, especially at those most used by tourists. For example, a large number of stations change money, provide general information about the town as well as railway matters, hire bicycles (see Chapter 5), handle luggage, etc.

Internal baggage

Of great value to walkers and cyclists is the facility to send luggage from all staffed stations (all but the smallest stations and halts) to any other station, where it will be kept until the appropriate numbered form is presented.

Luggage trolleys

Some of the largest stations, such as Geneva Aéroport and Zürich Flughafen, have luggage trolleys that are designed to go on to escalators. The first experience of wheeling a trolley on to one can be daunting, but rubber grips prevent movement once the handle is released to secure the brake. In particular these trolleys make the long haul from airport carousel to train much easier.

At stations of any size there are rows of trolleys both outside and at several points along the platform. A deposit of a SFr2 coin in a slide mechanism is required to release a trolley; it can be recovered by returning the trolley to a row and inserting the key into the adjacent trolley.

Left luggage

Most large stations have both an office for left luggage and banks of lockers. The latter are usually in two sizes: the smaller at SFr3 is suitable for smaller cases and items; the larger at SFr5 is for suitcases. The coin slots take SFr1, 2 and 5 coins. Many stations have lockers only.

Credit cards

Swiss Federal Railways (and most private railways) accept American Express, Diners Club, Eurocard/Mastercard and Visa.

Refreshments

Swiss railway stations are a hub of local life, and an astonishing number of even quite small stations have cafés of such quality that they are used by people not travelling by train. At the largest stations such as Olten and Chiasso, there are restaurants with table service. Most of the larger stations and junctions have at least a buffet, and all stations have vending machines that dispense fruit juice cartons, canned drinks, chocolate, biscuits and snacks.

It is very rare for an express train not to have at least a trolley selling hot and cold drinks, rolls, chocolate, etc. The more important trains on standard and metre gauge have restaurant cars.

Platform information

Timetables displayed on platform boards are colour coded: the yellow table shows departing trains (*Abfahrt, Départ, Partenza*); the white table shows arriving trains (*Ankunft, Arrivée, Arrivo*). Stations served by inter-city trains of some length have blue boards that show the composition of trains – where the first- and second-class coaches and any restaurant or sleeping cars may be found. This board should be consulted and the direction of travel established (it's usually obvious) so that you can wait in the appropriate sector of the platform (generally A–D). The legendary punctuality of Swiss trains depends upon station stops not being exceeded, and it is no pleasure having to race a trolley of cases down the platform at the last minute.

However, since seat reservations are neither possible nor necessary, except for groups of ten or more and for such trains as the Glacier Express (as detailed in the relevant descriptions in this book), it is usually a 'question only of finding the correct class of coach rather than a specified carriage.

Request stops

At some remote, unstaffed stations and halts, particularly on narrow-gauge railways, there is a system for passengers to indicate that they wish to board the train. A button has to be pressed to activate a signal that instructs the driver to stop to pick up passengers. Notes adjacent (usually in several languages) explain the procedure. If you do not follow the correct procedure, the train will not stop unless there are passengers wishing to get off. In the timetable such stations are marked by a small 'x'.

Postbuses

The Swiss postbus system has a network of over 600 routes covering about 8,000km (5,000 miles). It evolved from the 19th-century mail coach service which in 1913 was using 2,523 horses, 2,231 coaches and 1,059 sleighs, and on which the first motor service between Bern and Detligen was introduced in 1906.

Because the Swiss believe, quite rightly, that the only sensible way to organise public transport services is to achieve the maximum degree of integration between modes, bus services are complementary to the rail network. The majority of services therefore connect with trains, steamers or mountain cableways, 'so switching from one to the other is child's play' as the postbus timetable puts it, without exaggeration.

A map of the postbus network is available from tourist offices and the timetable is laid out in a similar manner to the rail timetable. Note that an 'R' in a square box means that seats have to be reserved, but this condition applies to very few routes, such as the popular service over the Grimsel Pass between Andermatt and Meiringen (table 470.75). Some of the routes over the passes can be operated during the summer months only.

The Swiss Pass allows unlimited free travel on postbuses, though there is a small supplement on some of the mountain pass routes that are patronised primarily by tourists. Most of the special tickets are applicable only to regular or commuter use, but regional 7-day Postbus Passes are available for the following regions: Appenzell, Toggenburg, Liechtenstein, Thusis/Andeer/Splügen, Ilanz and the Upper Valais, Sion, Sierre, the Saane region/Pays d'Enhaut, Les Ormonts and Mendrisiotto. The postbus Family Pass is available from all rail and postbus offices; it allows children up to 16 to travel free of charge. Without a pass, children under 6 travel free and those between 6 and 16 pay half fare. You can carry up to 30kg per person on buses, 50kg per person on postbuses – the latter operate most non-urban services and are painted in a distinctive yellow livery with red band.

Bikes are carried whenever there is room (which is normally the case), but a phone call to check is officially recommended – telephone numbers for operators are given alongside each table in the timetable.

It almost goes without saying that the quality of the buses and their cleanliness is extremely high.

Tourist offices

Besides providing information about what there is to see and do in an area, tourist offices (TO in text) usually provide excellent maps of the town or locality. Some also help with obtaining accommodation, though a small charge is normally made for this service.

In search of steam

Details of steam railways and steamers or other forms of preserved transport are given in an annual publication, *Schweizer Ferien mit Dampf und Nostalgie*, available free from Switzerland Tourism offices.

Using this book

Place names in headings that are in upper and lower case indicate the starting or finishing points of the train service but the section describes only the part of the line between places in capital letters (eg: LUZERN–AIROLO–Lugano–Chiasso). Place names in **bold** in the text refer to stations. Cross-referencing is usually by table, and a list of tables and page numbers is given on page 394.·

Crossing the Country

Besides the expresses that bisect Switzerland, there are a number of ways to travel from one region to another; some are less well-known trains, others have been devised specifically for tourists. All journeys except the William Tell Express can be made in either direction.

WILLIAM TELL EXPRESS: Luzern–Lugano/Locarno

One of the best-known tourist services is the William Tell Express which combines a paddle-steamer for the length of Lake Luzern with a reserved first-class coach on the train from Flüelen to Lugano or Locarno (change at Bellinzona). Included in the ticket is a good three-course lunch in the steamer's first-class restaurant, an English guide to the sights en route and a souvenir of the journey. The journey takes 6 hours to either destination. (See Chapter 14 and table 600 for the journey.)

STRESA EXPRESS: Interlaken–Stresa/Isola Bella

Operated by BLS once a week, the day excursion takes the Lötschberg route to Brig and continues through the Simplon Tunnel into Italy to the resort of Stresa, where there is a boat connection for the island of Isola Bella and its baroque palace. The ticket includes admission to the palace and the short boat journey back to Stresa in time for lunch (optional). The return journey takes a little under 12 hours. See tables 310 and 300 for the journey.

ZERMATT EXPRESS: Interlaken–Zermatt

Operated by BLS once a week, the day excursion leaves after an early breakfast, taking the Lötschberg route to Brig where you transfer to the metre-gauge Brig–Visp–Zermatt Railway train. You arrive in Zermatt in time for morning coffee and leave 4^1/2 hours later, allowing time for a trip up to Gornergrat. The return journey takes a little under 12 hours. See tables 310, 300 and 140 for the journey.

GOLDEN PASS ROUTE

One of the main promotions by Switzerland Tourism is the Golden Pass route which begins at Zürich and goes via Luzern, Interlaken, Jungfraujoch, Zweisimmen, Montreux (by the Panoramic Express) to Geneva. Nights can be spent at resorts of the traveller's choice. At present it is necessary to change trains at Zweisimmen and Interlaken Ost, but the installation of a metre-gauge third rail over the 53km (33 miles) between these stations will allow through running.

GOLDEN PASS PANORAMIC:
Montreux–Zweisimmen–Lenk

This name is given to the tourist trains operated by the Montreux–Oberland Bernois railway over its scenic route. The trains have observation cars at each end with an elevated driver's cab so that passengers have an unobstructed view of the track ahead or behind. The trains includes a lounge bar car. The service runs three times a day between July and October, and the journey takes just over 2 hours. Seat reservations, obtainable through offices of Switzerland Tourism, are strongly advisable in the high season. Booking for groups is obligatory. See table 120 for the journey. MOB website: www.mob.ch

GLACIER EXPRESS: Zermatt–St Moritz

The first Glacier Express between Zermatt and St Moritz ran on 25 June 1930, only a few weeks after the section between Visp and Brig was electrified. Originally a summer-only service, the train now runs all through the year, thanks to elaborate avalanche-protection works. See tables 140, 610 and 940 for the journey.

The Glacier Express is the slowest express in the world, averaging 36km/h (22mph), but it is such a remarkably scenic and varied journey that few passengers would want to lose a minute of the 8-hour journey. Indeed, it is probably the most popular of the tourist trains. There are two to three trains a day in each direction made up of special coaches with panoramic windows and restaurant car.

Rhaetian Railways also operates a luxury train named the Alpine Classic Pullman Express, which runs about ten times a year from St Moritz to Zermatt. The package includes three nights in luxury, first class hotels at either end and a gourmet lunch in the period dining-car en route. Contact Rhaetian Railways (tel: 081/254 91 04; fax: 081/254 91 05; email: contact@rhb.ch; web: www.rhb.ch).

PALM EXPRESS: St Moritz–Lugano–Locarno–Brig–Zermatt

The longest section of this 11-hour journey, from St Moritz to Locarno, is covered by PTT bus, taking a route southwest from St Moritz through the lovely Bregaglia Valley, which is not on the railway. The bus follows the shores of Lake Como and then Lake Lugano to Locarno. There, passengers transfer to the metre-gauge railway through the Centovalli to Domodóssola, where a bus awaits for the journey over the Simplon Pass to Brig. The final section is by the metre-gauge Brig–Zermatt railway. For those who have travelled on the Glacier Express, it is an attractive way to retrace one's steps, perhaps as far as Brig. See tables 620 and 140 for the journey.

BERNINA EXPRESS: Chur–St Moritz–Tirano–Lugano

This train takes in the final part of the Glacier Express route (travelling from Zermatt) and continues over the Bernina Pass, the highest rail crossing of the

Alps, to Tirano. The journey takes 4½ hours, so the return trip can be made in a day with over 2 hours in Tirano for lunch. In summer there is the option of continuing by bus to Lugano station and town centre, which takes a further 3 hours. See tables 940 and 950 for the journey.

HEIDILAND-BERNINA EXPRESS:
Landquart–Klosters–Tirano

First operated in 1995, this train serves the resorts of Klosters and Davos and like the Bernina Express makes possible a day excursion to Tirano with a little over 1½ hours for lunch. See tables 910, 940 and 950 for the journey.

ENGADIN STAR:
Landquart–Saglians (National Park)–St Moritz–Albula–Chur

Made possible by the opening of the Vereina Tunnel in November 1999, this train offers the fastest link from the national rail network to St Moritz.

VORALPEN EXPRESS: Luzern–Romanshorn

Linking two of Switzerland's largest expanses of water, lakes Luzern and Constance, the Voralpen Express runs at 2-hourly intervals, takes 2½ hours and has a bistro car. It provides connections for Einsiedeln at Biberbrugg and for the Appenzeller Bahn at Herisau and St Gallen. See tables 600, 670 and 870 for the journey.

The extraordinary rock formations in Val d'Hérens south of Sion

Walking and Cycling

WALKING

It would be hard to find a country with better provision for the walker than Switzerland. The superb public transport system takes you to even the remotest of places to begin a walk, and the country has over 50,000km (31,250 miles) of uniformly marked paths. Almost every station in the country has a number of suggested walks, indicated by small yellow signposts with black lettering listing destinations, usually with walking times. The use of yellow is perpetuated in the occasional use of an arrow where there is possible doubt about the direction of the path, and on small boards making special requests, such as not to leave the path through a nature reserve. Sometimes there is simply a sign saying *Wanderweg*, meaning footpath, without a destination being given.

Even on these paths, for which no particular knowledge or experience is required, it is advisable to wear at least proper walking shoes; trainers are not a good idea. It is always sensible to take weatherproof clothing appropriate for the season, sufficient food and drink for a longer walk, and a small first aid kit. In summer, and during all seasons at higher altitudes, it is wise to take a high-factor sunscreen or sunblock and to wear a hat – especially children with sensitive skin or fair hair. The lips should also be protected. Always take sunglasses or goggles. Don't attempt to do too much and try to maintain a steady even pace; walking fast with frequent stops induces fatigue.

The next category of path is the mountain route (*Bergweg*), denoted by a red horizontal flash at the end of the yellow signposts. For these walks it is necessary to be fit, well prepared and to have a head for heights, since sections of the paths may be narrow with long drops. Precautions to be borne in mind:

- hiking boots are essential;
- plan routes bearing in mind the limitations of the weakest member of the party, and do not go alone unless you are highly experienced;
- a first aid kit, provisions, protective clothing, a small torch and topographic maps are essential;
- a telescopic walking stick will help with descents;
- the weather in mountain areas can change rapidly, so it is advisable to obtain a forecast before setting out and to be prepared for a deterioration in conditions;

- always inform someone where you are going, and what time you expect to return;
- set off early and return early, allowing time to return if you encounter difficulties;
- be careful if lighting a fire, and never do so in dry weather;
- close gates behind you, be careful of plants and animals, and leave no litter.

The most difficult category of route is indicated by direction signs with a blue background and white typography. These are alpine walks which lead into trackless terrain, across snowfields and glaciers or up short sections of rock climbing. These should be attempted only by those who have experience of such terrain and are extremely fit; even then, it is unwise to go without a mountain guide who will be aware of localised dangers and the risk of avalanches. In addition to the above equipment, it is vital to take an altimeter and compass, rope and ice-axe.

Special walks or combined walking and cycling itineraries

Less commonly seen are brown signs with white typography; these denote cultural walks which might follow a Roman road, pilgrim route or pack-horse trail. Alternatively they may have a theme such as viticulture, castles or mills.

Some of these are very long routes that could form the basis of walking holidays taking several weeks or much shorter tours tackling a section of the route. Equally some can be covered by bike, using the railway to send your bike on when you come to a walking section, or by hiring a bike. Six of these longer-distance footpaths are:

- Roman roads, the route describing the letter 'n' through the country from the St Bernard Pass, through Martigny, Lausanne, Payerne, Murten, Augst (near Basel), Zürich and south to the Septimer Pass and Chiasso.
- The pilgrimage routes of St James, stretching from Geneva in the southwest to St Gallen in the northeast, with various branches and alternative routes.
- The Great Walser Route, which links the settlements of this nomadic tribe and takes in some of Switzerland's most lovely areas, from Zermatt and Saas Fee to the border with Austria beyond Klosters. This is a fairly taxing route for more experienced walkers.
- Mule tracks and long-distance trade routes, a series of suggested journeys rather than one itinerary. They take in some of the great mountain passes.
- The Swiss Path, the easiest and shortest, created to mark the 700th anniversary of the Swiss Confederation. Described in Chapter 14.
- Paths from the Steam Age. Three historical north–south routes, which give an insight into the industrial past, from Vallorbe–Bex, Basel–Lake Lugano, Winterthur–Sargans.

The PTT produces English-language leaflets describing walks that can be planned in conjunction with postal buses.

CYCLING

Cycling in Switzerland is not as laughable a proposition as the faint-hearted might think. There is plenty of gently undulating countryside and many of the alpine valleys have cycle routes along their bottom. Half the Swiss population – 3.5 million people – own a bicycle, and most cities and towns have good networks of cycle tracks and lanes. The highly developed environmental conscience evident in many Swiss people translates into a more considered choice of transport, so cycling in urban areas especially makes a real impact on reducing pollution. In Basel, for example, 40% of journeys using some form of mechanical transport are by bike (30% public transport, 30% car). In Canton Zürich there are spaces for 4,040 cars at stations – but accommodation for 12,000 bikes.

The consequence for the visitor is a developed infrastructure of cycle tracks, signs, maps and rental facilities. The railways, too, are keen to exploit the natural synergy between bike and train: most trains carry bikes, and there is covered accommodation for bikes at the majority of stations. On the Brünig line between Luzern and Interlaken, for example, the twice-daily Brunig Panoramic Express has an entire car adapted for cycle carriage. There are a few lines that do not carry bicycles, such as the Centovalli in Ticino and the lines in the Upper Engadine, so it is important to check. All SBB trains carry bikes except the few EuroCity trains (marked 'EC' in the timetable); the daily charge is under £4 for Regional trains, and under £7 for InterCity and Direct services. Cyclists have to present themselves at least 20 minutes before the scheduled departure time of the train.

Best of all, bikes can be hired at 180 railway stations; in 1999 they hired over 100,000 bikes. Three types of bike are available: a city/country (on-road) bike with 7 gears; a mountain bike with 21 gears; and a child's mountain bike with 7 gears. The bikes are of good quality with Shimano gears. It is advisable to reserve bikes a day or two ahead, especially in July and August, but not later than 18.00 the previous day. Rates are based on $\frac{1}{2}$, 1 or 7 day rentals. Bikes hired for a full day can be returned to a different station (enabling you to cycle downhill only) for which a small charge is levied; bikes taken for $\frac{1}{2}$ day have to be returned to the hiring station. A family package is available for the hire of two country bikes and one bike for a child under 16 years of age.

At many stations there are cycling information boards, usually denoted by a red 'i'. A map illustrates the area's cycling routes with gradients and other useful information. Bike routes are marked by red signs with white lettering.

Cycle routes

With so many cycle routes, it is almost invidious singling out a few for mention.

From the edge of Zürich there is a separate cycling path beside the River Glatt to Oberglatt, Höri, Niederglatt, Bülach, Glattfelden, Zweidlen and Eglisau. In the Bernese Oberland, there is a route from Kandersteg to Spiez which continues on through Thun, Bern, Aarberg, Solothurn and Olten to

Aarau. Also in the Bernese Oberland are some lovely paths through the valleys of the Black and White Lütschine to Grindelwald and Lauterbrunnen respectively, and some good paths around Interlaken.

Canton Solothurn has developed some attractive long-distance routes through easy cycling terrain, and, in common with most of the cycling initiatives in the country, there are good leaflets and maps to promote their use.

One of the best areas for cycling is the Upper Engadine and along the routes of the Rhätische Bahn in Graubünden. Two days' notice is all that is required to pick up a hire bike at any station on their system. Along the valley of the Upper Engadine between Samedan and Scuol-Tarasp is a 60km (37 miles) cycle route linking the villages along the valley – one of the loveliest in all Switzerland and a cyclist's dream.

Another, much longer journey in the area is between Thusis and Bellinzona. The old road is almost free of traffic now that a motorway has been unforgivably driven through this lovely series of valleys and tunnelled under the San Bernardino Pass.

Off-road cycling
Mountain-bikers will find Switzerland offers unique opportunities: the bike trails in the Bernese Oberland, for example, are surrounded by views that would be hard to beat anywhere you're likely to get a mountain bike. Dedicated mountain bike trails are indicated by roadside symbols similar to the conventional bike routes, but with the bike's front wheel raised.

The Swiss ask for bikers to follow a simple code:

- Mountain bike riders stick to existing tracks, roads and specially marked mountain bike route.
- Bikers give way to walkers in all circumstances and are polite and considerate towards them.
- Bikers respect all forms of plant and animal life, shut gates behind them and do not ride cross-country.
- Bikers do not leave litter behind.

Taking your bike to Switzerland
The easiest way is probably by Eurostar from London Waterloo to Gare du Nord in Paris, taking a quiet route (if you can find one) to Gare du Lyon and taking the TGV to Bern or Lausanne. Each Eurostar has space for eight bikes, but they must be reserved in advance. The only difference in the formalities at Waterloo is that bikes have to be checked in at the Euro Dispatch Centre (tel: 0990 850850) which is in Lower Road, on the opposite side of Waterloo from the International Station. Your bike is not guaranteed to travel on the same train, so dispatch some hours before you travel may be wise.

Bikes are accommodated on TGV and Corail coaches free of charge providing they can be folded or their wheels removed to fit into special covers that measure no more than 120 x 90cm. Bikes in these covers can be taken on the train as hand luggage. Most luggage vans on regional trains in France accept bikes, though the capacity of many is limited to three. Bikes are not allowed on the Paris Métro system or the central sections of the cross-Paris RER routes.

Alternatively you can take your bike on the Eurotunnel Shuttle trains from Folkestone to Coquelles. Eurotunnel uses a vehicle and trailer to ferry up to 12 bikes and their riders through the tunnel three times a day in each direction between the exhibition centres in Folkestone and Calais. Reservations are compulsory; tel: 08705 353535; fax 01303 288784; web: www.eurotunnel.com (Mon–Fri 07.00–23.00, Sat 08.00–18.00, Sun 08.00–19.00).

MAPS AND GUIDES FOR WALKING AND CYCLING

Switzerland's two principal cartographic companies, Kümmerly + Frey and the Federal Office of Topography, produce excellent ranges of maps for walkers and cyclists. These maps and other maps of the country may be obtained from Stanfords, 12–14 Long Acre, Covent Garden, London WC2E 9LP. For the mail order service, tel: 020 7836 1321; fax: 020 7836 0189; web: www.stanfords.co.uk

Walking

The Federal Office of Topography produces a set of 1:50,000 scale hiking maps in conjunction with the Swiss Hiking Federation. They show public transport as well as marked hiking and mountain trails:

Basel 213T	Avenches 242T	St-Cergue 260T
Liestal 214T	Bern 243T	Rochers de Naye 262T
Baden 215T	Escolzmatt 244T	Wildstrubel 263T
Frauenfeld 216T	Stans 245T	Jungfrau 264T
Arbon 217T	Klausenpass 246T	Nufenenpass 265T
Clos de Doubs 222T	Sardona 247T	Valle Leventina 266T
Delélemont 223T	Prättigau 248T	San Bernardino 267T
Zürich 225T	Tarasp 249T	Julierpass 268T
Rapperswil 226T	La Sarraz 251T	Genève 270T
Appenzell 227T	Buklle 252T	St Maurice 272T
Le Locle 213T	Gantrisch 253T	Montana 273T
Vallonde St-Imier 232T	Interlaken 254T	Visp 274T
Solothurn 233T	Sustenpass 255T	Val Verzasca 276T
Willisau 234T	Disentis/Munster 256T	Martigny 282T
Rotkreuz 235T	Safiental 257T	Arolla 283T
Lachen 236T	Bergün/Bravuogn 258T	Mischabel 284T
Val de Travers 241T	Ofenpass 259T	

The Kümmerly + Frey range of maps produced for walkers is very comprehensive and is to a scale of 1:60,000, except where stated. The list includes the ISBN number needed for ordering; this should be preceded by Kümmerly + Frey's identification number, 3-259-:

Bern and the Bernese Oberland
Berner Jura–Laufental–Seeland 00801-2
Berner Mittelland 00803-9
Emmental–Oberaargau 00802-0
Jungfrau-Region–Oberhasli 00804-7
Saanenand–Simmental–Frutigland 00805-5
Thunersee 00920-5 (1:33,333)
Zulgtal 00885-3
Berner Oberland 00901-9 (1:120,000)

Eastern Switzerland
Glarnerland–Walensee 00865-9
Schaffhausen–Winterthur 00861-6
St Gallen–Toggenburg–Appenzellerland 00864-0
Thurgau–Bodensee 00863-2
Zürich 00862-4

Ticino
Ascona–Losone–Ronco–Brissago 00333-9
Tessin (Ticino) 00904-3 (1:120,000)
Ticino (North)–Sopraceneri 00831-4
Ticino–Sottoceneri 00832-2

Graubünden
Hinterrheintäler 00812-8
Oberengadin 00815-2
Prättigau–Albula 00813-6
Surselva 00811-X
Unterengadin 00814-4
Region Lenzerheide 00312-6
Graubünden 00902-7 (1:120,000)

Northwest and Jura
Aargau–Basel-Stadt–Basel-Landschaft–Olten 00881-0
Chasseral–Neuenburg–Val de Travers–Ste-Croix 00883-7
Delsberg–Pruntrut–Biel–Solothurn 00882-9
Lausanne–La Côte–St-Cergue–Vallée de Joux 00884-5

Valais
Aletsch–Goms–Brig–Simplon 00821-7
Grand St Bernard–Dents du Midi–Les Diablerets 00824-1
Saastal, Saas Fee 00322-3 (1:40,000)
Simplon Süd 00323-1 (1:40,000)
Tour Monte Rosa 00321-5
Val d'Anniviers–Val d'Hérens–Montana 00823-3
Visp–Zermatt–Saas Fee–Grächen 00822-5
Wallis [Valais] 00903-5 (1:120,000)

Suisse romande

Freiburg–Gruyère–Lausanne–Yverdon 00841-1
Genève 00842-X
Schwarzseegebiet–Plasselb–Jaun 00342-8 (1:25,000)
Pays d'Enhaut 00326-6

Central Switzerland

Brunnen/Schwyzerland 00371-1 (1:40,000)
Flühli-Sörenberg and Oberer Brienzersee 00378-9 (1:40,000)
Kanton Uri 00873-X
Luzern–Obwalden–Nidwalden 00871-3
Schwyz–Zug–Vierwaldstättersee 00872-1
St Gotthard 00335-5

Miscellaneous

Parc Naziunal 00313-4 (1:45,000)

Cycling

Many of the cantons and urban areas produce their own maps showing cycle routes. For example, the regional tourist office for the Ticino produces a leaflet in four languages, including English, entitled *Cycling Itineraries in Southern Switzerland*. These are obtainable from tourist offices.

Kümmerly + Frey produces a national map to 1:275,000 scale showing various categories of roads and paths: bicycle paths, paved agricultural roads, roads with little traffic, roads without solid surfaces, bad paths, roads with medium traffic, dangerous connecting roads, and roads to be avoided at weekends. It also shows where there are steep gradients. Stations where bicycles may be hired are marked. The company also produces a large range of local cycling maps to 1:60,000 scale. The list includes the ISBN number needed for ordering; this should be preceded by Kümmerly + Frey's identification number, 3-259-:

Basel–Aargau 00507-2
Bern–Thun–Fribourg– Emmental 00510-2
Berner Oberland 00506-4
Biel–Solothurn–Oberaargau 00509-9
Bodensee–Thurgau 00503-X
Franches–Montagnes–Ajoie–Laufental 00511-0
Genève 00513-3
Goms–Aletsch 00596-X
Lausanne–Fribourg 00514-5
Lausanne–Vallée de Joux 00513-7
Locarno–Bellinzona–Lugano–Varese 00516-1
Luzern–Ob- und Nidwalden 00508-0
Neuchâtel–Pontarlier–Trois Lacs 00512-9
Sargans–Chur–Domleschg 00517-X

Schaffhausen–Winterthur–Wutachtal 00501-3
St Gallen–Appenzell Liechtenstein 00504-8
Sargans–Chur–Domleschg 00517-X
Zug–Schwyz–Uri–Glarus 00505-6
Zürich 00502-1

Part Two

The Guide

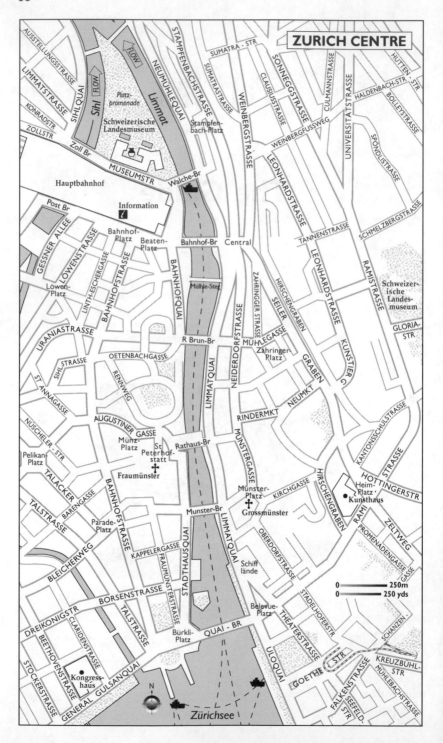

Zürich

Switzerland's largest city is probably not as well known as a tourist destination as it deserves to be. Its international reputation as one of the world's foremost financial centres has perhaps distracted attention from its other qualities. For those who know the city, it came as no surprise when Zürich came second among world cities for quality of life, in a 1999 poll conducted by one of the world's largest human resources consultancies. With a delightful old town straddling the Limmat River, some most attractive streets of good shops, 34 museums, 14 theatres, 51 cinemas, an opera house and many concert halls, the city has a great deal to offer the visitor.

The city's origins pre-date the birth of Christ: in 15BC the Romans established a customs post here, though the first record of Zürich as a town was in AD929. The government of the city was taken over by the guilds in 1336, and it joined the Swiss Confederation in 1351. It was in Zürich in 1523 that the great reformer Zwingli sparked off the Reformation in Switzerland. The first purely Swiss railway opened for traffic between Zürich and Baden in 1847, and 30 years later the city's stock exchange opened, growing to become the fourth most important in the world today. Zürich is the world's biggest gold trading centre.

Culturally the city's most vibrant years were probably around World War I when political and artistic refugees swelled the ranks of the intelligentsia. The most tangible product of that time was the founding of Dadaism in 1916 at the Cabaret Voltaire on Spiegelgasse.

The size of the city is modest (a population of 363,000) and the compact central area is easy to explore on foot. The region enjoys outstandingly good and well-integrated public transport, as well as facilities for cyclists. A measure of its efficiency is that public transport accounts for 60% of journeys to work and has cut by a quarter the number of people using cars. As a consequence Zürich's air quality is among the best in urban Europe.

Arriving in Zürich

Whether travelling by train from elsewhere in Switzerland, by international train or from the airport, passengers arrive at the imposing terminus of Zürich Hauptbahnhof (HB), opened in 1871. To reach the tourist office, go straight ahead from the end of the platforms, into what would be the choir of a cathedral, and the tourist office is on the left. Ask for a map of the S-Bahn network which shows all the railway lines and connecting bus routes on one side and on the other the tram network and connecting buses, as well as the train and bus network around Winterthur. The office supplies two maps: a Cityplan of the centre and a Stadtplan showing most of Zürich. Also ask for the fortnightly *Zürich News and Info*, which contains general information about the city as well as current events, and for a copy of the leaflet *Ride with us*.

Using public transport

Public transport in Zürich is organised by Zurcher Verkehrsverbund, which produces a leaflet explaining the ticket options and where and how to buy tickets. Single tickets are of course available, but the best value is the range of day or multiple day passes. The latter can be used by one person on six days, or by several people travelling together, invalidating one section of the pass per person. The city is divided into tariff zones, which are shown on the S-Bahn map. Children under six travel free, and those between six and 16 travel half price. Tickets cannot be purchased on trams or buses, and a fine of SFr50 is imposed on anyone travelling without a ticket.

Holders of Swiss and Flexi Passes can use the whole network and boat services free; Eurailpasses and Swiss Cards are valid on S-Bahn lines and on the lake.

S-Bahn, tram and bus services operate from 05.30 to 24.00.

Besides the railways, trams and buses, there are three funiculars in Zürich. From the area called Central – one of the principal tram junctions just the other side of Bahnhof Bridge from the station – a funicular ascends to the Institute of Technology and the university. From Römerhofplatz (on tram lines 3, 8 and 15) a funicular rises to the wooded Dolder where there are walks, tennis courts and a golf course. The largest area of woods above the city, on the Zürichberg, can be reached by funicular from Rigiplatz (tram lines 9 and 10 or bus route 33) to Rigiblick (so named because the Rigi can be seen from there).

Exploring the old town

The best way to see the old town is on foot, not least because many of its streets have restricted access for motor vehicles, though there is a sightseeing tram with refreshments available. The tourist office has a leaflet *Walks through Zürich* with four suggested itineraries, which take in most of the centre's main sights. The order is immaterial, but there are some streets and buildings that should not be missed.

Before leaving the station it is worth spending a few minutes admiring it and the statue outside to the right; this tribute to the great railway magnate Alfred Escher was created by Richard Kissling in 1889. You can reach the old town in minutes either by taking a tram (6, 7, 11 or 13) or by walking down Bahnhofstrasse, the city's principal shopping street which was built on the site of the city walls. Softened by trees and mostly free of traffic, it is a pleasure to walk along. Turn left into Augustinergasse which is lined with 17th- and 18th-century houses, many with bay windows. The street is broken by Münzplatz on which stands the Augustinerkirche, built in the late 13th century and secularised in 1525; its choir was later converted into the mint. The nave was returned to religious use in 1842 and the whole building was restored in 1958–9. There is also a fountain in the square, one of 1,030 in the city – locals insist the water is safe to drink. At No 9 Augustinergasse is Museum Strauhof (see below).

The street leads into the delightful St Peterhofstatt (St Peter's Square). Sitting in the quiet shade of its central tree, surrounded by historic buildings and the only sound coming from the modern sculptural fountain, it is hard to believe one is in the centre of the country's largest city. On one side is St Peter's, Zürich's oldest parish church, though this is the fourth building on the site. The tower dates from c1450 and has the largest clock face in Europe, at 8.7m (28½ft), which was installed in 1534. Restoration in the 1970s returned the church to its 1705 state when the nave was rebuilt. The barrel vault has fine stucco, the pulpit is oddly positioned in the arch of the apse, and stalls line the perimeter of the whole church. The church contains the grave of the theologian Johann Caspar Lavater (1741–1801) whose house (No 6) is on the opposite side of the square; he was visited here by Goethe. The pastor of St Peter's for 23 years, Lavater was shot by a French soldier while tending the wounded during the seizure of the city.

To the north of St Peter's Square is the Lindenhof, a raised area on which the Roman customs post was sited, followed by a ten-towered fort. This was enlarged c800 by Charlemagne into a palace that was occupied by German kings and emperors in the following century, law being administered from under the linden tree. The palace was destroyed in 1218 when Zürich became a free, imperial city. Today it is a park with a giant chess board and views across the Limmat.

To the south of St Peter's Square is the Fraumünster, founded in 853 as a convent for noble ladies by the German King Ludwig, whose daughter Hildegard was the first abbess. Having been suppressed in 1534 and adapted to become the Stadthaus, the convent has been reduced to a few remains: part of the Romanesque south tower, with blind arcading; part of the cloister; and most importantly the choir, with its screen of 1470, and the transept, both of which have stained glass by Marc Chagall, installed in 1970 and 1978. The keystones in the vaults of the transept are also noteworthy.

Adjacent to the Fraumünster is the Zunfthaus zur Meisen, the vintners' guild house that was built in rococo style in the mid-18th century. This now contains the ceramic collection of the National Museum (see below).

Across the Münster Bridge, at the end on the right is the neo-classical Helmhaus of 1791–4, which is now used for exhibitions. Adjacent to it towards the lake is the Wasserkirche, which was on an island until the extension of Limmatquai in 1839. The late Gothic church was built in 1479–84 on the site of a much earlier church. It was secularised in 1521, and for nearly 300 years from 1631 was used as the city library. It reverted to being a church in 1942 and has stained glass by A Giacometti.

Continuing into Münsterplatz, the Grossmünster is the largest church in the city, its twin towers with their octagonal lanterns dominating the skyline. Built on the site of an earlier building, the present Romanesque basilica was begun before 1100 and largely completed by 1230. It was here that Zwingli preached. The nave is unusually high, and the church contains complete and fragmented wall-paintings of the 13th and 14th centuries. In the crypt is a statue made in 1460 of Charlemagne, the founder of the original church on this site. The stained glass designed by A Giacometti was installed in 1932. The cloisters of c1200, which are now part of the university theological faculty, should not be missed for their mix of original and replacement sculptural decoration. (Open: Mon–Sat 10.00–16.00, Sun after services until 16.00.)

A little to the northwest is the Rathaus, built in 1694–8 on the barrel vault of the old one. Along the Limmatquai between Münster and Bahnhof bridges is a series of guildhalls, some with origins in the 13th century but mostly rebuilt in the 16th to 18th centuries.

Turning right up Mühlegasse to Zähringerplatz is the Central Library, built in 1915–17 on the site of a Dominican monastery. The state archives are housed in the adjacent former Predigerkirche, completed in 1269 with a Gothic choir added in the following century.

All the streets to the south of the Library are worth exploring, as nearly all have buildings of interest. Neumarkt and Rindermarkt form the longest street of the old town. Speigelgasse has a 14th-century tower (No 26). No 11 was the home of Lavater in the 1740s, and No 12 was the house in which the German poet Georg Büchner, author of *Wozzeck*, died in 1837 and also the home of Lenin until his portentous return to Russia in 1917.

Museums
Zürich has 34 museums, and a separate guide to them is available from the tourist office. Unless otherwise stated, entrance is free.

Swiss National Museum (Schweizerische Landesmuseum) As its name suggests, this is the most wide-ranging museum in Zürich, housed in a purpose-built neo-Gothic edifice designed to fuse various Swiss styles to resemble a castle. Completed in 1898, the museum has artefacts dating from the Stone Age to the 19th century. The entrance is to the left of the archway, just beyond the St Gotthard stage-coach. Its sections include pre- and early history, weapons, flags, uniforms and costumes, metalwork from pewter to gold, glass, jewellery, textiles, ceramics, sculpture, paintings, musical instruments, watches and farming implements. There are also entire rooms from medieval or Renaissance buildings that have been dismantled and reconstructed.
Museumstrasse 2 (adjacent to main railway station on north side, connected by subway). Trams 4, 11, 13, 14. Open: Tue–Sun 10.30–17.00. Tel: 01/218 65 11.

Zürich Art Gallery (Kunsthaus Zürich) The gallery has been successively enlarged since 1910 to house a large collection ranging from 15th-century religious works to late 20th-century paintings. Amongst the international artists represented are El Greco, Bellotto, Guardi, Canaletto, Hals, Hobbema, Cranach the Elder, Jan Breughel the Elder, Renoir, Courbet, Seurat, Manet, Corot, Bonnard, Rodin, Gauguin, Klee, Kandinsky, Chagall, Van Gogh, Picasso, Magritte, Ernst, Miró and Kokoschka. Swiss painters include Angelica Kauffmann, Böcklin, Füssli, Segantini, Anker and Hodler. There are changing exhibitions of international and local artists.

Among the best-known paintings is the *Gotthard Post*, painted in 1873 by Rudolph Koller, which was commissioned as a present for Alfred Escher, whose statue stands beside the station. It has been described as the most popular painting in Swiss art.
Heimplatz 1. Trams 3, 5, 8, 9 or bus 31 to Kunsthaus. Open: Tue–Thur 10.00–21.00, Fri–Sun 10.00–17.00. Tel: 01/251 67 55. Admission charge.

Museum Rietberg   Housed in a neo-classical mansion built in 1857, this collection of non-European art includes sculpture from India, China, Japan, Africa and South America.
Gablerstrasse 15. Tram 7 to Museum Rietberg. Open: Tue–Sun 10.00–17.00. Tel: 01/202 45 28. Admission charge.

E G Bührle Collection (Siftung Sammlung E G Bührle)   An important collection of the work of mainly French 19th- and 20th-century artists, including work by Gauguin. Special exhibitions.
Zollikerstrasse 172. Trams 2, 4 to Wildbachstrasse or bus 77 to Altenhofstrasse. Open: Tue and Fri 14.00–17.00, Wed 17.00–20.00. Tel: 01/422 00 86. Admission charge.

Foundation for Constructivist Art (Haus für konstructive und konkrete Kunst)   Changing exhibitions of Swiss and international artists of the constructivist movement.
Seefeldstrasse 317. Trams 2, 4, S-Bahn 7, Zolliker bus to Tiefenbrunnen. Open: Tue–Fri 10.00–12.00, 14.00–17.00, Sat–Sun 10.00–17.00. Tel: 01/381 38 08. Admission charge.

Collection of Prints and Drawings of the Federal Institute of Technology (Graphische Sammlung der ETH)   Large collection of woodcuts, etchings and engravings by European masters such as Mantegna, Dürer, Rembrandt, Canaletto, Piranesi, Goya and Picasso.
ETH, Rämistrasse 101 (entrance on Künstlergasse). Trams 6, 9, 10 to ETH-Zentrum. Open: Mon–Fri 10.00–17.00, Wed –20.00. Tel: 01/632 40 46.

Museum of Domestic Culture in Zürich (Wohnmuseum Bärengasse)   Situated in two re-erected houses of the 16th and 17th centuries, the museum's rooms are furnished to reflect the decorative arts from 1650 to 1840. Special exhibitions. Doll collection.
Bärengasse 20-22 (entrance on Basteiplatz). Trams 2, 6, 7, 8, 9, 11, 13 to Paradeplatz. Open: Tue–Fri, Sun 10.00–12.00, 14.00–17.00. Sat 10.00–12.00, 14.00–16.00. Tel: 01/218 65 58.

Porcelain and Faience Exhibition of the Swiss National Museum (Keramiksammlung Zunfthaus zur Meisen)   The setting of this museum is Zürich's most elegant guildhall, built by David Morf in 1752-7. Its

displays include 18th-century Swiss faience and porcelain produced in Zürich (1763–90) and Nyon (1781–1813).
Münsterhof 20 (first-floor entrance on Fraumünster side). Trams 2, 6, 7, 8, 9, 11, 13 to Paradeplatz. Open: Tue–Sun 10.30–17.00. Tel: 01/221 28 07.

Archaeological Collection of the University (Archäologische Sammlung) Collection of originals found in Egypt, Mesopotamia, Assyria, Persia, Greece and Etruria (objects found in Switzerland are in the National Museum). *Rämistrasse 73. Trams 6, 9 to ETH-Zentrum. Open: Tue–Fri 13.00–18.00, Sat–Sun 11.00–17.00. Tel: 01/634 28 11.*

North American Indian Museum (Indianermuseum) Containing 1,400 artefacts relating to the Indians of North America, this is the only museum devoted to the subject in western Europe. *Schilhaus Feldstrasse, Feldstrasse 89. Tram 8 or bus 31 to Hohlstrasse. Open: Wed, Fri and Sat 14.00–17.00, Thur 17.00–20.00, Sun 10.00–13.00. Tel/fax: 01/241 00 50.*

Museum of Arts and Crafts (Museum für Gestaltung) Changing exhibitions of everyday design and visual communication. Collection of graphics, design and 200,000 Swiss posters. *Ausstellungsstrasse 60. Trams 4, 13 to Museum für Gestaltung. Open: Tue–Fri 10.00–18.00, Wed –21.00, Sat–Sun 11.00–18.00. Tel: 01/446 22 11. Admission charge.*

Central Library (Zentralbibliothek Zürich) Reading room. Collection of manuscripts, maps and music. North American Library. *Zähringerplatz 6. Trams 4, 15 to Rudolf-Brun-Brücke. Tram 3, Bus 31 to Neumarkt. Open: Mon–Fri 08.00–20.00, Sat 08.00–17.00. Tel: 01/268 31 00.*

Thomas Mann Archives The study and library of the German novelist, with documents of his life and work. Mann left Germany for Switzerland in 1933 after expressing opposition to the Nazis; he lived in Küsnacht until moving to the United States before World War II. He returned to Switzerland after the war and died in hospital in Zürich in 1955. He is buried at Kilchberg. *Schönberggasse 15 (second floor). Trams 6, 9 to ETH-Zentrum, 5 to Kantonsschule. Open: Wed and Sat 14.00–16.00 or by telephone appointment. Tel: 01/632 40 45.*

Collection of the Cultural History of Coffee (Johann Jacobs Museum) Artefacts, books, paintings and special exhibitions on the history of coffee since the 16th century. *Seefeldquai 17/Corner of Feldeggstrasse. Trams 2, 4 to Feldeggstrasse. Open: Fri–Sat, 14.00–17.00, Sun 10.00–17.00. Tel: 01/388 61 51.*

Mill Museum (Mühlerama) Housed in a belle époque-style former brewery that was converted to a mill in 1913, the museum is devoted to the history of milling, following the course of the grain through the building's four storeys until it emerges as flour. Sections on nutrition and storage. *Seefeldstrasse 231. Trams 2, 4 to Wildbachstrasse or train/Zollikerbus to Tiefenbrunnen. Open: Tue–Sat 14.00–17.00, Sun 13.30–18.00. Tel: 01/422 76 60. Admission charge.*

Museum of Tin Figures (Zinnfiguren-Museum)   Collection of tin toys and figures, and Swiss history in tin figures.
Obere Zäune 19. Trams 4, 15 to Rathaus. Open: Mon, Tue, Sat 14.00–16.00, Sun 11.00–15.00. Admission charge. Tel: 01/262 57 20.

Zürich Toy Museum (Zürcher Spielzeugmuseum)   All manner of European toys from the end of the 18th to the early 20th centuries.
Ecke Fortunagasse 15 (fifth floor, lift). Trams 6, 7, 11, 13 to Renneweg/Augustinergasse. Open: Mon–Fri 14.00–17.00, Sat 1300–1600. Tel: 01/211 93 05.

Tram Museum   Collection of old trams (the oldest from 1897) with historical and technical exhibitions.
Limmatstrasse 260. Tram 4. Open: Wed 19.30–22.00, Apr–Oct first Sat of month 14.00–17.00. Tel: 01/341 50 58.

Zoological Museum of the University (Zoologisches Museum)   Exhibits depicting Ice Age mammals, birds and mammals of the world, insects, slide and film shows.
Künstlergasse 16. Trams 6, 9, 10 to ETH-Zentrum. Open: Tue–Fri 09.00–17.00, Sat–Sun 10.00–16.00. Tel: 01/634 38 38.

Anthropological Museum of the University (Anthropologisches Museum)   The foundations of human development portrayed in diagrams, charts, audio-visual presentations and videos.
Winterthurerstrasse 190. Trams 9, 10 to Irchel. Open: Tue–Fri 09.00–16.00, Sat–Sun 10.00–16.00. Tel: 01/635 54 11.

Paleontological Museum of the University (Paläontologisches Museum)   Collection of fossils of fishes and mammals.
Künstlergasse 16. Trams 6, 9, 10 to ETH-Zentrum. Open: Tue–Fri 09.00–17.00, Sat–Sun 10.00–16.00. Tel: 01/634 38 38.

Medical History Collection of the University (Medizinhistorisches Museum)   History of traditional and western medicine and surgery, with reconstructed rooms such as a children's ward of c1850 and a chemist of c1750.
Rämistrasse 69. Trams 5, 9 to Kantonsschule. Open: Tue–Fri 13.00–18.00, Sat–Sun 11.00–17.00. Tel: 01/634 20 71.

Collection of Geology and Mineralogy of the Federal Institute of Technology (Geologisch-Mineralogische Ausstellung)   Collection of minerals, rocks and fossils. Reliefs, maps and changing exhibitions.
Sonneggstrasse 5 (Floor E). Trams 6, 9, 10 to ETH-Zentrum. Open: Mon–Fri 10.00–18.00, Sat 10.00–16.00. Tel:01/632 37 87.

Parks

The city is well endowed with green spaces, of which the most notable are:

Belvoirpark, the largest (tram 7 to Billoweg).
Irchel (trams 9, 10 to Irchel and Milchbruck or 7, 14 to Milchbruck).
Rieterpark, with fine old trees (tram 7 to Museum Rietberg).

Muralengut, with rose garden (near Belvoir and Rieterpark).
Arboretum, part of lakeside gardens (tram 11 to Bürkliplatz, then walk in direction of Enge).
Quaianlagen, a delightful walk beside the lake from near Bellevueplatz (trams 4, 6, 8,.9, 15) to the rhododendron garden at the Zurichhorn.
City Hall Park, at Bürkliplatz (tram 11) where a flea market is held on summer Saturdays.

Of more specialist interest are:

Botanical Gardens of the University (Botanischer Garten) Large garden divided into areas according to the ecological zone or botanical theme. *Zollikerstrasse 107. Trams 2, 4 to Höschgasse or bus 31, tram 11 to Hegibachplatz. Open: Mar–Sep, Mon–Fri 07.00–19.00, Sat–Sun 08.00–18.00; Oct–Feb, Mon–Fri 08.00–18.00, Sat–Sun 08.00–17.00. Plant houses, daily 09.30–11.30, 13.00–16.00. Tel: 01/634 84 11.*

Municipal Garden, Display Garden and Greenhouses (Stadtgärtnerei) Peaceful park with conservatories and greenhouses of plants from all over the world, with a special display of orchids. *Sackzelg 25-27/Gutstrasse. Tram 3 or bus 89 to Hubertus. Open: daily 09.00–17.00, greenhouses 09.00–11.30, 14.00–17.00. Tel: 01/492 14 23.*

Municipal Succulent Collection (Städtische Sukkulentensammlung) Succulents from the old and new world, with over 25,000 cacti. *Mythenquai 88. Tram 7 to Brunaustrasse. Open: daily 09.00–11.30, 13.30–16.30. Tel: 01/201 45 54.*

Zoo (Zoologischer Garten) Over 1,500 animals of about 250 species with a rainforest hall, aquarium, big cats' area and a mini zoo for children. *Zürichbergstrasse 221. Trams 5, 6 to Zoo. Bus 751 to Dreiwiesen. Open: Mar–Oct, daily 08.00–18.00; Nov–Feb, daily 08.00–17.00. Admission charge. Tel: 01/252 71 00.*

Practical information

TO – Station concourse. Tel: 01/215 40 00; fax: 01/215 40 44; email: information@zurichtourism.ch; web: www.zurichtourism.ch Open: Apr–Oct, Mon–Fri 08.30–20.30, Sat–Sun 08.30–18.30; Nov–Mar, Mon–Fri 08.30–19.00, Sat–Sun 09.00–18.30. Guided tours.

The majority of central hotels are on the east bank of the River Limmat, and therefore a tram ride across the Bahnhof Bridge to Central (trams 3, 6, 7, 10). However, directly opposite the main exit from the station is the
Schweizerhof★★★★ (H), Bahnhofplatz 7, CH-8023. Tel: 01/218 88 88; fax: 01/218 81 81; email: info@hotelschweizerhof.com; web: www.hotelschweizerhof.com

A hotel only a little further away is the
St Gotthard★★★★, Bahnhofstrasse 87, CH-8023. Tel: 01/227 77 00; fax: 01/227 77 50; email: reservation@hotelstgotthard.ch; web: www.hotelstgotthard.ch

Most of the hotels are on or just off Limmatquai or in the fork between Limmatquai and Seilergraben, the closest to the station being
Central Plaza★★★★, Central 1, CH-8001. Tel: 01/251 55 55; fax: 01/251 85 35; email: guest-service@central.ch; web: www.astanet.com/get/centralhotel
Leonhard★★★, Limmatquai 136, CH-8001. Tel: 01/251 30 80; fax: 01/252 38 70.
Limmathof★★, Limmatquai 142, CH-8023. Tel: 01/261 42 20; fax: 01/262 02 17.

For those in search of a quiet hotel within a few minutes' walk of the old town, the Florhof has no passing traffic, a good restaurant and is an attractively restored building of 1576 (two stops to Neumarkt on tram 3 or bus 31)
Florhof★★★ (H), Florhofgasse 4, CH-8001. Tel: 01/261 44 70; fax: 01/261 46 11; email: info@florhof.ch; web: www.romantikhotels.com/zuerich

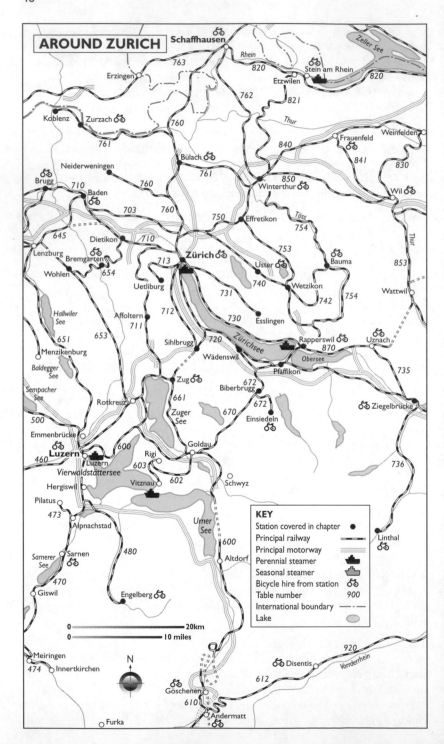

Around Zürich

7

There is plenty of scope for day excursions from Zürich, given the modest distances of most Swiss journeys and the efficiency of the railways. The tourist office suggests that day trips as far afield as Graubünden and the Ticino are perfectly feasible. The S-Bahn and outer suburban services from Zürich are frequent and some are operated by double-deck coaches that give excellent views from the upper level. For details of ticket arrangements around Zürich, see page 40.

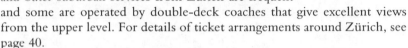

LAKE ZURICH (ZURICHSEE)

The lake is Switzerland's third largest completely within its borders, covering 88.5km² (34.2 square miles). Boat services on Lake Zürich operate from the pier at Bürkliplatz (trams 2, 5, 8, 9, 11) between the beginning of April and late October. A variety of trips is available: 1½-hour short excursions; half-lake tours of 2½ hours; and longer trips down to Rapperswil and beyond. There are 32 piers the length of the lake to Schmerikon, enabling travellers to devise circular journeys using rail for one leg.

Between mid-June and the end of August, two paddle steamers with restaurants, *Stadt Rapperswil* and *Stadt Zürich*, operate cruises between Zürich and Rapperswil. Evening jazz and dance cruises and even fondue cruises run on summer evenings.

Information and tickets are available at the tourist office or from the pier at Bürkliplatz.

ZURICH HB–UETLIBERG Table 713/S10

A short and pleasant way to reach woodland walks and enjoy panoramic views over the city and lake with the Alps in the distance is to take the standard-gauge rack railway up to the 871m (2,857ft) peak at Uetliberg.

Trains leave from the underground platforms on the west side of the station and follow the River Sihl for a short distance before starting to climb steeply after **Binz**. The suburbs of Zürich are soon left behind and the line climbs through woodland laced with footpaths.

From the summit terminus at **Uetliberg** (with buffet and adjacent children's playground), a path leads up through the woods to the summit hotel and terrace restaurant/café, built in 1879 in chalet style and recently refurbished. The path passes the first of the planets on a planetary trail that leads to Felsenegg, and on the left-hand side is the site of a huge Victorian hotel with cast-iron viewing tower and elaborate gardens; a picture of it may be seen in the small museum adjacent to the hotel which is devoted primarily to the Roman occupation of this strategic hilltop. A viewing platform on a huge telecommunications tower close to the hotel affords an even more impressive view for fit visitors – it is reached by stairs.

From Uetliberg it is a 1½–2-hour walk along the wooded ridge to Felsenegg, where there is a restaurant, for the cablecar down to Adliswil (table 2705). It is an eight-minute walk to Adliswil station on the S-Bahn line S4 to Sihlbrugg (table 712) for a train back to Zürich.

Practical information
Uetliburg
The hotel can be reached only by public transport so a peaceful location.
Berggasthaus Uto-Kulm★★★, Gratstrasse, CH-8143. Tel: 01/457 66 66; fax: 01/457 66 69; email: utokulm@uetliberg.ch; web: www.uetliberg.ch

ZURICH HB–SIHLBRUGG Table 712/S4
The exit from Zürich provides a depressing example of the way urban space has often been ruined by trying to cater for the motor car: for a mile or more beside the railway the River Sihl is in permanent shade from a monstrous viaduct carried on pillars sunk into the riverbed.

Once Zürich has been left behind, the attractiveness of the river valley progressively improves. At **Adliswil** a cablecar ascending to Felsenegg (table 2705) is eight minutes' walk from the station, and **Wildpark-Höfli** serves a wildlife park. Beyond **Langnau-Gattikon**, where many trains terminate, the valley is delightful with farming the predominant activity. A tree-shaded bicycle path follows the river; its gravel surface is better suited to off-road tyres. At **Sihlbrugg** numerous walks are signed from the top of the stairs from platforms 3/4, and a map indicates the routes.

A steam train with historic carriages hauled by two tank engines, of 1899 and 1911 vintages, can be hired for use between Giesshübel or Wiedikon stations in Zürich and Sihlbrugg. (Tel: 01/206 45 22; fax: 01/206 45 10.)

ZURICH HB–ZUG Table 720/S1
Zug is one of the towns served by the Zürich S-Bahn that well deserves a visit, with its lovely old town and lakeside setting.

This service shares with trains to Ziegelbrücke the line as far as **Thalwill** (also shown on table 720). At Thalwill the Zug line heads west through two long tunnels separated by a short stretch beside the River Sihl near **Sihlbrugg**. At the textile town of **Baar** St Martin's Catholic parish church has an attractive Romanesque tower with 17th-century cupola, and the half-timbered Rathaus on Hauptstrasse dates from 1676.

Low taxation in Canton Zug has encouraged many international companies to set up their European headquarters in the canton's capital. The mostly bland modern buildings that surround the station at **Zug** provide immediate evidence of the influx, but 10 minutes' walk brings you to one of Switzerland's loveliest and largely pedestrianised old towns. Zug is situated in the lee of the wooded plateau of Zugerberg, which has caused problems with periodic landslides, and at the northwest corner of the Zuger See, dominated at its southern end by Mount Rigi.

From the station, walk directly ahead down Alpenstrasse to reach the lake and walk along Seestrasse into Landsgegemeindeplatz, a pleasant tree-fringed square with cafés and restricted car access. Continue along Seestrasse to reach the old town, and turn left into Fischmarkt. Ahead you will see one of the old town's entrance towers, the Zytturm, built c1200, with blue and white tiles reflecting the canton's colours and incorporating an astronomical clock (open to visitors); on the right is the late Gothic Rathaus of 1505 with elaborate carving on the upper storey.

Running south from Fischmarkt are two parallel streets – Ober and Unter Altsadt (a third parallel street sank into the lake in 1435) – lined with delightful shuttered houses; their heavy overhanging eaves, dormer windows, window boxes and, in Ober, jetties along one side, give them a pleasingly homogeneous though not uniform character. Between the two streets are connecting walkways with fountains and trees, and at the southern end the streets meet beside the Liebfrauenkapelle. This church of c1266 was restored in a restrained baroque style in 1725–8, and has an imposing organ gallery at the rear of the nave.

On the other side of busy Grabenstrasse from the Liebfrauenkapelle is Zugerbergstrasse. The first turning on the left is St Oswald-Gasse on which there is a museum of masks and carvings from Central Africa (Afrikamuseum), housed in a painted house of c1540 (open: Mon–Fri 09.00–11.30, 14.00–17.30) and the Gothic St Oswald's Catholic church. Built between 1478 and 1545, the church is dedicated to the Northumbrian king and martyr, who gave to Bishop Aidan the island of Lindisfarne as a site for a monastery. The diffusion of the cult of St Oswald was largely due to the dismemberment of his body by the pagan king Penda, who defeated and killed Oswald in battle in 642. Inside the church at Zug is a painting of Oswald praying before this fatal battle. The late 15th-century choir-stalls are of exceptional quality and beauty.

Turn right into Kirchenstrasse to the half-timbered 13th-century castle, which contains the town and cantonal museum with displays of silver, gold, archaeology, arms and armour, paintings, costumes, furniture, pewter and stained glass. (Open: Tue–Fri 14.00–17.00, Sat–Sun 10.00–12.00, 14.00–17.00.) The stone making up the cylindrical tower of the castle is of diminishing size as the rough courses rise. On Dorfstrasse to the right of the castle is the Kunsthaus with a collection of largely 20th-century paintings, including work by Swiss surrealists. (Open: Tue–Fri 12.00–18.00, Sat–Sun 10.00–17.00.)

Return via Kolinplatz, on which there are some lovely town houses with a particularly fine carved stone doorcase dated 1689 on the corner with

Grabenstrasse, and Zeughausgasse for the Münz which housed the town's mint and the Master's residence.

Boats on the Zuger See serve various piers around the lake that make possible circular tours using trains for one leg of the journey; they include Cham, Oberwil, Walchwil, Arth and Immensee. Boats leave from the pier on Vorstadt, at the end of Alpenstrasse, directly ahead from the station. For information tel: 041/728 58 66; web: www.zugersee-info.ch

From Zug station buses serve the spectacular caverns of Höllgrotten (Hell's Cavern) (open: Apr–Oct, 09.00–12.00, 13.00–17.30) (table 660.30) and the funicular that ascends the Zugerberg from Schönegg (table 2562 for bus and funicular).

Practical information
Zug

TO – Alpenstrasse 16, CH-6304. Tel: 041/711 00 78; fax: 041/710 79 20; email: tourism@zug.ch; web: www.zug.ch/tourism Open: Mon–Fri 08.30–18.00, Sat 08.30–15.00, Sun 09.00–15.00. Guided tours.

A hotel five minutes' walk from the station is
Zugertor★★★, Baarerstrasse 97, CH-6300. Tel: 041/729 38 38; fax: 041/711 32 03; email: info@zugertor.ch; web: www.zugertor.ch

The next closest is
Parkhotel ★★★★, Industriestrasse 14, CH-6304. Tel: 041/727 48 48; fax: 041/727 48 49; email: phz@parkhotel.ch; web: www.parkhotel.ch

An attractive, quiet hotel overlooking the lake is
Löwen am See★★★, Landsgemeindeplatz 1, CH-6300. Tel: 041/711 77 22; fax: 041/711 67 41.

Bicycle hire from Zug station.

ZUG–ARTH-GOLDAU Table 600
This section of the through journey from Zürich to the Gotthard and Ticino is constantly in view of the Zuger See, with steep orchard- and vine-covered slopes to the left. **Walchwil** is a quiet fishing village served by lake boats. For **Arth-Goldau**, see table 600, page 208.

ZUG–ZURICH HB VIA AFFOLTERN Table 711/S9
A largely suburban route offering little of interest. At **Knonau** is a Gothic church and castle, both of the early 15th century, and at **Mettmenstetten** is an early 16th-century church with carved wooden ceiling. At **Affoltern** is a large model railway museum.

ZURICH HB–BRUGG Table 710/S12
The section of this route along the Limmat river valley as far as Baden was the first railway entirely within Switzerland, opened in 1847. It is probably the only railway in the world that received a nickname based on food: because of the penchant by Zürich

people for a particular type of roll made in Baden, a special train was run early each morning to convey fresh rolls. The line was consequently christened the Spanischbrötlibahn – the Spanish roll line.

As part of the main line between Zürich and Basel, this section is one of the busiest on Swiss railways, serving the industrial corridor through **Schlieren** to **Dietikon**, junction for the appealing tram to Wohlen (see table 654/line S17). A small tank engine is preserved under an awning on the north side of the line at Dietikon. At **Wettingen** is a former Cistercian abbey, founded in 1227 and now used as a school. The cloister has stained glass dating from the Renaissance to the baroque, and the choir of the church has some fine late Renaissance carving.

Although **Baden** has become an industrial centre, the old town remains relatively unspoilt and is largely traffic-free. The town's hot springs were used by the Romans and are still an attraction, with several hotels offering health programmes, but the town did not develop until the 13th century. Little remains of the fortifications except the 15th-century Gothic gate-tower, its corner turrets framing a clock. The arch of the tower leads to the Stadthaus, where the Old Confederation met between 1424 and 1712.

Although the castle of Stein above the town is a ruin, the Landvogteischloss (bailiff's castle) survives intact beside a covered bridge over the Limmat. Dating from the 13th century with later additions, it is now an historical museum with a collection of Roman finds, arms, furniture and local history (open: Tue–Fri 13.00–17.00 Sat–Sun 10.00–17.00). It also contains on loan an elaborate late 17th-century metal bowl depicting the town's fortifications that was owned by the American magnate J Pierpont Morgan.

In 1891 the Swiss-born son of a British engineer, named Charles Brown after his father, set up in Baden the now internationally famous Brown, Boveri & Co to make electrical railway equipment. A magnificent legacy of this decision is the Langmatt Foundation at Römerstrasse 30 which contains many French Impressionist paintings collected by Sidney and Jenny Brown since 1908, including works by Boudin, Bonnard, Cézanne, Corot, Courbet, Degas, Gauguin, Monet, Pissarro, Renoir, Sisley and Van Gogh. (Open: Apr–Oct, Tue–Fri 14.00–17.00, Sat–Sun 11.00–17.00; tel: 056/222 58 42.)

Children will enjoy the Swiss Children's Museum at Oelrainstrasse 29 which has displays of toys and learning materials as well as a programme of activities and playrooms. (Open: Wed, Sat 14.00–17.00, Sun 10.00–17.00.)

Brugg is situated on the River Aare close to the two places where it is joined by the rivers Limmat and Reuss. Three towers have survived, the Schwarze Turm, Archivturm and Storchenturm, and to the west of the town overlooking the Aare is Altenburg Castle, now a youth hostel. Adjoining the Schwarze Turm is the Gothic Rathaus of 1579, and around the cobbled Hofstatt is a cluster of former civic buildings such as the turreted arsenal (Zeughaus), salt store (Sallzhaus) and Kornhaus, as well as a local history museum. On the east façade of the former Latin School are allegorical wall paintings of 1640. The house where the educational reformer Pestalozzi (see page 246) died in 1827 still stands. The town's Roman connections are evident in the Vindonissa Museum (open daily: 10.00–12.00, 14.00–17.00); it is called Vindonissa after the name the Romans gave to the guardhouse and camp that they occupied from 15BC–AD260, which was across the river from Brugg in Windisch.

Beside this separate town are the remains of sections of wall, a 10,000-seat amphitheatre, the largest in Switzerland, and a gateway close to the abbey of Königsfelden. This was founded in 1310 by the widow of Albrecht of Habsburg on the spot where he was assassinated in 1308. Much of the original structure was demolished in 1868–71 to enlarge the mental hospital that the abbey had become in 1804, but the 14th-century church survived with its outstanding stained-glass windows of 1325–30 in the choir.

Practical information
Baden
TO – Bahnhofstrasse 50, CH-5400. Tel: 056/222 53 18; fax: 056/222 53 90; email: tourismus@baden-schweiz.ch; web: www.baden-schweiz.ch Open: Mon–Fri 08.30–12.00, 14.00–18.00, Sat 10.00–12.00. Turn left outside the station.

None of the hotels is close to the station, the majority clustering around Kurplatz on the bend of the Limmat. Those of historic or architectural interest include
Verenahof★★★★, Kurplatz 1, CH-5400. Tel: 056/203 93 93; fax: 203 93 94; email: verenahof@bluewin.ch
Schweizerhof★★★(H), Kurplatz 3, CH-5400. Tel: 056/221 03 25; fax: 056/221 58 04.
Atrium-Hotel Blume★★★(H), Kurplatz 4, CH-5400. Tel: 056/222 55 69; fax: 056/222 42 98. Listed building with unusual Roman-style atrium.

Brugg
TO – c/o Railway Station, CH-5200. Tel: 056/460 82 13; fax: 056/460 83 88. Open: Mon–Sat 08.00–17.00.

Bicycle hire from Baden and Brugg stations.

DIETIKON–WOHLEN Table 654/S17
This metre-gauge roadside tramway is a delight for connoisseurs of such forms of travel and serves the relatively undiscovered riverside town of Bremgarten.

The two-coach trains of the Bremgarten–Dietikon-Bahn leave from platforms 12 and 13 on the west side of **Dietikon** station. Contrary to several maps, trains leave the station in a northerly direction before turning west and climbing out of the town, houses on the outskirts betraying their rural origins by adjoining barns and orchards. After **Rudolfstetten Hofacker** the first of a series of exceptionally tight U-shaped curves takes the line steeply uphill until **Berikon-Widen** after which the line drops down through equally tortuous curves to **Bremgarten**.

Situated on the east bank of the Reuss, Bremgarten is well endowed with medieval and baroque buildings. Turn left outside the station (lockers and good buffet) until you see the sign to the Aldstadt where you turn right, soon passing a remnant of the town walls with covered wall-walk. Nearby is a handsome town house with coat of arms in the centre of a broken pediment and the date 1641 carved on the doorcase. Three towers survive, one of which, the Spittelturm at the head of Antonigasse, is dated 1557 and has a Renaissance coat of arms. The Catholic church of St Nikolaus is late Gothic, dating from the 13th century. The river is crossed by a covered wooden bridge incorporating two chapels originally built in the 1540s and restored in the 1950s. On the west bank is a church of 1618–21 that was once part of a Capuchin monastery that became a children's home in 1889.

A large number of walks is suggested from Bremgarten station, both on a map and by yellow signs. Amongst destinations with stations are Wohlen and Uetliberg (4³/₄ hours' walk), and the banks of the River Reuss offer attractive walks.

Leaving Bremgarten and just before crossing the river, the tram calls at a tiny halt which is only two minutes' walk from the main street and Hotel Stadthof. The line climbs steeply out of the Reuss valley to **Bremgarten West** and through attractive woods in which there is a small halt for walkers. The tram draws to a halt beside the SBB station in **Wohlen**, on the line between Lenzburg and Rotkreuz (see opposite).

Practical information
Bremgarten
TO – Marktgasse 7, CH-5620. Tel: 056/631 18 18; fax: 057/31 84 24. Open: Mon–Fri 08.00–12.00, 13.30–17.00, Sat 08.00–12.00, 13.30–18.30.

Sonne★★★ (H), Marktgasse 1, CH-5620. Tel: 056/631 12 40; fax: 056/633 50 85; web: www.sonne-bremgarten.ch
Stadthof (H), Antonigasse 22, CH-5620. Tel: 057/633 50 73; fax: 057/631 61 56.

Bicycle hire from Bremgarten station.

LENZBURG–ROTKREUZ Table 653
Most services over this line operate between Olten, Aarau and Zug.

For Lenzburg, see table 651. **Wohlen** is the junction for Dietikon to the east, and has a terraced buffet shaded by trees at the south end of platform 1. The line passes through gently undulating farmland and coniferous forests to **Muri** where there is an outstanding Swiss baroque church that once formed part of the Benedictine abbey founded in 1027. The nave of the Romanesque basilica was pierced in 1695–7 by an octagonal dome 25m (82ft) high, and the interior was lavishly decorated. The church has two early 17th-century baroque organs. Beneath the choir is an 11th-century crypt, and in the cloister is some recently restored Renaissance stained glass.

At **Sins** and **Oberrüti** are delightful timber-framed station buildings. **Rotkreuz** is the junction for Luzern, Arth-Goldau and Zug, and has a buffet on platform 1.

Practical information
Muri
Ochsen★★★, Seetalstrasse 16, CH-5630. Tel: 056/664 11 83; fax: 056/664 56 15; web: www.ochsen-muri.ch

ZUG–LUZERN Table 660
For Zug, see table 720. From Zug the train skirts the northern shore of the Zuger See, paralleling cycle and foot paths beside the lake. Close to **Cham** station is the Hirstgarten park overlooking the lake. On a promontory stands Schloss St Andreas and its chapel, the former first documented in 1282 but much altered and the chapel dating from 1488–9 with baroque alterations of 1675. The late baroque Catholic church of St Jacob, built in 1783–94, was given a zinc-covered spire in 1853 on a Gothic tower from an older building.

As the line makes for **Rotkreuz** (see table 653), it turns to the west away from the lake to follow the valley of the River Reuss which comes into view on the right before **Gisikon-Root**. At **Ebikon** at Luzernstrasse 63 is a museum of wildlife panoramas, but an appointment has to be made to visit it (tel: 041/420 46 18). Part of the Renaissance cloister of 1591 survives at the former Cistercian monastery. For Luzern see Chapter 13.

Bicycle hire from Cham and Rotkreuz stations.

ZURICH HB–ZIEGELBRUCKE Table 720/S2 and S8
Skirting the southern shore of Zürichsee and offering fine views over the lake, the line serves a number of villages at which steamers call, facilitating circular journeys. It is also the route to the magnificent monastery at Einsiedeln. Sit on the left.

Leaving Zürich HB, the line curves south through the striking station at **Zürich Enge**, its frontage being formed by a curving arched colonnade topped by a clock framed by two flying female figures. It was built in 1925–7 to the design of Otto and Werner Pfister. The writer Thomas Mann spent the last fifteen months of his life at No 39 Alte Landstrasse in **Kilchberg** and was buried here after his death in 1955.

Thalwil, once the centre of Switzerland's silk industry, is the junction for Zug to the west, the Ziegelbrücke line continuing along the lake. At **Oberrieden**, the Reformed parish church of 1761 is by Johann Ulrich Grubenmann, and at **Horgen** the Reformed parish church has an almost oval shape and idiosyncratic fenestration, dating from 1780–2.

At **Au** part of the small peninsula jutting into the lake is a nature reserve with orchards and vineyards; it is looked after by a college devoted to viticulture and fruit-growing which occupies the much-altered 16th-century castle in **Wädenswil**, a few kilometres to the south. Here, some timber-framed houses survive in the old town and the Reformed parish church of 1764–7 is another building by J C Grubenmann. The station is the junction for services to Arth-Goldau and Einsiedeln.

Besides a pretty, unspoilt centre, **Richterswil** has an interesting group of buildings around a mill that dates from the 13th century; they have been adapted to become a craft school. Of the boat piers on the west shore of the lake, Richterswil is closest to the island of Ufenau, on which the 12th-century Romanesque church of SS Peter and Paul stands on the site of a 1st- or 2nd-century Roman temple. The Chapel of St Martin was built in 1141 though its wall-paintings date from various centuries. Near the lake at Freienbach is a 13th-century castle which became the property of the abbey at Einsiedeln.

Pfäffikon is the junction for trains across the causeway to Rapperswil (see table 730). Just to the west of the station is the 13th-century fortified keep which housed part of the administration of Einsiedeln monastery; a moat and extensions were added in the 14th century. Leaving the town, a line forks off to the left to Rapperswil and the Zürichsee becomes the Obersee, connected by a channel through the causeway that divides the two.

Altendorf is served by boats on Obersee, as is Lachen where the large Catholic church was built in 1707–10, its twin towers surmounted by sugar-castor domes. Just before the junction at Ziegelbrücke the railway crosses the Linthkanal that connects Obersee with Walensee. Expresses continue beyond Ziegelbrucke to Chur, and branches go off to Uznach/Rapperswil and to Linthal.

Practical information
Thalwil
Thalwilerhof, Bahnhofstrasse 16, CH-8800. Tel: 01/720 06 03; fax: 01/722 29 77.

Horgen
Seehotel Meierhof★★★★, Bahnhofstrasse 4, CH-8810. Tel: 01/728 91 91; fax: 01/728 92 92; email: mail@seehotel-meierhof.ch; web: www.seehotel-meierhof.ch

Bicycle hire from Ziegelbrücke station.

ZIEGELBRUCKE–LINTHAL Table 736
This line keeps close company with the River Linth, which bisects the canton of Glarus, and serves some spectacular walking country around Linthal. It is one of those byways that deserves to be better known.

The northern part of the line is surprisingly industrial, the railway serving many factories as it heads south into the U-shaped ring of mountains that make up the southern part of the small canton. It is a 25-minute walk from Niederurnen to the small cablecar that goes up to Morgenholz (table 2825).

The town of Näfels (station Näfels-Mollis) is best known in Switzerland for the extraordinary victory won in 1388 by 600 men of Glarus over an overwhelmingly superior Austrian force; the losses were supposed to have been 54 and 2,500 respectively. The battlefield lies to the east of the railway. The town's Schlachtkapelle behind the baroque Catholic parish church of St Fridolin and Hilary (of 1778–81) was created as a memorial to the men who fell in battle. The cantonal museum is housed in the Freulerpalast, built as a house in 1642–7 with some fine Renaissance carving in stone outside and wood inside. The museum contains examples of printed textiles, an important industry in the canton. (Open: Apr–Nov, Tue–Sun 10.00–12.00, 14.00–17.30.)

Netstal has a concrete Catholic church built in 1933–4. The Linth is crossed just before the cantonal capital of **Glarus**, dominated by the 2,331m (7,646ft) high Glärnisch. The town's large neo-Gothic stone station of 1903 reflects the town's status rather than the needs of its relatively modest population. Zwingli, who was parish priest here for ten years from 1506, would recognise few of the buildings since fire fanned by the notorious Föhn wind laid waste the town in 1861. It was then rebuilt on a grid pattern, giving a neo-classical unity to much of the town's architecture.

A few buildings that survived the fire may be found around Landsgemeindeplatz, where the annual assembly takes place in May, and further away from the town centre. A fine example is the tall house built for the founder of the local textile industry in 1746–8, the Haus in der Wies. To the north is the Spielhofplatz where some of the civic buildings built after the fire may be seen, such as the courthouse and school. The Reformed church was built in 1864–5 to the design of Ferdinand Stadler. Near the Stadtpark, laid out in 1874–8, is the Kunsthaus with paintings by Swiss artists (open: Tue–Wed, Fri–Sat 14.00–17.00, Thu 14.00–21.00, Sun 11.00–17.00).

From late May to late October a bus service (table 735.50) from the station serves one of the area's scenic delights, the small Klöntalersee, ringed by precipitous slopes. The Russian General Suvarov came past the lake in 1799 on his way through the Pragelpass beyond, heading for Schwyz. A museum in Glarus commemorates Suvarov's epic journeys on Swiss soil; it is at Schwertgasse 2 (open: Tue–Fri 14.00–17.00, Sun 14.00–17.00).

Beyond Glarus the valley floor is formed of rolling hills between the high mountains on each side. During the 19th century **Ennenda** became a busy manufacturing village, and has some fine villas and housing of that era. While the train pauses at **Mitlödi**, you can admire the ducks and geese that live on a narrow strip between the station and river. The schoolhouse here is located in a neo-classical house of 1829–30, while on the hillside is a half-timbered house with façade paintings.

Schwanden is an industrial town, though the map at the south end of the station charts the extensive network of footpaths in the area. It was from Schwanden that Burkhardt Tschudi (1718–73) came to London and became one of the most eminent harpsichord-makers, providing instruments for Haydn, the Prince of Wales and Frederick the Great. John Broadwood, who later founded the piano-manufacturing firm, was an apprentice to Tschudi and married his daughter. It was also a native of Schwanden who introduced the potato to Switzerland from Ireland in 1697. Near Schwanden is the country's oldest wildlife reserve, the Kärpf, set up in 1569 to provide two chamoix for each man in the canton when he married. From the station a bus (table 736.70) goes up the valley of Sernftal to Elm, stopping at Matt from where it is a 5-minute walk to the cablecar up to Weissenberg (table

2835). Another bus from Schwanden (table 736.65) goes to Kies for the cablecar to Mettmen (table 2830). The Reformed church of 1753 at Schwanden is by J U Grubenmann.

Beyond the village of Luchsingen (station **Luchsingen-Hätzingen**) the valley narrows to reach **Linthal Braunwaldbahn**, where a new station links the SBB with the steep funicular through woods and a bare rock tunnel to Braunwald at 1,257m (4,123ft). It was in this traffic-free resort that the idea for the Society for Car-free Swiss Holiday Resorts was born. Built along a terrace affording marvellous views of the area's tallest mountain, the Tödi at 3,614m (11,854ft), Braunwald is popular for summer and winter sports, having eight hotels and many chalets. Besides 50km (31 miles) of footpaths through nature reserves, the resort has Europe's highest rose garden, which is a mass of colour when over 4,000 rose bushes of over 500 varieties are in bloom between July and September. From Braunwald a chairlift ascends to Kleiner Gumen (table 2841) and from nearby Niederschlacht a cablecar goes to Grotzenbüel (table 2843).

It is only a short distance to the terminus of the line at **Linthal**, head of the valley and gateway to the Urnerboden valley through which a road climbs across the border with Canton Uri to the Klausen Pass, Switzerland's longest pass. From the summit at 1,948m (6,389ft) the road drops down to the cantonal capital of Altdorf (see table 600). This is one of the most spectacular postbus journeys (table 600.29), the service connecting Linthal with Flüelen station and pier (see table 600), but it is necessary to reserve seats (tel: 055/643 12 03 at Linthal or 041/870 21 36 at Flüelen; fax: 041/870 94 74).

From the station at Linthal numerous walks are signed, most with the white and red markings indicating that heavy walking boots and appropriate clothing and equipment are required. Destinations amongst the high level walks include the Kisten, Richetli and Klausen passes, and there are a number of mountain lodges for hikers. In Linthal the Catholic church of 1906–7 has a tower that dates from 1283.

Many trains serving Linthal start or finish at Rapperswil.

Practical information
Glarus
TO – Burgstrasse 16, CH-8750. Tel: 055/640 15 06; fax: 055/640 33 03. Open: Mon–Fri 08.00–12.00, 13.30–17.00.

Glarnerhof ★★★, Bahnhofstrasse 2, CH-8750. Tel: 055/640 11 91; fax: 055/640 27 25.

Braunwald
TO – CH-8784. Tel: 055/653 65 85; fax: 055/653 65 86; email: tourismusinfo@braunwald.ch; web: www.braunwald.ch Open: Mon–Fri 08.30–11.45, 14.15–17.30, Sat 08.30–11.45.

Märchenhotel Bellevue★★★★, CH-8784. Tel: 055/643 30 30; fax: 055/643 10 00; email:info@maerchenhotel.ch; web: www.maerchenhotel.ch Supervised nursery.

Alpenblick★★★, CH-8784. Tel: 055/643 15 44; fax: 055/643 19 75; email: alpenblick@spectraweb.ch Environment-friendly philosophy (solar energy, compost, etc).

Alpina★★★, Postfach 8, CH-8784. Tel: 055/643 32 84; fax: 055/643 32 86.

Cristal★★★, CH-8784. Tel: 055/643 10 45; fax: 055/643 12 44; email: hotel.cristal@bluewin.ch; web: www.glarusnet.ch

Panorama★★★, CH-8784. Tel: 055/643 36 84; fax: 055/643 29 26; email cuharvey@swissonline.ch English/Swiss management.

Tödiblick★★★, CH-8784. Tel: 055/653 63 63; fax: 055/653 63 66.

Rubschen★★, CH-8784. Tel: 055/643 15 34; fax: 055/643 15 35.

Linthal

TO – Hauptstrasse, CH-8783. Tel: 055/643 15 22. Open: Mon–Sat 08.00–12.00, 14.00–18.00.

Bahnhof ★, CH-8783. Tel: 058/84 15 22.

Bicycle hire from Ziegelbrucke and Linthal stations. There is a signed bike route between Glarus and Linthal, much of it beside the river.

ZURICH HB–RAPPERSWIL Table 730/S7

Although this line serves commuter towns along the north shore of Lake Zürich, it has some attractive sections with good views over the lake and to the vineyards covering the hills inland. The elevated position of the upper level of the double-deck trains is a novelty for many visitors.

Trains thread through the suburbs to **Küsnacht** where a Romanesque keep has been adapted beyond recognition into a house, its top two timber-framed storeys built on a stone base of three storeys. Beside the lake is a venerable building called the Trottengebaüde where the villagers used to press the grapes. A former tithe barn that was once part of the Cistercian abbey of Kappel has frescos of c1410. Thomas Mann lived in Küsnacht at Schiedhaldenstrasse 33 from 1933 to 1938. He also lived at adjacent **Erlenbach** in 1953–4.

In Feldmeilen (**Herrliberg-Feldmeilen** station) is a 17th-century country house and estate named Landgut Mariafeld where the composers Franz Liszt and Richard Wagner were among members of the 'Round Table of Mariafeld'. Wagner completed his celebration of the simple man, *Die Meistersinger von Nürnberg*, while staying here. There follows a pretty stretch of line as it runs close to the lake shore.

It is worth breaking the journey at **Meilen**, where there are two fine 18th-century country houses, Seehalde and Seehof. Some of the wrought ironwork made for the latter is in the National Museum in Zürich; in the 1870s Seehof was the home of the poet and novelist Conrad Ferdinand Meyer. The Reformed parish church is a much extended building dating back to c700.

Rapperswil can also be reached by boat in 1³/₄–2¹/₄ hours depending upon route. The town was founded c1200 and the older part is attractively situated on a peninsula dominated by the late 12th-century castle. A circular walk can be made by first turning left outside the station and right at the end of Bahnhofplatz into Fischmarktplatz to walk beside the lake (the town's fish restaurants are renowned). Beyond the square, continuing beside the tree-fringed lake, is Seequai in which the tourist office can be found on the right near Hotel Schwanen.

The lakeside promenade becomes Bühler-Allee with a rose garden on the right, just before the much altered buildings of the Capuchin monastery begun in 1606. A flight of steps on the right leads up to the Lindenhof. At the top of the steps turn right through the trees towards the castle. Deer can be seen in the field that slopes down to the lake on the left.

Built c1230 by the Count of Rapperswil, the castle was destroyed by an army from Zürich in 1350 but quickly rebuilt. A square keep, round powder tower and five-sided clock tower are at the corners of the unusually shaped triangular courtyard (with all its castles, Britain has only one of this shape). Although the castle has been rather clinically restored – only the remnants of the gatehouse have the patina of antiquity – it contains an interesting museum illustrating the long-standing connections between Poland and Switzerland. A series of rooms illustrates the story behind Poland's struggle for independence and freedom between the 18th century and the rise of Solidarity from 1980 to independence in 1989. Many of the displays are devoted to Polish culture and arts, including a whole section on the pianist (and Prime Minister) Paderewski. Many Swiss craftsmen emigrated to Poland in the late 17th century and Swiss served at the Polish court until the mid-18th century. There were once 163 Swiss-run cafés in Poland. A Swiss designed the town hall in Poznan, of which there is a model in the museum. Set up in 1870, the museum at Rapperswil Castle became a bastion of Polish national aspirations and culture at a time when the country was partitioned by Prussia, Russia and Austria. The castle also houses a restaurant. (Polish Museum – open: Easter–Oct, daily 13.00–17.00; Mar, Nov–Dec, Sat–Sun 13.00–17.00.)

Leave the castle by walking beside its southern front, along the wall from which there are fine views overlooking the old town and lake, and walk through the tiny gatehouse. The smaller church on the left is the Liebfrauenkapelle, a late Gothic chapel of c1489 which serves the cemetery; the larger church on the right is the Catholic parish church of St Johannes; it was originally built in the 13th century, but had to be rebuilt after a fire in 1883. Its two asymmetrical towers were raised, rivalling in height those of the castle.

Between the parish church and the castle a double flight of stairs flanks a fountain to descend into the pedestrianised main square, Hauptplatz. On the right is Hintergasse, with arcaded buildings, and at No 16 the Bleulerhaus of 1606; this street leads down to Endingerplatz in which you can turn left along Marktgasse to return to Hauptplatz with the early 15th-century town hall on the corner. Turn right to return to Bahnhofplatz. The station building itself, with octagonal turret and asymmetrical gables, is worth a glance, though it has been insensitively extended.

The town also has a children's zoo (Knies Kinderzoo), which includes pigs, cows, rhinoceros, giraffes, zebra, emus, performing dolphins and elephants that give rides. Some may find the small size of enclosures and the repetitive behaviour of their occupants dismaying. Also on display is a small tank engine built in Winterthur in 1910. The zoo is ten minutes' walk from the station. Turn right outside the station and proceed past the bicycle racks, keeping as close to the railway as possible. A footbridge across the railway may be seen ahead. Cross it, proceed straight ahead at the foot of the stairs and a sign directs you down a street on the right to the entrance. (Open: mid-March–Oct 09.00–18.00, –19.00 in Jul–Aug.)

Practical information
Rapperswil
TO – Fischmarkplatz 1, CH-8640. Tel: 055/220 57 57; fax: 055/220 57 50. Open: Apr–Oct, Mon–Sun 10.00–17.00; Nov–Mar, Mon–Sun 13.00–17.00.

Schwanen****, Seequai 1, CH-8640. Tel: 055/220 85 00; fax: 055/210 77 77.
Du Lac*, Fischmarktplatz 1, CH-8640. Tel: 055/222 89 49; fax: 055/222 89 48.

Bicycle hire from Rapperswil station.

RAPPERSWIL–PFAFFIKON–ARTH-GOLDAU Table 670
WADENSWIL–EINSIEDELN Table 672
These routes form a letter 'X' and interconnect at Samstegern or Biberbrugg, enabling travellers from any direction to reach the monastery at Einsiedeln, one of the most important in Switzerland.

Taking the line from Rapperswil first, Lake Zürich was first divided by a wooden bridge in the 14th century which has been gradually rebuilt and enlarged into today's causeway with a channel for boats that serve Altendorf, Lachen and Schmerikon on Obersee. For **Pfäffikon**, see table 720. The line to Arth-Goldau and Einsiedeln, part of the Bodensee–Toggenburg-Bahn, climbs to the left through **Wollerau** where there is a lovely church on the left overlooking the railway.

If you have to change trains for Einsiedeln, it is better to do so at **Biberbrugg** rather than **Samstagern** since there is more shelter at the former. The line continues to climb through sparsely populated country on to a pastoral plateau. At **Rothenthurm** is a 13th-century tower left over from the conflicts between the monastery of Einsiedeln and Schwyz. Ten minutes' walk from **Sattel-Aegeri** is a chairlift to Mostelberg (table 2586.1). As the line begins to drop steeply down to Arth-Goldau, a magnificent view opens up to the south with Lake Luzern in the distance. For **Arth-Goldau** see table 600.

To return to the second route, from **Wädenswil**, the line climbs steeply to the junction at **Samstagern** (see above). Leaving Biberbrugg the **Einsiedeln** branch swings east through the sinuous valley of the River Alp, soon reaching the town made famous by its Benedictine monastery. Proceed slightly to the left out of the terminus to gain the main street and turn left; the tourist office is at Hauptstrasse 85 on the left-hand side. The monastery is at the end of this street, about ten minutes' walk from the station.

The monastic community at Einsiedeln grew up around the place where St Meinrad was murdered by robbers in 861. Meinrad was educated at the island monastery of Reichenau near Kreuzlingen and ordained there before taking his vows as a Benedictine monk. Later desiring solitude, he chose the hill of Etzel, a little to the northwest of Einsiedeln. A stream of visitors seeking advice drove him further into the forest where he lived by a spring; it was at his cell here that he was murdered.

The first community was founded on the site in 934, and the pilgrimage to it was blessed by papal bull in 964. The monastery received the protection of, successively, the counts of Rapperswil, the Habsburgs and the house of Schwyz. It was during the period of Habsburg protection, in 1314, that the monastery was sacked one night by a group of Schwýz men, angered by long-running disputes over grazing rights; they drank enough of the contents of the cellar to go on the rampage, smashing treasures and relics and departing the next morning with the monks and cattle as prisoners.

Perhaps the most famous priest here was Zwingli, in 1516–18. Fires and sparse information prevent a clear picture being given of the five or six successive buildings on the site until the late 17th and 18th centuries, when a growth in both the monastic community and the number of pilgrims necessitated expansion. The decision to build a new monastery was taken in 1702 and the work was planned by Brother Kaspar Moosbrugger, though he had to incorporate two relatively recent buildings, the confessional chapel and the adjacent choir. He created a cruciform ensemble and four courtyards enclosed within a huge rectangle, which bears comparison in size with the Escorial near Madrid.

By 1718 the monastery was finished and work began on the new church, again to plans by Moosbrugger. The convex west façade overlooking the square was finished in 1724, followed by the two flanking towers in 1726, but it was 1735 before the rest of the work was completed to allow consecration of the new church. The square in front, the Klosterplatz, was laid out in 1745–7.

The object of pilgrimage, the late 15th-century black madonna (replacing an earlier figure ruined by fire), stands in the octagon devised by Moosbrugger on the site of the ancient cell and first chapel. Although the monastery was plundered by the French in 1798, the madonna had been carried to safety in the Tirol by the monks.

The sumptuous decoration of the church, much of it by the Asam brothers from Munich, makes it one of the finest baroque buildings in Switzerland. Angels dangle legs over broken pediments while branch-waving cherubs gaze down on the congregation. The historian Edward Gibbon came here in 1755 and 'was astonished by the profuse ostentation of riches in the poorest corner of Europe; amidst a savage scene of woods and mountains, a palace appears to have been erected by magic'.

The courtyards should not be missed – those to the right of the entrance are open to visitors. Made up of barns and stables, some are still home to horses, their names or those of their predecessors given on enamel plates above the stalls. Through the archway at the end are rising hills with waymarked paths.

Einsiedeln has few other sights of note, but its oldest building is not even signed. Turn right out of the church along Klosterplatz, and straight ahead, over a traffic island, is a small stone church with tiny six-sided bell-tower. This is the chapel of St Gangolf, begun shortly after 1029.

From Einsiedeln station a bus (table 672.20) goes south along the valley of the River Alp to Brunni for the cable car up to Holzegg (table 2576), and a series of buses (tables 672.25/28/30) serves the villages beside the Sihlsee, now a reservoir. Amongst the villages served is Weglossen, where a cable car ascends to Seebli (table 2580).

Practical information
Einsiedeln

TO – Hauptstrasse 85, CH-8840. Tel: 055/418 44 88; fax: 055/418 44 80. Open: Mon–Fri 10.00–12.00, 13.30–17.30, Sat–Sun 10.00–16.00.

The closest hotel to the station is
Schiff, Hauptstrasse 10, CH-8840. Tel: 055/412 51 41; fax: 055/412 32 63.

Hotels overlooking the monastery, within ten minutes' walk of the station, are
Katharinahof★★★, Ilgenweidstrasse 6, CH-8840. Tel: 055/418 98 00; fax: 055/418 98 09; email: katharinahof@bluewin.ch
Linde★★★ (H), Schmiedenstrasse 29, CH-8840. Tel: 055/418 48 48; fax: 055/418 48 49; email: hotel@linde-einsiedeln.ch; web: www.linde-einsiedeln.ch
Zunfthaus Bären★★★ (H), Hauptstrasse 76, CH-8840. Tel: 055/418 72 72; fax: 055/418 72 70; email: info@hotelbaeren.ch; web: www.hotel-baeren.ch
Rot Hut★★, Hauptstrasse 80, CH-8840. Tel: 055/412 22 41; fax: 055/412 71 37.
Sonne★★, Hauptstrasse 82, CH-8840. Tel: 055/412 28 21; fax: 055/412 41 55.
St Josef★, Ilgenweidstrasse 2, CH-8840. Tel: 055/412 21 51.

Bicycle hire from Einsiedeln station.

RAPPERSWIL–WINTERTHUR Table 754/S26
Although part of Zürich's S-Bahn network, this line has not a trace of suburban character and passes through attractive countryside that offers good walking.

The exit from Rapperswil overlaps the final section of line S5 through Jona to Rüti (see table 740), where S26 curves sharply away to the east towards the pleasant market town of **Wald**, where the Reformed church of 1686–7 has a contemporary inlaid pulpit and balustraded gallery. Near **Steg** the line joins the River Töss which it follows for most of the way to Winterthur.

At **Bauma** a preserved railway to Hinwil (see table 740) is operated by the Dampfbahn-Verein Zürcher Oberland (DVZO) which has a collection of historic steam locomotives and electrics at Bauma. Three or five return trains are run on varying weekends between May and October over the steeply graded and scenic line (tel: 052/386 12 41).

The popularity of this hilly area for walkers is testified by the numbers that use stations such as **Wila** and **Turbenthal**. A little to the north of Turbenthal at Hutzlikon are the remains of an early 14th-century castle, Breitlandenberg Burg. At Zell (**Rämismühle-Zell** station) some mid-14th-century wall-paintings can be seen in the bell tower of the Gothic Reformed parish church.

From **Kollbrunn** it is a walk of about 2km (1½ miles) to the spectacular castle of Kyburg (though a longer distance, it can also be reached by postbus from the Zürich–Winterthur line, see below). The largest medieval stronghold in eastern Switzerland, Kyburg is positioned on a rock above the Töss and retains its 11th–13th century buildings. Now a museum with collections of furniture, arms and armour, it conveys a vivid impression of feudal life. The chapel has 13th–15th-century wall-paintings. (Open: Mar–Oct, Tue–Sun 09.00–12.00, 13.00–17.30; Nov, Jan–Feb, Tue–Sun 10.00–12.00, 13.00–16.00.)

For Winterthur, see table 750.

Bicycle hire from Bauma station.

ZURICH STADELHOFEN–ESSLINGEN Table 731/S18

More of a tramway than a suburban railway, the Forchbahn climbs into hills that offer walks through farmland. The generous space allowed for bicycles on the trams reflects the opportunity for cycling en route, for example a cycle route from Waldburg station to Zollikon.

The modern trams leave from an attractive leafy square outside **Stadelhofen** SBB station (on tram lines 11 and 15). The suburbs are soon left behind as the line enters wooded country with views over fields to Lake Zürich to the right, although there is a return to the urban tram with a long section of tunnel near **Zumikon**. Some of the line's historic vehicles, used on special occasions, may be seen at **Forch**, where many walkers leave the train at weekends.

Beyond **Scheuren** views open up to the east over Greifensee and the large town of Uster on its eastern side. From Sheuren the line falls towards the terminus, pausing at **Emmat** where walks are signed through neighbouring woods and farmland.

ZURICH HB–HINWIL/RAPPERSWIL
Table 740/S5 and S14

The departure from Zürich gives an attractive illustration of progressive lineside management: near **Zürich Wipkingen** is a deep cutting in which the vegetation is kept in check by goats and sheep. There is little else of interest until **Nänikon-Greifensee** where an attractive, early 12th-century castle, much rebuilt, is owned by the canton and privately let. In an angle of the lakeside town's walls is an unusual triangular church of c1350.

Above the industrial town of **Uster** stands the much-altered medieval stronghold built in the 11th century. The keep, topped by crow-stepped gables, is surrounded by mid-18th-century residential accommodation which is now a college of domestic science. Uster is also the start of a history trail that takes in sites of interest to industrial archaeologists on its way to Bauma.

Wetzikon is junction for the lines to Effretikon, Hinwil and Rapperswil, and has the remains of a medieval castle. **Hinwil** is the end of S-Bahn services and start of the historic steam trains that run to Bauma on two or three Sundays a month from May to October (see table 754).

Taking the Rapperswil line, at **Bubikon** is the impressive Ritterhaus (knights' residence), the only surviving Swiss Commandery of the Knights of Malta. Founded in 1192, it has been through such vicissitudes as becoming a cotton mill, but is now cared for by a local society which has also created a Crusader Museum. (Open: Apr–Oct, daily except Mon 09.00–11.00, 14.00–18.00.)

The Reformed parish church at **Rüti** incorporates parts of a Premailonstratensian monastery from which paintings of 1492 have become part of the choir. The Premailonstratensians are an order of canons, founded by St Norbert in 1119 at Prémontré near Laon. Beyond Rüti the line passes through a thickly wooded river gorge with craggy rock faces towards **Rapperswil** (see table 730).

Bicycle hire from Uster station.

WETZIKON–EFFRETIKON Table 753/S3

Leaving Wetzikon the line veers east to loop around Pfäffikonsee. A little inland on the outskirts of **Pfäffikon** are the well-conserved stone walls of the late 3rd-century Roman camp of Irgenhausen, their largest defensive site in Switzerland, with the remains of eight towers. The Reformed parish church of 1484–8 has late Gothic frescos.

ZURICH HB–WINTERTHUR Table 750/S12

Although the journey has little of note, Winterthur should not be missed. Despite its industrial background, it retains an attractive largely pedestrianised old city, and its prosperity has endowed the city with one of the world's finest art collections.

It is only 15 minutes by train from Zürich to **Winterthur**. In many countries, this proximity would militate against the smaller town having a vibrant cultural life. But Winterthur, with a population of only 89,000, can offer a variety and quality that would be the envy of much larger cities. Besides art collections, there is an aggressively modern theatre, a symphony orchestra that sometimes gives free concerts, and the Swiss Technorama.

The town's origins go back to a Gallo-Roman colony named Vitudurum, which was on the site of today's Oberwinterthur to the east of the centre. The present city was founded in 1170 by the Kyburgs, whose castles can be found in the surrounding countryside. Rivalry with Zürich has been a theme of its subsequent history, encouraging the entrepreneurship that gave Winterthur an early lead in Swiss industrial development. The city established a reputation first for textiles and then for heavy engineering; the name of Schweizerische Locomotiv & Maschinen- Fabrik, founded by a Middlesex-born Englishman, appears on the worksplates of steam and electric locomotives all over the world, while that of Sulzer can be seen in the engine-rooms of ships – including many of the steamers on Swiss lakes. The money made through industry and commerce found its way into civic projects and the arts, creating some fine buildings and the collections that enrich the city and attract visitors. Leaving the station by the main entrance, turn left into Bahnhofplatz; the tourist office is on the right-hand side at No 12. The old town lies immediately to the east of the station. Walk down Stadthausgasse from Bahnhofplatz; on the left is Museum Stiftung Oskar Reinhart (see below) and on the right is the Rathaus of 1782–4, which was altered in 1872–4 to create an elegant shopping arcade between this street and Marktgasse. In the latter is the Waaghaus, built in 1503 in a Moorish-Gothic style and now serving as an exhibition centre. Behind it in Kirchplatz is the Reformed town church with elements built between the 16th and 19th centuries.

Museums

Jacob Briner Museum   Landscapes, still lifes and portraits by 17th-century Dutch masters and their influence on English, French and German painters of the 19th century.
Rathaus, Stadthausstrasse 57/Marktgasse 20. Tel: 052/267 51 26. Bus 1 or 3 to Stadthaus (or 5 minutes' walk from station). Open: Tue–Sat 14.00–17.00, Sun 10.00–12.00, 14.00–17.00. Admission charge.

Art Gallery (Kunstmuseum)   The municipal collection has works by artists from the 19th century to the present, including Van Gogh, Bonnard, Léger, Fuseli, Kokoschka, Rousseau, Braque, Monet, Pissarro, Renoir, Vuillard, Gris, Klee, Mondrian and Arp.
Museumstrasse 52. Tel: 052/267 51 62. Bus 1 or 3 to Stadthaus (or 7 minutes' walk from station). Open: Tue 10.00–20.00, Wed–Sun 10.00–17.00. Admission charge.

Lindengut Museum   Museum of 18th- and 19th-century social life and culture, local history and Winterthur stoves. Toy Museum in the coach-house.
Römerstrasse 8. Tel: 052/213 47 77. Bus 1 to Obertor (or 10 minutes' walk from station). Open: Tue–Thu, Sat 14.00–17.00, Sun 10.00–12.00, 14.00–17.00. Admission charge.

Oskar Reinhart Collection (Sammlung Oskar Reinhart)   Winterthur's most important art collection was built up by the son of the head of the trading company Volkart Brothers, which was so successful that it spawned banks and insurance companies. Its Swiss headquarters were in Winterthur and its main trading office in Bombay. From 1924 until his death in 1965 Oskar Reinhart built up one of the world's finest collections, which he gave to the Swiss Confederation in 1958. The collection includes works by Cranach, Holbein, Brueghel, Rubens, Rembrandt, Hals, Poussin, Chardin, El Greco, Goya, Watteau, Constable (*Hampstead Heath*), Delacroix, Daumier, Corot, Courbet, Manet, Renoir, Cézanne, Van Gogh, Degas, Picasso and Gauguin.
'Am Römerholz', Haldenstrasse 95. Tel: 052/269 27 41. Bus 3 to Spital or 10 to Haldengut. Open: Tue–Sun 10.00–17.00. Admission charge.

Oskar Reinhart Foundation (Museum Stiftung Oskar Reinhart) A collection of over 500 paintings by Swiss, Austrian and German artists from the 18th to early 20th century, such as Friedrich, Böcklin, Hodler, Giacometti, Anker and Fuseli. *Stadthausstrasse 6. Tel: 052/267 51 72. Bus 1 or 3 to Schmidgasse (or 5 minutes' walk from station). Open: Tue 10.00–20.00, Wed–Sun 10.00–17.00. Admission charge.*

Photograph Museum (Fotomuseum) Located in a former factory, the museum hosts five large temporary exhibitions each year and is the only institution of its kind in the German-speaking part of the country. *Grüzenstrasse 44. Tel: 052/233 60 86. Bus 2 to Schleife. Open: Tue–Fri 12.00–18.00, Sat–Sun 11.00–17.00. Admission charge.*

Swiss Technorama (Technorama der Schweiz) Science and technology presented in an accessible and entertaining way, with sections on water, nature, physics, mathematics, automation, textiles, materials and music boxes. Plenty of interactive opportunities and historic industrial machinery, including operative steam engines. *Technoramastrasse 1. Tel: 052/243 05 05. Bus 5 to Technorama. Open: Tue–Sun 10.00–17.00. Admission charge.*

Practical information

TO – Bahnhofplatz 12, CH-8401. Tel: 052/267 67 00; fax: 052/267 68 58; email: tourist-service@win.ch; web: www.stadt-winterthur.ch Open: Mon–Fri 08.30–18.30, Sat 08.30–16.00.

The following hotels are within 5 minutes' walk of the station
Krone★★★ (H), Marktgasse 49, CH-8401. Tel: 052/213 25 21; fax: 052/213 48 08; email: info@kronewintherthur.ch; web: www.kronewintherthur.ch
Wartmann am Bahnhof★★★, Rudolfstrasse 15, CH-8400. Tel: 052/212 84 21; fax: 052/213 30 97; email: wartmann@wartmann.ch; web: www.wartmann.ch
Motel Wülflingen★★★, Riedhofstrasse 51, CH-8408. Tel: 052/224 44 44; fax: 052/224 44 88.

Bicycle hire from Winterthur station.

WINTERTHUR–BULACH–KOBLENZ Table 761/S41
A cross-country line that follows the Rhein for its western half.

Leaving Winterthur, the line briefly follows the River Töss as far as **Winterthur Wülflingen**, where there is a plain 17th-century manor house with crow-stepped gables now in use as a restaurant (open: daily except Wednesdays). The building was saved by a benevolent society in the early 20th century and presented to the city of Winterthur. The interiors have fine carved and painted panels and a coffered ceiling.

Although **Bülach** was documented as a town as early as 811, most of today's buildings in the old town date from after its third and last major fire in 1506. To the west the town walls survive in the form of a line of houses.

The Rathaus was built in 1672–3 incorporating parts of an older building, and the large half-timbered Gasthof Goldenen Kopf was carefully rebuilt after a fire in 1965–6.

Part of the riverside village of **Eglisau** was submerged when the level of the Rhein was raised artificially, but the group of half-timbered buildings and church by the riverside is delightful. The Romanesque church has a choir of 1350 and some late 15th-century frescos, and there is a well-restored almshouse of 1682. Leaving the village, the line to Schaffausen continues north as the Koblenz line turns west. Kaiserstuhl (**Weiach-Kaiserstuhl** station) was founded in the mid-13th century on an unusual triangular plan and has retained a medieval atmosphere with parts of the town wall, fortified towers and houses on Hauptgasse. At **Rümikon-Mellikon** are the restored remains of a 4th-century look-out tower.

Zurzach has long been an important crossing place of the Rhein. The Romans built a large fort, of which there are substantial remains. In the Middle Ages it became the venue of one of Europe's most important fairs, and since the discovery in 1955 of thermal springs has developed as the spa of Bad Zurzach. Its principal building of interest is the Collegiate church of St Verena, once the focus of pilgrimage to the grave of the Christian nurse who is thought to have come from Egypt with the Roman legions and died here in 344 after 20 years of work. The 10th-century Romanesque nave was unfortunately given a baroque refacing in the 18th century, but the choir and tower of 1294–1347 and the Gothic hall-crypt underneath were spared. A 19th-century manufacturer's house overlooking the Rhine has been converted into an art gallery with terraced restaurant.

Practical information

Bülach
Gasthof Goldenen Kopf***, Marktgasse 9, CH-8180. Tel: 01/860 39 31; fax: 01/862 01 51.

Zurzach
TO – Quellenstrasse 1, CH-5330. Tel: 056/249 24 00; fax: 056/249 42 22; email: info@badzurzach.ch; web: www.badzurzach.ch Open: Mon–Fri 09.00–12.00, 14.00–17.00, Sat 09.00–12.00.

Post***, Hauptstrasse 61, CH-8437. Tel: 056/249 22 44; fax: 056/249 24 82.
Bahnhof, CH-8437. Tel: 056/249 12 20.

Bicycle hire from Bülach and Zurzach stations.

ZURICH HB–NIEDERWENINGEN/–BULACH–SCHAFFHAUSEN Table 760/S5
The principal route to Schaffhausen (there is a secondary route via Winterthur) and the branch to Niederweningen share the same line as far as Oberglatt. The latter gives access to the medieval town of Regensberg.

On the branch to Niederweningen, the second station is **Dielsdorf**, from which a frequent bus (table 760.23) runs to Regensberg, founded in 1244 and situated on an attractive hill-top site. It has Switzerland's deepest well at 56m (184ft) and a castle with a circular keep – although the castle is a children's home, it is usually possible to climb the tower.

The line to Schaffhausen briefly crosses into Germany, taking a route through an area in which the border seems perversely sinuous. For **Bülach** and **Eglisau**, see above; for **Schaffhausen**, see table 820.

Bicycle hire from Bülach and Schaffhausen stations.

ZURICH–BADEN Table 703/S6

This suburban route to Baden (fast trains go via Dietikon) takes in one site of interest: about 7km (4 miles) from **Würenlos** is the Benedictine convent of Fahr, which has long been linked with the abbey of Einsiedeln. Both the convent church and buildings date from the 18th century. For Baden see table 710.

The Northeast

The northeastern cantons of Appenzell, St Gallen, Schaffhausen and Thurgau are not as well known as most other parts of Switzerland. Yet they have much to offer, both culturally and scenically. The Appenzell, for example offers some of the country's most attractive terrain for walking and cycling, and the whole region has many delightful towns and villages.

WINTERTHUR–ST GALLEN Table 850

Baedeker dismissed this principal route with the terse comment: 'The St Gallen railway is unattractive'. It is an unnecessarily harsh judgement on farming country of orchards, market gardens and woods dotted with characteristic farmhouses of red-painted timber framing.

For Winterthur see page 66. The first town of note after leaving industrial Winterthur is **Elgg** where the tall spire of the Reformed parish church dominates the late medieval town and its castle (not open to the public). The late Gothic church dates from 1508 to 1518, though the tower is thought to be c1370.

Midway between Winterthur and St Gallen is the large junction of **Wil**, from where lines to Frauenfeld and Weinfelden head north (see tables 841 and 830) and the line to Nesslau-Neu St Johann to the south (see table 853). Wil has some distinguished buildings in the old town. The outer oval ring of mostly domestic buildings stands fortress-like on a hill, similar to the north-eastern side of Avanches, while an inner ring has a section of arcades. At the centre is the largely 15th-century but much altered Catholic parish church of St Nikolaus, while to the north is the Hof. This late 12th-century castle was rebuilt in the 15th and 16th centuries and is joined to the town gate by the former residence of St Gallen Abbey, the late 15th-century Haus zum Toggenburg. Wil has the most important neo-classical house in the canton of St Gallen: the arcaded Baronenhaus of 1795 stands on Marktplatz and has a hipped roof and turrets.

Continuing east, the old choir tower of the Catholic parish church of Mariä Himmelfahrt at Henau (**Algetshausen-Henau** station) is considered the finest Gothic tower in the canton. Admirers of Arts and Crafts architecture can find an example of the work of the English architect M H Baillie Scott in

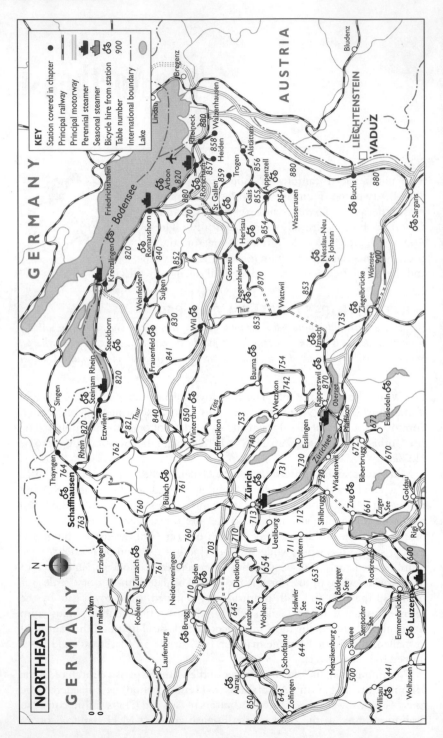

KEY

- Station covered in chapter
- Principal railway
- Principal motorway
- Perennial steamer
- Seasonal steamer
- Bicycle hire from station
- 900 Table number
- International boundary
- Lake

Uzwil, where he designed the Langhaus Waldbühl in 1907–11. From the station at **Flawil** it is only about 2km to the south to the beautifully situated Cistercian convent at Magdenau, founded in 1244 and periodically rebuilt and enlarged. About 2km to the east of Flawil is Burgau which has some fine 17th-century timber buildings, including the Rathaus which was built on to a 1632 farmhouse.

Gossau is a junction for the Appenzellerbahn (see table 854) and for Weinfelden. Within walking distance of the station is Schloss Oberberg. Built in the mid-13th century, it was rebuilt in 1406 after being destroyed in the Appenzell war. It later became the seat of the bailiffs of the Abbots of St Gall, and was restored after a fire in 1955.

For anyone interested in architecture, **St Gallen** deserves at least a day, with its old town and the cathedral with its magnificent library. The capital of the eponymous canton, its name is derived from the Irish monk Gall or Gallus, a pioneer of Christianity in Switzerland, who built a hermitage c612 in the Steinach valley. Between 719 and 752, an abbey was built on the site of his cell and flourished to become one of the most important religious communities in the area. The Benedictine abbey was encircled by a wall following a Hungarian invasion in 926, and by the second half of the 12th century markets were being held. The town's prosperity was founded on the linen and later cotton industries, its allegiance to the Abbot ending in 1454 when St Gallen joined the Swiss Confederation. The Reformation was brought to the town in 1524 by its mayor and great scholar, Vadian, whose statue, recalling the appearance of Henry VIII, dominates the junction of Marktgasse and Neugasse. The town wall was removed in the early 19th century, and the monastery was dissolved in 1805, becoming the cathedral of the new diocese of St Gallen in 1847.

Leaving the station by the main columned exit, go straight ahead across the square to the tourist office on the corner of Bahnhofplatz and St Leonhardstrasse. To reach the old town and cathedral, turn left out of the tourist office along St Leonhardstrasse towards the Broderbrunnen monument of 1894. Beside it turn right along Oberer Graben and almost immediately left into Webergasse to enter the largely pedestrianised quarter of the old town in Multergasse, straight ahead. Continue along Webergasse for Gallus-Platz; the cathedral is to the left.

The quality of St Gallen Cathedral and the surrounding buildings is reflected in their designation by UNESCO as a World Heritage Site. Several architects had a hand in designing the abbey which was built between 1755 and 1769, one of the last monumental buildings of the late baroque. The long nave and central rotunda were designed by Peter Thumb, and the imposing twin-towered east front was a collaboration between J M Beer, Brother Gabriel Loser and J F Feuchtmayer, who also designed the confessionals.

With no stained glass and the columns in off-white, the interior has a light, open feeling. The painting in the rotunda depicting the advent of Christ in the presence of the blessed and those representing the monastery's patron saints in the domes of the nave bays are by Joseph Wannenmacher. The elaborate pulpit is decorated with four figures, while each wooden pew end has different carved decoration. The intricate gilt wrought-iron choir screen was made in 1771 by J Mayer.

The interior of the adjacent Collegiate Library (*Stiftsbibliothek*) has been described as the country's most beautiful secular rococo interior. The ceiling of the two-storey room was again decorated by Joseph Wannenmacher. Built betwen 1758 and 1767 to designs by Peter Thumb, the library contains one of the most important collections in Europe; particularly rare amongst the 130,000 volumes, 2,000 illuminated manuscripts and 1,650 early printed works are some 7th–12th-century Irish manuscripts, early scores of Gregorian chant, an 8th-century Virgil and a plan of the abbey made c820. (Open: Dec–Mar, Mon–Sat 09.00–12.00, 13.30–16.00; Apr–Oct, Mon–Sat 09.00–12.00, 13.30–17.00, Sun 10.00–12.00, 13.30–16.00.)

Most of the buildings in the monastery precincts were built between the 17th and the first half of the 19th centuries.

The old town is a warren of narrow streets whose dominant feature is the profusion of glorious oriel windows – a most public-spirited display of one-upmanship. A rewarding hour or two can be spent ambling through these streets, in which there are plenty of cafés and restaurants. On the northeast side of the old town, in a broad street named Bohl, is the Waaghaus, a merchants' hall of 1584. From the adjacent Markt-Platz, Goliathgasse leads to the Reformed parish church of St Mangen, founded in 898 and rebuilt c1100. Its Gothic tower dates from 1505.

Amongst the town's museums in Museumstrasse are the Historical Museum (open: Tues–Sat 10.00–12.00, 14.00–17.00, Sun 10.00–17.00), which contains models of the town, paintings, reassembled rooms, furniture, sculpture, arms and armour, musical instruments and stamps. The Kunstmuseum contains works by Millet, Monet, Corot, Courbet, Pissarro and Sisley, and by eminent Swiss artists such as Angelica Kauffmann, Hodler and Boecklin as well as naive paintings by local artists. (Open: Tue–Sat 10.00–12.00, 14.00–17.00, Sun 10.00–17.00.) The Kirchhoferhaus contains furniture and items of local and archaeological interest (open: Tue–Fri 07.30–11.30).

In Vadianstrasse, off Oberer Graben, is the Textile Museum, devoted to lace, embroidery and linen (open: Nov–Mar, Mon–Fri 10.00–12.00, 14.00–17.00; Apr–Oct, Mon–Sat 10.00–12.00, 14.00–17.00).

For those staying in St Gallen, the town's opera is highly regarded in Switzerland, performing in the Stadttheater in Museumstrasse, built in 1968. The municipal orchestra plays in the Tonhalle opposite.

Practical information
Wil

TO – Bahnhofplatz 6, CH-9500. Tel: 071/913 70 00; fax: 071/913 70 09; web: www.stadtwil.ch Open Mon–Fri 09.00–12.00, 14.00–17.30, Sat 09.30–12.00.

Schwanen★★★, Obere Bahnhofstrasse 21, CH-9500. Tel: 071/911 01 55; fax: 071/911 66 27; email: schwanen.wil@bluewin.ch

Zum Ochsen**, Grabenstrasse 7, CH-9500. Tel: 071/911 48 48; fax: 071/911 83 41.

St Gallen

TO – Bahnhofplatz, CH-9001. Tel: 071/227 37 47; fax: 071/227 37 67; email:
info@stgallen-i.ch; web: www.stgallen-i.ch Open: Mon–Fri 09.00–12.00,
13.00–18.00, Sat 09.00–12.00.

Numerous hotels; close to the station are
Walhalla****, Bahnhofplatz, CH-9001. Tel: 071/222 29 22; fax: 071/222 29 66; email:
info@walhalla.ch; web: www.hotelwalhalla.ch
Metropol Garni***, Bahnhofplatz 3, CH-9001. Tel: 071/228 32 32; fax: 071/228 32 00.
Weissenstein***, Davidstrasse 22, CH-9000. Tel: 071/228 06 28; fax: 071/228 06 30;
email: hweisg@bluewin.ch; web: www.homenet.ch/weissenstein

Hotel of character in old town (10 minutes from station)
St Gallen*** (H), Bankgasse 12, CH-9000. Tel: 071/227 61 00; fax: 071/227 61 80;
web: www.hotel-st-gallen.ch

Bicycle hire from Wil and St Gallen stations.

ST GALLEN–TROGEN Table 859

*This delightful 10km (6¹/₄ miles) roadside tramway begins at a separate platform outside
and to the right of St Gallen station and is of particular use for walkers. Sit on the left.*

The streets through the town share the twin metre-gauge tracks with road
traffic until the outskirts at **Schülerhaus** where the tracks become single. The
line climbs for much of the way to Trogen, affording marvellous views to the
left over St Gallen and the increasingly deep drops into the valley floor. At
Schwarzer Bären signposts for walks radiate in all directions, some taking
you back to St Gallen, others sending you past the lake on the right. Soon after
Rank (more walks), Lake Constance comes into view. Just before
Schützerngarten is a good view to the left of the attractive church sited on a
knoll. The small health resort of **Speicher** has some good buildings, including
a neo-classical Reformed church, as well as the railway's headquarters and
depot.

Trogen is built on a hill and is the venue in even years of a meeting of the
Landsgemeinde (on the last Sunday of April) in which local people can vote
on the affairs of the half-canton of Appenzell Ausserrhoden – providing they
are wearing a sabre. The Dorfplatz where the meeting takes place is a
testimony to the town's prosperity since the 18th century, lined with affluent
houses and two double palaces. The Reformed church of 1779–82 in the
northeast corner is a highly regarded work by Hans Ulrich Grubenmann, one
of a family of master builders who built many churches in the region. To the
south of the town is a group of chalets known as Pestalozzidorf, named after
the Swiss educational reformer. This children's village was built between 1944
and 1957 for European orphans of World War II; it continues to fulfil a similar
role. The village has skiing in winter, including illuminated slopes.

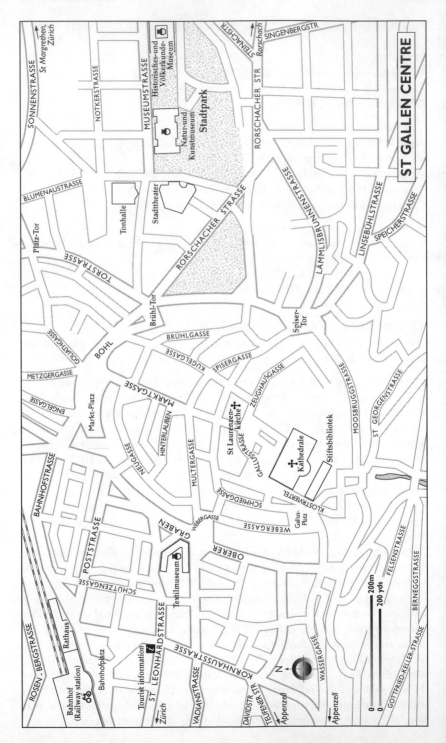

ST GALLEN CENTRE

From Trogen station a postbus (table 857.90) connects with some trains for the well-wooded journey to Heiden (table 857), enabling a circular tour to be made via Rorschach. There are also buses to Altstätten SG (table 880.60), Teufen and Herisau (table 870.55).

Practical information
Speicher
Appenzellerhof, CH-9042. Tel: 071/344 13 21; fax: 071/344 10 38.

Trogen
Krone* (H), Landsgemeindeplatz, CH-9043. Tel: 071/343 60 80; fax: 071/344 43 76.

ST GALLEN–WATTWIL–RAPPERSWIL Table 870
The eastern half of this line is part of the Bodensee–Toggenburg-Bahn, along which the Voralpen Express runs on its journey between Romanshorn and Luzern. It crosses the highest bridge in Switzerland and passes through one of the longest tunnels in the country.

Leaving St Gallen the train is soon above the level of the Winterthur line as it starts to climb up the deep gorge that carries the River Sitter down from the Appenzell towards Lake Constance. The railway crosses the river on the outskirts of the town by the tallest bridge in Switzerland. Opened in 1910, the steel truss span of 120m (394ft) is supported on two slender stone piers 99m (324ft) high.

Shortly after **Gübensee** the lake of the same name can be seen on the right, and the junction of **Herisau** is soon reached (see table 854 for the town). Here you can change on to the Appenzeller Bahn. An historic train and steam locomotive (Bodensee–Toggenburg-Bahn 2-6-2 tank No 9, built by Maffei in 1910) is kept here and runs special trains, entitled the 'Amor Express', to Nesslau–Neu St Johann between April and October. Leaving Herisau the line swings briefly to the north, crossing a long stone viaduct before weaving through a series of deeply folded and well-wooded valleys. To the right beyond the platform at **Degersheim** is a 2-6-2 tank engine built in 1910 on display; it once worked over the Bodensee–Toggenburg-Bahn. In the town is a Jugendstil Reformed church of 1908.

Immediately after **Brunnadern-Neckertal** the line enters the Wasserfluh Tunnel, at over 3.3km (2 miles) one of the longest of many tunnels on this railway. The train emerges at the junction of **Lichensteig**, a town founded c1200 by the Toggenburgs and built on an unusual triangular plan. Arcaded half-timbered houses and the former Rathaus can be seen in Hauptgasse. Close to the old town hall is the Toggenburger Heimatmuseum. To the north of the town is the Baroque Loreto chapel of 1677–80.

Wattwil is another junction, for Nesslau–Neu St Johann, and a better place to change trains than Lichensteig for northbound trains to Wil. The River Thur flows through this small textile town on its way to the Rhein. Regarded as the 'capital' of Toggenburg, Wattwil has a Reformed church of 1845–8 with the rare feature of a nave broader than its length. Ringstrasse has several timber-framed houses and an old people's home converted from a factory and given a Biedermeier-style roof. Above the town to the north are the walled Franciscan nunnery of St Maria der Engel, with a church of 1622–1780 and buildings of 1730–82, and the much altered and repaired Iberg Castle, built c1240.

Soon after turning southeast from Wattwil, the line enters the single-bore 8.6km (5¹⁄₃miles) Ricken Tunnel which developed a notorious reputation in the days of steam traction: a locomotive hauling a heavy freight train stalled on the gradient and the crew was asphyxiated.

At **Uznach** a line from Ziegelbrücke trails in from the left. Laid out in an oval form with two rings lined by houses, Uznach has two fine buildings built for travellers: the timber-framed Zum Hof inn of c1734 and the classical Linthhof, built as a hotel in 1834 but now offices. The Catholic church of the Holy Cross, built 1494–1505 and altered in 1775, has an integral polygonal choir.

The Obersee comes into view on the left at **Schmerikon**, after which the railway follows the lake shore to **Rapperswil** (see table 730).

Bicycle hire from Herisau, Uznach and Rapperswil stations.

ST GALLEN–ROMANSHORN Table 870

The line taken by the Voralpen Express on its last leg from Luzern to Romanshorn.

After a long tunnel entered on the outskirts of St Gallen, the railway passes **Wittenbach**, where the baroque Catholic parish church of St Ulrich was built c1675. To the east of the chapel of St Johannes Nepomuk of 1758 is a farmhouse that has been repeatedly altered to become Egg Castle.

Less than 2km (1¹⁄₄ miles) from **Roggwil-Berg** is the extraordinary castle of Mammertshofen (not open to the public) with a 16th-century wooden upper storey that overhangs the stone curtain wall. The keep dates from the 13th century. The castle can also be reached by a frequent bus service from St Gallen or Arbon stations (table 880.15).

From **Häggenschwil-Winden** station a bus (table 870.70) can be taken to Häggenschwil; about 2km (1¹⁄₄ miles) to the west of the village lies the ruined Burg Ramschwag on the bank of the River Sitter. The keep, a tower and a section of wall survive.

Another castle can be reached by bus from **Muolen** station: a service between there and Amriswil station (table 840.75) passes close to the moated castle of Hagenwil, first documented in 1264 and built by the Crusader Rudolf von Hagenwil. The half-timbered castle is built on stone walls. The gallery is a restaurant open daily except Wednesdays. For Romanshorn see table 820.

Bicycle hire from Wittenbach and Romanshorn stations.

ST GALLEN–GAIS–APPENZELL Table 855

Connecting with the Appenzeller Bahn from Wasserauen to Gossau at Appenzell, this line forms part of a near circuit of metre-gauge lines, offering good walks and cycling. The delightful countryside with snow-covered mountains in the distance is relatively undiscovered. At some intermediate stations on the Appenzeller Bahn, you need to indicate to the driver that you wish to catch the train by pressing a clearly marked button on the platform. Sit on the right.

Leaving from a separate platform outside and to the right of St Gallen station, adjacent to the Trogenerbahn, trains for Appenzell head southwest parallel to the main line for a short distance before swinging south. The rack mechanism is engaged and the train climbs through a series of horseshoe curves at a gradient that will astonish those still unaccustomed to the mountain climbing abilities of Swiss trains.

Once the upland has been reached and the train has emerged from steeply sloped woods, the open, rolling Appenzeller countryside is spread out to the south, with the dominant peak of Säntis in the distance. The train twists from one valley into another, past streams, waterfalls and small farms scattered over the hills. At **Niederteufen** is the Capuchin convent of Mariä Rosengarten founded in 1397; both church and monastery were rebuilt in 1687. It is worth breaking the journey at Teufen to explore this ribbon village, which is a good walking centre as well as a health resort. The Reformed church was rebuilt in 1776–8 by Hans Ulrich Grubenmann; in the old station is a museum celebrating the work of the Grubenmann family, who were also responsible for many of the wooden bridges that still span the Sitter and Wattbach rivers.

Bühler's main street is lined with solid stone houses of the 18th and 19th centuries; one incorporates the former Rathaus in Trogen, the upper part of which was dismantled and re-erected on a new base. **Gais** is the junction for Altstätten Stadt (see table 856) and a good centre for hiking and cross-country skiing. A fire in 1780 devastated much of the village so most of the houses date from this period, those around the village square displaying extraordinarily shaped gables.

Leaving Gais the line describes a 'U', passing the junction for Altstätten on the left, and drops down towards Appenzell. A characteristic of many of the farm buildings passed on the way is a T-shaped layout with the barn forming the vertical bar and the farmhouse the horizontal one. The line describes another horseshoe curve, with a great cliff of rock on the right-hand side of the valley, before crossing the River Sitter on a long girder bridge.

The first port of call in **Appenzell**, capital of the Catholic half canton of Appenzell Innerrhoden – the smallest in Switzerland – should be the tourist office in Hauptgasse, which is reached by walking directly north through Postplatz from the station. It has information on the whole of Appenzeller and exceptionally good information and maps about the area's cycle routes and 1,200km (750 miles) of footpaths. It also contains a new museum about the customs and history of the Appenzell region.

Although a capital, Appenzell is little more than a large village of 5,300 inhabitants and it enjoys a surprising range of holiday facilities for its size. Much of its centre is pedestrianised, enabling visitors to admire in safety the ornately decorated houses that line Hauptgasse and neighbouring streets. Many have intricately painted panels on the front and even painted, curved eaves. As so often in Switzerland, a fire in the village's history marks the start of a concentrated period of construction, in this case 1560. Having been spared another catastrophe, Appenzell now has an outstanding collection of later 16th-century houses.

Amongst other important buildings are the Catholic church of St Mauritius, dating from the 16th century with a nave of 1823; the Heiligkreuzkapelle of 1561 near to the Tourist office on Hauptgasse with a portico of 1787 and an immense organ that also fills the width of the church; the Capuchin monastery of Maria Lichtmess, dating from 1586–7, with a church rebuilt in 1688; and the Capuchin convent of Maria der Engel with a church of 1621–2. The Rathaus of 1561–3 is decorated with frescos on the façade depicting the history of Appenzell, painted in 1928.

It is in the Landsgemeindeplatz that the annual open-air meeting of the cantonal parliament takes place on the last Sunday in April, locals voting by a show of hands. Traditional dress is *de rigeur*, and many of the men wear swords or daggers. Other ceremonial occasions are the unspecified days when herdsmen move their cattle up to the Alpine pastures in early summer and back again in the autumn. This traditional procession takes place wherever this transhumance is practised in Switzerland, though the way the cattle are decorated and the particular details of the custom vary.

Practical information
Teufen
TO – In station. Postfach 220, CH-9053. Tel: 071/333 38 73; fax: 071/333 38 09. Open: Mon–Sun 08.00–12.00, 13.00–18.00.

Zur Linde★★★, Bühlerstrasse 87. CH-9053. Tel: 071/333 28 22; fax: 071/333 41 20; email: hotel.linde@swissonline.ch; web: www.appon.ch/linde
Anker, Dorf 10, CH-9053. Tel: 071/333 13 45; fax: 071/333 46 89.

Gais
Zur Krone★★ (H), Dorfplatz, CH-9056. Tel: 071/791 11 37; fax: 071/791 34 97.

Appenzell
TO – Hauptgasse 4, CH-9050. Tel: 071/788 96 41; fax: 071/788 96 49; email: ferein@appenzellerland.ai.ch; web: www.appenzellerland-ferein.ch Open: Jun–Oct, Mon–Fri 09.00–12.00, 14.00–18.00, Sat 09.00–12.00, 14.00–17.00; Nov–May, Mon–Fri 09.00–12.00, 14.00–17.00, Sat 09.00–12.00, 14.00–16.00.

Romantik Hotel Santis★★★★ (H), Landsgemeindeplatz, CH-9050. Tel: 071/788 11 11; fax: 071/788 11 10; email: saentis@romantikhotel.ch; web: www. romantikhotels.com/rhappen
Appenzell★★★ (H), Hauptgasse 37, CH-9050. Tel: 071/788 15 15; fax: 071/788 15 51; email: info@hotel-appenzell.ch; web: www.hotel-appenzell.ch
Adler★★★, Adlerplatz, CH-9050. Tel: 071/787 13 89; fax: 071/787 13 65.
Taube★ (H), Hirschengasse 8 am Postplatz, CH-9050. Tel: 071/787 11 49; fax: 071/787 56 33.

Gasthaus Hof, CH-9050. Tel: 071/787 22 10; fax: 071/787 58 83; email: hotel-hof@hotmail.com

Bicycle hire from Appenzell station.

GAIS–ALTSTATTEN STADT Table 856

Changes in the landscape are usually gradual, but this short journey provides a real surprise and passes through delightful farming country. Sit on the right.

Leaving Gais, the train turns sharply to the left and passes a couple of request stops before **Rietli** where an extraordinary panorama suddenly opens up to the right. The ground drops away steeply to reveal the broad valley of the Rhein, with mountains in the distance. The train engages the rack for the steep descent to Altstatten, and tilts down past farms with wood piles under the eaves, the logs stacked as carefully as the pieces of a mosaic. Outside a barn surrounded by orchards of pears and apples you may see sheep being sheared or a cluster of rabbit hutches.

Altstätten station is close to the centre of the attractive small town, with cobbled streets and arcades. Half-hourly buses link it with Altstätten SG station on the Rorschach–Sargans main line (table 880.57). Most of the town's houses date from the 18th century and one of the town's four gates, the Untertor, survives in Engelplatz. The local history museum on Obergasse occupies part of the Prestegg, the oldest part of which was built in 1488. In Merktgasse is the Placiduskapelle of 1646.

Practical information
Altstätten

TO– Railway Station (Stadt), CH-9450. Tel: 071/755 40 90; fax: 071/755 40 95. Open: Mon–Fri 08.30–11.30, 14.00–16.30.

WASSERAUEN–APPENZELL–HERISAU–GOSSAU Table 854

The Appenzeller Bahn connects with the service from St Gallen to complete the circuit back to the main line from Winterthur to Rorschach. It provides access to some of the finest parts of the Appenzell, including the Ebenalp and Säntis. The popularity of this area for walking and cycling is obvious from the number of hikers who use the trains and the cyclists on adjacent roads and tracks.

Travellers from either direction will pass through Appenzell on their way to Wasserauen, so this section of line will be described leaving Appenzell and travelling to Wasserauen.

The hills on either side of the line rise steadily as the journey progresses, until by the terminus at Wasserauen sunlight reaches the valley floor for only a few hours a day. At **Steinegg** the delightful small church of St Magdalena, consecrated in 1590, stands beside the level crossing, its windows deeply recessed and the doorway surrounded by painted decoration.

From **Weissbad** a bus to Brülisau (table 854.30) connects with certain trains. At Brülisau it is a minute's walk to the cablecar up the Hoher Kasten (table 2745) at 1,795m (5,889ft). From the summit you can see mountains in four countries. At **Schwende** is the Catholic parish church of St Martin, built as recently as 1928–9 by Alfred Gaudy, and combining Jugendstil (the German art nouveau) with the neo-baroque.

The approach to **Wasserauen** is dramatic as the valley sides close in and steepen into rock walls. On the opposite side of the road from the station is the cablecar for the eight-minute journey to Ebenalp (table 2740) at 1,923m (5,392ft). On the way up you can see the Wildkirchli perched on the edge of a cliff, the St Michael hermitage which was founded in 1658 and dissolved in 1853. Nearby is a series of caves in which the remains of pre-glacial bears, wolves and lions have been found, together with evidence of human occupation. Some of the finds are displayed in the hermit's dwelling. The Wildkirchli is reached by a short walk from the viewing platform at Ebenalp. Well-shod and equipped hikers can walk along the ridge to the highest mountain in the region, the Säntis at 2,503m (8,209ft) (see below) or descend to Wasserauen via the picturesque lake at Seealpsee.

Returning to Appenzell, the character of the country changes as the train heads west from Appenzell towards Urnäsch, the land being less densely farmed and woods crowning the hills. The pretty village of **Gonten**, where the neo-Gothic Catholic church of St Verena was built in 1863, derives its name from Gunton meaning mountain marshland. At **Jakobsbad** the cablecar station for the Kronberg (table 2725) at 1,663m (5,455ft) is adjacent to the Appenzeller Bahn.

The railway describes a 'U' to approach **Urnäsch**, a good walking centre with 120km (75 miles) of paths, and well endowed with colourful 17th- and 18th-century houses. The Reformed church was built on the foundations of an older church following a fire that devastated the village in 1641. The Säntis Skiing School complements the area's seven ski lifts. A museum of Appenzell folklore in Dorfplatz gives an introduction to the traditional wood-carving, dancing and music (open: Apr, Wed, Sat, Sun 13.30–17.00; May–Oct, daily 13.30–17.00).

A bus from the station climbs up to Schwägalp (table 854.20) for one of Switzerland's most impressive cablecar journeys, to Säntis (table 2730). It ascends the sheer precipice by a cable span of 960m (3,150ft), from a pylon close to the base to the first on top of the rock wall. The view from the 2,502m (8,208ft) summit of Säntis is spectacular, especially in mid-winter when the air is at its clearest: then you can see as far as the Jura in western Switzerland and even the Vosges in France. A network of paths gives various options for the return, including a walk for seasoned hikers along the ridge to Ebenalp via Seealpsee (4 hours). From Schwägalp a bus can be taken to the station at Nesslau-Neu St Johann (table 853.75) (see table 853).

Leaving Urnäsch the train follows the contours to **Waldstatt**, with its 1720–1 Reformed church, where the line drops down steeply into Herisau with a fine view to the left of the huge stone viaduct on the line to Wattwil. **Herisau** is the capital of the Protestant half-canton of Appenzell Ausserrhoden and was first documented in 837. An important textile centre, the town has some fine houses around the square, which was laid out following a fire in 1559. A small historical museum occupies the former Rathaus in Oberdorfstrasse (open: Apr–Oct, Sun 10.30–12.00). Buses from the station serve one of the few Appenzell towns not on the railway, Stein (tables 870.55 and 870.60). Besides its attractive central square, Grubenmann church of 1749, covered bridges and the highest footbridge in Europe, it has a working craft museum with demonstrations of embroidery and weaving, and a cheese centre with specialist restaurant.

From Herisau the line drops down to Gossau to connect with the Winterthur–St Gallen line.

Practical information
Weissbad
Gemsle Weissbad*, Weissbadstrasse, CH-9057. Tel: 071/798 90 30; fax: 071/798 90 49; email: gemsle@bluewin.ch

Schwende
Landgasthof Edelweiss, CH-9057. Tel: 071/799 11 59; fax: 071/799 13 74.
Gasthof Frohe Aussicht, CH-9057. Tel: 071/799 11 74; fax: 071/799 11 98.

Gonten
Jakobsbad*** (H), Hauptstrasse, CH-9108. Tel: 071/794 12 33; fax: 071/794 14 45; email: info@hotel-jakobsbad.ch; web: www.hotel-jakobsbad.ch
Bären, Hauptstrasse, CH-9108. Tel: 071/795 40 10; fax: 071/795 40 19.

Urnäsch
Krone** (H), Dorf, CH-9107. Tel: 071/364 15 15; fax: 071/364 23 81.

Schwägalp
Schwägalp*** (H), CH-9107. Tel: 071/365 66 00; fax: 071/365 66 01; email: kontakt@saentisbahn.ch; web: www.saentisbahn.ch

Herisau
TO – Oberdorfstrasse 24, CH-9102. Tel: 071/353 30 35; fax: 071/353 30 39. Open: Mon–Fri 08.00–12.00, 13.30–18.30, Sat 09.00–12.00.

Landhaus*** (H), Kasernenstrasse 29, CH-9100. Tel: 071/353 01 00; fax: 071/353 01 01.

Bicycle hire from Appenzell and Herisau stations.

St Gallen–GOSSAU–SULGEN–Weinfelden Table 852
Operated as a service from St Gallen to Weinfelden, this extraordinarily sinuous branch leaves the main line at Gossau and joins the Winterthur–Romanshorn line at Sulgen.

The 1664–5 country house of Oberes Schloss at **Hauptwil** is an early baroque design, but the setting leaves something to be desired. The village has some fine half-timbered houses of the 17th and 18th centuries.

The line between **Bischofszell Stadt** and **Bischofszell Nord** stations describes such a large horseshoe curve that there is an intermediate station between them, at **Sitterdorf**. Though a centre of brewing and the food industry, Bischofszell should not be missed: the delightful old town stands on high ground above the confluence of the Sitter and Thur rivers, the former spanned by an important late medieval eight-arched bridge of 1487. The town was fortified before 1000 by the Bishops of Constance, and as so often happened in Switzerland, the outer defensive wall of the town became the walls of a ring of houses. After a fire in 1743 destroyed about 70 buildings, the town was rebuilt to plans by the three Grubenmann brothers who were responsible for numerous buildings in the region.

Of the fortifications, the Bogenturm to the east became a bell and clock tower when this suburb was fortified in 1437, and the castle was once a 13th-century bishop's residence, with the upper part dating from the mid-15th century.

The Catholic church of St Pelagius is a basilica with rebuilt 15th-century nave and a 14th-century chapel. The pink baroque Rathaus of 1747–50 has a double staircase and ground-floor windows decorated by elaborate wrought ironwork.

Bicycle hire from Gossau station.

WIL–NESSLAU–NEU ST JOHANN Table 853
The line follows the River Thur all the way, mostly on the left-hand side.

Turning south from the Winterthur–St Gallen line, the branch quickly enters hilly country with the higher ground to the west. At **Lütisburg** the Catholic church of St Michael stands on the former castle mound and is partly built with stone from the remains. A wooden covered bridge of 1790 spans the river.

Between the junctions of **Lichtensteig** and **Wattwil** (see table 870), the branch joins the St Gallen–Rapperswil line. Between April and October steam-hauled trains, marketed as the 'Amor Express', are periodically run over this onward section to Nesslau; they start at Herisau (see table 870). At **Ebnat-Kappel**, in Eich, are some Toggenburg wooden houses and in Acker is a 1752 house that was re-erected here for Albert Edelmann, who founded the Heimatmuseum (open: Tue–Fri 10.00–12.00, 14.00–17.00; 2nd and 4th Sun in month, 14.00–17.00). **Krummenau** also has some Toggenburg wooden buildings. A footpath follows the wooded banks of the Thur.

The valley widens as the line nears the terminus at **Nesslau-Neu St Johann**, a good centre for walking and cycling, and for skiing. The former Benedictine abbey was moved to its present site in Neu St Johann in 1626; the baroque church was built 1641/4–80. Buses leave from the train station for Rietbad and Schwägalp (see bus table 853.75, train table 854) and for Wildhaus and Buchs station on the Rorschach–Sargans line (table 853.70).

The latter service calls at the small resort of Unterwasser where, four minutes' walk from the bus stop, a funicular followed by a cablecar ascends to

Chäserrugg (table 2767). At the larger resort of Wildhaus, the next major stop, the wooden birthplace of the liberal reformer Zwingli (1484–1531) can be visited (open: Jan–mid-Apr, mid-May–Oct, Tue–Sun 14.00–16.00) – it is behind Hotel Friedegg.

Practical information
Nesslau-Neu St Johann

TO – Toggenburgerstrasse 25, Nesslau, CH-9652. Tel: 071/994 17 22; fax: 071/994 10 02. Open: Mon, Tue, Thu, Fri 08.00–12.00, 14.00–18.00, Wed 08.00–12.00, Sat 08.00–12.00, 14.00–16.00.

For steam-hauled excursions, tel: 071/228 23 81.

Five minutes from the station is
Sternen***, Hauptstrasse, CH-9650. Tel: 071/994 19 13; fax: 071/994 26 67.

Wildhaus

TO – Lisighaus, CH-9658. Tel: 071/999 27 27; fax: 071/999 29 29. Open: Mon–Fri 08.00–12.00, 13.30–17.30, Sat 09.00–15.00.

Acker****, CH-9658. Tel: 071/999 91 11; fax: 071/999 20 11
Hirschen Wildhaus***, CH-9658. Tel: 071/999 22 52; fax: 071/999 25 25; email: hirschen@pingnet.ch; web: www.hirschen-wildhaus.ch
Sonne***, CH-9658. Tel: 071/999 23 33; fax: 071/999 23 57; email: beutler-hotels@bluewin.ch
Toggenburg***, Lisighaus, CH-9658. Tel: 071/998 50 10; fax: 071/999 38 69.
Friedegg**, CH-9658. Tel: 0714/999 13 13; fax: 071/999 10 24.

Bicycle hire from Nesslau-Neu St Johann station.

ST GALLEN–RORSCHACH Table 880

Heading east from St Gallen towards the Bodensee (Lake Constance), Schloss Sulzberg at **Goldach** was built c1230 but has been much altered for residential use. Rorschach is Switzerland's largest port on Bodensee, served by ferries that cross the lake to Lindau in Germany and along the Swiss shore to Arbon, Romanshorn and Kreuzlingen. **Rorschach** station is the junction where the line from St Gallen joins the Schaffhausen–Sargans line; it is also the junction for the rack railway to Heiden, although this service continues on to **Rorschach Hafen** station, along the line towards Schaffhausen.

Hafen serves the town centre and is situated on Hauptstrasse; on the corner with Mariabergstrasse to the right is the tourist office. To the left of the station is the Rathaus of 1681–9 and 1747, and close by are some fine oriel windows decorating houses of the 16th–18th-centuries. Equally close to the station is the Kornhaus, reached by turning right outside the station, crossing the railway and turning left. Picturesquely sited beside the harbour, the baroque Kornhaus in Hafenplatz was built in 1746–8 as a grain store but resembles a palace. Today it houses an art gallery and museum displaying lace and embroidery as well as exhibits about the town's history (open: Apr–Nov, Tue–Sat 09.30–11.30, 14.00–17.00, Sun 10.00–12.00, 14.00–17.00).

About a mile to the south of the station, directly at the end of Mariabergstrasse on which there are numerous baroque houses, is the former Benedictine convent. Regarded as one of Switzerland's finest late medieval monastic buildings, it was begun in 1487 and has magnificent stellar and net vaulting in the cloisters.

The town is dominated by the forest-covered slopes of the Rorschacherberg (3,000ft, 914m), which can be reached by postbus from the post office (tables 880.30 and 880.45). This is in Neugasse just outside the station across the road and to the right. Three castles stand on the Rorschacherberg: the 15th/16th-century St Anna-Schloss, the heavily rebuilt Schloss Wartensee and the equally altered Schloss Wartegg, now a hotel (see below).

There is a lovely walk or cycle ride along the shore to the west; it passes a garden and a children's playground before reaching Horn, where a train can be taken back to Rorschach.

Practical information
Rorschach
TO – Hauptstrasse 63, CH-9400. Tel: 071/841 70 34; fax: 071/841 70 36; email: info@tourist-rorschach.ch; web: www.tourist-rorschach.ch Open: Nov–mid-Mar, Mon–Fri 14.00–17.00; mid-Mar–Oct, Mon–Fri 09.30–12.00, 14.00–17.30; mid-Jun–mid-Sep, Sun 09.30–12.00.

Mozart★★★, Hafenzentrum, CH-9400. Tel: 071/841 06 32; fax: 071/841 99 38.
Schloss Wartegg, Rorschacherberg, CH-9404. Tel: 071/858 62 62; fax: 071/858 62 60; email: schloss@wartegg.ch; web: www.wartegg.ch Built in 1557 and situated in English-style parkland, the restaurant uses largely organic produce.
Hotel Rössli★★★, Hauptstrasse 88, CH-9400. Tel: 071/844 68 68; fax: 071/841 00 47; email:info@hotel-roessli.ch; web: www.hotel-roessli.ch
Hotel Rorschacherhof, Bahnplatz 15, CH-9400. Tel: 071/841 43 48.
Hotel Löwen, Hauptstrasse 92, CH-9400. Tel: 071/841 38 87; fax: 071/841 49 32.

Bicycle hire from Rorschach station.

RORSCHACH–HEIDEN Table 857
This rack line provides marvellous views over Lake Constance and serves a health resort noted for its Biedermeier houses. Apart from the Rigi system, it is the only standard gauge rack railway in Switzerland. Sit on the left.

Leaving from Hafen station and stopping at Rorschach's principal station, the trains of the Rorschach–Heiden-Bergbahn climb 394m (1,292ft) in 7km (4½ miles). It was one of the country's first rack-and-pinion railways, opening in 1875, using the Riggenbach rack system.

Trains ascend through vine-covered slopes near **Weinacht-Tobel**, past fields of pumpkins, orchards and farms, and through pretty woods as they near **Heiden**. A model of the station in the days when steam locomotives propelled trains up the hill can be seen in the booking hall. Turn left outside the station up the hill to reach the village square.

A large part of Heiden was badly damaged by fire in 1838, after which the town was laid out on a grid and the houses built in the Biedermeier style, which was in vogue in Germany and Austria between the Congress of Vienna in 1815 and the revolutions of 1848. The style emphasised the qualities of utility and good proportions at the expense of decoration or pronounced forms.

People have come here for over a century for health cures, which today include electrotherapy. The most celebrated health worker in Heiden was Henri Dunant (1828–1910) who was instrumental in founding the Red Cross after witnessing the plight of the wounded at Solferino in 1859 during the war between Austria and an alliance of France and Piedmont. Dunant was living in poverty when he received the first Nobel Peace Prize, in 1901. He died at Heiden, where a museum commemorates his work.

A postbus (table 857.40) leaves the post office in the main square for Walzenhausen, where the Bergbahn Rheineck–Walzenhausen (see table 858) can be taken down to Rheineck for a steamer down the Alter Rhein and along Lake Constance back to Rorschach. Buses also leave for Altstätten SG Rathaus (table 857.70), Heerbrugg station (table 857.60), Rheineck station (table 857.30), St Anton (table 857.80), St Gallen station (table 857.10) and Trogen station (table 857.90)

Practical information
Heiden
TO – Seeallee, CH-9410. Tel: 071/891 10 60; fax: 071/891 10 70; email: info@appenzellerland-bodensee.ch; web: www.appenzellerland-bodensee.ch Open: Mar–Oct, Mon–Sat 09.30–12.00, 14.00–17.00; Nov–Feb, Mon–Fri 13.30–16.30.

Buses (from post office): Walzenhausen station and St Margrethen station (table 857.40).

Krone★★★ (H), Biedermeier-Dorfplatz 9, CH-9410. Tel: 071/891 11 27; fax: 071/891 35 05; email: kroneheiden@bluewin.ch

Linde★★★ (H), Poststrasse 11, CH-9410. Tel: 071/891 14 14; fax: 071/891 53 65.

RORSCHACH–SCHAFFHAUSEN Table 820
A scenic delight since either the Bodensee or the Untersee is seldom out of view until the beginning of the Rhine at Stein am Rhein. Harbours for yachts punctuate the shore which is lined with market gardens and vineyards. Sit on the right.

Leaving Rorschach, the train passes a municipal garden with large fountains and water jets before entering a countryside of market gardens and fruit farms. A train can be taken back to Rorschach from **Horn** after a pleasant walk along the lake.

Although **Arbon** is an important industrial town, its Roman origins and development make it worth a visit, as their fort has been incorporated in the

13th-century castle. Turn left outside the station down Bahnhofstrasse (in which the tourist office is situated) to reach Hauptstrasse on which stands the Stadthaus, once the home of linen manufacturers but adapted to become the town hall in 1941. The Rathaus of 1791 in Promenadenstrasse is one of many half-timbered houses in the old quarter which lies to the west of the castle. The enclosure of the Roman fort, named Arbor Felix ('happy tree'), is preserved by the later castle walls. By the southeast tower is the Galluskapelle, marking the place where St Gallus/en and St Columban are said to have stepped ashore in 612. The chapel has a Romanesque nave and polygonal apse. The upper part of the keep was added in 1520 and can be easily distinguished from the 13th-century base.

A succession of fires and the industrial development of **Romanshorn** have left few buildings of note in the town, but it has a fine park and the ecumenical Old Church has 14th-century murals. The tower of the Catholic church of St Johann, built 1911–13, was based on St Mark's in Venice. The station is the junction for services to Winterthur (table 840) and St Gallen (see table 870).

At **Uttwil** is a much altered 17th/18th-century castle. **Kesswil** was the birthplace of the psychiatrist Carl Gustav Jung (1875–1961), and at **Altnau** the Landschlacht Chapel is notable for its 14th- and 15th-century murals. The chapel was built in the 11th–12th centuries on the pilgrim route between Constance and St Gallen. The former Benedictine nunnery at **Münsterlingen** was rebuilt in 1716 and now serves as a hospital, though the baroque church remains in use.

The town of **Kreuzlingen** is contiguous with Konstanz in Germany through which there is a railway line to Singen and Engen (table 830). Kreuzlingen is also the junction for trains to Weinfelden and Wil (also table 830), and the departure point for boat services to over a dozen piers in Germany. In Hauptstrasse is the former Augustinian monastery church of St Ulrich built in 1650–3; it was devastated by fire in 1963, but retains sumptuous rococo decoration and the 'Kreuzlingen Passion' of 1720–30, over 300 carved figures in wood, of which about 250 are original. The monastery buildings of c1660 have been converted into a teachers' training college.

Ermatingen offers no less than four castles: Hard, dating from 1520 but altered several times; Wolfsberg of c1571, altered and extended; Lilienberg, built in 1830; and at Fruthweilen (four minutes by bus from Ermatingen station, table 840.35) the partially half-timbered Hubberg of 1596. The town also boasts the oldest hotel in the canton of Thurgau, where Alexandre Dumas, Hermann Hesse, Thomas Mann and Graf Zeppelin (born in Konstanz) have dined.

The railway line is particularly close to the Untersee for the section to **Mannenbach-Salenstein** where even more illustrious castles can be found. Less than 1km from the station is Schloss Arenenberg. Originating in 1546-8, the castle was bought and rebuilt in 1817 by Hortense de Beauharnais, Napoleon's stepdaughter. She had been Queen of Holland through her marriage to Napoleon's third brother, Louis, who abdicated in 1810. Their son Prince Louis Napoleon, later Napoleon III, was brought up at Arenenberg.

Here Queen Hortense received Chateaubriand, Dumas père and Mme Récamier. After Napoleon III's death in exile in England, his widow Eugénie sometimes lived here until she gave the castle to the canton of Thurgau together with the Napoleonic collections. Today it is a museum (Napoleonmuseum) with fine portraits, Empire furniture and sculptures by Canova. (Open: Tue–Sun 10.00–17.00.) Also at Salenstein are Schloss Salenstein, much altered though with 11th-century remnants, and Schloss Eugensberg of 1821.

At the lovely village of **Berlingen**, with its lakeside timber-framed houses, the Untersee is at its greatest width of 8km (5 miles). A cycle route parallels the railway for much of its way beside the lake. **Steckborn** grew from a monastic farm into a town, receiving its charter in 1313 when the walls and Turmhof beside the lake were begun. Both survive, the latter as a local museum with Roman and Alemannic finds. (Open: mid-May–mid-Oct, Wed, Thur, Sat, Sun 15.00–17.00.) The half-timbered Rathaus was rebuilt in 1667, and Schloss Glarisegg was built in 1772–4.

The small lakeside village of **Mammern** is blessed with a large park surrounding Schloss Mammern, once the home of the abbots of Rheinau, described in the 1895 *Baedeker* as a 'Hydropathic Establishment' and still a clinic. The baroque chapel of 1749–50 has *trompe-l'oeil* decoration on the ceiling. Above the village is the ruined 13th-century tower of Neuburg.

Although the small town of **Stein am Rhein** is overrun by visitors in high season, they come for a good reason. Try to spend at least one night there; once the coach trippers have gone, those living or staying there reclaim the place and by late afternoon it is relatively quiet. It is only a short walk from the station to the centre: proceed straight ahead from the station, turn right at the T-junction and immediately left to cross the Rhine.

As you cross the bridge you can see to the left, reached by Bäregass, the landing stage for boats, while to the right is the Reformed church and former monastery of St George. Cars are excluded from much of the town centre, making it a pleasure to explore on foot the compact historic quarter, protected by 14th-century gate-towers. The centre of the town is Rathausplatz, reached by turning left at the T-junction shortly after crossing the bridge, where many of the house façades are graced with oriel windows and decorated with paintings depicting biblical or moral themes and subjects from Swiss history. The half-timbered upper storey of the Rathaus was added in 1745 above the two storeys of 1539–42, and the whole building restored in 1898–1900, by which time the value of Stein am Rhein's legacy of fine buildings had begun to be appreciated (earlier in the century a 17th-century star-shaped redoubt had been blown up).

Rathausplatz becomes Understadt, and at No 33 is the Museum Lindwurm, which should not be missed. In a building with elements dating from 1279, the rooms of the house have been superbly restored to illustrate the life of a bourgeois family and its servants in the mid-19th century. Each room has cards in English, French, Italian and Japanese to explain what you are looking at, and there is an even more detailed description which can be borrowed on request at the entrance. Reflecting the interest in 'below stairs' life, all the ancillary rooms such as the basement, laundry, tannery, nursery, attic with meat-smoking chamber, barn and wagon shed have been restored and opened to the public. (Open: Mar–Oct, daily except Tue 10.00–17.00.)

Down Chirchhofplatz (to the right of the Rathaus) and to the right is the Benedictine monastery of St George. Founded in 1005, the oldest monastery buildings date from the 11th century, including the Romanesque basilica which was altered in 1583–4 as a Reformed church. The monastery of 12th–16th-century buildings is now a local history museum with frescos and wood carving, but there are no guidebook or labels in English. The panelled interiors, old glass and decoration of the abbot's lodging are none the less worth seeing. (Open: Mar–Oct, daily except Monday 10.00–17.00.)

Another museum in Stein am Rhein is devoted to phonographs (Rathausplatz 6) (open: Mar–Dec, daily 10.00–17.00).

The town is overlooked by the well-preserved and largely intact castle of Hohenklingen, dating from the 11th century, though most of what stands is 16th-century. The walls and keep offer a panoramic view of the Rhine, and there has been a restaurant in the castle since 1865.

Beyond Stein am Rhein, the river is out of sight of the railway as it runs through a flat area of intensive market gardening. At **Etzwilen** is the junction for a branch line to Winterthur, though services run through to Stein am Rhein. **Diessenhofen** is noted for its 16th–18th-century houses and other buildings, many in Gothic style, and for its frequently rebuilt wooden bridge over the Rhine, more recently following its destruction by the Russians in 1799 and by American bombing during World War II. Surviving fortified buildings include, in Obere Kirchgasse, the much-rebuilt 12th-century Unterhof, and the Siegelturm of 1545–6, built as an inner gate.

The approach to **Schaffhausen** is impressive, crossing the Rhine on a tall viaduct and curving round the north of the town in a tunnel to enter the large station. The large historic quarter is straight in front of you, beginning on the other side of the road from the bus station, and it takes at least a day to do it justice. Cars are thankfully excluded from much of the area. To reach the tourist office, turn right outside the station parallel with the railway and turn left into Schwertstrasse; turn right into Fronwagplatz and the tourist office is in the Fronwagturm on the far side of the square.

Given its city charter in 1045, Schaffhausen owes its prosperity to one of its principal tourist sights: the nearby Rhine Falls. This impassable section of the river compelled carriers to unload their goods on to waggons at Schaffhausen; the expansion of trade during the Middle Ages encouraged its development as a centre of commerce and industry. The affluence of the town's merchants is reflected by the magnificent façades and oriel windows – over 170 of them – that decorate many of the older houses. Statues and fountains adorn many of the streets, helping to make the old town one of the loveliest in Switzerland.

The Falls in particular have attracted visitors for centuries. It was 1563 when the Holy Roman Emperor Ferdinand I visited the town, throwing the assembled burghers into confusion by arriving at the wrong gate following an impromptu detour to see the Falls. It was from Schaffhausen that Ruskin, as a child, had his first, distant view of the Alps and from where D H Lawrence set out in 1913 to walk the width of Switzerland, over the Gotthard Pass to Bellinzona and Lugano. His experiences are described in *Twilight in Italy and Other Essays*.

The best view of the town is had from the walls of the Munot, the largest circular fortress in Switzerland, which was built in 1564–85. It is unique in being the only castle based on the ideas of Albrecht Dürer, which he set out in his *Treatise on Fortification*, published in Nuremberg in 1527. The 5m-thick walls (16ft) of the Munot are reached by long flights of steps up a vine-covered hillside from either Bachstrasse or Unterstadt. Inside the dominant, cylindrical tower, with caretaker's flat under its pinnacled roof, is a spiral ramp which allowed cannon and carts of supplies to be taken up to the battlements. In summer, concerts, dancing and a Munot Ball are held in the open space inside the wall-walk.

Beneath the Munot and beside the Rhine on Freierplatz is the Güterhof of 1785–7, an imposing warehouse and reminder of the town's trading origins. Also recalling its mercantile past are the twelve guildhalls, some now restaurants. Most notable amongst the dozens of distinguished houses in the old town are: the Haus zum Ritter, No. 65 Vordergasse, with its scenes from Roman history and mythology by the town's native artist Tobias Stimmer – remnants of the originals can be seen in Allerheiligen Museum at All Saints; the Haus zum Goldenen Ochsen of c1600 in Vorstadt, which has one of the most ornate oriel windows and allegorical representations of the five senses on the 1609 Renaissance façade; and the Grosse Haus, with outstanding oriel window of 1685, on Fronwagplatz.

The largest of the churches is the Romanesque All Saints, founded in 1048, as part of the Benedictine abbey which was begun in the 11th century and extended between the 13th and 16th centuries. In 1052 Leo IX came to consecrate the abbey church, which was not completed until 1104. Today the abbey complex with its 12th-century cloisters houses a variety of activities. The Allerheiligen Museum has an exhibition of prehistoric, Roman and medieval antiquities, reconstructed rooms, ceramics, costumes, local industry, topographical and modern Swiss paintings, and 16th–20th-century copper engravings (open: daily except Mon 10.00–12.00, 14.00–17.00; May–Oct, Sat–Sun 10.00–17.00). The city library is housed in the former granary, while the sound of music may betray the presence of a music school. The air is often scented by fragrances from the medieval herb garden.

Just to the south of the abbey on the corner of Baumgartenstrasse and Klosterstrasse is a large former textile factory that has been converted into a gallery of international contemporary art, the Hallen für Neue Kunst. (Open: May–Oct, Sat 14.00–17.00, Sun 11.00–17.00.)

Beside Vordergasse is the Reformed parish church of St Johann, thought to have been founded in the 11th century. A 15th-century rebuild gave it a nave and pair of aisles, to which were added another two aisles, making it the third widest church in Switzerland, after Basel and Bern. On the fourth storey of the 1350 bell tower can be seen the crenellations of the former guard house.

Other fortified towers on the periphery of the old town are, to the north, the 14th-century Schwabentor, the successively raised 13th-century Obertor near the station, the Frontwagturm with its astronomical clock of 1564, and the Diebsturm to the southwest. To reach the Rhine Falls, take a bus (Schaffhausen has an excellent bus service) from outside the station to Neuhausen, from where it is a short walk. The sound of Europe's most powerful falls can be heard long before they are in sight. The volume of water is greatest in June and July when it is augmented by snow melt, and on 1 August (Swiss National Day) a firework display illuminates the sky above the falls. Statistics are impressive – an average of 1,200 tonnes of water a second, 700 cubic m (916 cubic yards) a second, 150m (492ft) wide – but it is no wonder that the experience of watching and listening to the cataract has inspired so many painters and poets. You can see the falls from several vantage points. Steps down from the bus stop at Neuhausen lead to a riverside walk past Restaurant Park to the former customs post at Wörth, thought to date from the 12th century and now a restaurant. Schloss Laufen (another restaurant and probably Europe's most dramatically sited youth hostel), has two nearby belvederes overlooking the falls; it can be reached by train (table 762), bus or by walking across the railway bridge taking the Schaffhausen–Winterthur line over the Rhine just above the falls. In season boats take visitors to a rock in the middle of the falls up which a staircase ascends to a viewing platform. The spray is such that waterproof clothing is needed for all vantage points except Schloss Laufen.

A journey east along the Rhine should not be missed, whether by boat (services to Kreuzlingen and Constance with many ports of call), bicycle or on foot, since this is one of the most highly regarded stretches of the Rhine.

Practical information
Arbon
TO – Bahnhofstrasse 40, CH-9320. Tel: 071/447 85 15; fax: 071/447 85 10. Open: Mon–Fri 08.00–12.00, 14.00–18.00, Sat 09.00–12.00.

Seegarten★★★, Seestrasse 66, CH-9320. Tel: 071/446 57 57; fax: 071/446 39 03.
Rotes Kreuz★★, Hafenstrasse 3, CH-9320. Tel: 071/446 19 14; fax: 071/446 24 85.

Romanshorn
TO – Railway Station, CH-8590. Tel: 071/463 32 32; fax: 071/461 19 80. Open: Mon–Sat 08.00–18.00, Sun 08.00–12.00, 14.00–18.00.

Schloss★★★ (H), Schlossbergstrasse 26, CH-8590. Tel: 071/466 78 00; fax: 071/466 78 01.
Bahnhof, CH-8590. Tel: 071/463 17 26; fax: 071/463 63 60.
Bodan, Bahnhofstrasse 1, CH-8590. Tel: 071/463 15 02; fax: 071/463 15 01.

Ermatingen
TO – c/o Hotel Ermatingerhof (see below).

Ermatingerhof★★★, Hauptstrasse 82, CH-8272. Tel: 071/663 20 20; fax: 071/663 20 30.
Adler, Fruthwilerstrasse 2+4, CH-8272. Tel: 071/664 11 33; fax: 071/664 30 11.

Stein am Rhein

TO – Oberstadt 9, CH-8260. Tel: 052/741 28 35; fax: 052/741 51 46. Open: Mon–Fri
09.00–11.00, 14.00–17.30.

The hotel nearest the station is about 10 minutes' walk
Rheinfels★★★ (H), Rhigass 178, CH-8260. Tel: 052/741 21 44; fax: 052/741 25 22.

In the old town is
Adler★★★ (H), Rathausplatz 2, CH-8260. Tel: 052/742 61 61; fax: 052/741 44 40.

Schaffhausen

TO – Fronwagturm, CH-8201. Tel: 052/625 51 41; fax: 052/625 51 43. Open:
Mon–Fri 10.00–12.00, 14.00–17.00; June–Oct, Sat 10.00–12.00. Besides dispensing
information, the tourist office organises 1½-hour town walks with English-speaking
guides on Mon, Wed and Fri between Apr and Oct.
Bahnhof ★★★★, Bahnhofstrasse 46, CH-8201. Tel: 052/624 19 24; fax: 052/624 74 79;
email: mail@hotelbahnhof.ch; web: www.hotelbahnhof.ch
Park Villa★★★ (H), Parkstrasse 18, CH-8200. Tel: 052/625 27 37; fax: 052/624 12 53.
Unspoilt 1900 villa in quiet street with park behind, 10 minutes' walk from station.

Bicycle hire from Arbon, Romanshorn, Kreuzlingen, Steckborn, Stein am Rhein and
Schaffhausen stations.

SCHAFFHAUSEN–ERZINGEN Table 763

The principal place of interest on this short line that runs to the German
border at Erzingen is **Neunkirch**. This delightful walled town was laid out on
a grid pattern in the later 13th century and retains much of its medieval
appearance. Defensive buildings include the Obertor of 1574 and the castle,
extended in the 16th century and now housing a local history museum (open:
Apr–Oct, first Sun in month 14.00–17.00). The high ground on which stands
the largely late 14th-century Reformed Bergkirche makes it a landmark for
miles around.

Also worth visiting is Wilchingen, a short walk to the southeast of the station
named **Wilchingen-Hallau**. A curious feature of this wine village is its
covered passages running between houses to connect adjoining roads or alleys.

SCHAFFHAUSEN–THAYNGEN Table 764

Local trains operate as far as **Thayngen** on this line to Singen in Germany.
The Reformed parish church of 1500–4 has a defensive tower on the north
side. The village was once well-endowed with guest houses: the Adler was
built in 1711–12, the Rebstock was documented in the Middle Ages and
enlarged in 1701, and the Sternen is a neo-classical building of 1792. At nearby
Kesserloch is a major paleolithic site; the items found in the caves are on
display in the Allerheiligen Museum in Schaffhausen.

SCHAFFHAUSEN–WINTERTHUR Table 762

Heading south from Schaffhausen, the train affords a glimpse of the Rhine Falls as it crosses the river on a stone-arched bridge before plunging into a tunnel. In summer trains stop at **Schloss Laufen am Rheinfall**. From **Marthalen** station, an hourly bus (table 762.20, line 620) serves the small town of Rheinau where a Benedictine abbey church and complex stands on a peninsula (once an island) on the Rhine. The largely baroque church is built on the grave of an Irish missionary from Leinster, St Fintan, who died here in 879. The church is considered one of Switzerland's finest examples of high baroque, having been rebuilt in the early 18th century. Besides the extensive abbey buildings are a covered bridge of 1804 over the Rhine and a Roman watchtower in Köpferplatz. Marthalen itself is worth an hour or two to admire its fine half-timbered houses.

The railway passes between vine-covered slopes to **Andelfingen**, centre of this wine-growing region. From the train you can see the Reformed parish church of 1666–7 with its colourfully tiled tower roof. In the centre the castle of 1780–2, now an old people's home, overlooks the River Thur across which there is a covered wooden bridge of 1814–15.

For Winterthur see table 750.

Bicycle hire from Winterthur station.

WINTERTHUR–ETZWILEN/STEIN AM RHEIN Table 821

A few minutes' walk from **Oberwinterthur** station is the attractive medieval stronghold of Hegi, in Hegifeldstrasse. The once moated castle has a keep dating from c1200 and now houses a youth hostel and museum (open: Mar–Oct, Tue–Thu, Sat 14.00–17.00, Sun 10.00–12.00, 14.00–17.00). At **Dinhard** is a late Gothic Reformed parish church of 1511–15. The line crosses the River Thur on the approach to **Ossingen** where there are some fine 16th–18th-century half-timbered houses around the Reformed parish church of 1651. The privately owned medieval Schloss Widen, to the west of the town overlooking the Thur, had to be rebuilt after a US bomber crashed here in 1944.

The station at **Stammheim** serves the separate parishes of Unterstammheim, around the station, and Oberstammheim, less than a kilometre to the east, served by bus from the station (table 840.25). Both are delightful villages with fine half-timbered vernacular buildings. The timbered Gasthof Hirschen at Oberstammheim has an unusual three-storey oriel.

For **Stein am Rhein** see table 820.

Bicycle hire from Stein am Rhein station.

WINTERTHUR–ROMANSHORN Table 840

The service shares the line as far as **Oberwinterthur** with trains to Stein am Rhein (see above) and then heads northeast to **Wiesendangen**, where the choir of the Reformed parish church of 1480 has 21 wall-paintings. About 2km (1.2 miles) to the northwest of the station, near the village of Stadel (no bus service), is the 11th–13th-century castle of Mörsburg. The large rectangular tower was taken over by the town of Winterthur as early as 1598 and is now a museum (Ortsmuseum, open: first Sunday in month except August 14.00–17.00).

Issikon began to develop as a centre of dyeing and fabric printing in the late 18th century, some of the buildings being in the Biedermeier style. Less than a kilometre to the northwest of the station, at Kefikon, is a much altered, formerly moated castle.

The origins of **Frauenfeld**, capital of canton Thurgau since 1803, go back to 1227 when the counts of Kyburg began to build their castle. To the keep were added residential buildings that now house the Thurgau Historical Museum (open: daily except Mon 14.00–17.00). However, the historical interest of the town was diminished by two fires in the late 18th century that laid waste most of the town. Neighbouring cantons came to the town's aid and helped to rebuild it, giving it a variety of baroque frontages that can be identified as the work of craftsmen from Zürich, Bern or Luzern. None the less some medieval buildings remain between the neo-classical Rathaus of 1790–4 and the Reformed church. In Oberkirch is the non-demoninational church of St Laurence, the oldest part of which is 10th-century; it has some important stained glass of c1330. At Freiestrasse 26 is a natural history museum (open: Tue–Sun 14.00–17.00). The railway station building itself at Frauenfeld is one of the country's older stations, built in 1855.

Near **Felben-Wellhausen** is Schloss Wellenberg with a 13th-century keep, 16th-century residential building and staircase tower of 1768. The village centre of **Weinfelden** has some interesting buildings, including the early baroque Gasthaus zum Trauben of 1649. On the Ottenberg to the north stands a castle with 12th-century keep and living quarters rebuilt in 1860. The station is the junction for trains to Kreuzlingen and Wil (see table 830 below for both).

The keep of the castle at **Bürglen** dates from the 12th–13th century. In 1888–9 it became a school and was further converted and enlarged in 1950–1. The River Thur is close to the line on the right after Bürglen, making it a pretty stretch. The Reformed church is the castle's chapel. **Sulgen** is the junction for St Gallen, though the train service starts at Weinfelden and runs through to St Gallen (table 852). The village of **Erlen** has half-timbered houses and a church of 1764 built by Johann Ulrich Grubenmann. **Oberaach** boasts one of the most elaborate half-timbered houses in Switzerland: the Gasthaus zum Goldenen Löwen has a courtroom on the first floor with coffered ceiling and intarsia work.

The industrial town of **Amriswil** has some half-timbered buildings and a modern Catholic church, built of concrete in 1939. The castle of Hagenwil (see table 870) can be reached by bus from the station (table 840.75).

For **Romanshorn** see table 820.

Practical information
Frauenfeld

TO – Railway Station, Bahnhofstrasse 75, CH-8500. Tel: 052/721 31 28; fax: 052/722 10 64. Open: Mon–Fri 09.00–12.00, 14.00–18.00, Sat 09.00–12.00.

Blumenstein★★★, Am Bahnhof, CH-8500. Tel: 052/721 47 28; fax: 052/721 91 35.

Weinfelden

TO – Pestalozzistrasse 18, CH-8570. Tel: 071/622 81 13; fax: 071/622 75 17. Open: Mon–Fri 08.00–11.00.

Rössli, Amriswilerstrasse 3, CH-8570. Tel: 071/622 30 90; fax: 071/622 78 90.

Gasthaus zum Trauben, Rathausstrasse 1, CH-8570. Tel: 072/622 44 44; fax: 072/622 44 35.

Amriswil

TO – Arbonerstrasse 2, CH-8580. Tel: 071/411 81 81. Open: Mon–Fri 08.00–12.00, 14.00–17.00.

Hirschen Landgasthof (H), Weinfelderstrasse 80, CH-8580. Tel: 071/411 79 71; fax: 071/411 79 75.

Bicycle hire from Frauenfeld and Romanshorn stations.

FRAUENFELD–WIL Table 841

This single-track metre-gauge roadside railway follows the River Murg for most of its 17km (11 miles), though it is seldom in sight and the scenery is unremarkable. Sit on the right.

The train for Wil leaves from a separate platform to the right outside Frauenfeld station. It weaves its way through the picturesque streets of the town, many of them pedestrianised. On the outskirts an area of immaculately tended allotment gardens can be seen on the right.

St Margaretha's chapel in **Münchwilen** dates from 1641 and has three baroque altars contemporaneous with the building. The train terminates at a platform outside **Wil** main station. For Wil see table 850.

Bicycle hire from Wil station.

WIL–WEINFELDEN–KREUZLINGEN–(Konstanz–Singen–Engen) Table 830

Although this route has the character of a branch line, it is operated as an international service into Germany, connecting with trains to Frankfurt and Kassel.

At **Bronschofen** is an exceptionally fine former parish church which was acquired by the monastery of Rüti in 1280. Becoming the pilgrimage church of Our Lady of Dreibrunnen, it was rebuilt in 1672 with an attractive demi-octagonal, colonnaded porch. Paintings of battles with the Turks at Lepanto and Vienna decorate the ceiling. At Tobel – alight at **Tobel-Affeltrangen** – is a Commandery of the Knights of the Order of St John, built in 1228 and successively rebuilt and enlarged. Buses leave from the station to Stettfurt (table 850.30), from which it is about 40 minutes' walk to the castle at

Sonnenberg. First documented in 1242, today's impressive structure is the result of rebuilding after a fire in 1596. It was acquired by the monastery of Einsiedeln (see table 672) in 1678 and remains in its possession, housing a museum and restaurant (open: daily except Thur).

The line weaves through rolling pastoral hills dotted with large farmhouses. On the approach to **Bussnang** a distinctive, almost circular modern church can be seen to the left.

Weinfelden (see table 840 above) is a junction on the Winterthur–Romanshorn line.

After a sinuous section of railway, the train reaches **Berg** where there are several notable buildings. The three-storeyed Schloss Pfauenmoos was built c1564 and altered in the late 18th century. The Grosser Hahnberg was built c1616 and rebuilt c1770, while the Kleiner Hahnberg is a 16th-century half-timbered building with tall staircase tower. The Catholic parish church of St Michael was rebuilt in 1775–6 incorporating the medieval tower.

Bicycle hire from Weinfelden and Kreuzlingen stations.

RORSCHACH–SARGANS Table 880

With sections of this route used by international expresses to such destinations as Vienna, Graz and Munich, there is a wide choice of trains through the Rhine valley, though the river is barely visible.

Heading east the first station of note is **Rheineck** close to the Rhine delta; this is the easterly end of Swiss lake services. Rheineck is the junction for the 2km (1¼ miles) rack line up to Walzenhausen (see table 858). The small town has a Rathaus of 1553–5, one of the country's first modern churches – the Catholic parish church of St Theresia, 1932–3 – and the baroque Custerhof of 1750–3 which has been an agricultural college since 1896. The huge three-storey Löwenhof, with mansard roof and dormer windows, was built in 1746–8 for a wealthy merchant.

St Margrethen is an industrial frontier village and junction for the line to Bregenz in Austria. At the junction to the east of the station, the line turns to the south to parallel the broad Rhine valley. On the site of an 11th-century fortress at **Heerbrugg** is a baroque residence of 1774–8 with a tower of 1911. Less than a kilometre to the southwest is Balgach which has a former Rathaus of 1566 and to the southwest again and visible from the railway is the rebuilt 13th-century Schloss Grünenstein.

Above the station at **Rebstein-Marbach** is the castle of Weinstein. First documented in 1375 and rebuilt in 1479, the castle is now a restaurant open daily. However, it is about 2km (1¼ miles) from the station, so a bus from Heerbrugg (table 880.55) may be preferred. For **Altstätten** see table 856.

From **Buchs** buses head east into Liechtenstein (the Swiss franc is the country's currency). The buses (table 880.90) run through Liechtenstein's capital of Vaduz on their way to Feldkirch on the main Aarlberg railway line to Innsbruck and Vienna. On the western edge of Buchs is the village and castle of Werdenberg, served by the bus from the station to Gams (table

880.78). Built beside an ornamental lake, the village is claimed to be Switzerland's, if not Europe's, oldest wooden housing settlement. Built around a market square dominated by a half-timbered house resting on three arches with huge pillars, the village is overlooked by the magnificent castle built c1230 by Count Rudolf of Montfort. It is now a museum with reconstructed rooms and 17th–18th-century furniture. (Open: Apr–Oct, Tue–Sun 09.30–17.00.)

Just to the west of **Sevelen** are the ruins of the 13th-century castle of Herrenberg. The village is connected to Liechtenstein by a wooden bridge. About a kilometre from **Weite** is the ruined 13th-century castle of Wartau; the five-storey keep survives with some residential buildings on a hill above the railway.

The approach to the junction of **Sargans** is dominated by the 13th-century castle that overlooks the town, its keep soaring above the cluster of residential buildings. The property of the town authorities since 1899, it now houses a Youth Hostel, restaurant and museum of local history, including an exhibition about the nearby Gonzen iron-ore mine (open: late Mar–mid-Nov, 09.30–12.00, 13.30–17.30). Few buildings in Sargans pre-date 1811 when a fire destroyed most of the town within the walls. Of note are the neo-classical Rathaus and the chapel of St Sebastian, dating from 1502. Sargans is on the Zürich–Chur main line (see table 900).

Practical information
Sargans
TO – Städtchenstrasse 1, CH-7320. Tel: 081/723 53 30. Open: Mon–Sat 08.00–17.00.

Zum Ritterhof★★★, Bahnofstrasse 12, CH-7320. Tel: 081/723 03 53; fax: 081/723 81 71.

Bicycle hire from St Margrethen, Buchs and Sargans stations.

RHEINECK–WALZENHAUSEN Table 858
Built to the unusual gauge of 1200mm (3ft 11¼in), this 2km (1¼ miles) line uses the Riggenbach rack system to climb up to the village and health resort of **Walzenhausen** overlooking Lake Constance. Before the railway opened in 1896, it took a diligence 1 hour 5 minutes; today it takes the train 6 minutes. A Capuchin monastery here was established in 1424 and rebuilt in 1724. A bus from the station (table 857.40) goes to Heiden, enabling a circular journey to be made back to Rorschach.

Practical information
Walzenhausen
TO – c/o Hotel Walzenhausen. Tel: 071/888 24 70; fax: 071/888 10 84. Open: daily 07.00–21.00.

A hotel adjacent to the station is
Walzenhausen★★★★, CH-9428. Tel: 071/886 21 21; fax: 071/888 10 84; email: info@hotel-walzenhausen.ch; web: www.hotel-walzenhausen.ch

Bern

Although Bern has been the capital of the Swiss Confederation since 1848, it is only the fourth largest city, after Zürich, Basel and Geneva, with a population of 134,000. Few cities in Europe can rival Bern for the way that it has kept its medieval centre intact; UNESCO has recognised this and placed the city on its list of world cultural landmarks, on a par with the centres of Rome, Florence and Havana. It is renowned for its fountains, towers and bridges, the profusion of geranium-filled windowboxes and the 6km (4 miles) of arcades that line many of the streets of greenish-grey sandstone buildings.

Its site on a high peninsula in a meander of the River Aare was chosen by Berchtold V, Duke of Zähringen, for its easily defensible position. Although he was certainly the city's founder, there was already a small settlement in existence by c1155, clustered around Nydegg Castle at the eastern end of the peninsula. Legend has it that the name came from Berchtold saying that the new settlement would have the name of the first wild animal caught on the peninsula. Whatever the validity of the story about the ensuing hunt, the bear has been the city's emblem since at least 1224 when it was used on the city's seal; it also gave rise to the tradition of keeping bears in the former moats from at least 1480 to 1857, when they were moved to the current bear pits beside the River Aare close to the Nydegg bridge.

The city grew in a westerly direction towards what is now Bahnhofplatz, two moats being successively filled in to form the north–south squares of Kornhausplatz and Bärenplatz/Waisenhausplatz and new walls built. On each occasion the main east–west street was extended. The first wall, built on Berchtold's orders, was divided by the Clock Tower; the main gateway-tower of the second wall, built c1250, was the Prison Tower; and the third wall, begun in 1346 on the site of today's railway station and completed in a mere 18 months, was dominated by the Christoffel Tower. The first two towers thankfully survive, but the last was torn down in 1865 after a referendum narrowly sanctioned its demolition.

From the completion of the third wall until the early 19th century, the city boundary did not alter, though defences were strengthened by a series of entrenchments built in the 17th century on the site of the present university. However, one event transformed Bern's appearance. At sunset on 14 May 1405, fire broke out near the Clock Tower. Fanned by a strong wind, the fire

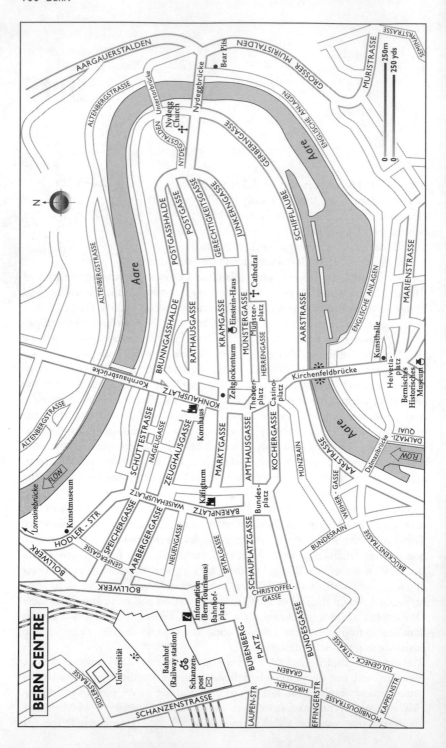

BERN CENTRE

N

250m
250 yds

Aare

Aare

Aare

FLOW

FLOW

AARGAUERSTALDEN

ALTENBERGSTRASSE

ALTENBERGSTRASSE

ALTENBERGSTRASSE

Untertorbrücke

NYDEGG (GSSTALDEN)

Nydegg Church

Nydeggbrücke

Bear Pits

GROSSER MUIRISTALDEN

MURISTRASSE

MATTENSTRASSE

AARSTRASSE

MURISTRASSE

GERBERNGASSE

ENGLISCHE ANLAGEN

MARIENSTRASSE

POSTGASSHALDE

POSTGASSE

GERECHTIGKEITSGASSE

JUNKERNGASSE

SCHIFFLAUBE

BRUNNGASSHALDE

RATHAUSGASSE

KRAMGASSE

Einstein-Haus

Cathedral

MÜNSTERGASSE

Münster-platz

HERRENGASSE

AARSTRASSE

Kornhausbrücke

KORNHAUSPLATZ

Zeitglockenturm

Theater-platz

Casino-platz

Kirchenfeldbrücke

Kunsthalle

Helvetia-platz

Bernisches Historisches Museum

SCHÜTTESTRASSE

NÄGELIGASSE

ZEUGHAUSGASSE

Kornhaus

MARKTGASSE

AMTHAUSGASSE

KOCHERGASSE

MÜNZRAIN

AARSTRASSE

Dalmazibrücke

DALMAZI-QUAI

Lorrainebrücke

Kunstmuseum

HODLER · STR

SPEICHERGASSE

AARBERGERGASSE

WAISENHAUSPLATZ

Käfigturm

BÄRENPLATZ

NEUENGASSE

SPITALGASSE

Bundes-platz

SCHAUPLATZGASSE

WEIHER · GASSE

BUNDESRAIN

BRÜCKENSTRASSE

SULGENECK · STRASSE

GENFERGASSE

BOLLWERK

BOLLWERK

Information (Bern Tourismus)

Bahnhof-platz

CHRISTOFFEL-GASSE

BUNDESGASSE

Universität

SIDLERSTRASSE

Bahnhof (Railway station)

Schanzen-post

SCHANZENSTRASSE

BUBENBERG-PLATZ

LAUPEN-STR

HIRSCHEN-GRABEN

MONBIJOUSTRASSE

EFFINGERSTR

SULGENECK · STRASSE

KAPPELENSTR

consumed 600 houses – almost all of the city's largely wooden structures. The city visitors see today is chiefly the product of the reconstruction in stone, clay and plaster that followed, helped by such neighbouring towns as Fribourg which sent 12 waggons and 100 people for nearly a month.

An equally harrowing experience was the occupation of the city by French troops in 1798 following defeat of the city's forces at Grauholz. The town was systematically plundered of all its treasures; even the bears were carried off. Its impoverishment was matched by a loss of political power which it did not regain until 1848 when Bern was chosen by the first Swiss Parliament as the capital of the Confederation. A legacy of the French occupation is the different coloured street signs and house numbers: many of Napoleon's soldiers could neither read nor write, so streets were coded red, green, blue and white to assist identification. The same system was used in Vienna.

The key to Bern's expansion has naturally been a series of bridges over the River Aare (see page 107). Until 1844 the only crossing was the Untertorbrücke, but the new structures made possible the construction of large civic buildings that could not have been accommodated in the old town without extensive demolition.

Regrettably the feature of Bern's environs that most impressed visitors was swept away when roads were adapted for motor traffic. Bern's prosperous families had country houses reached by roads radiating from the city that were often built for military purposes in the 17th century; these roads were characterised by avenues of elm trees planted to provide shade for travellers and the carriages of the landed families. Their destruction was keenly felt by the Bernese who had enjoyed walks out of the city.

Besides its exceptional buildings, Bern has numerous museums, art galleries and theatres, and a vibrant musical life, helped by being home to the Swiss Jazz School and an International Jazz Festival, held at the end of April/early May. The arcaded shopping streets have had a benefit that has become apparent only in the late 20th century: their modest proportions have kept out all but a few supermarkets, making the shops a delight even for those who normally abhor shopping. Besides specialist shops and antique dealers of all kinds, the residential use of the upper storeys throughout the old town has helped to retain grocers, delicatessens and cafés, as well as restaurants. The consequence is a variety of shops and entertainment that has been lost in many towns and cities thanks to anodyne out-of-town developments.

Arriving in Bern

The city's principal railway station, Bern HB, is perfectly sited on the western edge of the old town, and is the focal point of the tram and bus networks. The station's platforms are connected by a subway in which lockers are to be found, as well as a showcase of delightful mechanical toys of the 1930s between platforms 1/2 and 3/4.

The tourist office is situated in the bland complex erected over the station in 1970, which includes ticket and luggage offices and bicycle hire.

Using public transport

Trams and buses are operated by the municipal transport authority, Städtische Verkehrsbetriebe Bern (SVB). Several maps are available with varying degrees of detail showing just the urban network or the entire network of tram, bus and railway lines. For visitors without a Swiss Pass, tourist tickets covering the trams and buses are available for one, two or three days from the tourist office, hotels and SVB ticket offices.

Like Zürich HB, there is a separate underground station of four platforms, U1–U4, which serves an extensive metre-gauge suburban network with trains to Jegenstorf and Solothurn (line SE/J), Unterzollikofen (line Z) and Worb Dorf (line W). Line G to Gümligen and Worb Dorf starts just in front of the Casino at Zytglogge.

Using bicycles

Bern is particularly well suited to exploration by bicycle and has created a good 400km (250 miles) network of cycle lanes (marked on the road by yellow lines) and paths, which are marked on a special cycling map and by the usual red direction signs. For example, there are routes to Thun, Aarberg, Laupen, Olten and Biel/Bienne.

Reservation of bicycles hired from SBB at Bern HB is recommended (tel: 031/680 34 61). Another rental outlet is Ski- and Velocenter, Hirschengraben 7 (tel: 031/321 00 31).

Exploring the old town

Thanks partly to its modest size and partly to the confined location of the old town, Bern is a city that can be properly explored only on foot, by bicycle or by one of the horse-drawn carriages that rattles over the stone sets. The following walking itinerary takes in nearly all the principal buildings, and would take anything from half to one day depending upon the walker's interest in architecture. For the bridges, see the separate section on page 107. The tourist office has a very brief folded A4 sheet and a 56-page booklet on historic monuments in the old town.

A remnant of the old town can be seen even before leaving Bern HB: when the station was reconstructed in the 1970s, the decision was taken to preserve the foundations of the third of Bern's walls and the Christoffel Tower as part of the huge shopping area and station complex underneath Bahnhofplatz.

Above ground the square has two buildings of note. To the right of the station is the citizens' hospital (Burgerspital), a rectangular building with central courtyard like the Hotel des Invalides in Paris, built in 1734–42. Opposite is the Church of the Holy Ghost (Heiliggeistkirche), which has been described as the most important Protestant baroque church in Switzerland. The vast columns, stuccoed vaults and galleries were put up in 1726–9.

Leaving the church, turn left into Spitalgasse. Half-way down the street is the first of 11 Renaissance fountains for which the original figures were created in the mid-16th century. It is hard now to comprehend the importance of these water supplies, centuries before piped water was introduced into houses. For many of the population they would be the focus of street life, where news and gossip would be exchanged. The significance of the figure on the Piper Fountain is unknown.

In Bärenplatz is the Prison Tower (Käfigturm) which was built in 1641–3 on the site of the second west gate of 1256. It remained a prison until 1897. Turn right into Bundesplatz and straight ahead are the Houses of Parliament (Bundeshäuser), built in stages between 1851 and 1902. The interior is open to the public, including the two debating chambers when the flag is flying (45-minute guided tours on the hour; weekdays 09.00–11.00 and 14.00–16.00; Sundays 10.00–11.00 and 14.00–15.00).

From the south side of the Parliament building, walk along the terrace overlooking the Aare to the end of the Kirchenfeldbrücke at the south end of Casinoplatz, named after the Casino of 1909 on the opposite side of the road. Turn left (north) into Casinoplatz and proceed into the contiguous Theatreplatz, where the unusual single-storey, columned building with gabled roof was erected as a guard room in 1766–8 and became the police headquarters from 1832 until 1910. The square is dominated by the Hôtel de Musique, built in 1767–70 as a concert hall, theatre and venue for social gatherings by one of Bern's most successful and prolific architects, Niklaus Sprüngli.

Turn right into Münstergasse. On the corner is the City and University Library, which was built as a granary in 1755–60. The magnificent three-storey oriel window at No 62 is part of the May House, built in 1515 for Bartlome May.

Immediately on the right as you enter Munsterplatz is the Moses Fountain; the figure is a replacement of 1790–1 on the site of the 1544 original. The square in front of the cathedral is the old city's only purpose-built square (the others having been the result of filling in the moats). Bern's most impressive church was begun on 11 March 1421 on the site of an existing church which was gradually surrounded by the new edifice, but remained in use for over 30 years before being dismantled and carried out stone by stone through the new portal. Work began under Matthäus Ensinger, one of a family of cathedral builders from Ulm who had proved their worth at Ulm, Strasbourg and Esslingen. By 1517 much of the main work was finished, but during the Reformation many of its treasures were destroyed.

However, the magnificent tympanum over the principal entrance was spared, perhaps, it has been conjectured, because the extraordinary mélange of 238 individually sculptured figures includes the Last Judgement. The apostles and the wise and foolish virgins may also be seen. It was executed with a sense of humour, for the Lord Mayor of Bern is shown attaining paradise whereas his counterpart from Zürich is banished to hell! The condition of the figures is, of course, the result of restoration necessitated by the friable sandstone, and 47 of the original figures may be seen in the Historical Museum.

Inside, the reticulated vaulting over the nave contains 87 keystones, some incorporating the arms of old Bernese families. The figures on the choir-stalls are worth close attention: carved in 1523–5, they depict not only religious figures but also the tradespeople of contemporary Bern, such as the dairymaid, baker and tailor. Three of the nine cathedral bells were reused from the old church on the site and were rung in 1339 in celebration of the Bernese victory at the Battle of Laupen; they have been rung on comparable occasions in the city's history since then. One of the bells is the largest in Switzerland, weighing 10.5 tonnes and cast in 1611 with a frieze of dancing bears and cherubs.

Nearly all the stained glass in the choir dates from 1441 to 1450, except for the two to the right of the centre window, which date from 1868. The central window is known as the Passion window, that to its left is the Bible window, and left again is the Three Kings window, notable for its early depiction of landscape, then an unusual subject.

The 254 steps of the stair turret of the tower can be climbed to the first platform, followed by another 90 to the second, affording a magnificent view over the city. The tower was only half its present height at the Reformation and reached its height of 100m (328ft) only in 1893 with the addition of an octagon and spire, making it the highest church tower in Switzerland.

Leaving the cathedral, turn left and left again through the terraced garden beside it. Before turning left behind the east end, there is a fine view along the houses that line Junkerngasse, many of them having their main façades overlooking the Aare, like the fourth house along, Béatrice von Wattenwyl House, with its classical front of 1705. Turn right into Junkerngasse; on the right (No 59) is the plainer street front of Béatrice von Wattenwyl House, built in 1446–9. The house was given to the Confederation in 1934 and is used for receptions.

The imposing Erlacherhof at No 47 is the only courtyard house in Bern, built by Mayor von Erlach in 1746–52. It has been the seat of municipal government since 1832 and of the Federal Council for ten years from 1848.

At the end of the street, in a horseshoe of houses beside the west end of Nydeggbrücke, is the Nydegg Church; this was partly built on the site of Bern's original castle which predated the city's foundation and was pulled down c1260–70. Most of the late Gothic church was built between 1341 and 1500. Near the church is a statue of 1847 commemorating Berchtold V of Zähringen, the city's founder. To the left of the Untertorbrücke is the Messenger Fountain where men would wait to deliver messages brought over the bridge from the Bernese Oberland and Aarau – for long the only two roads to Bern. The figure is a replica of the original of 1545 which is in the Historical Museum.

Cross either bridge and turn right to the bear pits beside the end of the Nydeggbrücke. Cross the road and ascend a narrow footpath that veers to the left, passing in front of a few houses. This leads to the Rose Garden and one of the best views of the city. Much of the sandstone for Bern's reconstruction after the fire of 1405 was taken from the area below the Rose Garden, which accounts for the width of the road at the foot of the slope. Return across Nydeggbrücke and proceed straight ahead into Gerechtigkeitsgasse. The figure on the Justice Fountain holds the scales of justice and a sword with, at her feet, the pope, the sultan, the Holy Roman emperor and the mayor of Bern, respectively representing theocracy, monarchy, autocracy and democracy. Gerechtigkeitsgasse is lined with elegant classical façades built for Bern's patrician families. Notable are Marcaud House of 1741–2 (No 40) and Sinner House of 1767 (No 81). On the corner of Kramgasse (No 2) is the oldest pharmacy in Bern, established in 1571. Kramgasse also has several guildhalls, such as the Company of Merchants of 1720–2 (No 29) and the Butchers of 1769–70 (No 45). The figure of the Samson Fountain of 1544 is based on a fountain of the same name in Solothurn. A short distance before the Clock Tower is the Zähringer Fountain of 1535, another tribute to the city's founder, this time in the form of an armoured bear carrying the family coat of arms.

The Clock Tower (Zytglogge) is Bern's oldest building and probably its best known. It formed the main gateway to the town's first western wall, its earliest stonework dating back to the 12th century. The side facing the city was open and made of wood until reconstructed in stone after the fire of 1405. The clock was not only the official time by which other clocks were set, but also the point from which distances for cantonal mileposts were measured. In its archway are the standard measurements of meter and double meter, formerly 'Elle' and 'Klafter'. Guided tours of the tower are given daily at 16.30 from May to October (tickets from tourist office, hotels or at tower).

The tower's bell was cast in 1405 and rung by hand for 125 years. In 1530 Casper Brunner completed work at his workshop within the tower on the astronomical clock and mechanical figure play that have made the clock tower such an attraction for visitors ever since. The performance starts four minutes before the hour, beginning with a rooster and continuing with a procession of armed bears and various movements of a jester, Father Time, a knight in golden armour and a lion. The calendar displays the time of day, the day of the week and month, the month itself, the zodiac and the current phase of the moon.

On the right in Kornhausplatz is Bern's most gruesome fountain, the Ogre Fountain of c1544. The significance of the ogre devouring a child is a matter of conjecture: that it refers to the Greek myth of Cronus (who swallowed his children at birth to thwart a prediction that one of them would supplant him); that it alludes to the false accusation of ritual Jewish murder once thought to have been practised in the late 13th century; or that he is a carnival figure.

Continuing east towards the station, the figure of the Musketeer Fountain of 1543 in Marktgasse is an armoured commander. Further on is the Anna Seiler Fountain, supposedly named after one of the city's early benefactors who in 1354 gave her home and fortune to found the Insel Hospital with 13 beds (today it has about 1,000). However, the subject is more likely to be an allegory of moderation or temperance, with women mixing wine and water.

Turn right into Bärenplatz. Near the junction with Waisenhausplatz is the Dutch Tower: Swiss mercenaries serving in Dutch armies were particularly prone to acquiring the habit of smoking, but after the fire of 1405 smoking within the old town was banned, compelling them to congregate here to indulge themselves.

Turn right into Zeughausgasse for the French Church, which is on the left. Bern's oldest city church was built c1270–85 for the Dominican monastery founded in 1269, though the west front and south aisle date from 1753 to 1754. Paintings on the rood screen date from 1495. The huge building just beyond the church and fronting on to Kornhausplatz is the granary of 1711–18, rebuilt in 1894–8 and now housing one of the city's largest restaurants in its cellars and temporary exhibitions on upper floors (see below).

Continuing east into Rathausgasse, on the left is the Catholic parish church of SS Peter and Paul, built in 1858–64 to the designs of French architects as a result of a competition. Opposite is the town hall (Rathaus), with imposing double staircase, which was built in 12 years after the fire of 1405, though much altered and rebuilt in 1940–2. Nearby is the Ensign Fountain (Vennerbrunnen) of 1542. A 'Venner' was a flagbearer and inspector of arms, and the second most important official after the mayor. There were only four venners, one for each district into which the city was divided.

Further along Postgasse on the left is the state chancellery of 1526–5 (No 72) with lovely rib vaults in the arcade. No 66 was one of Switzerland's first post offices, built in 1686–94 for Beat von Fischer, the founder in 1675 of the Bernese postal service whose eponymous armorial device can be seen above the door. Mounted couriers rode to Basel, Geneva, Lausanne, Luzern, Neuchâtel, Thun and Zürich, later extending their services over the St Bernard and Simplon passes. On each side are the posthorn emblems of the post office. No 64 was a monastery until the Reformation; its basement later became and remains a Russian Orthodox Church. No 62 was built in 1492–1505 as the church of the hospital order of the Antonites and has subsequently been a granary, postal coach-house and antiques hall.

Return to the northwest quarter of the old city for the last few buildings, perhaps taking Postgasshalde, Brunngasshalde and Schüttestrasse which afford views over the Aare. On Waisenhausplatz is the Boys' Orphanage, built in 1782–6 for children of patrician families but since 1941–2 the police headquarters. Near the Museum of Fine Arts and below the Lorrainebrücke is the last remnant of the fourth stage of city fortifications, built c1458–73, with a rampart and gabled roof.

Finally in Aarbergergasse is the Ryffli Fountain of c1545–6, depicting a crossbowman with plumed headdress.

Markets

On Tuesday and Saturday mornings a produce market is held in Bärenplatz, Bundesgasse, Bundesplatz, Gurtengasse and Schauplatzgasse, while a general market is held in Waisenhausplatz each Tuesday and Saturday morning, and on Thursday from May to October. On the first Saturday of each month a handicrafts market is held in Münsterplatz, and on the third Saturday of the month from May to October a flea market is held on Mühleplatz. A geranium market is held on Bundesplatz on mornings only during mid-May.

The bridges

Until 1844 the only fixed crossing of the River Aare was by the stone Untertorbrücke of 1461–89 which replaced an earlier wooden structure. It still survives at the eastern end of the peninsula, along with the 13th-century gate tower on the east bank known as the Felsenburg, which was converted into a residence in 1862–4.

Opened in 1844 the Nydeggbrücke was the first high-level bridge across the river and was provided with a pair of customs' houses. It was followed in 1858 by the first railway bridge, which stood on the same site as the present reinforced concrete bridge put up in 1941.

A British company was responsible for the 230m-long (755ft) Kirchenfeldbrücke, which opened in 1883 and carries both motor traffic and trams. The Bern Land Company bought land south of the Aare, one of the three conditions of purchase being that it had to construct a bridge over the river.

The longest span across the Aare is the elegant Kornhausbrücke at 115m (377ft); this was completed in 1898 and also carries motor traffic and trams.

The reinforced concrete, 82m-span (269ft) Lorrainebrücke was the last road bridge to be built, completed in 1930.

Across the Aare

Development of the suburbs on the opposite banks of the Aare from the old town began in earnest in the second half of the 19th century. The most important such district for the visitor is Kirchenfeld to the south, where some of Bern's principal museums cluster around Helvetiaplatz.

Museums
The old town

Einstein House (Einstein-Haus) The Nobel prizewinner's apartment where he developed his general theory of relativity. Einstein lived in Bern from 1902 to 1909, publishing 32 scientific works, including in 1905 the *Quantum Thesis* for which he was awarded the Nobel Prize in 1921.
Kramgasse 49. Tram 12 to Zytglogge. Open: Feb–Nov, Tue–Fri 10.00–17.00, Sat 10.00–16.00. Tel: 031/312 00 91. Admission charge.

Kornhaus Temporary exhibitions and collection of 20th-century applied art held in the former granary.
Kornhausplatz 8. Tram 9 to Zytglogge. Open: Tue–Fri 10.00–19.00, Sat–Sun 10.00–17.00. Tel: 031/312 91 10.

Museum of Fine Arts (Kunstmuseum) Opened in 1879, this gallery has the world's largest collection of works by Paul Klee, who was born in 1879 in nearby Münchenbuchsee. It has works by the Bernese school of c1500, Fra Angelico, Renoir, Monet, Courbet, Delacroix, Utrillo, Pissarro, Cézanne, Toulouse-Lautrec, Braque, Matisse, Van Gogh, Modigliani, Picasso, Dalí, Magritte, Léger, Chagall, Kandinsky, Ernst, Miró, Mondrian, Rousseau and Rothko. A large section is devoted to the work of the Swiss artist Ferdinand

Hodler and to landscape painters such as Ludwig Aberli, Caspar Wolf, Franz Niklaus Konig and Mme Vigée-Lebrun.
Holderstrasse 12. Buses 11, 20, 21 to Bollwerk. Open: Tue 10.00–21.00, Wed–Sun 10.00–17.00. Tel: 031/311 09 44. Admission charge.

Across the Aare

Art Gallery (Kunsthalle)   This 1918 building is the attractive setting for changing exhibitions of contemporary art.
Helvetiaplatz 1. Trams 3, 5 to Helvetiaplatz. Open: Tue 10.00–21.00, Wed–Sun 10.00–17.00. Tel: 031/351 00 31. Admission charge.

Historical Museum of Bern (Bernisches Historisches Museum) Switzerland's second largest historical museum is housed in a purpose-built mock medieval castle designed by André Lambert and opened in 1894. It contains a marvellous variety of displays, ranging from prehistory and early history to dioramas of 19th- and 20th-century life. Rooms are devoted to Burgundy and the republic of Bern, the Christian view of life, the growth of the city, high society under the Ancien Régime and everyday life. There are large collections of coins, armour, jewellery, glass, ceramics, utensils, bronzes, mosaics, textiles and costumes, furniture in reconstructed rooms, maps and altars. One of the most unusual exhibits is an extraordinary series of 280 portraits of men and women of rural background conceived as a single ethnographic project in the 18th century.
Helvetiaplatz 5. Trams 3, 5 to Helvetiaplatz. Open: Tue–Sun 10.00–17.00. Tel: 031/350 77 11. Admission charge.

Natural History Museum (Naturhistorisches Museum)   Founded in the early 19th century, the museum is renowned for its 220 dioramas of Swiss animals and birds in their natural settings. It has an outstanding collection of rock crystals. A popular exhibit is the stuffed Saint Bernard by the very un-Swiss name of Barry, who saved the lives of over 40 people trapped in snow.
Bernastrasse 15. Trams 3, 5 to Helvetiaplatz. Open: Mon 14.00–17.00, Tue–Fri 09.00–17.00, Wed –20.00, Sat–Sun 10.00–17.00. Tel: 031/350 71 11. Admission charge.

Swiss Alpine Museum (Schweizerisches Alpines Museum)   A recently reorganised museum devoted to every aspect of the Alps, from geology, glaciology, climbing, tourism, maps, paintings, architecture, agriculture, costumes, flora and fauna, and ecology. Text accompanying the displays is in English, French, German and Italian, as is that on push-button screens which visitors can use to call up information on specific subjects. There are displays on the threats posed to the Alps by atmospheric pollution, largely caused by through road traffic and by unregulated tourism.
Helvetiaplatz 4. Trams 3, 5 to Helvetiaplatz. Open: Mon 14.00–17.00, Tue–Sun 10.00–17.00 (closed for lunch 12.00–14.00 mid-Oct to mid-May). Tel: 031/351 04 34. Admission charge.

Swiss PTT Museum   One of the world's largest stamp collections is combined with the story of postal communications and telecommunications, made fascinating by the challenges posed by Switzerland's climate and topography. Amongst many pictures, artefacts and models are the first St Gotthard post coach and the first Swiss telephone exchange. *Helvetiastrasse 16. Trams 3, 5 to Helvetiaplatz. Open: Tue–Sun 10.00–17.00. Tel: 031/357 55 55. Admission charge.*

Swiss Rifle Museum A large collection of firearms, including crossbows, complements the story of the country's shooting traditions, immortalised in the legend of William Tell. Also displayed are pictures and trophies, some of remarkable intricacy. *Bernastrasse 5. Trams 3, 5 to Helvetiaplatz. Open: Tue–Sat 14.00–16.00, Sun 10.00–12.00, 14.00–16.00. Tel: 031/351 01 27.*

Walks, parks and zoo
A walk along the outer bank of the Aare from Kirchenfeldbrücke to Kornhausbrücke is largely through woods and affords the best view of the Matte, the former artisans' quarter that lines the inner bank beneath the gardens of houses on Junkerngasse. The inner bank can be reached by a pedestrian bridge beneath Kornhausbrücke.

It takes about half an hour to reach Bern's 'mountain', the Gurten (858m, 2,815ft), from Bahnhofplatz. Take tram 9 in the direction of Wabern, alight at Gurtenbahn and take the funicular (table 2351). There is a children's playground at the top.

The Zoological Garden is situated beside the Aare at the southwestern end of the large wooded park of Dählhölzli. Take bus 19 from the railway station to Tierpark. The zoo has a collection of about 300 European species, some rare, including Przewalski's horse, musk-ox, moose, otter, wildcat, lynx, Syrian brown bear, golden vulture and various species of grouse. It also has a large collection of birds. (Open: daily Apr–Sept 08.00–18.30, Oct–Mar 09.00–17.00. Last admission half an hour before closing. Vivarium, summer only 08.00–18.30. Tel: 031/357 15 15. Admission charge.)

The Elfenaupark is an 18th-century Bernese garden adjacent to a park that can be reached from Bahnhofplatz by bus 19 in the direction of Elfenau. (Summer, daily 08.00–17.30; winter, daily 08.00–16.30. Greenhouses open: Mon–Sat 08.00–17.00. Tel: 031/352 07 13.)

Practical information
TO – Railway Station, PO Box, CH-3001 Bern. Tel: 031/328 12 12; fax: 031/312 12 33; email: info-res@bernetourism.ch; web: www.bernetourism.ch Open: Jun–Sep, Mon–Sat 09.00–20.30; Oct–May, Mon–Sat 09.00–18.30, Sun 10.00–17.00.

There are many hotels in the old town close to the railway station, but beware of those on or close to main squares – the combination of 24-hour underground car-parks, delivery lorries from 05.00 and late-night revellers on scooters can make for short and broken sleep. Ask for a quiet room. Those within easy reach of the station (but not necessarily in a quiet location) are Schweizerhof★★★★★, Bahnhofplatz 11, CH-3001. Tel: 031/326 80 80; fax: 031/326 80 90; email: info@schweizerhof-bern.ch; web: www.schweizerhof-bern.ch

Bären-Garni★★★★, Schauplatzgasse 4, CH-3011. Tel: 031/311 33 67; fax: 031/311 69 83; email: reception@baerenbern.ch; web: www.baerenbern.ch

Bern★★★★ (H), Zeughausgasse 9, CH-3011. Tel: 031/329 22 22; fax: 031/329 22 99; email: hotelbern@hotelbern.ch; web: www.hotelbern.ch

Bristol-Garni★★★★, Schauplatzgasse 10, CH-3011. Tel: 031/311 01 01; fax: 031/311 94 79; email:reception@bristolbern.ch; web: www.bristolbern.ch

Savoy-Garni★★★★, Neuengasse 26, CH-3011. Tel: 031/311 44 05; fax: 031/312 19 78; email: zghotels@smile.ch

City am Bahnhof★★★, Bubenbergplatz 7, CH-3011. Tel: 031/311 53 77; fax: 031/311 06 36; email: ambassador@ping.ch

Continental★★★, Zeughausgasse 27, CH-3011. Tel: 031/329 21 21; fax: 031/329 21 99; email: continental@hotelbern.ch; web: wwwhotelbern.ch

Krebs-Garni★★★, Genfergasse 8, CH-3011. Tel: 031/320 15 15; fax: 031/311 10 35; email: hotel-krebs@thenet.ch; web: www.hotelonline.de

Kreuz★★★, Zeughausgasse 41, CH-3000. Tel: 031/311 11 62; fax: 031/311 37 47.

Wächter Mövenpick★★★, Neuengasse 44, CH-3011. Tel: 031/321 15 21; fax: 031/321 15 16; email: hotel.waechter@moevenpick.ch

National★★ (H), Hirschengraben 24, CH-3011. Tel: 031/381 19 88; fax: 031/381 68 78; email: hotel@nationalbern.ch

Bern has a large number of good restaurants, listed in a leaflet available from the tourist office. Some in the old city have unusual entrances – angled double doors underneath the arches of the arcades, leading down into converted cellars.

The Eastern Bernese Mittelland

The Bernese Mittelland is the name given to the area
surrounding the capital. It takes in Lake Biel to the west,
the Schwarzen-burgerland to the southwest, extends
to Langenthal in the northeast and embraces the
Emmental almost as far as Luzern to the southeast.
Bern's relatively modest population means that there is
not the need for an S-Bahn network on the scale of Zürich. None the less the
city has numerous radiating lines that offer opportunities for day or overnight
excursions. They divide quite easily into railways that serve the eastern or
western parts of the region.

In the eastern half, the town that should not be missed by those interested
in architecture is Solothurn, while the best walking and cycling lies in the
picturesque Emmental.

In the immediate vicinity of Bern are the four-metre-gauge lines, each
denoted by a letter and operated by Regionalverkehr Bern-Solothurn
(RBS), which leave from four separate underground platforms at
Hauptbahnhof. Line Z to Unterzollikofen runs parallel for most of the way
with Line SE/J to Jegenstorf and Solothurn, but the other three deserve
description.

BERN ZYTGLOGGE/THEATERPLATZ–WORB DORF
Table 295/Line G

*Although it appears in the railway timetable, this suburban route is more of a long tram
line, operated by modern light rail vehicles. It starts at a platform near the cathedral and
concert hall.*

At **Gümligen** is a country house built in 1735–6 in the Louis XV style with
French garden for Beat Fischer who founded Bern's first post service (see
page 106). He was also responsible for the courtyard house of Hofgut which
has fine gardens; both the house and farm buildings have *trompe-l'oeil*
decoration.

Worb (**Worb Dorf** station) has two castles: the earlier, 13th-century castle
was completely rebuilt in 1535 after a fire. A 17th-century extension houses a
small museum of glassware. Schloss Neu-Worb was built in the mid-18th
century. The Reformed church of St Mauritius, built c1500, has glass
decorated with figures and coats of arms.

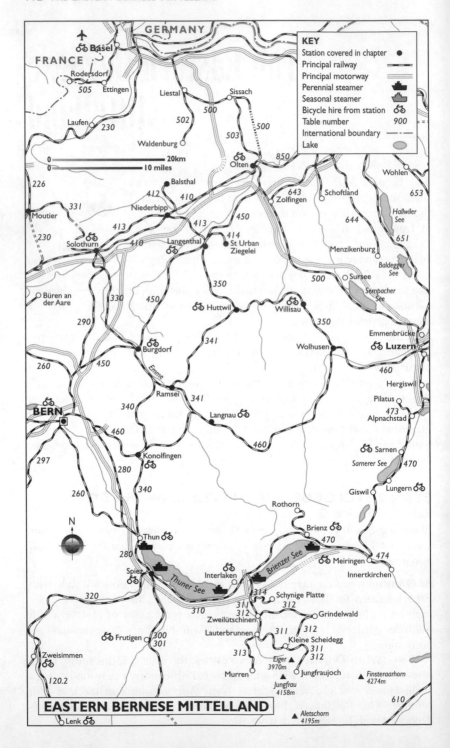

KEY

Station covered in chapter ●
Principal railway
Principal motorway
Perennial steamer
Seasonal steamer
Bicycle hire from station 🚲
Table number 900
International boundary
Lake

EASTERN BERNESE MITTELLAND

From Worb Dorf station a bus service to Grosshöchstetten (table 294.20) passes the attractively situated castle of Schlosswil. The 12th-century keep is incorporated into 16th-century residential additions.

Practical information
Worb

Löwen★★★ (H), Enggisteinstrasse 3, CH-3076. Tel: 031/839 23 03; fax: 031/839 58 77; email: loewen.worb@spectraweb.ch; web: www.meet.ch/loewenworb

BERN–WORB DORF Table 294/Line W

A surprisingly scenic metre-gauge line for a suburban service. Part of the route is mixed gauge to allow standard gauge access to factories.

At **Ittigen bei Bern** is the Thalgut, a symmetrically planned country house of 1668. **Bolligen** has a Reformed church with Renaissance pulpit and an adjacent tithe barn. As one leaves the timber-framed houses around the station behind, the train forges into the countryside with fine views of the Bernese alps to the southeast. From **Boll-Utzigen** a bus (tables 294.10/12) runs to Utzigen where there is an Italian late Renaissance style castle of the same name set in landscaped grounds. For **Worb Dorf** see above.

BERN–SOLOTHURN Table 290/Line SE/J

A delightful journey through rolling country with views of distant mountains to the east and south. The historic town of Solothurn should not be missed. RBS produces a leaflet of suggested walks from stations; though in German only, the maps and suggestions for sustenance en route can be easily understood.

Before Bern is left, at **Zollikofen** there is Schloss Reichenbach, another castle built for Beat Fischer who founded the first postal service in Berne. The first part of the castle was begun in 1688 and enlarged c1719.

The modern light rail vehicles that operate this metre-gauge line are soon out in open country, though there is a sense of suburbia until after **Schönbühl** (where there is a second station with the banal name of 'Shoppyland'). The castle at **Jegenstorf** is well worth breaking the journey to see. The early 12th-century keep has been incorporated into an 18th-century mansion in the style of Louis XIV and set in parkland. Now owned by a local foundation, it includes a museum of domestic furnishings. (Open: mid-May–mid-Oct, daily except Mon 10.00–12.00, 14.00–17.00.)

Another castle may be seen but not visited at **Fraubrunnen**, where a 13th-century Cistercian convent was rebuilt as a baroque mansion in the 18th century. It was at Fraubrunnen in 1376 that a contingent of English and Welsh mercenaries, intent on plunder under the leadership of the French noble Enguerrand de Coucy, was almost annihilated by a local force.

Bätterkinden is only a kilometre or two from the moated Schloss Landshut, which houses the Swiss Museum of Hunting and Wildlife Protection (see page 121). At **Biberist** the tower-house summer residence of the von Roll family, Schlösschen Vorder-Bleichenberg, is now a gallery of mostly local artists run by the Moos-Flury Foundation (tel: 032/672 2989).

Situated astride the River Aare, **Solothurn** was founded by the Romans c370 and became the northern cornerstone of the Burgundian kingdom where the kings were crowned. It became a free imperial city in 1218, and in 1481 became the eleventh canton to join the Confederation. Since then the number 11 has had a curious importance for the town, developed by the cathedral's architect, Gaetano Pisoni of Ascona in Ticino; noting also that the city's patron saints, Urs and Victor, were in the 11th Roman legion, that the town's fortifications had 11 towers, that there were 11 guilds and 11 fountains, Pisoni designed the cathedral to have 11 bells, 11 altars and three flights of 11 steps.

Although Biel/Bienne is supposedly the eastern boundary of the French language, Solothurn has long had strong connections with France and many of the town's inhabitants speak the language fluently. The town supplied mercenaries to the French kings for centuries; many returned with sufficient wealth and Francophile tastes to build houses in French style, and when the Protestant reformer Zwingli tried to abolish the practice of hired soldiers, the town opted to remain Catholic. As a consequence, from 1530 until 1792, Solothurn was the residence of French ambassadors to the Swiss Confederation.

Exploring the old town

It is a short and pleasant walk from the station to the largely pedestrianised and exceptionally picturesque old town, though bus lines 1, 3, 4 and 7 from the station cross the Aare into the old town. Cross the large area in front of the station by the underground walkway in which there is a sign to the centre (Zentrum). Walk along Hauptbahnhofstrasse to the bridge for pedestrians and cyclists only, the Kreuzackerbrücke; at the end of the bridge on the left is the Besenval Palace, built in 1701–6 for the mayor of that name for whom Schloss Waldegg was also built (see below). At the end of the bridge the street becomes Kroneng: on the right is the Natural History Museum, and behind it on Klosterplatz the 17th-century St Peter's church, on which site the town's patron saints were buried after their martyrdom c300. Proceed along Kroneng into the central area in front of the cathedral. The tourist office is to the right of the cathedral steps.

The Cathedral of St Ursus was built in 1762–73 of the local limestone known as 'Solothurn marble' on the site of a church founded c910. (Baedeker describes the material as Portland stone.) The first neo-classical church in Switzerland, the cathedral has ornate plasterwork and very pronounced capitals to the columns. The Treasury, containing historic chalices and vestments, and an illuminated manuscript of 983 called the Hornbach mass, can be visited by applying to the Sacristy at 75 Hauptgasse (or tel: 032/622 19 91).

At the foot of the cathedral steps turn right past the tourist office. Straight ahead at the east end of the cathedral is the Basel gate, a square gate-tower flanked by two bulbous cylindrical towers built in 1504–35. To the north is the largest remnant of the town's defences, begun in 1667 and continued until

Previous page The Landwasser Viaduct near Filisur, on the route of the Glacier Express, is one of the many dramatic bridges in the country. (ST)

Above left Among the areas which are home to the ibex is the Alpstein Massif in Appenzell, dominated by the 2,503m peak of Säntis. (ST)

Above right The Matterhorn is one of the country's best-known peaks, situated on the border with Italy. (ST)

Below On the scenic line from Chur to Arosa in the Graubünden, the Langweis bridge spans the Plessur river. When built in 1914 it was the longest reinforced concrete span in the world. (ST)

Above The distinctive castle of Vufflens can be seen from the Morges–Apples line, though regrettably the 15th-century building is not open to visitors. (ST)

Below Passengers on the Berninabahn to Tirano can travel in open carriages during the summer months. (ST)

Above The castle of Gruyères was completed by the 12th century and is now owned by the canton of Fribourg. (ST)

Below The Appenzellerbahn, seen here near Weissbad, serves an area of Switzerland that offers excellent walking and cycling. (ST)

1727 when work ceased; the wall encloses the Riedholz tower of 1548. Within sight of the wall-walk to the northwest is the Art Gallery.

In a square between the Riedholz tower and the cathedral is the Old Arsenal Museum; to the northwest of that lies the Gothic Franciscan church, built in 1426–36 as part of a Franciscan monastery; and on the south side of the square is the Rathaus. This elaborate building was begun c1476 with the central square tower, and the last alteration, the mannerist façade, was completed in 1711.

Return to the cathedral steps and proceed ahead along Hauptgasse past the neo-classical Hotel Krone on your left. Just past the hotel on the left is the baroque Jesuit church, built in 1680–1705, with elaborate stucco and a broken pediment supported on scagliola columns flanking the altar. Continue west along Hauptgasse to Marktplatz in which stand several fountains and the clock tower (Zeitglockenturm), one of the town's oldest buildings, variously dated from the 5th to 14th centuries! Often compared to Berne's famous clock, it has an astronomical dial and a mechanism operating a macabre figure of death, a king and a warrior. The hands of the clock are reversed: the longer is the hour hand, the shorter being installed much later when minutes began to count.

The beautiful oriel window in rich stone of No. 35 Hauptgasse should not be missed. From Marktplatz, either walk to the northwest up Gurzelngasse to the town's former western entrance, the 13th–14th-century Biel gate, and the nearby Buri tower of c1534, or continue along Hauptgasse. In Börsenplatz is the 1548 fountain of St George slaying the dragon. Turn towards the river to cross it by Wengibrücke. Looking east you can see on the left, jutting out into the Aare, the Landhaus of 1722 alongside which boats drew up to exchange cargo. On the south bank to the east is an attractive group of buildings, including the hospital church of the Holy Ghost (Spitalkirche zum Heiligen Geist), built in 1734–6 to the design of a French architect.

Beyond this group and the nearby Twisted Tower (Krumme Turm) is the landing stage for boats that operate excursions along the Aare to Biel/Bienne; they run at weekends in May and October and from Tuesday to Sunday between June and September (Lake Biel Navigation Company, tel: 032/322 33 22). Not only is the scenery attractive en route, but boats stop at Altreu, where Switzerland's largest stork colony of about 200 birds is only a few minutes' walk from the landing stage. The journey to Biel/Bienne takes under 2½ hours; if you would prefer to return by train, the railway station at Biel/Bienne is only a short walk from the pier.

A major attraction at Einsiedelei just to the north of Solothurn is the gorge where legend has it that St Verena lived and which now bears her name. Reached by an easy walk, the site of her hermitage is marked by two 17th-century chapels. A footpath to Langendorf (see below) for the train back to Solothurn provides an alternative to retracing your steps.

Museums

For a town of under 20,000 inhabitants, Solothurn has an outstanding collection of museums and galleries.

Fine Art Museum (Kunstmuseum)   The quality of this collection owes much to the generosity of private local collectors who have given paintings to the gallery. Although the museum now specialises in buying only the work of contemporary Swiss artists, it has paintings by Snyders, Cézanne, Van Gogh, Klimt, Renoir, Braque and Utrillo. There is a portrait of the Swiss composer Arthur Honegger, a Ferdinand Hodler of William Tell, and landscapes by the 19th-century Solothurn-born painter Otto Frölicher. Perhaps the gallery's most important painting is the Holbein Solothurn Madonna, painted in 1522, which shows the Virgin with St Martin and one of the town's patron saints, St Ursus.

Werkhofstrasse 30, CH-4500. Tel: 032/622 23 07. Open: Tue–Sat 14.00–17.00, Thu 14.00–12.00, 14.00–21.00, Sun 10.00–12.00, 14.00–17.00. Admission charge.

Natural History Museum (Naturmuseum)   A comprehensive display of the animals, plants, geology and fossils of the region with films and videos as well as plenty of hands-on exhibits that will entertain children.

Klosterplatz 2, CH-4500. Tel: 065/22 70 21. Open: Tue–Sat 14.00–17.00, Thu –21.00, Sun 10.00–12.00, 14.00–17.00. Admission charge.

Historical Museum   Housed in a château built c1725 in Régence style, the museum gives an insight into the life of the patrician class. On display are collections of pewter, glass, ceramics, musical instruments and religious objects.

Blumensteinweg 12, CH-4500. Tel: 065/22 54 70. Bus 4 to the Canton School (Kantonsschule) stop. Open: Tue–Sat 14.00–17.00, Sun 10.00–12.00, 14.00–17.00. Admission charge.

The Old Arsenal (Altes Zeughaus)   The political background to the Swiss Confederation meant that until at least the 18th century towns had to be as self-sufficient as possible in arms. Solothurn had its own gun foundry and gunpowder mill, and the arsenal has survived with the second largest collection of arms and armour in Europe. Built in 1609–14, the massively gabled building contains three floors of exhibits: heavy guns, including machine-guns, and ammunition; small firearms and light swords; and shafted weapons, heavy swords, armour (400 suits) and uniforms.

Zeughausplatz 1, CH-4500. Tel: 032/623 35 28. Open: May–Oct, Tue–Sun 10.00–12.00, 14.00–17.00; Nov–Apr, Tue–Fri 14.00–17.00, Sat–Sun 10.00–12.00, 14.00–17.00.

Kosciuszko Museum   Devoted to the Polish general Tadeusz Kosciuszko, who fought for his country's freedom and died in this house in 1817. The museum contains all kinds of artefacts relating to his life.

Gurzelngasse 12, CH-4502. Tel: 032/622 62 63. Open: Sat 14.00–16.00. Other days by appointment. Admission charge.

Castle Waldegg (Schloss Waldegg)   Built in 1682–1713 as the summer residence of Mayor Besenval, Schloss Waldegg is the largest and most beautiful of the town's many surrounding country seats. The baroque house contains

furniture and paintings from the 17th to 19th centuries, reflecting the influence of French taste. Appropriately a new museum is devoted to the links between Solothurn and France.
Feldbrunnen-St Niklaus bei Solothurn. Tel: 032/622 38 67. Bus 4 to St Niklaus or train to Niederbipp and alight at Feldbrunnen; 10 minutes' walk in each case. Open: mid-Apr–Oct, Tue–Thu, Sat 14.00–17.00, Sun 10.00–12.00, 14.00–17.00; Nov–mid-Dec, Feb–mid-Apr, Sat 14.00–17.00, Sun 10.00–12.00, 14.00–17.00. Admission charge.

Practical information
Solothurn
TO – Hauptgasse 69, CH-4500. Tel: 032/626 46 46; fax: 032/626 46 47; email: info@stadt-solothurn.ch; web: www.stadt-solothurn.ch Open: Mon–Fri 08.30–12.00, 13.30–18.00, Sat 09.00–12.00.

The nearest hotel to the station is
Ambassador★★★★ (H), Niklaus-Konrad-Strasse 21, CH-4500. Tel: 032/621 61 81; fax: 032/622 59 91; email: reception@ambassador-hotel.ch; web: www.ambassador-hotel.ch

Hotels in the old town are
Krone★★★★ (H), Hauptgasse 64, CH-4500. Tel: 032/622 44 12; fax: 032/622 37 24; email: reservation@hotelkrone-solothurn.ch; web: www.hotelkrone-solothurn.ch
Roter Turm★★★ (H), Hauptgasse 42, CH-4500. Tel: 032/622 96 21; fax: 032/622 98 65.
Zunfthaus zu Wirthen★★ (H), CH-4500. Tel: 032/626 28 48; fax: 032/626 28 58; email: zunfthaus@wirthen.ch; web: www.wirthen.ch

Solothurn prides itself on its gastronomy (another legacy of the French connection, no doubt) and a leaflet on the area's restaurants and their specialities is available from the tourist office.

Bicycle hire from Solothurn station. Canton Solothurn has developed excellent cycling routes and produces a leaflet describing not only these routes, but the links with paths in neighbouring cantons. The tourist office at Solothurn has this leaflet and one that it produces showing local cycling and walking itineraries.

SOLOTHURN–MOUTIER Table 331
This short line to the junction at Moutier provides access to the mountain closest to Solothurn, at Weissenstein.

A footpath from **Langendorf** to Einsiedelei provides access to the St Verena Gorge and chapels (see under *Solothurn* above). Also an object of pilgrimage is the church of Our Lady at **Oberdorf**, an elaborately decorated building of 1604 which incorporates a 15th-century chapel. Only a minute's walk from the station is the two-section chairlift to Weissenstein (table 2026) at 1,260m (4,134ft) from where there are spectacular views of the Alps from Säntis in the east right across to Mont Blanc. There has been a spa here since 1827, visited by Napoleon III, Alexandre Dumas and the Nobel prizewinner Karl Spitteler, who portrayed Weissenstein as a home for Gods in *Olympic Spring*. A network of paths takes in a botanical garden, a geological path and a five-hour hike of the solar system by walking to Grenchenberg along the 'Path of the Planets'. In winter the summit offers downhill and cross-country skiing and a toboggan run. From **Gänsbrunnen** station a postbus travels along the Dünnern valley to Balsthal station (table 412.10) (see table 412). For **Moutier**, see table 230.

Practical information
Weissenstein
Kurhaus Weissenstein★★★, CH-4515. Tel: 032/622 02 64; fax: 032/623 89 47.

SOLOTHURN–NIEDERBIPP–LANGENTHAL Table 413
This metre-gauge line links a series of villages in the lee of the Solothurn Jura mountains.

Trains depart from the street to the right outside Solothurn station and leave the town on a roadside tramway, crossing the River Aare and passing close to the Basel gate at **Solothurn Baseltor**. Heading east the line passes a number of fine classical houses built by the town's patrician families. **Feldbrunnen** station is 10 minutes' walk from Schloss Waldegg (see above).

With the tree-covered slopes of the eastern Jura to the left and a broad flat valley to the right, the railway retains sufficient height on the slope to give good views to the south. Founded in 1240, **Wiedlisbach** is one of the larger places en route, its original square now altered into two streets. A conically topped tower is all that survives of the fortifications; the walls have been incorporated into a line of houses that can be seen from the train. The 14th-century Katharinenkapelle contains frescos of the lives of St Catherine and St Dorothea, and there is a local museum in the granary.

At **Niederbipp** the train pulls into a platform beside the main Solothurn–Olten line and then reverses to corkscrew underneath the standard gauge to head southeast towards Langenthal. Beyond **Bannwil**, which has a particularly attractive station with date-stone of 1907, the line descends steeply through mixed woodland to cross the Aare with lovely views to the right down the valley. Close to **Aarwangen Schloss** is the gun-ported castle from which the station takes its name. The central 13th-century keep has been absorbed by 16th-century residential accommodation. At **Aarwangen** the 16th-century Gothic Reformed church has its original stained glass, and the Tierlihaus of 1767 is decorated with animals commissioned by its owner who had a travelling menagerie. A few miles of street running brings the train to **Langenthal** (see table 450).

SOLOTHURN–OLTEN Table 410
The line parallels the eastern Jura which lie to the north. The riverside town of Wangen is well worth a visit from Solothurn.

The first place of note after leaving Solothurn is **Deitingen** where a tower-house was created out of the moated Schlösschen Wilihof in 1680. **Wangen an der Aare** is a delightful small town, which arose around the bridge over the Aare on the Basel–Bern road. Today's covered wooden bridge of five spans was built mostly in 1552 and is the third on the site. At the four corners of the town's medieval square plan are the castle, the bridge gate, the chancellery and the clock tower, the tower and the priest's house. The last was once a Benedictine priory and was fortified. The 12th-century castle was rebuilt by Beat Fischer of Bern (see page 106), and the 14th-century Reformed church has contemporary frescos in the Gothic choir which was left unaltered by the rebuilding of 1825.

On the hillside above **Oensingen** is the castle of Neu-Bechburg, built c1200 and later enlarged. The station is the junction for Balsthal (see table 412), and the town has a priest's house of 1764 and an early stone baroque house of 1604, the Pflugerhaus, near the 15th-century Catholic church. A lovely 4-hour walk to Balsthal, through woods and pasture, is signed from the station. The path connects with a network of routes along the ridge that drops down to all the stations of **Egerkingen**, **Hägendorf** and **Wangen bei Olten**.

Olten is one of Switzerland's most important railway towns, with a large works. It became the principal railway junction of central Switzerland on the recommendation of Robert Stephenson who was invited to the country in 1850 to help plan the railway network. This choice has helped Olten to become one of the country's main conference centres. It was in Olten that the Swiss Alpine Club was founded in 1863.

The station, which has a buffet, restaurant and large grocery on platform 7, is situated on the south bank of the Aare. To reach the small old town, turn left outside the station to walk alongside the river (Bahnhofquai) and cross the river by the early 19th-century wooden bridge which leads directly into the old town. Continue straight ahead, down Hauptgasse, past the tourist office, and turn right at the end into Graben. The old town is built on the site of a Roman citadel. Just to the north and east of Hauptgasse is the 1807 Stadtkirche, and further at Kirchgasse 8 is the Kunstmuseum with landscape paintings by Hodler and Calame and the principal collection of the 19th-century Olten-born artist Martin Diseli. (Open: Tue–Fri 14.00–17.00, Sat–Sun 10.00–12.00, 14.00–17.00.)

A 45-minute walk from the town is the castle of Warburg-Säli, now a restaurant with terrace (open daily except Tuesdays and in February). Perched on a hill overlooking the town and the Aare, the castle has been a stronghold since the 13th century. However, the reconstruction into today's white-rendered fairy-tale pastiche was commissioned by the builder of the rack railway up Mount Rigi and inventor of the rack system named after him, Niklaus Riggenbach, whose grave may be found in the park in Olten.

Practical information
Wangen an der Aare
TO – Städtli 4, CH-3380. Tel: 032/631 50 70; fax: 032/631 50 90. Open: Mon–Fri 09.30–12.00, Mon, Thu 15.00–18.30, Tue, Fri 15.00–17.00.

Krone★★★, Städtli 1, CH-3380. Tel: 032/631 25 21; fax: 032/631 26 52..

Olten

TO – Klosterplatz 21, CH-4600. Tel: 062/212 30 88; fax: 062/212 70 18. Open: Mon–Fri 09.00–12.00, 13.30–18.00, Sat 09.30–12.00.

The closest hotels to the station are

Arte★★★, Riggenbachstrasse, CH-4600. Tel: 062/286 68 00; fax: 062/286 68 10; email: arte@konferenzhotel.ch; web: www.konferenzhotel.ch

Emmental★★, Tannwaldstrasse 34, CH-4600. Tel: 062/296 33 62; fax: 062/296 77 64.

A hotel in the old town is

Zunfthaus zum Löwen (H), Hauptgasse 6, CH-4600. Tel: 062/212 21 17; fax: 062/212 79 81.

Bicycle hire from Olten station which is on the excellent cycle network created by canton Solothurn.

OENSINGEN–BALSTHAL Table 412

A standard-gauge branch that affords access to two castles and closely follows the River Dünnern for most of the way .

The 12th–13th-century castle of Alt-Falkenstein is only ten minutes' walk from the station at **Klus**. Perched on a sheer cliff, the castle was the property of the Bishop of Basel before passing into the possession of Solothurn at the end of the Middle Ages, becoming a bailiff's seat. In 1922 it was bequeathed to the canton of Solothurn, and restoration of the neglected building began. The castle also contains a local history museum. (Open: Apr–Oct, Wed–Fri 09.00–11.00, 14.00–17.00, Sat–Sun 10.00–12.00, 14.00–17.00.)

The Roman origins of **Balsthal** may be glimpsed in the villa foundations of the 16th–18th-century Catholic church. The nearby chapel of St Antonius has early 17th-century vault paintings, and St Ottilien-Kapelle was founded in 1511. Herrengasse has some attractive buildings, including the early baroque Gasthof zum Kreuz and the Biedermeier 'Rössli'. A small paper museum has been installed in the 1773 paper mill. There is a pleasant walk to Oensignen station (see above).

Practical information

Balsthal

TO – Gemeindeverwaltung, CH-4710. Tel: 062/386 76 76; fax: 062/386 76 27. Open: Mon–Fri 09.00–11.30, Tue, Thu 15.00–18.30.

Kreuz-Rössli-Kornhaus,★★★ (H), Falkensteinstrasse 1, CH-4710. Tel: 062/386 88 88; fax: 062/386 88 89; email: kreuz@seminarhotelkreuz.ch; web: www.seminarhotelkreuz.ch

SOLOTHURN–BURGDORF Table 330

The first part of a sequence of connecting trains to Thun along the Emmental–Burgdorf–Thun-Bahn (EBT), the line traverses a flat, fertile plain through unremarkable scenery.

The River Emme, which rises near Mount Rothorn, is crossed before **Biberist**, one of two stations for the Moos-Flury Foundation gallery (see table 290 above). **Utzenstorf** station is close to the delightful Schloss Landshut which contains the Swiss Museum of Hunting and Wildlife Protection and an agricultural museum. Several rooms are furnished in 17th–19th-century style. The only moated castle in the canton of Berne, it is thought to have been built in the 12th century, although it was transformed in the 17th century. (Open: mid-May–mid-Oct, Tue–Sat 14.00–17.00, Sun 10.00–17.00.)

Near **Aefligen** the Emme is crossed again and now keeps close company most of the way to Burgdorf. At **Kirchberg** is a country house in Louis XVI style which is thought to have been designed by the Bernese architect Niklaus Sprüngli; the Tschiffeligut was commissioned by a musician and economist, Johann Tschiffeli. The village church of St Martin has early 16th-century stained glass. For **Burgdorf**, see table 450 below.

Practical information
Utzenstorf
Bahnhof* (H), CH-3427. Tel: 032/665 38 38; fax: 032/665 25 21; web: www.forum.ch/bahnhof-utzenstorf.htm

BURGDORF–KONOLFINGEN–THUN Table 340

A sinuous line through attractive rolling hills with streams fringed by birch in the western part of the Emmental.

Opposite the station at **Oberburg** is Restaurant Bahnhof, notable for its exuberant decorative woodwork. On the left after Oberburg is a covered wooden bridge across the river which is the longest of its kind in Switzerland; built in 1839 it has a span of 58m (190ft). At Hasle (the junction station of **Hasle-Rüegsau**, to which there is a very frequent service from Burgdorf, table 341), the baroque Reformed church of 1678–80 has 15th-century frescos from an earlier church that depict the life of St Benedict.

The Reformed church at **Biglen** was built c1521 and has an elaborately carved ceiling of fantastic creatures and foliage. From **Grosshöchstetten** station a bus (table 294.20) goes to the attractive castle of Schlosswil (see table 295). The line drops down steeply, the Bern–Luzern line coming into view far below before trains from the north twist down to cross it at the junction of **Konolfingen**. The small town has a village museum with Emmental farm, chemist shop of 1900 and collections of toys and tools.

A pretty valley with steep slopes to the west brings the line to **Oberdiessbach**, where old and new castles are within yards of each other. The old (Altes) was built c1546, the new (Neues) in 1666–8 in late French Renaissance style for Albrecht von Wattenwyl, to whom there is a monument in the 16th-century church.

The station at **Steffisburg** lies to the west of the town on the same side as the neo-classical country house known as Inneres Ortbühlgut. The Reformed church was rebuilt in 1681 but retains its Romanesque tower with wooden belfry. For Thun see table 280/310 on page 155.

Practical information
Konolfingen

TO – Bernstrasse 11, CH-3510. Tel: 031/791 15 16; fax: 031/791 15 16. Open: Tue–Fri 09.00–12.00, 13.30–19.00, Sat 09.00–16.00.

Close to Stalden im Emmental station, on the outskirts of Konolfingen is the attractive hotel Schloss Hünigen*** (H), CH-3510. Tel: 031/791 26 11; fax: 031/791 27 31; email: hotel@schlosshuenigen.com; web: www.schlosshuenigen.com 16th-century mansion in fine grounds.

Bicycle hire from Konolfingen station.

BERN–OLTEN Table 450

The route of trains from Geneva to Zürich skirts the northern edge of the Emmental, but is scenically the least inspiring of the lines through the area.

At **Hindelbank** is the baroque, horseshoe-shaped country house of 1722–5 built for Mayor Hieronymus of Erlach; it is now a women's prison. His tomb of 1751 may be seen in the Reformed church.

Burgdorf is regarded as the gateway to the Emmental, the fertile area to the east of the town synonymous with cheese. The region also offers good food and varied countryside highly regarded for both walking and cycling. The town and surrounding area is dominated by its magnificent castle, built on a hill with what is now the old town developing to its west, originally protected by walls punctuated with cylindrical towers. The castle was begun c1127 by Duke Konrad II of Zähringen, the keep and residential quarters being among the country's earliest brick buildings; they incorporate a Romanesque baronial hall and a chapel with frescos of c1330. In 1218 the town passed to the Kyburgs who sold it to Bern in 1384, a governor occupying the castle until 1798.

To reach the castle and old town, in which traffic is restricted, turn left outside the station. The tourist office is just past the bicycle park on the left. Turn right into Gotthelfstrasse, which curves round to the left, then turn right and immediately left into Kornhausgasse. The first building on the left is the Kornhaus, an imposing three-storey building with shutters painted in alternate waving bands of black and sienna. It now houses the Swiss Centre for Folk Culture with displays of traditional costumes from all the Swiss cantons, over 250 musical instruments, over 130 phonographs, gramophones and organs, and a film/audio-visual theatre. (Open: Nov–mid-Mar, Tue–Fri 13.30–17.00, Sat–Sun 10.00–17.00; mid--Mar–Oct, Tue–Fri 10.00–12.30, 13.30–17.00, Sat–Sun 10.00–17.00.)

On the opposite side of the street is the house, denoted by a plaque, where the educational reformer Johann Heinrich Pestalozzi founded his first regular school in 1798, moving to Yverdon six years later. At the end of the street, turn right into Metzgergasse up the rise, and then left into Staldenstrasse and Hohengasse in which there are some fine baroque and classical houses.

The castle also houses a local history collection with displays of ceramics, glass, church clock mechanisms, furniture and paintings. (Open: Apr–Oct, Mon–Fri 14.00–17.00, Sun 11.00–17.00.) At Kirchbühl 11 is a folk and ethnographic museum with sections on Asia and the Pacific, Africa and America (open: Wed–Sat 14.00–17.00, Sun 11.00–17.00), and just off the street is the Reformed church. This late Gothic building of 1471–90 has an exceptionally fine stone screen, unusually placed at the rear of the nave.

Crossing the Emme along Wynigenstrasse, the covered Inner Wynigen bridge of 1776 is a marvellous example of truss-framed construction.

Herzogenbuchsee used to be the junction for a short branch to Solothurn, but regrettably this has been replaced by a bus (table 410.50). The town's Reformed church was built in 1728 on the remains of a Roman villa and is decorated by 20 coats of arms and a Biedermeier pulpit. There is a local museum in the Gasthaus zum Kreuz.

The textile background of **Langenthal** and the surrounding area is reflected in the local history museum (Heimatmuseum) near the station (Bahnhofstrasse 11). The station is the junction for Solothurn (see table 413) and St Urban Ziegelei for the magnificent baroque church attached to the large Cistercian abbey (see below). A bus from the station (table 450.58/line 3) goes to the early 18th-century manor house (though referred to as a castle) at Thunstetten, built for a mayor of Bern, Hieronymous von Erlach, for whom the house at Hindelbank was also built (see opposite). The house is now used for concerts and banquets.

The Romanesque Reformed church of St Mauritius at Wynau (**Roggwil-Wynau** station) is a pillared basilica with frescos of c1400 built on the site of a medieval sanctuary. The last few miles before Olten are the most attractive of the journey as the line keeps close company with the River Aare, with the finest view looking back along the river with the white rendered castle of Wartburg-Säli on a hill in the background. For **Olten** see table 410.

Practical information
Burgdorf
TO – Poststrasse 10, CH-3401. Tel: 034/422 24 45; fax: 034/422 26 69. Open: Tue–Fri 08.30–12.00, 13.30–18.30, Sat 08.30–12.00.

No hotel is very close to the station. A little to the north of the station is
Gasthof Emmenhof, Kirchbergstrasse 70, CH-3400. Tel: 034/422 22 75.

Attractively and quietly sited in the old town, but a steep walk or taxi ride from the station is
Hotel Stadthaus★★★★★ (H), Kirchbühl 2, CH-3402. Tel: 034/428 80 00; fax: 034/428 80 08; email: info@stadthaus.ch; web: www.stadthaus.ch

Very close to Burgdorf Steinhof station (on the line from Burgdorf to Thun, table 442) is the attractive
Hotel Steinhof, Bernstrasse 61, CH-3400. Tel: 034/422 33 98.

Bicycle hire from Burgdorf, Herzogenbuchsee, Langenthal and Olten stations.

LANGENTHAL–ST URBAN ZIEGELEI Table 414

Operated by the Solothurn–Niederbipp-Bahn, this metre-gauge line provides access to the remarkable former Cistercian monastery and church of St Urban.

The line has the delightful character of a roadside tramway, leaving Langenthal to cross over the main line and turning east to **Roggwil Dorf** with its pretty church near the station and a small local museum in an 18th-century storehouse.

It is only a five-minute walk from **St Urban Ziegelei** to the monastery buildings, now a sanatorium. Founded in 1194 the monastery developed a healthy business producing decorated bricks, examples of which can be seen in surviving sections of late medieval wall. The early 18th-century baroque church was designed by the prolific Austrian architects Franz and Johann Michael Beer of the Voralberg school of artists who built many churches in Germany, Austria and Switzerland. The pilastered hall of the church is decorated with Louis XVI stucco and elaborate carving on the choir-stalls. The wooden rococo pulpit is richly gilded.

BERN–LUZERN Table 460

Expresses and stopping trains serve this main line through the Emmental with three different rivers for company and the delightful scenery for which the area is renowned.

Luzern-bound trains share the line to Thun as far as **Gümlingen** (see table 295), where they diverge to head east through fertile farming country, the rolling hills crowned with woods and the peaks of the Bernese Oberland in view to the south. **Worb SBB** is a mile or two from Worb Dorf (see table 295). The junction at **Konolfingen** (see table 340) provides connections for Thun and Burgdorf, and has a good buffet on platform 2.

The baroque priest's house of 1738 at **Signau** was built in the style of a Bernese country house. Both the compact streets and nearby farms have attractive vernacular buildings. To the east of the village the railway briefly follows the River Emme to **Emmenmatt** where it is joined by the Ilfis at a point near the railway junction with the line from Ramsei. Turning east the Ilfis is seldom out of view of the railway for the next dozen miles.

Langnau is the main market town of the Emmental. Besides its thriving dairies, it is known for ornamental ceramics which have been produced here since the 18th century and which can be seen in the Heimatmuseum in the Chüechlihaus on Bärenplatz. This museum is housed in a 16th-century wooden building known as a Blockbau in which the load-bearing walls are made up of horizontal timbers. Also on display are tools associated with the local timber trades and crafts, glassware and displays on local history (open: Apr–Oct, Tue–Sun 13.30–18.00).

The Hirschenplatz is a particularly fine, largely unspoilt square, and the pulpit and font in the Reformed church of 1673 have ornate baroque carving. The semi-circular wooden decoration under the gables that is characteristic of the area can be seen in some of the houses, and there are some Biedermeier houses. A bus from the station (table 460.30) takes the twisty road close to the

1,142m (3,747ft) summit of Lüderenalp (where there is an isolated hotel) and the former rail terminus of Wasen im Emmental, now regrettably served by a replacement bus (see table 341 below).

Trubschachen has some attractive buildings from the 17th to 19th centuries, some half-timbered, others with painted façades, like the Himmelhaus of 1738 which is decorated with pictorial devices and aphorisms.

Heading east, the river is periodically spanned by covered wooden bridges, and to the south waterfalls descend from hanging valleys into the increasingly steep-sided valley of the Ilfis. Even in summer, snow-covered mountains can now be seen to the east. At the attractive village of **Escholzmatt** the Ilfis turns south towards its source and is replaced on the left by another river, the Kleine Emme which the railway follows all the way to Luzern where it joins the Reuss.

The railway turns to the northwest along the Entlebuch valley, from which a band of peasants defeated a largely English force of 3,000 men in 1375. Under the command of Enguerrand de Coucy, who had married Edward III's daughter, the well-equipped army had invaded Switzerland in pursuit of Enguerrand's claim to a Habsburg inheritance through his mother. His force, known as the Free Companions, was defeated near Buttisholz, north of Wolhusen (see below). Sir Walter Scott refers to the battle in his novel *Anne of Geierstein* (1829), which is set largely in Switzerland.

From the station at **Schüpfheim**, the largest village in the Entlebuch, a bus (table 460.60) heads south along a spectacular road through the valley of the Waldemme to the resort of Sörenberg, where there is a small cablecar up to Rossweid (table 2503). The bus continues south to serve the cablecar from Sörenberg Schönenboden up to Brienzer Rothorn. There is a choice of returning from the summit of the Rothorn to catch the same bus service, continuing east over the Glaubenbuelen Pass at 1,611m (5,284ft) to the station at Giswil (see table 470), or proceeding down the south side of the mountain by the rack railway to Brienz (see table 475).

The railway reaches **Hasle** where the Gothic ossuary attached to the parish church contains a 17th-century painted Dance of Death. The Catholic church at the pretty village of **Entlebuch** is in the baroque style known as Singer-Purtschert, with shallow-vaulted ceiling and side altars in diagonal niches that link the nave and the choir. A bus from the station (table 460.75) goes to Stillaub, from where there is a walk over the Glaubenberg Pass at 1,543m (5,062ft) to Langis and Schwendi where there is a remote hotel and a bus (table 470.30) down to Sarnen station (see table 470).

Riverside paths offer delightful walking along a very pretty stretch of the Kleine Emme, with fine views of craggy peaks to the southeast. At the railway junction of **Wolhusen**, the Kleine Emme and the railway turn sharply to the east. A bus from the station (table 510.80) goes to the pilgrimage village of Buttisholz where there is a mound known as the 'English Barrow' in which the remains of Enguerrand de Coucy's English soldiers are said to have been buried in 1375 (see above).

In a glorious setting on the right, near **Werthenstein**, is a former Franciscan monastery founded in 1630 around the pilgrimage church of Unserer Lieben, which was built in 1608–13. Standing on a hill with cliffs behind and a wooden bridge of 1710 in the foreground, the monastery has a Tuscan-arched cloister decorated with frescos of 1779. As the line nears Luzern the valley broadens out. Beyond **Malters** on the right is an attractive group of white-rendered buildings around the pilgrimage church of St Jost, founded c1370. The tower and eastern part of the nave remain from the original church consecrated in 1391; the rest dates from the 16th to 18th centuries. For **Luzern** see Chapter 13.

Practical information
Langnau
TO – Dorfmühle, CH-3550. Tel: 034/409 95 95; fax: 034/409 95 98. Open: Mon–Fri 08.00–12.00, 13.00–18.00, Sat 09.00–16.00.

Bahnhof**, Bahnhofstrasse, CH-3550. Tel: 034/402 14 95; fax: 034/402 63 36.
Hirschen, Dorfstrasse 17, CH-3550. Tel: 034/402 15 17; fax: 034/402 56 23; web: www.forum.ch/hirschen-langnauie

Lüderenalp
Lüderenalp***, CH-3457. Tel: 034/437 16 76; fax: 034/437 19 80.

Trubschachen
Bahnhof, CH-3555. Tel: 034/495 51 22; fax: 034/495 52 63.

Bicycle hire from Konolfingen, Langnau and Luzern stations.

LANGNAU–BURGDORF Table 341/Line S4
A branch line through the heart of the Emmental, closely following the course of the River Emme nearly as far as Burgdorf.

Beyond the junction of **Ramsei** (for connections to Sumiswald and Huttwil see below) is Lützelflüh (station **Lützelflüh-Goldbach**). From 1832 the pastor at the Gothic Reformed church was Jeremias Gotthelf whose novels portray contemporary life in the Emmental. A museum of his life and works may be found next to the 1655 priest's house (open: mid-Apr–Oct, Mon 14.00–17.00, Tue–Sat 10.00–11.30, 14.00–17.00, Sun 10.30–11.30, 14.00–17.00). The village's former grain mill, built in 1821, is considered one of the region's finest and is now a cultural centre for the community. For the section of line beyond the junction of **Hasle-Rüegsau**, see table 440.

Practical information
Lützelflüh
Ochsen, CH-3432. Tel: 034/461 15 10; fax: 034/461 21 11.

RAMSEI–HUTTWIL Table 341/Line S44

Another branch through the heart of the Emmental which provides access to the market centre of Summiswald and to the Emmental Show Dairy.

The Gothic Reformed church at **Summiswald** was built in 1510–12 as a church of the Teutonic Order of Knights, with later stained glass depicting the founders and patron saints. An endowment of 1225 laid upon the Order an obligation to maintain a hospice for the poor and to offer hospitality to pilgrims. The Spittel is the outcome, though today's building, used as a nursing home, is the result of rebuilding following a fire in 1730.

From Summiswald it is less than a kilometre to the south to the village of Thrachselwald, where all the houses face south. The Reformed church of 1685 has a *trompe-l'oeil* painting based on part of Mantegna's fresco in the Camera degli Sposi of the Ducal Palace in Mantua. The oldest parts of the much-altered castle date back to the second half of the 12th century.

Summiswald used to be the junction for a short branch to Wasen im Emmental, but the train service has regrettably been the victim of 'bustitution' (table 341.10).

From **Affoltern-Weier** station a bus (table 343.20) runs to Affoltern where the Emmental Show Dairy (Emmentaler Schaukäserei) is situated. The cheesemaking process is demonstrated daily from 08.30 to 18.30 by the traditional method using a single vat and by the modern vat that makes four Emmental cheese wheels simultaneously. Audio-visual information is give in German, French, Italian and English. The dairy includes a bakery as well as confectionery, cheese and handicrafts shops and a restaurant. (Open: daily 08.30–18.30.)

Observant travellers will notice the large size of many farmsteads in the Emmental. This is largely the result of primogeniture, or at least single bequests, rather than the equal division of inheritances. This concentration of wealth has enabled farms to be run more like estates, with workers and other branches of the owning family living in a cluster of buildings around the farm rather than in neighbouring villages.

The village of **Dürrenroth** has several farms of this kind and two baroque Gasthofs, Bären and Kreuz, of the later 18th century. The Reformed church dates from 1486 but has been rebuilt in baroque style. For **Huttwil** see below.

Bicycle hire from Huttwil station.

WOLHUSEN–HUTTWIL–LANGENTHAL Table 350

Although not the prettiest of Emmental journeys, this cross-country line serves several attractive towns and villages.

Although **Willisau** has been destroyed by fire four times, the last in 1704, it retains some older buildings, such as the Obertor of 1551 – the Untertor at the east end of the delightful Hauptgasse has been rebuilt. Outside the Obertor is the early baroque pilgrimage chapel of 1674–5 known as the Heiliglut (Holy Blood) with biblical scenes painted on its wooden ceiling. On a hillock near the Obertor stands the neo-classical Catholic church; though rebuilt in 1804–10, it retains its 13th-century Romanesque bell-tower.

Above the town is the bailiff's castle, built in 1690–5 on to a watchtower in the town walls. Although used as a district court, school and for local administration, it is open for guided tours for groups on request at the tourist office (tel: 041/970 26 66; fax: 041/970 06 66).

From the station a bus (table 510.78) goes to Sursee on the Olten–Luzern line (see table 500), calling at Ettiswil and passing just before the village the picturesque castle of Wyher; once moated, this castle was built c1510 but has been much altered.

The Reformed church at **Zell** dates from the late 15th century but there has been a church on this site since 700; it was originally the tomb of a hermit. At **Hüswil** is an 18th-century granary with finely carved door.

A town since the 13th century, the junction of **Huttwil** has a unified neo-classical appearance following its rebuilding after fire. A branch line heads west to Ramsei, while the Langenthal line proceeds north, following the valley of the River Langeten. For **Langenthal** see table 450 above.

Practical information
Huttwil

TO – Railway Station, Bahnhofstrasse 44, CH-4950. Tel: 062/962 55 05; fax: 062/962 55 57. Open: Mon–Sun, 06.00–21.00.

Mohren★★★ (H), Markgasse 5, CH-4950. Tel: 062/962 20 10; fax: 062/962 20 11; email: info@mohren-huttwil.com; web: www.mohren-huttwil.com

Bicycle hire from Willisau, Huttwil and Langenthal stations.

The Western Bernese Mittelland

The area to the west of Bern is dominated by the three interconnected lakes of Biel, Morat and Neuchâtel, sandwiched between the southern range of the Jura Mountains to the north and the northwestern ranges of the Alps to the south. Despite the distance, the views of the latter on clear days can be dramatic.

It is a particularly good area for family cycling: the areas around the lakes have easy gradients, and there is an excellent network of signed, traffic-free cycle routes.

BERN–BIEL/BIENNE Table 260

A scenically unremarkable line that links the capital with a town that sees itself as the capital of watchmaking. Biel/Bienne has a lovely old town and some of the best sports facilities in Switzerland.

The Biel/Bienne line diverges from the main line to Olten and Zürich at Zollikofen, turning northwest to **Münchenbuchsee**, birthplace of the painter Paul Klee (1879–1940). A commandery of the Knights of the Order of St John was founded here in 1180; to the south of their surviving buildings is the Order's 13th-century Gothic church, now the Reformed church, which has stained glass of c1300. Nearby is the town bailiff's baroque castle.

Continuing through gently undulating farmland with sugar beet a major crop, the line reaches the junction of **Lyss**, a manufacturing town, where trains connect for Lausanne via Murten and Payerne to the southwest and Büren an der Aare (for buses to Solothurn) in the northeast.

Biel/Bienne is the only officially bilingual town in Switzerland, where the inhabitants switch with disarming ease from French to Schwyzerdütsch in mid-sentence and the street names appear in both languages. Founded between 1220 and 1230 by the Prince-Bishops of Basel, the town had semi-independent status for almost six centuries before being overrun by Napoleon's armies in 1789. It became part of the canton of Bern in 1815 and grew rapidly following the setting up of the watchmaking industry. The town is now its acknowledged centre and the home of Omega, Rolex and Swatch, the last of which sponsored an experimental car named 'The Spirit of Biel', produced by the Biel Engineers'

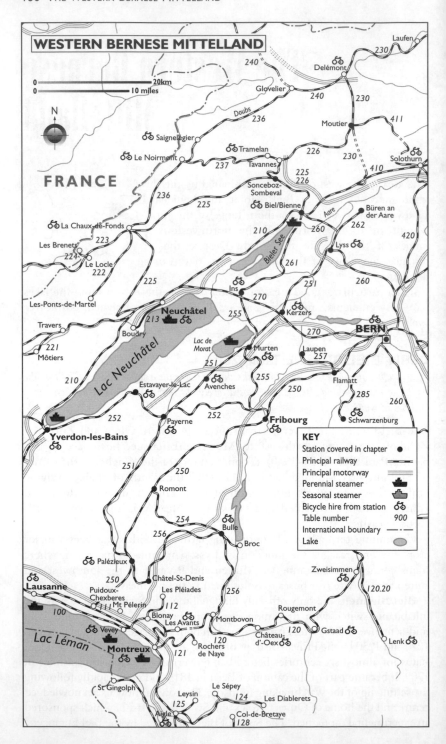

School. Swatch joined forces with Mercedes-Benz to produce the Smart production car, though Swatch has pulled out of the venture.

Before leaving the subway linking the station platforms, pause to look at the allegorical murals, painted by Philippe Robert, that decorate the waiting-room on the right. The tourist office is the small single-storey building at the edge of the bicycle park ahead and slightly to the right as you leave the station. It has to be said that the area around the station is not the best part of the town, even though many of the buildings in the area are the result of an architectural competition held c1930.

To reach the attractive and refreshingly understated old town, the principal area of interest, take bus 57 or walk directly ahead down Bahnhofstrasse to a major junction and then down Nidaugasse. The old town is the largely pedestrian quarter directly ahead at the end (about 15 minutes' walk). In Burggasse are the Fountain of Justice of 1714, the Zeughaus of 1589–91 – once the arsenal and today a theatre – and the Rathaus of 1530–4. Proceed into Obergässli to reach the Ring, the marketplace, which takes its name from the semicircle of town worthies which sat here in judgement on offenders. On the south side of the square is the Gothic Reformed Church of St Benedict; this dates from 1451 to 1492 and includes in the choir some stained glass of 1457 that depicts the life of St Benedict and Christ's passion. Also in the square is the Standard-bearer fountain of 1557 and, opposite the church, a magnificent three-storey oriel window.

Leading north out of the square is the arcaded Obergasse. Near the Fountain of Compassion is the Gasthaus zur Krone of c1582 where Goethe once stayed. Don't miss the lovely stone carving around the windows of No 64.

To the north again, up Brunngasse, may be found the station for the funicular up to Evilard/Leubringen (table 2023), a suburb surrounded by woods. Bus 51 from the station serves the funicular.

Three towers of c1405 and a suggestion of a moat are all that remain of the town's fortifications, on Jakob-Rosius-Strasse on the west side of the old town. The town's three museums are a short walk further west from these towers, right along Mühlebrücke and Seevorstadt. Museum Schwab at Seevorstadt 50 is named after the 19th-century colonel who revealed much about the region's 6,000-year-old lake settlements. These were discovered when the levels of lakes Biel, Murten and Neuchâtel were deliberately lowered during the 19th century to reclaim land and to reduce the risk of malaria. The museum contains artefacts from the lakes and tells the story of their communities. (Open: Tue–Sat 10.00–12.00, 14.00–17.00, Sun 11.00–17.00.) Museum Neuhaus at Schüsspromenade 26 portrays the life of 19th-century Biel, and Museum Robert (same address) contains work of the Robert family of painters depicting landscapes, plants and animals (open: Tue–Sun 11.00–17.00, Wed –19.00).

A second funicular (table 2022) leaves from the western end of Seevorstadt, near the park adjacent to the lake. A 20-minute walk from the station (or bus 53), this ascends to Magglingen/Macolin where there are some of the finest sporting facilities in Switzerland. The Swiss Sports School was founded in

1944 and is a combination of school and research centre, but most of the facilities are open to the public. The earliest buildings are notable examples of modern architecture.

A short walk from the station is the landing stage for vessels on Lake Biel and along the River Aare to Solothurn (see table 420). Turn left outside the station, pass underneath the railway and then bear right down Badhausstrasse to the lake. A wide range of day, gastronomic and evening cruises is available, some using rail travel in one direction and one taking in the connected lakes of Neuchâtel and Morat. Timetables from the tourist office or BSG, Rue des Bains 1, CH-2501; tel: 032/322 33 22.

Practical information
Lyss
TO – Marktplatz 9, CH-3250. Tel: 032/387 05 87; fax: 032/387 05 80. Open: Mon–Fri 08.30–12.00, 13.00–18.30, Sat 08.30–12.00.

Weisses Kreuz★★★, Marktplatz 15, CH-3250. Tel: 032/387 07 40; fax: 032 387 07 49.

Biel/Bienne
TO – Bahnhofplatz/Place de la Gare 12, CH-2501. Tel: 032/322 75 75; fax: 032/323 77 57. Open: Mon–Fri 08.00–12.30, 13.30–18.00; May–Oct, Sat 09.00–15.00.

The hotel closest to the station, but on a busy street, is
Elite★★★★, Bahnhofstrasse/Rue de la Gare 14, CH-2501. Tel: 032/328 77 77; fax: 032/328 77 70; email: hotelelite@swissonline.ch; web: www.hotelelite.ch

About 15 minutes' walk, but in quiet location with good restaurant is
Golden Tulip Plaza★★★★, 40 Neumarktstrasse/Rue du Marché Neuf, CH-2502. Tel: 032/328 68 68; fax: 032/328 68 69; email: info@gtplazabiel.goldentulip.nl; web: www.goldentulip.ch

Bicycle hire from Münchenbuchsee, Lyss and Biel/Bienne stations. Facilities for cyclists around Biel are exceptional: a brochure with five very different circular rides is available. Ranging from 38 to 62km, they include a circular tour of the lake, a riverside ride to Solothurn and a ride on the uplands above Biel to the Chasseral, the area's highest mountain at 1,607m (5,274ft). The tourist office produces a leaflet listing hotels in the area that hire bicycles or have secure covered accommodation for bicycles.

LYSS–BUREN AN DER AARE Table 262
Once part of a line on to Solothurn, the service beyond the small medieval town of Büren an der Aare has been replaced by a bus.

The principal building of interest in **Büren an der Aare** is the castle built for the governor c1620, which is flanked by huge projecting towers. The Reformed church has a Gothic nave of 1510 with a painted wooden ceiling.

BIEL/BIENNE–NEUCHATEL Table 210

A delightful journey beside Lake Biel through a series of wine-growing villages, most of which are also served by lake boats, enabling circular journeys to be made. On clear days the Bernese Oberland seems surprisingly close.

The line emerges from a long tunnel on the outskirts of Biel to come alongside the lake, which it follows closely throughout its length, paralleling the cycle and footpath that also follows the shore. On the right vineyards line the southern slopes of the Tessenberg, the terrace that forms the southern flank of the Chasseral, itself the southern ridge of the Jura Mountains. In places the vines come right down to the water's edge.

The picturesque village of **Twann** has been known for its wine since the Middle Ages. Some of the protruding roofs of the rendered wine growers' houses that line the main street have hoists and skylights. The Gothic Reformed church of St Martin has early baroque carved choir-stalls of 1666 and an inlaid pulpit. Near the station is a little harbour for yachts and a children's playground.

Ligerz is also a wine centre and has a museum of viticulture (Rebaum Museum) in a 1545 Gothic mansion a minute's walk to the left from the station (museum open May–Oct, Wed, Sat–Sun 14.00–17.00). Directly opposite the station is the Tessenberg Bahn (table 2016), an unusually sinuous funicular which climbs up through vineyards, woods and meadows to **Prêles**, where there is a breathtaking view of the Bernese Oberland on clear days (it is often hazy). Various halts en route give the option of walking part of the way, or visiting the Gothic Reformed church of St Imer and Theodul, which is surrounded by vines. Built in 1470–5, it has a carved wooden ceiling in the nave and stellar vaulting in the choir.

Soon after leaving Ligerz, St Peter's Island comes into view. This ceased to be an island when the lowering of the lake (see under Biel/Bienne) revealed a causeway linking the island with Jollimont near Erlach. The quality of the habitat for birds has caused the island to be designated a nature reserve. Its principal building is a former Cluniac monastery founded in 1127, which later became a hostelry and welcomed Goethe, Empress Josephine Bonaparte and the kings of Prussia, Sweden and Bavaria, as well as Jean-Jacques Rousseau with whom it is particularly associated. He described the two months he spent here in 1765 as 'the happiest time of my life', and a room in today's imaginatively restored hotel contains memorabilia connected with him. The Cornishman Thomas Pitt, 2nd Baron Camelford, so enjoyed the year of his youth spent on the island that he deposited £1,000 with a Bernese banker to buy him a plot of land in which he would be buried; he died in 1804.

The language frontier is crossed before the last station near the lake, **La Neuveville**, which serves the almost square-shaped town founded in 1312 by the Bishop of Basel. Besides many 16th–19th-century houses, the town still has remnants of several towers that were part of its first fortifications and a much altered and restored castle that predates the town, having been built in 1283. In the Hôtel de Ville, last rebuilt in 1541–69, is a museum containing historical artefacts, including cannon from the battlefield of nearby Grandson in 1476. The White Church to the east of the centre was built in 1345 and enlarged in the 15th century; it has 15th–17th-century murals.

Le Landeron is another historic town, founded in 1325 by the prince-bishops of Basel. At each end of the main street is a town gate and a fountain, while the houses flanking the street are mostly 18th-century. To the west of the clocktower is a 14th-century château, and most unusually one structure contains both the Hôtel de Ville and a chapel named the Ten Thousand Martyrs.

At Cressier is a château of 1609 now used as a parish hall and school, and the old village contains the late 16th-century lion fountain. Cornaux has some fine houses dating from the 15th to 18th centuries and a Reformed church with 14th-century choir tower.

For Neuchâtel, see Chapter 16.

Practical information
Twann
Fontana**** (H), Moos 34/36, CH-2513. Tel: 032/315 03 03; fax: 032/315 03 13; email: hotelfontana@bielstar.ch; web: www.hotelfontana.ch

Ligerz
A hotel very close to the station is
Kreuz (H), Hauptstrasse 17, CH-2514. Tel: 032/315 11 15; fax: 032/315 28 14.

St Peter's Island
St Peterinsel, CH-3235. Tel: 032/338 11 14/15; fax: 032/338 25 82.

La Neuveville
TO – Rue du Marché 6, CH-2520. Tel: 032/751 49 49; fax: 032/751 28 70. Open: Apr–Sep, Tue–Fri 09.00–12.00, 13.30–18.00, Sat 09.00–15.00; Oct–Mar, Wed–Fri 09.00–12.00, 13.30–18.00, Sat 09.00–12.30.

J-J Rousseau***, CH-2520. Tel: 032/752 36 52; fax: 032/751 56 23.

Bicycle hire from Neuchâtel station.

BIEL/BIENNE–LA CHAUX-DE-FONDS Table 225
A pretty journey through the St-Imier Valley, though part of it has been disfigured by roadbuilding.

The exit from Biel/Bienne is remarkably steep, quickly affording views to the right across the town. The line turns northeast into a well-wooded valley that joins the La Suze river, which the line follows to its source at La Creux, close to La Chaux-de-Fonds. The first station, **Frinvillier-Taubenloch**, provides access to the Taubenloch gorge, a narrow defile crossed by the railway immediately after it emerges from a tunnel. Consequently it flashes past in a glimpse, but it is well worth a special visit since a footpath was hewn out of the rock in 1890, enabling walkers to see the waterfall as well as the vertiginous gorge.

Apart from the villages and occasional town, the lovely St-Imier Valley is sparsely populated with few farms. **Sonceboz-Sombeval** is the junction for trains to Moutier and Delémont. Continuing up the valley, the predominance of mixed forest reflects the poor farming land. **St Imier**, home of Longines watches, once had a Benedictine monastery, but all that remains is the 12th-century Romanesque collegiate church. Twelve minutes' walk from the station is a funicular up to Mont-Soleil (table 2020), the peak which dominates the valley. At **Sonvilier** is the ruined 11th-century castle of Erguel with cylindrical keep. The early 17th-century dairy at the Auberge La Grande Coronelle has a vaulted kitchen with huge pillars.

A long tunnel precedes arrival at **La Chaux-de-Fonds** (see table 223).

Bicycle hire from La Chaux-de-Fonds station.

SONCEBOZ-SOMBEVAL–MOUTIER–Delémont Table 226

The line provides access to the eastern terminus of the metre-gauge branch of the Chemin de Fer du Jura at Tavannes.

From the junction with the Biel/Bienne–La Chaux-de-Fonds line, the branch to Moutier climbs to a long tunnel under the pass of Pierre Pertuis; this defile was enlarged by the Romans for the movement of their legions. The railway follows the La Birse river for much of the way. **Tavannes** is another watchmaking town where many houses have the generous glazing that indicates cottage industry, like those in early English textile towns. The Catholic church of 1929–30 has a mosaic of the Resurrection over the portal.

On the approach to the junction of Moutier are some impressive cliffs above the river to the left. For **Moutier** and the line on to Delémont see table 230 below.

Practical information
Tavannes
TO – Hôtel de Ville, Grand-Rue 1, CH-2710. Tel: 032/481 23 34; fax: 032/481 32 04. Open: Mon–Fri 08.00–12.00, 14.00–17.00.

Hotels very close to the station are
De la Gare, Rue de la Gare 4, CH-2710. Tel: 032/481 23 14; fax: 032/481 12 73.
De la Poste, Place de la Gare 1, CH-2710. Tel: 032/481 32 43.
Terminus, CH-2710. Tel: 032/481 23 50.

Bicycle hire from Delémont station.

BIEL/BIENNE–DELEMONT Table 230

Part of the main line from southwest Switzerland to Basel, the route crosses the southern massif of the Jura Mountains.

The first section to **Lengnau** shares the line to Solothurn (see table 410 below). At Lengnau the line turns north to pass through Grenchen before entering the 8.4km (5¼ miles) Grenchenberg Tunnel, opened in 1915, through the southern part of the Jura. The tunnel ends just before the junction of **Moutier**, a small industrial town which grew up around a monastery founded c640. The monks gave their name to one of Switzerland's best-known cheeses, Tête de Moine or Monk's Head, which is still produced in the locality and should be eaten in fine shavings. Nothing remains of the monastery, but the Great Bible of Moutier-Grandval is in the British Museum.

Although the town has some 16th–17th-century houses, the most interesting building lies just outside the town to the west, passed by a bus (table 226.25) from the station. The Romanesque Chapelle de Chalières has frescos of c1020, depicting the Apostles, Christ in Glory, and Cain and Abel.

Heading north, the railway weaves through the often spectacular rock formations that line the gorge of Val Moutier, or Cluses des Roches, so narrow that the line is often in shade. The clock tower at **Courrendlin** was built as a prison and has a clock dating from 1697. Emerging from the gorge, the train bowls through fertile countryside to the capital of canton Jura, Delémont. In the fork of the junction at **Delémont**, on the right as you approach the town, is an historic steam locomotive depot which was renovated for the 150th anniversary of Swiss railways in 1997, becoming a home for various preserved steam locomotives.

Founded by the bishops of Basel, Delémont has developed on a rectangular plan. Two of its gates survive, Porte du Porrentruy and Porte-au-Loup. Near the former is Maison Bennot, which houses the regional collection of Musée Jurassien (open: Mon–Tue 14.00–17.00). It is in front of this building that the town's public gatherings have been held. On the Grand-Rue is the early 18th-century horseshoe-shaped bishop's palace, which was used as a summer residence by church officials from Basel until 1815. Delémont's fountains date mostly from the 15th and 16th centuries.

Practical information
Moutier
TO – Av de la Liberté 26, CH-2740. Tel: 032/493 64 66; fax: 032/493 61 56. Open: Mon–Fri 08.00–12.00, 14.00–18.00, Sat 09.00–11.45.

Delémont
TO – Place de la Gare 12, CH-2800. Tel: 032/422 97 78; fax: 032/422 87 81. Open: Mon–Fri 09.00–12.00, 14.00–18.00, Sat 09.00–12.00, 14.00–16.00.

Le National★★★, Route de Bâle 25, CH-2800. Tel: 032/422 96 22; fax: 032/422 39 12.

Bicycle hire from Delémont station.

BIEL/BIENNE–SOLOTHURN Table 410
An underwhelming section of the Neuchâtel–Olten–Zürich main line which parallels the southern flank of the Jura Mountains.

The line climbs east out of Biel/Bienne, giving views over the town to the left. At **Lengnau** the line to Basel swings north, while the Solothurn line soon reaches the industrial and watchmaking town of **Grenchen**. Shortly before **Bellach** a loop of the River Aare can be seen to the right. For **Solothurn** see table 290.

Practical information
Grenchen

TO – Centralstrasse 12, CH-2540. Tel: 032/644 32 11; fax: 032/644 21 11. Open: Mon 13.30–18.00, Tue–Fri 08.30–12.00, 13.30–18.00, Sat 08.30–12.00.

Krebs**, Bettlacherstrasse 29, CH-2540. Tel: 032/652 29 52; fax: 032/652 29 85.

Bicycle hire from Solothurn station.

BIEL/BIENNE–INS Table 261

A metre-gauge line through pleasant, market gardening country along the southern shore of Lake Biel, though views of the water are limited.

The 21km (13 miles) Biel–Täuffelen–Ins-Bahn starts from an unprepossessing concrete bunker on the southern edge of Biel station. It can only get better. For a short distance out of Biel, the line is a roadside tramway. At **Nidau** is a formerly moated castle that dates from the late 12th century, though most of the present structure was built in 1627–36. The yellow-plastered Rathaus dates from 1756 to 1760.

The line crosses the River Aare and leaves the suburbs behind after **Ipsach**. Thereafter the line runs largely through the market gardens for which the area is renowned, though towards the southern end sugar beet dominates. The first walking signs appear at **Lattrigen** and views of the lake appear to the right as the line climbs through orchards and past venerable farm buildings to **Gerolfingen**, where there are two restaurants by the station.

From **Täuffelen**, where some historic vehicles adapted for use as buffet and bar cars on special trains are kept, the line drops down steeply through orchards, running alongside the road to **Hagneck** and a bridge over the canal of the same name. Dense woodland precedes open, intensively farmed country to **Ins Dorf**. It was here that the painter Albert Anker (1831–1910) was born and died. His popularity has led to him being described as 'the Norman Rockwell of 19th-century Switzerland', and it was from the people of Ins that he drew the subjects of many of his portraits. The fine town square is directly outside the station.

The line drops down steeply to the junction station of Ins, on the outskirts of the town, for trains to Neuchâtel, Bern and Murten.

Bicycle hire from Ins station.

LYSS–MURTEN–PAYERNE–PALEZIEUX–Lausanne
Table 251

A long cross-country line that links several major tourist destinations, including the enchanting town of Murten, the capital of Roman Helvetia at Avenches, and Payerne, which has one of the finest Cluniac buildings in Europe.

Leaving Lyss in a southerly direction through farmland largely devoted to sugar beet, the line nears the River Aare at **Aarberg** and crosses it to the southeast of the small town. The river is also crossed at this point by a four-arched wooden bridge of 1568, though the stone pillars have rested on dry ground since construction of the Hagneck Canal in the 1860s (see above). The town has a late 15th–16th-century Gothic Reformed church with six Renaissance stained-glass windows and a castle thought to have been built in the late 17th century.

Traversing flat intensively farmed land, the line reaches the junction of **Kerzers**, of interest to railway buffs for its unusual flat crossing of two lines and the rare old signal-box that towers over the lines. Platforms adjoining the crossing permit easy changes with trains between Bern and Neuchâtel.

Views across the flat terrain are broken by long stands of tall columnar trees, their serried ranks providing protection from the wind for the huge areas of vegetables growing in strips of subtly different greens or purple.

Murten is one of the best preserved medieval towns in Switzerland and should not be missed. Though now in the canton of Fribourg (a legacy of Napoleon's rule), it was once administered from Bern, and for a period was under the joint rule of both towns. Founded in the later 12th century on a site overlooking the lake of the same name, Murten still has most of the defensive walls built in the 12th and 15th centuries. They were put to the test in 1476 when 2,000 Bernese held off a siege by 20,000 troops under the Duke of Burgundy; for 12 days they withstood artillery fire and infantry assaults, enabling a relieving force of the Swiss confederation to engage the Burgundians and win one of the decisive victories on Swiss soil. Five hundred English archers died in the battle.

The walled town is about ten minutes' walk from the station. Turn right outside the station and left at the roundabout into Bahnhofstrasse, following the sign to 'Zentrum'. There is a children's playground in the park on the right. Near the top of the rise the road joins Lausannestrasse. Looking across the road to the left, you can see the grounds of the town museum, situated in an old mill. The leat to the mill still runs through the grounds, feeding at the side the unusual arrangement of a huge undershot wheel followed by an overshot wheel. The museum provides a good introduction to the history of the town and surrounding area, with displays on pre-history, folk art, iconography, stamps, military history (including a diorama of the Battle of Murten), dolls and enamelware. (Open: May–Sept, Tue–Sun 10.00–12.00, 14.00–17.00; Oct–Apr, Tue–Sun 14.00–17.00; Jan–Feb, Sat–Sun 14.00–17.00.)

Visitors interested in buildings should first visit the tourist office, which has available an outstandingly good booklet in English describing the town's many historic structures.

The old town is entered at the top of Lausannestrasse between the castle on the left and the law court. The oldest parts of the castle date from 1255, but much of the building dates from reconstructions in the 16th and 18th centuries. Once occupied by the bailiffs of Bern and Fribourg, it became in turn a barracks, prison and hospital during the French Revolution; since 1816 it has housed the district administration.

The walled town is compact, comprising three parallel streets and can only be explored on foot. The principal street, Hauptgasse, is lined with arcades similar to those in Bern, while the houses are a riot of colour with their profusion of windowboxes. A street market is held on the second Saturday of the month. The street leads to the Bernese Gate, a Baroque structure finished in 1778 incorporating a clock mechanism of 1712 made in La Chaux-de-Fonds. A pleasing touch along the battered (sloping) arcades is the incorporation of stone benches at the base of some of the piers. Of particular note at the west end of Hauptgasse is No 18 with its two enormous, superimposed dormer windows. Peculiar in the whole of Murten to this and the adjacent No 16 is the first-floor entrance; on No 18 the ogee-headed doorcase is matched by six lovely windows.

Construction of the walls began in 1238. They were periodically strengthened and extended until the havoc wreaked by the siege in 1476, after which the roof over the wall-walk became part of the rebuilding works. The twelve towers along the wall differ in date and design, and the Zerschossener (Riddled) Tower still bears the marks of the Burgundian artillery. Beneath the staircase to the wall-walk at the western end of Deutsche Kirchgasse is the huge mechanism of the former city hall clock built in 1816; its wrought-iron frame encases numerous brass cogs driven by heavy stone weights. The wall-walk provides a wonderful view over the town's remarkably homogeneous roofscape, the older chimneystacks having the common feature of curious open-ended gables with arched openings at the side.

Murten has separate churches for French and German speakers, the larger size of the German church close to the wall off Deutsche Kirchgasse reflecting the preponderance of German-speakers. Dedicated to St Mary, the German church was last rebuilt in 1518 and has choir-stalls of 1494–8 and some finely detailed stucco work on the ceiling. The pulpit is carved from a single trunk of oak and is dated 1484. Opposite the church is the German Rectory, built in 1730 by a Hungarian religious refugee.

Boats operate daily circular tours of Lake Murten from the end of May to the end of September. The landing stage is reached by leaving the old town through the Bern Gate, turning immediately left and crossing the road named Ryf down to the lake. Some boats also take in lakes Biel/Bienne and Neuchâtel and the River Aare to Solothurn, with the option of return by rail (tel: 032/725 40 12).

Leaving Murten, the line parallels the lake shore, though only brief glimpses of it can be seen across the fields of market gardening until **Faoug** where a large marina is close to the station. Under the Roman occupation, **Avenches** (Aventicum) was the capital of Helvetia and one of only three settlements in the province where full Roman citizens lived. It was made a colony by Vespasian after AD69, and grew to a town of 20,000 inhabitants surrounded by a wall four miles long, with four gates and 75 semicircular towers. Although the town never recovered from the destruction wrought by an attack in 260 by German tribes, followed by the Huns a century later, by the end of the 4th century it had one of the first Christian churches in western Switzerland, with a bishop. Despite being used as a quarry since the Middle Ages, Avenches has extensive Roman remains and the best preserved Roman amphitheatre in Switzerland.

The station is situated at the foot of the hill on which the town was built, but a bus meets trains for the short journey through today's town centre to the amphitheatre on the eastern edge of the town. Seating 12,000, the oval amphitheatre has a small section of original seating, but much of it has been replaced by concrete. Overlooking the amphitheatre is an 11th-century fortified tower which now serves as a museum containing Roman artefacts found locally, including a replica of a gold bust of Marcus Aurelius; this was found in 1939 close to the sole remaining Corinthian column of a temple that Byron describes in *Childe Harold* (he visited Avenches in 1816). To the east and northeast of the amphitheatre are remains of baths, a theatre, the east gate and the wall. (Museum open: Apr–Sep, Mon–Tue 10.00–12.00, 13.00–17.00; Oct–Mar, Mon–Tue 14.00–17.00.)

Avenches has many interesting buildings of later periods. Close to the amphitheatre is the castle, begun at the end of the 13th century by the bishops of Lausanne and enlarged by the Bernese governor in 1565–99 (Avenches fell to Bern in 1536) with Renaissance façade. The tall-spired staircase tower, with handrail carved into the stone, leads to a museum that combines old Avenches and the history of Swiss aviation. (Open: May–Sep, Sat–Sun 14.00–16.00.) The castle also contains an art gallery.

In the town centre is the three-storeyed town hall of 1438, though rebuilt in 1753–5; above its arcades is a triangular gable with two Moors holding the town's coat of arms. Nearby is the Reformed church of Ste Marie-Madeleine, the oldest part of which was built at the end of the 11th century and rebuilt in 1438 and 1753–5. It has crude wall-paintings and a curious flat ceiling with large coves. Parallel with the main street on the side opposite the station is Rue des Alpes in which can be found the 13th-century Benneville Tower, which was raised in the 15th century. Part of the walls have been incorporated in houses – this can best be seen by walking around the northwestern side of the town overlooking the railway. There is a children's playground near the post office at the top of the hill down to the station, and there is a Hippodrome for trotting races (tel: 026/676 61 11).

Continuing southwest, much of the flat country is given over to sugar beet, and in season tractors are a more common sight at level crossings than cars. **Payerne**, situated on the River Broye, is a junction for Yverdon and Fribourg, and was a town of great importance in the 10th and 11th centuries, though there was a chapel here as early as 587. The town has a tenuous link with Glyndbourne, for a direct ancestor of the opera's founder, John Christie, emigrated from here to England in 1788.

In the 10th century an abbey was founded, soon becoming a Cluniac property. After the Reformation the abbey became a barn and then a barracks, the choir a gymnasium, the westwork a prison; it is now a law court. Adjacent to it is the 11th-century abbey church of Notre-Dame, the largest Romanesque church in Switzerland and one of the finest examples of Cluniac architecture in Europe. Built on the site of a Roman villa and then an early church, the pillared basilica has a nave and two aisles with a tower topped by a slender 14th-century spire at the crossing. Of note are some interesting 11th-century capitals and wall-paintings of the 13th–15th centuries. Art exhibitions are sometimes staged in the abbey buildings, which also contain a local history collection. The town has some attractive 16th-century fountains.

Intensive agriculture continues to flank the line to **Granges-Marnand**, where there is a very pretty Romano-Gothic church of the 12th–15th centuries. On the right the River La Broye is seldom out of view, its channelled banks lined with trees. At **Henniez** is the source of the springs that produce Switzerland's best-known mineral water.

Above **Lucens** is a huge medieval stronghold with imposing cylindrical keep and numerous conical-topped turrets. Built in the 13th century by the bishops of Lausanne, it was burnt to the ground in 1476 but rebuilt and subsequently extended for the Bernese bailiff. A boys' college at the end of the 19th century, it is now used for exhibitions and displays of antiquities and pictures. It also contains a replica of Sir Arthur Conan Doyle's study in Baker Street. Opening hours have been irregular and need checking.

Moudon was a Celtic settlement before the Romans made it a staging-post on the road from Avenches to the St Bernard Pass. Little remains of the defences except the square 12th-century Tour de Broye in Rue de Château in the upper part of the town. However, the town's most notable building incorporates part of the former fortifications: the bell-tower of the Reformed church of St Etienne, which has been described as the most important Gothic structure in the canton of Vaud after Lausanne Cathedral, has a defensive belfry. The 13th-century church has many fragments of 13th–17th-century wall-paintings, finely carved choir-stalls and misericords of 1502.

The oldest part of the town, Quartier du Bourg, is on the hill and contains many attractive 16th- and 17th-century houses, some with turrets and pronounced overhanging roofs.

The valley narrows and impressive cliffs rise above the river on the right as the line climbs through thick woods to **Ecublens-Rue**. The latter village, on the opposite side of the valley, clusters round the hill-top castle, which was built in the 12th century, destroyed in 1237 and subsequently rebuilt and enlarged.

Equidistant between **Châtillens** and Oron station on the main line between Fribourg and Lausanne is the beautifully situated and unspoilt castle of Oron (open: Apr–Sep, Sat, Tue 10.00–12.00, 14.00–18.00). It is only a short walk from either station, but there is a bus service from Châtillens station (table 250.13). The same bus (table 250.13) going in the opposite direction (to Montpreveyres) from Châtillens station serves the large zoo at Servion, which is home to bison, lion, tiger, puma, lynx and many other species of mammals and birds. (Open: daily, 09.00–18.00, –17.00 in winter.)

The line continues to climb steeply, passing on the right near **Palézieux-Village** an interestingly designed modern school, with columned central

courtyard. The line joins the Bern–Lausanne main line to the north of
Palézieux station. For the section on to Lausanne, see tables 250/290 below.

Practical information
Murten

TO – Franz Kirchgasse 6, CH-3280. Tel: 026/670 51 12; fax: 026/670 49 83; email:
murtentourismus@bluewin.ch Open: Mon–Fri 09.00–12.00, 14.00–18.00, Sat
(May–Sep) 10.00–14.00, Sun (Jul–Aug) 10.00–14.00.

Only one hotel is close to the station
Bahnhof, Bahnhofstrasse 14, CH-3280. Tel: 037/71 22 56; fax: 037/72 13 36.

Hotels in the old town, only 10–15 minutes' walk from the station, are
Krone★★★ (H), Rathausgasse 5, CH-3280. Tel: 026/670 52 52; fax: 026/670 36 10.
Murtenhof ★★★ (H), Rathausgasse 1–3, CH-3280. Tel: 026/672 90 30; fax: 026/672 90
39. A medieval building with 18th-century wing and award-winning lake terrace
restaurant, built in 1991–2.
Weisses Kreuz★★★ (H), Rathausgasse 31, CH-3280. Tel: 026/670 26 41; fax: 026/670
28 66; email: info@weisses-kreuz.ch; web: www.weisses-kreux.ch
Ringmauer, Deutsche Kirchgasse 2, CH-3280. Tel: 026/670 11 01; fax: 026/672 20
83..

Avenches

TO – Place de l'Eglise 3, CH-1580. Tel: 026/676 99 22; fax: 026/675 33 93; email:
info@avenches.ch; web: www.avenches.ch Open: Mon–Fri 09.00–12.00, 14.00–17.00.

De la Couronne★★★, Centrale 20, CH-1580. Tel: 026/675 54 14; fax: 026/675 54 22.

Payerne

TO – Hôtel de Ville, CH-1530. Tel: 026/660 61 61; fax: 026/660 71 26; email:
tourisme.payerne@com.mcnet.ch; web: www.payerne.ch Open: Mon–Fri
08.00–12.00, 13.30–18.00.

De la Croix Blanche★★ (H), Grand Rue 42, CH-1530. Tel: 026/660 61 66; fax:
026/660 78 66.
De la Gare, CH-1530. Tel: 026/660 56 21; fax: 026/660 56 60.

Lucens

De la Gare, CH-1522. Tel: 021/906 81 48; fax: 021/906 82 04.

Moudon

TO – Place de la douane, CH-1510. Tel: 021/905 88 66; fax: 021/905 55 50; email
office.tourisme@moudon.ch; web: www.moudon.ch

Chemin de Fer, Place St Etienne 4, CH-1510. Tel: 021/905 70 91; fax: 021/905 70
92.
De la Gare, Av de la Gare 5, CH-1510. Tel: 021/905 11 76; fax: 021/905 11 20.

Bicycle hire from Kerzers, Murten, Avenches, Payerne, Palézieux and Lausanne stations.

BERN–NEUCHATEL Table 270

Apart from being the most direct route to Neuchâtel and providing connections to Murten and Avenches, the line has little of intrinsic interest.

The line heads due west out of Bern through hilly country, which proved costly for the railway builders — the viaduct before **Gümmenen**, from which there are fine views, is one of the largest in the country. This has been an important crossing point on the River Saane since at least the 12th century. From Gümmenen station buses leave for Laupen through the Saane valley; this service (table 257) is shown in the railway timetable as it has been a victim of 'bustitution'.

At **Kerzers** is the unusual flat crossing and connecting platforms with the Lyss–Palézieux line, protected by an imposing signal-box. The line continues across a plain of market gardening to **Ins**, where the metre-gauge line to Täuffelen and Biel/Bienne begins (table 261). To the west of **Zihlbrücke** station the line crosses the Zihl Canal that threads the isthmus between the lakes of Neuchâtel and Biel. **Marin-Epagnier** is the terminus of trolleybus route 1 from Place Pury in Neuchâtel and only a few minutes' walk from the tropical butterfly garden, Papiliorama (see under *Neuchâtel*, Chapter 16). From **St Blaise**, where there are some fine 16th- and 17th-century houses, the railway climbs from lake level to join the Biel/Bienne–Neuchâtel line from where are good views over the lake.

Bicycle hire from Bern, Kerzers and Neuchâtel stations.

INS–MURTEN–COURTEPIN–FRIBOURG Table 255

A short cross-country branch that connects several places of historic interest with the ancient city and cantonal capital of Fribourg.

From Ins the line bears away to the right from the main line to Bern, passing through attractive woods between **Sugiez** and the junction with the line from Lys and Kezers at **Muntelier**. In the village is an 18th-century château. At Murten (see table 251), the Fribourg line bears south to **Münchenwiler-Courgevaux** where a Cluniac priory was converted into a house in the mid-16th century. **Cressier** has a rebuilt 17th-century château opposite the church of St-Jean, rebuilt in 1842–4 from a building recorded in the 12th century.

At **Givisiez** the line from Yverdon and Payerne to Fribourg is joined (see table 252).

Bicycle hire from Murten and Fribourg stations.

BERN–LAUSANNE Tables 250/290

The route of IC expresses between St Gallen and Geneva Airport, it is also served by stopping trains working between Thun and Fribourg. Although the principal place of interest en route is Fribourg, the line also provides access to the lovely country around Bulle and Gruyères through the junction at Romont.

The early part of the journey has little of interest to offer. **Flamatt** is the junction for the lovely branch to Laupen (see table 257 below) and **Schmitten** has a massively towered Catholic church, rebuilt in 1706 from a late 15th-century building. The apse of the Romanesque St Luzius's church has wall-paintings that date from the second half of the 15th century. Between **Düdingen** and Fribourg the railway crosses the broad River Saane/Sarine by the Grandfey Bridge; the original 1857–62 iron bridge was encased in concrete in 1925–7 when the lower-level pedestrian walkway was retained.

Fribourg bears a number of resemblances to Bern. It was founded in 1157 by Berchtold IV of Zähringen, father of Bern's founder, and was also chosen for its easily defensible position on a river meander. Like Bern, too, its development was marked by successive lines of defence, but in contrast to the capital Fribourg retains 2km (1.2 miles) of wall with 14 towers, mostly on the south and east sides. Fribourg joined the Confederation in 1481, three years after the end of the Burgundy Wars, by which time the fortunes of the town's textile industry were already on the wane. However, a series of alliances, purchases and conquests helped the town to grow into a city-state ruled by a patrician oligarchy. Only with the French occupation in 1798 was a start made on introducing democratic structures and the formation of the canton of Fribourg. The city's conservative nature was both cause and effect of its adherence to Roman Catholicism during the Reformation. The bishops of Geneva and Lausanne both moved to Fribourg during the 17th century, and the city remains a bastion of Catholicism. Although the Jesuit College was disbanded in 1847 under pressure from the Swiss Confederation, a Catholic university was established in 1889. The bilingual city now has a population of 40,000.

The station at Fribourg is centrally located, but the city's hills may induce all but the fittest travellers to use the occasional bus – all bus routes serve the station. Although the walking/bus itinerary suggested below takes in most of the principal buildings, like most old cities Fribourg is best explored leisurely on foot. Good maps and guides to historic buildings and the museums are available from the tourist office.

To reach the oldest part of the city or the tourist office, bear left outside the station down Avenue de la Gare or take bus 2 or 6. The tourist office is at the end of Rue de Romont on the right, off Place Georges-Python. Continue on foot along Rue de Lausanne, or on buses 2 and 6, to St Nicholas's Cathedral on Place Notre-Dame.

St Nicholas's was begun in 1283 on the site of an earlier church. The choir was complete by 1343, but it was not until 1490 that the 74m (243ft) high tower was completed. It dominates the city, and its 365 steps may be climbed from mid-June to the end of September. Beneath the tower is the main entrance, which has a tympanum decorated with a late 14th-century relief of the Last Judgement. Beyond the nave and two aisles is the polygonal choir with stalls of 1462–4 and a wrought-iron screen of 1464–6. The richly carved stone pulpit is of 1513–16, and the highly regarded organ of 1824–31 was one of Fribourg's first tourist attractions. Buried at St Nicholas's is Clementina

Walkinshaw who was the mistress of Bonnie Prince Charlie, the Young Pretender, while he lived in Paris in the 1750s; she lived in Fribourg for ten years before her death in 1802.

In Place Notre-Dame is the Samson Fountain of 1547 which follows a design by Dürer. Opposite the cathedral, to the northwest, is Route de Morat along which, after a few minutes' walk, you come to the Romanesque Church of our Lady. This was built in the 12th century but remodelled in 1785–90; it retains choir-stalls of 1506, and in an early Gothic chapel at the foot of the tower is a painting of the Battle of Lepanto (1571), painted by Peter Wuilleret in 1635. Next door is the Franciscan church, which was completed by 1281 but rebuilt in the 18th century. Of particular note are the high altar painting of the Crucifixion of 1480 and the choir-stalls of 1280, which are amongst the oldest in the country.

Further along Route de Morat is the Art and History Museum, which is housed in three buildings: the Ratzé Mansion of 1581–4; the old slaughter house; and a building designed for temporary exhibitions. The mansion was built for Jean Ratzé who was commander of the Swiss guard at Lyons, it has been a museum since 1922 and houses paintings and sculptures, and many artefacts illustrating the political, social, military and religious life of Fribourg. The old slaughter house was built in 1834–6 and converted to a museum in 1979 for the display of religious statuary too fragile to remain in original locations; in contrast it has displays of Jean Tinguely's extraordinary mechanical creations. Tinguely was born in Fribourg in 1925, and one of only three 'waterworks' can be seen in the city's Grandes-Places (see below). (Museum open: Wed–Sun 10.00–17.00, Thur 20.00–22.00.)

The No 1 bus service continues along Route de Morat past the Capuchin church of 1622 to two more of the city's defensive towers: the Morat/Murten Gate (1410s) on the edge of a gorge and the Four-Pounder Tower (also 1410s), named after the cannon kept here in the 15th century.

Returning to Place Notre-Dame, turn right along Rue du Pont-Muré to the magnificent Town Hall (Hôtel de Ville), built in 1501–22. Until 1789 the ground floor was an arsenal, while above are the Grand Council Chamber and the Court Chamber, as well as the usual offices. In front of the building is the Morat linden tree, which is reputed to have been planted in 1476. Legend has it that the messenger bringing news of the victory over Charles the Bold at Murten/Morat expired as soon as he had gasped out the news; to commemorate his news they planted the twig of a linden tree that decorated his hat, and from this the present tree grew. His journey from Murten is commemorated by an annual race, started in 1934, from Murten to Fribourg on the first Sunday in October (there is also a signed footpath between the two towns, which takes 5½ hours to walk). On the south side of the Town Hall is a fine view overlooking the river.

From the cathedral, continue east along Rue des Chanoines and Rue des Bouchers on foot, or by buses 2 and 6, to the Zähringen Bridge which was the longest suspension bridge in the world for a few years after completion in 1834. It was replaced by a seven-arched iron and concrete structure in

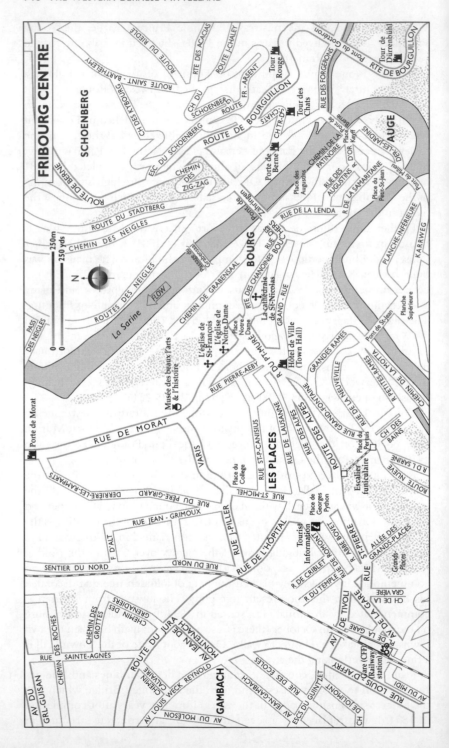

FRIBOURG CENTRE

1924 and affords views along the river, in a southeasterly direction to the covered Bern Bridge which dates from the mid-17th to mid-19th centuries. The oldest part of Fribourg is the area known as the Auge on the peninsula to the southeast of the Zähringen Bridge. It is worth exploring the streets on foot for this medieval quarter retains not only its street pattern but many of the Gothic façades to the houses. These were built to a strict building code set out in the late 14th century to reduce the risk of fire and hamper its spread. Streets that should not be missed are Goldgasse, Rue d'Or and Rue de la Samaritaine.

Across the Bern Bridge are five of the towers that protected the city: the Bern Gate (1270–90); the Cats' Tower (late 14th-century); the oldest and most impressive of the surviving towers, the Red Tower (mid-13th-century); the Gottéron Gate (15th- and early 16th-century); and the Dürrenbühl Tower (mid-13th-century).

At Derrière-les-Jardins 2 in Auge is a Puppet Museum with a large collection of puppets and theatres from Europe, Africa, Canada, China and the Far East. The museum can be reached by bus 4 from the station (alight at Place du Petit-St-Jean). (Open: Sat–Sun 14.00–17.00.)

Cross the river by the Middle Bridge of 1720 (or catch bus 4) and go up Karrweg to Planche-Supérieure. On the south-east side of the large triangular open space is the granary of 1762–7 with tall crow-stepped gable. It has been a winery, a barracks and a law academy, but is now a museum of archaeology. Beside the river and St John's Bridge (1746) is a group of buildings that formed the Commandery of the Knights of St John, established in 1224 and carrying out pastoral work until 1825. The church was consecrated in 1264 but has been much altered.

Across the river (a No 4 bus returns to the station from St John's Bridge and this walking route), bear left up Rue de la Neuveville, which has some especially attractive houses. Some had attics several storeys tall that were open at the sides for drying leather and textiles. On the right-hand side, approaching Place du Pertuis, is the Church of the Providence, built in 1749–62 with a Louis XV façade.

From the west side of Place du Pertuis, a funicular ascends the slope up to Route des Alpes. Turn left along Rue St-Pierre to the park of Grand-Places. At the end of Allée des Grands-Places is a fine view over the meandering Sarne/Sarine. Near the uninspiring pile of the Eurotel is Jean Tinguely's fountain. It was constructed in 1984 in memory of the sculptor's friend, the racing driver Jo Siffert, who was killed at Brands Hatch in 1971. The only other waterworks by Tinguely are in Basel and Paris.

From Grands-Places it is only a short walk back to the station via Avenue de la Gare.

Leaving Fribourg, the railway remains at a much higher level than the La Glâne river, which flows into the Saane/Sarine just to the south of Fribourg and which the line follows south almost to Vauderens. Following the contours of the hills at such a level, there are lovely views from the train over the river valley and surrounding uplands.

Romont is well worth a stop or day visit from Fribourg. Arrestingly sited on an exposed hill a little to the east of the station, this medieval market town was founded in 1239 by Peter II of Savoy, and retains its castle, waterwheel, tower, fortified walls and fountains. The castle was built by Peter II and still has three sides of its ring wall and cylindrical keep. The waterwheel in the courtyard dates from 1772. The Swiss Museum of Stained Glass has been housed in the 16th-century part of the castle since 1981; it organises regular exhibitions of precious works of art. (Open: Apr–Oct, Tue–Sun 10.00–13.00, 14.00–18.00; Nov–Mar, Sat–Sun 10.00–13.00, 14.00–17.00.)

Much of Peter II's town wall has also survived, and on the south side of the town is the 13th-century Tour à Boyer. The collegiate church of Notre-Dame-de-l'Assumption is largely mid-15th-century, though it incorporates part of the 13th-century church that survived the fire of Romont in 1434. The choir-stalls are of 1466–9, the screen of 1478 and the older glass of the 14th–15th centuries, though the twelve apostles were made in 1939.

Romont is also the junction for the network of branch lines to Bulle, Broc, Gruyères and Montbovon (table 254).

South of **Vauderens** fine views open up to the right. Only a short walk from **Oron** is the most attractive castle of the same name, built in the late 12th/early 13th centuries and now a museum (open: Apr–Sep, Sat–Sun 10.00–12.00, 14.00–18.00). There is also a bus from the station (table 250.13).

Dropping down through thick woods, the railway reaches **Palézieux**, the junction for Payerne, Murten and Lys (see table 251) and for Châtel-St-Denis and Bulle (table 256). A bus from Palézieux station (table 250.13) serves Oron Castle and the zoo at Servion (see table 251). Beyond Palézieux the line begins its steep descent to Lausanne, dropping 236m (775ft) in 16.4km (10¼ miles). At the junction of **Puidoux-Chexbres** (change for Vevey), the station building contains the largest private watch museum in Europe (open: mid-Mar–Sept, Sat–Sun 09.30–11.30, Oct–mid-Mar, second and last Sat and Sun of month 09.30–11.30, 13.30–17.30). After leaving Puidoux the line enters a tunnel and emerges to a breathtaking view of Lake Geneva, still 182m (600ft) below.

For **Lausanne** see Chapter 17.

Practical information
Fribourg
TO – Av de la Gare 1, CH-1700. Tel: 026/321 31 75; fax: 026/322 35 27; email: office.tourisme@fribourg.ch; web: www.FribourgTourism.ch Open: Mon–Fri 09.00–12.30, 13.30–18.00; May–Sep, Sat 09.00–12.30, 13.30–16.00; Oct–Apr, Sat 09.00–12.00.

Hotels closest to the station are
Alpha★★★, Rue du Simplon 13, CH-1700. Tel: 026/322 72 72; fax: 026/323 10 00.
Elite★★★, Rue du Criblet 7, CH-1700. Tel: 026/322 38 36; fax: 026/322 40 36.
Golden Tulip★★★, Grand-Places 14, CH-1700. Tel: 026/351 91 91; fax: 026/351 91 92; email: info@gtfribourg.goldentulip.nl; web: www.goldentulip.ch

Hotels close to the oldest part of the city are
Duc Berthold★★★★, Rue des Bouchers 5, CH-1700. Tel: 026/350 81 00; fax: 026/350 81 81.
Auberge de Zähringen (H), CH-1700. Tel: 026/322 42 36; fax: 026/322 69 08.

Romont

TO – Rue de Château 112, CH-1680. Tel: 026/652 31 52; fax: 026/652 47 77; email: office.tourisme@romont.ch; web: www.romont.ch

La Poularde, Route Fribourg 28, CH-1680. Tel: 026/652 27 21; fax: 026/652 14 72.

Bicycle hire from Fribourg, Palézieux and Lausanne stations.

FLAMATT–LAUPEN Table 257

Operated by the Sensetalbahn, this line threads the lovely Sense valley to the scene of a major battle in 1339 in which the Bernese vanquished a Burgundian coalition.

The short journey from the junction with the Bern–Lausanne main line has the River Sense for company on the left for most its length. The castle in the small town of **Laupen** has the distinction of being the oldest stone building in the canton of Bern, the oldest part dating to c930 when it was begun by, it is thought, King Rudolf II of Burgundy.

A connecting bus takes passengers on to Gümmenen on the Bern–Neuchâtel line (see table 220).

FRIBOURG–PAYERNE–YVERDON Table 252

A cross-country line of limited scenic value but linking several towns of great interest.

The line heads north out of Fribourg and leaves the main line to Bern on the outskirts to swing west. Just before **Belfaux** the branch to Murten/Morat turns off to the right. The church of St-Etienne at Belfaux is a large church dating from the 12th century, though rebuilt in 1841–52. After **Cousset** the rolling hills round which the railway has twisted start to peter out as the line descends to the fertile agricultural land to the southeast of Lake Neuchâtel. The village of **Corcelles** has many wooden and stone storehouses and the Reformed church is 11th-century with a Romanesque bell-tower.

For **Payerne**, the junction for Murten/Morat and Palézieux, see table 251. Passing through gently rolling farmland, the train pauses at the picturesque village of **Cugy** with its outsize church before reaching the lake at **Estavayer-le-Lac**.

This delightful small town has its origins in the late 11th century. Of its three castles, only one survives, but much of the walls erected between the three still stands, pierced by four gates. The remaining castle, Château de Chenaux, is one of the five largest castles in the country, built in the late 13th century and rebuilt in the last quarter of the 15th century after it had been badly damaged. It has three wings, a massive keep, barbican, covered bridge and two towers with machicolations. Unfortunately the castle is home to the cantonal police, though the exterior can be admired.

The Gothic collegiate church of St-Laurent was built between 1379 and 1525, though the staircase dates from 1859. The choir-stalls were carved in 1522–4 and there is some fine medieval stained glass. The church of Our Lady attached to the Dominican convent was built in 1697; the nave and two aisles are spanned by groin vaulting.

The town's museum in Rue du Musée has some decidedly odd attractions. It incorporates 108 sand-filled frogs arranged in human situations by an eccentric 19th-century military character named François Perrier. Housed in the attractive 15th-century Maison de la Dime, the museum also has displays of regional interest, a 17th-century kitchen, weapons, embroidery and a collection of over 200 railway lamps dating from 1880. (Open: Mar–Jun, Sep–Oct, Tue–Sun 09.00–11.00, 14.00–17.00; Jul–Aug, Mon–Sat 09.00–11.00, 14.00–17.00; Nov–Feb, Sat–Sun 14.00–17.00.)

The huge marina at Estavayer can be seen as the train turns southwest to parallel the lake shore, though it is some distance from the water. At the lakeside village of **Cheyres** is a château of 1773–4. Views of the lake diminish as the railway enters thickening woods before **Yverdon** (see table 210).

Practical information
Estavayer-le-Lac

TO – Place du Midi, CH-1470. Tel: 026/663 12 37; fax: 026/663 42 07; email: office.tourisme@estavayer-le-lac.ch; web: www.estavayer-le-lac.ch Open: Mon–Fri 08.30–12.00, 13.30–18.00, Sat–Sun in Jul/Aug 10.00–17.00.

Fleur-de-Lys★★, Rue de la Gare 12, CH-1470. Tel: 026/663 42 63; fax: 026/663 48 78.

Bicycle hire from Payerne, Estavayer-le-Lac and Yverdon stations.

ROMONT–BULLE Table 254
A standard-gauge branch that connects with a small metre-gauge network at Bulle with branches to Broc, Montbovon, Châtel-St-Denis and Palézieux. Bulle has an historic centre and notable museum.

The branch turns east from Romont towards the Gruyère district of Canton Fribourg. At **Mézières** is a château near the church with polygonal tower. **Vaulruz** has a much larger castle dating from 1302, though rebuilt in the 15th–16th centuries, with a tower on the northwest corner overlooking the square enclosure.

If the heart of **Bulle** conveys the impression of a venerable town, it is an illusion since few buildings survived a disastrous fire in 1805. The layout of the market square was retained, and the magnificent 13th-century castle survived. The latter was built on a square plan with dominant southwest keep and corbelled turrets on the other three corners. Near the castle another building which survived the fire is the chapel that was part of a demolished

Capuchin hospital; the church of Notre-Dame-de-Compassion was built in 1454 from the remains of a fire-damaged building.

Also near the castle in Place du Cabalet is the Gruyère Regional Museum (Musée Gruérien), housed in a striking modern building. An audio-visual of surviving local traditions provides an introduction to the displays of popular art, cowbells, butter moulds, utensils and reconstructed room interiors. Besides paintings of rural life by such artists as Courbet, Corot and Vallotton, there is a fine collection of naïve pictures of the Poya, the ceremonial journey to and from the alpine pastures at the beginning and end of summer.

The Gruyère region is the birthplace of the *ranz des vaches*, the cowherd's song, which is supposed to have exerted such a powerful nostalgic effect on Swiss mercenaries in French service that a minister banned it. It has also been incorporated into various operas by, amongst others, Weigl, Meyerbeer, Adam (whose *The Swiss Cottage* was performed for Queen Victoria at Windsor Castle) and Kienzl. (Museum open: Tue–Sat 10.00–12.00, 14.00–17.00, Sun 14.00–17.00.)

For the other lines from **Bulle** see table 256.

Practical information
Bulle
TO – Avenue de le Gare 4, CH-1630. Tel: 026/912 80 22; fax: 026/912 88 83; email: ot.bulle.environs@bluewin.ch; web: www.bulle.ch Open: Mon–Fri 09.00–12.00, 14.00–18.30, Sat 09.00–12.00.

Du Tonnelier*, Grand-Rue 31, CH-1630. Tel: 026/912 77 45; fax: 026/912 39 86.

Bicycle hire from Bulle station.

BERN–SCHWARZENBURG Table 285
A standard-gauge commuter line for Bern and curiously the only one that ends in a terminus rather than a junction with another line. It offers access to attractive walks in river valleys. Sit on the right.

The first part of the journey is unattractive, serving suburban stations surrounded by factories. The last station before the railway leaves the city behind is **Köniz**, where the Reformed church of SS Peter and Paul was once part of an Augustinian priory that was taken over by the Knights of the Teutonic Order in 1226. The Romanesque nave has a painted wooden ceiling of 1503. The nearby commandery was built as a castle in 1610.

Beyond Köniz the line climbs steeply along a ledge on the left-hand side of a valley to reach **Moos** where there are the first signed rural walks. Just beyond **Niederscherli** the line crosses a ravine, but the highlight of the journey is the breathtaking crossing of the Schwarz River by a tall bridge just before **Schwarzwasserbrücke**. Looking down to the right you can see a spectacular view of the Schwarz joining the River Sense. It is worth breaking the journey to see more than a glimpse of it, but there is also a signed walk from here to Thurnen, a station on the secondary line from Bern–Thun (table 298). The

walk passes Rüeggisberg, where there are the ruins of a Cluniac monastery founded in 1070, and Riggisberg where the Fondation Abegg has a collection of textiles and early decorative art of international importance. (Open: late Apr–mid-Oct, daily 14.00–17.30.) The walk takes about four hours; if Thurnen is not reached, there are buses from Riggisberg back to Bern (table 280.35).
From Schwarzwasserbrücke the line climbs steeply again with fine views to the right. The cheesemaking town of **Schwarzenburg** has a 16th-century castle, and the Reformed church of Maria Magdalena has a most unusual tower: built in the second half of the 15th century, the square, tapering tower is covered with wood shingles. To the right of the terminus is a map of about 20 marked walking routes. To the northwest of the town are the clifftop ruins of Grasburg castle, built in the 12th–15th century and abandoned in 1572.

Practical information
Schwarzenburg
TO – Dorfplatz 22, CH-3150. Tel: 031/731 13 91; fax: 031/731 32 11. Open: Mon–Fri 0830–1130.

Sonne**, Dorfplatz 3. CH-3150. Tel: 031/731 21 21; fax: 031/731 16 51.

Gasthof Bühl, Thunstrasse 1, CH-3150. Tel: 031/731 01 38; fax: 031/731 07 72..

Bicycle hire from Schwarzenburg station.

Bernese Oberland

The Bernese Oberland was one of the first areas of Switzerland to be 'discovered' by tourists, or travellers as they might legitimately be called, given the relative privations and difficulties that faced the first visitors. Their principal objectives were the glacier at Grindelwald and the waterfalls around Lauterbrunnen.

The first recorded visitors arrived in the 17th century but the first guidebook to the area did not appear until c1775, written by a clergyman from Bern, and it was the homes of clergymen that often provided accommodation for the earliest travellers: their houses were preferable to the few inns. Rousseau was one of the first to write of the region's beauty, and many writers followed in his wake, notably Goethe, Byron, Ruskin and Twain.

In common with most parts of Switzerland, it was during the 19th century that the economy of the area was transformed from being dependent largely on agriculture to a reliance on tourism. Thun was at first the town used by most visitors as a base, but with the opening of the railway through to Interlaken in 1893, the balance moved decisively in favour of the town that has remained the springboard for the network of railways that reaches into the high-alpine heart of the Bernese Oberland.

The region's mountains have been amongst the country's favourite challenges for climbers, the north wall of the Eiger being perhaps Europe's most notorious ascent. It also offers excellent facilities for winter sports, the area priding itself on the welcome it gives to families and the way it caters for their needs.

BERN–BELP–THUN Table 260
Known as the Gürbetal line, this commuter and local railway follows the broad valley of the River Gürbe for part of its length.

The railway shares the same exit from Bern as the Schwarzenburg line to a junction south of **Ausserholligen**, where the Thun line bears southeast. In **Kehrsatz** is a neo-classical manor house of 1782–3 known as Lohn. It was given to the Swiss Confederation in 1942 and is used as a guesthouse for visiting heads of state. The design of the park is a combination of French and English influences.

The largely Romanesque Reformed church of St Peter and Paul at **Belp** has

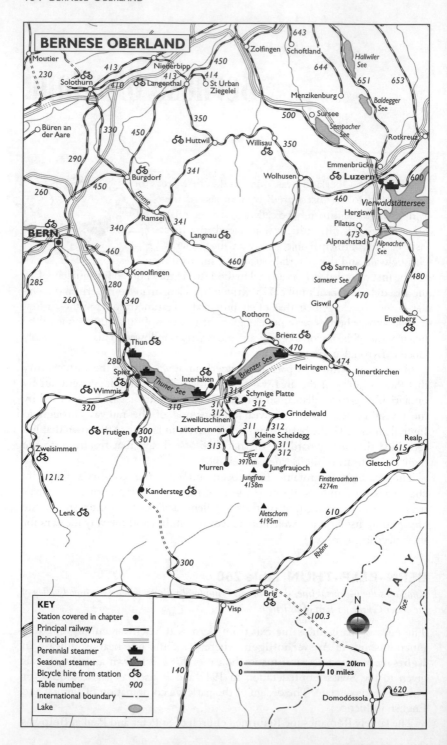

BERNESE OBERLAND

Moutier
230
Solothurn
413
410
Niederbipp
413
450
Langenthal
414
St Urban
Ziegelei
Zolfingen
643
Schoftland
644
Hallwiler
See
651
653
Büren an
der Aare
330
450
350
Huttwil
Willisau
350
Menzikenburg
500
Sursee
Sempacher
See
Baldegger
See
Rotkreuz
290
Burgdorf
341
Wolhusen
Emmenbrücke
Luzern
600
260
450
Ramsei
341
Langnau
460
Hergiswil
Pilatus
473
Alpnachstad
Alpnacher
See
Vierwaldstättersee
BERN
340
460
Konolfingen
280
460
Sarnen
Sarnerer See
470
Giswil
480
285
280
260
340
Rothorn
Brienz
470
Meiringen
474
Innertkirchen
Engelberg
Thun
280
Spiez
Wimmis
Interlaken
Thuner See
Brienzer See
314
Schynige Platte
320
310
311
312
312
Grindelwald
Realp
615
Frutigen
1300
301
Zweilütschinen
Lauterbrunnen
311
312
Kleine Scheidegg
Gletsch
Zweisimmen
313
311
312
121.2
Murren
Eiger
3970m
Jungfraujoch
Jungfrau
4158m
Finsteraarhorn
4274m
Kandersteg
610
Lenk
Aletschorn
4195m
300
Rhône
ITALY
Brig
100.3
Visp
N
Ticino
140
620
Domodóssola

KEY

Station covered in chapter	●
Principal railway	
Principal motorway	
Perennial steamer	
Seasonal steamer	
Bicycle hire from station	🚲
Table number	900
International boundary	
Lake	

0   20km
0   10 miles

Gothic frescos of c1455–60. At **Toffen** is a schloss of medieval origins rebuilt c1671. **Burgistein** also has a fortress, dating from the 13th century, that was rebuilt in the 16th century. At Burgistein the line turns east to **Thun** (see below).

Bicycle hire from Thun station.

BERN–THUN–SPIEZ–INTERLAKEN OST
Tables 280/Line S1/310

This was the first railway into the Bernese Oberland. Thun was reached via Münsingen in 1859, and two years later the line was extended to the lake at Scherzligen. It was not until 1893 that the railway along the shore of Lake Thun was opened, so Interlaken had to be reached by boat. However, from 1874 there was an extraordinary isolated railway through Interlaken connecting piers on lakes Brienz and Thun at Bönigen and Därligen respectively; called the Bödeli Railway, it used unique wine-red double-deck coaches, the upper one having open longitudinal seats so that passengers could enjoy the view. A model of one of the coaches can be seen in the Transport Museum at Luzern. Sit on the left.

Soon after leaving Bern a semicircle of mountains comes into view and dominates the horizon for much of the journey. The first part of the line passes through broad, flat farming country. To the left of the station at **Münsingen** is a small 14th-century castle, rebuilt in the 16th and 18th centuries.

At **Kiesen** is a dairy museum (Milchwirtschafliche Museum) which illustrates cheese-making (open: Apr–Oct, daily 14.00–17.00).

The site of **Thun** has been settled since 2500BC and is the largest town on the Thunersee, the lake which takes its name from the town, situated astride the River Aare where it meets the lake. During the early years of Swiss tourism, it was the principal starting point for visitors to the Bernese Oberland. The future Napoleon III came here in 1830 as a student at the artillery school (the town retains its role as an important military training centre), and Brahms lived in the suburb of Hofstetten in 1886–8, composing the *Double Concerto* among other works. Concerts are given in the castle, and an international festival of barrel organs is held in June.

The interchange between train and steamer could not be easier, the boats leaving from a pier only a few minutes' walk to the right as you leave the station, which houses the tourist office. The station restaurant features its own micro-brewery. To reach the old town and castle bear left outside the station along Bahnhofstrasse, crossing the river twice, to Hauptstrasse. Turn left along this street of two-tiered shops to reach Rathausplatz, which has a number of splendid buildings, notably the 16th–17th-century arcaded Rathaus and one of the town's oldest buildings, the 14th-century Casa Barba in the west corner. Open-air concerts and other events are held in the square during summer. Walking around Thun is made a pleasure by extensive pedestrianisation.

Reached partly by a covered stairway signed off Hauptgasse, the castle at Thun was begun in the 12th century by Berchtold V of the powerful Zähringer family and is the only one of their castles to have survived intact; the rectangular keep with four corner turrets has one of the country's largest baronial halls, partly furnished with the spoils of the Battle of Grandson in 1476. The castle is now a museum housing arms, altars, coins, toys, ceramics and folk art, and its towers offer extensive views over the lake and mountains (open: daily, Apr, May and Oct 10.00–17.00, Jun–Sep 09.00–18.00). Near the castle is the 18th-century baroque Reformed church of St Mauritius, which has a 14th-century polygonal tower.

In a building in Schadau Park between the station and the lake is a remarkable painting, the circular *Wocher Panorama*, painted in 1808–14 by Marquand Wocher; measuring 39 x 7.5m (128 x 25ft), it depicts the town in exceptional detail (open: May–Jun, Sep–Oct, Tue–Sun 10.00–1700; Jul–Aug Tue–Sun 10.00–18.00). Also in the park, close to the water, is Schloss Schadau, built on the site of a medieval castle in 1848–52 in a rather inharmonious mix of styles. Art exhibitions are held on the first floor in July and August; a restaurant on the ground floor is open daily from Good Friday until the end of September.

Most Swiss towns have good swimming pools but that at Thun deserves particular mention. It is a large complex with several pools catering for children and diving, but it is its location which makes it special – near the lake with lovely views of the mountains that ring Thunersee. The pool is at Strandbad to the south of the town.

There is a lovely walk back to Thun from **Gwatt**, passing through woods as well as skirting marshes on the lakeshore. At **Einigen** is the small 10th–13th-century Reformed church of St Michael. The line climbs steeply, providing broader views across the lake and an attractive wooded promontory before arrival at the junction of **Spiez**.

The view of the small town of Spiez as you step out of the station is enchanting, looking down over fields and vineyards to the small harbour and prominent castle. Agriculture, fruit-growing and viticulture were the town's mainstay before tourism.

As with so many comparable buildings, the architectural history of the castle is of a transformation from medieval fortress to patrician residence. Begun in the 10th century it was progressively enlarged and rebuilt up to the 16th century as the home of the von Bubenberg and later the von Erlach families. It is well worth a visit. The early kitchen has not been over-restored, and the dining-room has some very fine plasterwork of 1614 by the famous stuccoist from the Ticino, Antonio Castelli. The castle is now a museum. (Open: Easter–Jun, Sep–mid-Oct, Mon 14.00–17.00, Tue–Sun 10.00–17.00; Jul–Aug, Mon 14.00–18.00, Tue–Sun 10.00–18.00.)

The adjacent Romanesque church also dates from the 10th century, though it has been altered and the spire dates from c1625. It contains murals of the 11th and 16th centuries, and an oval, unsupported crypt which is unique in Switzerland.

A measure of Spiez as a resort is the welcoming party with illustrated talk that is held in the castle on Monday evenings from mid-May to September.

Swiss public transport is so comprehensive that it is easy to forget that some railway lines have been closed. An example is the tram that once linked Spiez station with its delightful waterfront. It was eloquently described by Bryan Morgan in 1955 before its demise: '[the Spiez tram] is one of the most perfect examples, rich in squiggling iron brackets and balconies and cornices. So evocative of lost Edwardian summers is it that electricity seems too harsh a medium for it, and it should surely be travelling its three-quarters of a mile behind an old horse in a sun-bonnet which would slowly plod through the chalet-lined streets shaded by lilac and chestnut and up to the station on the hill...'

Leaving Spiez the line begins to descend to the level of the lake. The former fishing village of **Faulensee** can be seen on the hillside above a cove. The lake is at its widest point here, stretching 3.8km (2¼ miles) across to Merligen. On the opposite side of the lake, a funicular can be seen rising up to Beatenberg (see page 161). By **Leissigen**, a small resort, the railway is right on the water's edge. At the well-wooded end of the lake, the entrance to the 2.75km (1¾ miles) canal to Interlaken, which opened in 1892, can be seen.

Interlaken West is only a few minutes' walk from the departure point for steamers on Lake Thun and the closer of the two stations to the centre of Interlaken. For the town of Interlaken see below.

The section of line between Interlaken West and Ost crosses the River Aare twice; there was no need for the bridges, the railway building them purely to thwart perceived competition by preventing steamers from sailing between the two lakes. **Interlaken Ost** is the end of the standard gauge and the junction for the metre-gauge lines to Luzern, Grindelwald and Lauterbrunnen.

Practical information
Thun
TO – Railway Station/Seestrasse 2, CH-3600. Tel: 033/222 23 40; fax: 033/222 83 23; email: thun@thunersee.ch; web: www.thuntourismus.ch Open: Mon–Fri 09.00–12.00, 13.00–18.00, Sat 09.00–12.00; Jul–Aug, Mon–Fri 09.00–19.00, Sat 09.00–12.00, 13.00–16.00.

None of the hotels is very close to the station. The most attractive hotels in the old town are
Krone★★★★ (H), Rathausplatz 2, CH-3600. Tel: 033/227 88 88; fax: 033/227 88 90; email: krone-thun@bluewin.ch; web: www.hauensteinhotels.ch
Emmental (H), Bernstrasse 2, CH-3600. Tel: 033/222 01 20; fax: 033/222 01 30.

Spiez
TO – Bahnhofplatz, CH-3700. Tel: 033/654 20 20; fax: 033/654 21 92; email:spiez@thunersee.ch; web: www.thunersee.ch Open: Mon–Fri 08.00–12.00, 14.00–18.00.

A hotel close to the station but on the main road is
Krone, Oberlandstrasse 28, CH-3700. Tel: 033/654 41 31; fax: 033/654 94 31.

A hotel overlooking the lake close to the site of the sadly demolished Spiezerhof Hotel and beside the steamer pier is
Aqua Welle★★★, Seestrasse 67, CH-3700. Tel: 033/654 40 44; fax: 033/654 76 75.

Leissigen

TO – Am Dorfplatz, CH-3706. Tel: 033/847 11 36; fax: 033/847 11 01. Open:
Mon–Fri 07.30–11.30, 14.30–18.00, Sat 08.00–11.00.

A hotel close to the station is
Kreuz★★★, Dorfstrasse, CH-3706. Tel: 033/847 12 31; fax: 033/847 12 56.

Bicycle hire from Thun, Spiez, Interlaken West and Interlaken Ost stations.

INTERLAKEN

Interlaken is built on the deposits of the River Aare and the Lombach stream
which, over millennia, separated the Wendelsee into lakes Thun and Brienz.
Interlaken is the principal town of the Bernese Oberland and has long been
popular as a base for day excursions in the region. Until 1891 it was known
as Aarmühle. It is an old settlement, however, growing up around an
Augustinian monastery founded in the early 12th century. After the
Reformation the monastery was converted into a residence for the Bernese
governor until its replacement in 1750 by a château that still houses the local
administration. To the west of Interlaken Ost station, the Gothic cloisters of
the monastery survive, the only such building in the Bernese Oberland. The
monastery chapel was built in 1452.

The Höhematte, a 14-hectare (35 acres) meadow in the middle of the town,
has been protected from development by law since 1864. Part of its purpose
was to ensure that the view of the Jungfrau remained unobstructed, the grand
hotels on the Höheweg benefiting from this early example of enlightened
town planning. Interlaken still has a few elegant 19th-century hotels which,
when sensitively modernised, have an ambience that their successors almost
invariably lack.

To the north of the Höhematte is the Kursaal (Casino), built in 1859 and
rebuilt several times. It is surrounded by an attractive garden and is the venue
for concerts and plays.

Unterseen is considered the loveliest part of the town, reached from
Interlaken West by crossing the River Aare by Bahnhofstrasse. Unterseen's
layout of two principal streets around the town hall square is the result of a fire
that destroyed a third street in 1470. In the centre of the square is the old town
hall, which served as a hostelry, Mendelssohn staying here in 1831. The
church dates from 1853, the previous one having collapsed under the weight
of snow, though the tower's foundations are early 14th-century. The
accoustics of the church are so good that concerts during the Interlaken Music
Festival (held in August) are given here. In the picturesque Unter den
Häusern near the Aare, an old smithy still produces ironwork.

Anyone interested in the history of the area or tourism should spend an
hour or two at the Tourism Museum in 26 Obere Gasse, Unterseen, a house
built in 1686. On the ground floor are a mail coach, the first bicycle
(velocipede) in Interlaken and other transport items. The upper floors
describe the 'discovery' of the Alps and all that contributed to it, shipping on

the lakes, the development of hotels and railways, and the growth of winter sports. (Open: May–mid-Oct, Tue–Sun 14.00–17.00.)

To the west of Interlaken on the shore of Lake Thun is Weissenau, where a castle guarded the approach to the Bernese Oberland and the Grimsel Pass; the ruins were restored in 1955. Beyond is the lakeside village of Neuhaus, once the steamer pier for Interlaken before the opening of the Bödeli Railway, and now known for its watersports.

Six minutes' walk from **Interlaken West** is the metre-gauge funicular to Heimwehfluh (table 2360), which operates from late April to late October. Turn right outside the station along Rugenparkstrasse. The walk up takes about 20 minutes. Lying on the northern slope of the Rugen, a wooded ridge to the southwest of the town, Heimwehfluh was described by the Swedish traveller Sven Hedin as 'one of the most beautiful places on earth'. The view from the observation tower is worth the ascent, and there is a restaurant, children's play area and O gauge model railway.

Also close to Interlaken West station, in Rugenparkstrasse (turn right outside the station), is a huge model railway exhibition (Modelleisenbahn-Treff) with up to 40 trains on the move. One of the networks has 350m (1,148ft) of track, and there are rack railways and cablecars as well as conventional trains. Railway videos are screened. (Open: late Apr–mid-Oct, daily 10.00–12.00, 13.30–18.00.)

Five minutes' walk from **Interlaken Ost** beside the Aare is the funicular up the Harder (table 2361), which opened in 1908 and leaves from its original well-preserved station to serve another period building, the summit restaurant and hotel. The peak at 1,322m (4,460ft) provides an excellent panorama and access to some superb walks, particularly enjoyed by Mendelssohn. In common with many hotel and mountain railway companies, the Harder Railway created many of the paths, the most notable perhaps being that to the east that reaches the Brünig Pass. The difficulty of building the railway is reflected in the fact that almost half its length is built on viaduct or bridge. Operation of the funicular is limited to May to mid-October.

Near the foot of the railway is an Alpine Wildlife Park with ibex and marmots (free admission). The massively horned ibex was hunted to extinction in Switzerland between the 16th and 19th centuries, and the colony here is the result of reintroduction in 1915. The park also has English-language leaflets to describe the 79 labelled trees and shrubs on the nearby Forestry Nursery Path (Waldlehrpfad).

Practical information

TO – Höheweg 37, CH-3800. Tel: 033/822 21 21; fax: 033/822 52 21; email: mail@InterlakenTourism.ch; web: www.InterlakenTourism.ch Open: Mon–Fri 08.00–12.00, 14.00–18.00, Sat 08.00–12.00.

Interlaken West

Hotels close to the station are
Eden-Nova★★★, Bahnhofplatz 45, CH-3800. Tel: 033/822 88 12; fax: 033/654 94 31.

Merkur***, Bahnhofstrasse 35, CH-3800. Tel: 033/822 66 55; fax: 033/822 66 16.
Bahnhof**, Bahnhofstrasse 37, CH-3800. Tel: 033/822 70 41; fax: 033/822 55 17.

Hotels of character in the town centre not far from Interlaken West station
Victoria-Jungfrau***** (H), Höheweg 41, CH-3800. Tel: 033/828 28 28; fax: 033/828
28 80; email: Interlaken@victoria-jungfrau.ch; web: www.victoria-jungfrau.ch
Interlaken's first grand hotel.
Interlaken****(H), Höheweg 74, CH-3800. Tel: 033/826 68 68; fax: 033/826 68 69;
email: interlakenhotel@bluewin.ch; web: www.interlakenhotel.ch Interlaken's oldest
hotel, this was once the monastic hostelry, and has a restaurant fitted out like a
dining-car.
Krebs****(H), Bahnhofstrasse 4, CH-3800. Tel: 033/822 71 61; fax: 033/823 24 65;
email: hotelkrebs@bluewin.ch; web: www.krebshotel.ch

Interlaken Ost
Hotels close to the staton are
Du Lac****(H), Höheweg 225, CH-3800. Tel: 033/822 29 22; fax: 033/822 29 15;
web: www.bestwestern.com/ch
Carlton***(H), Höheweg 92, CH-3800. Tel: 033/822 38 21; fax: 033/822 03 55;
email: carlton@tcnet.ch; web: www.interlaken_tourism.ch
Villa Europa***, Höheweg 94, CH-3800. Tel: 033/822 71 41; fax: 033/822 93 41.

LAKE THUN
The maiden voyage of the first steamship, the *Bellevue*, was made in July 1835.
The vessel was bought from Cave of Paris, brought to the lake in pieces by carts
and was named after the pension in Thun owned by the two purchasers of the
boat. Some British visitors would doubtless have been gratified that a barrel
organ on the *Bellevue* played 'God Save the King', not realising that the same
tune was used by the Swiss for their national anthem until the introduction of
the 'Swiss Psalm'; the instrument can be seen in the Castle Museum in Thun.

New vessels were added to the fleets of the two boat-operating companies,
which in 1913 came into the ownership of the Bern–Lötschberg–Simplon-
Bahn (BLS), which still runs them. The first motor vessels were introduced in
the 1920s, and there is now a fleet of 12 and one surviving paddler, the
Blumlisalp of 1906. BLS offers all kinds of tickets and special packages, including
such imaginative ideas as a two-day excursion from Thun to Mount Rothorn,
using the paddle steamers on lakes Thun and Brienz and steam-propulsion up
the mountain, with an overnight stay at the hotel on the summit.

There are numerous opportunities for sailing, water-skiing, windsurfing
and diving at the resorts around the lake.

Thun used to be the junction for a narrow-gauge line that ran along the
northern shore of Lake Thun to Interlaken; it has been replaced by a bus
service (table 300.70), and the principal villages of the northern shore are
also served by steamers. For places along the south shore of the lake that are
served by steamers, see the section on the railway between Thun and
Interlaken, above.

Hilterfingen   The French Renaissance-style Schloss Hünegg was built in 1861–3 by a Prussian baron and is now a museum of social history and interior decoration (open: mid-May–mid-Oct, Mon–Sat 14.00–17.00, Sun 10.00–12.00, 14.00–17.00).

Oberhofen   One of Switzerland's most romantic castles is built on the water's edge. The oldest part, the keep, dates from the 12th century, and it has been gradually extended, most recently in the mid-19th century. In 1940 it was transferred to the Oberhofen Castle Foundation by a lawyer from Pennsylvania, William Maul Measey. Apart from its important interiors, the castle houses collections of arms, toys and musical instruments. (Open: mid-May–mid-Oct, daily 10.00–12.00, 14.00–17.00; closed Mon am. Park: daily 09.30–18.00.) Nearby is a swimming pool with a statue of Sir Winston Churchill in the grounds. There is also a museum of mechanical musical instruments in Staatstrasse (open: mid-May–mid-Oct, Tue–Sat 10.00–12.00, 14.00–17.00).

Beatenbucht   The lower terminus of the funicular to the pretty village of Beatenberg (table 2355). Beatenbucht also provides access to the Beatus Cave, named after the 6th-century Irish monk St Beatus who is supposed to have lived in a hermitage at the entrance. Inside are the remains of a prehistoric house and some stalactites and stalagmites. (Open: late Mar – late Oct, daily 10.30–17.00.)

INTERLAKEN–ZWEILUTSCHINEN–LAUTERBRUNNEN
Table 311

The construction of the first railway into the heart of the Bernese Oberland and its opening in 1890 were not universally welcomed, many having reservations about the impact that tourism would have on life in the valleys. The Bernese Oberland Bahn (BOB) operates the lines to Lauterbrunnen and Grindelwald, which share the tracks from Interlaken as far as the junction of Zweilütschinen. The lines were built to metre gauge and electrified in 1914. As the means of reaching several car-free resorts and the Jungfraubahnen, it is a very busy line. Sit on the left.

Trains for Lauterbrunnen and Grindelwald operate as one unit as far as the junction at Zweilütschinen, where the two sections separate; there is not time to transfer at Zweilütschinen, so it is important to check at Interlaken Ost that you are in the right portion of the train. Almost invariably the front section goes to Lauterbrunnen, the rear section to Grindelwald.

Leaving Interlaken, trains describe a sharp curve to head south, crossing the flat Bödeli and skirting the site of a military airfield as they make for an opening in the valley walls. The airfield is being redeveloped into a theme park, Mysteries of the Universe, promoted by Eric von Däniken who wrote *Chariot of the Gods.*

At **Wilderswil** trains for Schynige Platte may be seen on the left. Beyond Schynige Platte-Bahn depot and over a covered wooden bridge across the river is the white church of Gsteig, where two daughters of Schumann and one daughter of Mendelssohn are buried. In the village is a working watermill built in 1513 which now houses a local history museum. To the north of Wilderswil is the ruined castle of Unspunnen, with cylindrical keep.

Approaching the junction of **Zweilütschinen**, the line crosses the Black Lütschine just before its confluence with the White Lütschine. At the railway workshops here, a former Rhaetian Railway tank locomotive is kept for special trains. Near the station are the remains of a 17th-century blast furnace.

Beyond the station the Lauterbrunnen line forks to the right along the valley of the White Lütschine, which steadily narrows, barely leaving room for the river, railway, cycle path and road. Two rack sections lift the line to the valley level on which Lauterbrunnen is built.

Lauterbrunnen is flanked by two remarkably perpendicular walls of rock, rising on one side to the shelf on which lies Wengen and on the other, Mürren. Although the village is famous for the Staubbach falls that inspired Goethe in 1779, there are 72 large and small waterfalls around the valley.

In a mill below the church is the Talmuseum, which houses a local history collection, re-created rooms, displays on iron-ore mining, lace, mountaineering and tourism, and the 'Lötscher Bell', cast in the Valais in 1486 (open: mid-Jun–mid-Sep, Tue, Thu, Sat, Sun 14.30–17.30). The building used to be a grocery store which had the valley's only supply of salt until the beginning of the 20th century. The inhabitants of outlying villages would purchase their salt after attending Sunday service.

A bus from the station goes to Isenfluh (table 311.20) from where a cablecar rises to Sulwald (table 2458). Unusually the cablecar was built to help farmers with the harvest rather than carry tourists, but it is now well used by hikers. There is a particularly fine walk from Isenfluh through alpine meadows and woods, and beside the Sausbach to Sausmatten and Winteregg where there is a restaurant.

Beyond Lauterbrunnen is Stechelberg, the bottom of a four-stage cablecar that ascends to Mürren and then on to the Schilthorn (table 2460). This can be reached by bus from Lauterbrunnen station (table 311.15) in 12 minutes. For description see Mürren, table 313 below.

Near Stechelberg station are the exceptionally spectacular Trümmelbach falls. They cascade through a chasm so narrow that it is not easy to appreciate the full spectacle, though a lift open from April to October helps visitors reach the different levels. The lift is complemented by tunnels, bridges and walkways to enable visitors to see the majestic force of the glacier falls at close quarters. The water drains the glaciers of the Eiger, Mönch and Jungfrau.

Practical information
Wilderswil

TO – Lehngasse, CH-3812. Tel: 033/822 84 55; fax: 033/823 33 35; email: mail@wilderswil.ch; web: www.wilderswil.ch Open: Mon–Fri 08.00–12.00, 14.00–18.00, Sat –17.00.

Numerous hotels; close to the station are
Jungfrau★★★, CH-3812. Tel: 033/822 35 31; fax: 033/822 72 92.
Gasthof Steinbock, Gsteigwiler, CH-3814. Tel: 033/823 30 01; fax: 033/823 30 15.

Lauterbrunnen

TO – Fuhren, CH-3822. Tel: 033/855 19 55; fax: 033/855 36 04. Open: Mon–Fri 08.00–12.00, 14.00–18.00 (Jul–Aug –19.00), Sat 09.00–12.00, 15.00–19.00; Sun 09.00–15.00.

Numerous hotels; close to the station are
Silberhorn***, CH-3822. Tel: 033/856 22 10; fax: 033/855 42 13; email: info@silberhorn.com; web: www.silberhorn.com
Bahnhof, CH-3822. Tel: 033/855 17 23; fax: 033/855 18 47.
Sternen, CH-3822. Tel: 033/855 12 31; fax: 033/855 44 31.

Bicycle hire in Lauterbrunnen from Crystal Sports (tel: 033/856 90 90) and Imboden Bike Adventures (tel: 033/855 21 14).

WILDERSWIL–SCHYNIGE PLATTE Table 314

This 800mm gauge Riggenbach-rack railway was opened in 1893 and taken over by BOB three years later. Although electrified in 1914, it still has a steam locomotive of 1894 for special trains. It is one of the most disorienting of mountain railways, its sharp curves, sometimes in tunnels, quickly destroying one's sense of direction. Its characterful though box-like locomotives are some of the oldest operating on Swiss railways, dating from 1910–14; some are second-hand from the Wengernalpbahn. The frequent change of direction leaves little to choose between seats on either side of the coaches.

Leaving Wilderswil on the continuous rack, the line crosses the Lütschine, running parallel with the line to Zweilütschinen before turning abruptly east and diving into the woods. The Rotenegg Tunnel takes the railway through a horseshoe curve to emerge in almost the opposite direction. There used to be a railway-owned hotel at **Breitlauenen**, but its seasonal opening and changing fashions led to closure in 1974.

The trees thin and the views become less impeded as the railway reaches alpine meadows. There are some tremendous drops from the train, and after Grätli Tunnel the train emerges to a spectacular view of the Eiger, Mönch and Jungfrau, which remain in sight all the way to the station at **Schynige Platte**. The view from the terminus must be one of the finest from any station in the world. At the beginning and end of the season, you may see cows being brought up or taken down the mountain by train, or sheep being transferred during the summer – the carriage of livestock by rail is now rare in Europe.

Near the summit station is the alpine garden that has delighted botanists and gardeners since 1929; with over 500 of the 620-odd plants that exist above the tree line, it has a growing season from June to October and is open all day.

A short walk above the station is the hotel that was one of the first on a Swiss mountain, opening in 1832. On two nights in mid-August walkers gather at the hotel an hour before midnight for a guided night hike to the peak of the Faulhorn, arriving in time for sunrise. The descent is via the gondola from First down to Grindelwald.

The mountain slopes around the station offer some wonderful walks with some of the finest views to be had of the Bernese peaks and over lakes Thun and Brienz. An easy circular walk takes in the extraordinary domed rock known as the Daube. Even in high season you can quickly escape the crowds by taking a footpath, and by 16.00 most people have left the summit. A path also descends through the woods to Gsteig and Wilderswil via Breitlauenen.

Practical information
Schynige Platte
Schynige Platte Kulm, CH-3801. Tel: 033/822 34 31; fax: 033/822 37 53.

LAUTERBRUNNEN–GRUTSCHALP–MURREN Table 313

When built, the section from Lauterbrunnen to Grütschalp was the steepest funicular in Switzerland; using the Riggenbach rack, the Bergbahn Lauterbrunnen–Mürren (BLM) was operated by the water/gravity principle until conversion to electric drive in 1901–2. Pincer brakes replaced the rack in 1948–50. Water was fed into a tank underneath the upper car and gradually emptied on the descent to counteract the growing weight of the descending car's cable and the lighter cable of the ascending car. It climbs in a straight line, partly on attractively arched stone viaducts. The line from Grütschalp to Mürren follows the contours along the top of the cliffs above Lauterbrunnen. Both lines were built to metre gauge, opened in 1891 and worked by the BOB from the outset. The inventor of one of the rack systems and for a time Inspector of the BOB, Emil Strub, described the impact of the view from the railway: 'The scenery from Grütschalp to Mürren becomes continuously wilder, more astonishing. The passengers rise involuntarily from their seats and, intoxicated with wonder, seek to assimilate the undreamt-of, magnificent spectacle...' Sit on the left on both lines.

A subway under the street links the BOB station at Lauterbrunnen with the station for Grütschalp. The ascent is largely through woods but there are momentary views over the Lauterbrunnen valley. At Grütschalp passengers and goods are transferred on to the adhesion line, a few yards from and at right angles to the funicular.

The short journey to Mürren is every bit as impressive as Strub's eulogy would suggest. The views over the valley and the range of towering peaks on the opposite side are unimpeded. Amongst the many walks in the area is a hike along the ledge back to Grütschalp, which offers a magnificent, changing panorama of the surrounding peaks. It soon becomes evident why **Mürren** is so popular: it is in an incomparable position on a broad shelf above the Lauterbrunnen valley, and it has arguably the finest views of the Eiger, Mönch and Jungfrau.

Mürren is one of the larger car-free resorts, reflected in the heavy traffic on the railway which carried 515,157 people and 7,401 tonnes of goods traffic in 1990. Inside the modern station is a relic from old Mürren: one of the 50cm-gauge trolleys that once ran for 450m through the village to take visitors and their luggage from the station to their hotel. Outside the station is a tablet commemorating one of the pioneers of alpine skiing, Sir Alfred Lunn (1888–1974), who had much to do with the promotion of Mürren as a winter resort.

At first the village was a summer only resort, patronised largely by British visitors, Tennyson amongst them. As early as 1869 an English visitor complained that the village was 'crowded to excess with English people'. The future Archbishop of Canterbury, E W Benson, was not pleased to see British people playing tennis within sight of the Jungfrau, evidently regarding such activity as little short of sacrilegious. (If this seems excessive, it was a view shared by many in the early to mid-19th century, including some of the painters of the Hudson River School: for the Bolton-born Thomas Cole, the attitude of many 'go-getting' Americans to beautiful landscapes as territory ripe for exploitation was akin to blasphemy. The redemptive power of landscape and natural forces was a recurrent theme in the works of Wordsworth and other Romantics.) The English church in Mürren was built in 1878 to the design of George Edmund Street (architect of the Law Courts in London). Amongst later eminent British visitors were Henry Morton Stanley, George Bernard Shaw, Joseph Chamberlain, Princess Mary and Field Marshal Montgomery.

In 1910 the railway was persuaded to operate a winter service for the first time; two years later, Sir Alfred Lunn officially inaugurated the first winter sports season at the Palace Hotel, where the Kandahar Ski Club was founded in 1924. The first of the now-famous Inferno ski runs from the Schilthorn took place in 1928, and three years later Mürren was host to the first world skiing championship.

The association of Mürren with ballooning goes back to 1910 when the first crossing of the Alps by balloon began here, ending in Turin. The first International High Alpine Ballooning Competition was held in 1957, and provides a colourful spectacle as the big balloons rise into the clear air. An Alpine Balloon Sport and Balloon Postal Service Museum, situated in the Resort and Sports Centre, tells the story of the sport and its use as transport.

In addition to an impressive range of sports facilities, including indoor pool, a nursery is provided – ask at the tourist office.

Above Mürren is the Allmendhubel, which can be reached by funicular (table 2463) from a station eight minutes' walk from the BLM station. Operating from August to mid-October, and for winter sports from mid-December to mid-April, the line climbs through a 183m (600ft) tunnel.

The most famous peak above Mürren is the Schilthorn, brought to world attention through its choice as the location for filming one of the most dramatic sequences of the James Bond film *On Her Majesty's Secret Service*, with Diana Rigg and George Lazenby. It was filmed just before the opening of the revolving restaurant known as Piz Gloria in 1969, which was rebuilt to increase capacity and the quality of its facilities in 1990. Now rotated by solar-power, the restaurant goes through a revolution once every hour. The complex must be one of the most spectacular sites in the world for a seminar or conference – up to 340 people can be accommodated. The daily catering requirements call for 4–6 service lifts at the end of each day to bring up supplies, including water, and the waste discharge pipe down to Mürren has to be heated to prevent freezing. If the weather is inclement, you can see a 10-

minute, multi-projector audio-visual of the surroundings and a 10-minute extract from *On Her Majesty's Secret Service*.

The summit of the Schilthorn is reached by the final stage of Europe's longest cablecar route that begins at Stechelberg (see under *Lauterbrunnen*, above) (table 2460) and ascends in four stages, the first to the mountain village of Gimmelwald, passing dramatically close to the Mürrenbach waterfall. The next section rises to Mürren and then to Birg before the final stage to the Schilthorn at 2,970m (9,744ft).

It is from the summit that the Inferno ski race down to Mürren takes place, the record being 15 minutes for the 15.8km (10 miles) descent that has been called 'the craziest ski race in the world'. Thrills of a different but equally crazy kind can be had by bungy-jumping out of a cablecar on the previous cablecar route between Stechelberg and Mürren, said to be the highest jump from a fixed installation in the world, at 180m (590ft).

The altitude of the mountain ensures that skiing remains possible long after lower slopes are closed. For walkers, a network of paths descends from the cablecar station, but the intermediate stations might be better starting points for the less experienced.

Practical information
Mürren

TO – CH-3825. Tel: 033/856 86 86; fax: 033/856 86 96; email: info@muerren.ch; web: www.mueren.ch Open: Mon–Sat 09.00–12.00, 13.00–18.30, Thu –20.30, Sun 13.00–17.30.

Hotels close to the station are
Eiger★★★★, CH-3825. Tel: 033/856 54 54; fax: 033/856 54 56; email: eiger@muerren.ch; web: www.muerren.ch/eiger
Guesthouse Eiger★★, CH-3825. Tel: 033/855 35 35; fax: 033/855 35 31.

The oldest hotel is the historic, though much rebuilt
Anfi Palace★★★★ (H), CH-3825. Tel: 033/855 24 24; fax: 033/855 24 17; email: palace@muerren.ch; web: www.mierren.ch/palace

Hotels perched on the edge of the cliff with stupendous views are
Edelweiss★★★, CH-3825. Tel: 033/855 13 12; fax: 033/855 42 02.
Alpina★★, CH-3825. Tel: 033/8/55 13 61; fax: 033/855 10 49.

Bicycle hire from the tourist office.

LAUTERBRUNNEN–KLEINE SCHEIDEGG Table 311
Opened in 1893, the Wengernalpbahn (WAB) was built to 800mm gauge rather than the metre gauge of the BOB, necessitating a change of train in a rare instance for Switzerland of poorly planned integration. It has the distinction of being the longest continuous stretch of rack railway in Switzerland, at 19.2km (12 miles). Using the Riggenbach rack, the railway was electrified in 1909–10, and of the 16 steam locomotives, only one of 1891 was saved, by sale to the Brienz–Rothorn Bahn. The early

coaches had open upper sections with cloth curtains that had to be opened in high winds to stop the carriages being blown over – like the injunctions in Indian narrow-gauge trains to lower the windows during storms. Thankfully most of the area served by the WAB is inaccessible to motor traffic so the railway still plays a vital role in carrying goods traffic as well as passengers. The Swiss Pass is valid only as far as Wengen, but trains wait for passengers not holding valid onward tickets to buy them, at a discount with the Swiss Pass. Sit on the right.

The views leaving Lauterbrunnen are superb. On the left is the huge massif of the Männlichen, Tschuggen and Lauberhorn, while to the right, above the valley of the White Lütschine to the south, is the great spout of water known as the Staubbach Falls, which has a drop of 274m (900ft). On the shelf of rock from which the falls descend is the village of Mürren.

At the passing loop of Witimatte, the railway divides, the right fork being the original line which climbs at gradients as steep as 1 in 4 through the woods and over some impressive viaducts to Wengen. Today it is used only by goods and service trains. The line to the left is the new line that was opened in 1910 with grades no steeper than 1 in 5.5. It ascends through woods and several tunnels to enter Wengen side by side with the older route.

Wengen is one of the largest car-free resorts, making it a perfect place for families. Like other resorts that have excluded traffic, the quality of air is an elixir for nostrils and lungs accustomed to urban pollution. The compact nature of the village makes it easy to walk everywhere, and small electric vehicles meet the trains to transport luggage and disabled people to their hotels. The tourist office is a two-minute walk from the station, taking a left turn by the Hotel Eiger.

The village is a particularly good skiing resort for families, catering for a wide range of skill in the 100km (62 miles) of runs, and there is a children's training area in the village. Wengen is the venue for the annual skiing contest on the Lauberhorn in late January. The village also has a natural and an artificial ice-rink, and the usual complement of tennis courts, heated outdoor swimming-pool and a curling hall.

A ten-minute walk from the station, past the English church dedicated to St Bernard, is the cablecar to the Männlichen (table 2455) at 2,230m (7,316ft). The cablecar station at the top is the start of numerous walks which help to clarify the complicated topography of the valleys. Particularly helpful is the view from the summit of the Männlichen, an easy 20-minute walk from the cablecar. One of the best walks takes you along the slopes of the Tschugen and Lauberhorn to Kleine Scheidegg (1½ hours). From there you can either take the train back or walk back to Wengen via Wengernalp (1½ hours). Another circular tour can be made by taking Europe's longest gondola down to Grindelwald (table 2445).

The climb out of Wengen takes you steadily closer to the chain of mountains ahead, pausing at **Allmend**, an isolated halt used by hikers, after which the tree line is crossed. By **Wengernalp** the train is so close to the massif that it induces the feeling you could almost reach out and touch the rock faces opposite. There is no other building near the station but the hotel, making it an exceptionally peaceful place to stay.

It was here that Byron wrote *Manfred*, which, on publication in 1817, brought the Bernese Oberland to the attention of many through its descriptions of Wengen, and the Scheidegg and Grindelwald glaciers. Tchaikovsky, Mendelssohn and Richard Wagner are amongst the guests that have stayed here in the frequently rebuilt hotel, though they would have arrived by sedan chair or on horseback.

Kleine Scheidegg is dramatically situated on the saddle between the Lauberhorn and the Jungfrau and is the junction for trains to Jungfraujoch and Grindelwald. The views down the valley towards Grindelwald in one direction and Mürren in the other, with the peaks of the Eiger, Mönch and Jungfrau on one side, are magnificent. The Lauberhorn to the north of the station provides one of the world's greatest skiing challenges, the World Cup Race, perpetuating the first British downhill ski races that were held here in 1921. The terrace at the station is a popular place to have lunch, and a collection of old signals adorns the station restaurant.

Practical information
Wengen
TO – CH-3823. Tel: 033/855 14 14; fax: 033/855 30 60; email: information@wengen.com; web: www.wengen.com Open: Mon–Fri 08.00–12.00, 14.00–18.00, Sat 08.30–11.30; high season, Sat and Sun 16.00–18.00.

Numerous hotels; close to the station are
Regina★★★★ (H), Dorfstrasse, CH-3823. Tel: 033/855 15 12; fax: 033/855 15 74; email: regina@wengen.com; web: www.wengen.com/hotel/regina
Hotel Silberhorn★★★★, CH-3823. Tel: 033/856 51 31; fax: 033/855 22 44; email: silberhorn@wengen.com; web: www.wengen.com/hotel/silberhorn
Eiger★★★, CH-3823. Tel: 033/855 11 31; fax: 033/855 10 30; email: eiger@wengen.com; web: www.wengen.com/hotel/eiger
Falken★★★ (H), CH-3823. Tel: 033/856 51 21; fax: 033/855 33 39; email: falken@wengen.com; web: www.wengen.com/hotel/falken Delightful character.

Wengernalp
Jungfrau-Wengernalp, CH-3823. Tel: 033/855 16 22; fax: 033/855 30 69.

Kleine Scheidegg
Scheidegg★★, CH-3801. Tel: 033/855 12 12; fax: 033/855 12 94.
Röstizzeria-Bahnhof, CH-3818. Tel: 033/855 11 51; fax: 033/855 11 52.

Bicycle hire from Imboden Bike Adventures (tel: 036/55 20 22 or 036/55 14 14).

KLEINE SCHEIDEGG–JUNGFRAUJOCH Tables 311/312
Many visionaries had toyed with the idea of a railway to the Jungfrau before Adolf Guyer-Zeller had a flash of inspiration while climbing the Schilthorn with his daughter in 1893. Staying at a hotel in Mürren, he spent much of the night sketching his ideas, which needed remarkably little alteration. Work began in July 1896, and the first section

to the mouth of the tunnel opened two years later. Thereafter it was a long, arduous process to bore the tunnel to successive stations, each provided with viewing platforms on the cliff face at the end of side tunnels. Guyer-Zeller, the driving force of the project, died in 1899 but his sons continued the work. As the railway lengthened, ticket revenue increased to help fund construction. Various disasters dogged construction, the worst in 1908 when 30 tonnes of dynamite exploded, shattering windows in Grindelwald and creating a noise supposedly heard in Germany. In all seriousness some papers reported the Eiger was wobbling. Europe's highest railway station, at 3,454m (11,333ft), opened on 1 August 1912. The metre-gauge railway was built with the Strub rack and has been electrically operated from the outset. The Swiss Pass obtains a discount on the high fares necessitated by the costs of maintaining such a railway. Because of the price, it is advisable to check that you are likely to have clear visibility from the summit. Warm clothing and sunglasses are vital. Sit on the right.

The first section of the line from Kleine Scheidegg as far as the first station is in the open, broken only by the occasional snow shelter. Beside the hotel and restaurant at **Eigergletscher** are the Jungfraubahn's husky kennels, home to the dogs which pull sledges at the summit. The station is one end of the Eiger Trail to Alpligen, a station on the line down from Kleine Scheidegg to Grindelwald (table 312). Beyond the station are the railway's workshops, the highest in Europe, and the portal of the 7,122m (4.43 miles) unlined tunnel that ends underneath the Jungfraujoch. The journey is broken by a five-minute stop at **Eiger Wall** where passengers can walk to the former viewing platform – now regrettably converted into a picture window – on the north face of the Eiger, which has a surprisingly pastoral aspect down to Grindelwald. Seven minutes later there is another halt, at **Eismeer**, from which there is a quite different view from the previous stop. Here the window overlooks the Grindelwald and Fiescher glaciers.

Passengers arriving at **Jungfraujoch** are warned of the effects of altitude on respiration and advised to walk slowly. From the glazed hall beside the station a lift provides access to the restaurants, Ice Palace, open-air verandas, exhibition gallery and the glacier outside, where a team of huskies gives sledge rides. A winter garden and an extension to the High Alpine Research Station were opened in 1996. The Jungfraujoch is also home to Europe's highest manned meteorological observatory, which measures about 25 weather elements every ten minutes. This information is analysed by computer, along with that from 60 other weather stations.

A multi-projector audio-visual with commentary in German or English describes the construction of the railway and facilities on the Jungfraujoch as well as the topography of the surrounding mountains. The present buildings were erected after fire destroyed the old hotel and restaurant in 1972 and incorporate the highest grid-connected solar power plant in Europe.

The view down the Aletsch glacier is spectacular, the great tongue of ice weaving its way downhill; at 21.6km (13½ miles) it is Europe's longest glacier, stretching south towards the Rhône valley close to the Brig–Andermatt railway.

ZWEILUTSCHINEN–GRINDELWALD Table 312

Opened in 1890, the line to Grindelwald threads the often narrow valley of the Black Lütschine, passing through the only two tunnels on the BOB.

From Zweilütschinen the Grindelwald line curves left round the BOB workshops to head up the valley of the Black Lütschine. A long rack section raises the line between **Lütschental** and **Burglauenen**, where the valley is so narrow that it is in shade for much of the day. Cliffs with trees covering the narrowest of ledges tower above the railway. To the left the fast-flowing river rushes down the valley, periodically crossed by covered wooden bridges. Beyond Lütschental the railway crosses the river. Another rack section follows after **Schwendi**, after which the valley opens out as the railway nears the terminus.

Grindelwald was burned to the ground in 1892, so its reconstruction was planned with tourism in mind. The local history collection in the Talhaus near the Reformed church of St Maria of 1793 provides an insight into the agricultural roots of the community, with a re-created alpine dairy and kitchen. It also has many items relating to early tourism, mountaineering and winter sports.

The modern sports centre has the usual facilities – indoor pool, sauna, skating hall, games room, table tennis and restaurant.

Found at the east end of the town, the two-section gondola to First (table 2440) is a ten-minute walk from the station and was the world's first fully automatic gondola cableway. The summit has a restaurant and is the start of some excellent walks, one of the most popular being to Bachalpsee, which takes about an hour. A path continues along the ridge to the Faulhorn and descends through Bussalp back to Grindelwald (about 5½ hours). Some of the best views to be had near First are from the Schwarzhorn at 2,928m (9,606ft), but this is a more difficult walk. To the east of the summit are popular ski slopes served by six lifts.

The station for the cablecar to Pfingstegg (table 2442) to the southeast is a 15-minute walk from the BOB/WAB station and close to the Firstbahn. There are several good walks from Pfingstegg. You can walk via the old marble quarries to the Lower Glacier, which at one time stretched down to the village; it can best be appreciated by the extraordinary walk through a canyon of rock and ice known as the Gletscherschlucht (1¼ hours). Alternatively you can stay at a higher level to reach Restaurant Stieregg overlooking the glacier (1 hour). In the other direction is the Upper Glacier, overlooked by Restaurant Milchbach (1 hour).

A bus from the station heads northeast through the Rosenlaui valley to Schwarzwaldalp (table 312.20) where connections are made with a service to Meiringen (table 470.65) on the Luzern–Interlaken line (table 470). A circular ticket can be bought for the bus journey to Meiringen, followed by a train journey to Interlaken and back to Grindelwald.

To the west of Grindelwald is the Männlichen, reached by a two-section gondola from Grindelwald Grund (table 2445). This is Europe's longest gondola cableway, at 6,240m (3.9 miles). From the summit there are marvellous walks along the ridge between the valleys of the Black and White Lütschine, which can help to put the complex topography of the area in perspective. Another cablecar descends to Wengen (table 2455).

Practical information
Grindelwald
TO – Sportzentrum, CH-3818. Tel: 033/854 12 12; fax: 033/854 12 10. Open: Mon–Fri 08.00–12.00, 14.00–18.00, Sat 08.00–12.00, 14.00–17.00.

Numerous hotels; close to the station are
Schweizerhof★★★★ (H), CH-3818. Tel: 033/853 22 02; fax: 033/853 20 04; email: schweizerhof@grindelwald.ch; web: www.grindelwald.ch/schweizerhof.html
Derby★★★, CH-3818. Tel: 033/854 54 61; fax: 033/853 24 26; email: derby@grindelwald.ch; web: www.grindelwald.ch/derby
Central Wolter★★★, Hauptstrasse, CH-3818. Tel: 033/854 33 33; fax: 033/854 33 39.
Steinbock★★★, Hauptstrasse, CH-3818. Tel: 033/853 10 10; fax: 033/853 34 94; email: mail@hotelsteinbock.ch; web: www.hotelsteinbock.ch/

Bicycle hire from Graf-Sport (about three minutes' walk from the station).

GRINDELWALD–KLEINE SCHEIDEGG Table 312
A short 800mm gauge line operated by the Wengernalpbahn that completes a circuit. Sit on the left so that you are on the right after reversal at Grindelwald Grund.

The railway drops down to the chalet-style station at **Grund** where the railway has its workshops and trains have to reverse, climbing out of the valley floor. The gradient is particularly severe on the ascent to **Alpiglen**, with a maximum of 1 in 4. The climb affords wonderfully open views across undulating pasture dotted with cow sheds and clumps of conifers that have survived clearance for pistes. The station is at one end of the Eiger Trail to Eigergletscher station. Although the railway is protected by snow shelters for a good length, the side to the right is open. For **Kleine Scheidegg**, see table 311.

SPIEZ–ZWEISIMMEN Table 320
The railway through the Lower Simmen valley is known as the Simmentalbahn and is operated by the Bern–Lötschberg–Simplon-Bahn (BLS). The heavily wooded valley is renowned for its distinctive style of chalets, and a leaflet is available describing a walk from Wimmis station to Erlenbach station taking in the finest examples; it is in German but the map and the gist of the text is readily decipherable. There is a proposal to lay a third rail to metre gauge between Interlaken, Spiez and Zweisimmen to permit throughrunning of metre-gauge trains between Luzern and Montreux. Sit on the left.

On leaving Spiez the Zweisimmen line shares the same route as the Thun line before turning southwest and crossing the River Kander ('the white one') soon after **Lattigen bei Spiez**. At **Wimmis** there is a 10th-century Romanesque church and an imposingly sited 15th-century castle.

The railway criss-crosses the River Simme ('the mighty one') which is also crossed by attractive covered wooden bridges. A bus from **Oey-Diemtigen** station goes along the secluded valley of Diemtigtal to Grimmialp (table 320.15). The valley won the 1986 Swiss Walker Prize for architectural heritage, Diemtigen itself having several fine farmhouses such as the Grosshaus of 1805, the largest private dwelling in Simmental.

Erlenbach im Simmental has some attractive wooden houses and a much rebuilt 10th-century church with 15th-century frescos. About 15 minutes' walk from the station is the cablecar up the Stockhorn (table 2370) from which there is a fine panorama over Thunersee, and alpine meadows renowned for their flowers. The summit has a restaurant and is particularly popular with hang-gliders for its take-off ramp. There are 70km (44 miles) of signed paths around the 2,190m (7,200ft) peak.

One of the valley's finest wooden houses is found in **Därstetten** – the magnificent façade of the Knuttihaus was built in 1756 in the combination of Ständerbau and Blockbau principles which is a characteristic of the area.

Beyond Därstetten the railway crosses an impressive viaduct and continues its course along a ledge on the right-hand side of the valley. **Oberwil im Simmental** is an attractive village, its Gothic Reformed church on a hill to the right. As the valley narrows near **Enge im Simmental** the railway drops down towards the level of the river before reaching **Boltigen**. From the station here a bus goes over a zig-zag route across the Jaunpass to Bulle station (table 254.21) (see Chapter 18).

For **Zweisimmen** see table 120.

Bicycle hire from Wimmis and Zweisimmen stations.

SPIEZ–BRIG Tables 300/301

The southern section of the Bern–Lötschberg–Simplon railway (BLS) is one of Switzerland's most spectacularly engineered railways, with 25 major bridges or viaducts and 24 tunnels, most notably the 14.6km (9 miles) long Lötschberg Tunnel. The final section from Frutigen to Brig opened in 1913 and was electrically worked from the outset. Sit on the right.

Leaving Spiez the line turns abruptly southeast to enter Hondrich Tunnel which leads into the Kander valley with the characteristic grey water of the glacial river on the right. A bicycle path runs close to the river all the way from Spiez to Kandersteg.

Adjacent to the station at **Mülenen** is the bottom of the two-section funicular that goes up to Niesen Kulm (table 2405), which opened in 1910. Immediately after departure the funicular crosses the broad River Kander. Alongside the track is a flight of 11,674 steps for maintenance workers that has the distinction of being the longest in the world.

The views from the summit are regarded as amongst the finest in the Bernese Oberland. From the summit at 2,362m (7,749ft) there is a lovely, partly wooded walk down which takes about 3½ hours. Other paths descend to Frutigen (3¾ hours), Wimmis (3½ hours) and Oey-Diemtigen on the

Spiez–Zweissimen line (see above). An attractive hotel at the summit enables guests to see dawn over the Bernese Alps.

At **Reichenbach im Kandertal** are some 18th-century timber buildings with carved decoration and painted façades. From the station at **Frutigen** an hourly bus goes up the steep-sided Engstligental to the popular resort of Adelboden (table 300.20). Half way to Adelboden the bus passes close to the cablecar from Elsigbach to Elsigenalp (table 2417), a popular area for walks with restaurants at both ends of the cablecar.

Leaving Frutigen the line passes on the right the ruins of Tellenburg Castle, which burned down in 1885, and then crosses an imposing viaduct before looping around the remains of Felsenburg Tower. The gradients steepen to 1 in 37 for much of the next 18km (11 miles) as the line describes two huge loops to gain the next step of the valley, using viaducts and tunnels to change direction. The storm of Boxing Day 1999 brought down so many trees in this area that the line can now be seen more clearly than for several decades. The spectacular ascent to Kandersteg, much more attractive scenically than the southern ramp, prompted BLS to create a footpath down to Frutigen, opened in 1993 (see below).

Kandersteg is a delightfully situated village that straggles over a broad flat expanse ringed by mountains. A summer and winter resort, the village is a good base for walking and mountaineering holidays. In the area are 350km (219 miles) of footpaths, and in winter there are 75km (47 miles) of cross-country ski trails and 13km (8 miles) of downhill runs. The village offers the usual indoor swimming and ice-rink, and has schools for mountaineering, paragliding and riding.

To the north of Kandersteg is the Blausee, a deep blue lake with crystal-clear water surrounded by a nature reserve and woodland. Boat trips are run on the lake which is also used as a trout farm, and St Bernard dogs are also bred here.

One of the best excursions from Kandersteg is to Oeschinensee: a chairlift (table 2410) 10 minutes' walk from the station takes you to the level of the side valley in which the lake is situated. It is a 20–30-minute walk to the lake, spectacularly sited in a bowl of rock that forms the 3,629m (11,908ft) peak of Blümisalp and overlooked by a hotel and restaurant. The water flows out of the lake underground and is used to generate electricity.

Also ten minutes' walk from Kandersteg station is the cablecar to Allmenalp (table 2411), where authentic cheese-making can be seen during the summer.

Much further away, about 40 minutes on foot from the station, is the cablecar to Sunnbüel (Gemmi) (table 2412), indicating the fact that the lift gives access to footpaths that lead past the Daubensee and over the Gemmi Pass to Leukerbad (see Chapter 19).

The Lötschberg Tunnel was constructed in 1906–12. It was planned as a straight bore, but after two years' work the tunnel was flooded with water and glacial debris from a fissure in the floor of the Gasterntal above. This forced the engineers to seal off 1,554m (5,100ft) of tunnel with a wall 10m (33ft) thick and build a curve to avoid the area of thin rock between the tunnel and the valley floor above. Camps for the 4,000 workers, mostly Italian, were built at Kandersteg and at **Goppenstein**, where the train emerges from the Lötschberg Tunnel. Shuttle trains for cars are run between the two stations. The first floor of the station has an exhibition about the AlpTransit projects to rid Switzerland of through lorry traffic by conveying it on piggyback trains through two new base tunnels. There is also a path to allow visitors to see the tunnel workings; boots are advisable.

The hamlet of Goppenstein is the start of the lovely Lötschental, though it is heavily visited. A bus from the station goes up the valley to Fafleralp (table 300.45).

Like its northern counterpart, the southern ramp of the BLS includes some of the steepest standard-gauge gradients in Switzerland with slopes of up to 1 in 37. Just after leaving Hohtenn Tunnel the line turns abruptly east to descend the north side of the Rhône valley; 400m (1,300ft) below is the SBB main line from Geneva to Brig.

The BLS has created a footpath along the southern ramp of the Lötschberg starting at **Hohtenn**. It is longer and very different in character from the northern walk, with impressive views over the Rhône valley. The section between Hohtenn and **Ausserberg** takes about three hours. A restaurant can be found at each end and at Ranerkumme en route. From Ausserberg runs one of the most attractive 'Bisses' referred to in Chapter 19 – the irrigation water courses that have sometimes become the focus of a walkers' path. This one irrigated the now protected Baltschiedertal. If you get tired, a bus links the post office in Baltschieder with Ausserberg and Visp stations (table 140.15). A small, quiet resort, Ausserberg has a climbing and riding school.

The footpath continues through **Eggerberg** to **Lalden**, the last station before Brig – see tables 100/100.2/100.3.

The BLS Adventure Trail

The northern section of this enterprising creation by BLS starts at Kandersteg station and ends at Frutigen station, taking advantage of the natural gradient. However, it is by no means as easy à descent as the railway, since the path naturally has to drop to the foot of viaduct piers and climb up to track level again, and it sometimes climbs over the top of tunnels. Stout shoes with good grips should be worn. The path is open between April and October (as is the southern section).

For anyone interested in the problems of operating an Alpine railway, there could be no better introduction. Information boards, for which an English translation can be bought at Kandersteg station, begin at the station but the majority are in the main section of the trail between the closed station at Blauseemailitholz and Kandergrund. It takes about two hours to walk from Kandersteg to Blauseemailitholz, an hour for the principal section, and a further two hours from Kandergrund to Frutigen. A bus runs every 1–2 hours from outside Kandersteg station to Mitholz (table 301.10), and you can return by the same service from Kandergrund.

The boards convey all kinds of information about the BLS and this section of track, but the most telling sight is the massive pillar of concrete that prevents an overhanging cliff from toppling into the valley, taking with it the railway's support. A platform goes round the pillar; make sure you go to the farthest point to look up at the inspection walks that have been created above. There is even a place about half way to have a barbecue: wood is provided with an axe (on a chain) to chop it up and a well-made grill with upended logs for seats.

If you want to take photographs, wait until after 11.00 as the line is entirely in shade before then.

Practical information
Niesen-Kulm
Berghaus Niesen-Kulm, Mülenen, CH-3711. Tel: 033/676 11 13; fax: 033/676 27 17.

Kandersteg
TO – Hauptstrasse, CH-3718. Tel: 033/675 80 80; fax: 033/675 80 81; email: info@kandersteg.ch; web: www.kandersteg.ch

Numerous hotels; closest to the station are
Schweizerhof**** (H), CH-3718. Tel: 033/675 19 19; fax: 033/675 19 27; email: schweizerhof.ksteg@bluewin.ch; web: www.strubel.ch/schweizerhof
Victoria Ritter**** (H), CH-3718. Tel: 033/675 80 00; fax: 033/675 81 00; email: info@hotel-victoria.ch; web: www.hotel-victoria.ch
Zur Post**, CH-3718. Tel: 033/675 12 58; fax: 033/675 22 58.

Oeschinensee
Oeschinensee**, CH-3718. Tel: 033/675 11 19; fax: 033/675 16 66.

Ausserburg
TO – CH-3938. Tel: 027/946 45 27; fax: 027/946 75 64. Open: Mon–Sun 09.00–22.00.

Sonnenhalde*** (H), CH-3938. Tel: 027/946 25 83; fax: 027/946 18 05; email: sonnenhalde@active.ch
Bahnhof**, CH-3938. Tel: 027/946 22 59; fax: 027/946 79 59.

Eggerberg
TO – CH-3939. Tel: 027/946 12 73; fax: 027/946 10 86. Open: Mon–Sun 09.00–22.00.

Bergsonne**, CH-3939. Tel: 027/946 12 73; fax: 027/946 10 86.

Bicycle hire from Frutigen, Kandersteg and Brig stations.

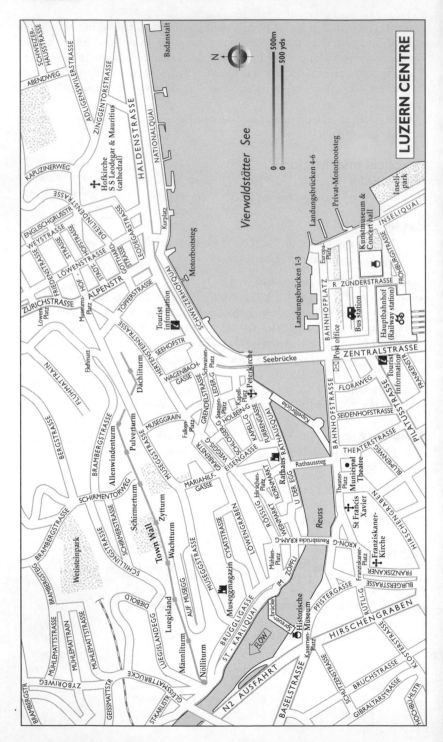

LUZERN CENTRE

Luzern

Luzern has become one of Switzerland's leading tourist centres largely thanks to its location. Not only is it beautifully situated in a fold of gentle hills on the edge of one of Europe's finest lakes, it is also close to several of the country's best-known mountains. It grew up around a Benedictine convent founded c750 and achieved some autonomy when it became a parish in 1178, but it was the opening of the Gotthard Pass to trade that acted as a catalyst to Luzern's growth. No road existed along the lake shore until the construction of Axenstrasse in 1856, so all goods had to be shipped by barge between Flüelen and Luzern. Wealthy merchants, ambassadors, pilgrims and carriers made Luzern a place of preparation for the crossing of the Gotthard or of recovery after it. By 1450 Luzern had 400 inns.

Although this role made Luzern a cosmopolitan town, its inhabitants remained conservative and adhered to the Catholic faith during the Reformation, and later even invited the Jesuits to 're-convert' the canton. Some of the first to fight for Swiss independence came from the area around the lake, and Luzern was the first town to join the country's fledgling cantons in 1332 when it formed an alliance with the Forest Cantons of Schwyz, Uri and Unterwalden.

Contact with other cultures perhaps inclined many from the district to seek mercenary service in foreign wars, one of Luzern's most visited monuments commemorating the Swiss who gave their lives in the defence of Louis XVI at the Tuileries in 1792 (see page 180). Another legacy of service abroad is one of Luzern's culinary specialities: the Kügelipastete, a creamed meat-filled pastry shell, was brought by returning mercenaries from Spain. Writers who came to Luzern as part of the 18th-century vogue for educational travel sometimes contributed to the town's fame, as did Goethe and Schiller, the latter using the William Tell legend to create a dramatic manifesto for political freedom (the play was the first production at Luzern's new theatre in 1838).

It was of course the construction of railways that increased significantly the number of tourists, the first railway opening from Basel in 1859. Luxurious hotels were built, many of them on Schweizerhofquai and Nationalquai along which a promenade was built. Part of this development was on land reclaimed from the lake, which entailed the destruction of a covered bridge similar in appearance to the famous Kapellbrücke. Some who had known Luzern for years were indignant at these changes. Turner chose Luzern as his base on several occasions in the 1840s and made numerous drawings and paintings of the town and the surrounding area. Retracing Turner's footsteps even in the 1860s, Ruskin could write of one of Turner's pictures as being 'a most precious drawing, all the more valuable, as the characteristic features of Lucerne are now being rapidly destroyed'.

These deplorable losses continued for much of the 19th century. Staggeringly there was a continual threat even to the Kapellbrücke. However, if Luzern's town planning was in less sensitive hands than Ruskin might have wished, much was in fact left to delight visitors a century and a half later.

Arriving in Luzern

Luzern station is a terminus, delightfully situated near the edge of the lake though only a single arch remains of the original handsome station which was damaged by fire and rebuilt in 1991. Though lacking the character of the old station, the new one is a model of convenience.

At the end of the platforms is a large concourse with the usual facilities. On a lower level, reached by escalator, and to the right are showers and banks of luggage lockers. For those catching a bus at the large terminal outside, a large board indicates the right platform (*Perron*) for the listed destinations. To the left on this lower level is a large shopping arcade and a pedestrian subway under the road to bring you up beside the post office on the corner of Bahnhofstrasse and Zentralstrasse.

The tourist office is reached by descending to the lower level under the concourse and bearing left to pass under the road, emerging near the corner of Frankenstrasse and Zentralstrasse. It has an excellent variety of publications on the city, including the *City Guide* (also found in most hotels). It is worth asking for special offers on, for example, a rail and cablecar excursion to Mount Titlis.

Using public transport

Steamers on the lake depart from quays on Bahnhofplatz, directly ahead from the end of the platforms and beyond the bus station.

Although bicycles can be hired from the station, Luzern is not an ideal city for cycling like Basel or Bern, partly because of the heavy traffic and lack of cycle paths, but also because it is easier to reach the main places of interest on foot. Bus tickets are discounted for more than one person, and a day card is available. The orange and white city bus is free and operates a circuit from the station to: Municipal theatre–Mühleplatz–Hirschenplatz–Schwanenplatz–Kapellplatz–station.

Bus route 1 goes to Kriens, where a funicular climbs up to Sonnenberg (table 2515) and a gondola rises to Fräkmüntegg (table 2516) from where a cablecar makes the leap up to Pilatus Kulm (table 2517). From there you can return to Luzern using the rack railway and either the SBB line or a steamer (see Chapter 14).

Exploring the old town

Luzern is a compact city, and most of its principal attractions can be reached on foot or by a short bus journey. The historic core of the city is pedestrianised and a booklet of suggested walks taking in the best buildings is available from the tourist office. Besides these buildings are scores of smaller vernacular buildings and small courtyards with fountains, which make a stroll round the traffic-free parts of Luzern such a pleasure.

The station (and tourist office) is only a few minutes' walk from Luzern's most famous attraction, the Chapel Bridge (Kapellbrücke); from both you can see the end of the main road bridge across the River Reuss where it leaves the lake. Make for it and the Chapel Bridge is to the left. Built in the first half of the 14th century and largely destroyed by a tragic fire in August 1993, the bridge formed part of the city fortifications and was named after St Peter's chapel at the northern end of the bridge. The Water Tower near the south end of the bridge was built c1300 and used at various times as a treasury, archive, prison and torture chamber.

Naturally the bridge had been rebuilt many times between its construction and the fire, but it was the loss of most of the paintings that decorated the bridge which was particularly sad. However, even these were the subject of repeated restoration and replacement. The originals were executed in the early 17th century and used Swiss history and Christianity as the principal themes. Although the bridge has been shortened by 44m (144ft) since it was built, it survived several threats of demolition during the 19th century. After the 1993 fire, the fabric of the bridge was restored within months, a decision being taken not to use distressed materials but to allow them to weather naturally.

From the southern, Bahnhofstrasse end of the bridge continue walking along the river bank away from the lake, past the Municipal Theatre to the Jesuit Church of St Francis Xavier. This was only one of many Jesuit buildings in Luzern, their college at one time teaching about 400 pupils. Work on Switzerland's first large baroque church began in 1666, and was consecrated in 1672. The identity of the architect is not known. Inside the shell niche on the façade stands a figure of St Xavier. The transition from the dark porch into the bright white interior is striking. The stucco-work and delicate colours are restrained, creating a beautiful interior, dominated by the monumental high altar built in 1681 of red stucco marble. A detailed English guidebook is available.

The building to the west is part of the old Jesuit college, adjacent to the Ritterscher Palast, and notable for its deeply chamfered rustication. It was built in 1557 for the mayor and now houses cantonal offices. Its lovely arcaded courtyard can be visited.

Behind the college and palace is the Gothic Franciscan church, built c1270–80. It has one of Switzerland's most ornate pulpits, early 17th-century stucco and frescos representing Luzern's military conquests.

Continuing along the river bank, at the end of the Spreuerbrücke is the Historical Museum (see below). The Spreuer Bridge was built in 1408 as part of the town's fortifications; in 1626-35 Kaspar Meglinger added a series of paintings representing the Dance of Death.

A worthwhile but time-consuming diversion here is a journey to Hotel Château Gütsch on the Gütschbahn, a funicular built specially to serve the hotel in 1884. To reach the bottom station, walk along Baselstrasse from the Historical Museum. It was at a pension on a site near Hotel Gütsch in 1868 that Queen Victoria stayed with Prince Arthur and Princess Louise. Its terrace is a marvellous place to have a drink while surveying the city and its walls rising up the hill opposite.

Returning directly to the river down Gütschstrasse, cross the river by the Geissmattbrücke and turn right to reach the lowest of the towers on the surviving stretch of town wall, the Nölliturm. The nine surviving towers and wall between them are a fragment of the town walls, built in 1350–1408 and largely torn down during the 19th century. The wall is a divide between old and new Luzern, and cows still graze the slopes to the north up which an enemy would have attacked. Some of the towers can be climbed; it is quite an ascent up the series of open steps but worth it for the view on a clear day. If you have time or energy only for one, the Zeitturm is probably the most interesting on account of its 16th-century clock; the mechanism is open to view, revealing its long pulleys and crude weights in the form of lumps of rock. The Watchturm provides access to the wall-walk, but its top is sealed off.

Following the walls to the end brings you to Museumsplatz. Cross over into Hofstrasse and left into Löwenstrasse, past the Bourbaki-Panorama (see *Museums*) to the Lion Monument. Mark Twain was usually ready to satirise or pour scorn on much that he saw in his travels, but he regarded this monument as 'the saddest and most moving piece of rock in the world'. The dying lion was carved out of the rock wall of a quarry in 1821 by Lukas Ahorn to a model by Bertel Thorwaldsen, to commemorate the 796 officers and men of the Swiss guard who died in 1792 defending Louis XVI and Marie-Antoinette when the Tuileries were stormed by the mob during the French Revolution.

Retrace your steps and turn left past the Old Swiss House restaurant and then right down Weystrasse to reach the cathedral, regarded as the most important Renaissance church building in Switzerland. The site on which the Hofkirche (of SS Leodegar and Mauritius) stands was used from the 8th century for a Benedictine monastery. The twin, finely tapering spires and their supporting square towers date from the 15th century and survived a fire in 1633 that destroyed the rest of the church. The replacement was consecrated in 1644 and contains some fine altars and carved pews. An arcaded churchyard surrounds the cathedral.

Proceed down the steps and directly ahead along Schweizerhofquai. The neo-classical Schweizerhof was built in 1845, the first of the large hotels after part of this area was reclaimed from the lake. Tolstoy stayed here in 1857 and wrote the short story *Lucerne*. Wagner stayed two years later while finishing *Tristan and Isolde*.

Bear left towards the bridge and turn right along the pedestrianised north bank of the river (most of this quarter of Luzern has been pedestrianised). The first building is the Zur Gilgen House; this ancient and much rebuilt house contains the country's oldest private library preserved in its original home. Its owner, the humanist Ludwig Zur Gilgen, died in 1577. The tower was once part of the town defences.

Just beyond the Kapellbrücke is St Peter's Church which gave the bridge its name. Dating from the 12th century but much rebuilt, St Peter's is the oldest church within the town wall.

On the right just before the pedestrian bridge is the open-arcaded Rathaus, built in 1602–6 in Italian Renaissance style but with a Bernese farmhouse roof. Markets are still held here in the arcades on Tuesday and Saturday mornings. Turn right here into Kornmarkt on which the Rathaus has a tower with six-sided turrets at the corners.

Another diversion can be taken to look at the enormous storehouse that can be seen from Château Gütsch. Turn left into Weinmarkt, briefly right into Kramgasse and left into Mühlenplatz. Looking west along the river, two roads lead out of the square. Take the upper road, Brüggligasse, and turn right into Museggstrasse to one of old Luzern's largest buildings. The huge Museggmagazin was built in 1685–6 to house supplies of corn and salt.

Returning to Kornmarkt, walk along Kapellgasse to Kapellplatz and the Seebrücke.

Markets

The colourful fruit and vegetable market is held under the arcades of the Rathaus beside the River Reuss. A handicrafts market is held on the first Saturday of the month (Mar–Dec) at Weinmarkt. A flea market is held every Saturday (May–Oct) on the Unter Burgerstrasse/Reusssteg, and a monthly market is held on the first Wednesday of every month.

Museums

Art Gallery (Kunstmuseum)   Adjacent to Luzern's concert hall, in which the International Festival of Music takes place, the Art Gallery was opened in 1933. The collection focuses on Swiss art from the 16th to 20th centuries, with smaller sections on Dutch and Flemish 17th-century paintings, 20th-century German and French expressionist works, and contemporary art. The subjects of its Swiss collection are primarily portraits and landscapes, providing an excellent insight into the way artists have seen the country through the centuries. A full catalogue is available with English text.
Robert-Zünd-Strasse 1. Immediately to the right of the station. Open: Tue–Sun 10.00–17.00, Wed –21.00. Tel: 041/410 90 40. Admission charge.

Swiss Transport Museum (Verkehrshaus)   Europe's largest transport museum could easily take a full day for anyone interested in the subject. Opened in 1959 and twice enlarged since, it attracts about half a million visitors a year. It includes not only rail, air, water and road transport but also space travel, telecommunications, tourism, a Cosmorama and Planetarium. Switzerland's first IMAX film theatre opened at the museum in 1996. The rail and water sections are understandably almost entirely Swiss-oriented, but the other sections are more international, with 35 aircraft from Britain, the United States, France and the Netherlands as well as Switzerland, and cars from a similar range of countries. Labels to exhibits are in four languages, including English, and an exceptionally informative 232-page guidebook is available in English, as well as other languages.

The railway section traces the history of railways in Switzerland from the first line into the country, across the border from France to Basel, to today's signalling system at Luzern station. Besides some superb, large-scale models and railway memorabilia, it has 60 original steam and electric locomotives, carriages, trams, funiculars and sectioned rack locomotive. There is a huge, working, scale model of the northern approach to the Gotthard from Erstfeld to Naxberg Tunnel that children (and lots of adults) are reluctant to leave. *Lidostrasse 5. Bus 6 or 8 from station to Wurzenbach. Open: April–Oct, daily 09.00–18.00; Nov–Mar, 10.00–17.00. Tel: 041/370 44 44. web: www.imax.ch Admission charge.*

Hans Erni-Haus Museum Over 300 works by this Swiss artist are on display, revealing the special relationship he had with technology. *Adjacent to Transport Museum. Same details.*

Picasso-Museum (Musée Picasso) A collection of important works by Picasso and over 200 photographs of the artist, mostly intimate portraits of the artist *en famille*, displayed in an attractive old house. *Furrengasse 21. Open: Apr–Oct, daily 10.00–18.00; Nov–Mar, daily 11.00–13.00, 14.00–16.00. Tel: 041/410 35 33. Admission charge.*

Bourbaki-Panorama This should not be missed by anyone interested in 19th-century history or epic canvases – it is the largest round mural in the world, covering 1,100m² (11,840sq ft). It depicts a poignant moment in the history of French arms when the Eastern Army under General Bourbaki sought asylum in Switzerland after its defeat at the hands of the Prussians in early 1871. About 88,000 exhausted men crossed the border at Les Verrières, west of Neuchâtel, where they were disarmed and given help by local people and by the recently founded Red Cross in its first act of humanitarian aid. This extraordinary canvas took seven painters two years to complete and came to Luzern in 1889 after ten years on display in Geneva. If you arrive when it opens, you are likely to have a private view and can request the English recorded commentary. *Löwenstrasse 18. Close to Lion Monument. Open: Mar–Apr, Oct–Nov daily 09.00–17.00, May–Sep 09.00–18.00. Tel: 041/410 01 15. Admission charge.*

Richard Wagner Museum Situated at Tribschen in a house overlooking the lake and still surrounded by trees and fields grazed by cows, the museum occupies the house Wagner rented from April 1866 until 1872. He married Cosima von Bülow (Liszt's daughter) in 1868, and the birth of their son Siegfried followed a year later. Wagner expressed his joy in the *Siegfried Idyll* which was given its first performance at Tribschen on Christmas Day 1870. The ground-floor rooms are filled with photographs, letters, scores, paintings and other memorablilia, all labelled in German, French and English. Oddly there is no general introduction to Wagner's time in Luzern, and the only guidebook is the price of a hardback. Upstairs there is a large collection of European, African and oriental musical instruments, but labels are in German only.

Richard Wagnerweg 27. Bus 6, 7 or 8 from outside station to Wartegg (10 minutes) then follow the signs (a pleasant 10-minute walk). Open: mid-Mar–Nov, Tue–Sun 10.00–12.00, 14.00–17.00. Tel: 041/360 23 70. Admission charge.

Historical Museum Situated in the old arsenal, this collection relating to Luzern's history includes arms and armour, sculptures, religious and secular artworks, glass and jewellery as well as a film (English commentary) about the city.

Pfistergasse 24. Open: Tue–Fri 10.00–12.00, 14.00–17.00, Sat–Sun 10.00–17.00. Tel: 041/228 54 24. Admission charge.

Glacier Garden (Gletschergarten) Discovered in 1872, the 'garden' contains various legacies of the last ice age, such as huge boulders, the largest glacial pot-hole ever found, with a depth of over 9m (30ft), and petrified palm leaves and seashells from 20 million years ago when Luzern had a subtropical beach on the sea. A museum contains a model of the city in 1792 and the oldest relief map of the country. A labyrinth of mirrors will delight childen.

Denkmalstrasse 4. Bus 1 from station to Löwenplatz. Bus 2 from Transport Museum to Luzernerhof. Open: Mar, daily 10.00–17.00; Apr–Oct, daily 09.00–18.00; Nov–Feb, Tue–Sun 10.00–17.00. Tel: 041/410 43 40. Admission charge.

Museum of Natural History The liveliness of the presentation at this museum has won it the European 'Museum of the Year' prize. It covers archaeology and geology as well as aquariums and terrariums, an educational forest path and special exhibitions.

Kasernenplatz 6. Open: Tue–Sat 10.00–12.00, 14.00–17.00, Sun 10.00–17.00. Tel: 041/228 54 11. Admission charge.

Festivals

The International Music Festival was founded in 1932 with the help of Arturo Toscanini who conducted the first concert. Held in August–September, the principal concerts are given in Luzern's magnificent new 1,840-seat concert hall in the Culture and Convention Centre, which opened in August 1998. The Festival attracts the world's best soloists, such as Heinrich Schiff and Maria Joao Pires, and orchestras of the calibre of the Royal Concertgebouw, Berlin Philharmonic and Vienna Philharmonic. The new Centre is very close to the station. Tickets are available from late March when the programme is published.

A five-day carnival is held in February, with colourful and noisy street processions, and in June or July the Altstadtfest gives an opportunity to hear local bands, dance and eat Swiss specialities.

Practical information

TO – Haldenstrasse 6, CH-6002. Tel: 041/410 71 71; fax: 041/410 73 34; email: luzern@luzern.org; web: www.luzern.org Open: May–Oct, Mon–Fri 08.30–18.00, Sat 09.00–17.00, Sun 09.00–13.00; Nov–Apr, Mon–Fri 08.30–12.00, 14.00–18.00, Sat 09.00–13.00.

Numerous hotels; close to the station are
Grand Hotel National*****, Haldenstrasse 4, CH-6002. Tel: 041/419 09 09; fax: 041/419 09 10; email: info@national-luzern.ch; web: www.national-luzern.ch
Flora****, Seidenhofstrasse 5, CH-6002. Tel: 041/229 79 79; fax: 041/229 77 77; email: flora@iac.ch; web: www.flora-hotel.ch
Monopol**** (H), Pilatusstrasse 1, CH-6002. Tel: 041/226 43 43; fax: 041/226 43 44; email: mail@hotel-monopol.com; web: www.hotel-monopol.com
Alpina***, Frankenstrasse 6, CH-6003. Tel: 041/210 00 77; fax: 041/210 89 44; email: hotel@alpina-luzern.ch; web: www.alpina-luzern.ch
Waldstätterhof***, Zentralstrasse 4, CH-6003. Tel: 041/210 54 93; fax: 041/210 09 59; email: hotelwaldstaetterhof@bluewin.ch

Luzern's main roads are busy and noisy with traffic, so hotels on quieter streets may be preferred. A few suggestions are
Château Gütsch**** (H), Kanonenstrasse, CH-6003. Tel: 041/249 41 00; fax: 041/249 41 91; email: frontdesk@chateau-guetsch.ch; web: www.chateau-guetsch.ch
des Balances**** (H), Weinmarkt, CH-6000. Tel: 041/410 30 10; fax: 041/410 64 51; email: balances@tic.ch; web: www.balances.ch
Rebstock**** (H), St Leodegar-Str. 3, CH-6002. Tel: 041/410 35 81; fax: 041/410 39 17.
Des Alpes***, Rathausquai 5, CH-6004. Tel: 041/410 58 25; fax: 041/410 74 51; email: hotel@desalpes-luzern.ch; web: www.forum.ch/des-alpes
Zum Weissen Kreuz*** (H), Furrengasse 19, CH-6004. Tel: 041/410 40 40; fax: 041/410 40 60.

Bicycle hire from the station.

Around Luzern

As Turner discovered, even before there was more than a rudimentary transport infrastructure, Luzern is unusually well placed for numerous excursions. Moreover, many of them are on the itineraries of first-time visitors to the country.

LAKE LUZERN (Vierwaldstättersee)

Lake Luzern's reputation as one of Europe's most beautiful stretches of inland water owes much to its irregular shape, creating constantly changing views, and to the grandeur of the mountains that encompass it. The shore ranges from vertiginous cliffs to gently undulating pasture grazed by cows. Although houses cover the eastern shore for some way after leaving Luzern and there are some unfortunate stretches of road visible between Brunnen and Flüelen, the lake remains remarkably unspoilt.

The lake is 38km (24 miles) long from Luzern to Flüelen, and its deepest point is 214m (702ft) between Beckenried and Gersau. It is fed principally by the River Reuss, at Flüelen, which flows out at Luzern, and less importantly by the rivers Engelberger Aa near Buochs and the Muota at Brunnen. Although the entire lake is referred to as the Vierwaldstättersee, strictly speaking the name applies to the main body of water, the section beyond the narrows between Brunnen and Treib being known as Urner See, or the Lake of Uri, and that beyond the bridge at Stansstad being the Alpnacher See.

Its German name means 'Lake of the Four Forest States' referring to the country's original cantons — Luzern, Schwyz, Unterwalden and Uri. The opening of the Gotthard Pass and the Schöllenen gorge to packhorses in 1230–40 made the lake a major artery for traffic between Italy and northern Europe. For centuries the boatmen, organised into guilds, enjoyed privileges granted by the cantons, and their business increased with the opening of a road over the Gotthard in 1830 and the subsequent mail coach services.

A threat appeared in 1837 in the form of the first steamship, which was greeted with a hail of stones at Flüelen and a threat to the captain of imprisonment if anyone dared to land. Sense prevailed and steamship services by various companies flourished, until 1869 when they amalgamated to form the company that still runs all services on the lake. The company has the world's largest fleet of passenger-carrying ships on an inland lake, with a capacity of 13,000 people. Besides the 15 modern vessels are five paddle

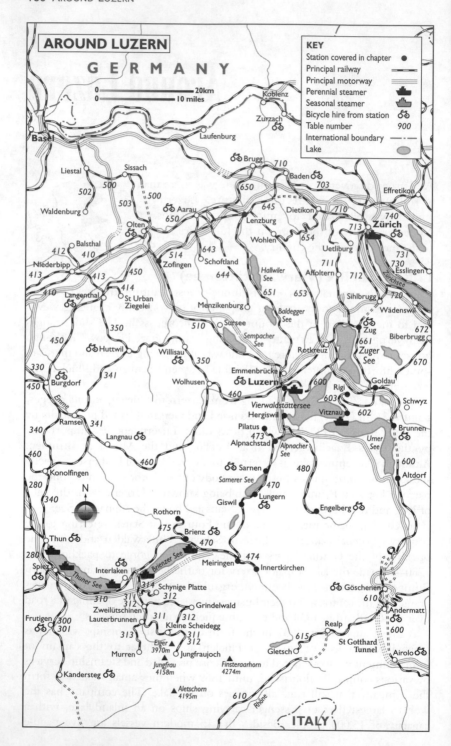

AROUND LUZERN

GERMANY

KEY

Station covered in chapter	●
Principal railway	
Principal motorway	
Perennial steamer	
Seasonal steamer	
Bicycle hire from station	🚲
Table number	900
International boundary	— ·· — ··
Lake	

0 — 20km
0 — 10 miles

Koblenz

Zurzach

Basel

Laufenburg

Brugg 710

Liestal   Sissach

Baden 703

502   500

650

645   Dietikon 710

Effretikon

740

Waldenburg

503   500

Aarau

Lenzburg

713   Zürich

Olten   650

Wohlen   654

Uetliburg

731

412   Balsthal
410

514   643
Zofingen   Schoftland

711   730
Affoltern   712   Esslingen

Niederbipp
413   450   450
410   413   414
Langenthal   St Urban
Ziegelei

644

Hallwiler
See

651   653

Sihlbrugg   720

Wädenswil

Menzikenburg

Baldegger
See

Zug   672
661   Biberbrugg
Zuger
See   670

350   510   Sursee

Sempacher
See

450   Huttwil   341
330   Burgdorf   450

Willisau   350

Rotkreuz

Emmenbrücke

Goldau

600   Rigi
603   Schwyz

Wolhusen   460   Luzern

340   Ramsei   341
460   Langnau   460

Vierwaldstättersee
Hergiswil

Vitznau   602

Brunnen

Pilatus
473
Alpnachstad   Alpnacher
See

Urner
See   600

280   Konolfingen
340

Sarnen   480

Altdorf

N   Sarnerer See   470

Giswil   Lungern

Engelberg

Rothorn
475
Thun   Brienz   470

Spiez   Interlaken   474
Meiringen   Innertkirchen

Göschenen   610

Frutigen
300   301
Zweilütschinen   312
310   312   Schynige Platte
314
311   312   Grindelwald
Lauterbrunnen

Realp   Andermatt
615   St Gotthard   600
Tunnel   Airolo

313   Kleine Scheidegg   311
312
Murren   Eiger
3970m   Jungfraujoch
Jungfrau   Finsteraarhorn
4158m   4274m

Gletsch

Kandersteg

Aletschorn
4195m   610   Rhone

ITALY

steamers: *Uri* (1901), which is the oldest working paddle steamer in Switzerland, *Unterwalden* (1902), *Schiller* (1906), *Gallia* (1913) and *Stadt Luzern III* (1929). Once coal-fired, all have been converted to oil-firing, but the engine rooms are open to view from a gallery above them and their immaculate condition is a tribute to the engineers who care for them. The *Uri* and the *Unterwalden* have telescoping funnels which enable them to pass under the rail and road bridge at Stansstad to reach Alpnachstad.

Two other paddle steamers survive as eating establishments: the *Wilhelm Tell* (1908) is moored at Luzern as a floating restaurant; and the *Rigi* (1848), which, unusually for a Swiss ship, was built in London by Ditchborne & Mare and may be seen serving as a café on dry land outside the Transport Museum (see Chapter 13).

Breakfast or lunch on the paddlers is a pleasure not to be missed; their Empire- or rococo-style dining-rooms have been sensitively restored and the food is remarkably good. Evening dinner cruises with music and dancing are also available on modern vessels.

The boats serve 33 points on the lake; most are substantial villages but some are delightfully small with a cluster of chalets and footpaths radiating from a tiny pier. Eight piers serve points on the Swiss Path between Rütli and Brunnen (see below). An entire holiday could be spent using the steamer services to reach the numerous attractions around the lake, some of which are suggested here, taking the lake in a clockwise direction from Luzern:

Verkehrshaus-Lido The pier serving Luzern Transport Museum (see Chapter 13).

Meggenhorn Schloss Meggenhorn was rebuilt in the style of a French Renaissance château in 1868–71 with adjacent Gothic chapel.

Meggen On a small island is a chapel dedicated to the patron saint of mariners, St Niklaus.

Küssnacht See Luzern–Airolo table 600, below.

Weggis Mark Twain spent several months of 1897 at this summer resort, bestowing the plaudit: 'This is the most charming place we have ever lived in for repose and restfulness.' Sheltered by Mt Rigi, it has a particularly mild climate, enabling it to supply Luzern with vegetables. A cablecar 15 minutes' walk from the boat goes to Rigi Kaltbad (table 2566).

Vitznau Another summer resort and the lower station of the Rigi Railway (see below).

Gersau This little town was politically independent from 1390 to 1798, the smallest republic in the world. It had its own laws, tax authorities and set of gallows. Some good stone and all-wooden houses can be seen.

Brunnen, **Sisikon** and **Flüelen** See Luzern–Airolo table 600, below.

Bauen A village of numerous wooden houses and the birthplace of Alberik Zwyssig, composer of the Swiss national anthem.

Rütli   The Rütli meadow, regarded as the cradle of Swiss democracy, can be visited only by boat and the tree-shrouded landing stage. According to tradition, it was here, on 7 November 1307, that representatives of the three founder cantons took an oath confirming the Everlasting league of 1291. Schoolchildren were primarily responsible for collecting sufficient funds c1860 to save the meadow from having a hotel built on it (little was sacred then in the pursuit of profit). Accordingly the Rütli is considered to belong to the children of Switzerland. It was the scene of a second symbolic meeting in 1940 when the Swiss general Henri Guisan summoned senior commanders to discuss the defence of the country against invasion. Between Rütli and Treib is the obelisk erected in 1859 to the memory of Friedrich Schiller; although the playwright never visited Switzerland, relying on his wife's recollections, it was his *Wilhelm Tell* of 1804 that did the most to propagate the legend, an invaluable contribution to 19th-century tourism in particular.

Treib   The boatman's house, inn and tiny harbour have offered boatmen sanctuary from storms since the 14th century. The present house dates from 1659. A funicular ascends from a station just by the jetty up to the small resort of Seelisberg (table 2590).

Beckenried   A pilgrimage chapel of 1700–1 above the lake is a landmark. Five minutes' walk from the boat is the cablecar to Klewenalp (table 2556), from which the Jura and Black Forest can be seen. Skiing in winter.

Kehrsiten-Bürgenstock   A minute's walk from steamer is the funicular up to the Bürgenstock (table 2554) where there are several exclusive hotels. The journey provides open views of the lake. Providing you have a reasonable head for heights, there is a dramatic path around the mountain from the summer resort. Known as the Felsenweg, the path towards the end looks down a sheer drop of 700m (2,296ft) before turning into the cliff face to give access to Europe's tallest lift. Named the Hammetschwand-Lift and built in 1903–5, this begins inside the rock but soon emerges, rising for 165m (540ft) inside a lattice steel structure that is bracketed out from the cliff, ending at the highest point of the mountain, 1,128m (3,700ft).

Stansstad   See Luzern–Stans–Engelberg table 480, below.

Alpnachstad   See Luzern–Meiringen table 470, below.

Tribschen   A convenient stage for Wagner's house (see Chapter 13).

Practical information

Lake Luzern Navigation Co, Werftestrasse 5, CH-6002. Tel: 041/367 67 67; fax: 041/367 68 68; email: info@lakelucerne.ch; web: www.lakelucerne.ch

Tickets

Special holiday season tickets valid for 15 days are available; these permit five days of unlimited travel and ten days at half price. Eurail, Swiss Pass and Swiss Card are also valid on the boats.

Weggis

TO – Seestrasse 5, CH-6353. Tel: 041/390 11 55; fax: 041/391 00 91; email: info@weggis.ch; web: www.weggis.ch Open: Mon–Fri 08.00–17.30, Sat–Sun 09.00–14.30.

Numerous hotels; close to the boat station are
Gotthard am See★★★ (H), Gotthardstrasse 11, CH-6353. Tel: 041/390 21 14; fax: 041/390 09 14; email: gotthard@gotthard-weggis.ch; web: www.gotthard-weggis.ch
Schweizerhof★★★, Gotthardstrasse 3, CH-6353. Tel: 041/390 11 14; fax: 041/390 00 15.
Seehof Hotel du Lac★★★ (H), Gotthardstrasse 4, CH-6353. Tel: 041/390 11 51; fax: 041/390 11 19; email: mail@hotel-du-lac.ch; web: www.hotel-du-lac.ch

Bürgenstock

TO – CH-6363. Tel: 041/610 55 45; fax: 041/610 76 88. Open: Mon–Fri 08.00–11.30, 13.00–17.30.

THE SWISS PATH

Few of Switzerland's thousands of footpaths are given a name but an exception was made in 1991 when this 35km (22 miles) route beside the Lake of Uri was created to mark the 700th anniversary of the Swiss Confederation. Each canton assumed responsibility for a section, their lengths determined by the population of the cantons. The well-signed path can be joined or left at eight steamer piers, three SBB stations, numerous bus stops and the Treib Seelisberg funicular. It is a wonderfully varied walk, some sections being beside the water, others giving wide panoramas over the lake and nearby mountains. Good walking boots or shoes are needed, and some sections are suitable for wheelchairs.

VITZNAU–RIGI Table 603

The Rigi is one of Switzerland's oldest tourist attractions, and has long been referred to as the Queen of the Mountains. Baedeker accorded it the seldom awarded two stars, and encapsulated the reason for its popularity: 'Owing to its isolated situation, the Rigi commands a most extensive view, 300 M[iles, 480km] in circumference, and unsurpassed for beauty in Switzerland.' However subjective the superlative, the Rigi has seen steadily greater numbers since peace returned to Europe in 1815, the first inn being erected on the Kulm in the following year. It is therefore appropriate that this line should have been the first rack railway in Europe, opened to Rigi Staffelhöhe in 1871 and to the Kulm in 1873. The standard-gauge Vitznau–Rigi Bahn (VRB) was engineered by Niklaus Riggenbach, who had been to the United States to see the world's first mountain railway up Mount Washington. The first locomotives were vertical-boilered, built at Riggenbach's Olten workshops, but were steadily converted to horizontal-boiler machines. The line was electrified in 1937 but the most modern steam locomotives, Nos 16–17 (1923 and 1925) were kept and still work special trains up the mountain. One of the 1873-built steam locomotives survives and has been on display at the Luzern Transport Museum, but was returned to working order for special runs up the mountain on the 125th anniversary of the railway in 1996. The summer and winter resorts served by the two railways (see Arth–Rigi, below) have the benefit of being traffic-free – there are no roads on the mountain. Circular tickets with various permutations are available from Luzern. Sit on the left.

The location of the station at Vitznau is idyllic: close to the lake shore at an elbow in the Vierwaldstättersee, it is only a couple of minutes' walk from the steamer jetty. The climb starts from the end of the platform, the ruling gradient being 1 in 4. The line curves up through woods and across the Schnurtobel Viaduct; this was built in 1957–8 to replace Riggenbach's structure which had itself been strengthened over the years. When Mark Twain crossed, it had only two supports:

> There is nothing to interrupt the view or the breeze; it is like inspecting the world on the wing. However, to be exact, there is one place where the serenity lapses for a while; this is while one is crossing the Schnurtobel Bridge; a frail structure which swings its gossamer frame down through the dizzy air, over a gorge, like a vagrant spider-strand. One has no difficulty in remembering his sins while the train is creeping down this bridge: and he repents of them, too; though he sees, when he gets to Vitznau, that he need not have done it, the bridge was perfectly safe.

Tiny platforms for milk churns may be seen beside the line, some with old-fashioned churns that still bring the milk down from the alpine cows. On the left just before **Romiti Felsentor** a huge tree trunk has been hollowed out to create a drinking trough for cattle. The woods and meadows are threaded by paths that tempt walkers to break the journey, and at **Rigi Kaltbad-First** a footpath has been created out of a railway that ran to Rigi-First and Rigi-Scheidegg (1 hour 50 minutes). Opened in 1874 as an excursion railway that afforded wonderful views, the metre-gauge 7km (4½ miles) line closed in 1931 and its three tank engines were sold. The railway went off to the right (east) of the VRB station. It makes a good walk, with a short tunnel at Weisseneg, a viaduct at Unterstetten and a bogie coach to be seen en route. From Scheidegg, the cablecar can be taken down to Kräbel (table 2568), a station on the Arth–Rigi Railway (see below). A series of walks for the area is suggested in an English-language leaflet, listed according to the duration of the walk.

Rigi Kaltbad became a larger resort than the Kulm, where limited space and the inappropriateness of large-scale building made expansion impossible and undesirable. The beneficial properties of the water at Kaltbad were discovered in 1585, but it was not until the 18th century that it became a health resort for pilgrims, the first hostelry being authorised in 1756. Flaubert came here on doctor's orders in 1874. A cablecar descends from Rigi Kaltbad to Weggis (table 2566) where it is a 15-minute walk to the steamer.

As the summit is approached, the line from Arth can be seen swinging in on the right, and the two run side by side into **Rigi Kulm**. The mountain actually has five summits, ranging in height from 1,551 to 1,800m (5,088 to 5,905ft).

In the 19th and early 20th centuries, most tourists wanted to see at least one sunrise from the summit of a mountain, doubtless influenced by the Romantic movement and the paintings of such artists as Caspar David Friedrich. Where better than from the Rigi, with its exceptional panorama. In autumn the valleys are often shrouded in mist, the peaks rising majestically from a blanket of cloud. It was on such a visit to the Rigi that Wagner heard the alphorn that inspired the herdsman's in the third act of *Tristan*. Turner made several paintings of the mountain.

The idea for a hotel on the Kulm came from the painter Heinrich Keller (1778–1862) who was staying down at Klösterli; he suggested to his landlord that he build a hotel at the top so that he wouldn't have to go up and down each day to paint. The landlord obliged and the first hotel opened in 1816. The grandest hotel on the Kulm was the Hotel Schreiber, completed in 1875 with accommodation for about 300 guests. Both Escoffier and Ritz worked there, Ritz having the idea of keeping guests warm by heating stones in the ovens and placing them under cushions. Ludwig II of Bavaria was an early guest, and the hotel flourished in the years before World War I. Sometimes families would come for the whole summer, bringing servants with them. On 8 August 1903, for example, 237 people were staying from 17 countries: 72 Germans, 47 French, 30 Americans, 21 Russians, 12 Dutch, 11 Swiss, 10 Austrians, 9 Italians, 6 Belgians, 5 English, 4 Poles, 2 Egyptians, 2 Spanish, 2 from then semi-independent Trieste, 2 Danes, 1 Brazilian and 1 Czech. In the same month the hotel required 14,100 small loaves of bread, 1,980kg (nearly 2 tons) of chicken and 4,500 litres of beer.

Changing fashions and economic circumstances meant that the capacity of the old hotel exceeded demand, so the present hotel was built in 1950–4 and the old one dismantled. Some of the fittings, such as mirrors and posters, from the old hotel were used in the new one. For those in search of quiet and a sense of being 'away from it all', a night on the bare mountain would be hard to better (once the last train has descended).

Practical information
Vitznau
TO – CH-6354. Tel: 041/398 00 35; fax: 041/398 00 33; email: info@vitznau.ch; web: www.vitznau.ch Open: Mon–Fri 08.30–12.00, 13.00–18.30, Sat 09.00–12.00.

Numerous hotels; closest to the station are
Rigi★★★, Seestrasse, CH-6354. Tel: 041/397 21 21; fax: 041/397 18 25; email: rigi.vitznau@bluewin.ch
Terrasse am See, CH-6354. Tel: 041/397 10 33; fax: 041/397 21 55.

Vitznau also has one of Switzerland's best hotels, dating from the Belle Epoque
Park Hotel Vitznau★★★★★ (H), CH-6354. Tel: 041/399 60 60; fax: 041/399 60 70; email: info@parkhotel-vitznau.ch; web: www.parkhotel-vitznau.ch

Rigi Katlbad-First
TO – CH-6356. Tel: 041/397 11 28; fax: 041/397 19 82. Open: Mon–Fri 09.00–12.00, 14.00–17.00, Sat 09.00–12.00.

Bergsonne★★★, CH-6356. Tel: 041/399 80 10; fax: 041/399 80 20; email: info@bergsonne.ch; web: www.bergsonne.ch

Alpina**, CH-6356. Tel: 041/397 11 52; fax: 041/397 14 50; email alpinarigi@csi.com; web: www.alpinarigi.ch.

Rigi First**, CH-6356. Tel: 041/859 03 10; fax: 041/859 03 11; web: www.minotel.com/hotel/ch319

Rigi Staffelhöhe

Edelweiss***, CH-6356. Tel: 041/399 88 00; fax: 041/397 11 36; email: edelweiss-rigi@bluewin.ch; web: www.edelweiss-rigi.ch

Rigi Kulm

Rigi-Kulm, CH-6410. Tel: 041/855 03 03; fax: 041/855 00 55; email: rigikulm@bluewin.ch; web: www.rigikulm.ch

ARTH–RIGI Table 602

For trains to Arth-Goldau, and the town, see Luzern–Airolo, below. Less well known than the ascent from Vitznau, the standard-gauge line from Arth was opened only two years after its rival, in 1875. It does not enjoy the open views of the Vitznau line until near the Kulm but it provides access to good walks and a different aspect of the Rigi. The railway has the oldest cogwheel railcar in the world, described as the Rigi-Pullman, which operates special trains. Sit on the right.

Passing the depot on the left, the line climbs through woods to **Kräbel** from where a cablecar ascends to Rigi Scheidegg (table 2568); the abandoned railway from there to Rigi Kaltbad can be walked (see above). The tall rock faces on the left indicate the amount of excavation required to build the railway. Numerous walking paths radiate from **Fruttli** and from a point just below the station.

A waterfall crashes down on the left just before the next tunnel (heralded by the carriage lights coming on). There is quite a village at **Rigi Klösterli**, with several hotels and a church. Several skilifts rise into the meadows above. The gradient steepens as the last woods are penetrated before emerging to marvellous views to the right before **Rigi Staffel**.

The Vitznau line joins from the left and the two run parallel into the terminus at **Rigi Kulm** (see above).

Practical information
Klösterli
Des Alpes (H), CH-6410. Tel: 041/397 11 08; fax: 041/397 11 08.

Rigi Staffel
Rigi-Bahn*, CH-6410. Tel: 041/855 00 40; fax: 041/855 00 41.

LUZERN–LENZBURG Table 651

The line skirts two minor lakes and provides access to two great castles. Passing through pleasant rolling hills, fields and woodland, the line provides connections with the main Geneva–Zürich line at Lenzburg. Running alongside or even on roads for much of the way, the railway is like an inter-urban tram.

Trains leave the terminus at Luzern in a southerly direction, but with one exception all loop round to head north, passing through the modern suburbs of the city. The Lenzburg branch turns off the main Olten line at **Emmenbrücke**, where trains for Lenzburg reverse, and reaches **Eschenbach**, where the rebuilt buildings and twin-towered church of a 13th-century Cistercian convent can be seen.

The Catholic church at **Ballwil** is something of a curiosity, being built in 1847–9 in a Romanesque style and regarded as the first ecclesiastical structure to be built in an historical style in central Switzerland. The industrial town of **Hochdorf** has an imposing mid-18th-century baroque Catholic church and adjacent priest's house and ossuary.

A glimpse of the Baldeggersee can be had to the west just before the village of **Baldegg**. The 5.6km-long lake is unusual in not having any significant resorts on its shore. At the northeastern corner of the lake is the pretty village of **Gelfingen**, above which is Schloss Heidegg, a medieval stronghold transformed into a residential pile in the early 17th century. Now a museum with displays of local history as well as furnishings, the schloss comprises a massive tower, chapel, outer wall, rose garden and attractive approach. The banqueting hall is particularly impressive. (Open: Apr–Oct, Tue–Fri 14.00–17.00, Sat–Sun 10.00–17.00; rose garden, Apr–Oct, daily 09.00–18.00.)

After leaving the lake the train comes to **Hitzkirch** where there is a former Commandery of the Knights of St John, founded in 1236 and rebuilt in the mid-18th century. Beyond **Mosen** the railway runs along the west shore of Hallwilersee, an attractive lake 8.4km (5¼ miles) long, and this station is the closest to the lake for intending walkers.

Beinwil am See used to be the junction for Beromünster, but the train has been replaced by a bus (table 651.60) which also serves Reinach. At Beromünster is a 14th-century tower in which the first book in Switzerland was printed in 1470; it is now a museum (open: May–Oct, Sun 15.00–17.00). The town of Beinwil has a baroque Catholic church of 1619–20 with fine ceiling paintings and stucco, and Schloss Horbin, a small mansion built c1700 as a rest home for Muri monastery. Trees screen the lake from view until the northern end, when the steamer that plies the lake may be seen. The boat can be caught from a pier which is 15 minutes' walk from the station at **Birrwil**. This is also the starting point for a signed 1 hour 20 minute walk to Schloss Hallwyl, which can also be reached by bus from the station at **Seon** (table 653.11). Schloss Hallwyl, near Seengen, is a magnificent and picturesque group of buildings that has been in the same family for over 800 years and is now open to visitors. One of the family's ancestors, Hans of Hallwyl, commanded the Confederate army at the battle of Murten in 1476. Built on two walled islands linked by drawbridge, the medieval castle comprises a ruined keep, residence, towers, gatehouse, granary and stables (open: Apr–Oct, Tue–Sat 09.00–11.30, 13.30–17.30, Sun 09.30–17.30).

Lenzburg was an important Roman town, as evidenced by the 1st-century theatre for 4,000 people on the northeast outskirts of the town. Today it is a centre of jam-making and canning of fruit of vegetables, but it has an attractive old town with elegant baroque houses and town hall — a fire in 1491 destroyed most older houses. The main reason for visiting the town, however, is its castle, a massive hill-top agglomeration of buildings that was begun in the 11th century. It can be reached from the station by bus 93 or by a 20-minute walk. Some of the buildings are strikingly positioned on overhanging rocks, and a perimeter walk gives a clearer idea of the various building periods. Built around a pretty courtyard with formal garden and trees, the castle was briefly the headquarters of the bellicose German emperor Barbarossa. The German dramatist Frank Wedekind lived here in 1886 when his father owned the castle. In 1892 it was bought by August Edward Jessup from Philadelphia, who restored the castle. Jessop was married to Lady Mildred Bowes-Lyon, daughter of the 13th Earl of Strathmore and Kinghorne from Glamis Castle in Scotland, and her monogram can be seen in the ceiling plasterwork above her bed. In 1911 the castle was bought by the wealthy Chicago mine owner and banker James W Ellsworth, and it was at Lenzburg Castle that his son, Lincoln Ellsworth, and Amundsen planned their 1920s polar expeditions. Besides the fortifications, the castle contains a large history collection of the canton of Aargau. A good English-language leaflet is available. (Open: Apr–Oct, Tue–Sun 10.00–17.00.)

Practical information
Lenzburg
TO – Bahnhofstrasse 5/Müli-Märt, CH-5600. Tel: 062/886 37 39; fax: 062/886 37 77; web: www.seetaltourismus.ch Open: Mon–Fri 08.30–18.30, Sat 08.30–16.00.

Several hotels; the closest to the station is
Haller★★★, Aavorstadt 26, CH-5600. Tel: 064/891 44 51; fax: 064/891 25 05.

LUZERN–OLTEN–Basel Table 510
A main line taken by trains from Italy to Basel, it serves several historic sites and towns, passing through gently undulating country.

It takes some time to leave Luzern behind, the line looping round **Rothenburg** before reaching the south end of the Sempachersee at **Sempach-Neuenkirch**. The station is equidistant between the two towns, and served by buses to Sempach and Sursee station (tables 510.85).

It was at Sempach in 1386 that one of the most famous battles on Swiss soil took place, marked by a monument in the church square and by the chapel of St Jakob near the village of Hildisrieden. A force of just 1,500 Swiss infantry defeated a larger force of Austrian knights in armour so heavy that the heat of the day helped to sap their fighting abilities. The Austrian commander, Archduke Leopold III, was killed in the battle, but historians have cast doubt on the main reason for the battle being so well known: a soldier named Arnold von Winkelried is supposed to have saved the day for the Swiss by deflecting enough of the long Austrian lances for the Swiss to break through. Unfortunately the story of this national hero seems to have been 'lifted' from a battle near Milan two centuries later.

The town of Sempach retains some of its medieval defences and a fine half-timbered Rathaus of the 17th century.

Neuenkirch is worth visiting for its medieval appearance and the remains of its fortifications in the form of parts of the town wall and a tower. The medieval castle, now a local museum, was enlarged in the 16th century and dominates part of the old town.

The railway now runs right beside the Sempachersee, an 8km-long lake, an example of what determined action to halt environmental degradation can achieve. The lake was badly polluted until strict laws were applied and the water artificially oxygenated.

Schloss Tannenfels at **Nottwil** is a hipped-roof house of 1688. Shortly after the lake is left behind, most trains stop at the attractive town of **Sursee**. Founded in the 13th century it still has two of its medieval towers, numerous fine houses of the 16th–18th centuries and a particularly splendid Rathaus of 1539–45.

On the hill above the village of **Reiden** stand the 16th–18th-century remains of a former Commandery of the Knights of St John, founded c1280.

Not much remains of the fortifications of **Zofingen**, but it has a palatial late baroque Rathaus of 1795, a market hall of 1725 and a Gothic Latin School of 1600–2 that now houses the library and archive. The Reformed church of St Mauritius dates from the 12th century and retains some stained glass of c1400 but has been substantially rebuilt. Zofingen is the junction for the branch that turns east to Lenzburg.

In a spectacular position above **Aarburg-Oftringen** stands the castle of Aarburg, built in the 17th century on the site of an older fortification. To the west of the town stands a wooden bridge across the River Aare that dates from 1568.

For **Olten**, see table 410.

Practical information
Sursee

TO – Bahnhofstrasse 45, CH-6210. Tel: 041/921 19 77; fax: 041/926 80 89. Open: Mon–Fri 08.00–12.00, 14.00–18.30, Sat 08.00–12.00.

Sursee★★★, Bahnhofstrasse 15, CH-6210. Tel: 041/921 50 51; fax: 041/921 00 50. Eisenbahn (H), Bahnhofplatz 5, CH-6210. Tel: 041/921 13 57.

Zofingen

TO – Marktgasse 10, CH-4800. Tel: 062/745 00 05; fax: 062/745 00 02. Open: Mon–Fri 09.00–12.00. 14.00–18.00, Sat 09.00–12.00.

Bicycle hire from Olten station.

ZOFINGEN–LENZBURG Table 514

A local line that crosses the two modernised metre-gauge branch lines running south from Aarau. At Suhr the line divides, one branch going to Aarau, the other to Lenzburg. It serves no tourist attractions of note.

LUZERN–STANS–ENGELBERG (LSE) Table 480

A pleasant journey up the Engelberger Aa valley to the monastery town of Engelberg. It serves funicular/cablecar excursions from Stans up the Stanserhorn and from Engelberg to Titlis. Sit on the right leaving Luzern.

Leaving from platform 15 at Luzern, the trains of this independent metre-gauge railway share the SBB line as far as **Hergiswil**, where the LSE turns east through a long tunnel and crosses Lake Luzern by the Achereggbrücke to reach the town of **Stansstad**. A crenellated square tower of 1280, the Schnitzturm, stands beside the harbour which has been a port since medieval times; it is now served by lake steamers.

Stans, capital of canton Nidwalden, has a fine central square, Dorfplatz, which is only five minutes' walk from the station. From the station subway follow the sign for the funicular to turn right up the stairs. Turn left to reach the main road and turn left again for the square, which owes its appearance to planning undertaken after a fire in 1713. Its dominant building is the early Swiss baroque Catholic church of St Peter, built 1641–7 and noted for its black and marble stucco. In the church is a tablet commemorating the death at the hands of the French of over 400 people from Nidwalden following their rejection of the Helvetian constitution in 1798. An orphanage was subsequently opened in Stans at the St Klara convent by Pestalozzi (see page 246). A painting of Pestalozzi and his children at Stans hangs in the Kunsthaus in Zürich. Beyond the square, in Engelbergstrasse, is the Winkelriedhaus, a cultural museum in a 16th–17th-century patrician home.

The town's principal museum is the Höfli on Alter Postplatz. Retrace your steps from the square towards the station and the museum is on the left-hand side of the main road. Its four floors contain historic paintings of the area, reconstructed rooms, military ephemera, coins and tiled floors and decorated ceilings. Beams cut by passing visitors activate video programmes in several rooms, but the commentary and the labels to exhibits are in German only. (Open: Apr–Oct, Tue–Sat 14.00–17.00, Sun 10.00–12.00, 14.00–17.00; Nov–Mar, Wed and Sat, 14.00–17.00, Sun 10.00–12.00, 14.00–17.00.)

From Stans you can take one of Switzerland's most delightful funiculars up the Stanserhorn at 1,924m (6,310ft) (table 2550). To reach this period piece, follow the sign in the station subway to turn right up the stairs. Turn left, cross the main road and then walk past the Höfli Museum into a carpark; the station is the sienna chalet-style building on the far left (five minutes' walk from LSE station). The 24-minute journey is in two sections: funicular to Kälti, an ascent of 263m (862ft); and a cablecar to the summit, rising another 1,184m (3,882ft). It operates from early-April to mid-November.

The funicular section has changed little since it was opened in 1893, its elderly wooden cars creaking softly as they crawl through orchards and farms. Two upper sections were also funicular until 1970 lightning struck a cable and set fire to the 100-bed hotel on the summit. It was decided to replace these two sections with a cablecar, and this opened in 1975, followed the next year with a new restaurant, open terrace and shop on the foundations of the hotel. The remains of the funicular and its tunnels can be seen from the cablecar. When it opened in 1893 the Stanserhornbahn was the world's first mountain railway to be powered by electricity. One of the partners, Franz-Joseph Bucher, was a farmer's son who went on to build railways and hotels all over the world, including the Semiramis in Cairo, and died in 1906 leaving a fortune of SFr14 million in cash alone. Although the Stanserhornbahn never paid a dividend, its shareholders proudly framed their share certificates — one can be seen on the wall of the buffet at Stans LSE station, along with historic photographs of the local railways.

The 360-degree panorama from the Stanserhorn is magnificent, the summit being ten minutes' walk from the station. Numerous paths descend from the summit, enabling you to gain solitude in minutes after your arrival. Amongst the signposted routes from the summit are walks to Alpnach (4 hours, station), Dallenwil (3 hours, station) and Wirzweli (3½ hours, cablecar to Niederrickenbach LSE).

Buses from Stans station can be taken to: Emmetten and Seelisberg station (table 480.10); Stansstad station and Obbürgen (table 480.12); Beckenreid and Flüelen station (table 480.15).

At **Dallenwil** is the Catholic parish church of St Laurentius, built 1697–8, with black stucco. It is a 15-minute walk to the cablecar for Wirzweli (table 2545) for signed paths to the Stanserhorn. From **Niederrickenbach** it is 2 minutes' walk to the east for the cablecar to the village of Niederrickenbach (table 2546); 15 minutes' walk to the west is the car to Wirzweli. Between these stations the line crosses the Engelberger Aa river, which remains on the right all the way to Engelberg, crossed by a series of wooden-covered bridges.

At the small resort of **Wolfenschiessen** (bus from station to Oberrickenbach, table 480.20) is the Catholic parish church of St Martin, built 1775–7. On the west bank of the river, before **Dörfli**, is a fine example of a lord's house dating from 1586: the Höchhaus has an attic room for entertaining like that in the Höfli at Stans — it can be viewed on request. Beyond Dörfli on the right is the dramatic Fallenbachfall, a three-stage waterfall. On the right, adjacent to the station at **Grafenort**, is the huge Herrenhaus of 1690, the summer residence of the abbots of Engelberg, and on the opposite side of the line is the curious octagonal Heiligkreuz chapel of 1689.

The valley narrows and the line curves more sharply as it approaches **Obermatt** where a rack section begins, the line climbing steeply through woods at a gradient of 1 in 4, the steepest section of Riggenbach rack line anywhere in the world. Work is underway to replace this section by a tunnel, built to a gradient that will not require rack working. Beyond **Grünenwald** (café/restaurant at Gasthaus Grünenwald is adjacent to the station) the valley opens out to give fine views of the mountains that surround **Engelberg**, the terminus of the line. The station bookstall sells maps of the area, and to the left of the station on the opposite side of Bahnhofstrasse is a map of the town with tourist information.

Engelberg is a summer and winter sports resort with good opportunities for walking and mountain biking. The first hotels were built in 1850 but it was the opening of the railway in 1898 that spurred its development. However, since 1120 it has been the site of a Benedictine abbey which gave the parish the status of an independent state until 1798. The abbey still dominates the town, the extensive buildings and monastery church dating from 1730 to 1737 when they were rebuilt after the third fire in the abbey's history. One of its 19th-century abbots founded two abbeys in the United States, at Conception, Missouri, and Mount Angel, Oregon.

The light, barrel-vaulted nave of the monastery church is flanked by side chapels, each with an altar, and its ceiling is decorated with seven frescos depicting scenes from the life of Mary. Smaller panels along each side are of the life of St Benedict. The spatial division between monks and laymen is marked by two altars which frame the high altar.

Tours of the monastery, one of only five Benedictine monasteries in Switzerland, at 10.00 and 16.00 (Mon–Sat) enable visitors to see the Great Hall, Library and the guests' refectory. The corners of the main building have *trompe-l'oeil* decoration to suggest chamfered rustication.

Near the tourist office (Klosterstrasse) at Dorfstrasse 6 is the Tal Museum in the Wappenhaus, which was built in 1786–7. The museum portrays the history of the town and the surrounding valleys through pictures, documents and a wide range of artefacts.

Most day visitors to Engelberg come to take the cablecar up Mt Titlis (table 2535), reached in 40 minutes. This excursion is on the coach trip circuit and is crowded even out of season; those who dislike tourist throngs might prefer the Stanserhorn. To reach the cablecar station, turn right outside the LSE station to pass in front of the Hotel Eden. Cross over the main road and then the river before turning right along a small path to follow a line of trees beside the river. The station is straight ahead, less than 10 minutes' walk. The first of three stages takes passengers to Gerschnialp at 1,300m (4,264ft) and to Trübsee at 1,800m (5,900ft) in 6-seater gondolas; doors open and close automatically, but remain seated at Gerschnialp unless you want to break the journey. The funicular which was superseded by the cablecars can be seen below; it has been retained to carry supplies up the mountain.

Beyond Gerschnialp, a second cablecar route offers bungy jumping with drops of 70 or 120m (230 or 394ft) between mid-April and mid-October (book through the Tourist Center in Engelberg, tel: 041/639 77 77; fax: 041/639 77 76; email: tourist.center@engelberg.ch). Both cablecars descend for a short distance over cow meadows before rising up to Trübsee, which takes its name from the lake close to the station. Although the lake is in a striking position, tarmac paths and rather ugly surrounding buildings mar its appearance. The chairlift to Jochpass (table 2537) is a 15-minute walk past the lake. From Jochpass you can take the chairlift down to Engstlensee (table 2538) from which there are footpaths down the Gental valley to Meiringen, and the train back to Luzern (table 470).

From Trübsee a larger gondola ascends to Stand (2,450m/8,000ft) for the final section to Titlis (3,020m/10,000ft) in the world's first revolving gondola, which was introduced in 1992. This is no gimmick, since it enables all passengers (near the windows) to enjoy the 360-degree panorama and to look down into the deep crevasses of the blue-grey Titlis glacier – like most Alpine glaciers in steady retreat. From Titlis station, you can walk in about 45 minutes to the summit.

The excursion to Titlis is one of the most expensive cablecar journeys, but its cost can be reduced by the usual discounts with various cards or by descending on foot from Stand (July–Sept only, 1¼ hours to Trübsee) or from Trübsee (1½ hours to Engelberg).

On the opposite side of the valley is the cablecar up to Brunni (Ristis) (table 2530). Turn left outside the LSE station and right into Dorfstrasse. Pass a park with children's playground on the left, and shortly after Hotel Engelberg turn left up Hinterdorfstrasse to the cablecar station (five minutes' walk). At the summit are a network of footpaths, a small children's zoo and several restaurants.

Practical information
Stans
TO – Bahnhofplatz 4, CH-6371. Tel: 041/610 88 33; fax: 041/610 88 66. Open: Jun–Sep, Mon–Fri 09.00–11.30, 14.30–17.30; Oct–Mar, Mon–Fri 14.30–17.30.

Linde★★★ (I I), Dorfplatz 7, CH-6370. Tel: 041/619 09 30; fax: 041/619 09 48.
Stanserhof★★★, Stansstaderstrasse 90, CH-6370. Tel: 041/619 71 71; fax: 041/619 71 72.

Engelberg
TO – Tourist Centre, Klosterstrasse 3, CH-6390. Tel: 041/639 77 77; fax: 041/639 77 66; email: tourst.center@engelberg.ch; web: www.engelberg.ch Open: Mon–Sat 08.00–18.30, Sun 08.00–18.00.

Hotels close to station
Crystal★★★, Dorfstrasse 45, CH-6390. Tel: 041/637 21 22; fax: 041/637 29 79; email: hotel-crystal@tic.ch; web: www.hotel-crystal.ch
Eden★★★ (H), Bahnhofstrasse 7, CH-6390. Tel: 041/639 56 39; fax: 041/639 56 30.
Bellevue-Terminus★★ (H), Bahnhofplatz, CH-6390. Tel: 041/637 12 13; fax: 041/637 44 49.

Trübsee
Berghotel Trübsee Hof★★★, CH-6390. Tel: 041/637 13 71; fax: 041/637 37 20; email: truebseehof@bluewin.ch; web: www.relaxresorts.com/truebseehof

Jochpass
Mountain hostel. Tel: 041/637 11 87.

Bicycle hire from Intersport, Klosterstrasse, opposite TO.

LUZERN–MEIRINGEN–Interlaken Table 470

The only metre-gauge line operated by Swiss Federal Railways (SBB) is one of the country's most popular journeys for visitors, passing through glorious scenery between the two major resorts. It provides access to the resort of Meiringen and two major mountain railways, up Pilatus and Rothorn. Golden Pass trains with special panorama cars and swivel armchairs are operated over the line. The railway opened fully between Luzern and Brienz in 1889, but it was not until 1916 that the section beyond Brienz to Interlaken was completed, passengers and freight being carried by steamer on Lake Brienz until then. Sit on the right.

Interlaken-bound trains share the same route out of Luzern as LSE trains to the junction and lakeside resort of **Hergiswil**, beyond which a tunnel takes SBB trains to the shore of the Alpnachersee with the Stanserhorn overlooking the far shore. Sheer cliffs can be seen rising out of the lake as the train approaches **Alpnachstad**, from where the rack railway up Pilatus begins (see below).

The railway follows the River Sarner Aa through rolling farmland and past the pointed spire of the Catholic church at **Alpnach** to the capital of the Forest canton of Obwalden at **Sarnen**. An early 13th-century foundation, Sarnen once had a castle on the west bank of the river and its ruins are the meeting place on the last Sunday in April of the Obwalden Landesgemeinde (open-air parliament). The imposing white building on the hill is a shooting lodge of 1752. The town is dominated by the diagonally placed towers of the hill-top Catholic church of St Peter, built by Franz and Johann Singer in 1739–42 on 11th-century foundations. An older church is the chapel of Maria Lauretana, its tower dating from 1556 and its last reconstruction in 1658–62. Near the lake is an early 17th-century convent and a Benedictine college of 1745–50, also by Jakob Singer. The Rathaus of 1729–32 contains the White Book of Sarnen, which is the oldest account of the inception of the Swiss Confederation, written c1470.

Soon after leaving Sarnen the lake of the same name comes into view on the right, a footpath following the shoreline. **Sachseln** is a good place from which to walk beside the lake. Boats can be hired and there is a children's playground beside the lake to the south of the station. The Catholic church of St Theodul, built in 1672–84, is well worth a visit for its extraordinary contrast in the use of black and white marble. The supporting columns of the arches and the archivolts are in black. The village also has numerous fine houses, such as the three-storey, half-timbered Alte Krone of 1673–4.

Beyond the reed-covered end of the Sarnersee is **Giswil**. Its Catholic church of 1630–5 stands on a mound once occupied by a castle — in 1629 the village was swept away by the Lauibach torrent. Buses from the station go over the Glaubenbüelenpass to Sörenberg Schönenboden (table 460.60), where a cablecar goes up the Brienzer Rothorn (table 2505). Above Giswil is the skiing village of Mörlialp. Giswil is the destination of steam-operated excursions from Interlaken that run on some Sundays during the summer; it is also the start of the climb to the Brünig Pass, trains engaging the Riggenbach rack soon after leaving the station.

The steep ascent provides lovely views looking back over the Sarnersee, and the almost turquoise water of the reservoir of Lungernsee soon comes into view to the right. The line climbs along a ledge with rock walls on the left to **Kaiserstuhl**, overlooking the lake. At the end of the lake is the charming small resort of **Lungern**. Just to the west of the village is a cablecar to Turren (table 2520.1) from where a gondola ascends to Schönbüel (table 2520.2). The lower cablecar is 20 minutes' walk from the SBB station, which is at a higher level than the village.

The line climbs into a remote, unspoilt valley with nothing more than a track and a few attractive farmsteads. From the summit station of **Brünig-Hasliberg**, a bus goes along the ridge through woods and meadows to Hasliberg Reuti (table 470.50), which serves the gondola from Twing to Käserstatt (table 2485.1). From there a chairlift continues to Hochsträss (table 2485.2). The area is popular with walkers and there is a tearoom opposite the station.

The Brünig Pass marks the cantonal boundary between Obwalden and Bern. As the train drops down to the valley of the Aare, glimpses open up between the trees of the Bernese Oberland peaks to the southwest. On the extraordinarily flat valley floor, the broad, channelled Aare can be seen flowing towards Lake Brienz, paralleled by the railway.

Meiringen is itself on the edge of the Bernese Oberland and a good place to break the journey, since there are some major attractions in the vicinity. The town is strategically situated between several mountain passes: the Brünig to the north, and the Susten and Grimsel passes to the east. The town's name was bestowed on the culinary creation of a local patissier named Gasparini: the French version, 'meringue', has become its usual name. Another reason for its fame and popularity with tourists is that Sir Arthur Conan Doyle chose the nearby Reichenbach falls as the setting for the death of his best-known creation, Sherlock Holmes. It has long been a popular resort for walkers and mountaineers, King Albert of the Belgians being a regular visitor on account of his love of rock-climbing.

When Hilaire Belloc passed through Meiringen on his way to Rome c1900, he encountered an aspect of tourism that has thankfully disappeared: he witnessed a crowd

> ...all bawling and howling with great placards and tickets, and saying, 'This way to the Extraordinary Waterfall; that way to the Strange Cave. Come with me and you shall see the never-to-be-forgotten Falls of the Aar,' and so forth. So that my illusion of being alone in the roots of the world dropped off me very quickly, and I wondered how people could be so helpless and foolish as to travel about in Switzerland as tourists and meet with all this vulgarity and beastliness.

Today the resort has good facilities for skiing and other sports, with indoor and outdoor swimming pools. However, it is probably walkers and mountain bikers who will find the area exceptionally attractive. The four-stage Meiringen–Hasliberg-Bahnen provides access to 300km (187½ miles) of footpaths along the Hasliberg: the cablecar station in Meiringen is ten minutes' walk from the railway. The first stage goes to Hasliberg Reuti (table 2480.1); the second and third are gondolas to Bidmi and Mägisalp (table 2480.2); and the final chairlift goes to 2,245m (7,385ft) at Planplatten (table 2480.3). Each level provides walks of a different kind, the higher the more rugged. For cyclists, the tourist office produces an excellent map showing the 420km (262 miles) of signed routes, some of which use flowers as symbols, as well as numbers. A well-produced English-language leaflet provides a guide to the distinctive farms and houses along the Hasliberg.

The town's connection with Sherlock Holmes is commemorated by a museum, appropriately situated in the basement of the English church near the Park Hotel. Its main feature is a reconstruction of the sitting-room of Holmes's house in Baker Street, but there are other fascinating items of memorabilia about Conan Doyle and Holmes's times, such as a large map of London c1840. An English-language guide is available. (Open: May–Sep, daily 13.30–18.00; Oct–Apr, Wed–Sun 15.00–18.00.)

The falls where Holmes plunged to his death after a struggle with Professor Moriarty lie to the southeast of the town and were chosen by Sir Arthur Conan Doyle because of their sheer impressiveness. They can be reached by a funicular (20 minutes' walk from the station) from Reichenbach to Reichenbachfall (table 2475), which operates from mid-May to mid-September. Besides taking passengers to the viewing platform where the duel took place, the funicular can be used for walks through the Rosenlaui valley to Gross Scheidegg, First and Grindelwald, the last stage of which could take advantage of the gondola down from First. Buses serve part of this route, running from Meiringen station to Schwarzwaldalp (table 470.65) for onward connection to Grindelwald (table 312.20). From Rosenlaui a path goes to the glacier gorge (Gletscherschlucht), offering spectacular views (open: May–Oct, admission charge).

To the east of Meiringen is the second magnificent natural feature close to the town. The Aare between Innertkirchen and Meiringen squeezes through a gorge of astonishingly narrow width, the sky often nothing more than a slit of colour between vertical rock walls only a metre or two apart in places. A footpath runs through the gorge, sometimes through a tunnel, and on to Innertkirchen, from where a train returns to Meiringen (see below). In July and August the gorge is lit on Wednesday and Friday nights from 21.00. There is a restaurant at the entrance to the gorge. (Open: Apr–Oct, daily, weather permitting. Admission charge.) A bus runs hourly from the station to the gorge in July to September.

Meiringen station is at one end of some notable postbus journeys. To the south a bus goes over the Grimsel Pass to Oberwald station on the Brig–Andermatt line and then on over the Furka Pass to Andermatt station (table 470.75). To the east a service crosses the Susten Pass to Göschenen and Andermatt stations (table 470.70). Finally, from early July to mid-October a bus goes up the Gental to Engstlenalp (table 470.80); from beside nearby Engstlensee you can either walk or take a chairlift up to the Jochpass (table 2537), from where you can walk or take a chairlift down to Trübsee and Engelberg (see above).

Of note in the town is one of the few buildings to survive the devastating fires of 1879 and 1891, the Reformed church of St Michael, which has the country's oldest dated bell (1351) in its Romanesque tower. The rest of the church was rebuilt in 1684 but incorporating fragmentary frescos of c1300 and 10th-century foundations, which are open to visitors beneath the floor of the church. Unusually the organ is placed directly behind the altar with the choir-stalls on either side. It is situated at the top of Kirchgasse close to the local history Hasli Museum (Museum der Landschaft Hasli) (open: Jun–Sep, Mon–Sun 14.00–17.00).

Practical information
Hergiswil
TO Seestrasse 24, CH-6052. Tel: 041/630 12 58; fax: 041/630 12 58. Open: Mon–Fri 09.00–17.00, Sat 09.00–12.00.

Sarnen
TO – Hofstrasse 2, CH-6060. Tel: 041/666 50 40; fax: 041/666 50 45. Open: Mon–Fri 08.00–12.00, 13.30–18.00, Sat 08.00–12.00 (Jun–Sep 13.30–16.00).

Sachseln
TO – Dorfstrasse 11, CH-6073. Tel: 041/660 26 55; fax: 041/660 94 51. Open: Mon–Fri, 08.00–11.30, 13.30–17.00.

Kreuz★★★★ (H), Dorfstrasse 15, CH-6072. Tel: 041/660 14 66; fax: 041/660 81 88.

Giswil
TO – Brünigstrasse, CH-6074. Tel: 041/675 17 60; fax: 041/675 25 62. Open: Mon–Sat 08.00–18.00.

Bahnhof, Brünigstrasse 48, CH-6074. Tel: 041/675 11 61; fax: 041/675 24 57; email: hotbahnhof@swissonline.ch

Kaiserstuhl
Kaiserstuhl, CH-6078. Tel: 041/678 11 89; fax: 041/678 17 16; email: contact@hotelkaiserstuhl.ch; web: www.hotelkaiserstuhl.ch

Lungern
TO – Brünigstrasse 105, CH-6078. Tel: 041/678 14 55; fax: 041/678 10 68. Open: Mon–Fri 09.00–12.00, 15.00–18.00, Sat 09.00–12.00, 14.00–16.00.

Meiringen
TO – Bahnhofstrasse 22, CH-3860. Tel: 033/972 50 50; fax: 033/972 50 55. Open: Mon–Fri 08.00–12.00, 14.00–18.00, Sat 08.00–12.00.

Numerous hotels; close to the station are
Alpin Sherpa★★★★, Bahnhofstrasse 3, CH-3860. Tel: 033/972 52 52; fax: 033/972 52 00.
Baer★★★, Bahnhofstrasse 2, CH-3860. Tel: 033/971 46 46; fax: 033/971 46 98.
Meiringen★★★, Bahnhofplatz 1, CH-3960. Tel: 033/972 12 12; fax: 033/972 12 19; email: meiringen@switzerland-hotels.ch; web: www.firstweb.ch/hotel.meiringen

Victoria***, Bahnhofplatz 9, CH-3860. Tel: 033/972 10 40; fax: 033/972 10 45; email: info@victoria-meiringen.ch
Brunner*, CH-3860. Tel: 033/971 14 23; fax: 033/91 31 98.

Bicycle hire from Sarnen and Lungern stations.

ALPNACHSTAD–PILATUS Table 473

This 4.3km (2¹/₂ miles) line has the distinction of being the world's steepest rack railway. Its fame makes it one of the busiest mountain railways, and deservedly so. Apart from the railway being a marvellous feat of engineering, the views from the summit are spectacular, and a variety of walks quickly takes unhurried visitors away from the crowds that throng the station area in season. The railway's operation is limited by snow to the months of mid-May to mid-November. Alpnachstad can be reached by rail or steamer from Luzern, and the return can be made by cablecar down to Kriens followed by bus 1. The Swiss Card obtains a 50% reduction, Eurail 35%. Dress warmly.

Visitors have been ascending Pilatus from long before the 800mm-gauge railway was opened in 1889, arriving by foot, horseback or even sedan chair, two hotels catering for their needs from 1860. Amongst the early visitors were Wagner, Tolstoy and Queen Victoria, who rode to the summit on a pony she had brought from England, accompanied by Highland attendants. The solution to the challenge of building a railway up Pilatus was found by the experienced railway builder Edward Locher. He devised an ingenious mechanism whereby the locomotive drive was transmitted by bevel gears to a pair of horizontal cog wheels; these engaged a double-sided rack placed centrally between the two rails. Underneath these cogs a disc overlapped the teeth to fit underneath the rack and prevent vertical movement. This mechanism gave sufficient power to lift the carriage up the fearsome gradient of 48% (1 in 2) and a safeguard against strong winds that might topple a train using one of the other types of rack mechanism. Unique steamcoaches – a locomotive combined with a coach on a chassis incorporating a water tank – struggled up the mountain until 1937 when the railway was electrified.

The journey starts at Alpnachstad where the Pilatus station is just across the road from the SBB station. The coaches are stepped so that passengers sit on the level; this is a common device on funiculars but not on rack and pinion lines. Sensational views vie with the railway's rate of ascent for attention as the cars climb through meadows, beech woods and a series of short tunnels to the loop at Amsigenalp, where the traversers at each end are original. Unless you can pose as a convincing shepherd, you are not allowed to get off the train here.

The final section to the top is awe-inpiring, the train clawing its way up a ledge blasted out of the face of a sheer wall of rock. The station is in the lee of the Esel, one of several peaks that form Mount Pilatus. Most unusually the point at the station throat rotates to change track. Directly outside is the Bellevue Hotel, built in 1963; it is neither an aesthetic nor good catering contribution to the mountain — at 11.00 on one visit there was not a clean table in the place, despite being nearly empty. The older

Pilatus Kulm Hotel, built in 1890, is a much more agreeable place to stay or eat, particularly after the creation of a new gourmet restaurant in 1999, incorporating sandstone arches and a glass wall overlooking the panorama of surrounding peaks.

One of the best vantage points is from the top of the Esel, which is reached by a path that begins beside the Bellevue Hotel. One of several paths continues past the Kulm Hotel along a gallery cut into the rock, part of it through a tunnel. To reach the other side of the ridge, you can climb through a passage hollowed out of the rock, past the observatory to a ledge looking west. Beneath, on the Klimsenhorn, is a tiny chapel, beside which the foundations of the hotel built in 1860 can just be made out.

An alternative way of returning to Luzern is to take the cablecar down to Fräkmüntegg (table 2517) from where a gondola descends to Kriens (table 2516). Bus route 1 takes you back to the main bus terminal beside the station.

Practical information
Pilatus-Kulm and Bellevue★★★, CH-6011 Kriens-Pilatus. Tel: 041/670 12 55; fax: 041/670 26 35.

MEIRINGEN–INNERTKIRCHEN Table 474
Opened as late as 1926 this 5km (3 miles) line was built in connection with the extensive hydro-electric works of the area to the east of Meiringen. Sit on the right.

The station of the Meiringen–Innertkirchen Bahn (MIB) is about five minutes' walk to the east of the SBB station. The train climbs gently up the valley with the River Aare on the right, diving into a long tunnel while the river negotiates the famous gorge (see above, table 470). The river is in exactly the same position on leaving the tunnel and is soon crossed by a covered wooden bridge. You may see llamas in a field near **Innertkirchen Hof**, the station close to the village's hotels. The line continues on to **Innertkirchen MIB** where the railway's shed contains some of the old trams and battery car that used to operate the line.

Practical information
Alpenrose★★★ (H), Hauptstrasse, CH-3862. Tel: 033/971 11 51; fax: 033/971 34 06.
Hof und Post★★, CH-3862. Tel: 033/971 19 51; fax: 033/971 44 17.

Luzern–MEIRINGEN–INTERLAKEN Table 470
Trains have to reverse at Meiringen, but since it is now better to sit on the left, through passengers from Luzern who have sat on the better, right side thus far will not have to move. The view of Lake Brienz looking west as the train approaches the large expanse of turquoise water is one of the loveliest views from a train in Switzerland. Brienz is the start of the mountain railway up Mount Rothorn and also the station for one of the country's finest museums.

The River Aare is not far away on the left as the train leaves behind the railway's workshops at Meiringen and bowls along the flat valley floor past orchards to the country's cleanest lake, once renowned for its oarswomen who rowed tourists to Giessbach for the falls. The first steamer was launched in 1839, and a paddle steamer, still plies the lake — the *Lötschberg* of 1914. The railway skirts the northern shore of the lake, the first station being the woodcarvers' village of **Brienz**. Apart from a tradition of woodcarving, Brienz has a school for making stringed instruments.

Opposite the station in this attractive village is the start of the Brienz Rothorn Bahn (see below). A bus meets all trains at Brienz to take visitors to the Swiss Open-Air Museum at Ballenberg (Freilichtmuseum), which opened in 1978 on a 80-hectare (198 acres) site. Over 70 buildings threatened with destruction on their original site have been carefully dismantled and re-erected to form a museum of rural architecture and décor. Drawn from almost all cantons, they have been placed in an appropriate setting that strives to be as authentic as possible — for example, using grasses or cereals that were once common but are no longer grown commercially.

The museum preserves not only buildings but also the crafts of the rural economy. Accordingly you may see demonstrations of such skills as the making of bread, baskets, lace, shingles, fountain troughs, pack baskets, brush bundles and woodcarving. Rare breeds can be seen in farmyards, a herb garden has been created behind a house, and there are various exhibitions explaining different aspects of the museum's work. The museum's three restaurants offer regional dishes, and there is an exceptionally good English-language guide. (Open: mid-Apr–Oct, daily 10.00–17.00. For daily programme, tel: 033/951 33 66.)

The museum name is given to occasional steam trains along this route, including the rack section, marketed under the name 'Ballenberg Dampfbahn'. Details from tourist offices or web: www.brienzersee.ch

The village of Brienz is in a delightful position beside the lake, its Reformed church with 12th-century tower standing on a knoll. Steamers from the pier near the station serve seven others, including Giessbach where a funicular near the jetty goes up to the celebrated falls from the end of May to late October (table 2470). Nearby is the historic Grandhotel.

Brienz West, a delightful chalet-style station festooned with hanging baskets, is popular with walkers. The village of **Oberreid am Brienzersee** has some characteristic wooden houses, and the 17th-century church on a knoll at **Ringgenberg** incorporates the masonry of a mid-13th-century castle.

Interlaken Ost is the more important of the town's two stations, being the interchange point between metre and standard gauges, and between the metre-gauge lines from Luzern and into the Bernese Oberland. However, Interlaken West is more convenient for the town centre. For Interlaken, see Chapter 12.

Practical information
Brienz
TO – Hauptstrasse 143, CH-3855. Tel: 033/952 80 80; fax: 033/952 80 88. Open: summer, Mon–Fri 08.00–18.30, Sat 09.00–12.00, 16.00–18.00; winter, Mon–Fri 08.00–12.00, 14.00–18.00.

Numerous hotels; close to the station are
Weisses Kreuz★★★, Haupstrasse 143, CH-3855. Tel: 033/952 20 20; fax: 033/952 20 21; email: hotel_weisseskreuz@tcnet.ch
Schonegg Garni★★ (H), Talstrasse 8, CH-3855. Tel: 033/951 11 13; fax: 033/951 38 13.

Giessbach
Grandhotel Giessbach★★★★ (H), CH-3855. Tel: 033/952 25 25; fax: 033/952 25 30; email: grandhotel@giessbach.ch; web: www.gliessbach.ch

Ringgenberg
TO – Hauptstrasse, CH-3852. Tel: 033/822 33 88; fax: 033/823 33 08. Open: summer, Mon–Sat 08.00–12.00, 14.00–18.30; winter, Mon–Fri 08.00–12.00, 14.00–17.30.

Milan★, Hauptstrasse, CH-3852. Tel: 033/828 15 20.

Bicycle hire from Brienz and Interlaken Ost stations.

BRIENZ–ROTHORN Table 475
This rack railway has the distinction of running the most steam locomotives in regular service of any Swiss railway, and is now one of the most heavily used mountain railways. It was not always so — the original company went bankrupt and the railway was closed between 1915 and 1930, doubtless contributing to the survival of the steam locomotives at a time when many other railways were adopting electric traction. It also has the distinction of climbing a greater vertical distance than any other railway in the country, 1,678m (5,505ft), in just 7.6km (4³/₄ miles). The railway operates only between early June and late October, and the single journey takes one hour.

The Brienz Rothorn Bahn (BRB) was built using the Abt rack system and formally opened to a station near the summit of the 2,350m (7,710ft) mountain in June 1892. The journey starts at the original delightful station at Brienz, which was carefully restored for the railway's centenary. Most departures are made up of several trains which form a procession up the mountain. Some are likely to be diesel-propelled, as the number of passengers often exceeds the capacity of its eight working steam locomotives. The five oldest steam engines (Nos 1–5) were built in 1891–2 though only three are currently in use, No 6 dates from 1933, No 7 from 1936, No 12 from 1992 and Nos 14 and 15 from 1996 — the last three in batches of new locomotives built in Winterthur for several railways in Switzerland and Austria.

Passing the railway's depot and workshops on the left, the railway twists up a series of horseshoe bends through farmland and deciduous woods with ever-broadening views over the lake. There is a passing loop at Geldried between two tunnels, but the only station is at **Planalp**, where there is a restaurant and from where numerous walks are signed. Steam locomotives take water here, so there is a chance to photograph them. The slopes above and below the railway are astonishingly steep after the trains have passed through the upper loop at Oberstafel and claw their way up the last switchback curves into the summit station, which was rebuilt in 1991.

Hotel Rothorn Kulm was opened in 1893 to replace an earlier structure destroyed by fire, though it has been rebuilt and extended so many times that it does not look its age. From the summit a cablecar descends to Sörenberg Schönenboden (table 2505), from where a bus (table 460.60) can be taken to either Schüpfheim station on the Bern–Luzern line (table 460), or to Giswil station (see above, table 470).

Practical information

BRB, CH-3855. Tel: 033/952 22 22; fax: 033/952 22 10.

Rothorn Kulm*, CH-3855. Tel: 033/951 12 21; fax: 033/951 12 21.

LUZERN–AIROLO–Lugano–Chiasso Table 600

A wonderfully varied journey that takes in several lakes and the Gotthard route through the Alps. The section from Flüelen to Lugano forms the railway part of the William Tell Express, so named because many of the places associated with the legend are served by this line. Sit on the right.

Leaving Luzern the train loops round the town to head east, running close to the shore of Vierwaldstättersee. The chapel of St Niklaus can be seen on its small island near **Meggen**, where Schloss Meggenhorn is built in the style of a French Renaissance château. Attached to it is an ornately decorated neo-Gothic chapel.

On the approach to **Küssnacht** is a chapel dedicated to the memory of Queen Astrid of the Belgians who was killed in a car crash near the site. The village has some fine half-timbered buildings, such as Gasthaus Engel in Hauptplatz. A 15-minute walk from the station is the cablecar to Seebodenalp (table 2565) from where there is a path up the Rigi.

It was near a chapel, the Tellskapelle, in a wooded, sunken lane outside Küssnacht on the way to Immensee that the Austrian Gessler was supposed to have been shot by William Tell. Goethe visited the site and suggested the story to Schiller, leading to Schiller's play (1804) and later to Rossini's opera (1829).

A line comes in from the north before **Immensee**, which overlooks the Zugersee. The lake remains in view for much of the way to the major junction of **Arth-Goldau**. The village of Goldau was destroyed on 2 September 1806 when part of the Rossberg collapsed to engulf the whole village, an event commemorated in Byron's verse drama *Manfred*, published in 1817. Turner painted the replacement village c1842–3. The Bergsturz-Museum near the Tierpark (see below) in Goldau describes the landslide, which was the first scientifically recorded collapse of its kind in the world (open: May–Oct, Tue–Sun 13.30–17.00).

When the railway was built, Goldau was simply a junction with a branch to the more important lakeside village of Arth; Arth had grown through being a port on the north–south Gotthard route, in much the same way as Flüelen on

Vierwaldstättersee. Today the branch to Arth is closed and Goldau is the larger of the two. The bus terminus in Arth (from Arth-Goldau station, table 660.36) is on the site of the old station, also indicated by Gasthof Bahnhof. Arth's Catholic church was one of the first large baroque churches to be built in central Switzerland, in 1695–6, though the Gothic tower is 14th-century.

Arth-Goldau station is the junction for services north to Zürich, northeast to Einsiedeln and Rapperswil, and for the Arth–Rigi Bahn. To reach the Rigibahn, walk along platform 5 towards sector A; trains for the Rigi leave from the platform built on a bridge over the main line. The trackbed of the line to Arth can still be seen from this bridge.

Only three minutes' walk from the station is the entrance to the Tierpark, a wildlife reserve for animals native to Switzerland. Some are wandering around freely, which always delights children, and in safe enclosures are bears, wolves, wild boar, lynx, racoons and marmots. (Open: daily, Mar and Oct 08.00–18.00, Apr–Sep 08.00–19.00, Nov–Feb 09.00–17.00.)

With views over the small Lauerzersee to the right, the train continues through **Steinen** to the capital of the eponymous canton of **Schwyz**. The station is poorly sited for the town, but numerous buses link the two (tables 600.14/16/17/20). The stop for the centre is Postplatz. The tourist office inside the post office has good leaflets on the town's exceptional wealth of patrician houses, two of which are open to visitors in summer.

The fame of the town rests on it giving the country its name and coat of arms. It was after the victory over the Habsburgs at nearby Morgarten in 1315 that Helvetia adopted the name of Schweiz, the canton being one of the three founders of the Confederation, the Forest Cantons of Uri, Unterwalden and Schwyz.

The cobbled main square (Hauptplatz) is the focal point of public life. On it stand the Catholic parish church of St Martin, built by the Singer brothers in 1769–74, and the Rathaus of 1643–5 with murals depicting events in Swiss history on two façades and some splendid interiors. To the south of the town hall, in the oldest building in Schwyz, the c1200 Archivturm (archive tower), is a museum about the canton's history (open: mid-May–mid-Oct, Tue–Fri 14.00–17.00, Sat–Sun 10.00–12.00, 14.00–17.00).

The most important collection in Schwyz is the Bundesbriefmuseum (Swiss Federal Archives) at Bahnhofstrasse 20. This contains all the charters of the Confederacy between 1291 and 1513, the copy of the very first charter being the only one in existence. Murals in the 1936 building illustrate seminal events and themes on Swiss history. (Open: daily, 09.30–11.30, 14.00–17.00.)

A museum near the post office, Forum der Schweizer Geschichte, traces the development of the Swiss lifestyle and what one might term the collective unconscious, including the attitude to nature and landscape (open: Tue–Sun 10.00–17.00).

A bus from Schwyz station and Postplatz goes to Rickenbach (table 600.20) where a nine-minute walk takes you to a two-section cablecar to Rotenfluh (table 2574). From the upper station there are several walks around the Large and Small Mythen (one requiring a head for heights) and down to Rickenbach or Schwyz.

Beyond Schwyz the line crosses the River Muota that flows into the lake to the west of **Brunnen**. Before the opening of the Axenstrasse in 1865, Brunnen was an important port where goods were transhipped between horse-drawn waggons and boats that plied between the town and Flüelen at the southern end of the lake. The opening of the Gotthard route in 1882 acted as a great stimulus to tourism in the area, and a number of new hotels were opened in Brunnen. Most of them tried to take advantage of the wonderful views over the lake, the town being situated at the elbow between the Vierwaldstättersee and the Urnersee.

Its position makes it an ideal centre for watersports – sailing, waterskiing and windsurfing.

It was here that Shelley and Mary Godwin almost ran out of money in 1814 and had to return to England after only two days. Turner spent a considerable time here and at Schwyz in 1843, painting one of his more detailed watercolours of Brunnen which is in a gallery in Williamstown, Massachusetts.

Above Brunnen is the alpine resort of Morschach, reached by bus from the station (table 600.25). This service passes the cablecar up to Stoos (table 2572) from where another car ascends to Fronalpstock (table 2571) for a view that almost rivals the Rigi's panorama.

The railway runs along the lake though the views are interrupted by numerous tunnels. From the station at the small resort of **Sisikon** a bus goes up a narrow gorge on the short journey to Riemenstalden (table 600.28). To the south of Sisikon is a small pier near the Tellskapell, the chapel built on the site where William Tell is supposed to have leapt to freedom from the floundering boat in which he was being taken to a dungeon in Küssnacht. A storm had blown up, and his captors had untied Tell so that with his knowledge of the lake he could steer them to safety. He said there was shelter to be had near the shore, and when near enough he grabbed his crossbow, leapt ashore and dived into the forest. The chapel was erected in 1879–80 on the site of an earlier commemorative building; the frescos of the legend are by the Basel painter Ernst Stückelberg. A painting of the earlier chapel by Turner hangs in the Yale Centre for British Art at New Haven, Connecticut.

Flüelen was once a thriving port for trans-shipping goods on the north–south road over the Gotthard. Today passengers on the William Tell Express leave the boat at this small resort and take the train on to Lugano. In the village are the disused church of SS George and Nikolaus, built in 1665–6, and the multi-gabled tower of Rudenz Castle; both buildings were prominent in one of Turner's watercolours of the settlement. When he stayed here, the marshes around the Reuss delta were regarded as a source of pestilence, which, according to Murray in 1838, gave the locals 'pale faces, crippled limbs, and goitred necks'.

A 15-minute walk from the station takes you to the cablecar to Eggberge (table 2592).

South of Flüelen the railway enters the broad valley of the Reuss, the land on either side a mix of arable and pasture overshadowed by the snow-covered pyramid of the Bristenstock. The mountains become so high that the valley floor is in shadow from mid-afternoon in autumn. The station for the cantonal capital of Uri, **Altdorf**, is on the edge of the town, but frequent buses link them (tables 600.34/35). The town's fame rests on the William Tell legend, for it was in the main square that Tell shot the apple from his son's head on the orders of the Austrian governor, Gessler, in 1307. A huge statue of Tell erected in 1895 stands in the square beside a 13th-century tower. Tradition has it that Tell was born in nearby Bürglen, where a museum has been set up in the 13th-century Wattigwillerturm telling the story of the legend over six centuries. (Open: May–Jun, Sep–Oct, daily 10.00–11.30, 13.30–17.00, Jul–Aug 09.30–17.30.) Bürglen can be reached by bus from Altdorf Post (tables 600.29/30).

Altdorf lost many of its older buildings in a fire which broke out in 1799 during the Revolutionary Wars, when the armies of France, Austria and Russia fought in and around the town. Among the older buildings that survived are Switzerland's oldest Capuchin monastery, of St Karl, founded in 1579 to the northeast of the town, and the mid-16th-century Suvarov House just off the main square to the southeast. This acquired its name from the Russian general who made it his headquarters in 1799 after forcing a passage of the Schöllenen gorge against fierce French resistance (see page 332).

A neo-Gothic building of 1905 at Gotthardstrasse 18 houses a regional museum with collections of art, porcelain, furniture, textiles and arms. (Open: Whitsun–mid-Oct, Tue–Sun 09.00–11.00, 13.00–17.00.)

A bus from Altdorf station goes to Schloss A Pro at Seedorf (table 600.35), an enchanting manor house built in 1556–8 which has been described as one of the finest mansions in Switzerland. Now owned by the canton of Uri, it has a display on minerals as well as changing exhibitions. (Open: May–Oct, Thu, Sat–Sun 13.00–17.00.)

With the Reuss still to the right, the railway reaches the railway town of **Erstfeld** where assisting engines were stationed for the northern ascent of the Gotthard which begins here. Over the next 28km (17³/₄ miles) the railway has to climb a vertical height of 634m (2,080ft). To achieve this it has to be taken through one spiral tunnel, the Pfaffensprung, and two horseshoe loops around the Catholic church at Wassen. The views as the railway forges up the gradient are spectacular, spoilt only by the new road. At Amsteg there is a fine view up the Kärstelenbach gorge to the east. The old packhorse route can be seen at several places, crossing the Reuss by elegant masonry arches. After the horseshoe curves the line enters the 1,570m (5,150ft) long Naxberg Tunnel which brings the railway to **Göschenen**, junction for the short rack line up to Andermatt (see Chapter 19).

The railway operates a marvellous scheme for those wishing to explore the ramps of the Gotthard: at Göschenen station you can hire bikes of various types, pedal down the old, almost traffic-free road through the valley to Flüelen and return by train. The same applies to the south ramp beteen Airolo and Biasca (see Chapter 20).

Immediately beyond Göschenen station the line enters the Gotthard Tunnel. Work began on the tunnel in June 1872, using compressed-air rock drills and working from both ends. For nearly eight years an average of 2,500 men toiled night and day to bore the 15km (9 miles 662yd) tunnel. Apart from a single curve at the southern end the tunnel is straight; when the tunnellers met up in 1880, the centre lines of the bores were only 18cm (7in) out horizontally and 10cm (4in) vertically. The tunnel opened to full traffic in June 1882. Tragically the tunnel's engineer, Louis Favre, died of a heart attack in the tunnel in 1879 and is buried in the cemetery beside the church at Göschenen.

It takes ten minutes to travel through the tunnel; before its opening the journey between Göschenen and Airolo took a whole day.

Practical information

Küssnacht

TO – Unterdorf 1, CH-6403. Tel: 041/850 33 30; fax: 041/850 34 30; email: kartvvk@bluewin.ch Open: Mon–Fri 08.00–18.30, Sat 08.00–16.00.

Du Lac Seehof★★★ (H), Seeplatz 6, CH-6403. Tel: 041/850 10 12; fax: 041/850 10 22; email: jtrutmann@bluewin.ch
Hirschen★★★ (H), Unterdorf 9, CH-6403. Tel: 041/850 10 27; fax: 041/850 68 80; web: www.hirschen-kuessnacht.ch

Arth

Seehotel Adler, Zugerstrasse 2, CH-6415. Tel: 041/855 12 50; fax: 041/855 28 79.
Hofmatt, CH-6415. Tel: 041/855 10 33; fax: 041/855 21 70.

Schwyz

TO – Oberer Steisteg 14, CH-6430. Tel: 041/810 19 91; fax: 041/819 34 88. Open: Mon–Fri 07.30–12.00, 13.45–18.30, Sat 08.00–11.00.

Brunnen

TO – Bahnhofstrasse 32, CH-6440. Tel: 041/825 00 40; fax: 041/825 00 49. Open: Mon–Fri 08.30–12.00, 13.30–18.00; Easter–Sep, Sat 09.00–12.00.

Numerous hotels; closest to the station is
National★, Bahnhofstrasse, CH-6440. Tel: 041/820 18 78.

A hotel overlooking the lake and adjacent to the steamer pier is
Waldstätterhof★★★★★ (H), Waldstätterquai, CH-6440. Tel: 041/825 06 06; fax: 041/825 06 00; email: info@waldstaetterhof.ch; web: www.waldstaetterhof.ch Winston Churchill stayed here on his honeymoon.

Sisikon

TO – Bachmattstrasse 3, CH-6452. Tel: 041/820 30 00; fax: 041/820 30 00. Open: daily 08.00–20.00.

Tellsplatte★★★, CH-6452. Tel: 041/874 18 74; fax: 041/874 18 75; email: tellsplatte@bluewin.ch; web: www.forum.ch/tellsplatte
Bahnhof, CH-6452. Tel: 041/870 12 84.

Flüelen

TO – Axenstrasse 18, CH-6454. Tel: 041/870 42 23; fax: 041/870 42 35. Open: Mon–Sat 08.00–12.00, 14.00–17.30; summer, Sun 09.00–17.00.

Several hotels; near the station is
Weisses Kreuz★★, Axenstrasse 2, CH-6454. Tel: 041/870 17 17; fax: 041/870 17 75.

Altdorf

TO – Rathausplatz 7, CH-6460. Tel: 041/870 04 50; fax: 041/872 04 51. Open: May–sep, Mon–Fri 09.00–11.30, 13.30–18.00, Sat 09.00–11.30; Oct–Apr, Mon–Fri 13.30–17.00, Sat 09.30–11.30.

Bahnhof★, Rynächstrasse, CH-6460. Tel: 041/870 10 32; fax: 041/870 99 32.

Bicycle hire from Brunnen and Göschenen stations.

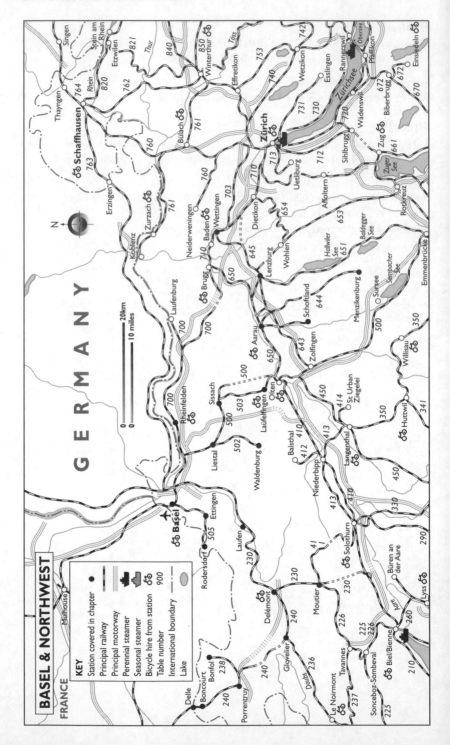

Basel and the Northwest

This populous corner of Switzerland has a concentration of heavy industry in some of the urban centres, such as Basel and Olten. But it also has the eastern end of the Jura Mountains and the Black Forest across the border in Germany, easily reached from the DB station in Basel. The main reason for visiting Basel is its museums, which are outstanding in scope and quality, especially in art.

BASEL

Basel is Switzerland's second largest city with a population of 200,000 and owes a long history of trading links to its strategic position on a bend in the Rhine between the barriers of the Jura and Black Forest ridges. Even by the time the town's first bridge (of wood) across the Rhine was opened in 1226, the place had established a reputation for scholarship. Its university was founded in 1460, and Basel became a part of the Helvetic Confederation in 1501. The city became a crucible of Humanism, adopting the Reformation in 1529 and providing a refuge for many skilled tradesmen exiled from France and Italy by the Counter-Reformation.

Basel was not only the first community in Switzerland to have a railway when the line from St Louis in France opened in 1844, it was the world's first international station. After the arrival of the last train each evening, the gates of the walled city were closed by a sentry paid for by the railway company. By the later 19th century Basel had become a major railway junction, and its chemical industries emerged as one of the city's principal activities. It is also a great centre for trade exhibitions and fairs, at which time hotel accommodation can be at a premium.

The Dutch Humanist Erasmus (1466–1536) spent about ten years of his life in Basel, where many of his books were published. Prince Charles Edward, the Young Pretender, spent the years 1754–6 here with his mistress Clementina Walkinshaw (who died in Fribourg) and their daughter Charlotte Stuart. Nietzsche was professor of classical philosophy at the university in 1869–79. Herman Hesse (1877–1962) spent much of his childhood here, becoming a bookseller and antiquarian in the city between 1895 and 1902.

It is said that the people of Basel, despite receiving influences from the three countries on their doorstep, are restrained and introspective. 'English understatement looks like megalomania when compared to that of the people of Basel', as someone put it.

Arriving in Basel

The airport is situated in France but frequent buses link it with the SBB station without border formalities. Basel is served by direct trains from Paris, Frankfurt, Cologne, Hamburg and Amsterdam. Trains for French and Swiss destinations use the SBB station on the south side of the Rhine; those for most German destinations leave from the DB station in Kleinbasel, linked with the SBB station by tram line 2 (destination Eglisee travelling to the DB station; destination Binningen travelling from the DB to SBB station).

The SBB station has all the usual facilities, including money change and a branch of the main tourist office (open: Mon–Fri 08.30–18.00, Sat 08.30–12.30; Apr–Sep, Mon–Fri 08.30–19.00, Sat 08.30–12.30, 13.30–18.00; Jun–Sep, also Sun 10.00–14.00).

Before leaving the station, spare a moment to look at the mechanical toy by Jean Tinguely in one of the concourses.

Using public transport

Basel has an outstandingly good public transport network with 11 tram lines and 46 bus routes. Clear maps are available free from the tourist offices or the city transport office in Barfüsserplatz.

Fares are determined by the zones, but most of the city is covered by zone 10 with outlying suburbs on the longer tram and bus lines covered by zones 11 and 12. Multi-journey cards are available, giving 12 journeys for the price of 10. Day cards offering unlimited travel are a better buy if you are making numerous journeys on a single day. Regional passes for the whole of northwest Switzerland are also available; these allow a one-way journey on a Rhine steamer between Basel and Rheinfelden (see below). All these cards have to be stamped in a ticket machine before commencement of the first journey by inserting them in the slot marked *Entwerten*.

The longer tram lines such as 10 to Rodersdorf and 11 to Aesch go out into the country.

Using bicycles

Cyclists in Basel enjoy one of the most comprehensive networks of cycle lanes in Europe. There are numerous segregated routes, and at junctions the needs of cyclists are not forgotten, overhead direction signs even having a separate sign for cycle lanes. Most one-way streets are open for two-way bicycle traffic, and speed humps have flat sections for cyclists.

These measures form part of a co-ordinated policy to reduce car traffic, especially by commuters. Only 21% of the population now travels to work by car.

The bike rental office at the station is open daily from 06.00 to 22.00.

Exploring the city

A good starting place is the Schifflände – the quay for steamers along the Rhine. A variety of cruises and excursions along the Rhine is offered by four boat operators, visiting such places as the Roman town of Augusta Raurica in Kaiseraugst and Rheinfelden (details from the tourist office). From outside the railway station take tram 1 (direction Schifflände, where it terminates) or 8 (direction Messeplatz). Much of the centre is pedestrianised, and there are colour-coded walking routes taking in the old town's historic buildings. Each walk is named after an historic figure associated with Basel, such as Erasmus or Holbein; details can be obtained from the tourist office, which also organises guided walks between April and October.

If time is short, the area to the southeast embraces Basel's principal old buildings, and it is a lovely walk parallel with the river, past timber-framed buildings, to the red sandstone cathedral on Münsterplatz. From Schifflände, walk up the narrow Rheinsprung. No 11 was an old university building where the Secretary of State to Elizabeth I, Sir Francis Walsingham, and the founder of the Bodleian Library in Oxford, Thomas Bodley, were educated.

As you approach the cathedral square you pass the Museum of Swiss Folk Art and the Museum of Natural History and Ethnography (see below).

The oldest part of the cathedral is a section of the choir's foundations, which date from an early 9th-century building destroyed by the Huns. The next structure was founded in 1019 by the Holy Roman Emperor Henry II, but fire in 1185 destroyed much of it. Reconstruction began in a part-Romanesque, part-Gothic style, but this was badly damaged by the severe earthquake of 1356 that brought down the tower situated at the crossing. This was dispensed with in the rebuilding that produced the building we see today (after various restorations): instead of a crossing tower, two slightly asymmetrical towers were put up at the west end, the northern tower dedicated to St George and the southern to St Martin. Equestrian statues of the saints can be seen at the foot of each tower. The west portal contains a statue of Henry II and his wife, Kunigunde, and of a Foolish Virgin and her seducer.

The interior of the nave has little decoration, except for the ornate pulpit on tapering base of 1486. At the east end of the choir are the Schaler chapel, in which Erasmus was reburied in 1928, and the Fröwler chapel with a relief of six apostles that dates from c1100.

At the east end of the cathedral is the tree-shaded Pfalz from which there is a fine view over the Rhine. South of the cathedral, along Rittergasse, is the Kunstmuseum (see below).

Parallel to Rheinsprung is Martinsgasse which leads, at its northern end, into Martinsplatz: the Reformed church of St Martin was built in the 13th–15th centuries on the site of a 6th-century church. It was here that the first Protestant services in Basel were held.

Steps beside the church lead down into Marktplatz, dominated by the sienna-coloured Rathaus. The three-storey central section with clock was built in 1503–7, the left-hand part with oriel window from 1606 to 1608 and the tower from 1898 to 1904. Its courtyard is decorated by frescos executed in 1608 by Hans Block.

South of Marktplatz, reached by Gerbergasse, is Leonhardskirchplatz, a small square in which stands the Reformed church of St Leonhard. Once part of an Augustinian foundation, the present Gothic church was built in 1481–1528. The interior has a fine stellar vault.

Slightly outside the pedestrianised part of the old city, at the end of Spalenvorstadt on tram route 3, is Basel's finest surviving city gate, the 14th-century Spalentor. Two round towers flank a massive square tower.

The career of Jean Tinguely began in Basel, so it is appropriate that the city has two works by the Swiss sculptor. One is in the station concourse; the other, his fountain of 1977, is outside the theatre on Theaterplatz.

Museums

Basel has 23 museums, including some of Switzerland's most important, in particular the Fine Arts Museum (Kunstmuseum) and Historical Museum. For visitors wishing to visit a number of museums, there is a three-day museum pass entitling the holder to free admission to permanent and special exhibitions in the canton of Basel-Stadt. The pass can be bought at the main and station tourist offices.

Museum of Fine Arts (Kunstmuseum) This contains the most distinguished collection of paintings in Switzerland and is one of the oldest galleries in the world. As early as 1679 the art historian Joachim von Sandrart could write: 'Of all the towns of the Swiss Confederation none deserves more praise than the City of Basel and its worthy elders for their great expenditure and diligence in collecting and highly honouring studies and the arts, especially excellent paintings, drawings and the like.'

The tradition was already two centuries old when von Sandrart was writing, for works had been bought from two artists resident in Basel in the 15th century: Konrad Witz, the first great Swiss painter, who lived in Basel from 1435 to 1446, and Hans Holbein the Younger who resided here from 1515 to 1532, when he moved to London and became the favourite court painter of Henry VIII.

The city of Basel bought 20 Holbeins in 1661, but these early collections have almost been eclipsed by the Kunstmuseum's modern art collection. This includes a small collection of Impressionists (but 200 works on paper by Cézanne), an outstanding collection of Cubist paintings and a large holding of American art.

Amongst the many other painters whose work can be seen are Altdorfer, Grünewald (there is a larger collection of his work across the border in Colmar, less than an hour on the train from Basel), Cranach, Holbein the Elder, David, Rembrandt, Teniers the Younger, Böcklin, Goya, Gauguin, Renoir, Van Gogh, Braque, Picasso, Chagall, Klee, Kline, Newman, Noland and Still. *St Alban-Graben 16. Tram 2 to Kunstmuseum. Open: Tue–Sun 10.00–17.00. Tel: 061/271 08 28.*

Museum of Contemporary Art (Museum für Gegenwartskunst) Built for the principal shareholder in the pharmaceutical firm Hoffman-La Roche, Maya Sacher, the museum's collection contains two Picassos bought in 1967 after a referendum; Picasso was so touched by the people's decision that he gave the museum several other canvases.
St Alban-Rheinweg 60. Tram 2 to Kunstmuseum. Open: Tue–Sun 11.00–17.00. Tel: 061/272 81 83.

Museum of Ancient Art (Antikenmuseum und Sammlung Ludwig) Housed in two adjacent mansions of 1826 and 1828, the museum contains Greek and Roman sculpture, glass, sarcophagi, vases, masks, caricatures and coins.
St Alban-Graben 5. Tram 2 to Kunstsmuseum. Open: Tue–Sun 10.00–17.00. Tel: 061/271 22 02.

Historical Museum The 14th-century Franciscan church was used as a salt store until conversion to a museum in 1894. It contains a heterogeneous collection relating to the history of Basel and the surrounding area, such as furniture, glass, pewter, metalwork, sculpture, arms and armour, medals and coins.
Barfüsserplatz. Trams 1 or 8 to Barfüsserplatz. Open: Mon, Wed–Sun 10.00–17.00. Tel: 061/271 05 05.

Historical Museum (Haus zum Kirschgarten) Near Theaterplatz is this large collection of porcelain, stoves, ironwork, glass, furniture (some in re-created rooms), tapestries, silver, musical instruments and shop-signs. A room tells the story of the remarkable life of the explorer Johann Ludwig Burckhardt, whose father originally owned the house. It was Burckhardt who 'discovered' Petra in 1812 and was the first European to make the pilgrimage to Mecca.
Elisabethenstrasse 27. Tram 2 to Bankverein. Open: Tue–Sun 10.00–17.00. Tel: 061/271 13 33.

Museum of Natural History and Ethnography (Naturhistorisches Museum) Notable collection of objects from Central and South America as well as Polynesia.
Augustinergasse 2. Trams 1 or 8 to Marktplatz. Open: Tue–Sun 10.00–17.00. Tel: 061/266 55 00.

The subjects of other museums include sports, applied arts, architecture, cartoons, paper, Swiss folk art, toys, cats, Jewish history, coaches and sleighs, cars, musical instruments, fire brigade, pharmacy, navigation and plaster cats.

Zoo
Close to the SBB station is the highly regarded zoo, which covers a large area and has some rare species amongst its 4,000 animals of 600 different species. At the entrance is a table of feeding times.
Binningerstrasse 40. Trams 10 or 17 to Zoo. Open: daily, Mar–Apr, Sep–Oct, 08.00–18.00; May–Aug, 08.00–18.30; Nov–Feb, 08.00–17.30.

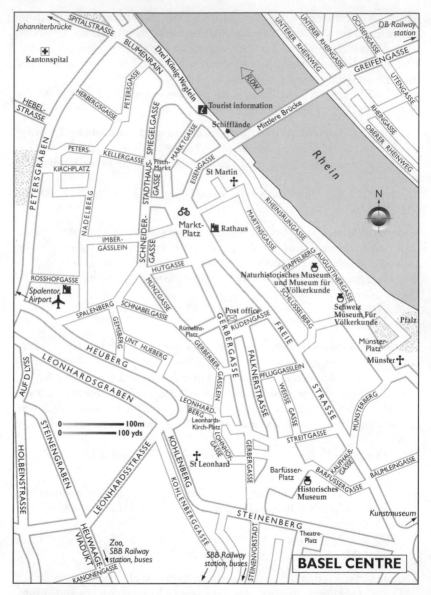

BASEL CENTRE

Festivals

Basel has what is probably the most idiosyncratic of Swiss festivals, the Fasnacht, which was first recorded in 1376. The atmosphere during part of this spring carnival is almost sombre, reflecting its self-deprecating and mocking undertones. The first event takes place in January when three mythological figures – the griffin (*Vogel Gryff*), savage (*Wilde Mann*) and lion (*Leu*) – appear to chase winter away. Then, at 04.00 precisely on the Monday after Ash Wednesday, all lights in the city are extinguished and the morning parade (*Morgenstreich*) begins. The shrill sound of piccolos contrasts with the rumble of heavy Basel drums as groups of outlandishly dressed musicians move through the streets. The music, weird masks and lanterns combine to create an eerie, timeless atmosphere, accentuated by the lanterns developed after open torches were banned in 1845. The festival continues for three days, fuelled by all-night opening of cafés and bars, where satiric verses are recited, and by the special trains operated by SBB to bring in more participants. Parades of floats take to the streets on Monday and Wednesday afternoons, and on Tuesday afternoons the children have their own parade.

Trade fairs
During the full calendar of trade fairs, the two most important (when hotel rooms are harder to find) are the Swiss Industries Fair in spring and the Autumn Fair at the end of October.

Practical information
TO – Schifflände 5, CH-4001. Tel: 061/268 68 68; fax: 061/268 68 70; email: office@baseltourismus.ch; web: www.baseltourismus.ch Open: Mon–Fri 08.30–18.00, Sat 10.30–16.00.

Numerous hotels; close to the station are
Euler*****, Centralbahnplatz 14, CH-4002. Tel: 061/272 45 00; fax: 061/271 50 00; email: reservation@hoteleuler.ch; web: www.hoteleuler.ch
Hilton*****, Aeschengraben 31, CH-4002. Tel: 061/275 66 00; fax: 061/275 66 50; email: basel@hilton.ch; web: www.hilton.com
St Gotthard****, Centralbahnstrasse 13, CH-4002. Tel: 061/225 13 13; fax: 061/225 13 14; email: hotelgotthard@access.ch
Schweizerhof****, Centralbahnplatz 1, CH-4002. Tel: 061/271 28 33; fax: 061/271 29 19.
Victoria am Bahnhof****, Centralbahnplatz 3–4, CH-4002. Tel: 061/270 70 70; fax: 061/270 70 77; email: hotel-victoria@bs.coop.ch; web: www.victoria.balehotels.ch

A hotel in the old city is
Drei Könige am Rhein***** (H), Blumenrain 8, CH-4001. Tel: 061/260 50 50; fax: 061/260 50 60; email: info@drei-koenige-basel.ch; web: www.drei-koenige-basel.ch
Claims to be Switzerland's oldest hotel. Built on the site of a house where in 1026 the Emperor Conrad II met the last king of Burgundy, Rudolf III. In a fine position overlooking the Rhine.

Bicycle hire from Basel station.

BASEL–RODERSDORF Table 505/Line 10
This is the longest of Basel's tram lines and takes you right out into the country.

Set in an attractive park at **Binningen** is a former moated castle built in the later 13th century. It is now a restaurant (tel: 061/421 20 55).

At **Bottmingen** is a magnificent moated castle. Thought to have been constructed in the 13th century, it was restored in baroque style in the 17th century and became a hotel and restaurant in 1890. Now the property of the city, it is still a restaurant and open to visitors every day except Sunday evening and Monday.

From the stop at **Flüh**, a bus runs to Mariastein (lines 113/117), the start of a 30-minute walk to the rebuilt medieval fortress of Rotberg. The castle was built in the 13th century and restored voluntarily by unemployed workers from Basel during the 1930s. Today it is a youth hostel and open to visitors (tel: 061/731 10 49).

BASEL–DELEMONT Table 230

The route of trains from Basel to Geneva follows the sinuous valley of the River Birse.

The first two stations on the line both serve suburbs of Basel which have a number of interesting buildings. At **Münchenstein** are the country houses of Bruckgut, built in1759–61, and the neo-classical Ehinger of 1828–31. On the St Alban pool is a large hammer mill.

The local history museum at Dornach (station **Dornach-Arlesheim**) is housed in the former Catholic church of St Mauritius. Between Dornach and Arlesheim is a curious ferro-concrete structure built in 1924–8 known as the Goetheanum which serves as the headquarters of the Anthroposophical Society founded by Rudolf Steiner. A 30-minute walk uphill from the town is the castle of Dorneck. The 13th-century castle was destroyed by an earthquake in 1356, rebuilt in 1360 and largely destroyed after it was sacked in 1798 during the French Revolution. However, there are extensive remains of the curtain walls, keep and various towers. (Open: May–Sep, Sun 10.00–12.00, 13.30–18.00.)

Some buildings have survived of the early 17th-century Schloss at **Aesch**, including the barn which is a local history museum (open: first Sun in month, 10.00–12.00, 15.00–17.00).

One of the area's most attractive and best preserved castles is at **Zwingen** where the walls rise above the River Birse which is crossed by a bridge that springs from the gatehouse-tower. The buildings date from the 14th to 17th centuries.

The railway continues through the well-wooded valley, which is a glorious kaleidoscope of browns and yellows in autumn, to **Duggingen**. On the cliff to the right the imposingly sited ruins of the castle of Pfeffingen can be seen; the keep and much of the walls remain of this 12th–13th-century fortress.

Laufen was founded in 1295 by the Bishop of Basel, and the town retains three gateways and a good length of the town walls. Near the Untertor is the baroque church of St Katharina with mid-18th-century rococo stucco.

Above **Soyhières** is the ruined castle of the same name, but buses from the village to Delémont (tables 230.15/20/21) can reduce the walk. The castle was built in the 11th century and destroyed during the Swabian War in 1499. It is privately owned and individual tours can be booked (tel: 032/422 22 35).

For **Delémont** see table 230.

Practical information
Dornach
Engel★★★ (H), Hauptstrasse 22, CH-4143. Tel: 061/701 96 60; fax: 061/701 96 64; email: office@hotel-engel.ch; web: www.hotel-engel.ch

Bicycle hire from Delémont station.

DELEMONT–PORRENTRUY–BONCOURT Table 240
An initially dull journey suddenly comes to life as the railway skirts the River Doubs. St Ursanne is an undervisited ancient town.

The only thing of interest on the scenically unexciting line between Delémont and Glovelier is the Catholic church of St Germain d'Auxerre in **Courfaivre**, which has stained glass of 1954 designed by Fernand Léger. At **Glovelier**, the metre-gauge line of the CF Jura leaves for La Chaux-de-Fonds from just outside the standard-gauge station. If you are changing trains, spend a minute and 20¢ in the waiting room (see table 236).

The long tunnel that follows after Glovelier provides one of those dramatic transitions that rail travellers soon become accustomed to in Switzerland. The line emerges high up on the right-hand side of the magnificent valley of the River Doubs as it describes a semicircle, with lovely views to the left as the line also sweeps round to the left across a huge viaduct. Just before another long tunnel, under the Col de la Croix, is **St Ursanne**, which is worth breaking the journey to see. The station has a buffet and terrace overlooking the valley.

The town beside the River Doubs is a 4-minute bus journey from the station (table 240.55). The settlement grew up around a monastic community based on the cell of the Irish monk Ursicinus, and the 12th-century concentric plan can still be seen, overlaid by the straight streets to the east created after fire swept through the town in 1403. The three town gates that were rebuilt in the 16th–17th centuries still survive, that of St Jean guarding the early 17th-century bridge across the river. The Romanesque collegiate church has a 12th-century choir under which there is a hall crypt that once held the bones of St Ursicinus. The tower dates from 1442, and the church has finely carved choir-stalls, pulpit and capitals.

The second tunnel provides another emphatic change in the landscape, the train emerging into farmland. The approach to **Porrentruy** is despoiled by a motorway that dominates the landscape, but the town, though industrial, has much of interest.

Dominating the old town is the castle, a stronghold built by the Bishop of Basel in the 13th century. The oldest part is the cylindrical Réfouss Tower, which is open daily from 08.00 to 18.00 (the rest of the buildings are used by local government). The residence, chancellery and Cock Tower (the cock was the bishop's emblem) were built in the 16th century. The castle ceased to be an ecclesiastical residence from 1792 and would have been demolished but for the intervention of local people.

The old town beneath the castle was built on an island in the river, but little of the fortifications remains other than the 16th-century French Gate. Even by the 11th century the town had two churches. The oldest today is the Romanesque Catholic church of St Germain, which dates from the 12th to 17th centuries and has a notable Gothic font.

The Catholic parish church of St Pierre is mid-14th-century Gothic with fine side altars, and the galleried church of the Ursulines dates from the early 17th century. The Hôtel-Dieu (former hospital) in Grand-rue houses the tourist office and a museum of local history.

North of Porrentruy the railway follows closely the River l'Allaine through an attractive valley, particularly between **Courchavon** and **Courtemaîche**. Beside the prettily sited station at **Buix** are a three-arched stone bridge across the river and the church, with striking coloured tiles. Most trains terminate at **Boncourt**, the last station on Swiss soil, but some trains run through to **Delle** for the benefit of passengers using the train to get to and from work. It is probably the least used international crossing on the Swiss network.

Practical information
St Ursanne

TO – Rue de 23-Juin 28, CH-2882. Tel: 032/461 37 16; fax: 032/461 37 16. Open: May–Sep, daily 10.00–17.00, Apr and Oct, Mon–Sat, 10.00–17.00; Nov–Mar, Mon–Fri 10.00–12.00, 14.00–16.00.

Demi-Lune** (H), Rue Basse 2, CH-2882. Tel: 032/461 35 31; fax: 032/461 37 87; email: demi-lune@econophone.ch

Porrentruy

TO – Grand-rue 5, CH-2900. Tel: 032/466 59 59; fax: 032/466 50 43. Open: Apr–Dec, Mon–Fri 09.00–12.00, 14.00–18.00, Sun 09.00–12.00; Jan–Mar, Mon–Fri 09.00–12.00, 14.00–18.00.

Hotels opposite the station are
Terminus**, Chemin de la Gare 22, CH-2900. Tel: 032/465 93 93; fax: 032/465 93 95. De la Gare, Chemin de la Gare, CH-2900. Tel: 066/466 20 30; fax: 066/466 81 80.

PORRENTRUY–BONFOL Table 238
An undistinguished branch that serves a military establishment beyond the terminus. Oddly it is operated by CF du Jura, though of standard gauge and quite separate from the rest of its system.

Leaving Porrentruy on a parallel course with the Delémont line, the branch then veers to the left through a mix of pretty woods and fields of sugar beet in season, with sparse habitation.

BASEL–OLTEN Table 500
A principal north/south artery, the line carries heavy passenger and freight traffic. Many of the places it serves depend on industry, and the only scenery of note is between Liestal and Sissach.

The suburbs of Basel are heavily industrialised but there is a surprising survival at **Muttenz**: in the centre of the upper village is a walled enclosure with a complex of largely 15th-century buildings surrounding the Romanesque and Gothic church of St Arbogast. In the choir of the church are some Renaissance murals. At Oberdorf 4 is a farmhouse museum (open: Apr–Jun, Aug–Oct, last Sun of the month 10.00–12.00, 14.00–17.00). Muttenz can also be reached by tram route 14.

The Schloss at **Pratteln** was built in the later 13th century and rebuilt in 1470–6. It survived use as a workhouse in the 19th century.

Liestal is the capital of the half canton of Basel-Landschaft (the 'rural' part of the canton as opposed to the city), and was the birthplace of the novelist and poet Karl Spitteler who was awarded the Nobel prize for literature in 1919. The station is the junction for Waldenburg (see below). The town's compact centre has some interesting buildings only a short walk from the station. On Rathausgasse, approached at the southern end by the medieval Obertor, is the Gothic Rathaus that dates largely from c1568. The Reformed church in Kirchplatz is largely 16th–17th-century, and the nearby 17th-century Zeughaus (arsenal) was later used as a granary.

In Zeughausplatz is the cantonal museum, which has archaeological, natural history and cultural collections (open: Tue–Fri 10.00–12.00, 14.00–17.00, Sat–Sun 10.00–17.00).

From the station at Liestal a bus runs to Reigoldswil (table 500.10/line 70) where a gondola ascends to Wasserfallen (table 2029).

The village of **Itingen** has some fine vernacular buildings of the 16th–19th centuries, and at **Sissach** is an opulent baroque country house built in 1773–5 and known as Schloss Ebenrain. It is approached by a long avenue and its grounds are landscaped in English style.

From **Gelterkinden**, which has an attractive village square, there is a good walk to the massive ruined fortress of Farnsburg, built c1320 and plundered by the local population in 1798 (open at all times).

Immediately before Olten is the second Hauenstein Tunnel through the Jura range, built in 1912–16; although at 8,134m (5 miles) it is considerably longer than the original tunnel on the Sissach–Olten line (see below), it avoids the steep 1 in 38 gradient of the earlier route.

For **Olten**, see table 410.

Practical information
Liestal
TO – Fischmarkt 14, CH-4410. Tel: 061/921 58 07; fax: 061/926 84 85. Open: Mon–Fri 09.00–12.00, 13.30–18.30, Sat 08.00–12.00.

Bicycle hire from Olten station.

LIESTAL–WALDENBURG Table 502/Line 19
The Waldenburgerbahn has the distinction of being the only 750mm (2ft 5¹/₂in) gauge railway in Switzerland. Opened in 1880 the 14km (8³/₄ miles) line serves the communities along the attractive valley of the River Frenke. The railway still has a tank locomotive built for the line in 1902 which operates special excursions.

The railway parallels the main line to the south as they leave Liestal before the narrow gauge turns southwest. In **Bubendorf** the Dinghof of 1600 has stepped gables and decorated windows. The valley gradually narrows, woods replacing fields of sunflowers. Above the small town of **Waldenburg** stand the remains of a late 12th-century fortress, which include a lofty crenellated tower.

Practical information
Bubendorf
Bad Bubendorf★★★(H), Kantonsstrasse 3, CH-4416. Tel: 061/935 55 55; fax: 061/935 55 56; email: info@badbubendorf.ch; web: www.badbubendorf.ch

SISSACH–OLTEN Table 503
A secondary line through the Homburgertal that was the original main line from Basel to Olten. The first Hauenstein Tunnel through the Jura was built by the British engineer Thomas Brassey in 1853–8. At the time it was the longest tunnel in Europe, at 2,495m (1¹/₂ miles).

The route holds little of interest other than the remains of castles at **Läufelfingen** and **Trimbach**.

OLTEN–BRUGG Table 650
The route of some Bern– and Biel/Bienne–Zürich trains, this is a busy stretch of line and serves the historic city of Aarau. It follows the valley of the Aare though is seldom in sight of the river.

In **Schönenwerd** the Romanesque former collegiate church of St Leodegar dates from the 11th century, though it has since been altered several times. In the town park is a reconstruction of a prehistoric lake dwelling. The Villa Felsgarten was once the home of the Bally family and now houses a museum of footwear (open: Jan–Jun, Aug–Nov, last Fri in month 14.30–17.00).

Aarau, the capital of canton Aargau, has long been an industrial town: its bell foundries are thought to have supplied a quarter of Switzerland's church bells. The town was founded in the mid-13th century and its early concentric plan may still be made out, helped by the survival of sections of the town walls and several towers. One of the latter has been incorporated into the largely 18th–20th-century Rathaus. Nearby is the 15th-century Reformed church. The surrounding old town has several streets of attractive 17th–18th-century houses, some with painted decoration on the upper façades and in the eaves.

The oldest building in Aarau is the small castle which was founded in the 11th century. Gradually extended over the next three centuries, the castle housed a boarding school in the 19th century and was given to the town in 1930 by the last private owners. Over 20 rooms are now open as a museum with re-created rooms and displays of weaponry, local history, handicrafts and industry, including Aarau pewter figures. (Open: Wed, Sat–Sun 14.00–17.00.)

The Kunsthaus in Aarauerplatz has a collection of mostly Swiss paintings by such artists as Ferdinand Hodler, Paul Klee and Giovanni Giacometti (open: Tue–Wed, Fri–Sat 10.00–17.00, Thu 10.00–20.00). Aarau is the junction for the branch lines to Schöftland and Burg-Menziken (see below).

Beyond **Rupperswil** the direct line to Zürich branches off to the south through Lenzburg while the Brugg line continues its easterly course to **Wildegg**. On a hill overlooking the village, about 20 minutes' walk from the station, is a fortress built c1200 by the Habsburg family. From 1484 until 1912 it was owned by 11 generations of the Effinger family who bequeathed it and most of the contents to the Swiss Confederation. Twenty-five rooms are now open, illustrating interior furnishings from the 16th to 19th centuries. (Open: mid-Mar–Oct, Tue–Sat 10.00–12.00, 14.00–17.00, Sun 10.00–17.00.)

About 20 minutes' walk from **Schinznach Bad** is a very large garden nursery, the Baumschule, in which there is a 3km (1.87 miles) railway in a figure of eight around the grounds. This 60cm (1ft 11½in) gauge line was built in 1928 to provide internal transport for the nursery, but now gives rides to visitors behind steam engines on Saturdays and Sundays between late April and early October, and diesels on Wednesdays. The locomotive fleet includes an articulated Beyer Garratt from South Africa and industrial engines from Poland and Germany.

The town of Schinznach Bad has the strongest sulphur baths in Switzerland, which are part of the health industry that has grown up around the medicinal spring. A classical semicircular building erected in 1828 and set in parkland is the principal hotel.

On the summit of the Wülpelsberg to the right of the line is the picturesque medieval stronghold of Habsburg. With an 11th-century keep and 16th-century residential wing, the castle became the property of the canton of Aargau in 1804 and shortly after a restaurant was opened in the residential part. It is still open (throughout the year), and the keep can be climbed for a fine view. It can be reached by bus from Brugg station (table 650.80/line 66).

For **Brugg**, see table 710.

Practical information

Aarau

TO – Graben 42, CH-5001. Tel: 062/824 76 24; fax: 062/824 77 50. Open: Mon 13.30–18.00, Tue–Fri 09.00–18.00, Sat 09.00–12.00.

Aarauerhof★★★★, Bahnhofstrasse 68, CH-5001. Tel: 062/837 83 00; fax: 062/837 84 00; email: aarauerhof@bestwestern.ch; web: www.bestwestern.ch/aarauerhof

Wildegg

TO – Gemeindehaus, CH-5103 Möriken. Tel: 062/893 12 70; fax: 062/893 12 45. Open: Mon–Fri 08.00–12.00, 14.00–17.00.

Aarhof★★★, Bahnhofstrasse 5, CH-5103. Tel: 062/893 23 23; fax: 062/893 15 04.

Schinznach Bad

Kurhotel im Park★★★ (H), CH-5116. Tel: 056/463 77 77; fax: 056/473 76 45.

Rössli, Aarauerstrasse 39, CH-5116. Tel: 056/443 11 23; fax: 056/443 34 54.

Bicycle hire from Aarau and Brugg stations.

AARAU–SCHOFTLAND Table 643

A metre-gauge line operated by modern light rail vehicles, which leave from platforms 13 or 14, simultaneously with the jointly operated line to Menziken-Burg (see below). The initials 'WSB' on the vehicles stand for Wynental- und Suhrentalbahn, named after the two valleys served by the lines.

After leaving the suburbs of Aarau, the line parallels the River Suhre to **Oberentfelden** where the line crosses the standard-gauge line from Zofingen to Lenzburg. At **Muhen** a 16th-century Ständerbau building (the walls having vertical wooden supports) with steeply angled thatched roof has been turned into a museum of rural life (Strohhaus) (open: Apr–Oct, first and third Sun in month 14.00–17.00).

The local administration at the terminus of **Schöftland** occupies a baroque Schloss of 1660.

AARAU–MENZIKEN-BURG Table 644

A metre-gauge line operated by modern light rail vehicles, which leave from platforms 13 or 14, simultaneously with the jointly operated line to Schöftland (see above). The initials 'WSB' on the vehicles stand for Wynental- und Suhrentalbahn, after the two valleys served by the lines. For much of the way the line is a roadside tram, well used by commuters and shoppers. Most stations are served by bike routes and footpaths, and covered accommodation for bikes is provided; the WSB is a perfect example of enlightened transport planning and provision.

At **Gränichen** is Schloss Liebegg, a mélange of the foundations of a castle, Gothic house of 1561–2, early 17th-century farm building and a neo-classical residence of 1817. Beyond Gränichen the suburbs recede and are replaced by pleasant farming country through which walks are signed from most stations.

The Romanesque church at **Unterkulm** has early 14th-century frescos that were revealed during restoration of the building in 1968. Various walks are suggested from **Menziken-Burg**, including paths to the lake at Sursee and to Beinwil on the Luzern–Lenzburg line (for both, see table 651).

AARAU–WETTINGEN Table 645

This regional service travels via **Lenzburg** (see table 651) on the route of Bern–Zürich trains to the junction of **Mellingen**. Situated on the River Reuss, the village retains parts of its 13th-century walls and towers and some attractive houses. For **Wettingen** see table 710.

BASEL–BRUGG–Zürich Table 700

Local trains on this main line serve one of Switzerland's most important Roman sites.

The service shares the same route out of Basel as the Olten line through **Muttenz** to **Pratteln** (for both, see above) where the lines divide. The Brugg line swings northeast to **Kaiseraugst**, a village on the site of the Roman town of Augusta Raurica, which was founded c15–10BC. During the 2nd century it developed into a flourishing commercial town with a population of 20,000 and opulent public buildings. It was destroyed by the Alemanni c260.

It is only 10 minutes' walk from the station to the reception area and Roman Museum, which is probably the best place to start. The museum contains the most interesting of the 900,000 items found on the site, the most notable being a hoard of 4th-century silver which is thought to have belonged to the commander of the nearby fortress on the Rhine. It was found in 1961–2 and contained 68 items of an ornate table service, a candelabrum, a statuette of Venus, three silver ingots and 186 coins and medallions. (Open: Mar–Oct, Mon 13.00–17.00, Tue–Sun 10.00–17.00; Nov–Feb, Mon 13.00–17.00, Tue–Sun 10.00–12.00, 13.30–17.00.)

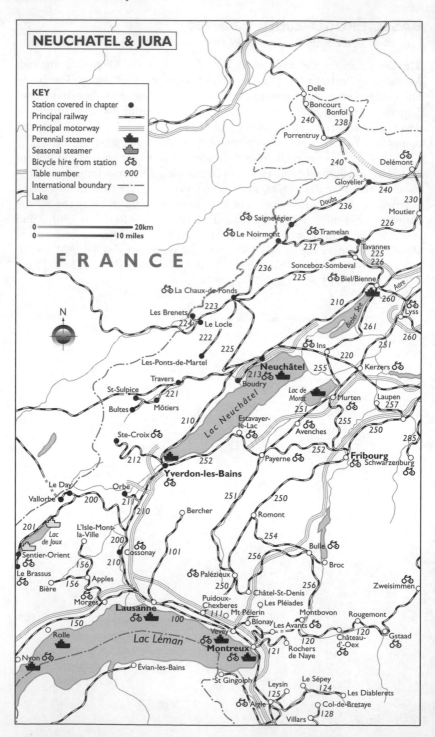

NEUCHÂTEL & JURA

KEY

Station covered in chapter	●
Principal railway	
Principal motorway	
Perennial steamer	
Seasonal steamer	
Bicycle hire from station	🚲
Table number	900
International boundary	
Lake	

0 ——————— 20km
0 ——————— 10 miles

FRANCE

N

Delle

Boncourt
Bonfol
240   238

Porrentruy

240   Delémont

Gloyelier   240

230

Doubs   236

Moutier
226

🚲 Saignelégier

🚲 Le Noirmont   237   Tramelan

Tavannes
225
226

Soenceboz-Sombeval
225   🚲 Biel/Bienne

Aare

🚲 La Chaux-de-Fonds   223

210   260
Lyss
Bieler See   261   260

Les Brenets
224   Le Locle   222

225   Ins   251
220

Les-Ponts-de-Martel

Travers   **Neuchâtel**   255   Kerzers 🚲

St-Sulpice   221   213 🚲
Boudry

Bultes   Môtiers   Lac de Morat   Murten   Laupen
210   251   257

Estavayer-le-Lac   255   250
Ste-Croix 🚲   Avenches   285

212   252   Payerne 🚲   **Fribourg**   Schwarzenburg
🚲

Yverdon-les-Bains
🚲

Le Day   Orbe
Vallorbe   200   211   251   250

210   Bercher

201   Lac de Joux   L'Isle-Mont-la-Ville   Romont

Sentier-Orient   156   200   Cossonay   101   254

Le Brassus 🚲   210   Bulle 🚲
Bière   156   Apples   256   Broc

Morges   Palézieux 🚲   Zweisimmen 🚲

Lausanne   250   256
Rolle   150   Puidoux-   Châtel-St-Denis
Chexbres   Les Pléiades   Montbovon   Rougemont   120

Vevey   111   Mt Pélerin   Blonay   Les Avants 🚲   Château-
Nyon 🚲   100   120   d'-Oex   Gstaad
Montreux   Rochers   🚲
Évian-les-Bains   121   de Naye
Lac Léman 🚲

St Gingolph   Leysin   Le Sépey
125   124   Les Diablerets
🚲 Aigle   Col-de-Bretaye
Villars   128

Neuchâtel and Jura

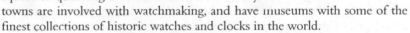

The western part of Switzerland lying close to the French border is probably one of the areas less well-known to tourists, with the exception perhaps of Neuchâtel. The proximity to France has given the area a legacy of fine castles, many to the Savoyard plan of a square or quadrangle with corner towers. Many of the towns are involved with watchmaking, and have museums with some of the finest collections of historic watches and clocks in the world.

Dominated by the Jura Mountains, the region offers wonderful walking country, with far fewer visitors than the Alps. The area around Les Chaux-de-Fonds known as the Neuchâtel Montagnes is excellent for cycling, with 1,760km (1,100 miles) of bike paths, and the country served by the CF de Jura from La Chaux-de-Fonds has many routes of varying difficulty signed from stations.

NEUCHATEL
The name of Neuchâtel appears for the first time in an act of 1011 when it was part of the Burgundian empire. During the 12th century the Counts of Neuchâtel emerged as the leading family, while the people of the town allied with the Swiss leagues. It was placed under the authority of the French sovereign until 1707 when a dispute arose over the succession, which was settled in favour of the Prussian king. Between 1752 and 1760 the city's governor was the exiled Jacobite Lord George Keith, 10th Earl Marischal of Scotland, thanks to his friendship with Frederick the Great. The Prussian connection was not ended until 1856–7, although the principality had become a Swiss canton from 1815.

Exploring the town
Arriving at the large station, built on the hillside overlooking the town, take bus 6 down to Place Pury, beside the lake. The tourist office is in Rue de la Place-d'Armes 7, at the southeast corner of the square.

Directly inland from Place Pury is the old city, which is largely pedestrianised and well worth exploring leisurely to appreciate the buildings, statues and market. From Place Pury proceed inland into Rue du Seyon and turn right into Rue du Temple-Neuf; on the right is the galleried Temple du Bas of 1695–6. The street leads into Place de l'Hôtel-de-Ville; the town hall was built in 1784–90 to the design of Louis XVI's architect, Pierre-Adrien Paris, and paid for by David de Pury. The gable of the neo-classical building has an allegory of war and peace. The ground floor is open to the public and contains a model of the 18th-century town.

Turn left into Rue de l'Hôpital, which has 18th-century houses and a fountain of justice carved in 1545–7, and proceed straight ahead into Place de la Croix-du-Marché. In the square is the Renaissance Hôtel du Banneret of 1609, with elaborately decorated door and first-floor windows, and Banner fountain of 1581. On the far corner with Place des Halles is Maison des Halles, a glorious building with corner oriel, polygonal staircase tower, and decorative banding and doorcase. Corn was sold on the ground floor, cloth above.

Walk up the steep Rue du Château out of the northwest corner of the square, following signs to the château. On the right-hand side of Escalier du Château is the 12th–13th-century Tour de Diesse, partly rebuilt in 1715. The château itself was founded in the 12th century but repeatedly altered and restored. The group of massive buildings is best appreciated from the railway to the west of the station; from below or the terrace beside the collegiate church it is hard to appreciate its size. It is now the seat of the cantonal government, but the courtyard is open to the public.

The collegiate church of Notre-Dame was begun before 1185 and dedicated in 1276. A fire that devastated part of the town in 1450 destroyed the church's timber-work, stained glass and ornaments. Further damage was inflicted during the Reformation, brought to Neuchâtel by Guillaume Farel (a statue of whom stands outside the west front), when soldiers returning from Geneva in 1530 sacked the chapels and altars. The rose window was created in the 18th century, and the spire of the steeple was added in 1869.

The three apses at the altar end of the church are notable examples of fine Norman decoration. The nave is surprisingly narrow for such an important church, and the heavy use of stained glass makes the interior dark, except where the tower lantern casts a pool of light. Under the arch of the choir is the church's great treasure – the cenotaph of the Counts of Neuchâtel, which was started in 1372 and represents knights and ladies of the city's ruling family.

Outside the terrace provides a wonderful view of the town, lake and the Bernese Oberland. Descend by steps beyond the statue of Farel to reach the Rue Jehanne de Hochberg. To the right, in Rue St Nicholas, is the Ethnological Museum; founded in 1834, it displays the finds of several local collectors and therefore reflects their interests – Africa, Bhutan and Oceania. (Open: Tue–Sun 10.00–17.00. Tel: 032/718 19 60.) Descending the hill along Rue Jehanne de Hochberg you pass a series of lovely houses with elegant street lamps.

Neuchâtel has three other museums. To the east of Place Pury, on the east side of the harbour, is the Museum of Art and History at 1 Esplanade Léopold-Robert. On the ground floor are exhibits of local interest – topographical pictures and portraits, silver, watches, coins, ceramics, furniture, jewellery, costumes, arms and glass. On the first Sunday of the month, on the hour at 14.00, 15.00 and 16.00, three incredibly intricate automata – the writer, the

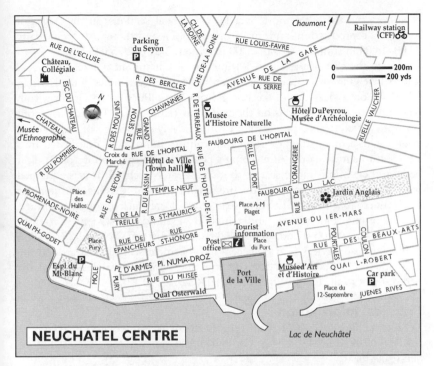

NEUCHATEL CENTRE

Lac de Neuchâtel

Map labels: RUE DE L'ECLUSE · Parking du Seyon · CH. DE LA BOINE · Chaumont · Railway station (CFF) · RUE LOUIS-FAVRE · Château, Collégiale · CHE DE-LA BOINE · R DES BERCLES · AVENUE DE LA GARE · RUE DE LA SERRE · 0 — 200m · 0 — 200 yds · ESC DU CHATEAU · CHAVANNES · R. DE TERREAUX · R. DE LA BOINE · Musée d'Histoire Naturelle · Hôtel DuPeyrou, Musée d'Archéologie · RUELLE VAUCHER · CHATEAU · Musée d'Ethnographie · R. DES MOULINS · R. DU SEYON · GRAND RUE · Croix du Marché · RUE DE L'HOPITAL · Hôtel de Ville (Town hall) · FAUBOURG DE L'HOPITAL · R'LLE DU PORT · RUE DE L'HOTEL-DE-VILLE · RUE DE L'ORANGERIE · R. DU POMMIER · Place des Halles · RUE DE SEYON · R. DU BASSIN · TEMPLE-NEUF · FAUBOURG DU LAC · Jardin Anglais · PROMENADE-NOIRE · R DE LA TREILLE · R. ST-MAURICE · Place A-M Piaget · AVENUE DU IER-MARS · QUAI PH-GODET · Place Pury · RUE DE EPANCHEURS · RUE ST-HONORE · Tourist information · Place du Port · RUE DES POURTALES · COULON · BEAUX ARTS · Espl du Mt-Blanc · MOLE · PURY · PL D'ARMES · PL. NUMA-DROZ · Post office · Musée d'Art et d'Histoire · QUAI L-ROBERT · Car park · RUE DU MUSEE · Port de la Ville · Place du 12-Septembre · JUENES RIVES · Quai Osterwald

musician and the draughtsman – created in the 18th century by three local watchmakers, come to life. The writer, for example, is animated by 120 revolving internal discs, assembled to tolerances of 0.1mm. On the first floor are rooms of Swiss paintings by such artists as Hodler, Anker and Amiet, and a collection of French, mostly Impressionist, pictures by Corot, Monet, Pissaro, Renoir and Sisley. (Open: Tue–Sun 10.00–17.00. Tel: 032/717 79 20.)

On the corner of Rue des Therreaux and Avenue de la Gare is the Natural History Museum, which has dioramas of Swiss birds and animals, displays of live fish and reptiles, and displays on animals of the world, minerals, fossils and rocks. (Open: Tue–Sun 10.00–17.00. Tel: 032/717 79 60.)

Just to the south of Avenue de la Gare at 7 Avenue du Peyrou is the Cantonal Museum of Archaeology, located at the back of a magnificent Louis XVI mansion designed by the Bernese architect Erasmus Ritter in 1765–7. The museum has some of the fascinating finds made at the sites of early dwellings along the shore of Lake Neuchâtel. (Open: Tue–Sun 14.00–17.00. Tel: 032/889 69 10.)

Trolleybus 1 from Place Pury goes to the station at Marin-Epagnier, which is a few minutes' walk from the tropical butterfly garden known as Papiliorama. It was set up in 1988 using knowledge gained from butterfly gardens in Britain to create a tropical environment inside a dome 42m (138ft) in diameter and 11m (36ft) high. This is inhabited by 40 species of butterfly, 600 plant species, including the world's largest waterlily (*Victoria amazonica*), 25 species of tropical birds (five of them humming-birds), tropical fish, turtles and a pair of miniature cayman. An insectarium contains lots of hair-raising creatures, and there are more overtly educational sections on the stages of butterfly reproduction and on tropical flora and fauna. (Open: daily 09.00–18.00 in summer, 10.00–17.00 in winter. Tel: 032/753 43 44.)

Also to the east of the city is a funicular to Chaumont where there is an unusual viewing tower from which there are magnificent views of the Bernese Oberland on a clear day. Take bus 7 from Place Pury to La Coudre from where the funicular ascends on the half-hour (table 2011). From Chaumont are some lovely walks, one of them to the lovely old village of Valangin (2 hours) with a main street of 16th–18th-century houses and dominated by a 12th–14th-century castle. After being a possession of the Bishops of Basel, it became the administrative seat of the Counts of Neuchâtel. It was equipped with several rooms used as torture chambers and prisons for persons condemned as witches. The fortress is now a local museum with furniture, arms, clothing, old kitchen, and temporary exhibitions. (Open: Mar–mid-Dec, Tue–Sun 10.00–12.00, 14.00–17.00. Closed Fri pm. Tel: 032/857 23 83.)

Finally boat services provide access to other places of interest around the lake, and on the connected lakes of Biel and Morat. Boats leave from the harbour just to the east of Place Pury (tel: 032/725 40 12).

Practical information

TO – Hôtel des Postes, CH-2001. Tel: 032/889 68 90; fax: 032/889 62 96. Open: Mon–Fri 09.00–12.00, 13.30–17.30, Sat 09.00–12.00; Jul–Aug, Mon–Sat 09.00–19.00, Sun 16.00–19.00.

The closest hotels to the station are
Eurotel★★★, Av de la Gare 15-17, CH-2000. Tel: 032/721 21 21; fax: 032/724 49 68; email: eurotel@ihtti.ch; web: www.ihtti.ch/eurotel.htm

A hotel in a lovely position beside the lake, but very expensive is
Beau-Rivage★★★★★, Esplanade du Mont-Blanc 1, CH-2000. Tel: 032/723 15 15; fax: 032/723 16 16; email: reception@beau-rivage-hotel.ch; web: www.beau-rivage-hotel.ch

Bicycle hire from Neuchâtel station.

NEUCHATEL–BOUDRY Table 213/Line 5

This metre-gauge line leaves from a terminus at Place Pury and is worked by state-of-the-art Light Rail Vehicles. As a separate system operated as part of the city's public transport network, it is something of an anomaly in that it appears in the railway timetable. It runs along the lake for much of the way.

The village of **Auvernier**, now part of the suburbs of Neuchâtel, is famous for the lake dwellings from the Neolithic and Bronze ages that have been excavated here. The attractively sited château dates from 1559 with late 17th-century extensions and wrought ironwork in the garden. The village has many 16th–17th-century houses.

The multi-towered castle at **Colombier** should not be missed. The huge building dates from the 12th to 16th centuries and was successively the property of the lords of Colombier and the Counts of Neuchâtel. Jean-Jacques

Rousseau was received here by Lord Georges Keith (see above) while he was governor of Neuchâtel. It now houses two museums: a military museum with a large collection of firearms (some from the 14th century) and uniforms; and a museum of printed fabrics. (Open for guided tours: Mar–Oct, Wed–Fri 15.00 and first Sun of month 14.00 and 15.30.)

Boudry was the birthplace of the chocolate manufacturer Philippe Suchard (1797–1884). The once-walled market town has two museums: one about wine and viticulture in the delightful 13th–16th-century castle (open: Thu–Sun, 14.00–17.00); and the Museum of the Areuse with a collection of local and African objects, and exhibitions on natural history (open: Mar–Sep, Sun 14.00–18.00).

NEUCHATEL–LA CHAUX-DE-FONDS Table 223

A short but spectacular line with a most unusual railway feature – a standard-gauge reversing point, necessitated by the need to cross the southern range of the Jura Mountains. The steep climb up the slope affords steadily more impressive views over Lake Neuchâtel to the Alps. Stopping and fast trains from Bern serve the line.

Trains head west out of Neuchâtel and bear right at a junction beyond **Corcelles-Peseux**; the main street of the former village of Corcelles has some fine 16th–18th-century houses and a 15th-century Reformed church, and Peseux has a 16th-century château with three polygonal towers. Climbing steeply, the line enters a tunnel and emerges high up on the hillside, passing through vineyards and then woods to the reversing station at **Chambrelien**.

Seven minutes are allowed for the locomotive to change ends. In the Andes and Himalayas, where narrower gauge railways employ a similar mountain-climbing device, the need for the locomotive to change ends is usually obviated by having a zig-zag so that the train can be propelled after the first reversing point and then continue with the engine at the 'right' end after the second.

The steepness of the climb is evident when the train pulls into **Les Geneveys-sur-Coffrane**, where level sidings are first seen above your carriage roof. Beyond the ski resort of **Les Hauts-Geneveys** the line enters a long tunnel, with the station at Convers sandwiched between it and another tunnel from which the train emerges on the outskirts of **La Chaux-de-Fonds**.

This city of 40,000 people is the highest (at 1,000m/3,281ft) in Switzerland and the third largest in the French-speaking part of the country. It is renowned as a centre of up-market watchmaking and as a prime example of 19th-century town planning and architecture. This was reflected in the Federal government classifying the city as being of national importance, with Switzerland's only significant collection of art nouveau.

Part of the reason for this heritage is that the village on the site was completely destroyed by fire in 1794; the town was then rebuilt on a grid pattern. The other reason is that one of the best-known figures of modern architecture was born here: Charles Eduoard Jeanneret (1887–1965), better known as Le Corbusier (the name of his maternal grandfather which he adopted in 1920). This pioneer of modern architecture studied and designed his first buildings here. He admired the English Arts and Crafts movement, and his first houses, built in 1906, incorporated decorative motifs based on the works of John Ruskin and Owen Jones. Later his designs were to exert a powerful influence on a whole generation of architects.

Leaving the large station, proceed directly ahead into the broad, tree-lined Avenue Léopold-Robert and turn right to reach the tourist office. Amongst the tourist literature available is a guide to the city's important modern buildings, such as the house built by Le Corbusier for his parents (the White House, 12 Chemin de Pouillerel).

Museums

Museum of Fine Art (Musée des Beaux-Arts)   This art deco construction was built in 1925–6 with a bas-relief of one of the architects, Ch. L'Eplatinier, on the façade. It contains portraits of and by Le Corbusier and furniture designed by him, as well as the work of other local and Swiss artists.
Rue des Musées 33, CH-2300. Open: Tue–Sun, 10.00–12.00, 14.00–17.00. Tel: 032/913 04 44.

The International Clock Museum (Musée International d'Horlogerie) This was founded in 1902 and contains over 3,000 items in a largely underground museum opened in 1974. Beginning with the sundial and concluding with the atomic clock, the museum traces the development of time pieces through paintings, machines and an outstanding collection of rare clocks and watches. There is also a restoration workshop where visitors can see craftsmen at work. In the park above ground is a unique Carillon in polished steel which comes to life every quarter hour with music, movement and changes of colour.
Rue des Musées 29, CH-2301. Open: daily except Mon, Jun–Sep 10.00–17.00, Oct–May 10.00–12.00, 14.00–17.00. Tel: 032/967 68 61.

The History Museum (Musée d'histoire)   This was set up in 1876 in a nobleman's residence, and includes reconstructed interiors, furniture, pewter, glassware, portraits, topographical pictures, coins and weapons as well as medals.
Rue des Musées 31, CH-2300. Open: Tue–Fri 14.00–17.00, Sat 14.00–18.00, Sun 10.00–12.00, 14.00–18.00. Tel: 032/913 50 10.

The Museum of Natural History (Musée d'Histoire Naturelle)   This museum has numerous dioramas of Swiss and African wildlife, as well as marine life, fossils and palaeontology.
Avenue Léopold-Robert 63 (in the post office building opposite the railway station), CH-2300. Open: Tue–Sat 14.00–17.00, Sun 10.00–12.00, 14.00–17.00. Tel: 032/913 39 76.

Museum of Farming and Crafts (Musée Paysan et Artisanal)   This is in the opposite direction from the other museums, to the southwest of the station, and is situated in one of the city's oldest buildings, a late 16th-/early 17th-century farmhouse. Furniture, tools, clothing and other artefacts illustrate the way of life of the *Montagnons* (mountain people). There is also an information centre on the preservation of the region's architectural heritage.

Eplatures-Grise 5, CH-2300. Bus 4 to Polyexpo on Rue l-J Chevrolet. Open: May–Oct, daily except Fri 14.00–17.00; Nov–Apr, Wed, Sat–Sun 14.00–17.00. Tel: 032/926 71 89.

In 'the wood of the small château' (Le Bois du Petit-Château) is a zoo and vivarium. Situated at the northwestern end of Rue Docteur-Coullery, it can be reached by bus 4 from the station.

Practical information
La Chaux-de-Fonds

TO – Espacité 1, CH-2302. Tel: 032/919 68 95; fax: 032/919 62 97. Open: Mon–Fri 09.00–1215, 13.30–18.00; Sat 09.00–12.15, 13.30 16.00; Jul–Aug, Mon–Fri 09.00–18.30, Sat 09.00–12.15, 13.30–16.00.

Hotels near the station are
Club★★★, Rue du Parc 71, CH-2300. Tel: 032/914 15 16; fax: 032/914 15 17.
De France, CH-2300. Tel: 032/913 11 16; fax: 032/913 18 49.

Bicycle hire from La Chaux-de-Fonds station.

LA CHAUX-DE-FONDS–LE LOCLE Table 223

The line forms the last section of express workings from Bern, providing connections with an international service across the French border to Besançon. Le Locle also provides access to the metre-gauge line to Les Brenets.

Heading southwest out of La Chaux-de-Fonds, it soon becomes apparent that the city and the railway are built on something of a plateau, for beyond **Le Crêt-de-Locle** the line drops steeply downhill to the watchmaking town of **Le Locle**.

It was here in 1709 that an anonymous travelling Englishman unwittingly provided the stimulus for the Swiss watch industry in this part of the country. Until then small numbers of very expensive watches had been produced in Geneva, but the ability to produce reliable, inexpensive watches was then largely the preserve of London clocksmiths. The traveller's watch had stopped working, so when he called at the blacksmith's shop of Daniel Jean-Richard in Le Locle and saw him mending a clock, he asked whether he could mend his watch; Jean-Richard did so, and made a drawing of the movement. He produced a replica and set up a business that dramatically undercut the competition in Geneva, spawning an industry that has been one of Switzerland's most important ever since. The town's debt to Jean-Richard is commemorated by a statue in the centre.

Like La Chaux-de-Fonds, Le Locle was largely laid waste by fire, in 1833, after which it was also rebuilt on a grid pattern. Only the 16th-century square tower with turret of the Reformed church is left of an earlier chapel, the nave being rebuilt in 1758–9. The Château des Monts of 1785–90, built for the watchmaker Samuel Du Bois, houses a Museum of Clocks and Watches (Musée d'Horlogerie), which displays some of the collection in appropriate room settings. There are also some automata, including an old lady shuffling with two sticks. (Open: May–Oct, Tue–Sun 10.00–12.00, 14.00–17.00; Oct–Apr, Tue–Sun 14.00–17.00.)

Near **Le Locle-Col-des-Rochers** station on the line to Besançon to the west of the town, but also served by some local trains, is a most extraordinary museum. At this point, the River Bied, which flows into the River Doubs (see below), flows for 2.5km (1½ miles) underground. In the mid-17th century Jonas Sandoz had the idea of harnessing this power and set about opening up huge caverns in the rock, sometimes creating waterfalls to extract more power. By the end of the century the mountain contained an oil mill, thresher, two flour mills and a sawmill. During the 19th century the sawmill was moved outside by the use of two 50m (164ft) wooden axles to transmit power, but shortly before 1900 the mills closed and the caverns began to fill in. In 1973 volunteers began to excavate them, and today visitors can walk through the galleries and see various exhibitions illustrating the mills and the power of hydraulics. (Open: May–mid-Jun, mid-Sep–Oct, daily 10.00–12.00, 14.00–17.30; mid-Jun–mid-Sep, daily 10.00–17.30.)

Trains for Besançon leave from platform 3. Buses leave from the station for Les Ponts-de-Martel and Neuchâtel (table 223.40).

Practical information
Le Locle

TO – Daniel Jean-Richard 31, CH-2400. Tel: 032/931 43 30; fax 032/931 45 06. Open: Mon–Fri 08.30–12.00, 14.00–18.30.

Des Trois Rois★★★★, CH-2400. Tel: 032/932 21 00; fax: 032/931 58 72.

LE LOCLE–LES BRENETS Table 224

Though short, this metre-gauge line should not be missed since it provides a glimpse of, and access to, the gorge known as Les Bassins du Doubs.

Trains leave from platform 4, which is at the west end of platform 2. The line passes through a very long tunnel before **Les Frêtes** from which there are numerous signed walks. The gorge can be seen through the trees to the left before the train dives into more tunnels, the last just before the station at **Les Brenets**. It is a 15-minute walk to the pier from which boats leave for a 1 hour 20 minutes journey between the limestone cliffs of Les Bassins du Doubs; at a point near the French border passengers disembark for a path to the spectacular Doubs waterfall (27m [88ft] high). The boats run from the end of May to the end of September (tel: 032/932 14 14). Alternatively it is a 1-hour walk from the station to the falls (Le Saut-du-Doubs)

LA CHAUX-DE-FONDS–GLOVELIER Table 236

The metre-gauge lines of the CF du Jura deserve to be much better known, since they serve some delightful walking, riding and cycling country. Besides its natural beauty, this area, known as the Franches-Montagnes, has some of the cheapest accommodation, largely because it is away from the Alpine honeypots. Nearly all the stations have large numbers of signed walks and many have cycle routes. A leaflet is available showing the routes marked from the stations at Le Noirmont and Saignelégier where bikes can be hired by telephoning the stations.

The railway leaves La Chaux-de-Fonds as though it was a tram line, mixed up with traffic, though on mostly quiet streets. It climbs steeply above the town, affording views to the left over it, and into woodland, reaching a summit at **Bellevue**. Most railways were built along valley floors, but this line clings to the higher contours, at this point at the same height as the top of the hills on the opposite side of a deepening valley.

The area is renowned for its Freiberger ponies, and it would be rare in clement weather not to see groups of riders from the train. The gentle nature of the region's horses has encouraged the setting-up of equestrian centres where horses can be hired by the hour or the week (see below).

The village of **La Ferrière** has a pretty little square, and cycle routes as well as footpaths signed from the station. Long avenues of mature trees become a feature of the almost entirely pastoral landscape, and the varied timbre of cowbells is sometimes the only sound to be heard as the train pauses at the smaller halts. Heavily booted walkers are the most likely passengers to board the train at **Le Creux-des-Biches**. The sparsely populated country is farmed from solid, often white rendered buildings, the door and window jambs and lintels of rough-hewn stone left unpainted as though to emphasise their strength.

Le Noirmont is the junction for the branch to Tavannes and a town of some importance. The Catholic basilica of St Hubert dates from the early 16th century, while to the east of the town is an aggressively modern church. The Tavannes line goes off to the south as the railway forges round the hills to the largest town on the line, **Saignelégier**, which is the railway's headquarters and the venue for an annual national horse show in early August. It was once the residence of the bishop's representative, who lived in the attractive 16th-century Préfecture which has a hipped roof and stone lock-up tower on one end. Numerous walks are signed from the station.

Beyond **Pré-Petitjea** a collection of elderly railway vehicles may be seen on the left-hand side, some from other metre-gauge railways. Shortly after, the character of the line changes quite suddenly, the railway plunging into woods with steep rock cuttings. **La Combe** offers woodland walks (and a reviving buffet by the station), and soon after a lake is passed near **Bollemont** the line enters the first tunnel. The railway joins a river fringed by rocky cliffs on the opposite side and drops down to the isolated station of **Combe-Tabeil**. Here the train reverses direction to continue its descent, burrowing down an exceptionally narrow, wooded valley that would seem familiar to anyone who has travelled the forestry railways of Transylvania.

The departure from beech woods is as sudden as the earlier entry into forest, the railway threading through farmland on the final leg of the journey to the junction with the standard-gauge at **Glovelier**. If you have a few minutes' wait for a connection here, the waiting room contains a delightful old music box; for a 20¢ coin three ladies dance round while three musicians at the back tap bells.

Practical information
La Ferrière
Auberge La Puce, CH-2333. Tel: 032/963 11 44; fax: 032/963 11 60.

Le Noirmont
De la Gare, CH-2775. Tel: 032/953 11 10; fax: 032/953 10 59.

A hotel also close to the station is
Du Soleil, CH-2775. Tel: 032/953 11 114; fax: 032/953 11 62.

Saignelégier
TO – Rue de la Gruère 1, CH-2350. Tel: 032/952 19 52; fax: 032/952 19 55. Open: Mon–Fri 09.00–12.00, 14.00–18.00, Sat 09.00–12.00.
Office du tourisme de Franches-Montagnes, Place du 23-Juin 1, CH-2726. Tel: 032/952 19 52; fax: 032/952 19 55. This tourist office covers the area of the Franches-Montagnes, and details of horse-riding holidays and facilities can be obtained from here.

De la Gare et Parc★★★, 4 Rue de la Gruère, CH-2350. Tel: 032/951 11 21; fax: 032/951 12 32; email: hotel-gare-parc@bluewin.ch
Bellevue★★, 13 Rue de la Gruère, CH-2726. Tel: 032/951 16 20; fax: 032/951 16 06.

Bicycle hire from Le Noirmont and Saignelégier stations.

LE NOIRMONT–TAVANNES Table 237
A steeply graded metre-gauge branch off the 'main line' of the CF Jura which drops down to a junction with the Moutier–Sonceboz-Sombeval–Biel/Bienne line.

Leaving Le Noirmont the line climbs sinuously across the rising valley floor in the first of two crossings of the ridges of the Jura Mountains that run southeast/northwest. Having crossed the open grassland, the train dives into woods before dropping down through delightful pasture, liberally broken up by spruce and Douglas firs. This is marvellous walking country, testified by the large numbers of walkers that use **Les Breuleux**.
The line climbs again to the attractive village of **Les Reussilles**, where there is a riding school near the station and a tea-room to fortify returning walkers. The line now begins a fearsome descent through a series of horseshoe curves to the large town of **Tramelan**. Falling more gently, the line crosses upland meadows and then finds a well-wooded narrow valley to reach the junction at **Tavannes** (see table 226).

Practical information
Tramelan

TO – Virgile-Rossel 1, CH-2720. Tel: 032/487 58 58; fax: 032/487 69 76. Open: Mon 13.30–18.30, Tue–Fri 08.00–12.00, 13.30–18.30, Sat 08.00–12.00, 13.30–16.00.

Bicycle hire from Tramelan station.

LA CHAUX-DE-FONDS–LES PONTS-DE-MARTEL
Table 222

A well-used metre-gauge line that serves a broad, flat-bottomed valley with heavily wooded hills to either side.

The line leaves from the metre-gauge platforms of the CF Jura at the eastern end of La Chaux-de-Fonds station. The line has to describe a 180-degree curve out of the town which it does by climbing steeply and twisting round over the standard-gauge lines to Biel/Bienne and Neuchâtel. For half a mile or so it keeps company with the latter before turning south-east down the curiously shaped valley towards Les Ponts-de-Martel. Despite the well-wooded slopes on each side of the valley, there are few trees on the valley floor, and those are usually in clumps.

The village of **La Corbatière** has some good examples of Jura houses and farms, with their characteristic heavy stone window and door lintels and jambs, the massive stones usually left unpainted in contrast to the coloured render of the walls. **La Sagne** has a late 15th-century Gothic Reformed church, its numerous vaults having carved keystones. It also has some fine houses, as does **Les Coeudres**.

The popularity of the valley for walking and cycling is evident from the large numbers of walkers who use the railway and in the generous provision for bicycles on the trains. At **Les Ponts-de-Martel** a cheese factory can be visited, and the surrounding peat bogs are now largely a nature reserve. A bus service from the station goes north to Le Locle and south to Neuchâtel (table 223.40).

NEUCHATEL–TRAVERS–BUTTES Table 221

A line of unexpected scenic beauty through the lovely valley of the River L'Areuse, with several sites of cultural and scenic interest. TGVs between Bern and Paris used to use the line as far as Travers where they climbed the north side of the valley slope to the border beyond Les Verrières, but now only secondary international trains use the route. Steam locomotives sometimes work special trains over the line between Travers and St Sulpice. The valley offers good walks and cycling routes. Sit on the left.

Heading west out of Neuchâtel, the line shares the same tracks as the Yverdon line as far as the junction west of **Auvernier**. This village has a main street of 16th–17th-century houses, and below it an attractive château of 1559 with 18th-century wrought ironwork in the garden.

Beyond **Bôle** the line enters a steeply sided valley with impressive views of mountains to the left. The River l'Areuse flows through the valley and is seldom out of sight all the way to Buttes. Clinging to the hillside on a shelf, the railway enters the spectacular limestone Gorge de l'Areuse, with waterfall near Pont-Dessus, which can be explored on foot from **Champ-du-Moulin**. At a nearby house Rousseau stayed in September 1764 (see below).

The valley opens out before **Noiraigue**, from where it is only a short walk to the Creux du Van. This extraordinary bowl, forming a natural amphitheatre in the mountains, should not be missed; its scale and the views over the surrounding countryside are stupendous, and it has been described as the most impressive feature of its kind in Europe. It is also the highest of the Jura peaks in the area, at 1,465m (4,806ft), and has a nature reserve for roe deer and chamois. There is a cycle route and footpath around it, forming part of a longer walk to Môtiers station (see below).

Travers is the junction for the lines to Butte and Les Verrières. A four-arched stone bridge of 1665 crosses the river, and there is a large 17th–18th-century château near the 13th–17th-century Reformed church. Just to the east of the village is a well-presented museum based on the asphalt mines that were in use from 1712 until 1986, for some of the time under British ownership. The story of this versatile substance is described, and 1km (⅝ mile) of the underground workings is open to visitors (warm clothing advised). The tunnels total about 100km (62 miles), and their ouptut was exported to places as distant as New York and Sydney. The museum also has an historic watchmaker's workshop and a restaurant in the miners' canteen; this offers local specialities, including the ham, wrapped in tinfoil, that the museum boils in asphalt for four hours at 220°C and serves with potatoes. (Open for guided tours: May–Oct, Mon–Sat 10.00 and 14.00, Sun 10.00, 14.00 and 16.00; Nov–Apr, Sun 14.00 and 16.00. Tel: 032/863 30 10.)

Leaving Travers the line crosses the river soon after the line to Les Verrières bears to the right. The river runs right through the centre of **Couvet**, which has some attractive 18th-century houses and a Reformed church of 1657. The town of **Môtiers** had a Benedictine priory from the 11th century; its secularised buildings and staircase tower form an attractive courtyard. The part Romanesque, part Gothic Reformed church dates from 1460–90, the choir and tower from 1669–79, while the lovely round-arched market hall was built in 1612. The town has no less than three museums, housed in a group of buildings just 5 minutes' walk from the station.

One of a number of fine 18th-century houses, Maison des Mascarons has become a local history museum with reconstructed rooms such as a cheese factory, absinthe distillery (produced in the area during the 19th-century from the locally grown wormwood), rustic kitchen, lace-making workshop and a bistro of 1900. The Jean-Jacques Rousseau Museum occupies the house where the political philosopher and essayist lived betweeen 1762 and 1765 after his expulsion from Geneva following the furore over the publication of his didactic novel *Emile*. While living in Môtiers under the protection of Frederick the Great, he was visited by James Boswell in 1764 and wrote *Lettres de la Montagne*. He left to take up an invitation to stay at

Wootton Hall near Ashbourne in Derbyshire. Amongst the exhibits associated with Rousseau is the desk at which he wrote, and visitors can see the peep-holes through which he could watch passers-by. (Open: Apr–Oct, Tue, Thu, Sat–Sun 14.00–17.00.) Close by is a Forestry Museum (Musée régional d'histoire et d'artisanat du val-de-Travers) with a collection of tools and documents, partly in memory of a local forester (open: May–Oct, Tue, Thu, Sat–Sun 14.00–17.00).

Outside Môtiers is a 14th–16th-century château that has an exhibition of paintings and sculpture by Léon Perrin (1886–1978). (Open: Feb–Dec, Tue–Sun, 09.00–19.00; tel: 021/721 13 91).

Fleurier is the junction where a branch to **St Sulpice** swings off to the right. The service over this line has been replaced by a bus (table 221.10, also shown in railway timetable) which serves some stations on the line between Travers and Pontarlier in France. It is now the only way to visit Les Verrières, the pine-forested border crossing where General Bourbaki's retreating and exhausted army sought asylum in February 1871 during the Franco-Prussian War. The scene of this epic event is depicted in the vast painting on display in Luzern (see page 182).

At St Sulpice is a railway museum depot which houses a large collection of steam locomotives, including massive examples from France and Germany. On various weekends of the year, special trains are operated over the line down the valley to Travers (Vapeur Val-de-Travers, tel: 032/861 36 78; fax: 032/861 40 53; email: info@vvt.org; web: www.vvt.org).

The hill above Fleurier to the west is known as Le Chapeau (hat) de Napoleon, from which there are fine views down the valley. From Fleurier station there is also a bus to the small skiing resort of La Brévine (table 221.15), known as the Siberia of Switzerland for its low winter temperatures, which has particularly good cross-country skiing. The French writer André Gide stayed here long enough in 1894 to write *Paludes* and some of *La Symphonie Pastorale*.

Walks back down the valley are signed from the terminus at **Buttes**. Le Chapeau de Napoleon can be reached in 1 hour 25 minutes, St Sulpice in 2 hours. A bus (table 221.20) leaves from the station for that at Ste-Croix (see table 212, below), passing through Mont de Buttes, the village beneath the eponymous peak.

Practical information
Travers
Crêt-de-l'Anneau, CH-2105. Tel: 032/863 11 78; 032/863 40 38.

Couvet
TO – Place de la Gare 16, CH-2114. Tel: 032/861 44 08; fax: 032/861 33 72. Open: 07.00–22.00.
De l'Aigle★★★, Grand-Rue 27, CH-2108. Tel: 032/863 26 44; 032/863 21 89; email: hotelaigle@bluewin.ch
Central, CH-2108. Tel: 032/863 23 81.
Du Pont, CH-2108. Tel: 032/863 11 15; fax: 032/863 37 13.

Fleurier

TO – Avenue de la Gare 16, Case postale 10, CH-2114. Tel: 032/861 44 08; fax: 032/861 33 72.

St Sulpice

Du Moulin, CH-2123. Tel: 032/861 26 98.

Les Verrières

De la Gare, CH-2126. Tel: 032/866 16 33; fax: 032/866 17 61.

NEUCHATEL–YVERDON Table 210

Part of a main route between Zürich and Lausanne/Geneva that follows the castle-lined lake shore for part of the way. It passes the site of one of the most celebrated military victories on Swiss soil, at the Battle of Grandson in 1476.

Leaving Neuchâtel there is a good view of the castle and collegiate church on top of the hill above the old town. For **Auvernier**, **Colombier** and **Boudry** see table 213 above (they are served by the light rail transit line to Boudry). The height of the railway above the lake continues to afford good views to the south, although the line turns away from the shore and begins to drop steadily to the water level.

At **Bevaix** is a baroque château of 1722 and a Reformed church of 1605 with Romanesque decoration on the west portal that was retrieved from the church of a nearby Benedictine priory. To the east of Gorgier (station **Gorgier-St-Aubin**) is a much altered 13th-century castle. **Vaumarcus** has an imposing 13th-century castle which was burnt after the Battle of Grandson but rebuilt with massive sloping buttress that reaches the machicolation under the roof. Beside the stronghold is a château that dates from 1773.

Look out to the right before the next station at **Concise** to catch a glimpse of a lovely château shaded by mature trees and screened to the north by woodland. Before the station, the railway has returned to the lake shore and runs alongside the water for most of the way to Yverdon. In the pretty village of Concise is an 11th–12th-century Romanesque Reformed church with late 15th-century Gothic additions. A bus from the church to Provence passes the site of the Battle of Grandson, commemorated by a stone and tablet; the bus starts at Yverdon station and calls at Grandson station (table 210.35).

The battle was fought in March 1476, war having broken out between the Austrians and the Burgundians in 1468 in which the Swiss sided with the Austrians. The castle of Grandson (see below) had been taken by the Burgundian forces under Charles the Bold, but two days later a Swiss force drawn from many parts arrived to give battle. It was an inconclusive fight in that it was a victory through Burgundian confusion rather than Swiss supremacy, and most of the French force quit the field to fight another day. However, they left behind loot so rich that one wonders what place it had in a military campaign. Today's Swiss museums are the beneficiaries, since many have on display trophies from Grandson. If a decisive victory eluded the Swiss at Grandson, Murten/Morat almost four months later was another matter (see page 138).

The station of **Onnens-Bonnvillars** serves the two villages. The Reformed church at the former has high Gothic wall-paintings of the Entombment and St Peter at the Gates of Paradise and Hell in the 14th-century choir.

Grandson should not be missed. The massive castle is one of the largest fortresses in Switzerland, dating from the 11th century though most of the present structure was built in the 13th. Its protection of three circular and two semicircular towers, gatehouse and outer defence works proved unable to withstand the assault of the Burgundian Charles the Bold in February 1476. Its garrison was put to death. Today a large part is open to the public (by courtesy of its private owner), with a display of arms and vintage cars (including a white Rolls-Royce owned by Greta Garbo), and a museum of military history. (Open: Mar–Oct, daily 09.00–18.00; Nov–Feb, Sat 13.00–17.00, Sun 09.00–17.00.)

The only part of a Benedictine monastery still to be seen at Grandson is the Reformed parish church (St-Jean-Baptiste). Once under the abbey of La Chaise-Dieu in the Auvergne, the 11th-century church owes much to the Auvergne Romanesque. The capitals of the columns have been described as some of the finest in the country.

Yverdon (-les-Bains) is the capital of the North Vaudois and has a long history of settlement going back to the 5th century BC, when Celts lived by the shore of the lake. It was strategically sited at the crossing on the main road between central France and Italy via Pontarlier, Vevey and the St Bernard Pass, and the short section of road between Yverdon and Vidy near Lausanne that linked the river systems of the Rhine, Aare and Rhone. The Romans named the town Eburodunum and established thermal baths to exploit the sulphurous springs on which stands today's impressive Thermal Centre.

The town lost its importance and for centuries was little more than a village until Peter II of Savoy chose it as the site of a new fortress in 1251 to defend the town on its most vulnerable side, the east. The castle was built in 1250–60 by one of England's most famous castle-builders, Master James of St George. He had been brought to Savoy when Peter finally returned to Savoy after 23 years at the English Court, during which time he was made Earl of Richmond and carried out diplomatic missions for Henry III. Master James was to return to England and become in 1286 Master of the King's Works in Wales, building many of the Principality's best-known castles and later becoming Constable of Harlech Castle.

After the castle was burnt in an accidental fire in 1378 and an intentional one in 1476 when the castle was embroiled in the Burgundian wars, it was conquered by the Bernese in 1536. Part of the castle became home to the first museum in the canton in 1761, and the building achieved some fame in

1805–25 as the home of Heinrich Pestalozzi's institute for poor or abandoned children.

Pestalozzi (1746–1827) is one of those historical characters whose reputation exceeds his achievements. Influenced by Rousseau and equally impractical (he once said that with 200 disciples he could change the world), his previous efforts at running homes at Stans and Burgdorf had not met with much success. However, his published writings had made him well known, and space in Yverdon Castle was offered to him. Here he was visited by educationalists and reformers such as Robert Owen and Henry Brougham, but the establishment was no more of a success than the others and it was forced to close.

Exploring Yverdon

Leaving the station, proceed directly ahead across the park (with children's playground) known as Place d'Armes, with the white, Belle Epoque-style Casino and Theatre of 1898 on the left. Cross Rue des Ramparts and proceed down Rue de Ruelle into Rue du Lac. Turn left to reach Place Pestalozzi, the heart of the old town. On the right is the tourist office, to its left the Town Hall of 1766–73 and to the left of that the castle.

Little remains of the moat that once surrounded the castle but otherwise it remains a fine and little altered example of a quadrangular Savoyard castle, with four cylindrical towers, one a massive keep. Today it houses an eclectic museum, the Pestalozzi Records and Research Centre, a theatre and conference facilities. Although labels in the museum are in French, a returnable English guide is available on request at the entrance. It includes displays on: the history of Yverdon, with a model of the Roman 4th-century AD fort, mosaics, decorative carvings, early pots, tools and utensils; weapons and firearms; bicycles; a collection of Egyptian remains, with the rather gruesome mummy and sarcophagus of Nesshou (3rd–1st century BC), the body still wrapped in a papyrus Book of the Dead and wearing amulets (shown by X-ray) to ward off evil spirits; and birds. There is also an independent museum of costumes, with a collection of several thousand garments. This can be seen as part of the tour through the castle. In the Guards' Tower is the carefully preserved living-room of Pestalozzi. (Open: Jun–Sep, Tue–Sun, 10.00–12.00, 14.00–17.00; Oct–May Tue–Sun 14.00–17.00.)

Opposite the castle at Place Pestalozzi 14 is a museum devoted to science fiction, called The House of Elsewhere (La Maison d'Ailleurs). Unique in Europe, it explores the great themes of the genre through magazines, comics, toys, works of art, posters, film stills and models. (Open: Tue–Sun 14.00–18.00.)

On the other side of the square is the striking baroque façade of the Reformed church of 1753–7, with a curved pediment above the blue-faced clock. The interior layout is unusual in that the altar is placed on the longest side, with a gallery around the three other sides; this contains an organ on one side and seating on the other two. There are some elaborately carved stalls of c1500 which came from an earlier Gothic church on the site.

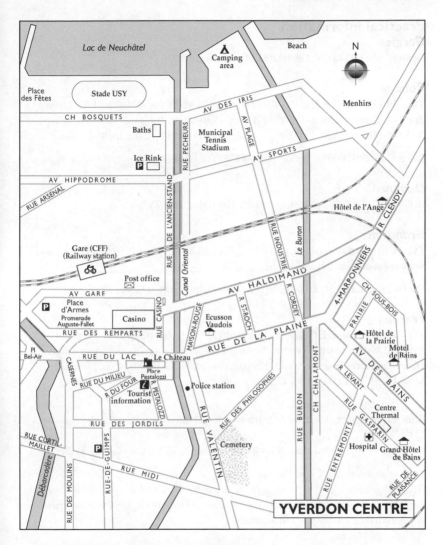

YVERDON CENTRE

The vernacular buildings on the square are a few of many lovely houses and old shops which line the streets of the pedestrianised old town. Rue du Four (No 17 has an almost Italian courtyard with murals, No 18 a curious corner extension with identical coats of arms above the door and window), Rue du Milieu, Rue du Lac and Rue de la Plaine (the last has traffic) are particularly well endowed with fine buildings.

The Centre Thermal off Avenue des Bains offers a wide range of treatments for various muscular and respiratory disorders, with indoor and outdoor pools supplied by water from 500m (1,640ft) below ground, and saunas and massage rooms. It is attractively designed and used by 1,200 people a day, making it one of Switzerland's most popular spas. (Open: Mon–Fri 08.00–22.00, Sat–Sun 09.00–20.00.)

Practical information
Gorgier
Des Tilleuls, CH-2023. Tel: 032/835 16 64; fax: 032/835 28 85.

Concise
TO – Place Pestalozzi 1, CH-1400. Tel: 024/423 62 90; fax: 024/426 11 22. Open: Apr–Jun, Sep–Oct, Mon–Fri 08.30–12.00, 13.30–18.00; Jul–Aug, Mon–Fri 08.30–18.00, Sat 09.00–12.00; Nov–Mar, Mon–Fri 08.30–12.00, 13.30–17.30.

Lac et Gare (H), Rue de la Gare, CH-1426. Tel: 024/434 18 36.

Onnens
Bellevue, CH-1425. Tel: 024/436 13 26; fax: 024/436 13 93.

Grandson
TO – Château de Grandson, CH-1422. Tel: 024/445 29 26; fax: 024/445 42 89; web: www.memsa.ch/grandson/

Du Lac, Rue Basse 36, CH-1422. Tel: 024/445 38 70; fax: 024/446 20 66.

Yverdon
TO – Place Pestalozzi, CH-1400. Tel: 024/423 62 90; fax: 024/426 11 22; email: tourism.info@yverdon-les-bains.ch; web: www.yverdon-les-bains.ch/tourisme Open: Apr–Oct, Mon–Fri 08.30–12.00, 13.30–18.00, Sat 09.00–12.00; Nov–Mar, Mon–Fri 08.30–12.00, 13.30–17.30.

No hotel is directly by the station, but the closest are
Ecusson Vaudois★★ (H), Rue de la Plaine 29, CH-1400. Tel: 024/425 40 15; fax: 024/425 44 85.
De L'Ange★, Rue Clendy 25, CH-1400. Tel: 024/425 25 84; fax: 024/426 31 20.

The hotel adjacent to the Centre Thermal is
Grand Hotel des Bains★★★★ (H), Avenue des Bains 22, CH-1400. Tel: 024/425 70 21; fax: 024/425 21 90; email: grand-hotel-des-bains@bluewin.ch; web: www.thermes-yverdon.ch The building is 18th-century.

Bicycle hire from Yverdon station.

YVERDON–STE-CROIX Table 212
This spectacular metre-gauge line climbs 631m (2,070ft) in just over 24km (15 miles) without any rack assistance. It climbs up a dramatic gorge and offers magnificent views, on clear days as far as Mont Blanc. Some of the trains are bizarrely decorated with clowns on the outside and like a nursery ceiling inside, with a starlit sky. Sit on the right.

The line leaves Yverdon on the same alignment as the Biel/Bienne line until it bears off to the left, passing the railway's workshops on the outskirts of the town. Some of the small stations are no longer staffed, but the title 'Chef du Gare' can still be seen in fading paintwork on the stone lintels.

The railway heads up a narrow valley, following a stream through orchards, before the country flattens out to reveal an agricultural plain leading gently up to hills on the right. Sugar cane is carried out by rail, huge standard-gauge wagons riding on diminutive bogies. A bus goes from **Essert-sous-Champvent** (table 212.10) to Champvent where there is one of the finest Savoyard castles in Switzerland, built in the 13th century and unusually sited on a hill. It is not open to the public but can be seen from the surrounding countryside. **Vuiteboeuf** is popular with walkers, and **Baulmes** is a delightfully unspoilt village. In the tower of the Reformed church is a Roman altar dedicated to Apollo, and the former Maison de la Dîme is a local history museum open on request (tel: 024/459 13 72).

Just before **Six-Fontaines** the line describes a 180-degree bend and climbs so steeply that passengers are looking down on the roof tops of Baulmes as the train passes by the village for the second time, in the opposite direction. There follows the breathtaking section of line that twists its way along a ledge on the edge of woods in which you may be lucky enough to glimpse a chamois near the isolated station of **Trois-Villes**. Shortly after, the line turns away from the views towards the Alps and heads up the deep Gorges de Coratanne in which the line is covered by the occasional avalanche shelter.

Suddenly the railway comes out of the trees on to an open plateau and into **Ste-Croix**. This ski and hiking resort lays claim to be the world capital of the music box and has a number of factories making them, so it is little wonder that there are two museums on the subject. The Automata and Music Box Museum (Musée d'Automates et de Boîtes à Musique) has a collection of exquisitely made early boxes, automata such as an acrobat with chairs and Pierrot the writer, and phonographs which were also made at Ste-Croix. An annexe houses craftsmen who preserve the traditional skills. The museum can be found at Rue de l'Industrie 2 and guided tours take about an hour (notes in English available). (Open: Sep–May, Tue–Sun 13.30–18.00; Jun–Aug, Tue–Sun 10.30–12.00, 13.30–18.00.)

Beyond Ste-Croix and reached by a bus from the station (table 212.30) through the Col des Etroits is the village of L'Auberson, close to the French border, where Musée Baud may be found. This family-run museum is the result of three generations practising the craft of making mechanical objects that reproduce music. Drawn from many countries, the huge collection ranges from a Gavoili fair organ and an extraordinary Phonoliszt Violina – a piano and three violins in an elaborate wood case – to a robotic accordionist made in 1930. Guided tours last about an hour. (Open: July–mid-Sep, daily 14.00–17.00; mid-Sep–Jun, Sat 14.00–16.00, Sun 10.00–12.00, 14.00–18.00.)

Around Ste-Croix/Les Rasses are 200km (125 miles) of marked footpaths, which include a stretch of the Jura Summits Path. Marvellous views can be had of the Alps from Mount Chasseron at 1,607m (4,833ft), about a two-hour walk from Ste-Croix. In February dog-sledding competitions are held here. From the station there is a bus service to the station at Buttes (table 221.20) (see table 221).

Practical information
Ste-Croix

TO – Rue de l'Industrie 2, CH-1450. Tel: 024/454 27 02; fax: 024/454 32 12; email: ot@st-croix.ch; web: www.ste-croix.ch Open: Mon–Sat 08.00–12.00, 14.00–18.00.

De France★★★ (H), Rue Centrale 25, CH-1450. Tel: 024/454 38 21; fax: 024/454 43 66; web: www.smuv.ch
Auberge de Jeunesse, CH-1450. Tel: 024/454 18 10; fax: 024/454 45 22.

Hotels in nearby Les Rasses, reached by bus from Ste-Croix station (table 212.25)
Grand★★★★ (H), CH-1452. Tel: 024/454 19 61; fax: 024/454 19 42.
Du Chasseron, CH-1450. Tel: 024/454 23 88; fax: 024/454 34 74.

Bicycle hire from Ste-Croix station.

YVERDON–LAUSANNE Table 210
Scenically unremarkable, but providing access to two interesting branches and the main line across the French border used by Lausanne–Paris TGVs.

For much of the way, the railway uses a broad valley with long stands of tall trees fringing the fields. At **Chavornay**, the junction for Orbe (see below), the main street has some attractive 16th–17th-century houses. Above the village of **Bavois** is a medieval castle rebuilt in the 19th century, and the village's part-Romanesque, part-Gothic Reformed church has a centrally placed belltower. Shortly after **Eclépens**, the line from France and Vallorbe trails in on the right.

The valley narrows at **Cossonay**, where the old town is on such a tall hill that it is served by a funicular from the station (table 2003). Although the original castle that was once home to a powerful local family has disappeared, Cossonay retains its old concentric plan and has an 18th-century château on the site. The largely 13th-century Reformed church has a tower surmounted by a 15th-century watch-tower, and the clocktower of a school in Petite Rue was once one of the town gates. Cossonay was the limit of the canal that Dutch engineers built from Yverdon, reaching here in 1648, when the goal of reaching Lake Geneva was abandoned. The canal was last used in c1829, but some impressive stone-lined stretches can still be walked.

For **Lausanne**, see Chapter 17.

Bicycle hire from Cossonay and Lausanne stations.

CHAVORNAY–ORBE Table 211
A very short branch, of only 4km (2¹/₂ miles), but serving an interesting town dating back to Roman times. The railway is independently operated and offers a remarkably full travel service, as well as carrying a healthy freight traffic. Most trains connect with services to and from Lausanne; fewer connect with services from Yverdon.

Known by the Romans as Urba, **Orbe** expanded from the 11th century and was the scene of a stout resistance by the Savoyard defenders in 1475 during the Burgundian wars, when the town was taken and largely destroyed by Bern. Little remains of the 13th-century castle but the cylindrical keep and a square wall-tower. The Reformed church dates largely from the 15th century, and has an extraordinary tower which was once part of the town walls; it was given a bellcote and four corner turrets (bartisans). Inside is some fine stone carving. The town has many attractive 18th-century buildings, including the Hôtel de Ville of 1786–9 which overlooks a banner fountain of 1543.

Just to the north of the town, about 2km (1¼ miles) out on the Yverdon road and served by buses from the post office at Orbe (table 210.10), are Roman mosaics that are claimed to be the most important in Switzerland. They were found at La Boscéaz in 1841 and date from the 3rd century AD. Four small pavilions also remain from the large villa. (Open: apply to the tourist office. Tel: 024/441 52 66.)

Practical information
Orbe
TO – Place de la Gare 7, CH-1350. Tel: 024/441 52 66; fax: 024/441 52 66. Open: Mon–Fri 06.30 12.00, 13.30–17.30, Sat 08.00–11.00.

Lausanne–COSSONAY–VALLORBE Table 200
The line is used by TGVs between Paris and Lausanne and by overnight trains between Paris and Brindisi as well as local trains. Travelling from the north, the first station south of the junction is Cossonay. The railway provides access to several places of interest and the branch along the Vallée de Joux.

From the junction to the north of Cossonay (see table 210, above), the line to Vallorbe turns to the northwest. At **La Sarraz** is a magnificent fortress dating back to the mid-11th century though the oldest surviving parts, including two square towers, are 13th-century. The castle was rebuilt after being badly damaged in 1475 and 1536, and was given by the family that had owned it for 850 years to a charitable society, which now runs it as a museum with collections of porcelain, silverware, furniture and antiquities. (Open: Apr–May, Sep–Oct, Sat–Sun 10.00–17.00; Jun–Aug, Tue–Sun 10.00–17.00.) In the attractive grounds of the castle is an Equestrian Museum (Musée du Cheval) which has a reconstructed smithy and saddlery, and displays of horse-drawn vehicles and smaller artefacts. It is open at the same times as the castle.

In the 14th-century church of St Antoine is the gruesome tomb of Franz I of La Sarraz, who died in 1363. The effigy of the naked man is carved in a state of decomposition which is being accelerated by nibbling toads and worms.

La Sarraz has one of Switzerland's last three bell foundries, and the abandoned canal from Yverdon to Cossonay (see table 210 above) passes by the village.

The line describes a long meander before **Croy-Romainmôtier**, which should not be missed by anyone interested in churches – the latter has the most important Romanesque monastery church in Switzerland. The church was part of the Abbey of St Pierre and St Paul, which is thought to have been founded in the 6th century. Today's building was begun in the early 11th century and retains many original features such as columns, capitals and the nave arcade. Frescos of the 14th-century decorate the vault of the porch, of the 15th-century the north chapel. Little of the cloisters remains, but the clocktower opposite the church was once part of the abbey's protective walls, and the former prior's house and the tithe barn, La Maison de la Dîme, survive. In the last is a tape/slide presentation (with English commentary as well as French and German) using nine projectors. (Open: Easter–Oct 09.00–12.00, 13.00–18.00; winter 10.00–12.00, 14.00–17.00. Tel: 024/53 14 65.)

Soon after **Le Day**, the junction for Le Brassus and the closest station to Vallorbe Fort (see below), the railway crosses the valley of the River Orbe and the river itself and swings to the west to reach the last station before France at **Vallorbe**. Its prosperity was created through the establishment of metallurgical industries, with the crude beginnings in the 13th century. By 1670 it had three blast furnaces and about 30 forges, developing into tool, nail, lock, gun and file manufacture. During the last century, Vallorbe turned to more sophisticated products, and today about 700 French people cross the border each day to work here.

The town has two notable museums. The Iron and Railway Museum (Musée du Fer and Chemin de Fer) is based on the site of Les Grandes Forges (at Grands Forges 11) and is only ten-minutes' walk from the station, near the bridge over the Orbe from which the foundry drew power and water. This site was first developed for metallurgy in 1495. Besides four large waterwheels, the smithy is still used to illustrate ancient skills and produce objects for sale. The railway part of the museum illustrates the strategic position of Vallorbe and the nearby Jougne Pass in the crossing of the Jura by the railway that arrived in 1870. There is a large exhibition of railway memorabilia and pictures, and an O-gauge layout of the station which is built to an exceptionally realistic standard. (Open: Palm Sunday–All Saints Day, daily 09.30–12.00, 13.30–18.00.)

Also of railway interest is a huge French steam locomotive (a 241P of 1948) near the stadium in the centre of Vallorbe. Another collection of railway memorabilia is open on request between May and October (tel: 021/843 18 75).

It is quite a hike to the other museum at Pré-Giroud – an hour from Vallorbe and 40 minutes from Le Day – but there is nothing else quite like it in Switzerland. Inside a mountain facing the Jougne Pass three connected forts known as the Vallorbe Fort were hollowed out in 1937–41, underground galleries linking observation posts, gun emplacements, magazines, control room, refectory, kitchen, dormitory and infirmary. It was abandoned and sold to the commune for 1 SFr as recently as 1988. The whole warren is open to visitors, for rather more. (Open: May–Jun, Sep–Nov, Sat–Sun 12.00–17.30; Jul–Aug, daily 12.00–17.30.)

To the southwest of the town is a half-hour walk through a gorge of the Orbe to the river's source at the foot of a cliff. The network of caves from which it emerges was opened to visitors in 1974; besides stalagmites and stalactites, panels provide information at stages in the underground circuit.

Practical information
Romainmôtier
TO – La Porterie, CH-1323. Tel: 024/453 14 65; fax: 024/453 14 86. Open: Mon–Sun 08.00–12.00, 14.00–18.00.

Au Lieutenant Baillival* (H), CH-1323. Tel: 024/453 14 58; fax: 024/453 18 30.

Vallorbe
TO – Grandes Forges 11, CH-1337. Tel: 021/843 25 83; fax: 021/843 22 62; email: vallorbe@iprolink.ch; web: www.lgi.ch/vallorbe Open: 09.30–12.00, 13.30–18.00.

Bicycle hire from Cossonay station.

VALLORBE–LE DAY–LE BRASSUS Table 201
A most attractive standard-gauge branch line of 13km (8 miles) that runs for most of its length beside Lac de Joux. Vallée de Joux means valley of forest, and much of the slopes are still covered in woods; the valley has developed a reputation for the high quality of its watchmakers. There are 250km (156 miles) of marked walks in the area, and Le Brassus and Le Sentier are ski resorts. Sit on the left.

From the junction at Le Day you can look back across the valley to Vallorbe and see the line climbing steeply towards the long tunnel underneath the Jura into France. From the broad open valley, the line enters a narrow valley with the cliffs from which the River Orbe emerges on the right.

Before the small resort of **Le Pont** the tiny Lac Brenet can be seen on the right. On the Vallorbe side of Le Pont is a park which is home to a herd of North American bison. From Le Pont, steam-hauled trains operate on certain days between June and September; they are hauled by one of two six-coupled tank engines dating from 1909 and 1915 (Le Brassus station, tel: 021/845 55 15; fax: 021/845 63 25; Le Sentier tourist office, tel: 021/845 62 57). From the station a bus crosses the Col du Mollendruz on summer Sundays only (table 150.80), terminating at Morges on Lake Léman. Le Pont is also the departure point for a boat service on Lac de Joux (Jun and Sep, Sat–Sun; Jul–Aug, daily; tel: 021/841 12 03).

As the line reaches the shore of Lac de Joux, the largest lake in the Jura, the huge tower at L'Abbaye can be seen across the water, all of any substance that is left of the Premonstratensian abbey.

Le Sentier is the largest town in the valley, both it and **Le Brassus** having specialist watchmaking industries. In 1969 a mammoth skeleton of c10300BC was found near Le Brassus; it may be seen in the Palais de Rumine in Lausanne. From Le Brassus station a bus runs on summer weekends to Nyon on Lake Léman, crossing the Col du Marchairuz (table 150.22).

Practical information
Le Pont
De la Truite***, CH-1342. Tel: 021/841 17 71; fax: 021/841 19 29.

Le Sentier

TO – Office du tourisme de la Vallée de Joux, CH-1347. Tel: 021/845 17 77; fax: 021/845 50 08. Mon–Fri 09.00–12.00, 13.00–18.00.

Du Lion d'Or★★★, Grand-Rue 17, CH-1347. Tel: 021/845 55 35; fax: 021/845 65 16. De Ville★★, CH-1347. Tel: 021/845 52 33; fax: 021/845 49 28.

Le Brassus

De France★★★, Route de France 8, CH-1348. Tel: 021/845 44 33; fax: 021/845 44 31. Modern, but very ugly, hotel.

De la Lande, CH-1348. Tel: 021/845 44 41; fax: 021/845 45 40. Family-run hotel in the centre of the town.

Bicycle hire from Le Sentier-Orient and Le Brassus stations.

Geneva and Lausanne

The southwestern corner of Switzerland is dominated by Lake Léman, commonly known as Lake Geneva, rather to the irritation of those living elsewhere along its shores. This French-speaking area has the benefit of the western end of the Jura Mountains as well as wonderful views across western Europe's largest lake to the French and Swiss Alps. It is also one of the most populous areas, partly due to the important international role played by Geneva and, to a lesser extent, Lausanne. The area's natural beauty has also attracted foreign visitors and affluent residents for centuries, and the tourist boards can call on a litany of famous names who have made their home in the area.

GENEVA

Geneva has long been Switzerland's most cosmopolitan city. For centuries, exiles from religious or political persecution have chosen the city as their refuge. Today, the headquarters of over 200 international organisations are based here, raising an always numerous foreign community to one-third of the population. The city is also a major banking centre – a 'city of wealth by stealth' as the British actor Robert Morley put it. These roles have contributed to it being an expensive city in which to live or stay, but it has much to offer the visitor, principally the old town and some fine museums.

Situated at the southwestern end of Lac Léman, Geneva is the departure point for lake steamers, and only an arrival by water can convey just how well sited the city is, with foreground hills against a backdrop of mountains.

There has been a settlement here since neolithic times, which became one of some importance in Roman times, judging by contemporary remains found near the cathedral. After becoming an imperial city under Emperor Conrad II in 1032, it was for five centuries the subject of a struggle for dominance between the local bishops and lords. Alliances with the cantons of Fribourg (1519) and Bern (1526) helped the city to achieve independence in 1530. This was reinforced by the adoption of Protestantism in 1535 and the arrival of the austere and intolerant theologian Jean Calvin, who lived here from 1541 until his death in 1564.

It was Calvin who fostered the birth of watchmaking in Geneva, but it was the influx of Protestant refugees, particularly Huguenots, that did most to develop this and other industries such as banking. Following the French

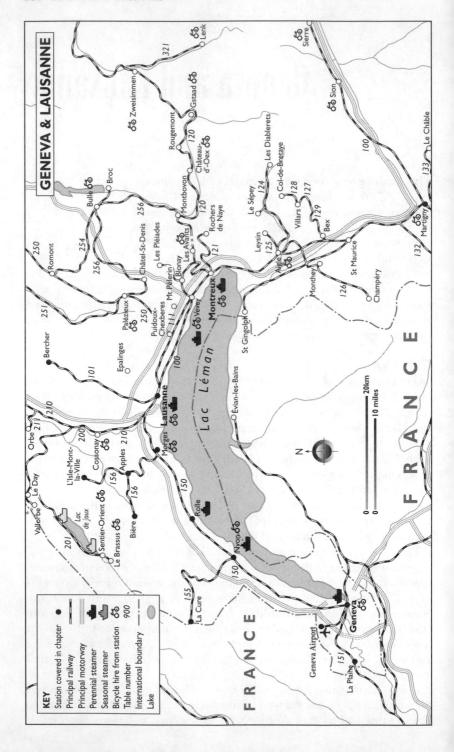

GENEVA & LAUSANNE

KEY

- Station covered in chapter
- Principal railway
- Principal motorway
- Perennial steamer
- Seasonal steamer
- Bicycle hire from station
- 900 Table number
- International boundary
- Lake

FRANCE

Lac Léman

Geneva
Geneva Airport
La Plaine

Nyon
Rolle
Morges
Lausanne
Évian-les-Bains
St Gingolph
Vevey
Montreux

La Cure
Le Brassus
Sentier-Orient
Lac de Joux
Vallorbe
Le Day
Le Day
Orbe
Bière
Apples
Cossonay
L'Isle-Mont-la-Ville
Bercher
Epalinges
Puidoux-Chexbres
Mt Pélerin
Palézieux
Châtel-St-Denis
Les Pléiades
Blonay
Les Avants
Rochers de Naye
Montbovon
Romont
Bulle
Broc
Zweisimmen
Rougemont
Château-d'Oex
Gstaad
Lenk
Sierre
Sion

Le Sépey
Les Diablerets
Leysin
Villars
Col-de-Bretaye
Bex
Aigle
St Maurice
Monthey
Champéry
Martigny
Le Châble

200
201
210
211
210
156
156
155
150
150
50
50
151
100
101
101
250
251
254
256
256
250
111
120
121
120
120
321
100
124
125
126
127
128
129
132
133

N

20km
10 miles
0
0

FRANCE

Revolution, Geneva became a part of France from 1798 until 1813, joining the Swiss Confederation the following year. The outcome of an international conference in 1864 was the Geneva Convention, which established the Red Cross and a code of conduct for the care of the victims of war by the Red Cross, using the Swiss flag with transposed colours as its emblem. In 1920 Geneva became the headquarters of the League of Nations, followed in 1946 by the European headquarters of the United Nations. Other international establishments here include the International Labour Organisation, the World Health Organisation and the International Telecommunications Union.

Geneva's reputation as a refuge for religious and political exiles led to many well-known figures making it their home or visiting friends who had. Amongst the hundreds that could be listed were John Knox (who became the first British pastor here in 1555), Robert Devereux (Elizabeth I's favourite), Milton, Richard Cromwell, Thomas Gray, John Evelyn, William Beckford, Disraeli, George Eliot, Tolstoy, Dostoyevsky (who wrote *The Idiot* here), General Ulysses Grant, Thomas Hardy, Lenin and Joseph Conrad. Sir Humphry Davy, who is credited with the invention of the eponymous mining lamp, is buried in the Plainpalais Cemetery.

Geneva's reputation, connected with the Academy established by Calvin (now the university), made the city a popular choice for the sons of prominent British families to finish their education, either formally or as part of the Grand Tour. During the 1730s, for instance, a group of such aristocratic visitors formed a loose club known as the Common Room, which put on plays and organised expeditions, notably to the Mer de Glace above Chamonix; they surveyed the little-known glacier and produced a pamphlet about it. Later Geneva became a popular refuge for Russian revolutionaries prior to the 1917 revolution, the life of anarchists in the area known as La Petite Russie being described in Conrad's *Under Western Eyes*.

Some visitors were highly critical of the destruction of ancient buildings during the 19th century. Ruskin, for example, spent many long visits to Switzerland trying to identify the precise subjects and angles of Turner's paintings; he was so angered by contemporary developments in Geneva that he included only one picture of the city in his exhibition catalogue of 1857, hoping that 'Geneva will be properly humiliated at being left out of the list, as too much spoiled to be worth notice'. However, if the universal ogre of insensitive redevelopment has destroyed much, the old town still has many lovely streets and squares of 18th-century houses, a good number thankfully pedestrianised.

The city straddles the Rhône, the northern part being referred to as the right bank (*rive droit*) and the southern the left bank (*rive gauche*).

Arriving in Geneva

Those arriving by air at Geneva have only a short journey from Geneva Airport station from which all Swiss expresses now depart rather than from the city's central and principal station at Gare de Cornavin, built in 1913–16. Cornavin has all the facilities one would expect, including an office providing details and tickets for public transport, operated by Transports Publics Genevois (open: daily 06.15–20.00). There is a press-button map with telephone to locate and book accommodation near the tourist office. The main locker area is adjacent to the main ramp to platforms 2–3, and another bank of lockers may be found by the ramp to platforms 4–6.

Most bus routes and the two tram routes serve the station from various stops close to Place de Cornvin, immediately outside the station. A map from the public transport office shows the precise locations.

Using public transport

It is advisable to pick up a map and guide to the bus and two tram routes at the separate public transport office at the station. Routes serving the city area are designated by a number; those reaching into the suburbs are given letters.

It is essential to buy tickets before you board a tram or bus – no tickets are sold on them and there is a penalty for ticketless travel. You can buy a ticket for one-hour's duration, irrespective of changes, from the vending machines at stops. For numerous trips, 1, 2 and 3 day passes can be bought from the office at Cornavin station or the Transports Publics Genevois office at Rond-Point de Rive. You must validate all tickets using the vending machines at stops.

The Swiss Pass covers all journeys.

Exploring the old town

The old town is a delightful area to explore on foot. The streets and squares comprise mainly 18th-century façades of dressed stone with restrained classical decoration. In common with many Swiss cities, the sound of water playing in fountains can be frequently heard. The tourist offices rent a special cassette player which gives a commentary about 26 sites of interest in the old town, lasting about $2^{1}/_{2}$ hours. Take bus 6, 8 or 9 from the station to the stops of Molard, Longemalle or Place du Port respectively.

The tourist office in Place du Molard is a good place to start, situated in a lively, pedestrianised square of flower stalls and numerous cafés that was once the city's economic centre. The tower was built in 1591.

The heart of the old town is the surprisingly small Cathedral of St Pierre, built between 1160 and 1289 on the site of a 4th–6th-century church. To the original Romanesque and Gothic elements was added a neo-classical portico in 1752–6. By this time, however, it had lost many of its ornaments and holy objects during the iconoclasm of the Reformation. As a consequence, there is an austere appearance to the body of the church, the decoration being limited to the capitals, some blind arcading and the chancel stained glass. So it is rather a shock to enter the Maccabean chapel: built in 1406, it was turned into a warehouse at the Reformation, but in 1878 it was refurbished in neo-Gothic style by the best-known French restorer, Viollet-le-Duc. The ceiling panels between the vault ribs have elaborate gilded decoration on blue and red grounds that would have appealed to the contemporary British Gothicist William Burges and his principal client, the 3rd Marquess of Bute.

If you feel energetic, a climb of 157 steps takes you to the top of the north tower from which there are fine views over the old town and lake (open daily until 17.30). The cathedral's carillons change their tune every month of the year.

Underneath the cathedral is an archaeological site that provides an insight into the cathedral's past, including the remains of a 4th-century baptistry and 5th-century mosaics (closed Mon).

Just to the southeast of the cathedral is Auditoire Calvin, once the 13th-century parish church of Notre-Dame-de-la-Neuve. Here Calvin lectured and Knox preached to the English and Scottish communities in 1554–9. It was in Geneva that Knox worked with Thomas Bodley (after whom the Bodleian Library at Oxford was later named) and others to revise the Coverdale Bible of 1535; the new version was first published in 1560 and known as the Geneva Bible.

To the west of the cathedral is Rue du Puit-St-Pierre in which is situated the 15th-century Town Hall (Hôtel de Ville), which houses Geneva's parliament. The Renaissance street façades date from 1617 to 1630. The cobbled ramp in the square tower of 1556–78 facilitated the arrival of dignitaries on horseback. Off the inner courtyard, in which concerts are held in summer, is the Alabama Chamber; it is named after the settlement by arbitration of the Alabama Dispute between Britain and the US in 1872, though this scarcely remembered incident was of little consequence compared with the signing eight years before in the same room of the first Geneva Convention. Outside the Town Hall in 1762, the public executioner burnt Rousseau's polemical novel on education, *Emile*, after which he was forced to flee Geneva for Môtiers (see page 242).

Opposite is the arcaded Armoury; this was built in the 16th century as a corn hall, altered in 1629–34, converted into an arsenal in 1720 and now houses the state archive. Under the pronounced eave is a pictorial frieze of 1893 telling the story of Geneva.

In the same street, at No 6, is Maison Tavel, the oldest private dwelling in the city and now a museum (see below).

To the east of the cathedral is Place du Bourg-de-Four, which is the oldest public square in Geneva and thought to have been built on the site of the Roman forum. To the east of the square is the Palais de Justice, with pronounced rusticated columns. Built in 1707–12 as a convent, it became a hospice until 1857 when it was converted into the judiciary.

Other sights on the left bank

To the south of the old town is a park, the Promenade des Bastions, in which stands the Reformation monument, a massive group of figures associated with the Reformation that was created in 1909–17. Knox and Oliver Cromwell are amongst them. It stands on a long wall with a moat below.

To the south again is the Parc des Bastions in which the university is situated, housed in a neo-classical building of 1868–72. To the northwest is

Place Neuve, a focal point of Geneva's musical life. The Grand-Théâtre of 1874–9 was inspired by the Paris Opera and is home to the Orchestra de la Suisse Romande, founded by Ernest Ansermet (1883–1969). The façade of the Florentine-style Conservatoire, built in 1857–8, is decorated with statues and niches. Just south of the square, in Rue Général-Dufour, is the Victoria Hall, a concert hall named after Queen Victoria.

Tram 13 from the station to Palettes will take you south across the River Arve to a district named Carouge (also the name of the bus stop) that was once the property of Sardinia. It was planned and designed in the 18th century by Piedmontese architects, and retains a Mediterranean feel. The main square, Place du Marché, is shaded by plane trees, and on its northeast corner, by Rue Vautier, is the former mansion of the Count of Veyrier which has a lovely courtyard.

In Cologny and Montalègre, reached by bus E from Rive (bus 8 from the station), are the villas where Byron, Shelley, Mary Godwin and her stepsister Claire Clairemont lived during the summer of 1816. Byron lived with his companion-physician John Polidori at Villa Diodati, 9 Chemin de Ruth; the others at Maison Chapuis, where Mary Godwin began *Frankenstein*, published two years later. The two households created some scandal, the result of which was Claire Clairemont having a child by Byron. The proprietor of the Hôtel d'Angleterre made money out of it by charging to look through a telescope trained on Byron's bedroom in the villa across the water from his hotel.

The right bank

Most of Geneva's international organisations are located near the Place des Nations, reached by buses F, V and Z from the station. The large park adjacent to the Place is dominated by the Palais des Nations, European headquarters of the United Nations and the largest building in Europe after the Palace of Versailles. It was designed by five architects of different nationality and built for the League of Nations in 1929–37. The lobby of the Council Chamber has bas-reliefs by Eric Gill. (Open for guided visits: daily from Apr–Oct; Nov–Mar, Mon–Fri.)

To the east of the Palais des Nations are the Botanical Gardens, which contain an aviary and llamas as well as rare plants (open: daily, Oct–Mar 09.30–17.00, Apr–Sep 08.00–19.30).

Musée Ariana and the Museum of the Swiss Abroad at Château de Penthes (see below) are both close by.

Continuing to the north by bus F you can cross the frontier into France to visit the château at Ferney-Voltaire where the French writer Voltaire lived from 1758 to 1778. His bedroom and antechamber contain their original furniture. He was visited at Ferney by Boswell in 1764, John Wilkes the following year, and Adam Smith in 1766.

On the western outskirts of Geneva is a Science and Technology Exhibition at CERN (European Council for Nuclear Research) where the world's largest scientific instrument is located. Built in 1983–9 the large electron-positron collider (LEP) is housed in a 17-mile tunnel that enables sub-microscopic particles to be accelerated to near the speed of light so that scientists can

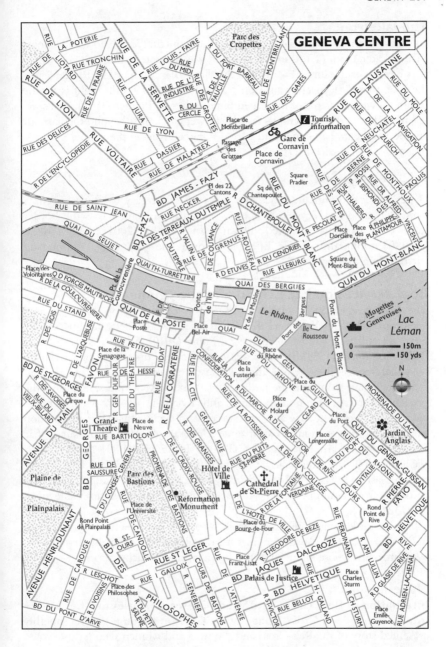

analyse the results. The Microcosm exhibition provides an insight into the science behind the machine and the whole field of space research and cosmology. It can be reached by bus 15 and Y from the station. (Open: Mon 14.00–17.00, Tue–Sat 09.00–19.00. Tel: 022/767 84 84; email: visits.service@cern.ch; web: www.cern.ch)

The lakefront

The view from any point is dominated by the fountain (*Jet d'Eau*) which shoots a jet of water 145m (476ft) into the air and was inaugurated in 1886; on windy days beware of the spray. From Pont du Mont Blanc, where the Rhône leaves the lake, there is a lovely walk along the south shore. To the right is the Ile Rousseau with its statue of the seated philosopher by Pradier (1835). You soon reach the Jardin Anglais with its famous flower clock. Just beyond the harbour are the large Parc La Grange and Parc des Eaux-Vives; in the former park is a fine neo-classical villa of 1766–7.

Mont Salève

Geneva's local mountain is actually in France, but easy to reach by bus 8 from the station to Veyrier. It is only a 10-minute walk across the border (take your passport) to the cablecar station (table 2001). The 1,100m (3,608ft) mountain affords fine views over the city, lake, Rhône and surrounding mountains.

Boat services on Lac Léman and the Rhône

The first steamer on the lake, in 1823, was owned by an American and inappropriately named *William Tell* (Lake Luzern has a better claim). Today there are still four paddle steamers: *La Suisse* (1910), *Savoie* (1914), *Simplon* (1920) and *Rhône* (1928). It is necessary to check the timetable (table 3150) to see which services they are operating, as most are worked by the 12 diesel ships.

Services leave from near the Jardin Anglais and serve 42 piers, including the French resorts of Thonon-les-Bains and Evians-les-Bains. Most services operate only between May and September, and excursions range in duration from one to eleven hours. Compagnie Générale de Navigation sur le Lac Léman, Postfach 116, Lausanne 6, CH-1000. Infoline: 084/881 18 48.

Cruises down the Rhône leave from Pont de Sous-Terre (bus 10 from the station), lasting 2¾ hours (Apr–Oct, daily at 14.15; on Wed, Thur, Sat and Sun departing from Pont de l'Ile on Quai des Moulins. Tel: Mouettes Genevoises 022/732 29 44).

It was while leaving Hôtel Beau Rivage to board a boat at Geneva that Elizabeth of Bavaria, wife of the Austrian emperor Franz Joseph I, was fatally shot in 1898 by an anarchist whose intended victim was a visiting French aristocrat.

Museums

International Red Cross and Red Crescent Museum (Le Musée International de la Croix-Rouge et du Croissant-Rouge) The superbly presented story of the Red Cross and the men and women who have devoted their lives to the service of mankind, with audio-visual presentations.
17 Av de la Paix, CH-1202. Bus 8 or F from station. Open: Mon, Wed–Sun, 10.00–17.00. Tel: 022/733 26 60. Admission charge.

Museum of Science History (Musée d'Histoire des Sciences) Unique to Switzerland, the subject of this museum is the numerous scientific instruments created by previous generations, their application and the story of the scientists who created and used them. Housed in a villa built in 1828–31, it focuses on Geneva and the particularly brilliant 18th century, when great progress was made in the city.

Villa Batholoni, 128 Rue de Lausanne, CH-1202. Bus 4 or 44 from station to Sécheron. Open: Apr–Oct, Mon, Wed–Sun 13.00–17.00. Tel: 022/731 69 85.

Natural History Museum (Musée d'Histoire Naturelle) Dioramas, collections of fossils, invertebrates and minerals, and live creatures in aquariums and vivariums.

1 Route de Malagnou, Case Postale 6434, CH-1211. Bus 6 or 8 from the station. Open: Tue–Sun 09.30–17.00. Tel: 022/418 63 30.

The Museum of Art and History (Musée d'Art et d'Histoire) has a collection so large that much is not on display or has been transferred to satellite museums. Probably the most notable picture is the *Miraculous Draught of Fishes*, which is the earliest European painting of an identifiable landscape. Painted in 1444, it depicts Lac Léman. Other subjects of interest are the Battle of Murten/Morat, portraits of Diderot, Maria Theresa and Rousseau, a hunt scene at Brockett Hall in Hertfordshire, and many topographical views of Switzerland as well as Geneva and its environs. There are works by Wouwerman, Maes, Pourbus the Younger, Jean-Etienne Liotard, Pieter Brueghel the Younger, Hobbema, Fuseli, Corot, Hodler, Cézanne, Renoir, Sisley, Monet, Calame and Félix Vallotton, who was born in nearby Lausanne. Some English portraits by Romney, Lawrence, Raeburn and Hoppner were bequeathed to the state of Geneva by Lord Michelham of Hellingly (1900–84), who lived in the city for 35 years. Other rooms contain furniture, arms and armour, pewter, stained glass and a substantial collection of archaeological finds (including Roman treasures from Martigny, see pages 306–7).

2 Rue Charles Galland, CH-1206. Bus 8 from station. Open: Tue–Sun 10.00–17.00. Tel: 022/418 26 00. Admission charge.

Petit Palais Modern Art Museum (Musée d'Art Moderne) Over 300 Impressionist and Post-Impressionist paintings dating from c1880 to c1930 with works by Renoir, Caillebotte, Monet, Cézanne, Utrillo, Chagall and less well-known artists.

2 Terrasse St-Victor, CH-1206. Bus 8 from station. Open: Mon–Fri 10.00–18.00, Sat–Sun 10.00–17.00. Tel: 022/346 14 33. Admission charge.

Collection Baur Situated close to the Art and History Museum, this exhibition of 8th–19th-century Chinese and Japanese treasures forms by far the most important collection of Far Eastern objects in Switzerland. Created by Alfred Baur (1865–1951), it includes ceramics, jade, laquerwork, prints, netsuke and ceremonial weapons.

8 Rue Munier-Romilly, CH-1206. Bus 8 from station. Open: Tue–Sun 14.00–18.00. Tel: 022/346 17 29. Admission charge.

Museum of clocks and enamels (Musée de l'horlogerie et de l'émaillerie)
Geneva was well known for its enamel painting as well as its watches and clocks; housed in a villa near the Natural History Museum, this museum combines the two crafts in an exceptional collection with many rare items. Besides the objects themselves is a reconstruction of a watchmaker's workshop.
15 Route de Malagnou, CH-1206. Bus 6 from station. Open: Mon, Wed–Sat, 12.00–17.00, Sun 10.00–17.00. Tel: 022/418 64 70.

Voltaire Museum and Institute (Institut et Musée Voltaire)   Voltaire owned this house from 1755 to 1765, living here for the first four years. Numerous books and objects associated with, and manuscripts by, Voltaire.
25 Rue des Délices, CH-1206. Bus 6 or 26 from station to Prairie. Open: Mon–Fri 14.00–17.00. Tel: 022/344 71 33.

Musée Barbier-Mueller   The first items in this collection were bought in 1907 by Josef Mueller, whose descendants continued to purchase items of classical and tribal sculpture, textiles and ornaments. The African and Indonesian collections are the largest. Close to the cathedral.
10 Rue Jean-Calvin, CH-1206. Bus 3 or 5 from station to Croix-Rouge. Open: daily 11.00–17.00. Tel: 022/312 02 70. Admission charge.

Musée Ariana   Seven centuries of ceramics, from Geneva and Nyon, elsewhere in Switzerland and from the Orient.
10 Av de la Paix, CH-1206. Bus F or Z to Place des Nations and then bus 18. Open: Mon, Wed–Sat 11.00–17.00, Sun 10.00–17.00. Tel: 022/418 54 50. Admission charge.

Museum of the Swiss Abroad (Musée des Suisses à l'Etranger)   The story of the Swiss abroad, focusing on the centuries when Swiss mercenaries were the most prized soldiers that could be hired. Other displays look at the achievements of Swiss architects, engineers, industrialists, explorers, etc. It is situated in a lovely house that was a family home until 1972, when it was sold to the state of Geneva. In the grounds is a pavilion containing a museum devoted to the military history of Geneva.
Château de Penthes, 18 Chemin de l'Impératrice, Pregny-Genève, CH-1292. Bus Z from station to Penthes. Open: Tue–Sun 10.00–12.00, 14.00–18.00. (Military museum Wed–Sun, same hours.) Tel: 022/734 90 21. Admission charge.

Museum of Old Geneva/Maison Tavel   Appropriately this museum is housed in the city's oldest dwelling. Although parts of the house were built in the 12th century, its façade dates from the 17th and there is a round tower on the northeast corner. The museum describes life in the city from the 14th to 19th centuries and has Switzerland's largest relief map on the top floor, illustrating Geneva when it was a walled city c1850.
6 Rue du Puits-St-Pierre, CH-1204. Bus 8 to Longmalle from station. Open: Tue–Sat 12.00–17.00, Sun 10.00–17.00. Tel: 022/310 29 00.

Car, Motorbike and Bicycle Museum (Musée Jean Tua de l'automobile, de la moto et du cycle)   Large collection of early cars, motorbikes and bicycles.

28–30 Rue des Bains. Bus 1 from station. Open: Wed–Sun 14.00–18.00. Tel: 022/321 36 37. Admission charge.

Practical information

TO – 18 Rue du Mont-Blanc, CH-1211. Tel: 022/909 70 70; fax: 022/909 70 75; email: info@geneve-tourisme.ch; web: www.geneve-tourisme.ch Open: mid-Jun–Aug Mon–Fri 08.00–16.00, Sat–Sun 09.00–18.00; Sep–mid-Jun Mon–Sat 09.00–18.00.

Hotels around Place de Cornavin, on to which the station fronts, are
Cornavin★★★★, Gare de Cornavin, CH-1201. Tel: 022/732 21 00; fax: 022/732 88 43; email: cornavin@iprolink.ch
Warwick★★★★, 14 Rue de Lausanne, CH-1201. Tel: 022/731 62 50; fax: 022/738 99 35; email: res.geneva@warwickhotels.com; web: www.warwickhotels.com
Arcades★★★, 14 Place Cornavin, CH-1201. Tel: 022/732 59 48; fax: 022/738 39 46; email: willacuma@mail.span.ch
Astoria★★★, 6 Place Cornavin, CH-1201. Tel: 022/732 10 25; fax: 022/731 76 90; web: www.bestwestern.com/best.html
Suisse★★★, 10 Place Cornavin, CH-1201. Tel: 022/732 66 30; fax: 022/732 62 39; email: reservation@hotel-suisse.ch; web: www.hotel-swiss.ch
Bernina★★, 22 Place Cornavin, CH-1201. Tel: 022/908 49 50; fax: 022/908 49 51.
Savoy★★, 8 Place Cornavin, CH-1201. Tel: 022/906 47 00; fax: 022/906 47 90.
Most hotels are modern or rather characterless, but in the old town are:
Les Armures★★★★★ (H), 1 Puits-Saint Pierre, CH-1204. Tel: 022/310 91 72; fax: 022/310 98 46; email: armures@span.ch; web: www.hotel-les-armures.ch

Hotels overlooking Lac Léman are
Beau-Rivage★★★★★ (H), 13 Quai du Mont-Blanc, CH-1201. Tel: 022/716 66 66; fax: 022/716 60 60; email: info@beau-rivage.ch; web: www.beau-rivage.ch
Des Bergues★★★★★ (H), 33 Quai des Bergues, CH-1201. Tel: 022/731 50 50; fax: 022/732 19 89; email: info@hoteldesburgues.com; web: www.hotelbesbergues.com

Bicycle hire from Cornavin station. Map showing cycle routes available.

LAC LEMAN

Its name derived from the Roman Lacus Lemanus, Lac Léman (or sometimes Lac Genève) is the largest lake in Switzerland and western Europe. Shaped like a croissant, the north shore is 72km (45 miles) long and its widest point is 14km (8³/₄ miles) across. Three-fifths of the lake belongs to Switzerland, the rest to France. In contrast to the blue-green of most Swiss lakes, Léman is much bluer. Its Swiss shore, to the east of Nyon particularly, is lined with terraced vineyards, backed by mountains that grow in height from west to east.

The marvellous views that are enjoyed from its northern shore, coupled with the attractiveness of the towns and villages between Geneva and the lake's eastern end at Villeneuve, have long made the region a favourite place to live for many eminent and famous people. Amongst those who have chosen the area to live in are: the composers Tchaikovsky, Lizst, Stravinsky, Ravel, Strauss and Hindemith; the writers Byron, Voltaire, Dickens, Tolstoy, Gibbon, Goethe, Simenon, Nabokov and Greene; film stars Charlie Chaplin, Noel Coward, Audrey Hepburn, Yul Brunner, Richard Burton, James Mason and Peter Ustinov; singers and musicians Arthur Rubinstein, Clara Haskil, Joan Sutherland, Barbara Hendricks and David Bowie; artists Kokoschka, Courbet and Balthus.

GENEVE-EAUX-VIVES–ANNEMASSE–LA ROCHE-SUR-FORON Table 4150

Only briefly in Switzerland, this service provides useful connections for St Gervais and Chamonix in one direction and to Annecy and Aix-les-Bains in the other.

The station at Eaux-Rives is reached from Gare Cornavin by bus 1 or 8 to Rive followed by tram 12.

GENEVA–LA PLAINE Table 151

Operated by light rail vehicles rather than conventional trains, this commuter line provides access to a few attractive villages, some surrounded by vineyards. A proposal has been made to extend the service to Bellegarde.

At the village of **Satigny** was a Benedictine priory founded in the 10th century. The Reformed church was attached to it, the Gothic choir dating from the 13th century. To the north of the church is a 15th–16th-century house and nearby, the 18th-century priest's house.

GENEVA–LAUSANNE–Brig Table 150

This is the first section of the important main line to Brig, where the line turns south through the Simplon Tunnel into Italy. It was built by the Irish engineer Charles Vignoles. Its scenic quality may be judged by the late Alan Clark, politician and historian, citing it as his favourite journey. There are many villages and towns of interest en route, and hardly a station does not afford access to at least one castle or château.

Leaving Geneva the railway affords few glimpses of the lake for the first few miles, and the western end of the journey depends upon the visibility of the French Alps to be inspiring. The line passes the Botanical Gardens with its large palm house visible to the right. At **Genthod-Bell** (also on bus line V from Cornavin station) are a number of 18th-century mansions, such as the Maison de Saussure, named after the alpinist Horace-Bénédict Saussure. A largely 17th-century château was the home of the lords of Genthod. A vain attempt was made to develop **Versoix** into a rival to Geneva when it was owned by France.

The small town of **Coppet** is graced by arcaded houses, but it is also worth a visit on account of the château of 1767 and its connection with the writer and political hostess Mme de Staël. She inherited the house from her father, Jacques Necker, who was born in Geneva and became Louis XVI's minister of finance. He was caught up in the maelstrom of the Revolution, but resigned in 1790 and retired to the château he had bought six years before. It was after his death in 1804 that Mme de Staël held the famous literary salons, like those she had held in Paris. Here they were attended by such figures as Genevese historian Sismondi, Mme Récamier and Chateaubriand. Byron visited her here in 1816. Set in a French-style park, the U-shaped house is approached through a courtyard with stables and orangery. (Open: Apr–Oct, Tue–Sun 14.00–18.00. Tel: 022/776 10 28. English-language tours.)

The Reformed church at Coppet was once part of a Dominican monastery; built c1500 it has 16th-century carved choir-stalls. In the late Gothic Maison Michel at Le Port, Grand Rue, is a regional museum (Musée Régional du Vieux-Coppet). (Open: mid-Apr–mid-Oct, Tue–Sat 14.00–17.00. Tel: 022/776 36 88.)

Château de Garengo at **Céligny** was built in 1722 and enlarged in the 19th century. Visible from the road at **Crans** is a large U-shaped château built in 1764–7.

Nyon was the first town to be founded by the Romans in western Switzerland, in 45BC by Julius Caesar, but it was destroyed by the Burgundians and was not revived until the 11th century. The 12th-century castle with five cylindrical towers was much altered in the 16th–18th centuries; today it houses a museum devoted to the history of the town and the products of its once-famous porcelain factory which turned out high-quality ware from 1781 to 1813. (Open: Apr–Oct, Tue–Sat 10.00–12.00, 14.00–17.00, Sun 10.00–17.00. Tel: 022/363 82 82.) The town's Roman past is well presented in the Roman Museum (Basilique et Musée Romains) in Rue Maupertuis near the castle. (Open: Apr–Oct, Tue–Sat 10.00–12.00, 14.00–17.00, Sun 10.00–17.00; Nov–Mar, Tue–Sat 14.00–17.00, Sun 10.00–17.00. Tel: 022/363 82 82.) Beside the lake at Quai Louis-Bonnard 8 is the Musée du Léman, which portrays the history and natural history of the lake and the vessels that have used it. (Open: same as Roman Museum. Tel: 022/361 09 49.) A ticket is available to cover all three museums.

The 12th–15th-century Reformed church has paintings on the north wall of the choir that date from c1300. The 18th-century building of the former porcelain factory still stands at 13 Rue de la Porcelaine.

Nyon is the junction for the line to La Cure (see below).

The 18th-century château at **Prangins** was briefly occupied in 1755 by Voltaire, and in 1814 by Napoleon's elder brother Joseph Bonaparte, who after Waterloo in the following year escaped to the United States, taking out citizenship and becoming a farmer in New Jersey. The château is now the museum for the French-speaking part of Switzerland, focusing on the cultural, social, political and economic aspects of the 18th and 19th centuries. (Open: Tue–Sun 10.00–17.00.) The attractive neo-classical Reformed church of 1761 in Prangins was given a bell tower in 1860.

The two villages of Gilly and Bursinel share a station (**Gilly-Bursinel**). Both have a château, Bursinel of medieval origin though largely 18th-century, and Gilly a modestly sized building with two low wings of 1724–93. On the lakeshore at **Rolle** is a late 13th-century castle that has been altered in the 16th and 18th centuries, but the medieval appearance of the four corner towers belies their years. The Grand-Rue has many fine 16th-century buildings. The obelisk on the tiny island is to Général César de la Harpe who secured independence from Bern for the canton of Vaud in 1798.

The Reformed church at **Perroy** dates back to at least the 12th century though the nave was altered c1828. There are two châteaux, of the 16th and 17th centuries, on the outskirts of the village on the road to **Allaman**, where a castle of the 15th–16th century was restored in the 18th as a rather austere château. Near the 14th-century Reformed church of St Jean is the fortified Maison de Rochefort, with cylindrical tower. A bus from the station goes to 'Aubonne, gare' (table 150.55), recalling the branch line that used to run from Allaman through Aubonne to Le Prunier-S, close to Gimel. According to Byron, Aubonne has 'by far the fairest view of the Lake of Geneva'; it also has a prominent château and well-preserved old town.

St Prex is a delightful lakeside town that was once walled. Only the entrance gate survives, and the château has also been reduced to a square tower and residence. The 12th–13th-century Reformed church of St Protais stands outside the settlement.

The town of **Morges**, junction for Bière and L'Islemailont-la-Ville, was founded in 1286 when work began on the huge square castle that sits right by the lake and was originally protected by moats. Modelled on Yverdon, the castle has four cylindrical corner towers, one acting as a keep and rising above the others. It is home to the Vaud Military Museum (Musée Militaire Vaudois) containing uniforms, weapons and an outstanding collection of lead toy soldiers. The cellars of the castle are an artillery museum with over 40 pieces on display. (Open: Sep–mid-Dec, Feb–Jun, Tue–Fri 10.00–12.00, 13.30–17.00, Sat–Sun 13.30–17.00; Jul–Aug, Tue–Sun 10.00–17.00. Tel: 021/801 85 56.)

Beside the castle is the harbour, today full of yachts and motor boats but built for naval vessels by the Bernese in 1696. The Hôtel de Ville in the square of the same name was built with a staircase tower in 1518–20 and given a baroque portal in 1682. At Grand Rue 54 is Musée Alexis Forel, a collection of furniture, tapestry and antiquities set in a 16th-century house that was rebuilt in baroque style in 1670. (Open: Tue–Sun 14.00–17.30. Tel: 021/801 26 47.)

It was on the Tolochenaz estate on the outskirts of Morges that the Polish statesman and pianist Paderewski, a prodigy from the age of three, spent the last years of his life. Stravinsky stayed here in 1915, completing *The Wedding*.

Beyond Morges the line soon enters the outskirts of Lausanne and is joined by the main line coming south from Yverdon and Neuchâtel. For **Lausanne**, see below.

Practical information
Nyon

TO – Av Viollier 7, CH-1260. Tel: 022/361 62 61; fax: 022/361 53 96; email: tourism@nyon.ch; web: www.nyon.ch Open: Jun–late Sep, daily 08.30–12.00, 13.30–18.00; late Sep–May, Mon–Fri 08.30–12.00, 13.30–17.30, Sat–Sun 09.30–12.00, 13.00–18.00.

A hotel very close to the station is
Des Alpes★★★, Av Viollier 1, CH-1260. Tel: 022/361 49 31; fax: 022/362 35 63; email: leperdtemps@smile.ch

Hotels overlooking the lake are
Beau-Rivage★★★★, Rue de Rive 49, CH-1260. Tel: 022/365 41 41; fax: 022/365 41 65.

Morges

TO – Rue du Château, CH-1110. Tel: 021/801 32 33; fax: 021/801 31 30; email: tourism@morges.ch; web: www.morges.ch/tourism   Open: Mon 14.00–18.00, Tue–Fri 09.30–12.00, 14.00–18.00; Sat 09.30–12.00.

Hotels in the pedestrianised old town are
De La Couronne★★★ (H), Grand-Rue 88, CH-1110. Tel: 021/801 40 40; fax: 021/802 12 97.
De Savoie★★★ (II), Grand-Rue 7, CH-1110. Tel: 021/801 21 55; fax: 021/801 03 29; email: savoie@span.ch

Hotels overlooking the lake are
Fleur du Lac★★★★, Route de Lausanne 70, CH-1110. Tel: 021/811 58 11; fax: 021/811 58 88; email: hotel@fleur-du-lac.ch; web: www.fleur-du-lac.ch
Mont-Blanc au Lac★★★, Quai du Mont-Blanc 1, CH-1110. Tel: 021/804 87 87; fax: 021/801 51 22.

Bicycle hire from Nyon, Morges and Lausanne stations.

NYON–LA CURE Table 155

A 27km (17 miles) metre-gauge line that opened as recently as 1916 and used to extend across the border with France to Morez. It serves some of the closest ski resorts to Geneva.

The line leaves from a point directly opposite the exit from the main line station, and curves underneath the Geneva–Lausanne line to head north, soon affording views over Lake Léman and the French Alps. Vineyards give way to beech and birch as the line climbs steeply towards **St Cergue**, which the scholar and Rugby headmaster Thomas Arnold credited with a view of the Alps he 'never saw surpassed' when he was here in 1829. After the skiing resort of **La Givrine** and the col of the same name at 1,232m (4,041ft), the line drops down through fields of yellow flowers to the terminus at **La Cure**. It is said that there was once a hotel here that straddled the border, enabling the proprietor to hire out a room to newly married couples who could then bemuse family and friends by saying that they spent their first night in different countries.

MORGES–BIERE/L'ISLEMAILONT-LA-VILLE Table 156

These metre-gauge branches divide at the junction of Apples, though on weekdays the service between Apples and L'Islemailont-la-Ville is replaced by a minibus. The line is little used by tourists but it serves a very different Switzerland from the popular resorts around Lac Léman. Traversing pleasant arable and well-wooded countryside, the line also affords a fine view of one of Switzerland's most idiosyncratic castles.

The huge, towering keep of the castle of Vufflens is visible for some distance before the train describes a U-shaped curve around it to reach the station of Vufflens-le-Château. Unfortunately the bizarre structure is not open to visitors. It was built of brick between 1395 and 1430 by Henri de Colombier, the keep echoed by four similar, smaller towers and linked by an inner courtyard to a rectangular residence with circular corner towers. The appearance of the two disparate parts is unified by the crenelles and the slender machicolations.

On the branch to L'Islemailont-la-Ville is Pampigny (station Pampigny-Sévery) where the late 15th-century Reformed church has contemporary wall-paintings in the choir. The village of Montracher had to be rebuilt after a fire in 1828, though a tower surviving from the defensive walls has been converted into a bell tower. At L'Isle (station L'Islemailont-la-Ville) is a château of 1696 which now serves as a school.

Practical information
Bière
Des Trois Sapins* (H), CH-1145. Tel: 021/809 51 23; fax: 021/809 59 27.

LAUSANNE
The capital of the French-speaking canton of Vaud is built on the slopes of Mont Jorat, though the earliest settlements were beside the lake; neolithic remains have been found at Vidy to the west of Ouchy. The Roman town on the lake was destroyed by the Alemans in 379, and the next settlement was on the hill where the cathedral now stands. The town gained in importance when Bishop Marius transferred his see here from Avenches in 590. The area was then part of the Burgundian kingdom, becoming part of the Holy Roman Empire in 1032.

Probably the greatest ceremony ever held in the town was in 1275 when the consecration of the cathedral was combined with the coronation of Rudolf of Habsburg, attracting secular and religious dignitaries from all over Europe, including Pope Gregory X. Having gained a degree of independence, the city was overrun by Burgundian troops in 1476. Protestantism was introduced after the Vaud was taken over by Bern in 1536, which retained its control until 1798. The bishopric was translated to Fribourg in 1663. Lausanne was made capital of the new canton of Vaud in 1803.

During the 20th century Lausanne hosted a number of international conferences, most notably that in 1922–3 in which Lord Curzon played a key role in achieving the Treaty of Lausanne (1923), which produced a post-war settlement between Turkey and Greece. In 1915 the city became the headquarters of the International Olympic Committee.

Lausanne's lovely position and its liberalism has for centuries attracted writers and artists. As the poet Robert Southey put it: 'were I to settle anywhere on the Continent, Switzerland would be the country, and probably

Lausanne the place'. In the 1750s Voltaire staged his plays at his home, to which the recently arrived Edward Gibbon was invited. It was in a summer-house in the city, on a June evening in 1787, that Gibbon wrote the final words of the most celebrated historical work in the English language, *The Decline and Fall of the Roman Empire*. Gibbon had lived for 15 years in a 'country which I have known and loved from my early youth. Under a mild government, amidst a beauteous landscape, in a life of leisure and independence, and among a people of easy and elegant manners.'

Dickens wrote much of *Dombey and Son* and *The Battle of Life* during six months in a villa overlooking the lake during 1846, where the family was visited by Tennyson, Thackeray and Marc Isambard Brunel amongst many others. Arnold Bennett wrote part of *Clayhanger* here in 1910. The final part of *The Waste Land* was written here in 1922 when T S Eliot came to convalesce after a breakdown.

Among notable natives of the city are J L Burckhardt (1784–1817), who 'discovered' Petra and was the first European explorer to enter Mecca, and the painter Félix Vallotton (1865–1925). The Russian jeweller Fabergé died here in exile in 1920.

Arriving in Lausanne

The main hall of the station has a branch of the main tourist office which is open daily (Apr–Jun 14.00–18.00; Jul–Sep 10.00–21.00; Oct–Mar 15.00–19.00). The Metro from Ouchy (see below) has a stop at the station before continuing to the northern, upper terminus at **Lausanne-Flon** close to the city centre.

The city has an excellent network of buses and trolleybuses, and there is a standard-gauge metro from Lausanne-Flon to Renens, serving 13 stations en route. Passes covering all public transport are available for a day or, for tourists, a three-day card.

Exploring the old city

Lausanne is a hilly city (to the benefit of women's legs, it is said), but the principal buildings and museums of the old city are not far from the station. From the station's main exit, in Place de la Gare, either use the Metro to Flon and walk along Rue du Grand-Chêne to Place St François, or proceed directly ahead into Rue du Petit-Chêne which climbs to the right to the square. It is dominated by the church of the same name, the sole remnant of a Franciscan monastery that was founded in 1258; however, it has been frequently rebuilt, and the main interest is the choir-stalls of 1387.

The post office opposite St François' church stands on the site of the house in which Edward Gibbon lived from 1783 and where stood the summer-house in which he completed *The Decline and Fall of the Roman Empire* in 1787 (Byron later sent a sprig of an acacia tree that grew in the garden to his publisher, John Murray).

From the northeast corner of Place St François take Rue de Bourg, turn left along Rue Caroline and left again on to Pont Bessières. This is one of a number of bridges that cross valleys to link the hills of Lausanne, here leading to Place de la Cathédrale. Lausanne's cathedral, still called Notre-Dame despite periodic Protestant objections, was begun in 1173 and consecrated by Pope Gregory X in 1275. It is regarded as one of the, if not the, finest Gothic building in Switzerland, though some critics have reservations about the exterior restoration work of Viollet-le-Duc which was begun in 1877 – he died in Lausanne two years later, but his plan was finally completed in 1926.

Built to a cruciform plan, with a nave and two aisles before a raised apsidal choir surrounded by an ambulatory and flanked by two side towers, the cathedral has a tower above the crossing. One tower of the main façade was never completed. The 13th-century southern entrance is referred to as the Apostles' Doorway or the Painted Portal and contains sculptures depicting the Death and Assumption of the Virgin Mary, Christ in Majesty, prophets and apostles. The richly decorated west doorway, though in the Gothic style, was not built until the 16th century.

The interior is austere and some monuments were damaged during the Reformation, but the sheer size of the building impresses. The glass in the rose window of the south transept is early 13th-century, and the choir- stalls placed along the south wall of the nave are also 13th-century, some of the oldest in Switzerland. From the south aisle a staircase ascends for 232 steps to a platform with stupendous views over the city, lake and Alps (open: Mon–Sat 09.00–11.00, 13.00–17.30, Sun 14.00–17.30; –16.30 in winter). Maintaining the tradition of the nightwatch, the hour is called by an 'All's well' from the cathedral tower between 22.00 and 02.00. To the southwest of the cathedral is the Historical Museum containing religious artefacts and views of old Lausanne (see below).

On the northeast corner of Place de la Cathédrale, Rue Cité Derrière runs north between attractive buildings to Place du Château, in which stands a huge square sandstone and brick building that was put up in 1397–1431 as the residence of the bishop. The Château St-Marie has four corner turrets and narrow machicolations. Enlarged and altered, the building became the seat of the Bernese governors and now that of the cantonal government.

From the southwestern corner of Place de la Cathédrale, Avenue de l'Université leads to Place de la Riponne on which stands the colossal Palais de Rimine, named after the benefactor who bequeathed the money to build it. The building houses the university headquarters and library, and various geological, zoological and palaeontological museum collections (see below).

Continuing south, Rue Madeleine leads to Place de la Palud, on which markets are held. On the west side of the square is the Renaissance-style façade of the rebuilt 17th-century town hall, with two storeys built over arcades. Mozart gave two concerts here when he was ten, in 1766.

Rue de la Louve leads south out of Place de la Palud, into Rue Centrale. Continue into Rue Pépinet to return to Place St François. By turning right to Le Grand-Pont of 1844, there is a good view of Pont Chauderon-Montbenon further west.

LAUSANNE CENTRE

Museums

The first five museums are all housed in the Palais de Rumine, Place de la Riponne 6, CH-1014. Buses 5, 6 and 9; alight at Riponne.

Museum of Fine Arts (Musée Cantonal des Beaux-Arts)   Includes French and Swiss artists of the 18th–20th centuries, including Anker, Bonnard, Ducros, Gleyre, Hodler, Marquet, Renoir, Utrillo, Vlaminck, Vallotton and Vuillard.
Open: Tue–Wed 11.00–18.00, Thu 11.00–20.00, Fri–Sun 11.00–17.00. Tel: 021/312 83 32. Admission charge.

Museum of Archaeology and History (Musée Cantonal d'Archéologie et d'Histoire)   A rich collection of neolithic and Bronze and Iron Age artefacts. It also has the golden bust of Marcus Aurelius that was discovered at Avenches in 1939.
Open: Tue–Thu 11.00–18.00, Fri–Sun 11.00–17.00. Tel: 021/316 34 30.

Geological Museum (Musée Géologique Cantonal)   Regional geology museum with a palaeontology room. Of particular interest is the skeleton of a mammoth dating from c10300BC found in 1969 near Le Brassus.
Open: Tue–Thu 11.00–18.00, Fri–Sun 11.00–17.00. Tel: 021/692 44 70.

Zoology Museum (Musée Zoologique Cantonal) Three galleries dealing with animals from all over the world.
Open: Tue–Thu 11.00–18.00, Fri–Sun 11.00–17.00. Tel: 021/312 83 36.

Medal Collection (Cabinet des Médailles) A collection of Swiss coins dating back to Roman times. By appointment.
Open: Tue–Thu 11.00–18.00, Fri–Sun 11.00–17.00. Tel: 021/316 39 90.

Olympic Museum (Musée Olympique) Opened in 1993, the museum stands in a park overlooking the lake and tells the story of the olympic idea and its revival by Pierre de Fredi, Baron de Courbetin in 1896. The quality of the displays and the techniques used to tell the history of a century of the games helped the museum to win the 1995 European Museum of the Year Award. It has special exhibitions on a wide range of subjects – from Technology in Sport to Sport in Art.
Quai d'Ouchy 1, CH-1006. Metro station Ouchy. Buses 2 (alight Navigation) and 8 (alight Musée Olympique). Open: Oct–Apr, Tue, Wed, Fri–Sun 10.00–18.00, Thu –20.00; May–Sep, Mon–Wed, Fri–Sun 09.00–19.00, Thu –20.00. Tel: 021/621 65 11. Admission charge.

Hermitage Foundation Changing exhibitions of paintings and sculptures, of a high standard, are held in this attractive old house.
2 Route du Signal, CH-1008. Buses 3, 8 (alight La Motte) and 16 (alight Hermitage). Open: variable hours. Tel: 021/312 50 13. Admission charge.

Elysée Museum Set in a 17th-century house within a park, this is Switzerland's principal museum of photography, illustrating both artistic and technical aspects.
Av de l'Elysée 18, CH-1006. Buses 2 (alight Croix-d'Ouchy), 4 and 8 (alight Montchoisi). Open: Tue–Sun 10.00–18.00, Thu –21.00. Tel: 021/617 48 21. Admission charge.

Historical Museum (Musée Historique de Lausanne) Housed in a remnant of the bishop's palace is a museum devoted to the city's history, which includes a huge model of the town in the 17th century, complete with sound and lighting effects. It also contains religious artefacts and a collection of pewter.
Ancien-Evêché, Place de la Cathédrale 4, CH-1005. Open: Tue, Wed, Fri–Sun 11.00–18.00, Thu –20.00. Tel: 021/312 13 68. Admission charge.

'Art Brut' Collection Created by a local painter Jean Dubuffet, this extraordinary collection of naïve art first opened in 1976. The creations are all by people on the margins of society and therefore idiosyncratic and highly original.
Château de Beaulieu, Av des Bergières 11, CH-1004. Buses 7 and 16 (alight St-Pierre/Pierre-Viret). Open: Tue–Sun 11.00–13.00, 14.00–18.00. Tel: 021/647 54 35. Admission charge.

Vidy Roman Museum A museum illustrating the Roman past of the area, with displays of tools, vessels, coins, ceramics and bronzes unearthed by digs.
24 Chemin du Bois-de-Vaux, CH-1007. Buses 1, 4 (alight Maladière) and 2 (alight Bois-de-Vaux). Open: Tue–Sun 11.00–18.00, Thu –20.00. Tel: 021/625 10 84. Admission charge.

Practical information

TO – Av de Rhodanie 2, CH-1000. Tel: 021/613 73 73; fax: 021/616 86 47; email: information@ lausanne-tourisme.ch; web: www.lausanne-tourisme.ch

TO – Railway Station, Place de la Gare. Open: daily, 09.00–19.00.

TO – Place de la Navigation (Metro, Ouchy). Open Apr–Sep, daily 09.00–21.00; Oct–Mar, daily 09.00–18.00

Hotels very close to the station are
Continental★★★★, 2 Place de la Gare, CH-1001. Tel: 021/320 15 51; fax: 021/323 76 79; email: reservation@hotelcontinental.ch; web: www.manzprivacyhotels.ch
Victoria★★★★, Av de la Gare 46, CH-1001. Tel: 021/342 02 02; fax: 021/342 02 22; email: info@hotelvictoria.ch; web: www.hotelvictoria.ch
A la Gare★★★, Rue du Simplon 14, CH-1006. Tel: 021/617 92 52; fax: 021/617 92 55; email: info@alagare.com; web: www.alagare.com
Elite★★★, Av Sainte-Luce 1, CH-1003. Tel: 021/320 23 61; fax: 021/320 39 63; email: elite@worldcom.ch; web: www.home.worldcom.ch/-elite
Jeunotel, Ch du Bois-de-Vaux 36, CH-1007. Tel: 021/626 02 22; fax: 021/626 02 26; email: jeunotel@worldcom.ch; web: www.jeunotel.ch This innovative concept offers no-frills but comfortable and modern accommodation, designed for young people on a budget.

See also under Ouchy, below.

Bicycle hire from Lausanne station.

LAUSANNE-FLON–OUCHY Table 103
This 1.8km (1 mile) standard-gauge line has the distinction of being the world's shortest metro, linking the centre of Lausanne with the lakeshore at Ouchy. It squeezes in three stops en route.

In most cities of the world, the view from such a line would be an eyesore, passing through embankments of litter and the ugly backs of buildings. Here they are planted with trees and shrubs. Trains run every 7½ minutes for most of the day, serving the main station en route, at **Lausanne-Gare CFF**.

It was at 9 Place du Port in Ouchy that Byron wrote *The Prisoner of Chillon*.

Practical information
Ouchy
Hotels close to Ouchy station on the lakeshore are
Château d'Ouchy★★★★ (H), 2 Place du Port, CH-1006. Tel: 021/616 74 51; fax: 021/617 51 37; email: hotel.chateau.ouch@worldcom.ch; web: www.chateau-d-ouchy.com
La Résidence★★★★ (H), 15 Place du Port, CH-1006. Tel: 021/613 34 34; fax: 021/613 34 35.
Mövenpick★★★★, 4 Av. de Rhodanie, CH-1006. Tel: 021/612 76 12; fax: 021/612 76 11; email: mphotel@movenpick-lausanne.ch; web: www.movenpick-hotels.com
Navigation★★★★, Place de la Navigation/Harpe 49, CH-1006. Tel: 021/616 20 41; fax: 021/616 70 80.
Aulac★★★ (H), Place de la Navigation 4, CH-1006. Tel: 021/617 14 51; fax: 021/617 11 30; email: aulac@cdmgroup.ch; web: www.aulac.ch

LAUSANNE–ECHALLENS–BERCHER Table 101

This 23km (15¹/₂ miles) line has the distinction of being Switzerland's first narrow-gauge railway, opening in 1873. Its original terminus in Lausanne, at Chauderon, has been superseded by a new station at Flon which is more convenient for the city centre. The line traverses scenery that is pleasant rather than spectacular, but there are good walks from some of the stations. Some of the 70 waymarked walks from the railway's stations are illustrated on side tables in the carriages and in a leaflet published by the railway. Steam-hauled trains are operated between Cheseaux and Bercher by an 0-6-0 tank engine of 1910, usually on two Sundays a month between June and September (tel: 021/886 20 15).

The line runs through the streets of Lausanne for a short distance before running alongside the Yverdon/Neuchâtel road. A large park overlooking the lake is served by the station at **Montétan**, but it takes several miles to leave behind the factories and suburbs of Lausanne.

From **Romanel** there are two walks to **Cheseaux** where a 17th-century château can be seen on the left-hand side of the train. It is not until after **Etagnières** that the last traces of Lausanne are left behind; once out into the country, the landscape is a broad plain of cultivated fields rarely punctuated by trees except in stands of woodland, reflecting the area's role in cereal production. The centre of this district is **Echallens** where the Wheat and Bread Museum (La Maison du Blé et du Pain) is a working museum at which you can bake bread or produce the perfect croissant yourself. Covering 8,000 years of agrarian activity, the museum is situated at 5 Place de l'Hôtel-de-Ville (open: early Jan–Christmas, Tue–Sun 08.00–18.00). The Hôtel de Ville itself was built in 1781 with a clock tower. Near it is a rebuilt castle of 1273 with two surviving cylindrical towers and a north wing of 1719.

The railway's depot is situated at Echallens and the historic carriages for the steam train, dating from 1873 to 1916, may usually be seen. It is worth noting the attractive station buildings on the line, with decorative keystones to the arched openings.

Numerous walks are signed from the terminus at **Bercher**, where there is a buffet on the station and Hotel/Restaurant de la Gare.

Practical information
Bercher
De la Gare, Place de la Gare, CH-1038. Tel: 021/887 70 50.

Bicycle hire from Echallens station (tel: 021/881 11 15).

LAUSANNE–VEVEY Tables 100/100.1

This section of the Geneva–Brig main line is dominated by terraced slopes of vines, which often reach right down to the water's edge. The western part of the line passes through the area known as the Lavaux, embracing the villages of Chexbres, Cully and Lutry in which the Lavaux wines can be sampled in the cellars of the vignerons. A network of footpaths threads the vineyards and links the caveaux and village inns. The line descends from the high level of Lausanne station down to the level of the lake, running right beside the water or separated from it by only a few feet of vines. Sit on the right.

Before leaving Lausanne, the line to the east divides, the northerly fork climbing towards Puidoux-Chexbres on its way to Fribourg and Bern, the Vevey line dropping down towards the lake. Local trains call at **Pully** (also reached by buses 4, 8 and 9 from Lausanne), where there is a restored Roman villa in Place du Prieurié; it contains the most significant 1st-century fresco discovered north of the Alps (open: Apr–Oct, Tue–Sun 14.00–17.00; Nov–Mar, Sat–Sun 14.00–17.00).

At **Lutry** the 13th–16th-century Reformed church has nave and choir vaulting painted in 1577, and on Rue du Bourg stands an imposing entrance to the 15th–16th-century castle. The gables of some of the older houses are decorated with monkeys' heads; this commemorates the occasion when Lutry was overrun by the Bernese, and the inhabitants, lacking any weapons, resorted to climbing trees and roofs and pelting the enemy with stones. This earned them the epithet *les singes de Lutry* (the monkeys of Lutry). In the vineyards to the south of the line stands a squat cylindrical tower, the Tour Bertholod. The vineyards in this area are interlaced by networks of monorails which help to transport the grapes up the steep slopes.

Cully has a delightful little harbour and a number of 16th–18th-century houses. To the north of the line, just beyond **Epesses** is the crenellated Tour de Marsens, documented since the 12th century but much restored in the 19th. As the train skirts the lake, you can see small gardens created on headlands that are reached by footbridges across the railway. To the east of **Rivaz** is the castle of Glérolles, thought to date back to the 12th century and once the summer retreat of the bishops of Lausanne.

St-Saphorin is renowned as one of the loveliest villages in the area; it also has one of the best sited stations in Switzerland from the point of view of waiting passengers – the westbound platform is right over the water of the lake. Amongst the village's old houses is the 16th-century arcaded priest's house, and the porch of the 16th-century Reformed church of St Symphorien is flanked by a 1st-century Claudian milestone and a Roman altar.

For **Vevey**, see Chapter 18.

Practical information
Lutry
De Ville et du Rivage★★★, Rue du Rivage, CH-1095. Tel: 021/796 72 72; fax: 021/796 72 00.

Cully
TO – Place de la Gare 4, CH-1096. Tel: 021/799 54 54; fax: 021/799 54 55. Open: Mon–Fri 09.00–12.00, 14.00–18.00.

Intereurope★★★, CH-1096. Tel: 021/799 93 93; fax: 021/799 93 88.
Auberge du Raisin (H), Hotel de Ville 1, CH-1096. Tel: 021/799 21 31; fax: 021/799 25 01; email: raisin@worldcom.ch; web: www.relaischateaux.fr/raisin A distinctive and beautifully appointed small hotel with excellent cuisine.
Au Major Davel, Place d'Armes 8, CH-1096. Tel: 021/799 94 94; fax: 021/799 37 82; email: aumajor@worldcom.ch; web: www.suisu.com/aumajor

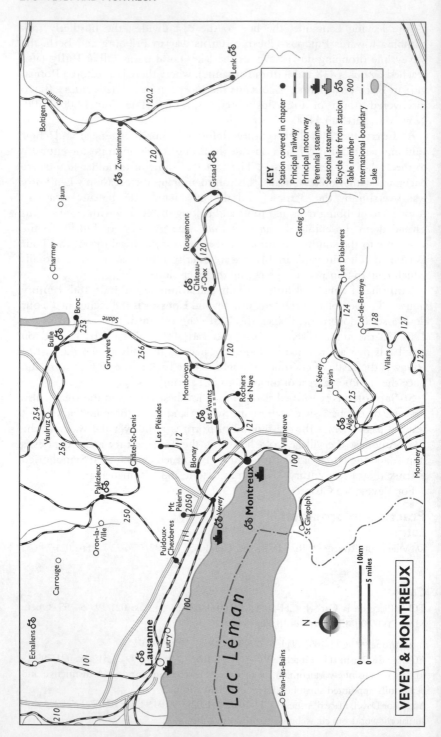

KEY

●	Station covered in chapter
│	Principal railway
▬	Principal motorway
🚂🚂	Perennial steamer
🚂	Seasonal steamer
🚲	Bicycle hire from station
900	Table number
─··─	International boundary
⬭	Lake

VEVEY & MONTREUX

N

0 ___ 10km
0 ___ 5 miles

Lac Léman

Lausanne
Lutry
Évian-les-Bains
St Gingolph
Monthey
Villeneuve
Montreux
Vevey
Mt Pèlerin
Puidoux-Chexbres
Blonay
Les Pléiades
Châtel-St-Denis
Oron-la-Ville
Carrouge
Palézieux
Vaulruz
Bulle
Broc
Gruyères
Montbovon
Les Avants
Rochers de Naye
Château-d'Oex
Rougemont
Gstaad
Gsteig
Zweisimmen
Boltigen
Lenk
Jaun
Charmey
Aigle
Le Sépey
Leysin
Villars
Col-de-Bretaye
Les Diablerets
Echallens

Sarine
Simme

100, 101, 210, 250, 254, 256, 253, 2050, 111, 112, 121, 100, 120, 120.2, 124, 125, 127, 128, 129

Vevey and Montreux

18

Few districts have as interesting a history of tourism or as much to offer today's visitor as the contiguous towns of Montreux and Vevey. Some of the country's best railway journeys are on their doorstep, the surrounding country offers excellent walking, both towns are served by lake steamers, there is a wealth of museums in the area, excellent food and local wines, and arguably Switzerland's best-known building – the castle of Chillon – is a short walk from Montreux.

In common with many of the towns and villages along the shore of Lac Léman, Vevey and Montreux have attracted foreign visitors and residents for centuries. These rich associations are developed in an English leaflet produced by the joint tourist office entitled 'On the Trail of Hemingway', which guides the visitor to places and buildings connected with 20 personalities in each town. Hemingway himself visited the area in 1922 and describes it in both *A Farewell to Arms* and *For Whom The Bell Tolls*.

Both towns are renowned for their international festivals, especially Montreux. Begun in 1961, the Golden Rose Festival has become one of television's major annual events, held in Montreux in May/June. The Montreux Jazz Festival follows in July, when Vevey hosts the International Film Festival of Comedy. In September the Montreux-Vevey International Music Festival is held.

Equally the area offers a host of sporting opportunities, from waterskiing to paragliding, and the combination of walking, cycling or journeys by train, bus and steamer offer a limitless range of excursions. The tourist offices have separate walking maps for the Vevey and Montreux regions.

VEVEY

The artist and author Edward Lear wrote in 1861 that 'Vevey...is Paradise, and I don't see how people there and at Lausanne can have the impudence to suppose that they can go to Heaven after death.' Most people have been attracted by the view of the lake and mountains, but for some of the earliest foreign residents, it was protection from extradition that drew them to Vevey. Several of the English regicides lived here from the 1660s, including Lt-Gen Edmund Ludlow (whose memoirs were published here in 1698) and Andrew Broughton, who read the death sentence to Charles I.

The town's origins go back to Roman times when it was called Vibiscum and was an important port, which it remained. Chocolate manufacture began in the 17th century, and the town is now the international headquarters of Nestlé. Henri Nestlé (1814–90) discovered in the 1860s how to make powdered milk, which made the company's fortune. He sold the company in 1874 and is buried in Vevey, with his wife Clementine. The area's vineyards are celebrated in an elaborate festival held every 25 years (next in 2024), the Fête des Vignerons, which takes place in the Grande Place beside the lake.

The literary and artistic associations with the town are numerous. Gogol began *Dead Souls* here. The novelist W M Thackeray wrote part of *The Newcomes* during a visit in 1852, and Henry James set in Vevey the opening chapter of the novel that established his reputation, *Daisy Miller*, following his stay here in 1872. In 1908 Arnold Bennett wrote *The Card* in Vevey. The musicologist and author of *The Oxford Companion to Music*, Percy Scholes, died here in 1958, as in 1977 did Charlie Chaplin, who had lived here since 1952, and Graham Greene in 1991.

Exploring the town

Close to the station is the Russian church, its gilded dome visible from passing trains. Turn left outside the station to reach it, in Rue des Communaux. The church was the gift of Prince Schouvalow and consecrated in 1878 (open: Tue 14.00–17.00). Musée Jenisch, of fine arts, is opposite (see below), and close by on a terrace is St Martin's church, repeatedly altered and rebuilt since its 13th-century origins, and included in Turner's 1841 watercolour of Vevey. Here is buried the regicide Andrew Broughton. The bell tower is distinguished by its balustrade and four bartisans.

In the Grand Place by the lake is the old grain market, the Grenette, of 1808. A market of local crafts is held in the square on Saturdays in July and August. The old town lies to the east of the square.

To the west of Vevey, at Route de Lavaux 21 in Corseaux, is the lakeside house built in 1923 by Le Corbusier for his parents. The Jeanneret family lived there until 1972. (Open: Wed 13.30–17.00 or by appointment; tel: 021/921 84 63.)

Notable walks from Vevey include a 10km (6¼ miles) hike beside the lake to Villeneuve known as the 'Flowered Path', for which a leaflet is available, giving the botanical name of many of the trees and rare flowers along the way.

Museums

Alimentarium (Musée de l'Alimentation)   Opened in 1985 and funded by Nestlé, the museum is devoted to all aspects of food. Its three sections focus on the scientific, ethnological and historical aspects of food. Temporary exhibitions, films and audio-visual programmes, and inter-active computers enliven the displays.

Rue du Léman. Open: Summer, Tue–Sun 10.00–17.00; winter, Tue–Sun 10.00–12.00, 14.00–17.00. Tel: 021/924 41 11. Admission charge.

Musée Jenisch: Musée des Beaux-Arts   Fanny Jenisch of Hamburg made her home in Vevey and bequeathed it to the town. It has a rich collection of Swiss paintings and a substantial part of the Oskar Kokoschka Foundation. *Av de la Gare 2. Open: Tue–Sun 10.30– 12.00, 14.00–17.30. Nov–Feb pm only. Tel: 021/921 29 50.*

Print Museum (Musée Jenisch: Cabinet Cantonal des Estampes)   A remarkable collection of art on paper, including woodcuts and engravings by Dürer, etchings by Rembrandt, Lorrain, Canaletto and Tiepolo, and contemporary lithographs and screenprints. Temporary exhibitions. *Av de la Gare 2. Open: as above. Tel: 021/921 34 01.*

Swiss Camera Museum (Musée Suisse de l'Appareil Photographique)   A strikingly designed museum about the development of the camera, photographic studios and processing, with inter-active exhibits and computer games. One floor is set aside for changing exhibitions of photographs. *Ruelle des Anciens-Fossés 6. Open: Tue–Sun 11.00–17.30; Nov–Feb 14.00–17.30. Tel: 021/925 21 40. Admission charge.*

Museum of Old Vevey/Museum of the Brotherhood of Wine Growers (Musée Historique du Vieux-Vevey/Musée de la Confrérie des Vignerons)   Housed in a château of 1599, these museums portray the district's past and its oldest industry. Restaurant. *Rue du Château 2. Open: Tue–Sun 10.30–12.00, 14.00–17.30; Nov–Feb pm only. Tel: 021/921 07 22.*

Practical information

TO – Grand Place 29/La Grenette, CH-1800. Tel: 021/922 20 20; fax: 021/922 20 24; email: tourism@vevey.ch; web: www.veveytourism.ch Open: Jul–mid-Sep, Mon–Fri 08.30–19.00, Sun 10.00–19.00.

Vevey has numerous hotels; those closest to the station are:
Pavilion et Résidence★★★★, Place de la Gare, CH-1800. Tel: 021/925 04 04; fax: 021/925 04 00.
De Famille★★★, Place de la Gare, CH-1800. Tel: 021/921 39 31; fax: 021/921 43 47; email: hotelfamille@bluewin.ch; web: www.minotel.com/hotelnet/182

Bicycle hire from Vevey station.

VEVEY–MONT PELERIN Table 2050

The station of this funicular is 15 minutes' walk from the main station, or five minutes by trolleybus. It takes you to a terrace with spectacular views over the lake on which several hotels have been built, set in a rural peace very different from the bustle of Vevey. During the 11-minute ascent, the funicular passes through lovely woods and pauses at the wine village of **Chardonne**. Numerous signed paths thread the woods and uplands, and the energetic can climb Mont Pèlerin at 1,080m (3,543ft).

Practical information
Mont Pèlerin

Le Mirador★★★★★, Ch du Mirador 5, CH-1801. Tel: 021/925 11 11; fax: 021/925 11 12; email: mirador@ibm.net; web: www.mirador.ch One of Switzerland's outstanding hotels.
Du Parc★★★★, 5 Ch de l'Hôtel du Parc, CH-1801. Tel: 021/921 23 22; fax: 021/923 52 18.

VEVEY–PUIDOUX-CHEXBRES Table 111

A useful link that obviates the need for passengers travelling from eastern Switzerland to go into Lausanne to head north, unless they are intent on catching an express. The line climbs steeply from Vevey to provide impressive views over Lac Léman and the Alps.

The one intermediate station of **Chexbres-Village** serves this wine-producing village and small resort, noted for its sunny position.

Practical information
Chexbres-Village

Cécil★★★ (H), En Genevrex, CP88, CH-1605. Tel: 021/926 64 64; fax: 021/926 64 65; email: minotelcecil@bluewin.ch; web: www.vevey.ch/tourisme/hotel/cecil/
Du Lion d'Or, CH-1605. Tel: 021/946 11 51.

VEVEY–LES PLEIADES Table 112

A journey not to be missed, climbing at almost alarming gradients to a terminus close to the summit of Les Pléiades. Sit on the right.

Trains leave from platform 7 at Vevey and turn through 90° to parallel the course of La Veveyse as it rushes down to the lake from its defile north of the town. The exit from Vevey is uninspiring, but after twisting through a tunnel the line emerges in orchards and vineyards with good views to the right overlooking Vevey.

Near **Hauteville** is a lovely avenue of trees leading to a mid-18th-century château with a pretty rotunda in the grounds; another avenue has been destroyed by the nearby motorway. **St-Légier Gare** used to be the junction for a metre-gauge line to Châtel-St-Denis, which closed in 1969. At the Reformed church of St Légier at **La Chiésaz**, the German composer Paul Hindemith is buried. The approach to **Château-de-Blonay** is dominated by the imposing building after which the station takes its name; the castle has been much altered and extended since it was begun in 1175 by the same family that still owns it. It is not open to the public.

Blonay is the starting point for the preserved CF-Musée Blonay–Chamby (see below). The rack section that continues all the way to Les Pléiades begins at the end of the platform at Blonay. There is a fine view of the castle as the train leaves, starting its formidable climb through woods. It sometimes stops at stations on a steep part of the line, as at **Bois-de-Chexbres**, demonstrating on restarting the extraordinary power of the rack mechanism. There are numerous walks waymarked through the woods (boots or walking shoes advised), and in winter the area provides plenty of skiing. Just beyond **Ondallaz-L'Alliaz** is a delightfully unspoilt chalet with chestnut roof tiles.

From **Lally** you can hire mountain bikes for an easy 9km (5½ miles) route taking less than an hour or a more challenging 37km (23 miles) route via Les Paccots and Châtel-St-Denis. A leaflet is available and the routes are signed. See below for bike hire.

The terminus at **Les Pléiades** is only a few minutes' walk from the summit and nearby children's playground and restaurant (closed Mon).

From the summit at 1,360m (4,462ft) there are panoramic views with only Rochers de Naye of the nearby peaks exceeding Les Pléiades in height. There are waymarked paths down to Blonay (1 hour 20 minutes), Montreux (4 hours 10 minutes) and Châtel-St-Denis (2 hours) (see table 256). One walk, down to Lally station, is known as the Botanical Path and takes 1½ hours.

Practical information
Blonay
Bahyse**, 11 Rte du Village, CH-1807. Tel: 021/943 13 22; fax: 021/943 48 10.
Les Sapins**, Route des Monts, CH-1807. Tel: 021/943 13 95; fax: 021/943 71 19; email: info@les-sapins-les-pleiades.ch; web: www.les-sapins-les-pleiades.ch

Les Pléiades
Les Pléiades, CH-1807. Tel: 021/943 11 23; fax: 021/943 12 55.

Bicycle hire
Lally: Dépôt Clio at Restaurant/Hotel des Sapins, CH-1807. Tel: 021/943 13 95; fax: 021/943 71 19. Reservation necessary.
Vevey: Altmann Sports, Rue de la Madelaine 22, CH-1800. Tel: 021/921 96 77.

BLONAY–CHAMBY
This is probably Switzerland's best-known preserved railway, operating trains on Saturday afternoons and Sundays from mid-May until the end of October. The museum buildings that house one of Europe's largest collections of metre-gauge steam and electric locomotives and rolling stock would be the envy of most preserved railways. The collection includes locomotives from France, Germany, Spain and Italy as well as Switzerland. Run entirely by volunteers, the line is only 3.2km (2 miles) but is full of interest with a tunnel, a graceful, curved masonry viaduct over the Baye de Clarens and a gradient of 1 in 20 that has steam locomotives barking noisily. The depot and museum, with café and shop, is at Chaulin near Chamby. Two hours should be allowed for a journey and museum visit.

Geneva–VEVEY–MONTREUX–Brig Tables 100/100.1
This short section is away from the lake and either largely screened from it by buildings or in a tunnel.

La Tour-de-Peilz, served by the first of three intermediate stations, is where the English writer, collector and builder William Beckford took up refuge at the château in 1785 to escape a scandal. Here he finished his novel *Vathek*, and later bought Gibbon's library in Lausanne. It is also where the painter Gustave Courbet died, having fled France to avoid punitive fines for his role in the Commune in 1871. A bust by him decorates the Fountain of Liberty near the church.

The Swiss Museum of Games (Musée Suisse du Jeu) is housed in the lakeside château, created in the 18th century out of a castle built by Peter II of Savoy in 1251–7. This unusual museum looks at the history of games throughout the world and at the various types of game, involving education, strategy, risk, memory, role-playing, etc. Visitors can play games both inside and in the garden, so the museum is ideal for children. (Open: Tue–Sun 14.00–18.00. Bus 1 from Vevey, to Place du Temple. Tel: 021/944 40 50. Admission charge.)

Clarens now forms the western suburb of Montreux. On the hill above Clarens is Châtelard Castle, the large 15th-century refuge built for the people of Montreux. Clarens has had its share of famous residents: the Russian anarchist Bakunin, Wagner, Tchaikovsky (the 4th Symphony was finished here) and Stravinsky wrote *The Rite of Spring* at his house in Clarens in 1913. It is also the setting for Rousseau's novel *Julie, ou la La Nouvelle Héloïse*, published in 1761, though it is impossible today to correlate places and descriptions. Adolf Loos built his first private house here, the Villa Karma, in 1904–6.

The station at **Montreux** is one of the very small number in the world that is served by railways built to three different gauges: the standard gauge of the main line; the metre gauge of the Montreux–Oberland Bernois Railway; and the 800mm gauge of the Montreux–Glion–Rochers-de-Naye line. For Montreux, see below.

Practical information
La Tour-de-Peilz
La Vieille Tour★★★, CH-1814. Tel: 021/944 96 96; fax: 021/944 98 96.

MONTREUX
The town of Montreux has been formed by the gradual joining of neighbouring villages that were once separated by vineyards. Montreux's past is portrayed in the Museum of Old Montreux (Musée du Vieux-Montreux). Situated at Rue de la Gare 40 in the former convent of Sâles, it traces the town's history from palaeolithic times with displays of Roman finds, local furniture and artefacts of everyday life, the growth of tourism and the way its environs have served as an inspiration for writers, artists and musicians. (Open: Apr–Oct, daily 10.00–12.00, 14.00–17.00. Tel: 021/963 13 53.) Hans Christian Andersen wrote *The Ice Maiden* here in 1861, and the painter Oskar Kokoschka died here in 1980.

The first two hotels opened their doors in 1835; before then visitors had lodged in private homes. The following year Hotel Byron opened. By 1850 the town offered 250 hotel beds, by 1860 there were 810 beds in 18 hotels, and by 1912 7,525 beds in 85 hotels. Part of the reason for Montreux's success, apart from its lovely position, was its comparatively mild winter and spring climate while being close to good skiing for those who wanted it. Funiculars and rack railways were built to provide access to mountain walks and ski slopes, and the Kursaal (casino) was opened in 1883.

World War I was a crushing blow to Montreux, and to Swiss tourism generally. The days of receiving families, and often their servants, for stays of months' duration from all over Europe and the United States were over, as were the days of SFr25 for £1. Some hotels closed or were adapted to other uses; some, like the National Hotel with its lovely interiors, still stand empty. Today there is less than half the 1912 number of beds.

Yet the popularity of the area for tourists remains, and the exceptional conference facilities have proved a tremendous success. Amongst such buildings is the Stravinsky Auditorium, named in honour of the Russian-born composer who spent many productive years here. The impressive and accoustically outstanding hall is now the setting for the annual jazz and classical music festivals and the Golden Rose television festival.

In the old Grand Hôtel et Hôtel des Alpes a museum has been set up devoted to the history of audio-visual communication (Musée Suisse de l'Audiovisuel 'Audiorama'). It contains over 500 radios and 600 televisions, as well as numerous other displays about the media. It can be reached from Montreux station by bus 1 in the direction of Villeneuve.

In Place du Marché by the lake is the well-restored market hall in which flea markets are held on Tuesday and Friday mornings. The older part of Montreux is up the hill from the station, reached by turning right from the station and right again into Rue de la Gare, continuing into Rue du Pont. The yellow building with covered staircase and a bear on a ledge (No 3) was an early hospital. One of the area's best walks begins (or, for those who prefer walking downhill, ends) off this street, in Rue de la Baye: turn right after crossing the river and follow the road round. Connecting the area of Les Planches with Les Avants, the signed path crosses a Roman bridge and threads the boulder-strewn gorge of Chauderon through which flows the Baye of Montreux. It is about 2 hours to Les Avants, 4 hours to the Col de Jaman and 5³⁄₄ hours to Les Rochers-de-Naye; there are restaurants at all three destinations.

Practical information

TO – Avenue du Théâtre 5, CH-1820. Tel: 021/962 84 36; fax: 021/963 91 13; email: tourism@montreux.ch; web: www.montreux.ch   Open: Apr–Oct, Mon–Sat 09.00–12.00, 13.30–18.00, Sun 09.00–12.00; Oct–Mar, Mon–Fri 09.00–12.00, 13.30–18.00, Sat 09.00–12.00.

Montreux has numerous hotels; the closest to the station are
Grand Hotel Suisse Majestic**** (H), 43 Av des Alpes, CH-1820. Tel: 021/963 51 81; fax: 021/963 35 06; email: suissemajestic@bluewin.ch

Parc et Lac★★★, Grand-Rue 38, CH-1820. Tel: 021/963 37 38; fax: 021/963 23 17.
Splendid★★★ (H), Grand-Rue 52, CH-1820. Tel: 021/963 64 66; fax: 021/963 75 04.

Bicycle hire from Montreux station.

Montreux (Territet)–Mont Fleuri/Glion Tables 2053/2054

These two funiculars ascend from the Montreux suburb of Territet (in which the English church, St John's, is situated); the SBB station, two minutes' walk from Territet funicular station, is off Rue de Chillon. From 1883 until 1975 the funicular to Glion used to be powered by water, a system designed by the great mountain railway engineer Niklaus Riggenbach. A tank under the car was filled at the top and emptied at the bottom, the amount of water required being determined by the number of passengers in each car. The number ascending was telephoned from the lower station to the operator controlling the volume of water at the top, who was able to calculate the quantity, knowing the number of descending passengers. The water also served to cool the rack and pinion mechanism, which was used as a brake.

This was not only the first mountain railway in the French-speaking part of Switzerland, it was also the first railway in the world to climb at a gradient as steep as 1 in 1.8. One of the cars survives at Territet station and another in the Transport Museum in Luzern.

The funicular to Glion links with a station on the line up Rochers-de-Naye (see below). Glion is the starting point for a signed walk of 1–2 hours called the Panoramic Path to the Heights of Caux, where there is a restaurant.

MONTREUX–ROCHERS-DE-NAYE Table 121

This 800mm (2ft 7¹/₂in) rack railway, known as the CF Montreux–Glion–Rochers-de-Naye (MGN), should not be missed. The 55-minute journey and the views from the summit are stupendous, and there is the added attraction of steam haulage on some trains. This was reintroduced in 1992, the railway's centenary. The new locomotive was one of a batch built for mountain railways by SLM in Winterthur. The Swiss Pass is valid as far as Caux; there is a 25% discount on tickets to the summit. Sit on the right.

The rack (Abt system) and steep gradient start as soon as the line leaves the station at Montreux, tunnelling under the town and soon climbing through woods and orchards to a tunnel that describes a semicircle before **Glion**. The reason for the large size of the station at Glion is not simply that this is the railway's headquarters, but also that this was before 1909 the start of the line up Rochers-de-Naye. Until then passengers reached Glion by the funicular from Territet (see above) and had to change trains; a link with Montreux station was then built. It was at Glion in 1926 that the Austrian poet Rainer Maria Rilke died, while attending a clinic.

Numerous walks are signed from Glion, including the Panoramic Path (see section on Glion funicular, above). From Glion, the line turns away from the lake, climbing along the ridge overlooking the deep valley of the Chauderon, on the other side of which the Montreux–Oberland Bernois Railway can be seen climbing to Les Avants. Huge revetments protect the MGN as it turns east, frequently crossing mountain streams and passing piles of neatly stacked logs protected by a sheet of corrugated iron. **Caux** is an old resort, which once had several large hotels. Today they fulfil other purposes. The enormous Caux Palace Hotel, for example, was opened in July 1902 with 350 bedrooms furnished by the Paris branch of Waring & Gillows of Lancaster. The hotel offered lawn tennis, tobogganing, skating, hydro and electric therapy, a telegraph, library and daily concerts. It was patronised by such people as John Rockefeller, the Maharajah of Baroda and the writers Scott Fitzgerald, Edgar Wallace and Kipling. The 1930s Depresssion, followed by World War II, ruined the hotel, forcing its closure. It was bought by a group of Swiss and is now a European centre of Moral Rearmament. Caux is also now a popular skiing centre.

The line climbs through pines in a fairly straight line towards the Dent de Jaman, by which time the tree line has been left behind. From Jaman a footpath known as the 'Riviera's High Road' follows the ridges to Les Pléiades, which takes about 5½ hours. Alternatively there is a shorter walk of 2 hours to Les Avants.

A tunnel takes you into a different world of often bare rock, the line protected by snow shelters and barriers. At this height you may be lucky enough to see chamoix or marmots, and in summer there is a myriad of butterflies. The train approaches the summit along a saddle of rock and describes a semicircle into the station at **Rochers-de-Naye** beside the hotel, discreetly tucked into a fold of the mountain beneath the summit. The view from the small viewing platform on the summit at 2,045m (6,709ft) is spectacular, encompassing the Swiss and French Alps, Lac Léman and even the Jura.

From the station a 220m (722ft) tunnel takes you under the peak to the Plein Roc restaurant with a wall of glass overlooking the views to the south. In bad weather screens descend over the windows and an eight-projector slide presentation shows what you're missing outside. One of many paths descending from the station turns upwards to one of the oldest alpine gardens, La Rambertia, founded in 1896. Allow 30–45 minutes to see the thousand-odd species, some extremely rare. It is about 15 minutes' walk from the station.

Practical information
Glion
Victoria★★★★, Rte de Caux, CH-1823. Tel: 021/963 31 31; fax: 021/963 13 51; email: victoria@worldcom.ch; web: www.relaiscahateaux
Righi Vaudois★★★★, CH-1823. Tel: 021/961 18 81; fax: 021/961 15 12; email: hotel-righi-glionvd@swissonline.ch; web: www.hotelbook.com/static/welcome_28559-html
Des Alpes Vaudoises★★★, Rue de Bugnon, CH-1823. Tel: 021/963 20 76; fax: 021/963/56 94; email: hotelalp@montreux.ch

Caux
Les Rosiers★, Ch de l'Impératrice, CH-1824. Tel: 021/963 61 73; fax: 021/963 61 73.

Hostellerie de Caux, Hauts-de-Caux, CH-1824. Tel: 021/963 76 08; fax: 021/963 25 00; email: hostelcaux@swissonline.ch; web: www.hostel-caux.ch

Rochers-de-Naye

Des Rochers de Naye, CH-1821. Tel: 021/963 74 11; fax: 021/963 86 20.

MONTREUX–ZWEISIMMEN–LENK Table 120

This is one of the best-known and most popular train journeys in Switzerland, reflected in the unique panoramic trains that operate some services. It forms a section of the Golden Pass Express between Zürich and Geneva, and serves some of the country's most popular ski resorts. At Zweisimmen trains connect with the standard-gauge branch from Spiez, while metre-gauge trains have to reverse there to reach Lenk im Simmental. Plans are in hand to lay a third rail between Zweisimmen and Interlaken Ost to enable metre-gauge trains to run all the way from Montreux to Luzern. It has always been a railway for tourists, opening in stages between 1901–5 and powered by electricity from the outset. Sit on the right for preference, though there is little in the choice.

The line is operated by the Montreux–Oberland Bernois Railway (MOB), a company which owns other railways in the Montreux area as well as eight hotels and restaurants. It has a long tradition of running luxury trains for tourists, having the distinction of running the only narrow-gauge Pullman service in Europe from 1931. However, it was a victim of the Depression, and the carriages were sold in 1939 to the Rhaetian Railway on which they still operate. Since the prototype panoramic coach appeared in 1976, the MOB has invested heavily in outstanding air-conditioned coaches, progressively improving the quality from the Panoramic to the Superpanoramic in 1985 and from 1993 the Crystal Panoramic Express, designed by Pininfarina. The train is now called the Golden Pass Panoramic. The trains have driving trailers at each end with the driver seated in a cockpit above a saloon; this allows passengers to enjoy a driver's-eye view of the line ahead (or behind). Reservation of seats in these trains is no longer mandatory, but advance booking is usually vital to secure a seat in the end coaches. The Panoramic stops at Les Avants, Château-d'Oex, Rougemont, Gstaad and Zweisimmen on its way to Lenk; the Crystal Panoramic (to Zweisimmen only) at Château-d'Oex and Gstaad.

There is also a Chocolate Train from Montreux, which visits a cheese factory at Château-d'Oex and a Nestlé chocolate factory at Gruyères-Broc. Stopping trains serve all stations between Montreux, Zweisimmen and Lenk and there are additional trains to various places at each end of the line, such as Les Avants from Montreux and Saanen from Zweisimmen.

Trains begin the 75.5km (47 miles) journey to Lenk in a spiral tunnel, climbing at 1 in 15 to escape the suburbs and reach the vineyards above Montreux. A series of horseshoe curves follows as the train climbs 575m (1,886ft) in height to Les Avants. At **Châtelard** is the 15th-century castle with its massive keep, built as a refuge for local people. The view becomes ever more spectacular as the train gains height; in the reverse direction the view from the summit of the climb is, without hyperbole, breathtaking.

At **Chamby** weekend travellers may be lucky enough to catch a glimpse of a steam train on the preserved line from Blonay. The train twists through more U-shaped curves, flanges squealing, to reach the winter resort of **Les Avants**. Noël Coward took the train to Les Avants in 1959 to look at a chalet that was for sale; he bought it and lived there until his death in 1973. From Les Avants, a funicular ascends every 20 minutes to Sonloup (table 2057), where the first bobsleigh championship was held c1929 though it had been a popular sport when the funicular opened in 1910. A circular 1½-hour walk begins here, known as the Narcissi Path, which is naturally best walked in the spring.

The gradient stiffens through pine and beech woods to the steepest on the entire line, an astonishing 1 in 13.7 – the MOB is entirely operated by adhesion. The train is still climbing as it enters the line's longest tunnel just beyond **Jor**; passing under the Col de Jaman it is 2,424m (2,560yds) long. The summit is reached just before the end of the mostly unlined tunnel, the line emerging at the lonely station of **Les Cases**. The tunnel often marks an abrupt change of weather, the train leaving grey skies on one side to emerge in bright sunshine – or vice versa! The descent from Les Cases is down one of the remotest valleys of the journey, the pasture dotted with only occasional unspoilt chalets linked by ribbons of unpaved tracks. Beyond **Les Sciernes** is one of the sharpest curves of the railway, the line crossing the River Hongrin before it joins the Sarine/Saane.

At the foot of the descent is the junction of **Montbovon** (change for Gruyère and Bulle), which Byron described as 'a pretty, scraggy village, with a wild river and a wooden bridge'. Below the neo-Romanesque Catholic church of St Grat, built in 1896–8, is a group of attractive old houses, one with an inscription listing the owners on its façade.

In places protected by avalanche shelters, the railway climbs through the wooded gorge of the Sarine to **La Tine**, entering the open valley known as the Pays d'Enhaut. After crossing over the Sarine/Saane and passing the tiny Lac du Vernex on the right, the railway reaches **Rossinière**, with some pretty chalets in the square and one of the largest and finest chalets to be found in Vaud. Built in 1754, it has 113 windows and is decorated with carvings, paintings and inscriptions.

The railway loops north away from the river to serve the winter and summer sports resort of **Château d'Oex**. Three churches, all on the right below the line, are passed before reaching the station: the first is the Catholic church, the second the English church of 1902, and beyond that the Reformed church of St Donat which is built on the site of, and probably using the masonry of, the castle from which the town takes its name.

Château d'Oex has made a speciality of hot-air ballooning, and in the last week of January the town hosts the world's leading hot-air championships. Visitors can experience the unique thrill of a balloon flight over the mountains, summer or winter (tel: 026/924 25 20; fax: 026/924 25 26).

Turning left outside the station and walking parallel with the railway, you come to the Pays-d'Enhaut Museum, with some fine reconstructed interiors and displays of local crafts such as lace-making and weaving (open: Tue,

Thu–Fri 10.00–12.00, 14.00–16.30, Sat–Sun 14.00–16.30). There are 250km (156 miles) of waymarked paths in the district, and the tourist office has maps for walkers and mountain bikers.

Close to the railway, beyond Hôtel de la Poste, is the bottom of the two-stage (cablecar and chairlift) cable journey up to La Montagnette (table 2060). Close by is Le Chalet, where demonstrations of cheese-making are given (the tourist office also organises overnight stays in genuine cheese-maker's chalets in the mountains); Le Chalet also contains a model railway and a fondue restaurant.

From the station a bus (table 124.10) makes a mountainous journey via L'Etivaz, where the cheese cellars storing the eponymous cheese can be visited, and the Col-des-Mosses, to the station at Le Sépey (see table 124). This service connects with another bus to continue to Leysin (table 124.14).

The line continues on its hillside shelf with good views across the valley to the right – one of the reasons for the popularity of the journey is the almost continuously high level at which the railway runs, affording far better views than any parallel roads below. A tributary of the Sarine/Saane is crossed by a viaduct just before **Flendruz**, and the end of the French-speaking area is reached at the last station in Vaud, **Rougemont**, the Sarine becoming the Saane.

To the west of this attractive village stands an 11th-century Romanesque church that was once part of a Cluniac priory dissolved in 1555. Concerts are held here as part of the Menuhin Festival (see Saanen below). The choir is 16th-century, the tower 17th-century. Near it is the château, built on the site of an 11th-century castle, but rebuilt several times, most recently after a fire in 1974; it retains a curtain wall punctuated by turrets. On the opposite side of the river, six minutes' walk from the station, is a two-section gondola lift up to La Videmanette (table 2062).

Saanen is another small village of wooden chalets, pronounced overhangs to the eaves being the local characteristic. The village is known in Switzerland for the quality of its Vacherin cheese and for the Menuhin Festival, which is held each year between late July and early September. Although the symphony concerts are held in Gstaad, most of the chamber or solo performances are given in the mid-15th-century church of St Mauritius. In the choir are frescos of the life of Mary and of St Mauritius.

The train bowls along the valley, making the most of the last stretch of fast track before the climbing starts in earnest after the well-known summer and winter sports resort of **Gstaad**. The resort is renowned for attracting the famous, though it is less exclusive than St Moritz and the better for it. Development has been carefully controlled, and the town's hotels are all of chalet style. The tourist office is on Hauptstrasse; turn right on to it from the station. The district around Gstaad has 71 skilifts and 250km (156 miles) of ski runs, mostly for intermediate levels of skill; the ski facilities are covered by the Gstaad Super Ski Pass. There is an exceptionally good sports centre with attractive indoor swimming pool, as well as an outside pool.

The area around Gstaad is known as the Saanenland and is a good centre for walking, the skiing infrastructure being equally useful in other seasons to reach alpine walks, such as the gondola lift to Höhi Wispile (table 2393), 20 minutes' walk from the station. The tourist office produces an excellent leaflet suggesting walks and giving details of the region's transport, including bus and train timetables, and mountain restaurants. Particularly recommended are walks in Lauenental; the pretty village of Lauenen (served by bus, table 120.20) has attractively carved and painted decoration to its 18th-century chalets and an early 16th-century Gothic church. Beyond the village is the tiny Lauenensee, served by some of the buses along the valley, southeast of which is a pair of impressive waterfalls at the head of a small valley, the Geltental.

Gstaad hosts a CinéMusic Festival in March, the Swiss Open Tennis Championships at the beginning of July, and the larger events in the Menuhin Festival and Alpengala, which combine to form a music festival from late July to early September.

From the station there are bus services to Les Diablerets (table 120.15) via Feutersoey and Gsteig.

The climb out of Gstaad is at 1 in 25, the line looping round to cross an imposing three-span truss viaduct that has been repeatedly featured in publicity material since the line opened. Only a few minutes' walk from the station at the small resort of **Schönried** are a chairlift to Horneggli (table 2388) and a two-section gondola to Rellerligrat (table 2389). From Horneggli there is a good walk around the Hornfluh. The summit of the whole line, at 1,275m (4,183ft), is reached before **Saanenmöser**, another small resort.

From there it is a steady descent down through the new Moosbach Tunnel, built after the previous tunnel was filled with debris washed down by a storm in 1983, to the junction for Spiez at **Zweisimmen**. This is the main village in the Simmental, and has a small folk museum at the Kirchstalden (open: Wed, Sat–Sun 10.00–12.00, 14.00–16.30). The mid-15th-century Reformed church of St Maria has late 15th-century frescos, and the village has some decorated wooden houses characteristic of the valley.

Just two minutes' walk, turning left from the station, is the longest gondola in Switzerland, at 5,102m (5,580yds), in two sections, up to Rinderberg (table 2375). There is a good walk back to the village. A bus from the station to Sparenmoos (table 320.20), where there is a restaurant, can be used as part of a lovely walk to or from the small Schwarzsee.

Attractive canopies with carved brackets shelter passengers at the multi-platformed station, at which trains for Lenk have to reverse. The line to Lenk opened in 1912, turning the small agricultural hamlet into a tourist resort. Near the first station, at **Blankenburg**, is a baroque schloss of 1767, built on the site of an older castle, and a covered bridge across the Simme may be seen soon after leaving the station.

The railway parallels an excellent signed bike route all the way to Lenk which is often on the other side of the river, the railway remaining on the east bank after crossing it on the outskirts of Zweisimmen. Evidence of the area's forestry can be seen at some stations such as **St Stephan**, where the church has a Romanesque nave and 17th-century wooden tunnel-vaulted roof.

On the approach to **Stöckli** a wonderful range of distant snow-covered mountains comes into view, growing as the train nears journey's end at **Lenk**, where the station is close to the centre. This summer and winter resort is attractively situated in a bowl of mountains dominated by the Wildstrubel at 3,243m (10,639ft) – 'a grand termination to the valley' as Baedeker puts it. Its location at the head of a valley means that it does not suffer from through traffic and is therefore quieter than most resorts. It offers a surprising variety of activities and events, and was a favourite resort of Field Marshal Montgomery, who stayed here (at Hotel Wildstrubel) in 1937 and again after the war.

The resort achieved recognition through its 'well fitted-up sulphur-baths and grounds', as Baedeker noted in 1895 (in those days Lenk was reached by an eight-hour journey by diligence from Thun). Astonishingly Lenk had already been a spa for over two centuries by then, having been authorised by Bern in 1689 to set up a spa to exploit the strongest alpine sulphur springs in Europe. Even today 30% of summer guests use the sulphur spa, which has the usual options of solarium, massages, beauty parlour and fitness training as well as specialist treatments.

There is a wide choice of sporting activities with indoor and open-air swimming pools, sports hall, open-air ice rink, tennis, fishing, river rafting, mountain biking and walking. Bike and walking route maps are available from the tourist office, and there is an alpine flower walk (Jun–Sep only) with English-language guide. During the winter there are 51 cablecars and chairlifts in the local skiing area, which includes Adelboden. An arrangement exists whereby a six-day pass entitles skiers to one free day ticket from a neighbouring area, such as Gstaad. This opens up access to 180 lifts and 610km (381 miles) of runs. The local area has a good balance between the three grades of ski runs, and there are also good cross-country routes. For those who eschew skis, 30km (19 miles) of paths are cleared for winter walks.

One of the finest walks in the area is to the impressive Simmenfälle and Siebenbrunnen, the seven springs, which is the source of the Simme; a bus from/to the station (table 320.27) can be used for one leg of the walk. This bus also takes you to the cablecar up to Metsch (table 2382). A two-section gondola to Betelberg (table 2380) is 10 minutes' walk from the station. There are also buses along a serpentine road to Bühlberg (table 320.25) and to Iffigenalp (table 320.26), which provides access to the highest waterfall in the area, the Iffigfall.

Sport is not the only attraction. For ten nights in July the town is given over to New Orleans jazz, with bands and guest musicians from other countries in Europe and from the United States. In late August/early September, the Summer Academy of Music brings together up to 200 students from all over the world who attend classes on individual instruments, workshops and lectures by visiting professors. Concerts are held every night.

Lenk makes a point of catering for families, with babysitting and kindergarten services, and even toy rental! It has also pioneered a concept for people with impaired hearing, providing a variety of inductive hearing systems in relevant buildings, training courses and staff trained in effective communication.

Practical information

Les Avants

De Sonloup★★ (H), Col de Sonloup, CH-1833. Tel: 021/964 34 31; fax: 021/964 34 80. Helioda★★, Rte des Narcisses, CH-1833. Tel: 021/964 39 50; fax: 021/964 39 50.

Montbovon

De la Gare, CH-1835. Tel: 026/928 10 88; fax: 026/928 10 88.

Rossinière

De Ville★, CH-1836. Tel: 026/924 65 40; fax: 026/924 79 52.

Château-d'Oex

TO – La Place, CH-1837. Tel: 026/924 25 25; fax: 026/924 25 26; email: chateau-doex@bluewin.ch; web: www.chateau-doex.ch Open: Mon–Fri 08.00–12.00, 14.00–18.00, Sat 09.00–12.00, 14.00–17.00.

Numerous hotels; close to the station are
Beau-Séjour★★★, CH-1837. Tel: 026/924 74 23; fax: 026/924 58 06.
De la Poste, CH-1837. Tel: 026/924 63 88; fax: 026/924 63 88.

Rougemont

TO – Bâtiment communal, CH-1838. Tel: 026/925 83 83; fax: 026/925 89 67; email: ot.rougemont@com.mcnet.ch; web: www.rougemont.ch Open: Mon–Fri 08.00–12.00, 14.00–17.00, Sat 10.00–12.00; in season, Mon–Fri –18.30, Sat 10.00–12.00, 16.00–18.00.

A hotel close to the station is
Valrose★★, Place de la Gare, CH-1838. Tel: 026/925 81 46; fax: 026/925 88 54.

Saanen

TO – Gstaad Saanenland Tourismus, CH-3792. Tel: 033/748 81 60; fax: 033/748 81 69; email: gst@gstaad.ch; web: www.gstaad.ch Open: Mon–Sat 08.00–12.00, 14.00–18.00, Sat –16.00.

Numerous hotels; close to the station are
Saanerhof★★★, CH-3792. Tel: 033/744 15 15; fax: 033/74; email: saanerhof@gstaad.ch; web: www.gstaad.ch/saanerhof
Bahnhof, CH-3792. Tel: 033/744 14 22.

Gstaad

TO – CH-3780. Tel: 033/748 81 81; fax: 033/748 81 83; web: www.gstaad.ch Open: Mon–Fri 08.30–18.30, Sat 09.00–18.00, Sun 11.00–15.00.

Numerous hotels; close to the station are
Bernerhof★★★★, Bahnhofstrasse, CH-3780 Tel: 033/748 88 44; fax: 033/748 88 40; email: bernerhof@gstaad.ch; web: www.gstaad.ch/bernerhof

Christiania★★★★, Hauptstrasse 1, CH-3780. Tel: 033 744 51 21; fax: 033/744 71 09; email: christiania@bluewin.ch; web: www.gstaad.ch/hotelchristiania
Sporthotel Victoria★★★, CH-3780. Tel: 033/748 44 22; fax: 033/748 44 20; email: sporthotel.victoria@bluewin.ch

Very expensive, but an historic hotel and the best in Gstaad is
Palace★★★★★ (H), CH-3780. Tel: 033/748 50 00; fax: 033/748 50 01; email: palace@gstaad.ch; web: www.palace.ch

Schönried
Bahnhof★★★, Hauptstrasse, CH-3778. Tel: 033/744 42 42; fax: 033/744 61 42; email: bruno.kernen@gstaad.ch; web: www.bruno-kernen.ch

Saanenmöser
Bahnhof★★, Hauptstrasse, CH-3777. Tel: 033/744 15 06; fax: 033/744 72 88; email: bahnhof.saanenmoeser@bluewin.ch

Zweisimmen
TO – Lenkstrasse, CH-3770. Tel: 033/72/2 11 33; fax: 033/722 25 85. Open: 08.00–12.00, 13.30–18.00, Sat 08.00–12.00, 13.30–17.00.

A hotel opposite the station in quiet position is
Post★★★ (H), CH-3770. Tel: 033/722 12 28; fax: 033/722 13 75.

Lenk
TO – Rawylstrasse, CH-3775. Tel: 033/733 31 31; fax: 033/733 20 27. Open: Mon–Fri 08.30–12.00, 14.00–18.00, Sat 08.30–12.00, 14.00–17.00.

All hotel guests at Lenk receive a Visitors Card, which gives discounts to a wide range of goods and services, including bike hire and free use of bus transport in the town.

Numerous hotels; close to the station are
Wildstrubel★★★★ (H), CH-3775. Tel: 033/736 31 11; fax: 033/736 31 51; email: wildstrubel@tcnet.ch; web: www.forum.ch/wildstrubel-len.ch
Sternen★★, CH-3775. Tel: 033/733 15 09; fax: 033/733 30 88.

Bicycle hire from Les Avants, Château d'Oex, Gstaad, Zweisimmen and Lenk stations.

MONTBOVON–GRUYERES–BULLE–PALEZIEUX Table 256
A metre-gauge line linking several major tourist towns, the first section through the district known as Haute Gruyère.

Leaving Montbovon, the railway careers down the streets of the town before reaching its own right of way on the outskirts. On the right is a small lake, one of several through which the River Saane/Sarine runs. **Lessoc** is a lovely village with an onion-domed fountain of 1796 at its centre; some of the farms in the village are decorated with poyas, naïve paintings of the celebrated transhumance of cows.

Beyond **Neirivue**, the river is just to the right of the railway for some miles, and a frequent sight on the parallel road is cows on their way to or from milking, cowbells clattering. The village of **Grandvillard** has many fine 17th-century houses and a 1930s church. Beyond **Enney**, with its wood-ceilinged early 17th-century church, railway and river part company as the former turns to the west into a narrower, more wooded valley.

It is best to try to visit **Gruyères** out of season. This deservedly popular medieval town is overrun in the summer months, when the town receives the majority of its one million anual visitors. An alternative is to stay the night to savour the atmosphere once the day visitors have left, but the limited accommodation puts a premium on the price of rooms. Needless to say cars have no place in such a town and are confined to the foot of the hill on which the walled town is built. It is a ten-minute walk from the station to the old town.

The town's walls and towers date from the 12th to 15th centuries and encompass an oval-shaped marketplace surrounded by some well-designed houses, mostly of the 15th–17th centuries. In summer the scene resembles a flower show in its profusion of window boxes and tubs. Older than most is the 14th-century Maison de Chalamala, which is believed to have belonged to a contemporary court jester at the castle. The church of St Théodule was founded in the 13th century but the tower dates from 1680, the choir from 1731 and the nave from 1860. The views from the town and castle are magnificent.

The castle was built by the 12th century for the Counts of Gruyère who held sway over the area until 1544 when the indebted Michael I was forced to sell the estates. The castle became the residence of the bailiffs and then prefects of Fribourg before being sold to the Bovy family in 1848. It was bought back by the canton of Fribourg in 1938 and opened to the public.

Of the original castle only the 13th-century dungeon and round Savoy keep remain, a fire in 1493 having destroyed the living quarters. It was reconstructed by the widow of Louis II; he had fought on the Swiss side at the Battle of Murten (1476) and brought back as booty the three copes bearing the arms of defeated Charles the Bold which now hang in the Burgundy Room. On the ground floor are the guardroom and kitchen. On the first floor are Gobelin tapestries in the Count's Room, landscape paintings by Corot and original 17th-century painted décor in the Bailiff's Room. The second floor has some good pieces of Louis XV furniture. The Arsenal Room is used for temporary exhibitions, and the lovely Chapel of St John has 15th-century stained glass. (Open daily: Jun–Sep 09.00–19.00, Mar–May and Oct 09.00–12.00, 13.00–17.00, Nov–Feb Mon–Fri 09.30–12.00, 13.30–16.00, Sat–Sun 10.30–12.00, 13.30–17.00.)

The name of Gruyères is famous because of cheese, though it is the area rather than the town that lends its name to the product. Opposite the station is a dairy open to visitors free of charge. Although open daily from 08.00 to 19.00 (18.00 in winter), production takes place usually from about 09.00 to 11.30 and 13.00 to 16.00. Since it takes 12 litres of milk to produce 1kg of cheese, it's no wonder that the dairy uses 13,000 litres of milk a day. A tape/slide show with English commentary illustrates the process in which milk is warmed and stirred before rennet is added to curdle the milk. The firm mass is cut into tiny granules that float in whey before being pumped into round presses for compaction. A day's submersion in a saline bath is followed by ripening, which can take anything from four months to a year. (Tel: 026/921 84 00; web: www.lamaisondugruyere.ch) A bus from Gruyères station runs to Moléson-Village (table 254.35) where there is another dairy open to visitors (daily: mid-May–mid-Oct 09.30–19.00; tel: 026/921 10 44). Only a minute from the bus stop is the small cablecar up Le Moléson (table 2045).

On a rock at **La Tour-de-Trême** stands a large 13th-century tower which protected the village founded by the Counts of Gruyère. On the outskirts of **Bulle** the branch line from Broc trails in on the right. Change here for Broc and Romont. For the town of Bulle see table 254.

A few miles after leaving Bulle, the line turns to the southwest into the area known as the Veveyse, in which the largest town is **Châtel-St-Denis**. The neo-Gothic church of St Denis was built in 1872–6. Near the church are the remains of a 13th-century castle, which was incorporated in 18th-century alterations. A walking map showing signed routes in the area is available from the tourist office. A bus from the station serves the winter resort of Les Paccots (table 256.10) which has a network of skilifts.

Practical information
Gruyères

TO – [chapel in main street], CH-1663. Tel: 026/921 10 30; fax: 026/921 38 50; web: www.gruyeres.ch Open: Mon–Fri 09.30–12.00, 13.30–17.00, Sat–Sun (May–Sep) 09.30–12.00, 13.30–17.00.

Hostellerie des Chevalliers***, CH-1663. Tel: 026/921 19 33; fax: 026/921 25 52.
Hostellerie St-Georges*** (H), CH-1663. Tel: 026/921 83 00; fax: 026/921 83 39.
Hôtel de Ville**, CH-1663. Tel: 026/921 24 24; fax: 026/921 36 28.
Fleur-de-Lys**, CH-1663. Tel: 026/921 21 08; fax: 026/921 36 05.

Châtel-St-Denis/Les Paccots

TO – Les Paccots, CH-1619. Tel: 021/948 84 56; fax: 021/948 07 66; email: office.tourisme@les-paccots.ch; web: www.les-paccots.ch Open: Sep–Jun Mon–Sat 09.00–12.00, Jul–Aug Mon–Fri 09.00–12.00, 15.00–17.00.

Corbetta*, CH-1619. Tel: 021/948 71 20; fax: 021/948 72 00.

Bicycle hire from Bulle and Palézieux stations.

BULLE–BROC Table 253
A metre-gauge branch line that serves the resort of Broc on the south tip of Lac de la Gruyère.

Broc-Village is best known for the Nestlé chocolate factory founded in 1898 by Alexandre Cailler. Factory visits have had to be replaced by a film. At the entrance to the village is a 14th-century fortified house, Château-d'En Bas. Near Lake Gruyère is Electrobloc, an information centre on energy (open: Mar–Dec, Mon–Fri 08.00–18.00, Sat 09.00–17.00). A bus from the station goes up the east side of the lake to Corbières (table 254.10), where there is a château in the centre of the village.

From the station a bus service goes to the beautifully situated village of Charmey (and on to Jaun) (table 254.20) past the artficial Lac de Montsalvens. In the woods above stand the impressive ruins of the 12th-century castle of the same name that was abandoned in 1671. The chalet that houses the tourist office at Charmey also contains a museum of rural artefacts, particularly those relating to the dairy industry and cheese-making, weapons, flora and local history (open: Tue–Fri 14.00–18.00, Sat 14.00–16.00, Sun 14.00–18.00). Two minutes from the bus stop is a chairlift to Vounetse (table 2042). At Jaun is a ruined castle, destroyed in 1407.

A second bus service (table 254.21), which begins at Bulle station, calls at Jaun before proceeding over the Jaunpass to Boltigen station on the Spiez–Zweisimmen line (see table 320).

Practical information
Charmey
TO – Bâtiment du Musée, CH-1637. Tel: 026/927 14 98; fax: 026/927 23 95; email: office.tourisme@charmey.ch; web: www.charmey.ch Open: Mon–Fri 08.00–12.00, 14.00–18.00, Sat –16.00.

Geneva–MONTREUX–AIGLE–Brig Tables 100/100.1
This section of the main line between Geneva and Brig covers the transformation from the eastern end of Lac Léman to the fertile Rhône valley, along which orchards of apples and pears cover the broad valley floor while vines climb the eastern slopes. It passes close to the world-famous Castle of Chillon, immortalised by Byron's poem.

The first station, **Territet**, is a suburb of Montreux from which two funiculars ascend, to Glion and Mont-Fleuri (see above). **Veytaux-Chillon** is the station adjacent to the castle, but there is a delightful footpath along the lakeshore from west of Clarens through Montreux to the castle and beyond.

Even if Byron had not written *The Prisoner of Chillon*, the castle would still be the outstanding attraction it has become; not only is its position on a peninsula strikingly picturesque, but it is one of Europe's best preserved examples of medieval military architecture. The rock on which it is built has supported a settlement since the Bronze Age, the Romans fortified it, and the defences were developed in the 9th century. The present castle was begun in the mid-13th century by Peter II of Savoy (London's Savoy takes its name from him) who employed the military architect Pierre Mainier to create strong defences on the side of the road and mountain with the residential parts overlooking the lake.

The castle was held by the lords of Savoy until 1536 when an army of 6,000 Bernoise and some vessels from Geneva forced the castle's surrender. It was this that effected the release of Chillon's most famous prisoner, the prior François Bonivard (1493–1570). A supporter of the Reformation and of Geneva in its struggles with the Catholic dukes of Savoy, Bonivard was imprisoned in Chillon in 1530, spending four of the six years incarcerated in the dungeons, chained to a pillar. It was his plight, and the poem Bonivard wrote ('Lamentation in Captivity at Chillon'), that inspired Byron to write his poem following a visit to the castle with Shelley in 1816.

After the seizure by the Bernois until the early 18th century, Chillon was the residence of the Bailiff of Vevey. The castle was then used as a prison and hospital before being restored at the end of the last century, having become one of the most visited, painted and engraved castles in the world. Flaubert waxed lyrical about seeing Byron's name carved in the stone of the dungeon; he was deluded – it is a forgery.

There is an excellent English-language guide to the castle, which has 28 rooms and areas open to visitors, with a fine banqueting hall and collection of armour. The castle can be very crowded in summer, but it is justly popular. The best viewpoint of the castle was probably from the lake until marred by one of the country's most insensitively sited motorways (regrettably it is not without serious competition), which rises on piers out of the wood behind the castle. There is a landing stage by the castle for lake steamers. (Open: hours vary slightly almost every month, extending gradually from core hours of 10.00–12.00, 13.30–16.00 to 09.00–1815 in high season.)

Villeneuve was for centuries an important staging post on the route from Italy to Gaul over the Grand St Bernard Pass. As late as 1800 Napoleon used it as his advance base for getting the Army of Reserve across the Alps at the start of what became the Marengo campaign. Remains of fortifications can be seen near the church.

At Le Bouveret, along the shore towards the French border and where the Rhône enters Lac Léman, is the Swiss Vapeur Parc: up to ten trains at a time are in use on 1.5km (1,640yds) of superbly laid-out 5in- and 7$\frac{1}{4}$in- gauge track, with scale buildings, tunnels, viaducts and an impressive variety of locomotives based on prototypes from different countries. Children (and most adults) are invariably reluctant to leave. (Open: mid-Mar–mid-May, Wed, Sat–Sun 13.30–18.00; mid-May–mid-Sep, daily 10.00–18.00; mid-Sep–Oct, weekdays 13.30–18.00, Sat–Sun 10.00–18.00.)

Unfortunately Vapeur Parc is no longer easy to reach by rail since most trains on the branch line between Monthey and St Gingolph, serving Bouveret, have been replaced by buses. The easiest way to reach it from the west is by steamer, since it is only a short walk to the Steam Park from the pier at Bouveret. The more difficult alternative is to take a bus from Villeneuve station (table 100.20) and change at Vouvry (walking from the stop at the post office to the station) to catch the replacement bus (table 130 of the railway timetable).

There is also a steam train, the 'Rive-Bleu Express', over the standard-gauge line from Bouveret to St Gingolph and across the border to the well-known source of bottled water, Evian. The scenery along the 22km (13$\frac{3}{4}$ miles) is superb, the train running along the lake for most of the way interrupted by the odd tunnel and cutting. The trains are hauled by a SLM-built 0-6-0 tank engine of 1893 and operate on Sundays from the end of May to mid-September and on Tuesday, Thursday and Saturday in July and August (tel: 024/481 51 21; fax: 024/481 43 40).

As Lac Léman comes to an end, there is a sudden transition as the line enters the broad Rhône valley, the hills to the west lined with vineyards and orchards of apples and pears. For **Aigle**, see Chapter 19.

Practical information
Villeneuve

TO – Grand-Rue 10, CH-1844. Tel: 021/960 22 86; fax: 021/968 10 13; email: tourism@villeneuve.ch Open: Mon 13.30–18.00, Tue–Fri 09.00–12.30, 13.30–18.00, Sat 09.00–12.30.

Du Port★★★, Rue de Quai 6, CH-1844. Tel: 021/960 41 45; fax: 021/960 39 67; email: hotel@duport.ch; web: www.duport.ch

Du Quai★★, Quai 4, CH-1844. Tel: 021/960 18 81; fax: 021/960 17 96.

Château de Chillon beside Lac Léman to the southeast of Montreux

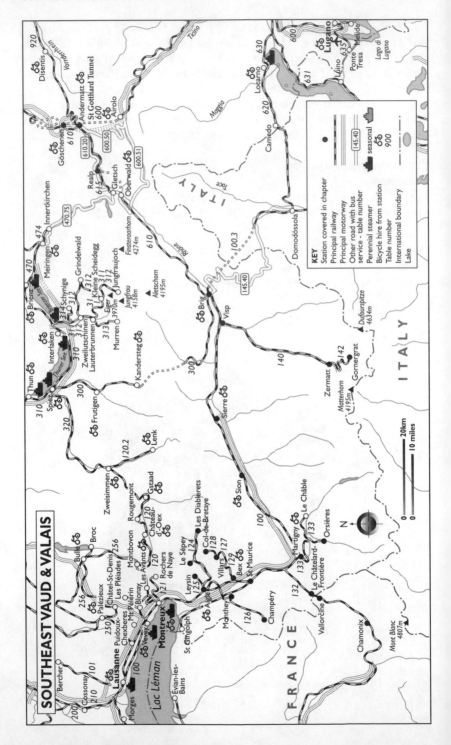

SOUTHEAST VAUD & VALAIS

KEY

- ● Station covered in chapter
- Principal railway
- Principal motorway
- Other road with bus service - table number
- Perennial steamer
- Bicycle hire from station
- 145.40 Table number
- International boundary
- Lake
- seasonal
- 900

Southeast Vaud and the Valais

This region contains many of Switzerland's best-known ski resorts, mostly situated in the mountains that line the Rhône valley and easily reached by railway, cablecar and postal bus. One-fifth of the canton of Valais is covered by glacier so it is little wonder that there should be such good skiing, served by an extensive network of cablecars and skilifts. Fifty-one of the mountains in the canton are over 4,000m (13,000ft) high. It is also one of the finest areas for walking, with tens of thousands of kilometres of paths.

The area produces the largest quantity of Swiss wines, and the regional dish of raclette (melted cheese with potatoes) is found in many restaurants. The Valais has one of the lowest rainfall rates amongst the Swiss cantons, and the need to bring water to the vines and other crops has created a feature found in many valleys; the *Bisses* are irrigation channels that were created as long ago as the 13th century. Some are in extraordinarily vertiginous locations, and many are in such attractive settings that they are often followed by walkers' trails.

AIGLE

This centre of viticulture is a major junction, the yard outside and to the east of the main line station being the start of three metre-gauge railways that serve resorts in the mountains above the Rhône valley. Each has a very different character, both scenically and in the resorts at their terminus – Leysin, Les Diablerets and Champéry. Sometimes pulling a four-wheel van for post and newspapers, the trains play an important transport role in valleys whose roads are slow and dangerous in winter. The three branches from Aigle, and the line from Bex–Villars, are marketed by Transport Publics du Chablais, which offers a Regional Pass (see Chapter 3).

The town of Aigle dates back to Roman times and was held by Savoy from 1076 until the Bernese captured the town and destroyed the 11th-century castle in 1475. After being rebuilt the castle was the residence of the governor until 1798, becoming a prison until 1972. The following year work began on its restoration and conversion into a magnificent museum of the vine and wine, with some of the state rooms adapted for dinners. The museum looks at the industry's history, equipment, bottles, barrels and the position of wine in society using reconstructed rooms as well as displays (open: Apr–Jun, Sep–Oct, Tue–Sun 10.00–12.30, 14.00–18.00; Jul–Aug, Tue–Sun

10.00–18.00). The castle itself is one of the most picturesque in the canton, situated on the outskirts of the town surrounded by vines and a vast 17th-century barn.

The town itself has a pedestrianised centre, and the medieval German Reformed church of St James was where the famous Reformer Guillaume Farel (whose statue stands beside the Collegiate Church at Neuchâtel) preached when he lived in Aigle. The unusual arcades of the attractive alley named Rue de Jérusalem should not be missed.

Practical information
Bicycle hire from Aigle station.

AIGLE–LEYSIN Table 125
Serving the summer and winter sports resort of Leysin, the line is the shortest of the three private railways from Aigle, at 6.2km (4 miles).

For anyone unfamiliar with street-running trams, the line to Leysin will be an eye-opener in the way the train glides through the streets of Aigle before a horseshoe bend brings it to the railway's depot. Here it reverses, engages the rack and begins the fierce climb through vineyards and then forest to **Leysin**.

This was a completely isolated village, accessible only by footpath until a road was built in 1875. Its people were largely self-sufficient, growing nearly all their food and even making wine. Their long life-expectancy came to the notice of the British economist Thomas Malthus who devoted six pages of his *Essay on the Principle of Population* to the village. Its healthy climate and reputation attracted people in search of a cure, and the first large hotels were clinics, especially for those suffering from tuberculosis; the large balconies on which beds could be wheeled and protective glass screens can still be seen on many of Leysin's buildings. Oskar Kokoschka came here in 1909, painting a view of the Dents du Midi.

The railway opened in 1900 to Leysin-Feydey, being extended 15 years later to the present terminus at Grand Hôtel. During World War II Leysin was one of the places where British servicemen who managed to escape to Switzerland were interned. It was only after the war that Leysin became a major winter sports centre with the construction of chairlifts and cablecars. In 1962 the American School moved to Leysin, boosting demand for the excellent sports facilities the town has progressively developed. Amongst them, and ten minutes' walk from the station, are gondola lifts up the Berneuse (table 2070) and to Mayen (table 2071).

Plans are in hand for a 3.87km (2½ miles) extension of the railway from the Grand Hôtel to the Berneuse where it would terminate in an underground station beneath the Kuklos (Greek for turning) revolving restaurant, which is situated on the peak of the Berneuse at 2,048m (6,719ft) above sea level and provides a wonderful panorama of the surrounding Alps in its 90-minute revolution. The restaurant is said to have been designed to mirror the shape of two nearby mountains, the Tour Mayern and Tour d'Ai, in order to blend into the natural surroundings; some visitors may feel the simple structures of earlier generations, using a local stone, do less to announce their presence.

Practical information
Leysin
TO – Place Large, CH-1854. Tel: 024/494 22 44; fax: 024/494 16 16; email: tourism@leysin.ch; web: www.leysin.ch Open: Mon–Fri 08.00–21.00, Sat–Sun 09.00–21.00.

Numerous hotels; close to the station is
Classic★★★★, CH-1854. Tel: 024/493 06 06; fax: 024/493 06 93; email: classic.hotel@leysin.ch; web: www.leysin.ch

AIGLE–LES DIABLERETS Table 124
Probably the most scenic of the three lines from Aigle, it serves the smallest population and, despite the gradients, the climb through the Ormont valley is made without rack assistance. The cablecar journeys from the winter and summer sports resort of Les Diablerets are particularly impressive. Sit on the left.

Like the line to Leysin, the railway to Les Diablerets leaves Aigle through the streets, passing, even in the town, tiny stone-walled areas of vines, as though no patch of ground can be wasted that might produce grapes for the celebrated white wines that Aigle *vignerons* produce. Shortly after the station it crosses the line to Champéry at a right angle on the level. As soon as the railway's depot is passed on the right, the castle comes into view. The railway describes a series of horseshoe curves to gain height, affording marvellous views of three sides of the castle.

A tunnel leads into the thickly wooded, steep-sided valley of the Grande-Eau, the railway keeping to its southern flank except where it crosses the river on a long bridge to reach Le Sépey. Passing through pine and beech with sheer rock cuttings, the drop to the valley floor becomes progressively more spectacular. Small mountain farms are linked by paths, some discreetly signed, as from **Les Fontanelles**.

Les Planches is a junction, though served by only a tiny hut. Here alternate trains proceed to the small resort of **Le Sépey** where they reverse, return to Les Planches and proceed up to Les Diablerets; the other trains are met at Les Planches by a postbus for Le Sépey, the train proceeding directly to Les Diablerets. From Le Sépey station a bus runs to Château d'Oex over the Col des Moses (table 124.10).

Streams tumble down from side valleys to join the Grande-Eau as the line drops down to **Les Aviolats**, after which the valley narrows before the first skilifts are seen at **Vers-l'Eglise**. The lovely church after which the village is named was built c1456 with a square stone tower, but was altered in the 18th century. The line drops down further to **Les Diablerets**, where the station is close to the unspoilt village centre. In summer the resort offers various sports such as climbing, tennis, swimming, riding, rafting and mountain biking.

There are numerous good walks: to Col de Bretaye in 3 hours 20 minutes, Gryon in 4 hours 40 minutes and L'Etivaz (boots essential) in 5 hours 20 minutes, for example.

The bus from the station to Gstaad (table 120.15) stops at Col-du-Pillon for the three-section gondola and cablecar up to the Glacier-des-Diablerets (table 2085); this should not be missed – the views are exceptionally fine, and there is almost year-round skiing at this height (3,000m, 9,843ft). The glacier is also served by a two-section cablecar that comes up from Reusch (table 2398), which is on the same bus route. Only six minutes' walk from Les Diablerets station is the gondola lift to Isenau (table 2080), and there is a bus over the Col de la Croix to Villars (table 127.15).

In winter Les Diablerets offers 120km (75 miles) of varied ski runs with 50 lifts, skating and curling rinks and an indoor swimming pool.

From Les Diablerets you can experience what it is like to build and sleep in an igloo. A bus from the town goes to the cablecar in the Pillon Pass from which you ascend to 3,000m (9,843ft). Guides take you across the glacier to the Quille du Diable (Devil's Bowling Skittle) where you are instructed in the art of ice construction, with the incentive of having to spend a night in the result. A traditional alpine meal helps to fend off the cold before bed, and the trek down after breakfast takes in the beauties of the Martisberg nature reserve. Details from the tourist office.

Practical information
Les Diablerets

TO – Rue de la Gare, CH-1865. Tel: 024/492 33 58; fax: 024/492 23 48 email: diablerets@bluewin.ch; web: www.alpes.ch/diablerets Open: Mon–Sat 08.30–12.30, 15.00–18.00, Sun 09.00–12.30; high season Mon–Sun 08.30–18.30.

Numerous hotels, though none is adjacent to the station. Within five minutes' walk are
Grand Hotel Les Diablerets★★★★, CH-1865. Tel: 024/492 35 51; fax: 024/492 23 91; email: grandhotel.diableret@worldcom.ch
Le Chamois★★★, Rue de la Gare, CH-1865. Tel: 024/492 26 53; fax: 024/492 26 06.
Auberge de la Poste★ (H), CH-1865. Tel: 024/492 31 24; fax: 024/492 12 68; email: auberge_tfp@bluewin.ch

Opposite the station, Restaurant Le Terminus has excellent local dishes, such as wild mushrooms.

AIGLE–CHAMPERY Table 126

The principal place on the line is the industrial town of Monthey, where the train reverses to head up the Val d'Illiez through which runs La Vieze. The Strub rack system is employed on the steeper sections to the ski resort at the terminus. Sit on the right.

Crossing on the level the line to Les Diablerets soon after leaving Aigle, the train for Champéry runs alongside the road for much of the way to Monthey. Above **St-Triphon-Village** are the substantial remains of a ?12th-century castle destroyed in 1476 during the Burgundian wars. Just to the north are the ruins of an 11th–14th-century chapel.

The line climbs sharply up to the attractive village of **Ollon**, where the Reformed church has a 15th-century frieze depicting the apostles. From the post office in Ollon a bus goes up to Panex (table 126.10) where the remains of Switzerland's first salt mine, operated between 1554 and 1797, can still be seen, including the Maison des Salines.

Dropping down, the railway traverses the Rhône valley, crossing the Geneva–Brig railway and the river which forms the boundary between the cantons of Vaud and Valais. Near these crossings an extraordinary Italianate villa can be seen to the right perched on a large outcrop of rock. After crossing over the line to St Gingolph, the railway turns abruptly south along the main street of **Collombey**, overlooked by the Monastery de Bernardine. The 17th-century buildings were built on to the keep of a 13th-century castle.

The train enters the modern terminus at **Monthey**, passing the railway's depot, which also maintains its buses. Near the station is a château rebuilt in the 17th century incorporating a medieval tower; it now houses a museum about old Monthey (open: Thu 14.30–17.00). The town also has several interesting defensive buildings, including an arsenal and a walled residence in Avenue du Crochetan.

The train reverses (do not change sides – the best views are now to the left) and swings west to engage the rack and climb steeply out of the town to reach the Val d'Illiez, along which it holds to the west bank at a height that provides good views for most of the way to Champéry. Just before **Hôpital (Monthey)** on the right is a huge rock precariously balanced on another with wedges to prevent it from moving. Near **Croix-du-Nant** is an attractive small church with tiny bell tower. Beyond the station is a viaduct across the Val de Morgins which joins the main valley at this point. Morgins is a ski resort close to the French border, reached by a bus (table 126.25) that starts at Monthey station and calls at **Troistorrents** station before tackling the hairpin bends up to Morgins at 1,400m (4,593ft).

Glorious views of the Dents du Midi can be seen to the left, and the chalets thin out as the valley sides steepen, those on the opposite side being reached by zig-zag tracks. On the right before **Fayot** is a lovely old bridge with the characteristic shrine incorporated into a parapet. **Val d'Illiez** is a picturesque village with ornately carved decoration to the chalet balconies; its white-rendered Catholic church has a distinctive spire to the façade tower. A bus ascends from Val d'Illiez to the tiny village of Champoussin (table 126.35). Before **La Cour** there are stupendous views down to the river hundreds of metres below, though the valley is wooded and the views in summer are more limited.

The station at **Champéry** was rebuilt in the mid-1990s, the line being slightly extended to incorporate the cablecar station to Planachaux (table 2110), from where there are marvellous views of the Dents du Midi, Dents Blanche and other ranges. Many other lifts on the slopes to the west of the resort cater principally for skiers capable of intermediate runs.

Practical information
Champéry

TO – CH-1874. Tel: 024/479 20 20; fax: 024/479 20 21. Open: Mon–Sun 08.00–12.00, 14.00–18.00.

Numerous hotels. None is adjacent to the station. Within 10 minutes' walk are Beau-Séjour★★★, CH-1874. Tel: 024/479 17 01; fax: 024/479 23 06. De Champéry★★★, Grand Rue, CH-1874. Tel: 024/479 10 71; fax: 024/479 14 02. Suisse★★★, Grand Rue, CH-1874. Tel: 024/479 07 07; fax: 024/479 07 09. La Rose des Alpes★★, CH-1874. Tel: 024/479 12 18; fax: 024/479 17 74.

Geneva–AIGLE–MARTIGNY–Brig Tables 100/100.1

This fast stretch of the main line runs almost north–south, paralleling the Rhône once south of Bex. It is best to keep the eyes on the valley slopes and mountains beyond, as industrial activity is evident along the valley floor for much of the remaining journey to Brig. The railways that branch off the Rhône valley are all more attractive.

The first station, at **Bex**, is the junction for the delightful rack railway to Villars. The station is on the outskirts of the town, which can be reached by trains to Villars or by the delightful Bex–Bévieux tramway (see below).

Soon after crossing the Rhône the railway reaches **St Maurice**. Tradition has it that the warrior-saint Maurice was martyred here for refusing to fight fellow Christians. The abbey named after him was built on the site of a 4th-century chapel erected on the tomb by St Theodore, first bishop of the Valais, and is the oldest Christian site in the country. A monastery was founded in 515 by the Burgundian King Sigismund, the kings residing in the town until the ninth century. The monastery became an Augustinian possession in 1128. Situated in the north of the town, the abbey has been repeatedly rebuilt but contains several important examples of ecclesiastical art.

In the castle is the cantonal museum of military history, focusing on the development of arms, uniforms and regimental colours from 1815 to the present (open: Tue–Sun 10.00–12.00, 14.00–18.00).

In 1863 a huge underground lake fed by a waterfall was discovered at St Maurice. The Grotte aux Fées is open to visitors, but wear a pullover – it's cold 914m (3,000ft) inside the rock. (Open: daily, mid-Mar–Jun, Sep–mid-Nov 10.00–18.00, Jul–Aug 09.00–19.00. Rest of the year by reservation. Tel: 024/485 10 45.)

The approach to **Martigny** is heralded by the cylindrical keep of the castle at La Batiaz on a rock to the right of the train. Situated on an elbow of the Rhône and at its junction with the Drance valley that leads to the Great St Bernard Pass, Martigny has been an important crossroads for 2,000 years. Little remains of the Roman capital of the region, except for the foundations of an elliptical ampitheatre for 5,000 spectators (see below). Christianity arrived c300, and the first bishopric in Switzerland was established here.

Previous page The Swiss National Museum in Zürich is housed in a neo-Gothic building finished in 1898. (AL)

Above The village of Mürren is built on a ledge overlooking the massif of the Eiger, Mönch and Jungfrau. (AL)

Right The *Stadt Luzern* is the most modern of the five paddle steamers on Lake Luzern, being built in 1929. (ST)

Below The Chapel Bridge (Kapellbrücke) is only a few minutes' walk from Luzern station and one of Switzerland's best-known landmarks. (AL)

Above Switzerland's mountain railways are an indispensable part of the skiing infrastructure. This is the Wengernalpbahn to Kleine Scheidegg. (ST)

Left Stein am Rhein is an architectural gem, with many oriel windows and painted façades. (AL)

Below left The steepest rack railway in the world ascends Mount Pilatus near Luzern, with a gradient of 1 in 2. (AL)

Below right The preserved Blonay–Chamby line above Montreux and Vevey. (AL)

Above Biedermeier houses in Heiden, terminus of a branch from Rorschach in canton Appenzell. (AL)

Below left The postbus network connects with the railway system and operates with the same precision and efficiency. A bus passes the town hall of 1539–45 in Sursee. (ST)

Below right The castle at Tarasp near Scuol dates from the 11th century and is open to visitors. (AL)

The town's oldest building is the 13th-century castle of La Batiaz, which was painted by Turner. It can be reached by crossing the Drance on a covered bridge. The first part of the castle was built by the Bishop of Sion, but the cylindrical keep was commissioned by Peter II of Savoy. The castle was sacked in 1475 and slighted after a siege in 1518. At the foot of the hill to it is the Notre-Dame de Compassion chapel of 1595 with a collection of beautiful 18th- and 19th-century votive pictures.

In the centre of the town is the 17th-century baroque Catholic church of Notre-Dames-des-Champs, with fine carved door, and behind it the Provostry where Napoleon stayed in 1800. At Place Centrale 7 (near the tourist office) is the much altered, mid-16th-century Grande-maison, a former hotel that welcomed Rousseau, Goethe, Stendhal, Byron and Alexandre Dumas, amongst others.

Martigny's principal attraction, however, is close to Martigny-Bourg station on the branch to Orsières/Le Châble (see table 133 below). The Pierre Gianadda Foundation would be worthy of a city and is a surprise to many visitors. It is the creation of Leonard Gianadda, a civil engineer who was building housing in Martigny when his brother Pierre was killed in an air crash in Italy. When a Roman temple was discovered on the site of the housing, Leonard Gianadda decided to create a memorial to his brother on the site. The result is a cultural centre that hosts exhibitions of an astonishing quality, sometimes in association with museums of the stature of the Metropolitan Museum of Art in New York, and concerts in an impressive hall. On an upper level is a Gallo-Roman museum displaying artefacts found in the town, notably a three-horned bull.

A passage underneath the adjacent road is used as a photographic gallery and links the main building with the largest collection of Swiss-made motor cars, including a Martigny. The Delaunay-Belleville was built to order for Tsar Nicholas II, intended for use on hunting expeditions, but never delivered because of the October Revolution. All are in working order. There is a small section devoted to the Swiss inventor Isaac da Rivaz (1752–1828), who came up with the idea of an explosion in a cylinder and who died in nearby Sion.

In the park around the Foundation are sculptures by Giacometti, Modigliani, Rodin, Toulouse-Lautrec and others, and a swimming pool. (Foundation open: daily; Mar–May 10.00–18.00; Jun–Oct 09.00–19.00; Nov–Feb 10.00–12.00, 13.30–18.00. Tel: 027/722 39 78.)

On the other side of the branch line, on Rue du Levant, are the remains of the amphitheatre, where the annual cowfight takes place in early October. Locals are adamant that there is no cruelty involved and that the cows are very seldom hurt in this popular event. The amphitheatre is one of the places on the archaeological walk that starts at the tourist office (leaflet available) and takes in the various sites of interest.

Martigny is a good centre for walking with three railway branch lines up surrounding valleys, which provide access to the gorges of the Durnand, Trièg and Trent (see below). Asparagus and apricots are grown in quantity in the area, and there is an annual Apricot Market in early August.

Practical information
St Maurice

TO – Grand Rue 48, CH-1890. Tel: 024/485 27 77; fax: 024/485 32 11 Open: Mon 14.00–18.00, Tue–Fri 10.00–12.00, 14.00–18.00, Sat 09.30–11.30.

Martigny

TO – Place Centrale 9, CH-1920. Tel: 027/721 22 20; fax: 027/721 22 24; email: info@martignytourism.ch; web: www.martignytourism.ch Open: Sep–Jun, Mon–Fri 09.00–12.00, 13.30–18.00, sat 09.00–12.00; Jul–Aug, Mon–Fri 09.00–18.00, Sat 09.00–12.00, 14.00–18.00, Sun 10.00–12.00, 16.00–18.00. From the station, proceed directly ahead along Av de la Gare.

Numerous hotels; close to the station are
Forclaz-Touring★★★, 15 Rue du Léman, CH-1920. Tel: 027/722 27 01; fax: 027/722 41 79.
Near Martigny-Bourg station is
Forum★★★, Av Grand S-Bernard, CH-1920. Tel: 027/722 18 41; fax: 027/722 79 25.
Excellent restaurant.

Bicycle hire from Martigny station.

BEX–BEVIEUX–VILLARS Tables 127/129

This is one of the loveliest of Switzerland's mountain railways, with great character for those who appreciate such things. Indeed, the tramway service that runs from Bex to Bévieux, sharing the line with Villars trains, must be one of the last of its kind in Europe.

Trains leave from directly outside the station at Bex (pronounced Bé), the Villars train standing at right angles to the main line. If you intend to explore the town of Bex, it is worth waiting for the Bévieux tram service for the experience of riding in a vehicle that has been plying the route for most of the 20th century.

The train proceeds directly up the road to the town centre, twisting through narrow streets to **Bex-Place-du-Marché**. The prosperity of Bex was built on salt, which the Bernese began to exploit in the 16th century. In the 19th century this was augmented by the development of the town as a spa – its full name is Bex-les-Bains – which was patronised by Victor Hugo, Tolstoy and Rimski-Korsakov. The huge tower of the Reformed church of St Clément is the oldest part, dating from 1501; the classical nave and choir are early 19th-century.

The line continues as a roadside tramway to **Bévieux**, where the railway's depot is situated on the right and the tram service terminates. To the left is one of Switzerland's most unusual and fascinating museums. The subject of salt may not sound enthralling, but the experience of riding on a mine train through 3.2km (2 miles) of the 48km (30 miles) of tunnel, and seeing the vast, ingeniously lit and interpreted chambers, will never be forgotten. Although the salt deposits were discovered in the 16th century, the first tunnel was not dug until 1684, and the mines were developed with painful slowness because of the hard rock and limited tools of the time. For example, there is an unfinished passage of 734 steps 1,500m (1,640yds) long that was abandoned after 13 years' digging. The reason for such Herculean endeavour was, of course, the price of salt which was compared with gold. The toll on health was severe: miners started work at the age of 12 and seldom lived beyond 35.

The salt was dissolved in underground chambers and then piped along larch logs to intensifying plants where it was boiled, requiring huge amounts of timber, followed by evaporation. The discovery of salt-impregnated rock in 1867 and cheaper methods of extraction was a breakthrough. Today nine men produce about 40,000 tonnes of salt a year, half of which goes to the chemical works of Ciba-Geigy and most of the other half to the kitchens of Switzerland. About 10 million tonnes of salt remain.

Conducted tours begin in a huge chamber with a central pillar of rock supporting a 30m- (100ft-) wide roof; in the centre is a model of the mines in a lake of brine, and around the perimeter are dioramas of the extraction process. A three-projector tape/slide presentation about three centuries of salt mining is shown (with headphone commentaries in English, French and German), followed by the train journey into the heart of the mine for a walk through some of the tunnels and such demonstrations as the flammability of methane gas. The tour lasts just over two hours. A pullover should be worn as the temperature is a constant 17°C (63°F). It is a 3.2km (2 miles) walk from Bévieux station to the mine; the only alternatives are a bicycle hired from Bex station or a taxi. (Open: Apr–mid-Nov, daily 09.00–16.00. Tours can be pre-booked; tel: 024/463 03 30.) There is also a restaurant at the mine, 400m below ground, open from Feb–mid-Nov.

The first section of Abt rack starts just beyond Bévieux station, the line heading into a gorge with sheer walls of rock on the other bank of the river. The fields in spring and summer are a mass of wild flowers, appearing days after the last crystals of snow have soaked into the ground so that residual tongues of melting snow can be surrounded by brilliant colours. The line twists so much that it is difficult to keep track of the compass, tunnels sometimes masking the passage from one valley to another.

Gryon is a small resort, principally of interest for winter sports but a good base for mountain walks, notably that to the ancient and isolated village of Taveyannaz. Besides its local slopes, Gryon is connected with the Villars ski runs. The lovely chalet-style station has a restaurant and café with a view that would be hard to beat. The village also has a passenger-carrying miniature railway, Roby Vapeur Parc.

Just before Gryon the railway joins the road to Villars and continues running alongside it all the way to the terminus. During the summer a bus leaves **La Barboleuse** (table 127.10) for the remote village of Solalex from where there is a path to Derborence for a postbus to Sion (table 135.15). Five minutes' walk from the station at La Barboleuse is a gondola to Les Chaux (table 2089), from which it is a short walk to Taveyannaz.

Villars is a major skiing resort with 120km (72 miles) of signed pistes, mostly for beginner to intermediate levels, served by 45 skilifts, with 44km (27½ miles) of cross-country trails. However, there is much to do in summer with riding, climbing, paragliding, tennis, ice-skating, swimming and 300km (187 miles) of signed walks on offer. The ski kindergarten here is excellent. The main access to the pistes is by the rack railway to Col-de-Bretaye (see below), and four minutes' walk from the station there is a gondola to Roc-d'Orsay (table 2090) from which you can walk to one of the area's principal viewpoints at Le Chamossaire at 2,113m (6,932ft).

Practical information
Bex
TO – Rue Central 14, CH-1880. Tel: 024/463 30 80. Open: Mon–Fri 08.00–12.00, 14.00–17.30.

Gryon
TO – Place de la Barboleuse, CH-1882. Tel: 024/498 14 22; fax: 024/498 26 22; email: gryon@swissonline.ch; web: www.gryon.ch Open: Mon–Sat 08.00–12.00, 14.00–18.00.

La Crémaillère**, Place de la Barboleuse, CH-1882. Tel: 024/498 21 55; fax: 024/498 40 52.

Villars
TO – Rue Centrale, CH-1884. Tel: 024/495 32 32; fax: 024/495 27 94; email: villars@pingnet.ch; web: www.villars.ch Open: high season, Mon–Sun 08.00–19.00; low season, Mon–Sat 08.00–12.00, 13.30–18.00, Sun 10.00–16.00.

Numerous hotels; close to the station are
Du Golf & Marie Louise*** (H), Rue Centrale, CH-1884. Tel: 024/495 24 77; fax: 024/495 39 78.
Les Papillons* (H), Av Centrale, CH-1884. Tel: 024/495 34 84; fax: 024/495 42 31.

VILLARS–COL-DE-BRETAYE Table 128
This short line is a scenic delight at any season, though it is busiest in winter ferrying skiers to the principal pistes near Villars. In summer you may see milk churns being loaded on to a wagon attached to the train, a sight long since vanished from most European railways. The Swiss Pass is not valid for the journey.

The climb starts from the end of the platform at Villars, which is adjacent to that for trains from Bex. Climbing through woods the train reaches **Col de Soud**, where the *auberge*/restaurant overlooks the valley. Shortly beyond is what must be one of the world's most majestically sited golf courses, though some may prefer to see it in winter when the clubhouse is concealed under a blanket of snow. It is so peaceful up here that in summer you may see a fox content to stand in a field as the train passes.

At the summit the train swings through a right angle to the terminus, unusually crossing over a skilift on the approach. The walks from here are legion, and there is a lovely old chalet hotel beside one of the three small lakes for those who wish to make the most of them.

Practical information
Col de Soud
Auberge du Col de Soud, CH-1884. Tel: 024/495 26 40; fax: 024/495 26 50.

Col-de-Bretaye
Hôtel du Lac (H), CH-1884. Tel: 024/495 21 92; fax: 024/495 77 55.

Sion–ST MAURICE–ST-GINGOLPH Table 130
The usefulness of this line has been much reduced by the replacement of most trains by buses.

The branch leaves the Geneva–Brig main line just north of St Maurice station and proceeds north along the west bank of the Rhône. For **Monthey** see table 125 above. At **Vouvry** the bell tower of the 15th-century church stands near the neo-classical Catholic church built in 1820; the older building has some original stained glass.

Unless approaching from the south, it is much easier to visit the Steam Park at **Bouveret** (see above) by steamer, since the pier is close to the park. Steam trains operate over the line from Bouveret to Evian in France (see tables 100/100.1).

MARTIGNY–VALLORCINE–Chamonix–St Gervais Table 132
This international metre-gauge railway deserves to be better known as one of Switzerland's great mountain railways. The views along the valley of Le Trient are stupendous, and it provides access to numerous walks and to some of the best views of the highest mountain in the Alps, Mont Blanc. New trains obviate the need to change trains at the frontier, at either Le Châtelard-Frontière or Vallorcine. The service is marketed as the Mont-Blanc Express, and an excellent leaflet is available describing some of the best walks, sometimes using a combination of train and bus, including the Orsières/Le Châble lines which are operated by the same company. Sit on the left.

Trains for Vallorcine leave from a bay platform at the west end of Martigny station. For the first section the line parallels the main line to Geneva, passing the castle of Le Batiaz on the left, orchards and rows of poplars. At **Vernayaz**, where the main depot is on the right, a footpath bracketed out from the rock heads up the extraordinarily narrow defile of the Gorge du Trient down which the water boils in its rush to join the Rhône. The path leads up to the next station at Salvan (the descent is obviously easier). The line swings southwest, engages the Strub rack and climbs at an almost alarming gradient. Twisting through tunnels and sheer rock cuttings, the line affords impressive views down the Rhône valley before reaching the summit of the climb and the end of the rack section before the pretty station at **Salvan**.

From the station here, a bus goes up to Van-d'En-Haut (table 132.10) from which it is a short walk to Lac de Salanfe. Five minutes' walk from the station at **Les Marécottes** is an alpine zoo with most species of mammals in a generous natural setting; it also has a large natural swimming pool with nearby restaurant. (Open: high season, daily 09.00–dusk; low season Wed–Sun 09.00–dusk; restaurant –23.00.) Seven minutes' walk from the station is the gondola to La Creusaz (table 2140), from where there is a walk to Emaney and back down to Les Marécottes.

Trétien is a delightful village clinging to the mountainside, its roofs a marvellous mélange of stone. From here a footpath goes up the Gorges du Triège, a spiral staircase giving access to a spectacular waterfall and to three caves. Trétien is the start of the most spectacular part of the journey as the line is perched on a ledge with a sheer drop of 426m (1,400ft) to the valley floor. Its scale is made all the more breathtaking by the short tunnels from which the train emerges with no visible means of support.

From **Finhaut** you can either take a bus from the station (table 132.15) or walk to Col-de-la-Gueulaz for the dam at Emosson (see below). On the opposite side of the Trient, hanging valleys can be seen descending from the peak of Pointe Ronde at 2,655m (8,711ft). Some of the railway's historic vehicles are kept in the tunnel before **Châtelard**. A funicular 2 minutes' walk from the station provides another way of reaching the Emosson dam (table 2143); the funicular was built by Swiss Federal Railways in 1920 to take materials up to build the Barberine dam, which generated electricity for the railways. However, the dam was itself submerged by the construction in 1967–75 of the huge Emosson dam.

The funicular to Château-d'Eau is a 22-minute journey. From there, an electric 60cm-gauge 'panoramic' train takes you on a 10-minute journey along the course of a steam railway that was built during construction of the Barberine dam. The views of the Mont Blanc range and the Gorges du Bouqui are magnificent. The Emosson-Minifunic then takes you up to La Gueulaz near the top of the dam, providing an impressive view of the curving dam wall. There is a restaurant here, and numerous walks, including a one-hour walk to the largest dinosaur footprints in Europe, which are on the path beside the shore of the lake to the old Emosson dam (Barrage de Vieux-Emosson). From La Gueulaz you can take the bus down to Finhaut (see above).

In the days before through trains, transfer to SNCF trains took place either at **Le Châtelard-Frontière** or amongst the lupins on the platform at **Vallorcine**, the two stations a contrast in appearance. From Le Châtelard, a bus returns to Martigny via Col-de-la-Forclaz (table 100.41), offering spectacular views and access to strenuous walks. The railway proceeds to Chamonix, where the CF Chamonix–Montenvers rack line climbs 5.4km (3⅓ miles) to the terrace over the Mer de Glace; this sinuous glacier is overlooked by the Grandes Jorasses at 4,206m (13,799ft). Beyond is Chamonix, and journey's end at St Gervais-les-Bains-Le-Fayet. This large station offers connections with the standard gauge for trains to Annecy and Lyons, and with the Tramway du Mont-Blanc to Le Nid d'Aigle for spectacular views of Mont Blanc.

Practical information
Salvan
TO – As for Les Marécottes.
Bellevue, Place Central, CH-1922. Tel: 027/761 15 23.

Les Marécottes
TO – Place de la Télécabine, CH-1923. Tel: 027/761 31 01; fax: 027/761 31 03. Open: 08.30–12.00, 13.30–17.30; high season, Mon–Sun; low season Tue–Sat.

Jolimont, CH-1923. Tel: 027/761 14 70; fax: 027/761 14 76; web: www.salvan.ch/jolimont.
Aux Mille Etoiles, CH-1923. Tel: 027/761 16 66; fax: 027/761 16 00.

Finhaut
TO – CH-1925. Tel: 027/768 12 78; fax: 027/768 18 08. Open: Tue–Sat 09.30–11.30.

Beau-Sejour**, CH-1925. Tel: 027/768 11 01; fax: 027/768 13 60.

Le Châtelard
TO – as for Finhaut.

Suisse**, CH-1925. Tel: 027/768 11 35; fax: 027/768 11 35.
Les Touristes*, CH-1925. Tel: 027/768 11 45.

MARTIGNY–ORSIERES/LE CHABLE Table 133
These standard-gauge branches share the same line between the bay platform at the east end of Martigny station and the junction at Sembrancher. Since the branch to Orsières serves the larger community, trains are normally run through from Martigny while passengers for Le Châble have to change at Sembrancher. The ski resort of Verbier is reached by cablecar or bus from Le Châble.

Leaving Martigny the River Drance is on the right as the train skirts the town to **Martigny-Bourg**, close to the Foundation Pierre Gianadda and the amphitheatre. As the train begins to climb, the valley bifurcates; the railway takes the right-hand valley but there are lovely views along the cliffs of the left-hand valley along which a road ascends the Col des Planches, served by a bus from Martigny station (table 100.43). Ten minutes' walk from **Bovernier** is the hamlet of Les Valettes, where a footpath can be taken to the Gorges du Durnand. This canyon of rock, through which a noisy torrent of water cascades over 14 waterfalls, was made accessible in 1877 by the construction of a gallery bracketed out from the rock. It takes about an hour to explore the gorge, either returning by a footpath or continuing up a steep road to Champex and its lake (see below).

The line criss-crosses the river to the junction at **Sembrancher**, where the village has some attractive stone houses and, overlooking the village to the south, the ruins of a 12th-century castle destroyed in 1575.

The **Orsières** line enters a tunnel and turns south up the Val d'Entremont to the attractive town. From the station a bus climbs up to Champex (table

133.20) where the resort is clustered round a smallish lake. A botanical garden has been created on the shore. Ten minutes' walk from the bus is the chairlift to La Breya (table 2150). This has the distinction of being the steepest chairlift in Switzerland, climbing at an angle of almost 45°.

Another bus from Orsières station continues along the Val d'Entremont and provides an international service to Italy over the Great St Bernard Pass. It was through this valley that Napoleon's Army of Reserve passed on its epic crossing of the pass in 1800 at the beginning of the Marengo campaign against Austria. Stendhal was amongst the 40,000 men, who had to carry sufficient provisions to last from the army's supply base at Villeneuve near Montreux to the Aosta valley. However, the unexpectedly doughty defence by just 300 soldiers of Fort Bard, which commanded the road down the Aosta valley, threatened the whole campaign. Supplies could not be brought up because the army blocked the track through the pass, which was only 45cm (18in) wide in places. The fort finally surrendered, but Napoleon's difficulties suggest that the Gotthard would have been the better pass to have chosen.

Before the bus enters the tunnel under the pass, it stops at Bourg-St-Pierre where the tower of the Catholic church dates from c1000 and there is an alpine garden. Further on, at the Col du Grand St Bernard, is the famous hospice where about 20 of the even more famous breed of dog can be seen at the museum. They were used by the monks to seek out lost travellers, saving hundreds of lives. The hospice is supposed to have been established in the 11th century by St Bernard, archdeacon of Aosta, but the buildings have been much altered and rebuilt over the centuries. The older buildings, which may be visited, contain a library, a chapel and room with a Broadwood piano presented by Edward VII in 1904. Some visitors are dismayed by the extent to which the remaining monks, bereft of their original function of saving lives, have succumbed to 'market forces'. The museum tells the story of the pass, the hospice and the natural history of the surrounding area. The bus continues over the border to Aosta, a station on the line from Pré St-Didier to Turin.

The branch from Sembrancher to Le Châble crosses the river and starts to climb steeply up a broad pleasant valley with snow-covered peaks ahead. **Le Châble** is the station for the car-free ski resort of Verbier, reached by a gondola (table 2160) from a huge circular building adjacent to the station, which has a café/restaurant on the platform. Buses leave from the station to Verbier (table 133.35), Bruson and Moay (table 133.40), and up the Val de Bagnes to a protected area that is closed in winter due to avalanches, but glorious in summer. At the end of the valley is the Mauvoisin dam, the tallest concave dam in the world.

The relatively new resort of Verbier has one of the largest skiing areas in Europe, with 400km (250 miles) of runs served by 100 lifts. It also boasts Europe's largest cablecar, which can take 150 passengers up to Mont Fort at 3,000m (9,843ft), and it is a good base for walking in summer when accommodation is cheaper.

Practical information
Orsières
TO – 90 Ferdinand Rausis, CH-1937. Tel: 027/783 16 43; fax: 027/783 33 03. Open: Mon–Fri 09.00–12.00, 14.00–18.00, Sat 09.00–12.00.

A hotel adjacent to the station is
Terminus*** (H), CH-1937. Tel: 027/783 20 40; fax: 027/783 38 08.

Verbier
TO – Place Centrale, CH-1936. Tel: 027/775 38 88; fax: 027/775 38 89; email: verbiertourism@verbier.ch; web: www.verbier.ch Open: Mon–Fri 08.30–12.30, 14.00–18.30, Sat 08.30–19.00, Sun 09.00–12.00, 16.00–18.30.

Numerous hotels. Near the cableway from Le Châble are
De la Poste***, CH-1936. Tel: 027/771 66 81; fax: 027/771 34 01.

Geneva–MARTIGNY–BRIG Tables 100/100.2/100.3
This fast stretch of line along the Rhône valley serves some of Switzerland's most popular skiing resorts, reflected by the through TGV service with Paris on winter Saturdays. The broad valley itself alternates between fruit growing and industry, while the slopes are largely planted with grapes.

At the attractive village of **Saxon** the partly Romanesque chapel of St Maurice stands beneath the ruins of the castle. Shortly after Saxon the magnificent ruined walls of the castle at Saillon may be seen on a hill to the left. Regarded as one of the best preserved 13th-century fortifications in Switzerland, it was partly built by Peter II of Savoy to the design of Chillon's architect, Pierre Meinier. Next to the Catholic church is a 13th-century priest's house.

Eight minutes' walk from **Riddes** is the cablecar to Isérables (table 2173), a village perched on a ledge of rock 610m (2,000ft) above the valley. Below the village are some venerable wooden granaries. A bus also takes a serpentine road from the station to Mayens-de-Riddes from where it is a ten-minute walk to the gondola from Tzoumaz to Savoleyres (table 2171). From there another gondola continues to Le Creux (table 2170) which is 20 minutes' walk from Verbier. There is also an easy 5¹/₂-hour walk from Mayens-de-Riddes (where food is available) following the course of the ancient Saxon *Bisse* through Boveresse to Col des Planches, from where there is a bus to Martigny (table 100.43).

The station named **Chamoson** is some way from the village of that name but close to St-Pierre-de-Clages, where the eponymous church is one of the most highly regarded Romanesque buildings in the Valais. Thought to have been built in the early 12th century, the triple-apsed church had an octagonal tower added over the crossing later in the century. Remains of another castle built by Peter II of Savoy can be seen at Conthey (station **Châteauneuf-Conthey**).

It would be quite wrong to judge **Sion** by the view from the railway: apart from the castles on top of the two hills that overlook the town, Sion looks a bland, modern town. In fact, the main town of the Valais has an historic centre and much of interest to visitors. Evidence of a settlement here dates back to 3500BC, but it was the choice of Sion as the political and ecclesiastical capital of the Valais in the 6th century that created the status it still enjoys.

To reach the tourist office, proceed directly ahead from the station along Av de la Gare, and the office is on the right in Place de la Planta. As the town map reveals, the principal places of interest are close together and easily visited on foot. The furthest away are the two castles, Tourbillon to the north, Valère to the south. The latter is the older and more extensive group of buildings, the castle dating from at least the early 10th century and the Romano-Gothic Collegiate church of Notre-Dame from the 12th to 13th centuries. The church contains fine 12th-century carved capitals, a 13th-century rood screen, decorative choir-stalls of 1662–4 and some remarkably well-preserved, gruesome early 15th-century wall-paintings, one depicting the martyrdom of St Sebastian. The pulpit-like structure jutting out from the rear wall is claimed to be the oldest playable organ in the world, dating from the 14th century and used for occasional concerts. Its restoration in the early 1950s was begun by an English music teacher from Eton, and it is played on Saturdays in July and August at 16.00. A guided tour is the only way to see the church following vandalism of a 15th-century wall-painting.

In the castle is the Cantonal Museum of History and Ethnography, which has some rare medieval chests and sculptures as well as a good collection of arms and armour (open: Tue–Sun 10.00–12.00, 14.00–18.00).

Tourbillon Castle was built c1294 and frequently rebuilt or altered until 1788 when it was ruined by fire, which destroyed most of the castle but left the walls. It is quite a steep climb to the castle but the view from the hill towards Brig is impressive. (Open: mid-Mar–mid-Nov, Tue–Sun 10.00–18.00.)

Returning to the old town via Rue des Châteaux, you pass on the right the Cantonal Art Museum (Musée Cantonal des Beaux-Arts), which is housed in a 16th-century episcopal building and concentrates on work by Valaisian artists from the Middle Ages (open: Tue–Sun 10.00–12.00, 14.00–18.00). Almost opposite is the Archaeological Museum (Musée d'Archéologie) which has finds dating back to the neolithic period, Roman glass, jewellery and sculptures (open: Tue–Sun 10.00–12.00, 14.00–18.00).

On the corner with Rue du Grand-Pont is the Hôtel de Ville of 1657–65 in which is displayed one of the oldest Christian inscriptions, and the oldest in Switzerland, dating from 377. Outside is an astronomical clock of 1667 and decorative downpipes at the corners.

Nearby, in Rue de Conthey, is Maison Supersaxo, built in 1503–5 for a local potentate. A Gothic staircase leads to its chief feature, the lavishly decorated ceiling of a second-floor hall. (Open: Mon–Fri 08.00–12.00, 14.00–18.00.)

A little to the north is the Cathedral Notre-Dame-du-Glarier, a largely 15th-century building incorporating a 12th-century bell tower, and close by the Catholic church of St Théodule. This early 16th-century building in the Flamboyant style was built on much older foundations and has good vaulting in the choir and carved angels at the foot of the pillars of the triumphal arch. Curiously all the glass is modern.

To the northwest of these churches is the last remnant of the town's 12th-century fortifications, the Tour des Sorciers. Round the corner from it, at the north end of Avenue de la Gare, is the Natural History Museum, which focuses on the flora and fauna of the Alps (open: Tue–Sun 14.00–18.00).

Sion boasts the largest postal bus station in Switzerland, reflecting the number of side valleys that join the Rhône valley, and can be reached by bus from the station. Amongst the services are ones to the Sanetsch See over the Col du Sanetsch at 2,251m (7,385ft) (table 135.23); Dixence (table 135.66), where the world's tallest dam towers 284m (932ft) above the valley floor and requires a cablecar to take visitors to the Lac-des-Dix (table 2190); the remote valley of Derborence (table 135.15), from where there is a path over the Pas de Cheville to Solalex for a bus to La Barboleuse (see tables 127/129 above); and buses to a string of delightful villages in Val d'Hérens (tables 135.70–2), including the larch-wooded resort of Arolla, passing through the extraordinary pyramids of rock at Euseigne.

Characteristic of many of these valleys are the *Bisses*, water courses built for irrigation as long ago as the 13th century. The walking on offer in the region is astonishing: there are 7,000km (4,375 miles) of signed paths.

Finally, an excursion to the east from Sion that should not be missed: the lake of St Léonard, which was discovered as recently as 1943. The station that once served the village has been closed but a bus (table 100.80) from Sion station goes to the largest underground lake in Europe, on which rowing boats are used to explore the illuminated chambers (open: mid-Mar–Oct, daily). Wear warm clothing.

Continuing east along the valley, with the Rhône close to the railway on the right, the line reaches **Sierre**. Smaller than Sion, the town has some buildings of note and the tourist office has a leaflet, *Promenade des Châteaux*. They include the 16th-century Château des Vidames with a massive square tower, and the 13th-century Tour de Goubing in a vineyard southeast of the town. Off Avenue du Château is the 15th-century Church of Notre-Dame-des-Marais with 16th-century frescos.

In the northeast of the town, reached by Rue du Manoir, is Château de Villa, which forms one part of the Valaisian Wine Museum (open: Mar–Oct, Tue–Sun 14.00–17.00; Nov–Feb, Fri–Sun 14.00–17.00). The exhibition features wine presses, the cellar, and the social aspects of wine; it is linked to the other part in the well-preserved village of Salgesch by a Wine Path. This meanders through vineyards with 45 explanatory panels about viticulture and its associated buildings. The walk takes about two hours.

To the left of the station, seven minutes' walk away, is the lower station of a two-stage funicular that has the distinction of being the longest single haulage cable of any funicular in Switzerland, from Sierre–Montana-Vermala (table 2225). The first section has 1½ miles of moving cable, and the two stages lift passengers up a vertical height of 930m (3,054ft) to the modern winter and summer sports resort of Montana-Vermala. It spreads inseparably along the mountain side to Crans, the two places being marketed as Crans Montana and projected openly as an 'up-market' resort. Its stature as a winter sports centre was confirmed by hosting various world ski championships. It has the usual broad range of sports facilities, but is especially proud of its three golf courses.

Buses run from Sierre station to Crans Montana and from the top of the funicular to Crans and a host of neighbouring villages (tables 100.70–1). There are some particularly spectacular gondola and cablecar journeys from Crans Montana, for example to Bellalui (table 2221), from which there are stupendous views of the Valaisian Alps, to Glacier de la Plaine-morte (table 2231) and Cry-d'Er (table 2227).

Buses serving the south side of the Rhône valley include the lake at Moiry (table 100.77) and the long Val d'Anniviers through eight picturesque villages to Zinal (table 100.78). From Zinal a cablecar ascends to Sorebois (table 2203). A six-day walking package through the valley is available in pre-arranged hotels with luggage transferred between them.

Leaving Sierre the railway parallels the Wine Path to **Salgesch**, where the second part of the Wine Museum is situated in the Zumofen House, focusing on viticulture rather than wine. (Open: Mar–Oct, Tue–Sun 14.00–17.00; Nov–Feb, Fri–Sun 14.00–17.00.) This district reputedly produces the best Swiss reds, and wine-tastings can be laid on at the vintners.

Between Sierre and Leuk the railway negotiates a section of the Rhône valley which has been engulfed by massive landslides. The undulating topography has helped to keep the area in a state of relative wildness, and the Bois de Finges is now regarded as one of the most important pine forests in Europe. A path through it has been created by the Swiss League for the Protection of Nature.

Around **Leuk** (or **Loèche**) the language changes to German, marking the former border between the Burgundians and the Alemanni. The town is some way from the station, but there is a good bus service between the two (table 100.82). The town has some remarkably fine buildings, on some of which the town's symbol of a dragon carrying a sword may be seen. The square-towered Bishop's Palace is a much altered 15th-century building that houses a local history and folk museum (open: Jul–mid-Sep, Sat 14.00–16.00). Another massive tower, with corner turrets, is the Rathaus, formerly the Château des Vidamcs, which was founded c1254 and last rebuilt in 1541–3.

The Ringackerkapelle is regarded as one of the canton's most outstanding baroque buildings. Constructed in 1690–4, it has a most unusual arcaded porch that belies the building's role as a church. Inside are lavish stucco decoration, an imposing high altar and a baroque organ. The Catholic church of St Stéphane was built c1497 incorporating a fine 12th-century Romanesque bell tower.

Buses from Leuk station serve the popular spa and sports resort of Leukerbad (table 100.82). It offers a variety of baths and pools, some fed by pipes of hot spring water that have been cleverly channelled under the road to keep the street near the church free of snow. Mark Twain described the sight of valetudinarians in the baths here, submersed for hours up to their chins and occupied by floating trays of coffee, books and chessboards. (There is a picture depicting such scenes in the museum at Valère castle in Sion.) Around Leukerbad are 60km (37½ miles) of signed walks, 16 skilifts and two cablecars, to Gemmipass (table 2240) and Rinderhütte (table 2242). The summit of the former is close to the small lake of Daubensee, an easy walk, and it is possible to return to Leukerbad by an exciting path with handrail for the difficult parts.

Continuing east from Leuk, the line crosses the duck-egg blue Rhône, remaining on the south bank of the river all the way to Brig. The next station, **Turtmann**, is five minutes' walk from the cablecar to Oberems (table 2246) from where there is a walk up Turtmanntal to the glacier of the same name. From **Gampel-Steg** it is a 15-minute walk to the cablecar to Jeizinen (table 2247). Looking up to the left the south ramp of the Bern–Lötschberg–Simplon Railway (BLS) can be seen beginning its descent to Brig.

In the graveyard beside the 16th-century Catholic parish church of St Romanus at **Raron** is buried the Austrian poet Rainer Maria Rilke, who spent the last five years of his life in the Valais. He died in 1926. The church is in a spectacular hilltop position next to the 12th-century tower that was once the seat of the lords of Raron. In the nave of the church is an early 16th-century painting of the Last Judgement.

Less than ten minutes' walk from Raron station are the cablecars to Eischoll (table 2250) and Unterbäch (table 2253) in the Augstbord region; the latter is an excellent centre for walking with 500km (312½ miles) of hiking trails and for mountain biking with 60km (37½ miles) of trails.

At **Visp** the metre-gauge Brig–Visp–Zermatt Railway (BVZ) curves in from the south to run parallel with the standard gauge to Brig. Between 1250 and 1365 Visp was under Italian control, but there are only two buildings from that time: the much rebuilt Catholic church of Heiligen Drei Könige ('The Three Wise Men') with Romanesque bell tower and the square tower of the Lochmatterturm. The area around this and the Catholic church of St Martin has some attractive 14th–16th-century houses.

Brig has been an important road junction for centuries, and its history is inseparable from its location at the upper end of the main Rhône valley and at the junction of the roads over the Furka and Simplon passes. Even the town's most imposing building was financed from the profits of trade: the Stockalper Palace was built in 1658–78 by Kaspar von Stockalper, by all accounts an arrogant and autocratic man who so alienated the people of Brig that he was forced to leave the town and seek refuge in Italy. Much of his money came from salt, but also from a trade in mercenaries, especially with France.

None the less the building he left behind is the most important baroque palace in Switzerland and was the country's largest private residence. The palace takes the form of two- and three-storey arcades of different heights arranged around a courtyard, which is overlooked by three tall square towers crowned by bulbous gilded onion domes. The tallest is nine storeys high, and they are said to recall the three wise men. The living quarters are arranged on four floors with two levels of cellars beneath. The palace is connected to a rebuilt 16th-century house put up by an ancestor, Peter Stockalper. Various rooms including the chapel are open to visitors, there is a local museum on an upper floor and a horse-drawn postbus from the Grimselpass route in the courtyard. (Open by guided tours on the hour, Tue–Sun: Jun–Sep 09.00–11.00, 14.00–17.00, May and Oct 10.00–11.00, 14.00–16.00.)

It is worth spending an hour wandering through the attractive alleyways and pedestrianised streets of the old part of Brig. Much of the town had to be restored in 1993, following a devastating flood on 24 September after which people could walk on compacted mud at first-floor level. The town is well endowed with churches, the most notable being the 17th-century Catholic Collegiate church of Spiritus Sanctus on Simplonstrasse and the Chapel of St Sebastian of 1636–7 in the central square that takes its name. Also in the square is a statue and fountain in memory of the Peruvian pilot Georges Chavez, who crashed and was killed after being the first person to fly over the Alps, in 1910.

It is worth taking the postbus over the Simplon Pass (table 145.40) and returning to Brig by train from either Iselle or Domodóssola stations at which the bus stops (see below). Another bus route serves the region at the foot of the Aletsch glacier, starting from beneath the Jungfrau, as it curves southwest towards Belalp. The bus goes from Brig station through the historic village of Naters to Blatten bei Naters (table 145.35). From here a cablecar ascends to Belalp (table 2325) for a fine view of the glacier. The first non-Swiss known to have visited Belalp was Ruskin, in 1844.

Practical information
Saxon
De la Gare, CH-1907. Tel: 027/744 18 78; fax: 027/744 38 78.

Sion
TO – Place de la Planta, CH-1950. Tel: 027/322 85 86; fax: 027/322 18 82; email: info@siontourism.ch; web: www.siontourism.ch Open: Mon–Fri 08.30–12.00, 14.00–17.30, Sat 09.00–12.00.

Numerous hotels; closest to the station are
du Rhône★★★, Rue du Scex, CH-1950. Tel: 027/322 82 91; fax: 027/323 11 88.
Elite★★, Avenue du Midi 6, CH-1950. Tel: 027/322 03 27; fax: 027/322 23 61.

Sierre
TO – Place de la Gare, CH-3960. Tel: 027/455 85 35; fax: 027/455 86 35; email: sierre-salgesch@vsinfo.ch Open: Mon–Fri 08.00–19.00, Sat 08.00–12.00.

Numerous hotels; close to the station are
Terminus★★★, 1 Rue du Bourg, CH-3960. Tel: 027/455 11 40; fax: 027/455 23 14; email: minotelterminus@bluewin.ch
Central★★★, 17 Rue du Bourg, CH-3960. Tel: 027/55 15 66; fax: 027/56 49 66.

Crans Montana
TO – Case postale 372, CH-3962. Tel: 027/485 04 04; fax: 027/485 04 60; email: information@crans-montana.ch; web: www.crans-montana.ch Open: Mon–Sat 08.30–12.15, 14.00–18.30, Sun 10.00–12.00, 16.00–18.00.

Leukerbad

TO – Rathaus, CH-3954. Tel: 027/472 71 71; fax: 027/472 71 51. Open: Mon–Fri 09.00–12.00, 13.30–18.00, Sat 09.00–12.00, 13.30–17.00, Sun 09.30–12.00.

Unterbäch

TO – Dorfplatz, CH-3944. Tel: 027/934 56 56; fax: 027/934 56 57; email: info@unterbaech.ch; web: www.unterbaech.ch Open: Mon–Sun 08.30–11.00.

Visp

TO – La Poste-Platz, CH-3930. Tel: 027/948 33 33; fax: 027/948 33 35; email: visp@rhone.ch; web: www.visp.ch Open: Mon–Fri 09.00–12.00, 13.30–18.30; Jun–Aug, Mon–Fri 09.00–18.30, Sat 09.00–16.00.

Hotels close to the station are
Visperhof★★★, Bahnhofstrasse 2, CH-3930. Tel: 027/946 34 91; fax: 027/946 10 36; email: visperhof@reconline.ch; web: www.reconline.ch/visperhof
Touring★★★, Bahnhofplatz 3, CH-3930. Tel: 027/948 05 00; fax: 027/948 05 05; email: info@hotel-touring.ch

Brig

TO – Bahnhofplatz, CH-3900. Tel: 028/23 19 01; fax: 028/24 31 44. Open: Mon–Fri 08.30–12.00, 13.30–18.00, Sat 09.00–12.00, 14.00–16.00.

Numerous hotels; close to the station are
De Londres, Bahnhofstrasse 17, CH-3900. Tel: 027/922 93 93; fax: 027/922 93 94.
Victoria★★★ (H), Bahnhofstrasse 2, CH-3900. Tel: 027/923 15 03; fax: 027/921 21 69; web: www.bestwestern.ch
Europe★★★, Viktoriastrasse 9, CH-3900. Tel: 028/923 13 21; fax: 028/923 13 23; email: info@hotel-europe-brig.ch; web: www.hotel-europe-brig.ch

Bicycle hire from Sion, Sierre and Brig stations.

BRIG–DOMODOSSOLA Table 100.3

Trains from western and northern Europe for Milan converge on Brig where the northern portal of the Simplon Tunnel is entered shortly after leaving the station. The first Simplon Tunnel was opened in June 1906, completing the Simplon Railway to Italy, and was followed by a second slightly longer bore in 1922. It remains the longest railway tunnel in Europe, at 19,823m (12.55 miles), but has been easily eclipsed in the world listings by Japan's Siekan Tunnel at 53,850m (33.8 miles). The Swiss/Italian frontier is about half way through. Besides through passenger and freight trains, the tunnel handles car-carrying trains between Iselle di Trasquera and Brig. Bicycles are also carried on these shuttles.

At Domodóssola, connections are made with trains over the marvellous Centovalli line to Locarno (see table 620).

BRIG–DOMODOSSOLA Bus table 145.40

One of the country's most impressive roads, enlarged in 1801–8 from a track by 30,000 labourers working to Napoleon's orders, though the current road takes a different route in many places. Besides the pass at 2,006m (6,581ft), the road negotiates the Gondo Gorge on the descent into Italy. It was after crossing the pass in 1646 that the diarist and author John Evelyn nearly died in Brig, having been given the bed of the innkeeper's sick daughter and promptly contracting smallpox. During the 1810s, a former London–Dover mail coach was in use, still with its English route painted on the panels. Sit on the right.

The climb starts almost immediately to offer ever more impressive views over the Rhône valley and the dramatic rock formations that overlook the road. The old road built by Napoleon can be seen below; it makes a perfect route for cyclists. Small mountain villages can be seen as the bus approaches Rothwald, one of a number of places where the bus driver drops off and picks up a sack of mail. The road passes through a succession of avalanche shelters, which are camouflaged by grass on their roofs to minimise their intrusion on the landscape.

At the summit is the hospice begun in 1801 but not completed until 1831 by the canons of Great St Bernard. It replaced a hospice that dated from 1235. The Simplon eagle commemorates the mobilisation of the country in 1939–45, to defend Switzerland against attack by the Axis countries.

Hardly a house in Simplon Dorf is without geranium-filled window boxes. The descent through the narrow Gondo gorge is spectacular and very different in character from the northern ascent. Black striations on the rock look as though a giant has taken a tar brush to the defile.

The peaceful station at Iselle is a more pleasant place to wait for a train, and there are a good café and restaurant on the platform.

BRIG–ZERMATT Table 140

The western section of the Glacier Express route is operated by the Brig–Visp–Zermatt Railway (BVZ) and was constructed between 1886 and 1891 when the first steam train pulled into Zermatt station. During the 1880s, when it was possible to reach Zermatt only by mule track, the village received 12,000 visitors a year. In the first year of the railway, it received 33,695 people. The reason for its fame was, of course, the tragic first ascent of the Matterhorn by Edward Whymper in 1865, coupled with the magnificent views of the striking mountain that can be had from Zermatt. Of the 44km (27½ miles) between Brig and Zermatt, 7.7km (4¾ miles) are rack assisted, the steepest gradient being 1 in 8. Sit on the left.

The metre-gauge trains of the BVZ parallel the main line to Geneva as far as **Visp** (see tables 100/100.2/100.3 above) where they turn south to follow the River Vispa through a narrow, steep-sided valley with vines on the slopes.

Stalden-Saas has long been an important crossing point of the valley, testified by the graceful stone bridge that has for centuries carried travellers across the river. The village is situated at the confluence of the Matter Vispa and Saaser Vispa rivers, the latter flowing down the Saastal that leads up to the car-free resort of Saas-Fee. Above the railway are the highest vineyards in Europe.

Frequent buses leave from Stalden-Saas station (table 145.10) for a resort that some believe would have eclipsed Zermatt in fame had it not been for the Matterhorn. Saas-Fee lies in a glorious position at the foot of the highest mountain entirely within the Swiss frontier, the Dom at 4,545m (14,911ft) – the higher Dufourspitze is shared with Italy. Although the first hotels were built in the mid-19th century, the first road to Saas-Fee was built only in 1951, on condition that the village itself would remain traffic-free. Consequently it has a quality of air and an atmosphere of tranquillity that are unknown to many visitors and a distant memory to others. Luggage is transported by electric vehicles, and concern for the environment extends to other facets of tourism in Saas-Fee.

It has become a popular winter resort, offering 100 km (62½ miles) of ski runs, winter hiking trails, cross-country runs, day and night toboggan runs and the usual range of all-weather sports facilities. The world's highest underground railway takes skiers to the Mittelallalin at 3,500m (11,482ft), where there is an Ice Pavilion explaining glaciers and their significance. There are also five cablecars and gondolas from Saas-Fee (tables 2300–1, 2303–6). In summer 280km (175 miles) of paths are open for hikers and mountain bikers, and the height of Saas-Fee makes summer skiing possible – the US national ski teams spend several weeks of the summer here.

The final part of the road up to Saas-Fee climbs from Saas Grund, the starting point for a bus up to the dam and lake of Mattmark (table 145.15). There are some marvellous walks from here, including one over the Monte Moro Pass from which you can take a cablecar down to Macugnaga in Italy.

Another bus service from Stalden-Saas takes the incredibly sinuous road to Moosalp (table 140.50), and the three-section cablecar to Staldenried and Gspon (table 2270) provides excellent views along the Saastal and Mattertal.

Continuing south from Stalden-Saas, the train begins its journey up the Mattertal. The quality of the landscape and sheer size of the mountains that tower above the train soon explain the reason why the Glacier Express is one of Switzerland's most popular journeys. From **Kalpetran**, which has an attractive station building, a cablecar ascends to Embd (table 2272) where the steeply sited village quarries green quartzite roofing slates and pavement slabs. Ropeways lower 5,000 tonnes a year. From Embd another cablecar continues to Schalb (table 2273) where there is a restaurant. From Kalpetran there is a walk of almost six hours to the Augstbordpass at 2,894m (9,495ft).

The railway continually changes river bank, waterfalls periodically drop to the Matter Vispa and the first scree slopes appear as the valley broadens out. From the station at **St Niklaus**, buses serve Gasenried (table 140.60) and Grächen (table 140.54–5) where two gondolas begin from this sun terrace, to Hannigalp (table 2275) and Seetalhorn (table 2276).

On the left you may glimpse a small barn elevated by staddle stones to deter nibbling mammals, and a modern chalet with a huge mural of St Niklaus. The sound of cow bells may be heard beyond **Herbriggen**, where, on the right, you may see the vast hole in the flank of rock that descends from the Brunegghorn; here, in 1991, part of the mountain collapsed, necessitating construction of a new alignment for the railway and road.

Randa is a village rich in mountaineering traditions and the starting point for several ascents. The vulnerability of this part of the valley is reflected in the number of times that Randa has been damaged by glacial slides. The valley broadens again before the village of **Täsch**, beyond which access by motor vehicles is severely restricted as part of the necessity of making Zermatt a car-free resort. The huge area of car and coach parking is not a pretty sight. A shuttle service operates between Täsch and Zermatt, supplementing the through trains from Brig. This section through the narrow Nikolai valley is the most vulnerable to avalanches – hence the numerous shelters over the line.

Journey's end at **Zermatt** is in a large new station fronting on to a square in which the tourist office is situated, on the right. It contains an illustrated accommodation board that displays the availability of rooms and enables you to make immediate bookings.

The reason why Zermatt now has 113 hotels and accommodation for 13,500 guests goes back to 1865, when the rivalry between British and Italian climbers to be the first to plant their national flag on the summit of the Matterhorn was finally ended by Whymper's successful climb. Human nature being what it is, his achievement would probably not have achieved the same publicity had four of his party not plunged to their deaths on the descent. The controversy that surrounded the fatalities kept the name of Zermatt in the news, and tourists from all over the world came to see the scene of the tragedy and the objective of the fateful climb. Amongst them was Thomas Hardy who came in 1887 and wrote a sonnet about Whymper entitled *To the Matterhorn*.

One may speculate on whether an Italian village would have become as popular as Zermatt had the Italian climber J A Carrel beaten Whymper to the summit. But Zermatt's appeal lies not only in its historical associations and tradition, but of course its location. Tourism had begun in 1820, and the first inn opened in 1838. As Baedeker put it, with admissible hyperbole: 'In no other locality is the traveller so completely admitted into the heart of the Alpine world, the very sanctuary of the "Spirit of the Alps".' The views of the Matterhorn from Zermatt itself are splendid enough, but a network of mountain railways and cablecars allows an exceptional choice of viewpoint.

As for the town itself, it has retained a surprising number of unspoilt buildings and in places still retains the character of an alpine village – no mean achievement given its long history of mass tourism. It is consequently a real pleasure to explore on foot, quite unlike some modern resorts that offer little but the bland trappings of tourist retailing. Anyone interested in the story of the climbers and the objects of their endeavours should not miss the fascinating Alpine Museum, which contains the varied memorabilia collected by the Seiler family (famous hoteliers), as well as displays on natural history, geology, social history – with some reconstructed rooms – and some helpful relief models of the region. It includes a photograph of Winston Churchill who climbed Monte Rosa in 1894. The museum is in the Seiler Garden down a path beside the Mountain Guides Office and Ski School (almost opposite Hotel Mont Cervin) on Hauptstrasse, and guides in English are available. (Open: Jun–Oct, daily 10.00–12.00, 16.00–18.00; mid-Dec–May, Mon–Fri, Sun 16.30–18.30.) Immediately behind the museum is the English church, which was consecrated by the Suffragen Bishop of Dover in 1871 and still has Sunday services at 09.15 and 20.30.

Zermatt's narrow streets and the sheer number of visitors make it immediately apparent why motor vehicles had to be excluded from the town. It inevitably adds to the pleasure of walking around the town, the only 'threat' being from horse-drawn carriages or sleighs and the electric vehicles that ferry luggage between station and hotels. Towards the arrival time of trains, the square outside the station is lined with these vehicles, slightly smaller than British milkfloats, which each serve a particular hotel. The drivers wear identifying caps, and load the luggage on to the back platform while passengers seat themselves in the cab. The two 5-star hotels (Mont Cervin and the Zermatterhof) have horse-drawn open carriages, which are lavishly decorated with flowers for newly married couples.

The area is famous for the length of the skiing season, having the largest all-year skiing area in the Alps. In winter there are 230km (140 miles) of runs for all degrees of skill, served by an exceptional network of 73 mountain railways and cableways of various kinds. A kindergarten is available. In summer there are 388km (242½ miles) of walking routes, and sports facilities in abundance.

The network of transport up the adjacent slopes is impressive. In addition to the Gornergratbahn, there is an underground railway called the Sunneggabahn which opened in 1980 (table 2290). From here there is a three-section cablecar to the Rothorn (table 2291). Others climb from Zermatt to Schwarzsee (table 2280) and by a three-section cablecar to Klein Matterhorn (table 2285), the second part being the highest altitude cableway in Europe, at 3,820m (12,533ft).

It is still possible to travel by steam on the BVZ: one of the eight original rack tank locomotives, No 7 *Breithorn* built by SLM in 1906, survives and can be chartered.

Practical information
Saas-Fee
TO – CH-3906. Tel: 027/958 18 58; fax: 027/958 18 60; email: to@saas-fee.ch; web: www.saas-fee.ch Open: Mon–Fri 08.30–1200, 14.00–18.30, Sat 08.00–19.00, Sun 09.00–12.00, 15.00–18.00.

Täsch
TO – CH-3929. Tel: 027/967 16 89; fax: 027/967 21 18. Open: Mon–Sat 09.00–12.00, 14.00–18.00.

Täscherhof-Bahnhof★★★, Bahnhofstrasse, CH-3929. Tel: 028/967 18 18; fax: 028/967 58 20; email: t-hof@bluewin.ch; web: www.taesch.ch/taescherhof

Zermatt
TO – Bahnofplatz, CH-3920. Tel: 027/967 01 81; fax: 027/967 01 85; email: zermatt@wallis.ch; web: www.zermatt.ch Open: mid-Apr–mid-Dec, Mon–Fri 08.30–12.00, 13.00–18.00, Sat 08.30–12.00; mid-Dec–mid-Apr, Mon–Fri 08.30–12.00, 14.00–18.30, Sat 08.30–19.00, Sun 09.30–12.00, 16.00–19.00.

Hotels close to the station are
Schweizerhof****, Bahnhofstrasse, CH-3920. Tel: 027/967 67 67; fax: 027/967 67 69; email: schwezerhof@zermatt.ch; web: www.zermatt.ch/schweizerhof/
Gornergrat***, Bahnhofplatz, CH-3920. Tel: 027/966 39 20; fax: 027/966 39 25; email: gornergrat@reconline.ch; web: www.gornergrat.com

Hotels of character and interest are
Mont Cervin***** (H), CH-3920. Tel: 027/966 88 88; fax: 027/967 28 78; email: montcervin@zermatt.ch; web: www.zermatt.ch/montcervin/ Originally built in 1852.
Zermatterhof***** (H), Bahnhofstrasse, CH-3920. Tel: 027/966 66 00; fax: 027/966 66 99; email: zermatterhof@zermatt.ch; web: www.zermatt.ch/zermatterhof/ Built in 1879.
Monte Rosa**** (H), Bahnhofstrasse, CH-3920. Tel: 027/967 33 33; fax: 027/967 11 60; email: monterosa@zermatt.ch; web: www.zermatt.ch/monterosa/ Built in 1855, Zermatt's first hotel and where Whymper stayed before his ascent of the Matterhorn.

ZERMATT–GORNERGRAT Table 142

This remarkable metre-gauge railway was Switzerland's first electric rack and pinion line, opened in 1898 and climbing a vertical distance of 1,484m (4,868ft) in 9.4km (5.9 miles). There are five tunnels, five bridges and five viaducts, one of which is a particularly impressive structure – the Findelenbach, which is 50m (164ft) high. It is the most popular mountain railway in Switzerland, carrying up to 3.3 million people a year, but less busy after mid-afternoon. It is advisable to wear sunscreen on a bright summer day. The Swiss Pass obtains a 25% discount. Good views on both sides.

The station of the Gornergratbahn (GGB) in Zermatt is just to the left of the BVZ station. Trains quickly climb above the rooftops of the town and into spruce trees, huge drops opening up as the railway sails over mountain torrents with vast boulders beneath. The line twists up through tunnels and horseshoe curves, pausing at four intermediate stations, including **Riffelalp** to serve several wonderfully positioned hotels. A 600mm tramway built by Alexander Seiler once served his isolated Riffelalp Hotel, because the local authorities would not sanction a road – an early instance of green local planning. The tram has been replaced by a tiny caterpillar dray that takes cases, but not people, to the hotel.

Gornergrat is the highest open-air station in Europe, at 3,092m (10,145ft). The solidly built and crenellated building at the summit is close to the combined hotel and observatory, surrounded by balconies from which can be seen 29 of Switzerland's 34 peaks over 4,000m (13,123ft). However, the hotel management has strung up loudspeakers outside the hotel, as though the experience of seeing these mountains could not be complete without pop music at ghetto-blasting volume. Given the Swiss concern with the environment, it is a wonder that such a flagrant example of inappropriate aural pollution has not been dealt with.

During the summer a weekly trip is operated to enable visitors to watch the sun rise from Gornergrat. Breakfast is available at the hotel.

From the Gornergrat a cablecar ascends to Hohtälli (table 2296), continuing in a second section to the Stockhorn at 3,407m (11,117ft) while another cablecar links Hohtälli with Rote Nase (table 2297).

Practical information
Riffelalp
Riffelalp★★★, CH-3920. Tel: 027/966 46 46; fax: 027/967 51 09; email: riffelalp@zermatt.ch Opened in 1884, but the original hotel tragically burnt down during restoration. New hotel in traditonal style.
Riffelberg★★★, CH-3920. Tel: 027/966 65 00; fax: 027/966 65 05; email: riffelberg@zermatt.ch; web: www.zermatt.ch/riffelberg/ First opened in 1854 and since extended.

Gornergrat
Kulm Gornergrat, CH-3920. Tel: 027/966 64 00; fax: 027/966 64 04; email: gornergrat.kulm@zermatt.ch; web: www.zermatt.ch/matterhorn-group/ The highest hotel in the Alps.

BRIG–ANDERMATT Table 610
This section of the Glacier Express continues up the Rhône Valley into the eastern part of the Upper Valais known as the Goms, with the first spiral tunnel of the journey. Opened as late as 1926, it is operated by the Furka-Oberalp-Bahn (FO), taking its name from the Furka and Oberalp passes which the railway has to cross or tunnel under. All the way to the Furka Tunnel, the railway forges up a broad, steep-sided valley with numerous side valleys that afford excuses to break the journey at almost every station. The river is a constant companion on the south side of the line. Along the ridge to the north of the railway is the lovely Arolla pine forest of Aletsch, which offers fine walking. Some of the villages are also small ski resorts. It is also on this section that lunch is served on eastbound trains. If you are fortunate, you may have the pleasure of eating in the 1925-built coach that was originally built for the Montreux–Oberland Bernois Railway. It has beautful walnut panelling, brass bottle-holders, hooks, lights and racks, and each section of roof is coved. Sit on the right.

At present, trains have to reverse at Brig but plans to rebuild part of the station and the depot facilities are expected to permit through running. For Brig and the first station at **Naters**, see tables 100/100.2/100.3. To the right leaving Naters, you may see the northern portals of the great Simplon Tunnel.

The much-rebuilt medieval Catholic church at **Mörel** has 16th- and 17th-century wall-paintings, and a walk of one or three minutes from the station are two cablecars to the car-free-resort of Riederalp (tables 2330 and 2331), where there is an alpine dairy and a small museum in an authentically furnished 17th-century chalet. Two chairlifts continue to Moosfluh (table 2333) and Hohfluh (table 2334).

Just before **Betten** the train engages the first FO rack section and the line crosses the Rhône by the Nussbaum Viaduct. Above the valley and reached by a cablecar from near the station (table 2337) is another car-free resort,

Bettmeralp, forming with Riederalp Europe's largest pedestrian area! The area is also noted for its large number of days of sunshine. Bettmeralp is a good summer and winter sports resort, especially for those with children. The rack continues to **Grengiols** where the train crosses the FO's highest viaduct just before entering a spiral tunnel to gain height.

You emerge to a marvellous view looking down on Grengiols Viaduct and the confluence of the Rhône and Binna rivers, while the train continues on the rack as far as **Lax**, another good departure point for walks. To the right you can look up the Binntal, a lovely valley of particular interest for its terminal moraines left by the retreating Fiescher glacier. It can be reached by bus from the next station, at **Fiesch** (table 610.15). The buses stop at Ernen, regarded as one of the Valais' most beautiful villages with many 15th–18th-century houses and a sumptuously decorated and wonderfully sited Catholic church of 1510–18, which has a notable organ of 1679 on which recitals are given. The south front of the Tellenhaus of 1576 is decorated with the earliest known representation of the William Tell legend. The bus continues through a nature reserve (because of the outstanding flora) and a long tunnel to Binn, another delightful village with a small museum; it contains some fine crystals for which the area is renowned.

Five minutes' walk from Fiesch station is the cablecar to Eggishorn (table 2343) from which there are outstanding views along the Great Aletsch glacier, Europe's longest at about 24m (15 miles). In contrast to the view of the glacier from Jungfraujoch, from here you get a much better idea of its immense size.

Leaving Fiesch another rack section climbs through the Fiesch forest to **Fürgangen-Bellwald** from where a cablecar ascends to Bellwald (table 2345), a sports resort which claims to have protected itself from 'real estate madness'. The hamlets that make up Bellwald have no less than eight chapels, mostly of the 17th–18th centuries, and the village is at one end of the hiking trail along the Goms ridgeway that leads to Oberwald (see below). At the village of Mühlebach across the Rhône is one of the oldest wooden buildings in the Valais, which was the birthplace of Cardinal Matthäus Schiner, the Bishop of Sion and Pope Julius II's military leader; he campaigned in Italy and became a familiar figure at European courts.

The valley now becomes broader still, with the village of Steinhaus to the right before the train reaches **Niederwald**. This was the birthplace of the famous hotelier César Ritz (1850–1918), who managed the Savoy in London soon after it opened, then went on to build the Ritz in Paris and lend his name to the Ritz in London. Edward VII called him 'the hotelier of kings and king of hoteliers'. Ritz was but one of several people from the area who emigrated in the 19th century, many to the USA. The Catholic church of St Theodul has an elaborate baroque interior, and the village has many attractive traditional buildings.

The onion-domed baroque Catholic church at **Reckingen** has an ossuary with a gruesome skeleton decorated with glass medallions, and the village has some fine agricultural buildings, the oldest of which dates from the 17th century. The village once had a bell foundry, casting many of the bells that can still be heard in cantons Valais, Uri and Luzern, and there is a covered bridge across the river just beside the railway. **Münster** is another picturesque village with vernacular buildings as old as the 15th century. The mill's waterwheels may still be seen and some of the buildings are mounted on staddle stones. The white-painted Catholic church of St Maria has a Gothic altar of 1509 that is regarded as second in beauty only to that of Chur Cathedral in all Switzerland. It also has a fine ceiling and choir-stalls of 1670. The area offers river-rafting and excellent opportunities for mountain-biking.

The valley floor is now broad and flat, and you may see herds of goats on the track beside the railway. More dark-wood houses and barns can be seen at **Geschinen**. From **Ulrichen** station you can take one of the most impressive bus journeys in Switzerland (table 600.51), over the Nufenen Pass at 2,478m (8,129ft) to Airolo station at the south end of the Gotthard Tunnel in the Ticino. The bus starts in Oberwald (see below).

The different appearance of the village at **Obergestein** is due to the fire that devastated it in 1868. Some of it was rebuilt in stone rather than the wood characteristic of Goms. **Oberwald** is the highest village in the Upper Valais, and one end of the Goms ridgeway path that extends all the way to Bellwald (see above) and the riverside path along the Rhône down to Ernen. There is also a notable cross-country skiing trail from here to Niederwald. The station is a stop on the spectacular bus route between Meiringen and Andermatt that takes in the Grimsel and Furka passes (table 470.75).

The passes crossed by the road beyond Oberwald open only in the summer months, so for eight months of the year the car-carrying trains through the Furka Base Tunnel are the only way to proceed east. The single-bore 15km (9½ miles) tunnel was opened in 1982 and was the longest metre-gauge tunnel in the world, with two passing places, until eclipsed by the Vereina Tunnel (see page 373). It avoids the notorious climbs up to the old Furka Tunnel, which were susceptible to avalanches and forced the railway to close in winter. Above the new tunnel are the headwaters of the Rhône, the boundary between Valais and Uri, and the intersection of old east–west and north–south trade routes, the Grimsel Pass leading north towards Meiringen.

The train emerges from the tunnel into a very different landscape, with few trees and fewer farms, and the hills covered with gorse. One could be in a Scottish glen. Soon after returning to daylight, the train passes **Realp**, the start of a steam-operated preserved railway over part of the old line to the Furka Tunnel and down to Gletsch (see table 615 below).

The young River Reuss appears on the left as the train bowls along the Urseren Valley, past the tiny hamlet of Zumdorf and across the Richleren bridge to **Hospental**, where the 12th-century tower of the Hospental family stands. Part of the village is not visible from the train, but it contains a large baroque church of 1705–11.

Andermatt is an important railway junction, providing a connection with the Zürich–Milan main line at Göschenen where the main line enters the northern portal of the Gotthard Tunnel, the route of which lies directly underneath the FO station at Andermatt.

The town is both a summer and winter resort, helped by a reputation for sun and clear air: with 500km (312 miles) of paths, it is an excellent centre for walking, and there is canoeing, hang-gliding, fishing and mountain-biking, as well as the usual facilities for such sports as swimming and tennis; in winter 56km (35 miles) of ski runs are served by ten lifts, a chairlift to Nätschen (table 2596.1) and Stöckli (table 2596.2), and a cablecar to the impressive viewpoint of Gemsstock (table 2597), at 2,961m (9,714ft). About 600 peaks can be seen from the mountain. In summer there is a path back to Andermatt from the Gemsstock, which takes about 5½ hours.

Andermatt's attractive arcaded Rathaus of 1767 incorporates part of an older building, and the town has a 17th-century baroque Catholic parish church. On the southern outskirts of the town is the pilgrimage church of Maria-Hilf, built in 1739–42 and standing in a commanding position overlooking the town. From the chapel a path leads southeast to the Gurschenbach Falls. The sound of small arms fire is periodically heard around Andermatt as the district is an army training centre – as is usually obvious by military movements on the railway and roads – and some areas are off-limits.

Andermatt offers some of the best postbus journeys in Switzerland. It is linked to Meiringen by the splendid bus journey over the Furka and Grimsel passes (table 470.75), affording magnificent views over the Rhône glacier, which is at its best in early summer when the shoulders of the valley are bright with alpine flowers. To the south is a journey over the Gotthard Pass (see below).

For the next section of the Glacier Express, see table 920 on page 361.

Practical information

Fiesch

TO – CH-3984. Tel: 027/970 60 70; fax: 027/970 60 71. Open: Mon–Fri 08.00–12.00, 13.30–18.00, Sat 08.00–12.00, 13.30–17.00.

Des Alpes★★★, Furkastrasse, CH-3984. Tel: 027/971 15 06; fax: 027/971 36 28; email: des-alpes@rhone.ch; web: www.des-alpes.ch

Münster

TO – CH-3985. Tel: 028/973 17 45. Open: Mon–Fri 10.00–12.00, 15.00–18.00.

Croix d'Or & Poste★★★ (H), CH-3985. Tel: 027/974 15 15; fax: 027/974 15 16; email: post.muenster@bluewin.ch Goethe stayed here.

Andermatt

TO – Gotthardstrasse 2, CH-6490. Tel: 041/887 14 54; fax: 041/887 01 85; email: verkehrsverein-andermatt@bluewin.ch; web: www.andermatt.ch Open: Mon–Sat 09.00–12.00, 14.00–18.00.

Numerous hotels; closest to the station is
Badus★★, Gotthardstrasse 25, CH-6490. Tel: 041/887 12 86; fax: 041/887 03 38; web: www.forum.ch/badus-andermatt.htm

A hotel in the town centre is
Kronen★★★, Gotthardstrasse 64, CH-6490. Tel: 041/887 00 88; fax: 041/887 18 38; email: kronen.hotel@bluewin.ch; web: www.centralnet.ch/publipage/kronen/hotel.htm

Bicycle hire from Oberwald and Andermatt stations.

REALP–GLETSCH Table 615

When the old section of line between Realp and Oberwald closed for the last time in October 1981, it seemed as though that would be the end of rail access to the Rhône glacier.

The reason for building the new Furka Base Tunnel was to end the seasonal availability of the line, which had had to be closed in the winter, and a particularly vulnerable bridge, the Steffenbach bridge, dismantled until the threat of snow damage had passed in the spring.

However, a preservation society was formed, the Dampfbahn Furka Bergstrecke (DFB), which took over the line and commenced operations to Tiefenbach in July 1992, followed by reopening to Furka, the entrance to the tunnel, in July 1993. In July 2000 the section through the 2km-long tunnel and down to Gletsch was opened. The rack line is worked by three steam locomotives: two that were built for the line in 1913, sold to Vietnam when the FO was electrified, and repatriated in 1990; and a third locomotive that was built for the Brig–Visp–Zermatt Railway. The railway operates mid-Jun–early Oct, Fri–Sat; mid-Jul–mid-Aug, daily. In bad weather services are reduced, and the round trip takes 3–3¹/₂ hours. Tel: 027/973 33 73; web: www.net4u.ch/dfbfurka Sit on the left to the summit tunnel and then move to the right.

The DFB station at Realp is a ten-minute walk from the FO station, following the road on the north side of the line that parallels the railway towards the new tunnel. Trains are made up of four-wheel coaches, one a more generously windowed bar coach. They do not have lights so the passage through the tunnels is atmospheric for those close to the locomotive, the orange glow of the fire illuminating the swirling steam.

The scenery is truly spectacular, the railway forging up a desolate, steep-sided valley that is like a Scottish glen writ large when mist obscures the mountains that tower over the line to the north. The postbus route over the Furka Pass can be seen snaking its way round the contours hundreds of feet above the railway. The Furkereuss river keeps close company with the railway all the way to the summit, periodically tumbling over boulders beneath a sturdy bridge. There is a loop at **Tiefenbach** and trains take water there, enabling passengers to photograph the train. At the summit station, **Furka**, passengers can patronise the buffet, set into the hillside to protect it from snow.

The single-bore tunnel under the pass is 1,874m (6,148ft) long, and the line emerges at Muttbach station to begin the descent to **Gletsch**, offering a magnificent panorama over the Rhône Glacier to the right.

Practical information
Gletsch
Glacier du Rhône★, CH-3999. Tel: 027/973 15 15; fax: 027/972 29 13.

ANDERMATT–GOSCHENEN Table 610

This useful link between the Furka–Oberalp-Bahn and the Zürich–Milan main line is also an extraordinary if short journey and worth doing just for the experience. The rack railway drops down the Schöllenen gorge past the famous Teufelbrücke (Devil's Bridge). Sit on the right.

Trains for Göschenen leave Andermatt in an easterly direction and turn north immediately to enter the exceptionally narrow and deep defile of the Schöllenen gorge in which there is only just room for the railway and road. The first path through the gorge was created by suspending planks from the valley sides. The construction of the bridge across the River Reuss that flows through the gorge was a crucial event in opening up north–south communications. Two successive old bridges can be seen on the right at the head of the gorge: the still usable (by pedestrians and cyclists) 1830 bridge and below it the fragments of its 15th-century predecessor which was swept away. The falls near here sometimes send spray over the Devil's Bridge, so named because legend has it that the structure was built through a Mephistopholian pact whereby the devil would have the soul of the first to cross the bridge; the builder sent a goat. In 1799 the sound of the falls would probably have been drowned out by the clash of arms as Austrian and Russian troops under Suvarov fought two savage battles here against the French.

Although the railway clings to the west bank and is often protected by avalanche shelters, there are occasional long views down the gorge. However, the best way to appreciate the gorge is on foot or by bicycle. Another graceful stone arch can be seen over the river at the lower end of the Schöllenen, and just before Göschenen, the train twists over the river into the station with the northern portal of the Gotthard Tunnel on the right. For **Göschenen**, see table 600.

Bicycle hire from Andermatt and Göschenen stations.

OBERWALD–MEIRINGEN Bus table 470.75

The postbus journey over the Grinselpass is regarded as one of the most spectacular, requiring a double-decked postbus to meet demand. But it also serves a useful purpose in linking two east–west railways separated by the massif that parallels the northern flank of the Rhône. Sit on the left.

From Oberwald the bus climbs alongside the track of the old railway over the Furka Pass, which is gradually being reopened by a preservation society (see Table 615 above). On the approach to Gletsch the spiral tunnel can be seen on the right. The bus winds its way through a seemingly endless succession of hairpin bends, its unique horn demanding the right of way as it takes up the full width of the road to negotiate the turn. At the summit the bus stops long enough for passengers to have a beverage in the summit café or hotel.

The air is so clean at this altitude that the rocks covering the hillsides of the descent are covered in pale green lichen. Two dammed lakes are passed before the bus has to make a deviation around a tunnel too low for the large bus.

Practical information
Grimselpasshöhe
Grimsel-Blick★★★, CH-3864. Tel: 027/973 11 77; fax: 027/973 14 22.

OBERWALD–AIROLO Bus table 600.51
A postbus journey to the south of Oberwald takes the route over the Nufenen pass completed as recently as 1969. The broad valley sides on the northern side are covered in hardy bushes and rocks. The bus passes the Griesser reservoir on the right, beyond which is the Griespass, an old 'wine road' between Switzerland and Italy. The bus stops at the summit for refreshment in the café-restaurant, before the long, straight descent down the Val Bedretto to Airolo. A small force of French retreated this way and north over the Nufenen Pass in 1799 after being defeated by Suvarov's superior Russian army.

AIROLO–ANDERMATT Bus table 600.50
The Gotthard Pass is perhaps the most famous of the Swiss alpine passes and for centuries has been associated with hazardous and punishing travel. As long ago as 1402 Adam of Usk crossed the pass in an ox-cart with eyes blindfolded. The coach road was built in 1819–30, heralding the era of epic postbus journeys, replaced by postal sleighs when conditions were so bad that coaches could not get through. The importance of the road diminished when the rail tunnel was opened in 1882.

The climb out of Airolo begins immediately, the old road twisting its way upwards to the east as the newer and less sinuous new route uses tunnels and shelters to gain height with fewer bends.

At the 2,108m (6,916ft) summit is a group of buildings of mostly 19th-century origin that derive from the first use of the pass in the 13th century. A hospice and chapel were built by Capuchin fathers, who assisted travellers until 1799. One of the buildings houses the National St-Gotthard Museum, which vividly portrays the history of the pass, its geographic significance and the hard life of those who provided transport over it. An excellent guidebook and history of the Gotthard in English is available. (Open: Jun–Oct, 09.00–18.00. Tel: 091/869 15 25.) For bus tickets or bookings (advisable in high season), apply at the tourist office.

An alternative to the postbus during July and August is a full-size replica of the old horse-drawn coaches that worked the route. The journey can be done in a southerly direction only and takes about eight hours, after which the three horses and coach are driven back to Andermatt. The coach seats eight people, attended by four postilions, and a stop is made at the summit. Details from Historia Swiss Tours, Postfach 239, Brunnen, CH-6440. Tel: 041/820 12 41; fax: 041/820 62 30; email: historia@bluewin.ch

ANDERMATT–FURKA–OBERWALD Bus table 610.20
Although this postbus journey parallels the old route of the Furka–Oberalp railway, now reopened to Gletsch, the views offered by the higher road are different enough to justify the experience of both.

The ascent to the Furka Pass affords good views over the railway and the very Scottish character of the scenery in the valley of the Furkareuss. Near the summit is the massively built, traditional Hotel Belvedere. To the right is the Rhône Glacier, one of the most photographed of glaciers, though it has shrunk considerably since it was first recorded on glass plates. The road follows the railway down to Gletsch, the current terminus of the DFB (see above), to Oberwald station.

The station for Pilatus at Alpnachstad

The Ticino

The only Swiss canton to lie wholly on the southern side of the Alps, Ticino was the result of a consistent policy by the Confederation to incorporate the area south of the great trade route across the mountains. The canton became part of the Confederation in 1803 and is the fourth largest. It is noted for the extraordinary variety of its flora and fauna which inevitably reflect the exceptional difference in altitude between the lowest and highest parts – from just under 200m (656ft) to over 3,400m (11,155ft).

AIROLO–LUGANO Table 600

The southern section of the Gotthard main line is one of the busiest arteries in Europe, handling 118 passenger and freight trains a day in each direction. As the Alpine Museum in Bern puts it, 'since the opening of the Gotthard motorway in 1980, the magical word "Gotthard" has lost its lustre. It has become a synonym for transit and queues, and arouses feelings of anger and loss'. The unobtrusive railway remains a marvel of engineering, but the view of stark concrete road viaducts from the train window is a sad reminder of misplaced priorities. The pollution caused by the motorway was one of the reasons behind the referendum vote in favour of building new railway tunnels through the Alps to rid the country of transit lorries.

The Gotthard Tunnel crosses the boundary between the cantons of Uri and Ticino and marks the transition between the German- and Italian-speaking parts of the country. Trains emerge from the tunnel at the station of **Airolo**, the highest on the Swiss Federal Railways' network, at 1,142m (3,747ft). The town grew up as a staging post for packhorse trains, wagons and coaches crossing the perilous Gotthard Pass. The town was almost totally destroyed by fire in 1877, while tunnelling work was in progress, and was devastated by a landslide in 1898, so few old buildings survive. On the left near the station buildings is the bronze monument by Vincenzo Vela to the 177 men who died building the tunnel.

Buses from Airolo station travel through the dramatic Val Bedretto and over the Nufenen Pass to Oberwald station on the Brig–Andermatt line (table 600.51) and over the Gotthard Pass to Andermatt (table 600.50) (see Chapter 19). The funicular from Piotta to Ritom (table 2603) can be reached by bus from Airolo station (table 600.53); built in 1921 in connection with a hydro-

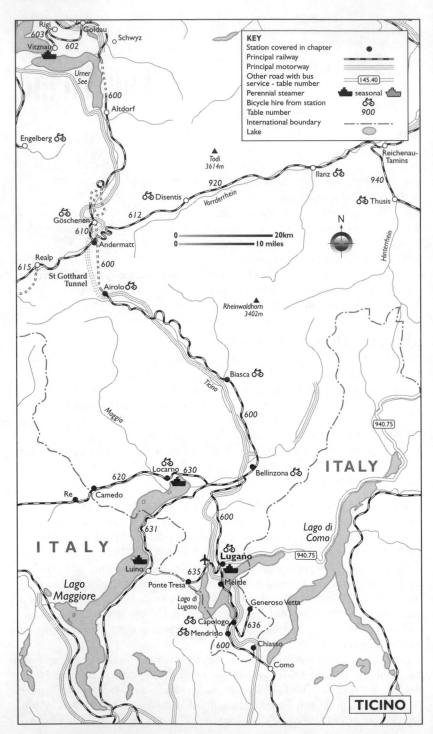

KEY
Station covered in chapter
Principal railway
Principal motorway
Other road with bus
service - table number
Perennial steamer   seasonal
Bicycle hire from station
Table number   *900*
International boundary
Lake

145.40

Rigi
603
Goldau
Vitznau
602
Schwyz
Urner
See
600
Altdorf
Engelberg
Todi
3614m
Reichenau-
Tamins
920
Ilanz
940
Vorrderrhein
Disentis
612
Göschenen
610
Thusis
Realp
Andermatt
600
615
St Gotthard
Tunnel
Airolo
Rheinwaldhorn
3402m
N
0   20km
0   10 miles
Ticino
Biasca
Maggia
600
940.75
ITALY
Locarno
630
620
Bellinzona
Re
Camedo
600
ITALY
631
Lago di
Como
Luino
Lago
Maggiore
Lugano
635
940.75
Ponte Tresa
Mélide
Lago di
Lugano
Generoso Vetta
Capologo
636
Mendrisio
Chiasso
600
Como

TICINO

electric project, the country's steepest funicular serves a sanatorium, the village of Altanca and the artificial lake of Ritóm, on the shore of which is an alpine park with an estimated 500 species of flora. The railway takes 12 minutes to rise 785m (2,575ft).

As with the north ramp, the volume of traffic over the Gotthard route leaves no paths for local trains so an hourly bus serves the smaller communities down to Bellinzona (railway table 600.2). However, a good way to explore the villages as far as Biasca is to avail oneself of the special bicycle hire system at Airolo whereby combined tickets cover bike hire and a return journey by train. Bicycles are returned to Biasca station. (The same facility exists between Göschenen and Flüelen; see Chapter 14.)

Walking routes can be followed along both sides of the valley to Biasca: the eastern one known as the Strada Alta is the more developed (with the regrettable and thankfully rare use of asphalt for sections of the path); the western route passes through villages such as Prato and Chironico, which has a beautiful Romanesque church with frescos of 1338.

The south ramp of the Gotthard is gentler than the northern approach, with a vertical drop down to Biasca through the Val Levintina of 849m (3,747ft) in 45.6km (28½ miles). None the less it calls for four spiral tunnels and gradients of 1 in 37, as well as repeated crossings of the River Ticino, which the railway follows all the way to Giubasco. Both pairs of spirals were required by steep falls in the valley at points where the river crashes through gorges. The first pair of tunnels is just below Rodi Fiesso on the approach to **Faido**.

The principal town of the Val Levintina, Faido, has some fine 16th-century wooden houses as well as typical Ticinese stone dwellings. To the south of the town is a Capuchin monastery and church of San Francesco, built in 1608. Samuel Butler stayed here in 1880 while writing *Alps and Sanctuaries of Piedmont and the Canton Ticino*, published two years later.

South of Faido chestnut and mulberry trees and vines appear as the train approaches the second pair of spiral tunnels beyond the closed station of Lavorgo. Three levels of track can be photographed together as the tightly compressed loops skirt the adjacent river as it gushes through the Biaschina ravine.

The descent from the Gotthard is marred by the ugly motorway that has been ruthlessly driven down the valley without regard to the landscape. The Val Levintina is a textbook example of the way railway engineers were able to integrate their narrow threads of steel into the landscape, building bridges of elegance out of local materials, whereas the functional concrete motorway structures obtrude horribly into what was a lovely valley. Moreover, the electric railway produces no pollution while traffic on the St Gotthard route emits 30 tonnes of nitrogen each weekend. As a result the air quality in many alpine valleys bordering the motorway is now worse than that in cities like Zürich and Basel.

It is well worth making the effort to visit Giornico. It was here in 1478 that a Swiss force outnumbered 10 to 1 defeated a Milanese force. But the reason for visiting the village is its two famous churches, especially San Nicolao, which is regarded as the loveliest Romanesque church in the canton. Dating from the second half of the 12th century, the doorway is guarded by sculptured beasts, and 15th-century frescos decorate the raised choir. Up the hill the church of Santa Maria di Castello stands beside the ruins of a Milanese castle destroyed in 1518; it too has 15th-century frescos. The 16th-century Casa Stanga contains a museum about the Levintina (open: Apr–Oct, Tue–Sun 14.00–17.00).

The valley has widened by the time **Biasca** is reached at the foot of the descent. This is the southern ramp equivalent of Erstfeld where an additional locomotive was attached for the ascent. Looking up the valley side to the east, you can see a spectacular waterfall which may be reached by a panoramic path called the Via Crucis. It begins at the collegiate church of Santi Pietro e Paolo, which is thought to have been built between the end of the 11th and 12th centuries and contains an exceptionally fine collection of frescos. Ask for the key at the parsonage before climbing the hill.

The Via Crucis takes you over a Roman bridge to the oratory of St Petronella and continues past several lovely waterfalls, the remains of an aqueduct carved out of rock and the ruins of Orelli Castle.

Buses from Biasca serve the Blenio Valley along which a metre-gauge railway used to run to Acquarossa-Comprovacco. Year-round services reach Olivone (table 600.72) and Ludiano (table 600.70), but between mid-June and mid-October the Olivone bus is extended all the way to Disentis station between Andermatt and Chur (table 600.73). The Blenio Valley is noted for its walking, and maps and suggested itineraries are available from the Biasca tourist office.

From **Castione** a preserved electric railway operated by Ferrovia Mesolcinese FM runs up Val Mescolcina to Cama. Trains usually run on varying Sundays, Apr–Oct (tel: 079/681 05 59; web: www.marmotech.com/aafm).

Leaving Biasca the train races along a straight section to the capital of the Ticino at **Bellinzona**, which developed from Roman times thanks to its strategic position at the entrance to three passes – Gotthard, Lukmanier and San Bernardino. To reach the tourist office from the station, turn left along Viale Stazione to arcaded Piazza Nosetto on which the office may be found. This, with the adjacent Piazza Collegiata, is the heart of the old town in which a colourful market is held on Saturday mornings. The latter takes its name from the large collegiate church of Santi Pietro e Stefano, a much rebuilt largely Renaissance church which has elaborate 17th–18th-century stucco.

Beside the church is a pedestrian alley that climbs the hill to one of Bellinzona's three castles, all of which have survived largely intact and which constitute some of Switzerland's most important military buildings. The three are also known by the names of the three cantons which prosecuted the policy of bringing the canton under Swiss hegemony and which installed their bailiffs in them. The Castello di Montebello (Castle of Schwyz) was begun at the end of the 13th century and progressively enlarged to consist of two multi-towered curtain walls surrounding a rectangular five-storey keep and a gate tower. The fortress's slender and uniform machicolations belie the different building periods. It houses the Civic Museum of archaeological and historical artefacts (open: Feb–Dec, Tue–Sun 10.00–12.30, 13.30–17.30). (Castle open: daily 08.00–18.00.)

On the other side of Piazza Collegiata is Castel Grande (Castle of Uri), the oldest and largest of the three, dating from the 12th century. The castle is dominated by two tall 13th-century towers, one a keep, the other residential (open: daily). The third castle, Castello di Sasso Corbaro (Castle of Unterwalden), lies outside the old town and is approached by a winding road. Reputed to have been built in just six months by the Milanese after their defeat at Giornico (see above), this large structure houses a museum of folk art. (Castle open: Feb–Dec, Tue–Sun 10.00–12.30, 13.30–17.30.)

Along Via Lugano is a church that once came under a Franciscan monastery: Santa Maria delle Grazie was built in 1481–5 and has an exceptionally intricate fresco decorating the rood screen. The central scene of the Crucifixion and 15 surrounding scenes of the life of Christ were executed by an unknown artist in the late 15th century, but they have been compared with the fresco by Bernardino Luini in the Santa Maria degli Angioli in Lugano.

Not far from Santa Maria delle Grazie, on the other side of the railway, is the 13th-century church of San Biagio, with a huge 14th-century fresco of St Christopher on the façade and 14th–15th-century frescos inside.

One of the country's longest postbus journeys leaves from Bellinzona station for Thusis and Chur stations (table 900.80), crossing the San Bernardino Pass.

Beyond **Giubiasco** is the junction where the lines to Locarno and Luino (in Italy) veer to the right, while the line to Lugano and Chiasso climbs to the south. Five minutes' walk from **Rivera-Bironico** is the gondola up to Alpe Foppa (table 2640) on Monte Tamaro where there are good walks with views over lakes Maggiore and Lugano.

Practical information

Airolo

TO – Via Stazione, CH-6780. Tel: 091/869 15 33; fax: 091/869 26 42. Open: Mon–Fri 0815–1215, 14.00–18.00, Sat 0815–1315.

Forni★★★, Via Stazione, CH-6780. Tel: 091/869 12 70; fax: 091/869 15 23; email: info@forni.ch; web: www.forni.ch Opposite station.

Biasca

TO – Contr. Cavalier Pellanda, CH-6710. Tel: 091/862 33 27; fax: 091/862 42 69. Open: Mon–Fri 08.30–12.00, 14.00–18.00; May–Oct, Sat 08.30–11.30.

Nazionale★★, Bellinzona 24, CH-6710. Tel: 091/862 13 31; fax: 091/862 43 62; email: nazionale@swissonline.ch; web: www.exposwiss.ch/expo/nazionale Opposite station.

Bellinzona

TO – Palazzo lat Posta, Viale Stazione 18, CH-6500. Tel: 091/825 21 31; fax: 091/825 38 17; email: tourism-ticino.ch Open: Mon–Fri 08.30–18.30, Sat 09.00–12.00.

Unione★★★, Via G Guisan 1, CH-6500. Tel: 091/825 55 77; fax: 091/825 94 60; email: info@albergo-unione.ch; web: www.albergo-unione.ch
Internazionale★★★, Piazza Stazione 35, CH-6501. Tel: 091/825 43 33; fax: 091/826 13 59.

Bicycle hire from Airolo, Biasca, Bellinzona and Lugano stations. A good cycle track runs from Bellinzona to Lake Maggiore, Locarno and Ascona, running beside the River Ticino

LUGANO

Lugano is the principal resort of Ticino, Switzerland's third banking city thanks to its proximity to Italy, and a good base for exploring one of Switzerland's two Italian-speaking cantons. Visitors are attracted by its extremely mild climate, glorious scenery and luxuriant vegetation. The Swiss record for hours of sun is held by the nearby hill village of Agra, but the humidity of July and August does diminish visibility. Its location on the oddly shaped lake of the same name is complemented by a long, tree-shaded promenade along the water's edge, created in the later 1840s by sweeping away numerous villas and gardens; a few relics survive, such as the bust of George Washington that once graced the garden of a villa built by a returning emigré. The views are dominated by the peaks of Monte Bré to the east and Monte San Salvatore to the south.

The locals share the Italian love of showing off in motor cars, so traffic levels and accident rates are high. However, extensive pedestrianisation makes the historic core of the city a delight to walk round: trees, shrubs and fountains enhance the attractive stone sets, and many of the old villas and arcades have been carefully conserved. Guided walks are organised daily except Saturday and Sunday from early May to late October (tel: 091/913 32 32). Lugano has also become a centre of modern architecture, and the tourist office has an illustrated leaflet for a walk taking in its contemporary buildings. The city is particularly proud of its most famous modern architect, Mario Botta, who has designed buildings in North America as well as Europe. In Lugano he has designed one of the many banks, several residences and the library of the Capuchin monastery. Although his work and some other modern structures in Lugano are striking and exciting, others – especially some of the banks – are as sadly lacking in merit as their counterparts the world over, despite, in some cases, their position next to an historic building.

The station is on high ground overlooking the city and connected to the pedestrian centre by a frequent funicular that runs from under the platform canopy as you leave the station down to Piazza Ciocarro. Alternatively, across the main road and directly ahead is a zig-zag path that drops down the hill, past the Federale Hotel and the Cathedral of San Lorenzo to the pedestrian area. This walking route is a delight, the streets graced by fountains, trees and tubs of flowers and shrubs. Arcades line many of the shopping streets. Markets are held in the main square of Piazza della Reforma on Tuesdays and Fridays.

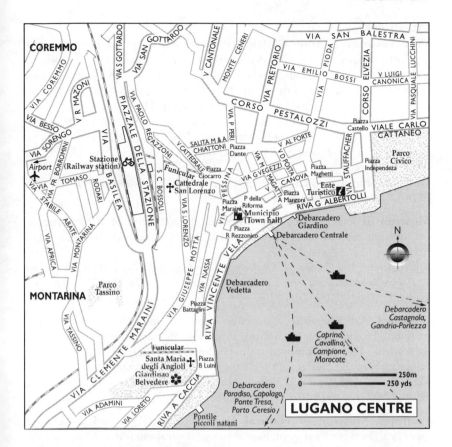

Amongst Lugano's many churches are two that should not be missed. A church has stood on the site of the Cathedral of San Lorenzo since at least the 9th century, but the Romanesque building has been progressively enlarged. The fine Renaissance façade dates from 1500 to 1517, and the interior has frescos in varying states of completeness from the 13th to 16th centuries.

Overlooking the lake on Piazza B Luini and best reached from the pedestrian area by walking along Via Nassa is the Santa Maria degli Angioli. Once part of a Franciscan monastery, the church was built in 1499–1515. Its crowning glory is the vast fresco that occupies the whole wall above three arched openings that link the nave and choir. Painted by Bernardino Luini (c1475–1532) towards the end of his life, the fresco portrays the Passion and Crucifixion of Christ. The church has other frescos, some also by Luini.

Near the church are the Belvedere Gardens (Giardinao Belvedere) in which works by local and international sculptors stand beneath sub-tropical trees. Another park worth visiting is Parco Tassino (on bus routes 9, 10), just to the southwest of the railway station. Once owned by Swiss Federal Railways, it is laid out in the form of an English garden and contains 300 rose bushes of 80 varieties. It also contains some red and fallow deer and a children's playground.

Museums

Villa Favorita Picture Gallery (Fondazione Thyssen-Bornemisza)
The collection of the Thyssen-Bornemisza family is one of the finest private collections created this century. The family owes its fortune to a huge iron and steelworks at Mülheim in the Ruhr. Unfortunately many of the old masters have been loaned until 2002 to the Prado in Madrid. The residual collection is largely 19th- and 20th- century works by European and American artists. Over 50 of the 150 works on display date from 1835 to 1900 by exponents of Luminism, the Hudson River School of Painting and American Impressionists.
Castagnola. Bus 1 from Lugano. Open: Easter–Oct, Fri–Sun 14.00–18.00. Tel: 091/972 17 41. Admission charge.

Museum of Extra-European Cultures A collection of statues, masks, photographs and other objects from Melanesia, Polynesia, Indonesia and Africa.
Villa Helenum, Via Cortivo 24. On footpath from Castagnola (steamer pier) and buses 1, 2. Five minutes' walk from Villa Favorita. Open: Tue, 14.00–17.00 Mar–Oct, Wed–Sun 10.00–17.00. Tel: 091/971 73 53. Admission charge.

Cantonal Art Museum Collection of 19th- and 20th-century artists, including Hodler, Klee, Nicholson, Degas and Renoir, as well as numerous local artists. The museum is also the headquarters of the Swiss Photography Foundation in the canton, and regular exhibitions of its collection are held.
Via Canova 10 (off Pixxa della Reforma). Bus 4. Open: Tue 14.00–17.00, Wed–Sun 10.00–17.00. Tel: 091/910 47 80. Admission charge.

Cantonal Museum of Natural History Collections and displays of zoological, botanical, palaeontological and geological interest.
Viale Cattaneo 4. Near Parc Civico, buses 1, 2, 11, 12. Open: Tue–Sat 09.00–12.00, 14.00–17.00. Tel: 091/911 53 80. Admission free.

Fondazione Galleria Gottardo Temporary exhibitions of paintings, applied arts, photographs, ethnography and archaeology in conjunction with other museums and cultural foundations.
Viale Stefano Franscini 12. Bus 4. Open: Tue–Sat 10.00–17.00. Tel: 091/808 19 88. Admission charge.

Monte San Salvatore (table 2652)

The attractive station at the foot of the two-stage funicular can be reached from the first station south of Lugano, Lugano-**Paradiso**, or by buses 9 and 10. It opened in 1890 and operates from mid-March to mid-November. Unusually the funicular crosses over the standard-gauge Chiasso line close to Paradiso station. The second stage is especially steep, climbing through woods and rock cuttings. Although the top of the mountain is disfigured by a huge communications mast, it is an excellent place from which to work out the complicated shape and topography of Lake Lugano. Standing close to the 912m (2,992ft) summit is a chapel of 13th-century origin; the present building dates from 1705, the materials having been carried up the mountain by the women of Pazzallo and Carabbia as voluntary offerings. The church has an adjacent tower and viewing platform; walk round the side of the chapel to the stairs.

An Italianate villa at the top has a restaurant and picnic terrace. During July and August dances are held at the restaurant, with the last funicular down at 23.00. There is a good walk to Carona (for the bus back to Lugano, table 633.60) or down to Melide with the possibility of returning by steamer or train.

Monte Brè (table 2653)

Monte Brè has the distinction of being the sunniest mountain in Switzerland, and the two-section funicular operates from February to December.

Buses 1, 2 and 11 pass the end of Via Pico on which the funicular station is situated, only a few minutes' walk from the bus. A restaurant and terrace at the summit offer panoramic views as far as the Valais and Bernese Alps, and a network of paths descends to Castagnola and Gandria; both places have piers for a return journey by boat.

Regional pass

Passes giving either free travel or discounts of 25-50% on all public transport in the Lugano/Locarno area are available from local transport companies, Swiss Railways, travel agents, hotels and the tourist office (TO). Available for 7 days or 3 days in a week with discounts on the other 4 days. Milan is an easy day trip, being just 1½ hours by train.

Practical information

TO – Palazzo Civico, Riva Albertolli, CH-6901. Tel: 091/913 32 32; fax: 091/922 76 53; email: info@lugano-tourism.ch; web: www.lugano-tourism.ch Open: Apr–Oct, Mon–Fri 09.00–18.30, Sat 09.00–12.30, 13.30–17.00; Nov–Mar, Mon–Fri 09.00–12.30, 13.30–17.30.

Numerous hotels; closest to the station are
Continental-Parkhotel★★★, Via Basiea 28, CH-6903. Tel: 091/966 11 12; fax: 091/966 12 13; email: info@continentalpark.ch; web: www.continentalpark.ch
Federale★★★, Via Paolo Regazzoni 8, CH-6903. Tel: 091/922 05 51; fax: 091/923 29 88; email: reservation@hotel-federale.ch; web: www.hotelfederale.ch Quiet location.

Bicycle hire from Lugano station.

LAKE LUGANO

Motor ships serve 14 points on the lake. There is a variety of options, with lunch, tea and dinner cruises as well as excursions to piers that offer connections with buses and trains. For example, Ponte Tresa is the terminus of a branch from Lugano (see below), and two trains a day up Monte Generoso connect with boats from Lugano at Capolago pier. There are even shopping expeditions to Italy for those in need of retail therapy. Services are operated by the Navigation Co of Lake Lugano (tel: 091/971 52 23; fax: 091/971 27 93; email: lakelugano@bluewin.ch).

Passing through Lugano c1900, Hilaire Belloc observed boats that 'were strange, unlike other boats; they were covered with hoods, and looked like floating waggons. This was to shield the rowers from the sun.'

A footpath skirts most of the lake. Taking the villages in a clockwise direction from Lugano:

Gandria One of the most charming villages of the Ticino, helped by being car-free, Gandria is best reached on foot or by boat. Since the village clings precariously to a steep slope from the water's edge, it has no roads, only twisting alleyways along which all provisions have to be carried. Out of season this is delightful; choose a quiet time (early or late) during the high season.

Cantine di Gandria The unusual *Swiss Customs Museum (Museo Doganale Svizzero)* can be reached only by lake steamer (13.00 departure from Lugano Giardino) or by footpath. It is housed in a four-storey building that served from 1865 to 1948 as a barracks for frontier guards. The displays, some interactive, cover such subjects as the history of frontier protection, smuggling and ways of combating it. Limited English interpretation. (Open: Palm Sunday–mid-Oct, daily, 14.30–17.30. Free admission.)

Campione An enclave of Italy surrounded by Switzerland. Swiss money is preferred and there are no border formalities though it is wise to take your passport. The pilgrimage church of Santa Maria dei Ghirli dates principally from the 13th to 14th centuries and contains some important 14th- and 17th-century frescos.

Bissone The birthplace of Francesco Borromini (1599–1667), described as the most original genius of high baroque architecture in Rome. Much of the picturesque village remains unspoilt. Casa Tencalla is a typical and beautifully furnished 17th-century Ticinese house, but is no longer open to visitors.

Capolago The start of two trains a day up Monte Generoso (most start at the junction station with the main line), see below. Only a short walk from the pier is the very old settlement of Riva San Vitale (see Lugano–Chiasso, table 600 below).

Brusino Two minutes' walk from the jetty is the cablecar to Serpiano (table 2680), a health resort and the start of woodland walks and with good views over the lake.

Ponte Tresa, **Caslano** and **Agno** See Lugano–Ponte Tresa table 635 below.

Morcote One of the most delightful villages of the Ticino, which lies at the foot of the Ceresio peninsula. A pretty row of buildings lines the waterfront, many of the villas decorated with elaborate stucco or frescos. The campanile of the much rebuilt 14th-century church of Santa Maria del Sasso towers above the houses; it is decorated with 16th-century frescos. The chapel of San Antonio Abate is part of a group of medieval buildings and has 15th-century frescos. Parco

Scherrer is an extraordinary park, founded by the proprietor of an embroidery business from St Gallen who died in 1956. He had opened the park to the public and his widow donated it to the municipality of Morcote. Besides the fine cedars, Mexican pines, camphor trees, Chinese magnolias and palms, the park is full of original works and copies of objets d'art from around the world, such as a Siamese tea house, Greek statues and an Arab house (open: mid-Mar–Oct, daily 10.00–17.00; Jul–Aug –18.00).

Melide   For the village, see Lugano–Chiasso, table 600. There is an attractive lakeside walk starting near the pier which passes Swissminiatur.

Practical information
Gandria
Moosmann***, CH-6978. Tel: 091/971 72 61; fax: 091/972 71 32.

Morcote
Carina-Carlton*** (H), Via Cantonale, CH-6922. Tel: 091/996 11 31; fax: 091/996 19 29. Close to pier.
Bellavista ** (H), Strada Da Vigh 2, CH-6921. Tel: 091/996 11 43; fax: 091/996 12 88.

AROUND LUGANO
The tourist office in Lugano organises a series of guided walks of half and full day duration throughout the surrounding area, some with a particular theme.

Parts of the Malcantone to the northwest of Lugano, and the Ceresio (the peninsula to the southwest of the town), can be reached only by bus from Lugano. Many bus routes start in Via San Balestra and call at the station before leaving the town.

Cademario in the Malcantone is served by the bus to Aranno (table 633.15) and its botanical garden is home to Switzerland's finest collection of cacti. Just below the village of Cademario is the church of San Ambrogio, which dates from the 12th century and has some exceptional wall-paintings from the first half of the 13th century. Continuing on to Aranno, the village has an old water-powered forge with the only trip hammer in the Ticino. Malcantone means 'area of hammer mills', for the area was once famous for its water-powered ironworks. The region has some exceptionally fine walks, including two – the Trail of Wonders (*Sentiero delle meraviglie*) and the Green Trail (*Sentiero verde*) – that follow the banks of the Magliasina; details can be obtained from the tourist office in Caslano, a station on the line from Lugano to Ponte Tresa (see below).

To the northeast of Lugano is the village of Tesserete, once the terminus of a branch line from Lugano and now served by bus (table 633.29). Just before Tesserete is Ponte Capriasca where the Catholic parish church of San Ambrogio has a 1550 copy of Leonardo da Vinci's Last Supper; it is of great value to art historians because the original masterpiece in the Refectory of Santa Maria delle Grazie in Milan is badly damaged.

To the south of Lugano is the hilltop village of Carona, reached by bus from the main bus station in Via San Balestra (table 633.60). Carona is notable for

Botanical Park San Grato, which is open free all year and has large collections of conifers, azaleas, rhododendrons and heathers. Carona also has three fine churches: San Giorgio with 15th-century relief sculptures; Santa Marta with 15th-century frescos; and the picturesquely sited pilgrimage church of Santa Maria d'Ongero with mid-16th century stucco.

Admirers of the novels of Hermann Hesse can see his house (privately owned) at Montagnola and his grave at nearby San Abbondio di Gentilino, both of which are served by the bus from Lugano to Agra (table 633.55). Hesse lived in Montagnola from 1919 to 1926, and a rare piece of film records his fear that excessive motor traffic would one day damage the quality of life around Lugano. The conductor Bruno Walter is also buried at San Abbondio.

LUGANO–PONTE TRESA Table 635

Opened in 1912, this metre-gauge railway provides access to the area lying to the north of the line known as the Malcantone. This beautiful area is made up of the main and side valleys of the River Magliasina which flows from Mount Lema into Lake Lugano at Magliaso. Gold has been mined in the area on and off for two centuries, with little success, but it has left a rich legacy of industrial archaeology in a glorious setting. The regional tourist office in Caslano produces a map of the area's footpaths and an exceptionally good English guide to a circular walk from Novaggio, taking in many sites of historic and archaeological interest. Bicycles cannot be carried on this line.

The station for Ponte Tresa is on the opposite side of the main road outside the main station at Lugano and a minute's walk to the right. There is an attractive café in the station. The railway dives underneath the main line and soon leaves the town behind, though it serves a populous area all the way to the Italian border. Near **Sorengo** the line skirts the small Laghetto di Muzzano in which the fish are dying; no explanation has been found for their demise. The lake is unusual in that no streams flow in or out.

From **Cappella-Agnuzzo** there is a walk along the ridge of the Collina d'Oro to the hilltop village of Agra, which holds the Swiss record for hours of sunshine. The railway then drops down and describes a U-bend around Lugano airport to reach the largest town on the line at **Agno**. Here the railway reaches the shore of Lake Lugano where Garibaldi landed after his troops were defeated near Varese in 1848.

From **Magliaso** station a bus goes to Lisone (table 635.20), stopping at Miglieglia, where the church of San Stefano has a fine Romanesque tower and Gothic frescos. The paintings of the 12 apostles form part of a service conducted here at least seven or eight times a year at the request of infertile couples. Candles are lit in front of each of the apostles; following mass, a special prayer is said on behalf of the couple who then vow to give the anticipated child the name of whichever apostle is the last to be lit by a candle.

A bus from Magliaso serves Curio (table 635.21) where the attractive old high school, built in 1855, has been converted into a local history museum (open: Apr–Oct, Thu and Sun 14.00–17.00). The bus continues to Novaggio, the start of a signed, circular walk, the *Sentiero delle meraviglie*. An illustrated leaflet in English describes the walk and objects of interest on the way, such as mills (including the Aranno forge), mines, kilns, woods, agricultural terraces and a castle. The walk takes four to six hours depending how long one lingers. Curio can also be reached by bus from Ponte Tresa (table 635.25).

From Miglieglia a chairlift goes up Monte Lema (table 2660) at 1,624m (5,328ft) from which there is a panorama over the Malcantone to Lake Lugano and to the Grisons and Bernese Alps. You can walk along the ridge from Monte Lima to Monte Tamaro, where a gondola descends from Alpe Foppa to Rivera (table 2640), five minutes' walk from Rivera-Bironico station on the Bellinzona–Lugano line.

Zoo 'Al Maglio' at Magliaso has over a hundred animals from all over the world (open: daily, Apr–Oct 09.00–19.00, Nov–Mar 10.00–17.00). Leaving Magliaso the railway cuts across the golf course on the way to the resort of **Caslano** where there is a museum that chocaholics should not miss, though it's rather short on interpretation and long on sales promotion. Astonishingly Schokoland Alprose is the only museum in Switzerland devoted to the subject and is situated alongside a factory producing 12,000 tonnes a year under the brand name Alprose. (Open: Mon–Fri 09.00–18.00, Sat–Sun 09.00–17.00. Admission charge.)

Ponte Tresa is Switzerland's smallest municipality, with an area of only 0.28 km² (69 acres), and the bridge over the River Tresa, which flows from Lake Lugano into Lake Maggiore, is the border. From Ponte Tresa station a bus goes to Luino (table 633.40), following the river for much of the way. Bridges periodically cross the river, each one a border post. The border of the bus route is a few miles before Luino on Lake Maggiore; from there a steamer or train can be caught to Locarno in the north (see below) or Sesto Calende in the south.

Practical information
Magliaso
Villa Magliasina★★★★ (H), CH-6983. Tel: 091/611 29 29; fax: 091/611 29 20; email: mail@villa-magliasina.ch; web: www.villa-magliasina.ch

Caslano
TO – Piazza Lago, CH-6987. Tel: 091/606 29 86; fax: 091/606 52 00.

Gardenia★★★★ (H), Via Valle, CH-6987. Tel: 091/606 17 16; fax: 091/606 26 42; email: albergo-gardenia@bluewin.ch; web: www.albergo-gardenia.ch

Ponte Tresa
Del Pesce★★★, Via Cantonale, CH-6988. Tel: 091/611 27 00; fax: 091/611 27 09; email: info@delpesce.ch; web: www.tinet.ch/delpesce

LUGANO–ST MORITZ Bus table 940.75
The Palm Express leaves from a bus stop just outside the station and to the right. Almost half the journey is through Italy, and the stop for refreshments is in Italy. Reservations are

required (Lugano, tel: 091/807 85 20; fax: 091/923 69 39. St Moritz, tel: 081/837 67 64; fax: 081/837 67 60). Sit on the right.

The journey begins along the north shore of Lake Lugano, overlooking the lakeside villas and villages. The bus squeezes through gaps barely wider than its wing mirrors. The border is crossed before the end of the lake, and a series of unremarkable Italian towns preceeds the first glimpse of Lake Como as the bus descends to the pretty lakeside town of Menággio.

The bus then follows the lake shore for much of the way to its northern end, through the town of Dongo where Mussolini and other Fascists were caught in April 1945. The isthmus between Como and Lago di Viezzola is crossed before turning north to the historic town of Chiavenna, which thrived while the road over the Splügenpass was still an important international artery. The town is the terminus of a branch railway from Cólico with the odd through train to Milan. A stop is made here for refreshments.

The road follows the River Mera on the south side of the road. The stone bridge in Promontogno dates from 1390, and many of the village houses are decorated with sgraffito. Vicosoprano is just off the main road and has several good restaurants. Deciduous woodland gives way to conifers as the bends tighten during the bus's climb to the Malojapass at 1,815m (5,955ft). The stretch of road alongside Silser See is delightful, with a rugged shoreline on the opposite shore and streams tumbling down the hills.

Sils Maria benefits from being off the main road, and has numerous hotels. The smaller Silvaplaner See is followed by the even smaller Champfèrer See, after which the road drops down towards St Moritz.

LUINO–CADENAZZO–Bellinzona Table 631
A delightful journey for most of which Lake Maggiore is constantly in view. Sit on the left.

Although the line follows the lakeshore all the way, the railway remains at a level high enough to afford good views over the lake, looking down on tiny harbours like that at **Maccagno** or on the villas that occupy some of the headlands. The station at **Pino-Tronzano** is particularly delightful, its well-tended garden screened by palms and shrubs. The border is crossed before **Ranzo-San Abbondio**, which is followed by a string of lakeside villages before the line drops down to the Bolle of Magadino. This protected marshland that surrounds the deltas of the Ticino and Verzasca rivers is an area of great ecological interest, forming a transitional zone between land and water that is home to 300 kinds of birds and many rare species.

For Locarno, change trains at the junction of **Cadenazzo**.

BELLINZONA–LOCARNO Table 630
Although obviously of less importance than the Lugano line, the branch to Locarno has through trains to such cities as Nürnberg, Schaffhausen, Basel and Zürich.

The Locarno line bears to the right leaving Giubiasco as the Chiasso line climbs away to the left. Market gardening is much in evidence as the train follows the River Ticino across the broad Magadino Plain to **Cadenazzo**, the junction station for the line along the eastern shore of Lake Maggiore into Italy. The Locarno line swings to the right, crossing the wide river, and is soon amongst the suburbs of Switzerland's principal town on the lake. **Locarno** station is situated right in the centre, only a few minutes' walk from the lake and many of the hotels.

Bicycle hire from Locarno station.

LOCARNO

Like Lugano, Locarno was once the property alternately of the bishops of Milan and Como, becoming a part of Switzerland in 1512 with a victory by a force from cantons Uri, Schwyz and Unterwalden. The town earned a place in the history books through hosting the Locarno Peace Conference of 1925, but is best known today for its International Film Festival. The mildness of the climate has spawned a rash of developments around Locarno and Lake Maggiore; few have done the appearance of the area any favours.

The centre of the town is Piazza Grande, a few minutes' walk west of the station; en route is the tourist office, which organises a 1¾-hour walking tour of the old town, starting at 09.45 on Monday. Attractive houses over arcades line the north side of the piazza, in which films are screened in the open during the festival. To the west of the square is Via F Rusca off which narrow streets to the right lead to Via Cittadella and Piazza Castello, where the medieval palace that was once the home of the ruling Visconti family can be found. Work on the building is thought to have started in 1342, though conflict and rebuilding have substantially altered the structure. The museum it houses contains Bronze Age and Roman items, a fine collection of medieval glassware and an exhibition on the Locarno Treaty (open: Apr–Oct, Tue–Sun 10.00–17.00).

The town's oldest church is San Vittore, just north of the railway along Via Collegiata. Although much altered, the church dates from at least the 9th century. The 11th-century Romanesque crypt has sculptured capitals, and the tower has a marble relief of St Victor brought from the castle.

The patrician house of Casa Rusca on Piazza San Antonio is now an art gallery with work by Jean Arp and by Ticino and French artists (open: Tue–Wed, Fri–Sun 10.00–12.00, 14.00–17.00, Thu –22.00).

Locarno is on the route of the Palm Express to Zermatt or St Moritz (see Chapter 4).

Practical information

TO – Lago Zorzi 1, CH-6600. Tel: 091/791 00 91; fax: 091/792 10 08. Open: Apr–Oct, Mon–Fri 09.00–18.00, Sat 10.00–16.00, Sun 10.00–14.00; Nov–Mar Mon–Fri 09.30–12.30, 14.00–18.00.

Numerous hotels; close to the station are
Muralto★★★★, Piazza Stazione 8, CH-6602. Tel: 091/743 01 81; fax: 091/743 43 15; email: info@hotelmuralto.com; web: www.hotelmuralto.com

Rosa-Seegarten★★★, Lungolago Verbano 25, CH-6600. Tel: 091/743 87 31; fax: 091/743 50 02; email: rosa-seegarten@bluewin.ch; web: www.rosa-seegarten.ch
Zurigo★★★ (H), Viale Verbano 9, CH-6602. Tel: 091/743 16 17; fax: 091/743 43 15; email: info@hotelmuralto.com; web: www.hotelmuralto.com

Locarno–Madonna de Sasso (table 2620)

The funicular to Locarno's most important group of religious buildings is two minutes' walk from Locarno station; from the end of the platforms turn left and the funicular station is on the right.

The first halt is for the Grand Hotel, the town's oldest hotel and the building in which some of the meetings leading to the Locarno Peace Treaty of 1925 were held, confirming the German borders of France and Belgium and the demilitarisation of the Rhineland. Mussolini and Austen Chamberlain stayed at the hotel during the conference. The halt is linked to the hotel by an elegant iron bridge. The second halt is for Hotel Belvedere.

Construction of the Franciscan monastery beside the terminus at Orselina must have been a difficult task. As you near the top of the funicular you can see the supporting arches built on near perpendicular rock. The monastery was founded in 1480 after a monk had had a vision of the Virgin Mary and was reached by pilgrims ascending a path from the lakeshore representing the Way of the Cross. On the way up to the church, a room with grille door contains life-sized terracotta figures that once occupied the shrines along the path. Attributed to Francesco Silva, they date from 1625 to 1650.

The church itself was built in the 16th–17th centuries but much altered at the beginning of the 20th. Its low ceiling painted blue-black makes the church dark and the frescos difficult to see. On the high altar is a miraculous image of the Madonna of 1485–7, and in the south aisle a 1522 painting by Bramantino of the flight to Egypt.

A small museum containing religious treasures is attached to the monastery (open: Easter–Nov, Mon–Fri 14.00–17.00, Sun and holidays 10.00–12.00, 14.00–17.00).

Beyond the church and sanctuary is the cablecar to Cardada (table 2621) followed by a chairlift to Cimetta (table 2622) from where there is a splendid panorama over the Alps and over Lake Maggiore to the Italian plains.

Practical information

Belvedere★★★★, Via ai Monti 44, CH-6601. Tel: 091/751 03 63; fax: 091/751 52 39; email: ptaylor@tinet.ch; web: www.hotel-belvedere.com
Grand Hotel★★★★ (H), Via Sempione 17, CH-6600. Tel: 091/743 02 82; fax: 091/743 30 13; email: grand-hotel@bluewin.ch

LAKE MAGGIORE

A fifth of the 212 km^2 (82 sq miles) of Lake Maggiore is in Switzerland, and it stretches for 66km (41 miles) from Magadino in the north to Sesto Calende in the south, the points at which the River Ticino enters and leaves the lake respectively. The lake water's cleanliness makes it a great centre for watersports, but local winds sometimes make navigation difficult for the vessels on Lake Maggiore run by Navigazione Laghi Maggiore (tel: 091/751 61 40). The company has an unusually diverse fleet of vessels, ranging from the 1908 paddle steamer *Piemonte* to the 1989 hydrofoil *Lord Byron*, though most of its boats are conventional motorships. Day passes are available (unusually, the Swiss Pass is not valid), and boats operate from early April to late September. The services call at 28 places on the lake, and there are some outstanding attractions. It is advisable to take your passport. There is a range of cruises and special offers, some involving rail travel, such as the Lago Maggiore Express which takes the Centovalli (see table 620 below) from Locarno to Domodóssola where a Milan-bound Cisalpino is caught to Stesa for the boat journey back to Locarno via Isola Bella.

Taking first the places in Switzerland served by boat from Locarno, in a clockwise direction:

Magadino   A nature reserve of particular interest to ornithologists: the Bolle di Magadino is an area of marsh and waterways in which live over 300 species of bird. A path enters the reserve from the village of Magadino. Tours of the reserve are operated from Locarno by Gambarogno Turismo every Monday in July and August at 09.00 (tel: 091/743 62 65).

Brissago   On the lakeshore stands the baroque Palazzo Baccalà, built in 1740–50. In the middle of the village is the Renaissance Catholic parish church of Santi Pietro e Paolo, 1526–1610. The Italian operatic composer Leoncavallo (1858–1919) made his home here. Offshore are the islands of the same name; on the main island of San Pancrazio is a botanical garden (open: Apr–Oct, daily 09.00–18.00) and a 1927 villa that houses a small museum of African ethnography. The church on the smaller island dates from the 11th to 12th centuries. Boat trips are run to the islands every hour from Brissago and every half hour from Porto Ronco.

Places of interest on the Italian part of the lake include, again in clockwise direction from the northeast:

Laveno   where the 18th-century buildings along the waterfront have retained a homogeneous appearance.

Stresa   A resort since the mid-19th century, with many elegant 18th-century villas. The Sanctuary of Santa Caterina on the other side of the lake from Stresa is built on a shelf of rock in sheer cliffs; a separate boat service takes visitors from Stresa. Stresa offers marvellous views over the lake and the three Borromeo Isles, which are linked with Stresa by a half-hourly boat.

Isola Bella, probably the lake's *pièce de résistance*, has an outstanding mansion and 17th-century garden created by the Borromeos. The palazzo has a gallery with works by Tiepolo and Zuccarelli amongst others, and the garden is a series of ten terraces arranged as a pyramid. (Open: Mar–Oct, daily 09.00–12.00, 13.30–17.30.)

Isola dei Pescatori The first of the three islands to be inhabited, by fishermen. Today it is a labyrinth of alleys, houses covering the tiny island to the extent that there is barely room for a dozen trees.

Baveno The garden shore has attracted many famous guests, such as Byron, Lamartine, Wagner, Queen Victoria and Churchill.

Isola Madre was transformed in the mid-16th century by Lancillotto Borromeo's villa and garden, described by Flaubert as 'a terrestrial paradise'.

Pallanza Nearby is the island of San Giovanni where for several decades the conductor Arturo Toscanini had his summer residence in a 17th-century palace.

Villa Taranto, between Pallanza and Intra, was created by a Scot, Captain Neil MacEacharn, who donated to the Italian state in 1939 one of Europe's richest botanical gardens with over 30,000 specimens. (Open: Mar–Oct, daily 08.30–18.30, last admission 18.30.)

Italian railways serve Stresa, Arona and Laveno, and both Luino and Maccagno are on the line that runs up to Bellinzona.

AROUND LOCARNO

Ascona, easily reached by bus from Locarno (table 630.30), by boat or on foot along the lake, should not be missed. Made famous by the patronage of writers and intellectuals such as Carl Jung, Hermann Hesse, James Joyce and Erich Maria Remarque and more recently by film stars, Ascona has retained the attractiveness of the old village by the careful conservation of its buildings and extensive pedestrianisation of the old quarter and the piazza on the lakeshore. Art galleries, antique shops and craft shops proliferate.

The church of Santa Maria has 15th–16th-century frescos, and the Collegio Papio to the south of it has a lovely two-storeyed cloister of the 16th–17th centuries.

Amongst the subjects of Ascona's festivals are New Orleans jazz (end of June), classical music (late August–early October) and puppets (September). In the Palazzo Pancaldi at Via Borgo 34 is a modern art gallery which includes works by Paul Klee, Hans Arp and Ben Nicholson (open: Mar–Dec, Tue–Sat 10.00–12.00, 15.00–18.00, Sun 10.00–12.00).

Buses continue beyond Ascona to Porto Ronco and Brissago (table 630.30/line 21); for both places, see Lake Maggiore, above. A free bus service connects the two villages every hour.

To the northeast of Locarno is the Verzasca valley, reached by bus from the station (table 630.55). The relatively unspoilt valley encapsulates vineyards, chestnut forests, beechwoods and pine forest with views of the valley's tallest mountain, Pizzo Barone, at 2,864m (9,396ft). At Vogorno the church of St Bernard has Byzantine-style frescos of c1200. It is worth stopping off at Bivio per Corippo, at the northern end of Lago di Vogorno, to take the track up to the village of Corippo, designated a national landmark for the cluster of carefully restored houses on a mountain ledge. A little further up the valley, at Lavertezzo, is a double-arched medieval bridge across the River Verzasca with an adjacent 18th-century chapel. The church of Santa Maria at Brione has some highly regarded frescos of c1350, depicting scenes from the Life of Christ, including the Last Supper. The 17th-century castle of Marcacci near the church is now a restaurant. In the village of Sonogno at the end of the valley is a local museum in Casa Genardini (open: May–Sep, daily 11.30–16.30). A footpath, the *Sentierone*, runs the length of the valley, and there are good walks into lonely side valleys, such as Val d'Osola from Brione.

Practical information
Ascona

TO – Casa Serodine, CH-6612. Tel: 091/791 00 91; fax: 091/792 10 08; email: locarno@ticino.com; web: www.lagomaggiore.org Open: Apr–Oct, Mon–Fri 09.00–18.00, Sat 10.00–16.00; Nov–Mar, Mon–Fri 09.00–12.00, 13.30–17.00.

Numerous hotels; in traffic-free area on lakeside promenade is
Castello Seeschloss**** (H), Piazza Motta, CH-6612. Tel: 091/791 01 61; fax: 091/791 18 04; email: castello@romantikhotel.ch; web: www.romantikhotel.ch/17 Delightful hotel, part of which is converted from a medieval castle.

Hotels also in quiet locations are
Giardino*****, Via Segnale, CH-6612. Tel: 091/785 88 88; fax: 091/785 88 99; email: giardino@bluewin.ch; web: www.giardinaqo.ch
Ascona****, Via Signor in Croce 1, CH-6612. Tel: 091/791 35 11; fax: 091/791 17 48; email: booking@hotel-ascona.ch; web: www.hotel-ascona.ch
Acapulco au Lac***, Via Cantonale, CH-6612. Tel: 091/791 45 21; fax: 091/791 19 51; email: acapulco@nikko.ch
Al Porto***, Piazza G. Motta, CH-6612. Tel: 091/785 85 85; fax: 091/785 85 86; email: info@alporto-hotel.ch; web: www.alporto-hotel.ch
Tobler**, Via Collina, CH-6612. Tel: 091/791 31 57; fax: 091/791 05 69; email: info@hotel-tobler.ch; web: www.hotel-tobler.ch

LOCARNO–DOMODOSSOLA Table 620
From either end this glorious journey starts unpromisingly in a concrete bunker. Opened as recently as 1923, the metre-gauge international line is known as the Centovalli – a hundred valleys – which refers to the numerous side valleys that join the main valley of the River Melezza. These forced the railway's builders to span them with 17 major bridges or viaducts that are as impressive today as they must have been to the local people when new – it is their spectacular locations as well as the engineering that attracts admiration. The elements in the area can be destructive – in 1978 a storm did so much damage to the line that it was shut for three years, the opportunity being taken to modernise it. This must have caused real hardship to the communities along the railway for it is a vital lifeline to many isolated communities as well as one of Switzerland's finest journeys for tourists. The line is operated by the Ferrovie Autolinee Regionali Ticinesi, which uses the unfortunate acronym. Nine of the 12 stations in Switzerland are request stops, requiring intending passengers to press a button in the shelter, or if there is none to give a

hand signal to the driver. Bicycles cannot be taken on the trains. Sit on the left to Camedo,
then on the right.

The bunker in Locarno, with its statue of the patron saint of miners, St
Barbara, may be reached by steps from platform 3. For the first few miles, the
railway has the character of a modern light rail transit, with two more
underground stations before the modern train rushes up a steep gradient into
the open. Soon after the first above-ground station at **San Martino**, the
railway joins the River Maggia which it follows to the point where it is joined
by the Melezza.

Ponte Brolla is at the confluence of the Maggia with the Melezza, the
defile beneath the bridge a jumble of enormous rocks. The excellent
Restaurant della Stazione is another good excuse to break the journey here.
The railway's historic 1923 train, which can be hired for special occasions, is
kept here.

Ponte Brolla used to be the junction for a branch up the Valle Maggia to
Bignasco that has sadly closed. Trains have been replaced by buses, and the
beauty of the valley makes it an outstanding excursion. The main bus
service up the valley leaves from the station at Ponte Brolla (table
630.60/line 10) to Cavergno. The village of Maggia has a notable church, St
Maria della Grazia, with some early 16th-century frescos. From Cevio,
shortly before Cavergno, there is a bus service which climbs up a side valley
to Cerentino where the road again divides: the southern arm goes to
Cimalmotto (table 630.67); the northern fork goes to the highest village in
Ticino and the only place where German is the principal tongue,
Bosco/Gurin (table 630.65). The area is made up of larch-forests, and one
of the village's oldest houses accommodates a local museum (open:
Easter–Oct, Tue–Sat 09.45–11.30, 13.30–17.00, Sun 13.30–17.00).

In Cevio is the Valmaggia Museum, housed in two elegant buildings that
were once home to Chancellor G A Franzoni (open: Apr–Oct, Tue–Sat
10.00–12.00, 14.00–18.00, Sun 14.00–18.00). Continuing up the main valley of
the Maggia, at the former railhead of Biagnasco, the valley bifurcates, the
western fork following the River Bavona to San Carlo (table 630.70) where a
cablecar goes up to Robiei (table 2627) from June to early October. The
Bavona valley is inhabited only in summer. The eastern fork goes up the valley
of the Maggia to Fusio (table 630.72) and Piano di Peccia (table 630.74),
renowned for its white marble.

The Maggia valley is of interest to ecologists because its vegetation is an
unusual amalgam of alpine and sub-tropical, the former brought down by
flood waters. Consequently the woods comprise oak, birch, lime, ash and
chestnut, the last best seen during blossom time in late June.

Returning to the Centovalli, the line soon reaches **Tegna** where the villas
exhibit the stucco and painted decoration that can be seen along the valley. The
tree-covered hills to the north rise higher and higher, bare patches of rock
outcropping amongst the trees. At **Verscio** the church of San Fedele, topped
by an octagonal tower, is clearly visible from the train just before the station.

The 13th–14th-century building was rebuilt in 1743–8 into a lovely baroque church with liberal use of marble. The choir of the old church, with its intricate and beautifully coloured 15th-century Gothic frescos, was incorporated into the new building.

The railway has climbed high above the river by **Cavigliano**, beyond which an immense bridge can be seen ahead; this is the first of several spectacular iron bridges, leaping 91m (300ft) across the River Isorno 70m (230ft) below. The railway organises bungy jumping from this bridge (contact either the railway, see below, or the tourist office in Locarno). On the hill overlooking the bridge is the village of **Intragna**, where the church tower of San Gottardo is the highest in Ticino at 65m (213ft). Five minutes' walk from the station is the cablecar to Costa (table 2624) from where there is a 2½-hour walk through a wood of walnut trees to the hamlet of Cremaso and down through the village of Pila back to Intragna. If there is a wait for the next train, visit the museum in the 17th-century Casa Maggetti devoted to the Centovalli, which includes paintings, agricultural implements, re-created rooms and costumes (open: Easter–Oct, Tue–Sun 14.00–18.00). There is also a lovely walk along the river to Corcapolo.

Beyond Intragna the valley becomes remoter and even more densely wooded, the occasional farm isolated in a clearing in the forest. The river can be glimpsed below, the banks periodically joined by stone arches with a shrine at the apex of their parapets. Waterfalls punctuate the great folds of hills that stretch into the distance, the intensity of their colour receding to a misty horizon. The trees are mostly deciduous, so the valley clothed in the colours of autumn is spectacular.

Right by the station at the picturesque village of **Verdasio** is the cablecar up to the unspoilt hill village of Rasa (table 2625), which is inaccessible to motor traffic and whose tiny church has the oldest playable organ in Ticino. From Rasa you can walk in an easterly direction down to the earlier station at Corcapolo. Leaving Verdasio the views down to the river hundreds of feet below are breathtaking.

Some of the houses in the village of **Palagnedra** are decorated with paintings, and the largely 17th-century church of San Michele has late 15th-century Gothic frescos from an earlier building. Below the railway are the turquoise waters of an artificial lake which winds along the valley floor to **Camedo**, the last station in Switzerland and the site of another huge iron bridge on the eastern approach. The walking possibilities from Camedo are legion, indicated on the walking map at the station. Sustenance before or after walks can be had at Restaurant Vittoria, which is reached by a flight of steps at the end of the platform and which produces ham sandwiches with slices of meat as thick as the bread. One of the walks, taking about four hours, climbs briefly to Lionza and then follows an old mule path through Verdasio down to Intragna.

The railway somewhat redeems its refusal to carry bicycles by hiring them at Camedo for a return on two wheels to Ponte Brolla. Since the track/road is at a much lower level than the railway it gives a very different perspective.

Half a mile beyond Camedo, through a broader stretch of the valley, the railway comes to the border with the old road bridge on the right. Once in

Italy the line goes through a long stretch of shelters which interrupt views of the boulder-strewn river before the Vigezzo valley opens out at **Folsongo-Dissimo**, where some attractive villas can be seen from the train.

Leaving the large station at **Re** the pilgrimage church can be seen on the hillside; for 500 years pilgrims have come here following the miracle when the Madonna is supposed to have shed blood for 21 days after an enraged young man threw a stone at her forehead. Some of the farm buildings in the area have the distinctive characteristic of stone steps leading to the first floor. The highest station on the line is reached at **Santa Maria Maggiore**, the largest community served by the railway. The village's popularity as a home for artists is evident from the number of galleries, and the square is bordered by some elegant palazzi. It has a tiny museum devoted to, of all things, chimney-sweeps. It was also the home of the inventor of eau de Cologne, Giovanni Maria Farina (1685–1766).

Conifers replace deciduous trees and the hills diminish in height as the train presses west to the delightful village of **Gagnone-Orcesco**. The homogeneous character of the stone-walled buildings, usually roofed in stone too, is a feature of a succession of villages as the river threads another gorge and the hillsides steepen. The natural beauty of this area is reflected in the name given to the valley, 'Valley of Painters'. After the pretty village of Marone the line starts to descend, twisting down the contours to the level of the first vines, at **Verigo**.

Near the station at **Trontano** is a fine group of religious buildings with separate, tall bell tower. Beyond the village the railway and the Val Vigezzo join the broad valley of the River Toce, Val Antigório, though the railway is still high above the valley floor, requiring a tortuous, flange-squealing descent through horseshoe curves. One of the curves circumscribes the lovely garden of a tower-house that stands in a commanding position on the valley slope.

Once reached, the valley floor is unattractive, the train passing through a mile or so of scruffy industrial activity before reaching the terminus in a bunker beside the main Simplon line at **Domodóssola**. Here direct trains can be caught to Brig, Thun, Bern, Olten, Basel, Sierre, Montreux and Lausanne to the north, and Milan, Genoa, Florence and Rome to the south. The old town is delightful and well worth exploring

Practical information

FART, Via Franzoni 1, CH-6601. Tel: 091/751 00 31.

Tegna

Barbate, CH-6652. Tel: 091/796 14 30; fax: 091/796 25 30. Peaceful, good food and close to station.

Intragna

Antico★★ (H), CH-6655. Tel: 091/796 11 07; fax: 091/796 31 15; email: paris@nikko.ch
Intragna, CH-6655. Tel: 091/796 10 77; fax: 091/796 31 15; email: paris@nikko.ch

Bicycle hire from Camedo station.

LUGANO–CHIASSO–Milan Table 600

The line offers excellent views over Lake Lugano, but beyond the junction for Monte Generoso at Capolago the line passes through a series of industrial towns to the border station at Chiasso.

Trains leaving Lugano's hillside station provide good views along the eastern limb of the lake as they descend through **Lugano-Paradiso**, where the San Salvatore funicular crosses over the line, to the water's edge. For much of the way to Melide the train skirts the lakeshore. **Melide** is famous for the Swissminatur Parc, which contains many of the country's most famous buildings in one-twenty-fifth scale, with examples from all the cantons. The railway that threads the park comprises a network of 3.5km (1.87 miles) of track and includes rack railways and cablecars. There is also a passenger-carrying miniature railway and a children's playground. (Open: early Mar–Oct, daily 09.00–18.00; mid-Jul–mid-Aug 09.00–22.00.)

From Melide the railway crosses the man-made causeway, built in the 1840s, over the lake to proceed along the eastern shore of the lake to **Capolago-Riva San Vitale**. A short walk from the station, the village of Riva San Vitale has Switzerland's oldest surviving Christian building. The baptistery dates from c500 and has an octagonal interior and drum dome although its ground plan is square. Until the 9th or 10th century, baptisms were performed by immersion in the octagonal basin in the centre; the huge font was then installed. Niches around the apse contain 12th-century paintings. Adjacent to the baptistery is the Catholic parish church of San Vitale, a 10th-century (or earlier) foundation rebuilt in 1756–9. The Catholic church of Santa Croce, designed by G A Piotti, is regarded as one of the country's finest Renaissance buildings, and has a prominent rotunda with drum dome.

The station is the junction for the rack line up Monte Generoso, although two trains a day run over the short section down to the boat pier to connect with sailings from Lugano. The run on to **Mendrisio** is uninspiring, though Monte Generoso and the railway up it can be seen to the left. The large town of Mendrisio is an old settlement with some fine houses in the square and a bell tower that may date from the 12th century. The Catholic church of Santi Cosma e Damiano is a vast 19th-century structure, its rather fussy façade and portico leading to a colossal rotunda with octagonal dome and lantern.

A preserved steam-worked railway operates from Mendrisio station to Valmorea, across the border in Italy – a rare example of an international heritage railway. (Tel: 051/227 95 15 [Mendrisio station] or 091/646 57 61 [Mendrisio tourism].)

The much altered 12th-century church at **Balerna** has an adjacent baptistery in which there is a 16th-century fresco of the Virgin and Child and a Renaissance triptych of c1500. Immediately beyond **Chiasso** the railway enters a tunnel which marks the border with Italy. Milan is only 40 minutes away.

Practical information

Melide

Del Lago★★★ (H), Lungolago G Motta 9, CH-6815. Tel: 091/649 70 41; fax: 091/649 89 15. Art Deco building.
Seehotel Riviera★★★, Lungo Lago G Motta 7, CH-6815. Tel: 091/649 79 12; fax: 091/649 67 61; web: www.hotel-riviera.ch

Mendrisio

TO – Via Angelo Maspoli 25, CH-6850. Tel: 091/646 57 61; fax: 091/646 33 48. Open: Sep–May, Mon–Fri 08.00–12.00, 14.00–18.00; Jul–Aug, Mon–Sat 08.00–19.00.

Stazione★★★, Piazza Stazione, CH-6850. Tel: 091/646 22 44; fax: 091/646 82 27.

Chiasso

Centro★★★, Corso S Gottardo 80, CH-6830. Tel: 091/683 44 02; fax: 091/683 44 58.

Bicycle hire from Capolago and Mendrisio stations.

CAPOLAGO–GENEROSO Table 636

The only rack line in the south of the country was opened in 1890 with steam propulsion. The 800mm-gauge railway suffered financial difficulties during the 1930s and closed in 1939, to be reopened two years later under the new ownership of the founder of the supermarket chain Migros, Gottlieb Duttweiler. Diesel replaced steam in 1953, but the line was not electrified until 1982. A steam locomotive, built by SLM in 1890, and a diesel survive for special workings. The railway operates between May and October, and the journey takes 35 minutes. Sit on the right.

To connect with steamers from Lugano, the 9km (5.6 miles) railway begins at **Capolago Lago** on the lakeshore. Using the Abt rack even on almost level sections, trains have to travel only a few hundred metres to the junction with the Lugano–Chiasso line at **Capolago-Riva San Vitale**. Near the station is a display of the different types of rack system used in Switzerland. The Monte Generoso line then twists over the standard gauge and climbs steeply up the hillside away from the lake. As so often happens on mountain railways, a tunnel masks a transition into very different terrain by describing a horseshoe bend to take the railway into another valley.

The station at **San Nicolao** is named after the nearby grotto, which is a 15-minute walk. A climb through thick woods interlaced with paths brings the railway to **Bellavista**, where there is an alpine garden on the south flank of the mountain. Its slopes are of particular interest to botanists as it is home to flowers that are rare or seen only here in Switzerland. The station has a restaurant with terrace and a kiosk adapted from an old tramcar. Numerous paths are signed from the station area. The views become much more open as the railway approaches the summit, for a while traversing the ridge to give views in both directions.

The summit at 1,704m (5,590ft) offers unrivalled views over the Ticino, northern Italy and the Tyrolean Alps, but the hotel and restaurant building is devoid of character. Amongst many routes from the summit there is a walk down the eastern flank of the mountain towards Scudellate and Muggio which gives an insight into the past and present of the rural economy and way of life. You pass mills, wash-houses, bird-hunting towers and water troughs. A bus from Muggio takes you along the Ticino's southernmost, unspoilt valley to Chiasso station (table 639.11). A booklet is available suggesting 25 other walks.

Practical information
Monte Generoso
Vetta Monte Generoso, CH-6825. Tel: 091/649 77 22; fax: 091/649 77 91.

The compact village of Splügen in Graubünden

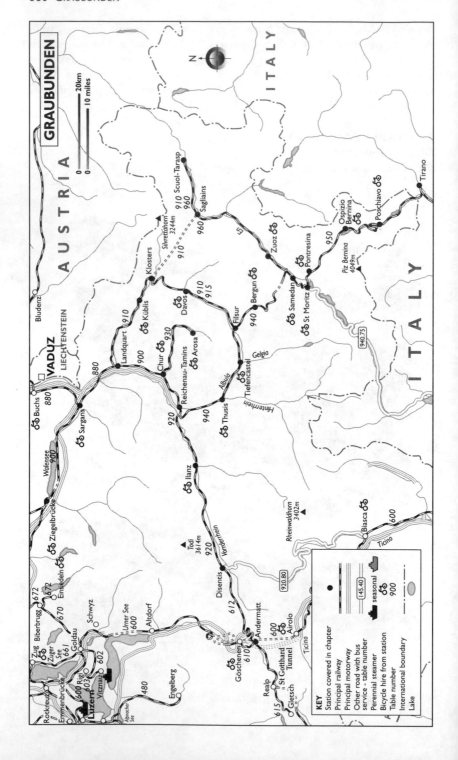

GRAUBUNDEN

0 ____ 20km
0 ____ 10 miles

AUSTRIA

ITALY

ITALY

VADUZ
LIECHTENSTEIN

Bludenz

Buchs 880
Sargans
Walensee 900
Ziegelbrücke
Einsiedeln 672
Biberbrugg 672
670
Rotkreuz
Emmenbrücke 600 Rigi 603
Zug Zuger See 661
Luzern
Goldau
Schwyz
Vitznau 602
Engelberg
Alpnacher See
480

Landquart 910
900
Klosters
Silvrettahorn 3244m
910
Küblis
Davos 910
915
Chur 930
Reichenau-Tamins
Arosa
920
940
Thusis
Tiefencastel
Albula
Gelgia
Bergün 940
Filsur
Ilanz
Vorderrhein
Todi 3614m
920
Disentis
612
Rheinwaldhorn 3402m
Hinterrhein
940.75
920.80
Andermatt
Göschenen 610
Realp
Gletsch 615
St Gotthard Tunnel
Airolo 600
Ticino
Biasca
600
Ticino

Scuol-Tarasp 910
960
Sagliains
960
910
Zuoz
Pontresina 950
Samedan
St Moritz
Piz Bernina 4049m
Ospizio Bernina
Poschiavo
Tirano

KEY

● Station covered in chapter
Principal railway
Principal motorway
Other road with bus
service - table number 145.40
Perennial steamer   seasonal
Bicycle hire from station
900 Table number
International boundary
Lake

Graubünden

The history of Graubünden, or Grisons, reflects its location at the crossroads of different cultures to the north and south of the Alps. The Alpine passes gave it an importance difficult to appreciate today, though the scenic grandeur that surrounds them now makes the canton one of the most visited by tourists. Graubünden became a canton in 1803 and is the largest in Switzerland, though also the most sparsely populated. About one-seventh of the inhabitants speak Romansch, the language derived from vernacular Latin.

The canton has many of the most popular winter sports resorts, such as St Moritz, Arosa, Klosters and Davos (the metre-gauge Rhätische Bahn which serves them once had a special hospital-car for those injured in skiing accidents); it also has wonderful opportunities for cycling, ranging from hard-going climbs for mountain-bikers to easy routes through the Engadine valley. An excellent map showing recommended cycling routes in the canton is available from tourist offices.

Graubünden was also the last canton to hold out against the motor car, refusing on eight occasions to allow the 'precarious vehicle' on to its territory, finally relenting in June 1925.

ANDERMATT–CHUR Table 612/920

The next section of the Glacier Express continues on the Furka–Oberalp-Bahn (FOB) as far as Disentis where the Rhätische Bahn (RhB), translated as the Rhaetian Railway, takes over. The line passes through remote country, entering the area in which Switzerland's fourth national language, Rhaeto-Romansch, is spoken. Sit on the right.

The departure east from Andermatt is nothing if not dramatic – eastbound trains can be watched from the platform for about ten minutes as they snake their way up four half spirals, three of which are through a tunnel. The views from the train are magnificent as it climbs higher than the summits of some chairlifts. Shingle-roofed farm buildings dot the fields of tussock grasses, tiny streams and bogs glint fleetingly in the sun. It is for sections of climb like this 1 in 9 ascent that the restaurant car has special glasses with angled stems so that they can be turned to avoid spilling the wine (they are also sold as souvenirs).

The rack continues through **Nätschen**, past Lake Oberalp on the right and beyond it the summit of the Pazzolastock, to the summit of the Oberalp Pass, the highest point on the FOB at 2,033m (6,670ft) and the boundary between cantons Uri and Graubünden. At this point there is a station, **Oberalppasshöhe**, from which there is a fine walk to the source of the Rhine at Toma Lake; where the branch of the Rhine known as the Vorderrhein leaves the small lake you can cross it in a single step. In winter the snow can be so high here that the train passes through a sheer-sided canyon of it that almost blocks out direct light, and the line is shielded by periodic avalanche shelters.

From the pass the line drops down, still on the rack, into a long tunnel. This is the moment the head waiter on the Glacier Express often chooses to do his party trick – pouring grappa with a metre gap between glass and bottle. The train emerges into daylight at **Tschamut**, the first village on the Rhine, which enters a narrow defile visible from the train. To the south the dam holding back the waters of Lai da Curnera can be glimpsed up a side valley. Young forests overlook the line, planted as a protection against avalanches as the line continues to drop down the attractive valley of the Vorderrhein, twisting through sharp curves and rock cuttings to the winter and summer sports resort of **Sedrun**. The church here dates back to 1205 and has a fine baroque altar.

A branch line drops down to the AlpTransit base tunnel workings to the east of **Bugnei**. It is sufficiently steep to require rack working.

Locomotives are changed at the summer and winter resort of **Disentis**, a town dominated by the imposing white Benedictine monastery of St Martin, said to have been founded by an Irish monk named Sigisbert c700. The baroque monastery church was completed in 1712 to the design of Caspar Moosbrugger of Einsiedeln. Today the monastery has 40 fathers, brothers and novices.

From the post office a series of postbuses, starting with the service to Lukmanier Passhöhe (table 920.80), heads south through attractive valleys to Biasca on the Gotthard route. The cablecar to Caischavedra (table 2905) is 15 minutes' walk from the station.

The desolate character of the line since Andermatt gives way to pasture and more woodland as the train descends at a higher speed through several small stations, with the Rhine close to the line on the right, to **Trun**. Near the station is the baroque chapel of St Anna, built in 1704; inside is a wall-painting which was executed to mark the 500th anniversary of an important local event that took place beside the maple tree outside in 1424. In that year an alliance of farmers was formed, for the first time giving political ascendancy to the communes over feudalism. The tree that stands today is actually a cutting of the original tree, which was destroyed by a storm in 1870. Meetings of the confederation took place in the attractive Disentiser Hof at the west end of the village which is now the Museum of the Grey League (open: mid-Apr–mid-Nov, Mon, Wed, Sat 14.00–17.00).

On the hillside above the village of Brigels (**Tavansa-Breil/Brigels**) is the small, white-rendered pilgrimage church of St Sievi which has exterior and interior wall-paintings of the 15th century.

Before **Ilanz** the railway crosses the Vorderrhein (the Glacier Express booklet, incidentally, is wrong in showing it on the south side of the line here).

Ilanz has been a town since the late 13th century and is the first town on the Rhine. Two towers of its fortifications have survived. The Reformed church of St Margarethen was finished in 1518, incorporating an earlier defensive tower that had been adapted as a bell tower in 1438. Some fine 15th–16th-century houses testify to the town's early prosperity.

From the station a bus goes to Waltensburg (table 920.60) where the Reformed church of c1100 has wall-paintings dating from the 14th to 15th centuries, one showing a gruesome martyring of St Sebastian. Two castles are each within about 30 minutes' walk of Waltensburg: the curious 12th-century stronghold of Kropfenstein which incorporated a cave into the structure; and the substantial and dramatically sited remains of Jörgenberg, which was first mentioned in 765 and last inhabited in the late 16th century.

Leaving Ilanz the valley broadens and arable fields break up the pasture. If there is a spare seat on the left-hand side of the train, take it. Near **Valendas-Sagogn** the valley divides, the railway following the Rhine along the right-hand valley which soon becomes one of the scenic highlights of the journey. The dimensions of the gorge of Flims are exceptional, huge, almost white cliffs towering over the railway on its ledge above the river, the rock faces above often contorted into peculiar shapes. If you want to explore the gorge on foot, local trains stop at **Versam-Safien**.

Soon after **Trin** the railway from St Moritz can be seen to the right swinging in to join the line to Chur shortly before the confluence of the Vorderrhein and Hinterrhein, which can be seen on the left. Hereafter the river is known simply as the Rhine. On the opposite bank of the river is Reichenau Castle, which dates from the early 17th century. A century later it became a school for the upper classes where the future king of France, Louis-Philippe, taught in 1793–4, before he went to the US for four years and then to England. Although **Reichenau-Tamins** is the junction station, it is usual for Glacier Express coaches on the direct service to St Moritz to proceed to Chur and return here on a St Moritz-bound train. The Glacier Express that runs to Davos continues through Chur to Landquart.

The train now races along a broad valley past a huge chemical works to **Chur**, the capital of Graubünden. Admirers of London's Waterloo International station may want to spare time to look at the similar, striking new station roof at Chur, which won for Ove Arup & Partners the 1994 Brunel Award for outstanding visual design in rail transportation in the Major Civil Engineering Projects category. The bus station is accommodated on a raft built over the platforms.

There has been a settlement on the site of Chur since neolithic times, c2500BC. It was an important Roman town and became a bishopric by the end of the 4th century. As princes of the Holy Roman Empire, the bishops ruled the town until forced to surrender their power in 1464. The Reformation was accepted in 1524.

Chur was the birthplace of the painter Angelica Kauffmann (1741–1807) who in 1766 emigrated to England where she had a brilliant career as a portrait painter, becoming a Royal Academician. Her birthplace, at Reichsgasse 57, still stands.

To explore the principal sites of the old town, the tourist office organises a guided tour every Monday from February until the end of October at 14.30 (no booking required). Alternatively it can supply an English-language leaflet to inform you about the most important buildings, reached by following green and red footprints and signs. With plenty of pedestrianised areas and numerous old houses, the old town is a pleasure to wander round.

To reach the tourist office proceed directly ahead from the station along Bahnhofstrasse and then left into Grabenstrasse. On the right of Grabenstrasse, retracing your steps, is the Bündner Kunstmuseum (Art Gallery). Housed in a villa of 1874–6, it contains pictures and sculptures from the 16th century, a self-portrait by Angelica Kauffmann, a Hodler landscape, and works by Giovannia, Augusto and Alberto Giacometti. There is a portrait of Alberto, the most famous of the three, whose surrealist work achieved international acclaim.

To continue to the old town, which is grouped around Martinsplatz, return to Bahnhofstrasse and turn left into Poststrasse. On the left is the arcaded Rathaus – two buildings of 1464 linked by a hall with groin vaulting of 1540. Further south is the Reformed parish church of St Martin, largely completed in 1491 though the tower was added in 1526. On the right as you enter are three windows painted by Augusto Giacometti in 1919.

Beside the church is the Rätisches Museum at Hofstrasse 1 in a house put up in 1675 for the family of Baron Paul von Buol. Since 1876 it has been a museum about the canton's archaeology, history and culture. It has neolithic, Bronze Age and Roman finds, paintings and maps of the area, and collections of arms and armour, silver, furniture, pewter, costumes, woodcarvings, pottery and musical instruments. (Open: Tue–Sun 10.00–12.00, 14.00–17.00.)

To the east of the museum is the Hof-Torturm, the entrance tower to the court beside the 17th–18th-century palace of the bishops of Chur. The cathedral was founded in the 8th century; fragments of this Carolingian-style building were incorporated into the present cathedral, built in 1150–1272. Largely Gothic, it has some Romanesque embellishments, and the tower with baroque dome was added c1600. Beyond the massive piers of the nave, the choir is at an unusually higher level. The vault of the crypt is supported by a single column that rests on a man squatting on a lion.

To the east, on a vine-covered hill, stands the former monastery church of St Luzi, an often- and over-restored partly Romanesque building of the 12th century.

For the next section of the journey to St Moritz or Tirano, see table 940 below.

Practical information
Sedrun
TO – Sedrun Disentis Tourism, Via Alpsu 62, CH-7188. Tel: 081/920 40 30; fax: 081/920 40 39. Open: Mon–Fri 09.00–12.00, 14.00–18.00, Sat 10.00–12.00, 16.00–18.00.

Disentis
TO – as above.

Trun

Casa Todi★★★ (H), Hauptstrasse, CH-7166. Tel: 081/943 11 21; fax: 081/943 18 28.

Ilanz

TO – Bahnhofstrasse 22, CH-7130. Tel: 081/925 20 70; fax: 081/925 24 74. Open: Mon–Fri 08.00–12.00, 13.30–18.00.

Casutt★★ (H), Glennerstrasse 20, CH-7130. Tel: 081/925 11 31; fax: 081/925 41 47.

Chur

TO – Grabenstrasse 5, CH-7002. Tel: 081/252 18 18; fax: 081/252 90 76; email: info@churtourismus.ch; web: www.churtourismus.ch Open: Mon 13.30–18.00, Tue–Fri 08.30–12.00, 13.30–18.00, Sat 09.00–12.00.

Numerous hotels; closest to the station are
ABC Terminus★★★★, Ottostrasse 8, CH-7000. Tel: 081/252 60 33; fax: 081/252 55 24; email: abc@hotelabc.ch; web: www.hotelabc.ch
Duc de Rohan★★★ (H), Masanserstrasse 44, CH-7000. Tel: 081/252 10 22; fax: 081/252 45 37; email: ducderohan@gr-net.ch; web: www.churtourismus.ch

Hotels with character in or near the old town are
Freieck★★★ (H), Reichsgasse 44/50, CH-7002. Tel: 081/252 17 92; fax: 081/253 34 19; web: www.minotel.com
Stern★★★ (H), Reichsgasse 11, CH-7000. Tel: 081/252 35 55; fax: 081/252 19 15; email: stern@romantikhotel.ch; web: www.romantichotel.ch/09
Rebleuten★★ (H), Pfisterplatz 1, CH-7000. Tel: 081/257 13 57; fax: 081/257 13 58.

Bicycle hire from Ilanz and Chur stations.

DISENTIS–BIASCA Bus table 920.80

The Lukmanier Pass at 1914m (6280ft) is one of the lower of the alpine passes but quite different and varied in character from the others, being far more wooded on the lower slopes. Sit on the right.

The departure south from Disentis follows the fast-flowing Medel river as it rushes down to join the Rhine. The landscape is pastoral with the occasional tended herds of goats and sheep. Long avalanche shelters are pierced by openings to allow something of a view. Spruce and pines cover the hillsides around Olivone, where the 12th-century Romanesque tower of the church survived an 18th-century rebuilding.

At Acquarossa the bus pauses at the former railway station on the line that ran up the Val Blenio. The journey ends at Biasca station, to the east of which is a large waterfall visible from the platform.

CHUR–AROSA Table 930

A railway journey that has much of interest and some marvellous walks from its stations. It opened as late as 1914, by which time Arosa was already a thriving resort with 16 hotels. Before the railway the twice-daily diligence took six hours from Chur; the railway takes one hour. Sit on the right.

Trains for Arosa leave from outside the station at Chur and are found standing in the road like a tram. Indeed, for the first couple of miles the train behaves like a tram, ploughing through the streets to the road that follows the tree-lined banks of the River Plessur. There was a plan to re-route the railway to avoid this street running but it seems that better ways have been found of spending the money than eradicating a feature of character just to save a few seconds on a car journey.

Between the street halt at **Chur Stadt** and **Sassal** the line parts company with the road and begins to climb up the immensely impressive gorge of the Schanfigg Valley with the River Plessur often far below as the railway gains height along its ledge on the steep valley side. Short tunnels and avalanche shelters periodically interrupt the view of the long drops to the meandering river. Eventually upland meadows are reached, affording some views to the left. It is worth breaking the journey at **Lüen-Castiel** to savour the landscape and to visit one of Switzerland's oldest churches in Lüen; the small Reformed church dates from 1084 and has wall-paintings of c1350. Unobstructed views take the train to **St Peter-Molinis** where the village can be seen below the pretty station. It is quite a climb up from the station at **Peist** to the village above. Tiny wooden-roofed huts and barns dot the landscape as a huge bridge comes into view. **Langweis** is a particularly attractive village from which there are good walks, including one to the Büelenbach gorge and waterfalls, and vantage points over the Langweis bridge. When first built, this was the longest reinforced concrete span in the world, with a 96m (315ft) span and a total length of 287m (942ft).

After leaving the station, the line turns sharply south to cross the bridge, followed by a long climb through woods away from the river. The train pauses at **Litzirüti** before continuing to climb through horseshoe curves set in pine woods to the tunnel that precedes arrival at **Arosa**.

In 1851 the population of Arosa was just 56. Within 50 years it had become a major resort with sanatorium as well as hotels, and skiing had begun. Today it is best known as a skiing resort with 70km (44 miles) of downhill runs and 25km (15 miles) of cross-country routes, along with the usual ice rinks, indoor swimming pools and even balloon flights. However, in summer it offers 200km (125 miles) of walking paths, horse-riding, mountain-biking, golf and tennis. Between July and October, the tourist office offers special hiking packages, starting in Lenzerheide or Davos, in which your luggage is taken care of by hotels en route and carried by train or bus to your next destination. Maps, route descriptions and vouchers for cablecars and mountain railways are included.

The station is close to the Obersee, one of Arosa's three lakes, which help to give the town a village atmosphere by spreading out the town's hotels – it never looks big enough to have 6,000 beds. There is a small local history museum in the Egga House (open: Jan–Mar, Tue and Fri 14.30–16.30, mid-Jun–mid-Sep, Mon, Wed, Fri 14.30–16.30).

Close to the station is a two-section cablecar up the Weisshorn (table 2910) from where you can walk over the Carmenpass and down to Tschiertschen to catch a postbus to Chur station (table 900.73) for the train back to Arosa. A free bus service around Arosa makes it easy to reach the gondola to Hörnligrat (table 2912); the bottom is a 40-minute walk from the station.

Arosa has few old buildings but the walk up to the famous mountain chapel at Innerarosa built in 1492–3 should not be missed. The walls are battered (tapered) and above the wooden roof shingles rises a wooden tower.

Practical information
Litzirüti
Ramoz, CH-7058. Tel: 081/377 10 63.

Arosa
TO – Poststrasse, CH-7050. Tel: 081/378 70 20; fax: 081/378 70 21; email: arosa@arosa.ch; web: www.arosa.ch Open: Mon–Fri 09.00–18.00, Sat –17.30.

Numerous hotels; close to the station are
Posthotel★★★★, CH-7050. Tel: 081/377 01 21; fax: 081/377 40 43; web: www.posthotel-arosa.ch
Vetter★, Seeblickstrasse, CH-7050. Tel: 081/377 17 02; fax: 081/377 49 19.

Hotels in a quiet location are
Astoria★★★, CH-7050. Tel: 081/378 72 72; fax: 081/378 72 70; web: www.astoria-arosa.ch.
Panarosa Herwig★★★, CH-7050. Tel: 081/378 75 75; fax: 081/378 75 70.

Bicycle hire from Arosa station.

CHUR–ST MORITZ Table 940
As though the journey of the Glacier Express thus far has not been dramatic enough, the final leg surpasses the earlier sections both in terms of railway engineering and in scenic splendour. In fact the final part of the continuous climb to the Albula Tunnel has been described as one of the railway engineering wonders of the world. Appropriately the climax comes towards the end, as it does for the westbound working with the prospect of the Matterhorn at journey's end. One of the astonishing aspects of this part of the journey is that there is not a single rack section – all the climbs are achieved by adhesion. This is also the first part of the Bernina Express which runs between Chur and Tirano. Seat reservations and a surcharge are required on both trains. In November 1999 the 18.4km (11¹/₂ miles) Vereina Tunnel opened to provide a direct railway link between Klosters and the St Moritz–Scuol line at Saglains/Susch. This has greatly reduced the fastest times between Chur and St Moritz, though passengers wanting the most scenic route should choose the slower trains using the Albula line. There is a good service of stopping trains between Chur and Thusis and between St Moritz and Filisur. Sit on the right.

The Glacier Express retraces its steps to **Reichenau-Tamins** (see above), swings to the left at the junction and starts climbing steeply, affording good views along the Vorderrhein valley to the right. The railway stays on the west bank of the Hinterrhein as it heads south into a fertile area known as the Domleschg. The throat of the valley was guarded by several castles on the east slope, the ruins of which can be seen from the train. **Rhäzüns** has three churches, all worth visiting: the Catholic parish church of 1697 has an unusual octagonal nave and polygonal choir; and the churches of St Paul and St Georg both have particularly good wall-paintings.

More castles can be seen to the east as the valley narrows, but none is open to visitors. **Thusis** has a large new station and is an attractive town, divided into an area that survived the fire of 1845 and a new village. A remarkable postbus journey leaves from Thusis station, threading the Via Mala (see below) and crossing the San Bernardino Pass, ending at Bellinzona station (table 900.80).

Leaving the station, the train climbs and turns to the east to cross the Hinterrhein, allowing a quick glimpse of the Via Mala to the right. This extraordinary road was first built in 1473, negotiating a defile barely 10m (33ft) wide with sheer cliffs of limestone soaring above. Murray's *Hand-book* described it as 'the most sublime and tremendous defile in Switzerland', and Turner made several paintings of it. The view from Thusis has been ruined by a utilitarian motorway bridge thrown across the gorge, seemingly without regard for the beauty of the surroundings. Indeed most of the section between here and Tiefencastel has been spoilt by ruthless upgrading of the road.

On the right-hand side, but too high to be seen easily, is the 12th-century castle of Hohenrätien which appears in at least two of Turner's paintings. It is quite a climb from the lovely village of **Sils im Domleschg** – about an hour's walk – but the view from the ruins is well worth it. In the village of Sils is a former palace with Italian-style terraced garden. A 15-minute walk to the south of the village is the castle of Ehrenfels, now a youth hostel, which may be visited (tel: 081/651 15 18).

The train passes through a succession of tunnels along the wild Schyn ravine, which is shared with the Albula river. The railway crosses the river immediately after **Solis** by a graceful masonry arch of 42m (138ft) at a height above the river of 89m (292ft), the arch being approached on either side by viaduct. The comparison with the slabs of concrete that form the parallel motorway bridge says little for the aesthetics of some modern civil engineering.

After further tunnels there are glorious views to the right as the valley opens out on the approach to the prettily sited village of **Tiefencastel**, dominated by the spire of the baroque Catholic parish church of St Stefan, built in 1650–2. A postbus from Tiefencastel (starting in Chur) goes south to Bivio and over the Julierpass at 2,284m (7,493ft) to St Moritz (table 900.85).

The valley grows wilder and more heavily forested, trees seeming to crown every ledge. Near **Surava** a waterfall can be seen to the right, and a mile or so after **Alvaneu** is a structure on which miles of film must have been expended. The combination of a spectacular location and an elegant, curving design have given the Landwasser Viaduct a rare status for a railway viaduct. The final arch is sprung from the wall of rock into which the train burrows to reach the junction of Filisur, where the line from Davos trails in on the left. (For Filisur–Chur, see below.)

Filisur is in a pleasant position and the village itself has some attractive houses decorated in the Engadine style with painted motifs, sgraffito and window grilles. Its hotels make a perfect base for walkers, not least because the footpath that has been created to view the civil engineering triumph of the railway is only a few miles to the south.

Leaving Filisur the train begins the climb to the Albula Pass, negotiating a single spiral tunnel, though the real drama does not begin until after **Bergün**. This mountain village has a 12th-century Reformed church with Romanesque nave and wall-paintings of c1500. Even earlier wall-paintings, of the early 14th century, can be seen by taking a bus from the station to Stugl/Stuls (table 940.60) to see the Reformed church. Preserved in the station drive at Bergün is one of the old 'Crocodile' electric locomotives that once hauled trains over the line.

To reach the Albula Tunnel without rack assistance, the railway's engineers contrived an ingenious series of loops and spiral tunnels, raising the line a vertical height of 416m (1,364ft) in 13km (7.9 miles). The 8km (5 miles) historic rail trail from Bergün to the next station at **Preda** enables walkers to see the four spirals, two galleries and seven viaducts at close quarters, with information boards and seats at suitable points. Immediately after the station at Preda the line enters the Albula Tunnel, which took a thousand workers four years to build from 1898 and is 5,865m (3.6 miles) long. In winter, sledges can be hired at Preda station so that people can toboggan down the most popular run in the canton along the road to Bergün, which is closed to traffic. In order to offer the special experience of a moonlit run, with lamps at intervals, the railway obligingly ferries passengers up to Preda until 01.30!

Emerging at the extraordinarily isolated and attractive station of **Spinas**, from where there is a cycle and footpath down to Bever, the train drops down the Val Bever to join the Engadine. A small river, the Beverin, joins the River Inn at **Bever**, eventually flowing into the Danube near Passau in Germany and ultimately into the Black Sea. At Bever, the line from Scuol-Tarasp trails in from the left. The church here has an exterior wall-painting of a knight fighting a dragon, painted in the 14th–15th centuries.

The upper Engadine is quite different in character from the narrow valleys since leaving Reichenau-Tamins, being much broader and with gentler contours to the lower mountains. **Samedan** is another junction, where a curve goes off to Pontresina and Tirano, forming a triangle of lines with the direct line from St Moritz to Pontresina. The village has some imposing houses, including one that belonged to the influential Planta family and is now a Rhaeto-Romansch cultural centre.

Leaving Samedan you can see to the left a partially ruined group of church buildings, standing in a picturesque setting of trees on a low hill. The church of San Gion (John the Baptist) dates from the 11th to 12th centuries, though the taller tower was added in 1478. In 1682 it was struck by lightning and never restored. Inside the choir are some 15th-century wall-paintings. The key is held at Celerina tourist office. The church is closest to Celerina Staz station on the line between St Moritz and Pontresina.

About six minutes' walk from Celerina is the gondola to Marguns (table 2976). Celerina is the bottom of the Olympic bob-run and Cresta run, on which speeds of 140km/h (87mph) have been reached. A short tunnel precedes arrival at the world-famous resort of **St Moritz**.

There is some evidence that the springs for which St Moritz became famous were used in pre-Roman times, and by 1519 Pope Leo X promised full absolution for every Christian visitor to the spa. But it was not until the 1830s that visitors began to come here in some numbers. Even then, accommodation was limited until the first hotel of consequence was built in 1856–9 by Johannes Badrutt. It was he who began the vogue for the British to winter in Switzerland by offering a group of British tourists free winter accommodation to prove that winter in the mountains could be a pleasure. They agreed to both propositions, and thousands followed. (Badrutt also switched on the first electric lightbulb in Switzerland at his Engadine Kulm Hotel.)

Curling was introduced from Scotland, and in 1884 the Cresta run was built through the initiative of three Englishmen. In 1928 and 1948 St Moritz hosted the Winter Olympic Games. It has become immensely fashionable, in part because of its marvellous winter climate, when four months of mostly uninterrupted clear, dry weather are the norm. However, exclusivity has its price, and if it is Switzerland you have come to see, rather than other people, one of the neighbouring resorts is likely to be cheaper and less rarefied. It is also less likely to be choked with traffic and fumes, which have become serious problems for St Moritz at certain times of year.

Of interest in the town is the leaning tower of 1672 that was once part of the former parish church of St Mauritius. The Engadine Museum in Via dal Bagn gives a good idea of what life was like in the area through a number of reconstructed rooms and collections of furniture and stoves (open: Dec–Apr, Mon–Fri 10.00–12.00, 14.00–17.00, Sun 10.00–12.00; Jun–Oct, Mon–Fri 09.30–12.00, 14.00–17.00, Sun 10.00–12.00). The Segantini Museum in Via Somplaz is devoted to the paintings of Giovanni Segantini (1858–99) who specialised in mountain landscapes (open: Jun–mid-Oct, Tue–Sat 09.00–12.30, 14.30–17.00, Sun 10.30–12.30, 14.30–16.30; Dec–Apr, Tue–Sat 10.00–12.30, 15.00–17.00, Sun 15.00–17.00). The museum was renovated for the 100th anniversary of Segantini's premature death.

In the centre of the town, 15 minutes' walk from the station, is the two-section funicular to Corviglia followed by a cablecar to the top station at Piz Nair (table 2970), from which it is a short walk to the 3,055m (10,026ft) summit and panoramic views.

The River Inn near St Moritz offers some of the best canoeing and river-rafting waters in Europe, and there are over 500km (312 miles) of signed walking routes. Local walking and cycling maps are available.

In January/February each year a Gourmet Festival is held in St Moritz, attracting leading chefs from all over the world. Taking a lead from this festival, the Rhaetian Railway operates regular gourmet excursions during the winter from Chur to St Moritz using a special dining-car, which can also be chartered.

From St Moritz there are several outstanding postbus journeys. By the Palm Express postbus to Lugano (table 940.75) you can reach the Italian town and railway terminus of Chiavenna (see pages 347–8). The road passes the two lakes of Silvaplanersee and Silsersee (which has Europe's highest lake boat service), and serves the village of Sils-Maria where the house in which Nietzsche spent his summers is open to visitors in high summer. It contains a collection of memorabilia. The bus also stops at the village of Stampa, home of the Giacometti family, where there is a museum with works by Giovannia, Augusto and Alberto (open: Jun–mid-Oct, daily 14.00–17.00). Several postbus journeys operate only on certain days of the week. The tourist office has a list of them on a board, and it is worth asking for recommendations.

Practical information
Thusis
TO – Neudorfstrasse 70, CH-7430. Tel: 081/651 11 34; fax: 081/651 25 63; email: vvthusis@spin.ch; web: www.graubunden.ch/thusis Open: Mon–Fri 08.30–12.00, 14.00–18.00, Sat 09.00–12.00.

Weiss Kreuz★★★, Neudorfstrasse 81, CH-7430. Tel: 081/651 29 55; fax: 081/651 48 65.

Tiefencastel
TO – Julierstrasse 42, CH-7450. Tel: 081/681 18 71. Open: Mon–Fri 08.00–12.00, 14.00–18.00, Sat 08.00–12.00.

Filisur
TO – c/o Railway Station, CH-7477. Tel: 081/404 21 27; fax: 081/407 14 04. Open: Mon–Sun 06.00–21.00.

Grischuna, Am Bahnhof, CH-7477. Tel: 081/404 11 80; fax: 081/404 24 80.
Rätia, Bahnhofstrasse, CH-7477. Tel: 081/404 11 05; fax: 081/404 23 53.

Bergün
TO – Hauptstrasse, CH-7482. Tel: 081/407 11 52; fax: 081/407 14 04. Open: Mon–Fri 08.00–12.00, 14.00–18.00, Sat 09.00–12.00, 16.00–18.00.

Weisses Kreuz★★★, Hauptstrasse, CH-7482. Tel: 081/407 11 61; fax: 081/407 16 86.
Albula★, Hauptstrasse 70, CH-7482. Tel: 081/407 11 26; fax: 081/407 14 83.

Samedan
TO – Haus Bernina, CH-7503. Tel: 081/852 54 32; fax: 081/852 53 88; email: samedan@compunet.ch; web: www.samedan.ch Open: Mon–Fri 08.30–12.00, 14.00–18.00, Sat 09.00–12.00, 15.00–17.30.

Numerous hotels; closest to the station is
Bernina★★★★ (H), Plazzet 20, CH-7503. Tel: 081/852 12 12; fax: 081/852 36 06.

Celerina
TO – Kreisel, CH-7505. Tel: 081/830 00 11; fax: 081/830 00 19; email: info@celerina.ch; web: www.celerina.ch Open: Mon–Fri 08.30–12.00, 14.00–18.00, Sat 10.00–12.00, 15.00–17.00.

Numerous hotels; closest to the station is
Posthaus★★★, Bahnhofstrasse 15, CH-7507. Tel: 081/833 22 22; fax: 081/833 41 07.

Hotels of character are
Cresta Palace★★★★ (H), Hauptstrasse 91, CH-7506. Tel: 081/836 56 56; fax: 081/836 56 57; email: mail@ crestapalace.ch; web: www.crestapalace.ch
Chesa Rosatsch★★★ (H), CH-7505. Tel: 081/837 01 01; fax: 081/837 01 00; email: hotel@rosatsch.ch; web: www.rosatsch.ch
Stüvetta Veglia (H), Celerina/Schlarigna, CH-7505. Tel: 082/833 80 08; fax: 082/833 45 42.

St Moritz

TO – Via Maistra 12, CH-7500. Tel: 081/837 33 33; fax: 081/837 33 66; email: information@stmoritz.ch; web: www.stmoritz.ch Open: Mon–Fri 09.00–18.30, Sat 09.00–18.00, Sun 16.00–18.00.

Numerous hotels; closest to the station are
La Margna★★★★ (H), Via Serlas 5, CH-7500. Tel: 081/832 21 41; fax: 081/833 16 72; email: info@lamargna.ch; web: www.lamargna.ch Delightful period hotel.
Waldhaus am See, Via Dim Lej 6, CH-7500. Tel: 081/833 76 76; fax: 081/833 88 77; email: waldhaus.am.see@bluewin.ch Quiet location overlooking lake, with the largest selection of whiskies in the world (according to the *Guinness Book of Records*). Also voted best three-star hotel in Switzerland.
Bellaval★★, Via Grevas 55, CH-7500. Tel: 081/833 32 45; fax: 081/833 04 06.

Bicycle hire from Thusis, Tiefencastel, Bergun, Samedan, Celerina and St Moritz stations.

ST MORITZ–SCUOL-TARASP Table 960

The railways travelled by the Glacier and Bernina expresses quite rightly receive lavish praise and promotion. But this line through the Upper and Lower Engadine deserves to be far better known: although the landscape is less obviously dramatic, it has about it a softer, immensely pleasing quality that is hard to convey. The broader views, gentler slopes, forests, river and delightful villages with distinctive Engadine style of architecture combine to produce an idyllic setting. It is the perfect valley to explore by bicycle, with a cycle route for much of its length. Sit on the right.

The train shares the railway with services to Chur as far as the junction just beyond **Bever**, the Scuol line following the River Inn the whole way and keeping to the north side of the valley. The first station building at **La Punt-Chaumes** is typical of those that follow, with attractive round-headed doors and windows, usually festooned with bright window boxes. The white Reformed church at La Punt has an octagonal choir, and the large white rectangle of Casa Mereda, with crenellated gables, is an example of the combination of farm buildings and living accommodation under one roof that is common to the Engadine.

Zuoz was once the main village of the Upper Engadine, and the original home of the influential Planta family whose curious three-storey tower can be seen near the ugly new station. This was part of their mansion, one of many patrician houses in the village which is well worth exploring. The bear's claw crest of the Planta family can be seen on buildings throughout the area. The Gothic Reformed church has glass of 1929–33 by Augusto Giacometti, and the now secularised chapel of St Sebastian, which was built c1250, has some fine 15th-century wall-paintings.

Several houses in **S-chanf** have the sgraffiti decoration characteristic of the Engadine. Also known as scratch work, this process entails overlaying a coat of coloured plaster with a white coat which is then scratched off to create a pattern out of the colour underneath. Access to the western end of the huge National Park, described under Zernez below, can be gained to the east of S-chanf station.

Shortly after **Cinuos-chel-Brail**, which also affords access to the park, the railway crosses the river on a single-span bridge across a deep gorge. A section with tunnels and mushroom-covered cuttings follows before **Carolina**. After a few miles, the railway turns sharply to the west, crossing the River Spöl, which flows into the Inn just before **Zernez**. The uniformity of this village is the result of a fire in 1872, after which similar square houses with gently pitched roofs were built as replacements. The Reformed church incorporates a Romanesque tower of c1200 and has fine stucco work in the choir and a pierced wooden parapet to the gallery. Schloss Wildenberg was the home of the Planta family for 450 years from c1400, and is arranged around a court with a corner tower of 1280. The headquarters of the Swiss National Park, the country's largest reserve, are situated here (see below).

A postbus from Zernez post office goes over the Ofenpass to Müstair (table 962.20), almost on the Italian border.

Between the attractive station at **Susch** and **Sagliains** is the triangular junction for the Vereina Tunnel line to Klosters. In high summer 3,000 cars an hour used to cross the Flüela Pass, and the tunnel enables car-carrying trains to reduce this unacceptable level of pollution. For Scuol the impact has been dramatic, reducing the journey time by train with Zürich from 4 hours 50 minutes to 2 hours 40 minutes. It is to be hoped that such fast train journeys will encourage most people to leave their car at home so that the special character of the Lower Engadine is not destroyed by the traffic levels sometimes received at the other end of the valley.

After **Lavin**, where the Reformed church of c1500 has extensive wall-paintings in the choir, the scenery becomes even more attractive. A covered bridge crosses the tree-lined Inn with forest and mountains beyond. **Guarda** is another typical Engadine village which is well worth wandering round; in 1975 it won the Walker Prize for architecture. **Ardez** has as many buildings of interest and a marvellous view from the hillside nearby. Sgraffiti and woodcarvings decorate many of the houses in the village which climbs up the hill above the station. The village has received European recognition for the way it has conserved its heritage. The best viewpoint is from the ruined keep of Steinsberg Castle on its knoll of rock which can be seen to the right as the train leaves Ardez.

The line drops steeply to a tunnel from which the train emerges to glorious views over the valley with a glimpse of Tarasp Castle, surely one of the most beautifully sited castles in all Europe. A longer tunnel follows to bring the train to **Ftan**, the station some way below the village which is served by a bus from Scuol (table 960.50). From Ftan you enjoy a clear view of Tarasp Castle on its rocky eminence, before proceeding to journey's end at Switzerland's most easterly station, **Scuol-Tarasp**. Trains arriving between 07.20 and 18.20 are met by a shuttle bus serving the town and hotels.

Scuol is the main town of the Lower Engadine and is one of the country's most celebrated spas. It is also a skiing resort, with the longest downhill run in the Engadine, and enjoys 300 days of sunshine and only 1.4 days of fog a year. Mountain bikes can be hired to explore the designated routes, and there are 1,000km (625 miles) of footpaths in the area. River-rafting and white-water canoeing are available on the Inn. From a building close to the station a gondola rises to Motta Naluns (table 2993).

A new spa and health centre, Bogn, has recently been built, and the result is spectacular. Clever use of daylight, materials of the highest quality, such as north Italian marble, and the subtle use of the six colours of Graubünden have produced an exciting yet restful building. All the equipment is state of the art, with computer-programmed whirlpools. Apart from the benefits to be derived from the ten different types of mineral springs, part of the purpose of the spa is to promote preventive medicine, with diet one of several areas on which advice is available. The spa has the only Roman-Irish bath in Switzerland in which steam and water baths are alternated, followed by soap-and-brush massage and relaxation periods. One of the pools leads outside, enabling you to soak up the mountain scenery as well as the salts.

Scuol is divided into upper and lower parts; both are worth exploring on foot, having numerous elegant houses with sgraffiti, paintings and even coats of arms for decoration. The old centre of upper Scuol is delightful: farm buildings are still interspersed with houses of massive walls, their deeply recessed windows splayed like gunports. Some have balconies supported by poles, and oriel windows are a feature of the village, perhaps the finest being on La Plazzetta. There, a fountain offers two types of drinking water: normal and red, iron water. The nearby street named Somvi also has some attractive houses. The Reformed church in the lower part dates from 1516 and has been little altered since.

Beside the river, on the opposite side from Scuol Palace Hotel in Nairs, is the neo-classical Trinkhalle, built in the 1840s for people to drink a specifically prescribed mineral water. The interior is rather like a temple, with malachite obelisks and arched doorways in front of each of the waters.

A good bus service from Scuol post office to the pretty village of Tarasp (table 960.55) makes it easy to reach the castle. Built c1040 by the lords of Tarasp, the castle was briefly the summer retreat of the bishops of Chur before becoming for several centuries an Austrian possession. Following the upheaval of the Napoleonic Wars, ownership passed to the newly created canton of Graubünden, but the cost of upkeep prompted its sale in 1827. A series of irresponsible owners allowed its fabric to deteriorate, and the contents were gradually sold off or dispersed. Salvation came in 1900 with its purchase by a wealthy German from near Dresden, Dr Karl Lingner, who had made his money principally from a mouth freshener named Odol. He spent a fortune restoring the building, but tragically he died just as he was about to take up residence, in 1916. The castle was bequeathed to the King of Saxony, but for practical reasons he declined it. It was then offered to a grandson of Queen Victoria, Grand Duke Ernest Ludwig of Hesse, who accepted it, and it remains in the care of his family.

The interior is as fascinating as one would hope from such a romantic edifice. Guided tours begin with the shrine dedicated to St John of Nepomuk which was built in 1720. Then follows the armoury near the entrance, stuffed with muskets, crossbows, pikes, halberds and helmets. The tour takes in the chapel, with 15th-century frescos, the water cistern fed by the castle's inward-sloping roofs, staircase, a room used as an assize court, dining-room, now used for organ recitals and concerts, concert room, battlements, bedrooms and kitchen. The castle has been restored by using salvaged ceilings, panelling, doorcases, locks and other items of the highest quality, which extends to the sympathetically chosen collection of furniture and paintings. An excellent English guidebook is available. Open-air concerts are sometimes given in the courtyard. (Open: Jun–mid-Oct, daily guided tours; tel: 081/864 93 68.)

Practical information
La Punt-Chaumes-ch
Albula (H), CH-7522. Tel: 081/854 12 84; fax: 081/854 35 55.

Zuoz
TO – Via Maistra, CH-7524. Tel: 081/854 15 10; fax: 081/854 33 34. Open: Mon–Fri 09.00–12.00, 15.00–18.00, Sat 09.00–11.00.

Numerous hotels; closest to the station is
Bellaval★★★, Bahnhofstrasse 63A, CH-7524. Tel: 081/854 14 81; fax: 081/854 31 41.

Cinuos-chel-Brail
Accommodation
Veduta, CH-7526. Tel: 081/854 12 53; fax: 081/854 26 75.

Zernez
TO – Chasa Fuschina, CH-7530. Tel: 081/856 13 00; fax: 081/856 11 55. Open: Jul–Oct Mon–Fri 08.30–12.00, 14.00–18.30, Sat 08.30–12.00, 14.00–16.00, Nov–Jun Mon–Fri 08.30–12.00, 14.00–17.30.

Bettini★★★, Haupstrasse 51, CH-7530. Tel: 081/856 11 35; fax: 081/856 15 10; email: hotel.bettini@engadin.net; web: www.engadin.net/bettini
Filli-Bäckerei★★★ (H), Roeven 61, CH-7530. Tel: 081/851 51 51; fax: 081/851 51 00; email: fillibaeck@bluewin.ch; web: www.engadin.net/filli
Gasthof Bahnhof, CH-7530. Tel: 081/856 11 26; fax: 081/856 19 47.

Guarda

TO – Società da trafic, CH-7545. Tel: 081/862 23 42; fax: 081/862 21 66. Open: Jun–Oct Mon–Fri 10.00–11.00, 15.30–17.30, Nov–May Mon–Fri 16.00–17.30.

Meisser★★★ (H), Dorfstrasse 42, CH-7545. Tel: 081/862 21 32; fax: 081/862 24 80; email: meisser@mirus.ch; web: www.tourismus.ch/tour

Ardez

TO – CH-7546. Tel: 081/862 23 30; fax: 081/862 25 16. Open: Mon–Fri 16.00–18.00.

Aurora★★★, CH-7546. Tel: 081/862 23 23; fax: 081/862 22 04.
Alvetern★★, CH-7546. Tel: 081/862 21 44; fax: 081/862 22 09.

Scuol

TO – Stradun, CH-7550. Tel: 081/861 22 22; fax: 081/861 22 23; email: scuol@spin.ch; web: www.scuol.ch Open: Mon–Fri 08.00–12.00, 14.00–18.30, Sat 10.00–12.00, 14.00–18.00, Sun 16.00–18.00.

Numerous hotels; closest to the station are
Bellaval★★★, Ftanerstrasse, CH-7550. Tel: 081/864 14 81; fax: 081/864 00 10; email: bellaval@span.ch; web: bellaval-scuol.ch
Panorama Garni★★★, Ftanerstrasse 491A, CH-7550. Tel: 081/862 10 71; fax: 081/864 99 35.

Hotels of character are
Belvedere★★★★ (H), CH-7550. Tel: 081/861 06 06; fax: 081/864 90 72; email: belvedere@spin.ch
Engiadina★★★ (H), Rablüzza 152, CH-7550. Tel: 081/864 14 21; fax: 081/864 12 45.

Bad Tarasp-Vulpera

Schlosshotel Chasté, CH-7552. Tel: 081/867 17 75; fax: 081/864 99 70.

Bicycle hire from Zuoz station.

THE SWISS NATIONAL PARK

Although Switzerland has numerous nature reserves, it has only one national park. It was created in 1914 after eight years of discussion, becoming Europe's first national park. It now covers 17,000 hectares (289,113 acres) around the Ofenpass in the Lower Engadine, thanks to periodic additions from the surrounding communes, and there are plans to enlarge it still further. A much higher level of protection is given to the park than its equivalents in either Britain or the United States. No grazing of animals is allowed, no trees have been felled and visitors must stick to the 80km (50 miles) of authorised, marked paths. No camping is allowed, and the customary country codes of not picking fruit or flowers, or disturbing animals, etc, are enforced. Walking in the park is permitted as soon as the snow melts in late spring and forbidden once snow covers the footpaths in autumn.

The result is a unique environment in which nature has been allowed to take its course unchecked by human intervention. There are over 600 plant species in the park, thanks to the great difference in altitude and the variety of rock types within the park. Larch, spruce, mountain pine, dwarf pine, alpine alder, alpine rose bush and the majestic cembra pine dominate the forest. Among the flowers are spurred violet, gentian, catch-fly, saxifrage, alpine ranunculus, mountain crowfoot, hawkweed, yellow Rhaetian mountain poppy, bearberry, androsaca and primroses. June and early July are the best times for flowers. Visitors may see red and roe deer, ibex, marmot, bearded vultures, common vipers and nutcrackers, but the last lynx was shot in 1872 and the last bear in 1904.

Camp sites are provided just outside the park, and it is possible to stay within the park at Chamanna Cluozza, an old inn set amid larches above Ovada Cluozza, or on the edge of the park at Hotel Il Fuorn on the Ofenpass road. Booking is essential. A visit to the exhibition at the National Park House in Zernez (tel: 081/856 17 40; fax: 081/856 17 40; web: www.nationalpark.ch) is strongly recommended before venturing into the park (open: Jun–Oct, daily 08.30–18.00, Tue – 22.00). There is also an exhibition on bears and mining at S-charl (open: mid-Jun–mid-Oct, Tue–Fri, Sun 14.00–17.00). S-charl can be reached by bus from Scuol (table 960.60).

Practical information

Hotel Il Fuorn (H). Tel: 081/856 12 26.
Chamanna Cluozza. Tel: 081/856 12 35 or 081/856 16 89.

Booking can be made through the tourist office at Zernez (see above).

ST MORITZ/SAMEDAN–TIRANO Table 950

This line is the highest rail crossing of the Alps, helping to make it one of Europe's outstanding train journeys. Where else can you travel from glaciers to palm trees in two hours? In summer open-air cars enable passengers to experience the views and glorious air without the interference of glass, making it perfect for photographers. The climb is made even more astonishing by the fact that it is achieved without rack assistance, compelling the builders to devise tortuous loops and spirals to gain or lose height. Sit on the right.

Leaving St Moritz, the train crosses the River Inn, curving away from the Samedan line to head for Pontresina through the Charnadüra Tunnel, at 888m (2,913ft) the longest on the line. The line passes close to the church of San Gion (see Celerina, above) which can be reached from **Celerina Staz** (though the keys are held at Celerina tourist office); the chalet station building here has the date 1720 carved on it, a very rare instance of a much older building being adapted for use as a station. The halt at **Punt Muragl Staz** is only a short walk from **Punt Muragl** station on the chord between Samedan and Pontresina. From Punt Muragl a funicular climbs up to Muottas Muragl (table 2980) from which there are commanding views over the Upper Engadine.

From Punt Muragl the two lines run parallel to the large year-round resort of **Pontresina**, an excellent base for wintersports, walking, cycling and mountaineering. In winter there are 350km (219 miles) of ski slopes served by 60 cablecars and skilifts, and 150km (94 miles) of cross-country runs. The first inn was opened in 1850 and had become a sufficiently popular resort by 1879 for an English church to be opened. It was here that Elizabeth Gaskell wrote *Wives and Daughters*.

A path from the upper town leads to the town's principal building of interest, the Reformed church of Sta Maria on which an informative booklet in English is produced by the tourist office. It has some quite exceptional wall-paintings dating from c1230 and 1495. Nearby is a pentagonal Moorish tower.

The Alpine Museum in Via Maistra is a fascinating collection of photographs, furniture, alpine equipment, natural history, reconstructed rooms and a tape/slide presentation about the area (showings at 16.30 and 17.15). (Open: Dec–mid-Apr, Jun–mid-Oct, Mon–Sat 16.00–18.00.)

Leaving Pontresina the train climbs through woods of larch and sweet-scented cembra pine with the River Bernina on the left. A few minutes' walk from **Surovas** is an open-air concert site in the Tais Forest where an orchestra plays daily from mid-June to mid-September from 11.00–12.00, weather permitting.

Bicycle and walking routes are liberally provided in the area, and one of the most popular walks is the half-hour stroll to Morteratsch glacier from **Morteratsch**. From the glacier you can climb to viewing points on either side. A waterfall plummets down on the right as you leave the station, where the railway describes a horseshoe bend, providing a lovely view of the glacier. Beyond are the snow-covered peaks of the Bernina range, the tallest of which is Piz Bernina at 4,049m (13,284ft).

From **Bernina Diavolezza** a cablecar ascends over the green waters of the eponymous lake to Diavolezza (table 2985) where there is a 'view of surpassing grandeur', as Baedeker puts it, along the Bernina range and over the ice field that merges with the Morteratsch glacier. Another cablecar goes southeast from Curtinatsch near **Bernina Lagalb** to Piz Lagalb (table 2987) from where you can look over Lago Bianco towards Italy.

Now above the tree line, the terrain is desolate and rugged, and it is little wonder that this pass was seldom used until a road was built to replace a bridlepath in the mid-19th century. As the train climbs towards the summit, it begins to skirt the large, dammed lake known as Lago Bianco, its pale green water only a few feet from the train. Some of the rocks around the lake are covered in lichens, a sign of unpolluted air – the road over the range takes a different valley. The solidly built summit station of **Ospizio Bernina** at 2,253m (7,329ft) is popular with walkers, and there is a fine two-hour walk on to the next station at Alp Grüm, passing en route Restaurant Sassal Masone. As the highest rail crossing of the Alps, this can be spectacular in winter when the train can pass through walls of snow, the track cleared by rotary snowploughs. Near the summit is Galleria Scala, the first of many snowsheds.

The descent into Italy begins gently but steepens as the train drops down through two tunnels to **Alp Grüm**, another popular place to break the journey. The main reason to do so is the viewing point over the Palü glacier and down Val Poschiavo. The station has a restaurant and adjacent terrace from which the view can be savoured while you have lunch. The descent to Poschiavo is one of the greatest sections of railway in the world. Without rack, trains drop down at the astonishingly steep ruling gradient of 1 in 14, negotiating curves so severe and numerous that the direct distance between the two points is doubled by rail. In many places the railway follows the route of an old Roman road. The experience is, of course, made exceptional by the views, though the elbows of the curves are often in tunnels and trees cover the slopes in a landscape very different from the barrenness of the pass. With flanges squealing on the curves, the train reaches a short flat section through **Cavaglia**. The most sinuous part of the descent follows **Cadera**, the line resembling a child's fantasy as it twists through tunnels and crosses numerous watercourses by viaduct. Italian-influenced buildings are now in evidence and the linguistic divide is crossed. At Ospizio Bernina you may see the station official rush in to get his binoculars to see a rare bird; here you are more likely to see hunting rifles.

As the railway approaches **Privilasco**, the road over the pass can be seen on the left, later joining the railway in following the Poschiavino river down the valley. Before they meet, the railway arrives in the valley's main town, **Poschiavo**. Linking the Engadine to the north and the Italian Valtellina to the south, it is not surprising that the valley of Poschiavo has been fought over by Etruscans, Romans and the troops of the bishops of Como and Chur. It became part of Graubünden in 1494.

Curiously the Reformation was brought to Poschiavo by two Italians in the first half of the 16th century, when the second printing press in what is now Switzerland was set up here, printing the first Romansch translation of the Bible. Catholics and Protestants used the same church. In 1803 the Graubünden joined the Swiss Confederation.

Architecturally, Poschiavo is a gem. The fountained central piazza (in which the tourist office is situated) is surrounded by many fine patrician houses as well as the old town hall with square Romanesque tower of c1300. Behind it is the Reformed church of 1642–9 with tall tower. On its south side is the Catholic church of San Vittore with rose window and tracery of 1503. On the west side is Albergo Albrici, built in 1682, which has old furniture and portraits, tunnel-vaulted corridors and a coffered ceiling.

On the opposite side of the river is Palazzo Mengotti, built in two stages between the mid-17th and early 18th centuries, which now houses a local museum with all kinds of artefacts, some in reconstructed rooms (open: mid-end Jun, Sep–mid-Oct, Tue, Fri 15.00–17.00; Jul–Aug, Tue 14.00–17.00, Fri 15.00–17.00), as well as the police station and local administration.

In the southern part of the town is the delightful Spanish quarter, built c1830 with the savings of returning emigrants who had made money as hotel-keepers, brewers and pastrycooks. Standing alone to the south of the town is the baroque Catholic church of Sta Maria Assunta. Built in 1692–1709 it has a *trompe l'oeil* painting in the dome and an outstanding Renaissance pulpit of 1634.

The tourist office has numerous printed suggestions for walks, one to the station of Brusio (see below).

The train runs right beside the road through the cultivated, fertile valley beyond Poschiavo, woods covering the steep mountain slopes. At **Le Prese** the railway reaches Lake Poschiavo, overlooked by the superbly sited Le Prese Hotel, which is close to the station. The railway skirts the western shore of the lake with nothing more than a cycle- and footpath between water and railway. Looking north from **Miralago** where the lake ends, there is a lovely view of the mountains the railway has descended.

Since Poschiavo, the gradient has been gentle, but beyond Milagro it joins the river in a headlong descent to Tirano. Twisting down the hill with vines, tobacco, corn and maize appearing beside the line, the railway reaches **Brusio**, dominated by two tall campaniles. Beyond the station is the famous open-air spiral, in which the line crosses itself on a steeply angled nine-arched viaduct, looping around three modern sculptures. **Campocologno** is the last station in Switzerland, but border formalities are carried out on the train.

The valley opens out to join the Valtellina, the train then drops steeply down through orchards and market gardens to **Tirano** where the railway runs through the streets before terminating alongside the FS station (no luggage lockers). From here trains can be taken to Colico on Lake Como and on to Milan.

Tirano's streets are shaded by palm trees, in extraordinary contrast to the landscapes of the 61km (38 miles) from St Moritz. There are plenty of restaurants and hotels close to the station.

Practical information
Pontresina
TO – CH-7504. Tel: 081/838 83 00; fax: 081/838 83 10; email: pontresina@compunet.ch; web: www.pontresina.com Open: Mon–Fri 08.30–12.00, 14.00–18.00, Sat 08.30–12.00, 16.00–18.00, Sun 16.00–18.00.

Numerous hotels; closest to the station
Bahnhof*, Via de la Stazium, CH-7504. Tel: 081/838 80 00; fax: 081/838 80 09; email: hotel-bahnhof@bluewin.ch; web: www.hotel-bahnhof.ch

Ospizio Bernina
Ospizio-Bernina, CH-7710. Tel: 081/844 03 03; fax: 081/844 10 39.
Buffet RhB (rooms available), CH-7710. Tel: 081/844 03 07.

Alp Grüm
Belvedere, CH-7710. Tel: 081/844 03 14; fax: 081/844 10 67.
Bahnhofbuffet, CH-7710. Tel: 081/844 03 18.

Poschiavo
TO – Piazza Comunale, CH-7742. Tel: 081/844 05 71; fax: 081/844 10 27; email: valposchiavo@gr-net.ch; web:www.valposchiavo.ch Open: summer, Mon–Fri

08.00–12.00, 14.00–18.00, Sat 09.00–12.00, 14.00–17.00; winter, Mon–Fri
09.00–12.00, 14.00–17.00.

Numerous hotels; closest to the station are
Suisse★★★ (H), Via da Mez, CH-7742. Tel: 081/844 07 88; fax: 081/844 19 67; email:
hotel.suisse@bluewin.ch; web: www.forum.ch/suisse/
Croce Bianca★★, Via da Mez, CH-7742. Tel: 081/844 01 44; fax: 081/844 12 70; email:
croce.bianca@swissonline.ch; web: www.croce-bianca.ch
Albrici a la Poste (H), CH-7742. Tel: 081/844 01 73; fax: 081/844 09 98; email:
albricihotel@gr-net.ch; web: www.schweizferein.ch 17th-century mansion.

Li Curt
Pension Apollo 12, CH-7745. Tel: 081/844 15 03.

Le Prese
Le Prese★★★★ (H), CH-7746. Tel: 081/844 03 33; fax: 081/844 08 35; email:
info@hotelleprese.com; web: www.hotelleprese.com Spa hotel built in 1857 close to
station.

Bicycle hire from Pontresina, Ospizio Bernina and Poschiavo stations.

FILISUR–DAVOS–CHUR Tables 915/910
Serving the two major skiing resorts of Davos and Klosters, this line is busy in winter.
The section between Landquart and Klosters will become still busier when the Veraena
Tunnel opens to the Upper Engadine in 2000. It provides access to some fine walks,
especially from Wiessen and Cavadürli stations. Sit on the left.

Leaving Filisur in a northerly direction, the line soon turns to the northeast
along the south bank of the River Landwasser, which gives its name to the
famous bridge on the Thusis line. The railway remains at a high level through
the gorge, providing fine views to the left, culminating in the crossing of the
great masonry arch at **Wiesen** with wonderful views to either side. Beside the
station is a café to serve the many walkers who come to enjoy the spectacular
walks along the valley, following the footpath beside the river.
    The railway enters a long tunnel and by its end the river is only 50m (164ft)
below the line. Davos must be one of Switzerland's most linear communities,
strung out along the valley for miles, but this side of Davos is relatively
unspoilt with old chalets dotting the slopes. Near **Davos Monstein** is the
Bergbaumuseum devoted to the history of mining (open: mid-June–mid-Oct,
Wed 14.00–16.00, Sat 14.00–16.00). **Davos Glaris** is opposite the cablecar to
Jatzmeder (table 2878) for the Rinerhorn. After **Davos Frauenkirch** (where
the Reformed church has a wedge-shaped avalanche deflector on one wall)
and **Davos Islen**, the train finally arrives at the famous skiing resort's principal
station, **Davos Platz**.
    Davos was a large village until the 1860s when a Dr Alexander Spengler
promoted its favourable climate for the cure of tuberculosis – dry, sunny,
sheltered from wind and with clear air. Sanatoria and hotels were put up,

winter visitors arrived and with them the first pair of skis, brought by a Colonel Napier in 1888.

Davos was not short of famous visitors from the beginning: *Treasure Island* was finished here while Robert Louis Stevenson was convalescing in 1881. He first came to Davos the year before, when there was still no railway, so the final leg of the journey was an eight-hour sleigh ride. Conan Doyle, too, wrote here while accompanying his consumptive wife, and laid out the first golf course. It was during a visit in 1912 that Thomas Mann conceived the story of *The Magic Mountain*, based on Davos and published in 1924.

The town has remained a prime destination thanks to the quality of its skiing, boasting some of the longest downhill runs and enough hardware on the slopes to carry 35,000 people an hour. It has also built a vast skating rink, conference facilities that cater for the kind of gatherings that appear on the main television news, and a good array of other sports facilities. Yet the situation of the town lacks the beauty of so many other Swiss resorts, and there are few buildings to lift the spirits. Even the Rathaus of 1564 was spoilt by a hamfisted reconstruction during the 1930s.

From Davos Platz station a bus goes over the Flüelapass to Susch (table 910.75) on the St Moritz–Scuol railway (see table 960 above).

Close to Davos Platz station is a cablecar to Ischalp and Jakobshorn (table 2875) at 2,580m (8,464ft). However, the highest peak is ascended by a funicular from near the next station towards Chur, **Davos Dorf**. The Parsennbahn (table 2865) has unique 140-seater double cars and is the highest funicular in Switzerland, reaching 2,663m (8,737ft) at Weissfluhjoch, from where a cablecar goes up to the top of the Weissfluh, Weissfluhgipfel (table 2866), at 2,844m (9,331ft).

The railway continues around the edge of the small Davoser See through more stations named after Davos, though the town has been left behind: **Davos Wolfgang** and **Davos Laret**. Open country with clumps of conifers precedes the Wolfgangpass, where the line drops down steeply through woods which surround the sunflower-gardened station at **Cavadürli** from which there is a choice of woodland walks. The mountain farms beyond are delightful, ancient barns housing goats and horses in scenes that seem light years from dreary factory farming.

After a horseshoe loop **Klosters** comes into view below, the train passing the northern portal of the Vereina Tunnel on the right just before the station. Like Davos, Klosters is divided into Platz around the station and Dorf served by another station towards Chur. Unlike Davos, Klosters has much more of the atmosphere of an alpine village, though it attracts large numbers for skiing, and the resort is Prince Charles's favourite.

The tourist office is to the right outside the station, and opposite is the Gotschnabahn, a two-section cablecar to Gotschnagrat (table 2860) that crosses over the railway on its way to the 2,293m (7,523ft) summit, where there is good walking and one of the most dangerous ski runs in the world, the Gotschnawang. A free bus service for guests links Klosters with the spa of Serneus, which has indoor sulphur baths. A regional ticket expands the local skiing to the Davos area, producing a total of 480km (300 miles) of runs.

The railway drops quite steeply to **Klosters Dorf**, which has retained more of its older chalets than the area around Platz. A tunnel underneath the road outside the station leads to the gondola lift to Madrisa (table 2855). The railway now descends the wooded Prättigau valley, following the River Landquart down to its confluence with the Rhein. A waterfall can be seen on the right just before **Saas** where there are lovely views across the valley, small villages being perched on bluffs that protrude from the slopes.

The old part of **Küblis** can be seen from the train, the Rathaus and Gothic Reformed church of 1472, with fine interior vaulting, clustered around the square. A lovely section of line follows the crossing by the railway of the Landquart, the river now flowing through a gorge on the right, white water frothing. The valley broadens out and becomes more populous as the train nears **Grüsch**, where the huge mid-17th-century patrician house known as the Haus zum Rosengarten contains a local history museum (open: Apr–Nov, Sat–Sun 14.00–17.00). A long tunnel precedes the wine-growing village of **Malans**, with many 17th-century houses, a Rathaus of 1690 and the huge Schloss Bothmar. Its garden is regarded as the finest surviving French baroque garden in the country. From the station it is a 20-minute walk to the gondola lift to Alpli (table 2848).

The valley broadens still further until the train is speeding through a flat landscape with the mountains steadily more distant. The railway joins the standard-gauge line from Zürich at **Landquart**, where the workshops of the Rhätische Bahn are situated and the railway's three surviving steam locomotives are kept (these and a vintage train with period Pullman coaches can be hired). Although metre and standard gauge follow a roughly parallel course, they are separate, the RhB serving local stations while the main line expresses press on to journey's end at Chur.

In the village of **Igis** is the canton's only moated castle, with corner towers; although built in the 13th century, most of the structure dates from the 17th. **Zizers** has two schlosses, the lower one an imposing square 17th-century building with a five-storey, domed octagonal tower. The upper schloss is late 17th-century. It was in a convent here that Zita, the widow of the last Habsburg emperor, Karl I, who had died in 1922, herself died in 1989.

The metre gauge crosses over the main line just before **Untervaz**. The last station before Chur, **Haldenstein**, has a 16th–18th-century schloss, partly commissioned by a French ambassador. Above it, on a pinnacle of rock, stands the ruined keep of the 12th-century castle of Haldenstein. For **Chur**, see table 920.

Practical information

Davos Platz

TO – Promenade 67, CH-7270. Tel: 081/415 21 21; fax: 081/415 21 00; email: davos@davos.ch; web: www.davos.ch Open: summer, Mon–Fri 08.30–18.00, Sat 08.30–16.00; winter, Mon–Fri 08.30–18.00, Sat 08.30–17.00, Sun 10.00–12.00.

Numerous hotels; close to the station are
Bahnhof Terminus★★★, Talstrasse 3, CH-7270. Tel: 081/413 25 25; fax: 081/413 71
77; email: bahnhof-terminus@bluewin.ch; web: www.bahnhof-terminus.ch
Bethanien★★★, Bahnhofstrasse 7, CH-7270. Tel: 081/415 58 55; fax: 081/415 58 56;
email: bethanien@vch.ch; web: www.vch.ch/bethanien

Davos Dorf
Numerous hotels; close to the station is
Derby★★★★, Promenade 139, CH-7260. Tel: 081/417 95 00; fax: 081/417 95 95; email:
derby.davos@bluewin.ch; web: www.derby.ch

Klosters
TO – Alte Bahnhofstrasse, CH-7250. Tel: 081/410 20 20; fax: 081/410 20 10; email:
info@klosters.ch; web: www.klosters.ch Open: summer, Mon–Fri 08.30–12.00,
14.30–18.00, Sat 08.30–12.00, 14.30–17.00; winter, Mon–Sat 08.30–12.00,
14.30–18.00, Sun 09.00–11.30, 15.30–18.00.

Numerous hotels; close to the station is
Alpina★★★★, Bahnhofstrasse 1, CH-7250. Tel: 081/410 24 24; fax: 081/410 24 25;
email: hotel@alpina-klosters.ch; web: www.alpina-klosters.ch

Küblis
Bahnhof, CH-7240. Tel: 081/332 13 43.

Malans
Weisskreuz★★ (H), Rathausgasse, CH-7208. Tel: 081/322 81 61; fax: 081/322 81 62;
email: gtinguely@weisskreuz.com; web: www.weisskreuz.com

Bicycle hire from Davos Dorf, Küblis and Chur stations.

CHUR–ZIEGELBRUCKE–Zürich Table 900
*Chur can be reached by direct train from Amsterdam, Hamburg and Brussels, as well as
numerous connections through Basel and Zürich. The line is seldom out of view of
mountains through a part of Switzerland less frequently visited by tourists. Sit on the right.*

For the section between Chur and the junction with the Rhätische Bahn at
Landquart, see tables 915/910 above. **Maienfeld** has some fine houses and
Rathaus, but its main attractions are two large schlosses: Brandis began as a
medieval castle of which the 13th-century residential tower survives; and the
largely 17th–18th-century Salenegg, fronted by a baroque garden. Nearby is
Steigwald where the 'Heidi' novels of Johanna Spyri (1827–1901) are set.

Before **Bad Ragaz** the railway crosses the cantonal boundary into St
Gallen. The town has some interesting buildings, such as the Chapel of St
Leonhard with unique (for Switzerland) Italianate painting of 1414–18 in the
choir, and the spa hotel that was converted from a Benedictine monastery
building in 1840. But the principal reason for breaking the journey here is to
explore the extraordinary gorge of the River Tamina.

A bus from the station to the small resort of Vättis and Gigerwald (table 900.62) goes up the wooded defile, in which there is barely room for river and road, to Bad Pfäfers. This village has a huge monastery church built in 1688–93 and spa buildings of 1704–18. Beyond is the Taminaschlucht in which hot springs rise; early patients were lowered into the gorge by ropes. There is a signed walk back to Bad Ragaz, via Pfäfers, with fine views over the Rhein valley, and the ruins of 13th-century Wartenstein Castle.

A five-minute walk from Bad Ragaz station is the gondola lift to Pardiel (table 2800.3) for good views over the Rhein valley and surrounding mountains.

The railway and Rhein part company, the river turning east before continuing north to the Bodensee while the railway heads northwest. For the junction of **Sargans** see table 880. Change here for trains to Rorschach. **Mels** has numerous good 18th–19th-century buildings. Opposite the station is the Gothic Heiligkreuz chapel with wall-paintings of the late 15th century. The Landsgemeindeplatz (the main square) is remarkably unspoilt; it includes a mid-17th-century Capuchin monastery and a row of 17th-century wooden buildings.

The village of **Flums** still has evidence of the iron smelting that was carried on here in the surviving ironmaster's house (Eisenherrenhaus) of 1567. The Romanesque former parish church was rebuilt in the 12th century and has 15th-century painting in the choir. From the station a bus twists up a hairpin road to Flumserberg Tannenbodenalp (table 900.42) from where a gondola ascends to Maschgenkamm (table 2792) for views over the Walensee. A cablecar descends from Tannenbodenalp to Unterterzen (table 2790) beside the lake and only one minute from the railway station.

To the northwest of Flums is the spectacularly sited ruined castle of Burg Gräpplang and the St Jakob chapel with wall-paintings of c1300.

Passing through pleasant farming country along the level floor of the valley, the railway reaches **Walenstadt** and the eastern end of Walensee, which the railway skirts part of the southern shore. The views across the lake are dramatic, since steep cliffs rise directly out of the lake along the northern shore, culminating in the Churfursten ridge. A cycle-path and footpath run along the south shore of the lake, on which there are boat services in summer.

From **Unterterzen** a cablecar climbs to Tannenbodenalp (table 2790, see above), and at **Mühlehorn** a working water-powered hammer can be seen as a relic of the 18th-century iron industry. A long tunnel brings the railway to **Weesen**, a resort at the western end of Walensee. The Catholic Heiligkreuz church dates from the 13th century and forms an attractive group with the Dominican convent buildings, which were last rebuilt c1690.

A bus from Weesen post office (starting at Ziegelbrücke station) climbs up on to the western end of the Churfirsten at Amden (table 900.20), another small resort. There is also a good walk from Weesen along the northern shore of the lake to Betlis, and from there to the Serebach Falls.

For **Ziegelbrücke** and the journey on to Zürich see Chapter 7.

Practical information
Maienfeld
Falknis Landgasthof, Bahnhofstrasse, CH-7304. Tel: 081/302 18 18 fax: 081/302 66 24.

Bad Ragaz
TO – Maienfeldstrasse 5, CH-7310. Tel: 081/302 10 61; fax: 081/302 62 90; email: badragaz@spin.ch; web: www.badragaz.ch Open: Mon–Fri 09.00–18.00, Sat 09.00–12.00, 13.00–16.00.

Numerous hotels; close to the station is
Bristol**** (H), Bahnhofstrasse 38, CH-7310. Tel: 081/302 82 61; fax: 081/302 64 94; web: www.bristol-bad-ragaz.ch

Walenstadt
TO – Bahnhofstrasse 19, CH-8880. Tel: 081/735 22 22; fax: 081/735 22 22. Open: Mon–Fri 07.30–12.00, 14.00–18.00, Sat 08.30–11.00.

Curfirsten***, Bahnhofstrasse, CH-8880. Tel: 081/736 44 44; fax: 081/736 44 45.

Weesen
Parkhotel Schwert am See*** (H), Hauptstrasse 23, CH-8872. Tel: 058/616 14 74; fax: 058/616 18 53; email: parkhotel.schwert@bluewin.ch; web: www.gamag.ch Building dates from the late 14th century.

LANGUAGE
Days and months

	German	French	Italian
Sunday	Sonntag	dimanche	domenica
Monday	Montag	lundi	lunedì
Tuesday	Dienstag	mardi	martedì
Wednesday	Mittwoch	mercredi	mercoledì
Thursday	Donnerstag	jeudi	giovedì
Friday	Freitag	vendredi	venerdì
Saturday	Sonnabend	samedi	sabato
January	Januar	janvier	gennaio
February	Februar	février	febbraio
March	März	mars	marzo
April	April	avril	aprile
May	Mai	mai	maggio
June	Juni	juin	giugno
July	Juli	juillet	luglio
August	August	août	agosto
September	September	septembre	settembre
October	Oktober	octobre	ottobre
November	November	novembre	novembre
December	Dezember	décembre	dicembre

Numbers

1	eins	un(e)	uno/una
2	zwei	deux	due
3	drei	trois	tre
4	vier	quatre	quattro
5	fünf	cinq	cinque
6	sechs	six	sei
7	sieben	sept	sette
8	acht	huit	otto
9	neun	neuf	nove
10	zehn	dix	dieci
11	elf	onze	undici

	German	French	Italian
12	*zwölf*	*douze*	*dodici*
13	*dreizehn*	*treize*	*tredici*
14	*vierzehn*	*quatorze*	*quattordici*
15	*fünfzehn*	*quinze*	*quindici*
16	*sechszehn*	*seize*	*sedici*
17	*siebzehn*	*dix-sept*	*diciassette*
18	*achtzehn*	*dix-huit*	*diciotto*
19	*neunzehn*	*dix-neuf*	*diciannove*
20	*zwanzig*	*vingt*	*venti*
100	*hundert*	*cent*	*cento*
1000	*tausend*	*mille*	*mille*

Useful vocabulary

arrivals	*Ankunft*	*arrivées*	*arrivo*
departures	*Abfahrt*	*départs*	*partenza*
information	*Auskunft*	*renseignements*	*informazioni*
left luggage	*Gepäckauf-bewahrung*	*consigne*	*il deposito bagagli*
platform	*Bahnsteig, Perron*	*quai*	*binario*
station	*Bahnhof*	*gare*	*stazione*
ticket office	*Fahrkarten-schalter*	*bureau de vente des billets*	*l'ufficio prenotazioni*
timetable	*Kursbuch*	*horaire*	*orario*

German words used in text

Bad	spa, bath
Bahnhof	station
Burg	castle, citadel
Brücke	bridge
Dorf	village
Fälle	waterfall
Gasthaus	guesthouse
Gasthof	inn
Gondelbahn	gondola lift
Graben	trench, often site of former moat
Hauptgasse	main street
Heimatmuseum	local/folk museum
Hauptbahnhof	main station
Jugendstil	German/Austrian form of Art Nouveau
Kirche	church
Kulm	summit, peak
Luftseilbahn	skilift
ober	upper, main
Perron	platform

Platz	square
Rathaus	town hall
Rhoden	medieval tax district
Schloss	castle
See	lake
Standseilbahn	funicular
Stöckli	accommodation for retired farmers
Tal	valley
Tor	gate
Turm	tower
Turmhof	tower-house
unter	lower/secondary
Verkehrsbüro	tourist office
Zentrum	centre
Zeughaus	arsenal
Zunfthaus	guildhall

French words used in text

hôtel de ville	town hall
train à grande vitesse	high-speed train

A train seat with a fine view, a yellow bus in a mountain village en route to the heart of the country, a gently rocking paddle steamer.
The Swiss Pass, a timeless journey, the freedom of Switzerland.

The freedom of Switzerland can be yours for less than £140 for 8 days with the Swiss Pass.

Journey unrestricted on the whole 16,000kms of the Swiss Travel System. On any train in the world's finest railway system, including the famous panoramic routes (with the exception of mountain summit railways, where major reductions are offered.)

By paddle steamer and postbus throughout Switzerland. And by tram and bus services in 36 towns and cities.

And with the free Family Card, any of your children up to the age of 16 can travel with you free.

For information on the Swiss Pass, Flexi-Pass and Swiss Card call the Swiss Travel Centre on 00800 10020030 (Freephone), 00800 10020031 (Freefax). Or e-mail: stc@stlondon.com
Internet: www.MySwitzerland.com

Your holiday. Switzerland.

Appendix

USEFUL ADDRESSES
Switzerland Tourism offices

Austria Schweiz Tourismus, Postfach 34, A-1015 Wien; tel: 0043 1 512 74 05; fax: 0043 1 513 93 35; email: stwien@schweizferien.ch

Belgium and Luxembourg Suisse Tourisme, Boîte postale 213, B-1060 Bruxelles 6; tel: 0032 2 345 54 45; fax: 0032 2 345 35 52; email: stbruxelles@switzerlandvacation.ch

Canada 926 The East Mall, Etobicoke (Toronto), Ontario M9B 6K1; tel: 0041 416 695 2090; fax: 0041 416 695 2774; email: stnewyork@switzerlandtourism.com

Egypt c/o Swissair, 22 Sharia Kasr el Nil, Cairo; tel: 0020 2 393 7955; fax: 0020 2 391 6080; email: chswrkbk@ibmmail.com

France Suisse Tourisme, Porte de la Suisse, 11 bis, rue Scribe, F-75009 Paris; tel: 0033 1 44 51 65 51; fax: 0033 1 47 42 43 88; email: stparis@suissevacances.ch

Germany
Berlin Schweiz Tourismus, Haus der Schweiz, Unter den Linden 24, Friedrichstr 156–6, D-10117 Berlin; tel: 0049 30 201 20 50; fax: 0049 30 201 20 51; email: stfrankfurt@schweizferein.ch
Düsseldorf Schweiz Tourismus, Wilhelm-Marx-Haus, Heinrich-Heine-Allee 53, D-40213 Düsseldorf; tel: 0049 211 83 07 242; fax: 0049 211 83 07 393; email: stfrankfurt@schweizferein.ch
Frankfurt Schweiz Tourismus, Postfach 16 07 54, D-60070 Frankfurt; tel: 0049 69 256 00 10; fax: 0049 69 256 00 138; email: stfrankfurt@schweizferein.ch
Hamburg Schweiz Tourismus, Rathausmarkt 5, D-20095 Hamburg; tel: 0049 40 33 07 31; fax: 0049 40 32 39 00; email: stfrankfurt@schweizferein.ch
München Schweiz Tourismus, Brienner Strasse 14/11, D-80333 München; tel: 0049 89 286 59 903; fax: 0049 89 286 59 904; email: stfrankfurt@schweizferein.ch

Hong Kong Switzerland Tourism, Admiralty Centre, Tower 2, 8th Floor, 18 Harcourt Street, Hong Kong; tel: 00852 2865 1013; fax: 00852 2528 995; email: sthongkong@switzerlandtourism.com

Israel c/o Swissair, 1 Ben Yehuda Street, 63801 Tel Aviv; tel: 00972 3 511 66 66; fax: 00972 3 510 29 93

Italy Svizzera Turismo, Centro Svizzero, Piazza Cavour 4, I-20121 Milano; tel: 0039 02 76 01 31 14; fax: 0039 02 76 00 11 63; email: stmilano@svizzeravacanze.ch

Japan Toranomon Daini Waiko Building 3F, 5-2-6, Toranomon, Minato-ku, Tokyo 105-0001; tel: 0081 3 5401 5426; fax: 0081 3 5401 5427; email: tourist@switzerlandtourism.or.jp

Netherlands Zwitserland Toerisme, Postbus 75387, NL-1070 AJ Amsterdam; tel: 0032 2 345 54 45; fax: 0032 2 345 35 52; email: stamsterdam@switzerlandvacation.ch

Spain/Portugal Suiza Turismo, c/o SERGAT ESPANA SL, Pau Casals 4, E-08021 Barcelona; tel: 0034 9 3 414 5874; fax: 0034 9 3 201 8657; email: sergat@sergatspain.com

United Kingdom Swiss Centre, Swiss Court, London W1V 8EE; tel: 0044 20 7734 1921; fax: 0044 20 7437 4577; email: stlondon@switzerlandvacation.ch

United States 222 Sepulveda Boulevard, Suite 1570, El Segundo, CA 90245; tel: 001 310 335 0125; fax: 001 310 335 0131; email: stnewyork@switzerlandtourism.com

European railways

French Railways (SNCF) Rail Europe Travel Shop, 179 Piccadilly, London W1V 0BA; tel: 08705 848848

German Rail 18 Conduit Street (no callers), London W1R 9TD; tel: 020 7317 0919; fax: 020 7491 4689; Int: www.bahn.de

Swiss Federal Railways Swiss Centre, Swiss Court, London W1V 8EE; tel: 020 7734 1921; fax: 020 7437 4577

Miscellaneous

Inghams Travel 10–18 Putney Hill, London SW15 6AX; tel: 020 8780 4400; web: www.inghams.co.uk

Kuoni Travel Kuoni House, Dorking, Surrey RH5 4AY; tel: 01306 742500; fax: 01306 744222; web: www.kuoni.co.uk

Plus Travel 52 Ebury Street, London SW1W 0LU; tel: 020 7259 0199; fax: 020 7259 0190; email: sales@plustravel.freeserve.co.uk

Swiss Travel Service Ltd Bridge House, High Road, Broxbourne, Hertfordshire EN10 7DT; tel: 01992 456123; fax: 01992 448855; email: swiss@bridge-travel.co.uk

The Swiss Railways Society Membership Secretary, Dave Howsam, 3 Balmain Road, Davyhulme, Manchester M41 5TR

Appendix 3

FURTHER READING

Allen, Cecil J *Switzerland's Amazing Railways*, Thomas Nelson & Sons, 1953.
Bonjour, E, Offler, H S and Potter, G R *A Short History of Switzerland*, Oxford, 1952.
Brown, Karen *Swiss Country Inns & Itineraries*, Travel Press, 1984.
Lieberman, Marcia and Philip *Walking Switzerland The Swiss Way*, The Mountaineers (Seattle), 1987.
Morgan, Bryan *The End of the Line*, Clever-Hume Press, 1955.
Robertson, Ian *Switzerland, Blue Guide*, A & C Black,1992.
Rossberg, Ralf Roman *The Jungfrau Region*, Hallwag Edition, 1991.
Rubli, Walter H *Bern, Lausanne*, 1954.
Soloveytchik, George *Switzerland in Perspective*, Oxford University Press, 1954.
Wade, Paul, and Arnold, Kathy *Charming Small Hotel Guide: Switzerland*, Duncan Petersen, 1993.
Warrell, Ian *Through Switzerland with Turner*, Tate Gallery Publications, 1995.
Wraight, John *The Swiss and the British*, Michael Russell, 1987.

Switzerland, Insight Guides, 1993
Switzerland, A Phaidon Cultural Guide, Phaidon, 1985.
Zermatt U Guides, 1995.

Appendix 4

RAILWAY AND POSTBUS ROUTES BY TIMETABLE NUMBER
Railway

Table	Page	Table	Page	Table	Page
100	276, 283,	211	250	301	172
	297, 306,	212	248	311	161, 166,
	315	213	234	311	168
100.1	276, 283,	221	241	312	168, 170
	297, 306	222	241		171
100.2	315	223	235, 237	313	164
100.3	315, 321	224	238	314	163
101	276	225	134	320	171
103	275	226	135	330	120
111	282	230	135, 222	331	116
112	282	236	239	340	121
120	288	237	240	341	126, 127
121	286	238	224	350	127
124	303	240	223	410	118, 138
125	302	250	143	412	120
126	304	251	137	413	118
127	308	252	149	414	124
128	310	253	296	450	122
129	308	254	150	460	124
130	311	255	143	470	200, 205
132	311	256	294	473	204
133	313	257	149	474	205
140	322	260	129, 153	475	207
142	326	261	136	480	196
150	266	262	132	500	224
151	266	270	143	502	225
155	269	280	155	503	226
156	269	285	151	505	221
200	251	290	113	510	194
201	253	294	113	514	195
210	133, 244	295	111	600	52, 208,
210	250	300	172		335, 357

Table	Page	Table	Page	Table	Page
602	192	710	52	853	84
603	189	711	52	854	81
610	327, 332	712	50	855	78
612	361	713	49	856	81
615	331	720	56	857	86
620	353	730	60	858	98
630	348	731	65	859	75
631	348	736	57	870	77, 78
635	346	740	65	880	85, 97
636	358	750	66	900	384
643	228	753	66	910	381
644	228	754	64	915	381
645	228	760	69	920	361
650	226	761	68	930	365
651	192	762	94	940	367
653	55	763	93	950	377
654	54	764	93	960	372
655	53	820	87	2050	281
660	56	821	94	2053	286
661	49	830	96	2620	350
670	62	840	94	2652	342
672	62	841	96	4150	266
700	229	850	71		
703	70	852	83		

Postbus

470.75	332	600.51	333	920.80	365
600.50	333	610.20	333	940.75	347

MEASUREMENTS AND CONVERSIONS

To convert	Multiply by
Inches to centimetres	2.54
Centimetres to inches	0.3937
Feet to metres	0.3048
Metres to feet	3.281
Yards to metres	0.9144
Metres to yards	1.094
Miles to kilometres	1.609
Kilometres to miles	0.6214
Acres to hectares	0.4047
Hectares to acres	2.471
Imperial gallons to litres	4.546
Litres to imperial gallons	0.22
US gallons to litres	3.785
Litres to US gallons	0.264
Ounces to grams	28.35
Grams to ounces	0.03527
Pounds to grams	453.6
Grams to pounds	0.002205
Pounds to kilograms	0.4536
Kilograms to pounds	2.205
British tons to kilograms	1016.0
Kilograms to British tons	0.0009812
US tons to kilograms	907.0
Kilograms to US tons	0.000907

5 imperial gallons are equal to 6 US gallons
A British ton is 2,240 lbs. A US ton is 2,000 lbs.

Temperature conversion table

The bold figures in the central columns can be read as either centigrade or fahrenheit.

°C		°F	°C		°F
−18	0	32	10	50	122
−15	5	41	13	55	131
−12	10	50	16	60	140
−9	15	59	18	65	149
−7	20	68	21	70	158
−4	25	77	24	75	167
−1	30	86	27	80	176
2	35	95	32	90	194
4	40	104	38	100	212
7	45	113	40	104	219

Index

Page numbers in **bold** numerals indicate the principal entry for places that
are repeatedly mentioned in the text

Aarau 226–7
Aarberg 138
Aarburg 195
Aarwangen 118
Adelboden 172
Adliswil 50
Aesch 222
Affoltern (Emmantal) 127
Affoltern (Zürich) 52
Agno 344
Aigle 301–4
Airolo 335–6
Albula Pass/Tunnel 369
Allaman 268
Alp Grüm 378
Alpnachstad 200, 204
Altdorf 211
Altendorf 57
Altnau 88
Altstätten 81
Amriswil 78, 95
Andelfingen 94
Andermatt 203, **329**, 332, 333, 361
Annemasse 265
Appenzell 79–80
Aranno 343
Arbon 87–8
Ardez 373
Arlesheim 222
Arosa 366–7
art galleries 4, 42, 43, 51, 53, 58, 67, 68, 74, 85, 91, 107, 108, 116, 119, 151, 181, 218–19, 227, 232, 236, 263, 273, 281, 307, 316, 342, 364
Arth 49
Arth–Goldau 192, **208**
Ascona 352–3
Au 57
Aubonne 267
Ausserberg 174
Auvernier 234, 241

Avenches 139–40

Baar 50
Bad Pfäfers 385
Bad Ragaz 384
Baden 53
Balerna 357
Ballwil 193
Balsthal 120
banks 9
Basel 215–227
Bätterkinden 113
Bauen 187
Baulmes 249
Bauma 65
Baveno 352
Bavois 250
Beatenberg 160
Beatenbucht 161
Beckenreid 188
Beinwil am See 193
Belfaux 149
Bellavista 358
Bellinzona 338–9
Bellwald 328
Belp 153
Bercher 276
Berg 97
Bergün 369
Berlingen 89
Bern **99–113**, 150
Bernina Diavolezza 378
Beromünster 193
Bettmeralp 328
Bevaix 244
Bever 369
Bévieux 308
Bex 306, **308–9**
Biasca 338, 365
Biberist 113–14, 121
Biel/Bienne 129–32
Bière
Biglen 121
Binningen 221

Binz 47
Birrwil 193
Bischofszell 84
Bissone 344
Blankenburg 291
Blonay 282, 283
Bolligen 113
Boltigen **172**, 296
Boncourt 224
Bonfol 224
Boniswil 193
Bosco/Gurin 351
Bottmingen 221
Boudry 235
Bovernier 313
Braunwald 59
Bremgarten 55
Brienz 206, 207
Brig 26, 319
Brissago 351
Broc–Village 296
Bronschofen 96
Brugg 53
Brünig Pass 159, 201
Brünig–Hasliberg 201
Brunnen 210
Brunni (Nidwalden) 199
Brunni (Schwyz) 64
Brusino 344
Brusio 380
Bubendorf 226
Bubikon 66
Buchs 97
Bühler 79
Bülach 69
Bulle **150–1**, 172, 295
Büren an der Aare 132
Burgdorf 122–3
Burgistein 155
Bürglen 95
Bursinel 267
Buttes 243, 249
Buttisholz 124

Cademario 345
Cadenazzo 349
Camedo 355–6
Campione 344
Capolago-Riva San Vitale 357, 358
Capologo 344
car-free resorts 7, 59, 164, 167, 190, 323, 324, 327–8
Carona 345
Carouge 259
Caslano 343, **347**
Castione 338
Caux 287
Cavigliano 355
Celerina Staz 377
Céligny 267
Cevio 354
Cexbres-Village 281
Cham 56
Chambrelien 235
Chamby 283
Chamonix 312
Chamoson 315
Champ-du-Moulin 242
Champéry 305
Champex 313
Charmey 297
Chäserrugg 82
Château d'Oex 289–90
Château-de-Blonay 282
Châtel-St-Denis 296
Châtelard (Vaud) 288
Châtelard (Valais) 312
Châtillens 141
Chaumont 234
Chavornay 250
Cheseaux 276
Chiasso 357
Chiavenna 348
Chillon 297
Chur 27, **363–5**, 367, 379, 380
Clarens 284
Col-de-Bretaye 310
Col de Soud 310
Col-du-Pillon 303
Collombey 305
Cologny 259
Colombier 234
Combe-Tabeil 239
Concise 244
Conthey 315
Coppet 266
Corcelles 149
Corcelles-Peseux 235
Cornaux 134

Cossonay 250
Courfaivre 222
Courrendlin 136
Couvet 242
Crans Montana 317
Cressier 134, 143
Creux du Van 242
Croy-Romainmôtier 251
Cully 277
cycling 31–3, 35–6

Dallenwil 197
Därstetten 172
Davos 363, **381–2**
Degersheim 77
Deitingen 118
Delémont **136**, 222
Delle 224
Dielsdorf 70
Diemtigen 171
Diessenhofen 90
Dietikon 53, 54
Dinhard 94
disabled, travel and access for the 8
Disentis 362, 365
Domodóssola 321, 356
Dornach 222
Dürrenroth 127

Ebenalp 82
Ebikon 56
Ebnat-Kappel 84
Echallens 276
Eglisau 69
Eigergletscher 169
Einigen 156
Einsiedelei 114, 116
Einsiedeln **63–4**
electric current 9
Elgg 71
Elm 56
embassies 10
Engelberg 197–9
Engstlenalp 203
Ennenda 58
Entlebuch 125
Erasmus 215
Erlen 95
Erlenbach 60
Erlenbach im Simmental 172
Ermatingen 88
Erstfeld 211
Escholzmatt 125
Essert-sous-Champvent 249
Esslingen 63
Estavayer-le-Lac 149–50

Etzwilen 90

Fahr 68
Faido 337
Farnsburg 225
Faulensee 157
Felben-Wellkausen 93
Feldbrunnen 118
Feldmeilen 58
Fiesch 328
Filisur **368**, 381
Finhaut 312
First 169, 202
Flamatt 144, 148
Flawil 73
Fleurier 243
Flüelen 25, 57, **210**, 2122
Flüh 222
Flums 385
Fly-Rail 21
Forch 65
Fräkmüntegg 179, 205
Fraubrunnen 113
Frauenfeld 95
Frederick the Great 56, 243
Fribourg 144–7
Frinvillier-Taubenloch 134
Frutigen 173, 174
Fruttli 192
Ftan 374
Furka Base Tunnel 329
Furka Pass 202, 331, 332

Gagnone-Orcesco 356
Gais 79
Gampel-Steig 319
Gams 97–8
Gandria 344
Gänsbrunnen 118
gardens and parks 45, 46, 109, 156, 163, 169, 183, 287, 345, 346, 351, 352, 376–7
Gelfingen 193
Gelterkinden 225
Generoso 358–9
Geneva 25, 255–66
Genthod-Bell 266
Gersau 187
Gilly 267
Giornico 337
Giswil **200**, 208
Giubiasco 337
Glarus 58
Glaubenbuelen Pass 125
Glauenberg Pass 125
Gletsch 331

Glion 286–7
Glovelier 223, 240
Goldach 85
golf courses 310, 318, 382
Gonten 82
Goppenstein 174
Gornergrat 326
Göschenen 203, **211**, 332
Gossau 73
Gotthard Pass 330
Gotthard Tunnel 212
Grafenort 198
Grandson 245
Grandvillard 295
Granges-Marnand 141
Gränichen 228
Greene, Graham 279
Grimsel Pass 203, 329
Grindelwald **170**, 202
Grosshöchstetten 113, 121
Grotzenbüel 59
Grund 170
Grüsch 383
Grütschalp 163
Gruyères 295–6
Gryon 309
Gstaad 290–1
Guarda 373
Gümligen 111
Gümmenen 143

Hagenwil **78**, 94
Häggenschwil 76
Haldenstein 383
Hasle 125
Hasle-Rüegsau 121
Hauenstein Tunnel 225, 226
Hauptwil 83
Hauteville 282
health 10
Heerbrugg 97
Heiden **86–7**, 96
Henau 71
Hergiswil 196
Herisau 77, **82**
Herrenberg 96
Herzogenbuchsee 122
Hilterfingen 161
Hindelbank 122
Hinwil 66
Hitzkirch 193
Hohenklingen 88
Holzegg 64
Horgen 56
Hospental 329
hotels and accommodation 5
Hüswil 128

Huttwil 128

Igis 383
Ilanz 359
Immensee 49, **208**
industrial archaeology 44, 68,
    98, 242, 250, 251, 252,
    309, 345, 347, 385
Innertkirchen 205
Ins 137, 143
insurance 10
Interlaken 25, 157,**158–9**, 206
Intragna 355
Irgenhausen 64
Isenfluh 162
Isola Bella 351
Isola dei Pescatori 352
Isola Madre 352
Issikon 95
Itingen 225
Ittigen bei Bern 113

Jakobsbad 82
Jaun 297
Jaunpass 172, 297
Jegenstorf 113
Jochpass 198, 202
Jungfraujoch 169

Kaiseraugst 229
Kaiserstuhl 69
Kalpetran 323
Kandersteg 173–4
Kehrsatz 153
Kehrsiten-Bürgenstock 188
Kerzers **138**, 143
Kesswil 88
Kies 56
Kiesen 155
Kilchberg 56
Kirchberg 121
Kisten Pass 57
Klausen Pass 57
Kleine Scheidegg 168
Klosters 27, **382**
Klus 120
Knonau 52
Kollbrunn 65
Köniz 151
Konolfingen 121, 124
Kräbel 190, 192
Kreuzlingen 88
Kriens 205
Krummenau 84
Küblis 383
Küsnacht 60
Küssnacht 208

Kyburg 63

L'Auberson 249
La Barboleuse 309
La Brévine 243
La Chaux-de-Fonds 235–41
La Chiésaz 282
La Combe 239
La Corbatière 241
La Cure 269
La Ferrière 239
La Givrine 269
La Neuveville 133
La Punt-Chaumes 372
La Roche-sur-Foron
    265
La Sagne 241
La Sarraz 251
La Tour-de-Peilz 284
La Tour-de-Trême 296
Lachen 57
lake and river services 52, 57,
    61, 85, 87, 115, 132, 155,
    160, 185–8, 234, 267, 343,
    350
Lally 283
Landquart 27, **379**
Langendorf 117
Langenthal 118, 123
Langis 124
Langnau 124
languages 9
Langweis 366
Lauenen 290
Läufelfingen
Laufen 222
Laupen 148
Lausanne 270–6
Lauterbrunnen 162
Laveno 351
Lax 328
Le Bouveret 298, 311
Le Brassus 253
Le Châble 314
Le Châtelard
Le Day 252
Le Landeron 134
Le Locle 237
Le Noirmont 239, 240
Le Pont 253
Le Prese 380
Le Sentier 253
Le Sépey 303
Leissigen 157
Lenk 25, 292–3
Lenzburg 193–4
Lenzerheide 363

Les Avants 284, **289**
Les Brenets 238
Les Diablerets 303
Les Marécottes 312
Les Paccots 296
Les Pléiades 283
Les Ponts-de-Martel 238, **241**, 242
Les Verrières 183
Les Verrières 243
Lessoc 294
Leuk 318
Leukerbad 318
Leysin 302–3
Lichensteig 77
Liechenstein 95
Liestal 225
Ligerz 133
Linthal 59
Locarno 25, 26, 349–53
Lötschberg Tunnel 173
Lucens 141
Lüderenalp 125
Lüen-Castiel 363
Lugano 25, 26, 27, **340–8**, 354
luggage facilities 21, 22
Luino 345
Lungern 201
Lütisburg 84
Lutry 277
Lützelflüh 126
Luzern 25, 27, **177–84**, 185–213
Lyss 129

Magadino 351
Magdenau 71
Maggia 351
Maggiore, Lake 350–1
Magliaso 346
Maienfeld 384
Malans 379
Malters 126
Mammern 89
Mammertshofen 75
Mannenbach-Salenstein 88
maps 33
Mariastein 222
Marin-Epagnier 143, **233**
Martigny 306–8
Marthalen 94
Matt 59
Matterhorn 321
Matzingen 94
Meggen 187, 208
Meggenhorn 187

Meilen 61
Meiringen 170, 199, **201–3**, 332
Melide 344, **357**
Mels 385
Mendrisio 357
Menziken-Burg 228
Mettmen 59
Mettmenstetten 52
Mézières 150
Miglieglia 344
Miralago 380
Mitlödi 58
money 7, 9
Mont Pèlerin 281
Montalègre 259
Montbovon 289, 294
Monte Brè 343
Monte Generoso 358–9
Monte San Salvatore 342
Monthey **305**, 310
Montracher 270
Montreux 25, 284–8
Morcote 344
Mörel 327
Morges 253, **268**
Mörialp 201
Morschach 210
Morteratsch 378
Mostelberg 62
Môtiers 242–3
Moudon 140–1
Moutier 134, 136
Muhen 228
Mühlebach 328
Mühlehorn 385
Mülenen 172
Münchenbuchsee 129
Münchenstein 222
Münchenwiler-Courevaux 143
Münsingen 155
Münster 329
Münsterlingen 88
Muri 55
Mürren 164–6
Murten 138–9
Muttenz **224**, 229

Näfels 58
Nänikon-Greifensee 66
Naters 320, 327
National Park 376
Nesslau-Neu St Johann 84–5
Netstal 58
Neuchâtel 231–4
Neuenkirch 194

Neunkirch 93
Nidau 137
Niederbipp 118
Niederrickenbach 197
Niederschlacht 57
Niederteufen 79
Niederurnen 57
Niederwald 328
Niesen Kulm 172
Noiraigue 242
Nottwil 195
Nufenen Pass 328, 335
Nyon 253, **267**, 268

Oberaach 95
Oberalp Pass 362
Oberburg 121
Oberdiessbach 121
Oberdorf 117
Obergestein 329
Oberhofen 161
Oberrieden 56
Oberwald 203, **329**, 332–3
Oberwil 49
Oberwinterthur 94
Oensingen 119
Oey-Diemtigen 172
Ollon 305
Olten 119, 225
Onnens-Bonnvillars 245
Orbe 250
Oron 141, 148
Orsières 313–14
Ospizio Bernina 378
Ossingen 94
Ouchy 274

paddle steamers 160, 185–7, 206, 262, 351
Palagnedra 355
Palézieux 141, 148
Pallanza 352
Pampigny 270
Panex 304
Payerne 140
Perroy 268
Pfäffikon 57, 66
Pfingstegg 170
Pilatus Kulm 179, **204–5**
Planalp 207
Ponte Brolla 354
Ponte Tresa 347
Pontresina 378
Porrentruy 223
Poschiavo 379
postbuses 23
post offices 10

Prangins 267
Pratteln **225**, 229
Pré-Giroud 252
Pré-Petitjea 239
Preda 369
Puidoux-Chexbres 148
Pully 277
Punt Muragl Staz 377

rail passes 12–3, 17–20
Ramsei 126
Randa 323
Rapperswil 45, **61–2**
Raron 319
Re 356
Realp 329, 331
Rebstein-Marbach 95
Reckingen 328
Regensberg 70
Reichenau-Tamins 363, 367
Reichenbach 202
Reiden 195
Reigoldswil 225
Rhäzüns 364
Rheinau 94
Rheineck 87, **97**
Rheinfelden 229
Rhäzuns 367–8
Richetli Pass 57
Richterswil 57
Rickenbach 209
Riddes 315
Riederalp 327
Riffelalp 326
Riggenbach, Niklaus 118,
    190, 285
Riggisberg 151
Rigi Kaltbad 190
Rigi Klösterli 192
Rigi Kulm 190
Rinderberg 291
Rivaz 277
Rivera-Bironico 337
Rochers-de-Naye 287
Roggwil 123, 124
Roggwil-Berg 78
Rolle 267–8
Romainmôtier 251
Roman sites/museums 50, 53,
    54, 66, 69, 88, 89, 91, 139,
    140, 193, 229, 267, 274,
    277, 306, 364
Romanshorn 27, **88**
Romont 148
Rorschach 85–6
Rossinière 289
Rotenfluh 209

Rothenthurm 62
Rothorn 124, 201, **208**
Rotkreuz 56
Rougemont 290
Rue 141
Rüti 66
Rütli 188

S-chanf 373
Saanen 290
Saas-Fee 322
Sachseln 200
Sagliains 373
Saignelégier 239
Saillon 315
Salenstein 86
Salgesch 318
Salvan 311
Samedan 369
San Bernadino Pass 368
Santa Maria Maggiore 356
Sargans **98**, 385
Sarnen 200
Satigny 266
Sattel-Aegeri 62
Saxon 315
Schaffhausen 90–2
Schilthorn 164–5
Schinznach Bad 227
Schloss Landshut 119
Schlosswil 111
Schmerikon 45
Schmitten 143
Schöftland 228
Schönegg 52
Schönenwerd 226
Schönried 291
Schüpfheim **125**, 208
Schwägalp 80
Schwanden 58
Schwarzenburg 152
Schwarzwasserbrücke 151
Schwende 82
Schwendi 124
Schwyz 209
Schynige Platte 163–4
Scuol-Tarasp 374–5
Sedrun 362
Seebli 64
Seedorf 211
Seengen 193
Sembrancher 313
Sempach 194
Serneus 379
Sevelen 98
shopping hours 6
Sierre 317

Signau 124
Sihlbrugg 50
Sils Maria 348, 371
Simplon Pass 320, 321–2
Simplon Tunnel 321
Sion 315–17
Sisikon 210
Sissach 225
Solalex 309
Solothurn 114–117
Sonceboz-Sombeval 135
Sonloup 288
Sonnenber 179
Sonvilier 135
Sörenberg 125
Sörenberg Schönenboden
    201, 208
Soyhières 222
Speicher 75
Spiez **156–7**, 171, 172
Spinas 369
St Bernard Pass 297, 313
St Cergue 269
St Gallen **73–5**
St Gingolph 298
St Imier 135
St Légier Gare 282
St Léonard 317
St Margrethen 97
St Maurice 306
St Moritz 26, 370–2
St Niklaus 323
St Oswald 48
St Peter's Island 132
St Peter-Molinis 366
St Pierre-de-Clages 315
St Prex 268
St Saphorin 277
St Stephan 291
St Sulpice 243
St Triphon-Village 304
St Urban Ziegelei 124
St Ursanne 223
Stalden-Saas 322
Stammheim 94
Stans 196
Stanserhorn 197
Stanstaad 196
station facilities 21
Ste-Croix 244, **249**
steam railways/locomotives
    24, 45, 50, 62, 77, 136,
    181, 206, 207, 225, 243,
    252, 276, 283, 286, 298–9,
    331, 338, 357
Stechelberg 162, 165
Steckborn 89

Steffisburg 120
Steg 63
Stein (Appenzell) 83
Stein am Rhein 89–90
Steinegg 81
Stettfurt 94
Stockhorn 171
Stoos 210
Stresa 25, 351
Sulwald 162
Summiswald 127
Sursee 195
Susten Pass 202
Swiss Path 189

Täsch 324
Taubenloch 134
Tavannes 135, 240
Taveyannaz 309
Tegna 354
telephones 10
Territet 286, 297
Tesserete 345
Thalwill 56
Thayngen 93
Thrachselwald 126
Thun 155–6
Thunstetten 122
Thurnen 150
Thusis 368
Tiefencastel 368
timetables 19, 21
Tinguely, Jean 145, 146, 216, 218
Tirano 27, 380
Tobel 96
Toffen 155
Tolstoy, Leo 181
tourist offices 24, 389
Tramelan 240
Travers 242
Treib 188
Trétien 312
Trimbach
Trogen 75
Trontano 356
Trubschachen 125
Trübsee 198–9
Trun 362
Turtmann 319
Twann 133

Uetliberg 49, 52
Ulrichen 329
Unterkulm 228
Unterseen 158
Unterterzen 381

Unterwasser 82
Urnäsch 82
Uster 66
Uttwil 88
Utzenstorf 121
Utzigen 113
Uznach 78
Uzwil 73

Vaduz 95
Val d'Illiez 305
Valangin 233
Vallorbe 252
Vallorcine 312
Vaulruz 150
Vaumarcus 244
Verbier 314
Verdasio 355
Vernayaz 311
Vers-l'Eglise 303
Verscio 354
Vevey 276, 279–84
Villars 309–10
Villeneuve 298
visas 7
Visp 319, 321
Vitznau 190
Vouvry 311
Vufflens-la Château 270
Vullierens 267

Wädenswil 57
Walchwil 52
Wald 64
Waldenburg 226
Waldstatt 82
Walenstadt 385
walking 29–30, 33–5
Walzenhausen 84, 98
Wangen an der Aare 118
Wasserauen 82
Wattwil 77
Weesen 385
Weggis 187, 191
Weglossen 64
weights and measures 6
Weinfelden 93
Weissbad 81
Weissenberg 56
Weissenstein 117
Wengen 167
Wengernalp 167
Werdenberg 95
Werthenstein 126
Wettingen 53
Wettingen 228
Wetzikon 66

Wiedlisbach 118
Wiesen 381
Wil 71
Wilchingen 93
Wildegg 227
Wilderswil 161
Wildhaus 82
Wildpark-Höfli 50
Willisau 127
Wimmis 171, 172
Windisch 51
Winterthur 36, 66–7, 69
Wittenbach 78
Wohlen 55
Wolfenschiessen 197
Wolhusen 125
Wollerau 62
Worb 111, 124
Würenlos 70
Wynau 123

Yverdon 245–7, 248

Zell (Zürich) 65
Zell (Emmental) 128
Zermatt , 25, 26, 324–6
Zernez 370
Ziegelbrücke 57, 381, 385
Zizers 383
Zofingen 195
Zollikofen 113
Zug 51
Zugerberg 49
Zuoz 372
Zürich 25, 39–47, 54
Zurzach 69
Zweilütschinen 162, 169
Zweisimmen 26, 291
Zwingen 222